MW01044761

Loss in French Romantic Art, Literature, and Politics

An interdisciplinary examination of nineteenth-century French art pertaining to religion, exile, and the nation's demise as a world power, this study concerns the consequences for visual culture of a series of national crises—from the assault on Catholicism and the flight of émigrés during the Revolution of 1789, to the collapse of the Empire and the dashing of hope raised by the Revolution of 1830.

The central claim is that imaginative response to these politically charged experiences of loss constitutes a major shaping force in French Romantic art, and that pursuit of this theme in light of parallel developments in literature and political debate reveals a pattern of disenchantment transmuted into cultural capital. Focusing on imagery that spoke to loss through visual and verbal idioms particular to France in the aftermath of the Revolution and Empire, the book illuminates canonical works by major figures such as Eugène Delacroix, Théodore Chassériau, and Camille Corot, as well as long-forgotten images freighted with significance for nineteenth-century viewers. A study in national bereavement—an urgent theme in the present moment—the book provides a new lens through which to view the coincidence of imagination and strife at the heart of French Romanticism.

The book will be of interest to scholars working in art history, French literature, French history, French politics, and religious studies.

Jonathan P. Ribner is Associate Professor in the Department of History of Art & Architecture at Boston University.

Cover: Hippolyte Flandrin, *Nude Young Man Seated at the Edge of the Sea*, 1835–36, oil on canvas, 98 x 124 cm. Paris, Musée du Louvre. Photo: Michel Urtado. © RMN-Grand Palais /Art Resource, NY.

Routledge Research in Art History

Routledge Research in Art History is our home for the latest scholarship in the field of art history. The series publishes research monographs and edited collections, covering areas including art history, theory, and visual culture. These high-level books focus on art and artists from around the world and from a multitude of time periods. By making these studies available to the worldwide academic community, the series aims to promote quality art history research.

Italian Painting in the Age of Unification
Laura L. Watts

East-West Artistic Transfer through Rome, Armenia and the Silk Road
Sharing St. Peter's
Christiane Esche-Ramshorn

Interpreting Modernism in Korean Art
Fluidity and Fragmentation
Edited by Kyunghee Pyun and Jung-Ah Woo

Representing the Past in the Art of the Long Nineteenth Century
Historicism, Postmodernism, and Internationalism
Edited by Matthew C. Potter

Greek and Roman Painting and the Digital Humanities
Edited by Marie-Claire Beaulieu and Valérie Toillon

Loss in French Romantic Art, Literature, and Politics
Jonathan P. Ribner

The Visual Culture of Meiji Japan
Negotiating the Transition to Modernity
Edited by Ayelet Zohar and Alison J. Miller

For more information about this series, please visit: https://www.routledge.com/Routledge-Research-in-Art-History/book-series/RRAH

Loss in French Romantic Art, Literature, and Politics

Jonathan P. Ribner

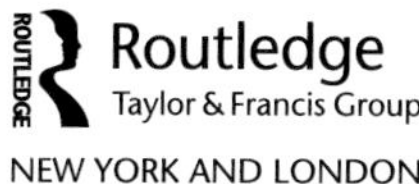
NEW YORK AND LONDON

First published 2022
by Routledge
605 Third Avenue, New York, NY 10158

and by Routledge
2 Park Square, Milton Park, Abingdon, Oxon, OX14 4RN

Routledge is an imprint of the Taylor & Francis Group, an informa business

Library of Congress Cataloging-in-Publication Data
A catalog record for this title has been requested

ISBN: 978-1-032-02703-6 (hbk)
ISBN: 978-1-032-02704-3 (pbk)
ISBN: 978-1-003-18473-7 (ebk)

DOI: 10.4324/9781003184737

Typeset in Sabon
by codeMantra

For Susan, Lauren, Alex, Hanna, and Norah

Contents

List of Figures ix
Acknowledgments xv

Introduction 1

1 Amid the Debris of Our Temples 19

2 Agony in the Garden 57

3 Banished 98

4 "He's Not Dead!" 143

5 Heroism Lost 177

Epilogue: After the Terrible Year 215

Bibliography 233
Index 255

Figures

I.1 François-Joseph Heim, *Transfer of the Remains of the Kings from the Place Called "Cemetery of the Valois," in a Cave, the Eighteenth of January 1817 at Saint-Denis*, 1817. Sceaux, Musée du Domaine départemental de Sceaux 6

I.2 *Le Conservateur des ruines*, 1819. Paris, Bibliothèque nationale de France 7

I.3 Jean-Baptiste Greuze, *A Girl with a Dead Canary*, 1765. Edinburgh, National Gallery of Scotland, Bequest of Lady Murray of Henderland, 1861 13

1.1 *King of Judah*, head no. 12, formerly Notre-Dame cathedral, Paris, West Façade, Gallery of Kings, 1220–30. Paris, Musée de Cluny, Musée national du Moyen-Âge 20

1.2 Hubert Robert, *The Demolition of the Church of Saint-Jean-en-Grève in 1800*, ca. 1800. Paris, Musée Carnavalet 21

1.3 Jacques-Louis David, *Emperor Napoleon Crowning Himself*, ca. 1805. Paris, Musée du Louvre 24

1.4 *Father Forgive Them, for They Know Not What They Do*, ca. 1803. Paris, Bibliothèque nationale de France 25

1.5 François Gérard, *Saint Theresa*, 1827. Paris, Infirmerie Sainte-Thérèse 29

1.6 François-Joseph Navez, *Saint Veronica of Milan*, 1816. Ghent, Museum of Fine Arts 31

1.7 Jean-Victor Schnetz, *The Vow to the Madonna*, Salon of 1831. Paris, Musée du Louvre 32

1.8 Pierre Langlumé, *Liberty of Religion under Charles X*, 1827. Paris, Bibliothèque nationale de France 33

1.9 Denis-Auguste-Marie Raffet, "The Archbishop Was Always a Joker." In *La Caricature*, no. 35 (24 February 1831). Paris, Bibliothèque nationale de France 34

1.10 Théodore Chassériau, *Dominque Lacordaire, of the Order of Preaching Friars*, 1840. Paris, Musée du Louvre 40

1.11 André-Jacques-Victor Orsel, *Good and Evil*, 1829–32. Lyon, Musée des Beaux-Arts 43

1.12 Hippolyte Flandrin, *Christ's Entry into Jerusalem*, 1842–44. Paris, Saint-Germain-des-Prés 45

1.13 Cham (Amédé de Noé), Caricature of Lamennais, 1850. In Auguste Lireux, *Assemblée nationale comique, illustré par Cham* (Paris: Michel-Lévy Frères, 1850), 127. Paris: Bibliothèque nationale de France 47

2.1 Eugène Delacroix, *Christ in the Garden of Olives*, 1824–26. Paris, Saint-Paul-Saint-Louis 58
2.2 Eugène Delacroix, Study for *Christ in the Garden of Olives*, ca. 1824. Paris, Musée du Louvre 59
2.3 Théodore Chassériau, *Jesus in the Garden of Olives*, ca. 1839–40. Lyon, Musée des Beaux-Arts, formerly in the church of Saint-Jean-d'Angély 61
2.4 Théodore Chassériau, *Jesus in the Garden of Olives*, Salon of 1844. Souillac, Sainte-Marie 62
2.5 Eugène Delacroix, *Christ in the Garden of Olives*, 1851. Amsterdam, Rijksmuseum, on deposit in Amsterdam, Van Gogh Museum 66
2.6 Pierre-Paul Prud'hon, *Christ on the Cross*, 1822. Paris, Musée du Louvre 67
2.7 Eugène Delacroix, *Christ on the Cross*, 1846. Baltimore, The Walters Art Museum 69
2.8 Eugène Delacroix, *The Lamentation* (*Christ at the Tomb*), 1847–48. Boston, Museum of Fine Arts, Gift by contribution in memory of Martin Brimmer 71
2.9 Louis Janmot, *Christ in the Garden of Olives*, 1840. Lyon, Musée des Beaux-Arts 78
2.10 Louis Janmot, *The Paternal Roof* (*Le Toit paternel*), from *The Poem of the Soul*, ca. 1848; signed and dated 1854. Lyon, Musée des Beaux-Arts 80
2.11 Louis Janmot, *The Evil Path* (*Le Mauvais sentier*), from *The Poem of the Soul*, 1850. Lyon, Musée des Beaux Arts 81
2.12 Louis Janmot, *The Nightmare*, from *The Poem of the Soul*, 1850. Lyon, Musée des Beaux Arts 82
2.13 Louis Janmot, *On the Mountain*, from *The Poem of the Soul*, 1851. Lyon, Musée des Beaux Arts 83
2.14 Louis Janmot, *The Passage of Souls*, from *The Poem of the Soul*, ca. 1838; signed and dated 1854. Lyon, Musée des Beaux Arts 84
2.15 Louis Janmot, *Sursum Corda*, from *The Poem of the Soul*, 1879. Lyon, Musée des Beaux Arts 86
3.1 Léonor Mérimée after François Gérard, *Belisarius,* 1797. Los Angeles, The J. Paul Getty Museum at the Getty Center 99
3.2 Pierre-Narcisse Guérin, *The Return of Marcus Sextus*, 1797–99. Paris, Musée du Louvre 100
3.3 François Gérard, *Corinne at Cape Miseno*, ca. 1819–21. Lyon, Musée des Beaux-Arts 105
3.4 Henry Monnier, *The Exile* (*L'Exilé*) after Béranger, 1828. Paris, Bibliothèque nationale de France 106
3.5 Ary Scheffer, *Greek Exiles on a Rock Look over at their Lost Fatherland*, ca. 1825. Enschede, Rijksmuseum Twenthe, on deposit from Amsterdam, Amsterdam Museum, C.J. Fodor Bequest 107
3.6 Tony Toullion, *Mickiewicz*, 1847. Paris, Bibliothèque nationale de France 109
3.7 *Adam Mickiewicz*, 1853. Paris, Bibliothèque nationale de France 110

3.8 Antoine-Jean Gros, *Portrait of Julian Ursyn Niemcewicz*, 1833–34. Krakow, National Museum/ Princes Czartoryski Museum 111
3.9 Eugène Delacroix, *Portrait of Frédéric Chopin as Dante*, ca. 1843–46. Paris, Musée du Louvre 114
3.10 Eugène Delacroix, *The Babylonian Captivity*, ca. 1842. Paris, Musée du Louvre 115
3.11 Eugène Delacroix, *Ovid among the Scythians*, 1859. London, National Gallery 116
3.12 Claude Lorrain (Claude Gellée), *Landscape with Hagar and the Angel*, 1646. London, National Gallery, Presented by Sir George Beaumont, 1828 118
3.13 Jean-Baptiste-Camille Corot, *Hagar in the Wilderness*, 1835. New York, Metropolitan Museum of Art, Rogers Fund 119
3.14 Jean-Gilbert Murat, *Hagar in the Desert*, ca. 1842. Guéret, Musée d'Art et d'Archéologie 121
3.15 Jean-François Millet, *Hagar and Ishmael*, 1848–49. The Hague, Rijksmuseum H.W. Mesdag 122
3.16 Charles-Adolphe Richard-Cavaro, *The Exiles* (*Les Exilés*), 1848–49. Besançon, Musée des Beaux-arts et d'Archéologie 124
3.17 Georges Jacquot, *Cain Cursed by God* (*Caïn maudit*), 1820. Nancy, Musée des Beaux-Arts 125
3.18 Antoine Étex, *Cain and His Race Accursed of God* (*Caïnet sa race maudits de Dieu*), 1839 (after a plaster exhibited in the Salon of 1833). Lyon, Musée des Beaux-Arts 126
3.19 Antoine Étex, "Cain." In *L'Artiste*, 1st ser. 5 (1833). Paris, Bibliothèque nationale de France 127
3.20 Henri de Triqueti, *Thou Shall Not Murder*, 1834–41. Paris, Church of the Madeleine 128
3.21 François-Nicolas Chifflart, *Conscience*, ca. 1885. Paris, Maison de Victor-Hugo 130
3.22 Charles Hugo, *Victor Hugo on the Rock of the Proscribed*, summer 1853. Guernsey, Maison de Victor Hugo-Hauteville House 131
3.23 Alphonse-Xavier Monchablon, *Portrait of Victor Hugo*, 1880. Épinal, Musée départmental d'art ancien et contemporain 133
4.1 Antoine-Jean Gros, *Napoleon on the Bridge of Arcole*, 1796. Paris, Musée du Louvre 144
4.2 Antoine-Jean Gros, *Napoleon on the Battlefield of Eylau*, 1808. Paris, Musée du Louvre 145
4.3 Bernard Poyet (design), François-Honoré-Georges Jacob-Desmalter (woodwork), and Augustin-François-André Picot (embroidery), Throne of Napoleon I for the Corps législatif, 1804–05. Paris, Musée des Arts Décoratifs 147
4.4 Horace Vernet, *The Barrière de Clichy, Defense of Paris on 30 March 1814*, 1820. Paris, Musée du Louvre 149
4.5 Horace Vernet, *Peace and War*, or *The Soldier Plowman* (*Le Soldat laboureur*), 1820. London, Wallace Collection 150

4.6 Théodore Géricault, *The Swiss Guard at the Louvre*, 1819. Paris, Bibliothèque nationale de France 151
4.7 François Rude, *Napoleon Awakening to Immortality*, 1846. Paris, Musée du Louvre, on deposit in Paris, Musée de l'Armée 160
4.8 Horace Vernet, Frontispiece to Robert-Augustin Antoine de Beauterne, *Conversations religieuses de Napoléon, avec des Documents inédits de la plus haute importance où il révèle lui-même sa pensée intime sur le christianisme* (Paris: Chez l'auteur, Olivier-Fulgence, and Debécourt, 1841). Paris, Bibliothèque nationale de France 163
4.9 Émile Bayard, "Napoleon the Little Superimposes Himself on Napoleon the Great," from *Napoléon le petit, edition illustrée par MM. J.P. Laurens, É. Bayard, E. Morin, D. Vierge, Lix, Chifflart, Garcia, H. Scott, Brun, G. Bellenger* (Paris: Eugène Hugues, 1879). Paris, Bibliothèque nationale de France 166
5.1 Honoré Daumier, "France at Rest" ("Repos de la France"). In *La Caricature* (28 August 1834). Paris, Bibliothèque nationale de France 177
5.2 Théodore Géricault, *The Return from Russia*, 1818. Paris, Bibliothèque nationale de France 183
5.3 Nicolas-Toussaint Charlet, *Episode from the Russian Campaign*, 1836. Lyon, Musée des Beaux Arts 185
5.4 Joseph-Fernand Boissard de Boisdenier, *Episode from the Retreat from Moscow*, 1835. Rouen, Musée des Beaux-Arts 187
5.5 Édouard-Alexandre Odier, *Episode from the Retreat from Moscow (1812)—Dragoon of the Imperial Guard*, 1832. Amiens, Musée de Picardie 188
5.6 Théodore Chassériau, *The Punishment of Cain* (or *Cain Accursed*), 1836. Cambridge, MA, Harvard Art Museums/Fogg Museum, Gift of Eric Seiler AB '78, AM '82, JD '82 and Darcy Bradbury AB '78, MBA '82 in honor of Matthew Rutenberg 191
5.7 Théodore Chassériau, *Self-portrait*, 1835. Paris, Musée du Louvre 192
5.8 Théodore Chassériau, *The Return of the Prodigal Son*, 1836. La Rochelle, Musée des Beaux-Arts 193
5.9 Théodore Chassériau, *Self-portrait Holding a Palette*, 1838. Paris, Musée du Louvre 195
5.10 Hippolyte Flandrin, *Nude Young Man Seated at the Edge of the Sea*, 1835–36. Paris, Musée du Louvre 196
5.11 Hippolyte Flandrin, *Dante, Led by Virgil, Offers Consolation to the Souls of the Envious*, 1834–35. Lyon, Musée des Beaux-Arts 197
5.12 Jean-Germain Drouais, *The Dying Athlete*, 1785. Paris, Musée du Louvre 198
5.13 Léon Noël after Eduard Bendemann, "Jeremiah on the Ruins of Jerusalem". In *L'Artiste*, 1st ser. 13 (1837). Paris, Bibliothèque nationale de France 199
5.14 Théodore Chassériau, *Lamentations of Jeremiah*, ca. 1836–37. Paris, Musée du Louvre 199
5.15 Théodore Chassériau, *Venus Anadyomene* (*Vénus marine*), 1838. Paris, Musée du Louvre 200

5.16 Théodore Chassériau, *Susanna Bathing*, 1839. Paris, Musée du Louvre 201
5.17 Théodore Chassériau, *The Trojan Women* (*Les Troyennes*), 1841. Destroyed, originally in the collection of Ferenc Hatvany, Budapest 202
5.18 Théodore Chassériau, Study for *The Trojan Women*, 1840–41. Beauvais, MUDO, Musée de l'Oise, Donation Chancerel-Gobineau, 1974 203
5.19 Théodore Chassériau, *Tomb Project for Napoleon I*, ca. 1840. Paris, Musée du Louvre 204
5.20 Gustave Moreau, *The Young Man and Death*, 1856–65. Cambridge, MA, Harvard Art Museums/Fogg Museum, Gift of Grenville L. Winthrop, Class of 1886 205
E.1 Honoré Daumier, "France-Prometheus and the Eagle-Vulture." In *Le Charivari*, 13 February 1871. New York, Metropolitan Museum of Art, Elisha Whittelsey Collection, Elisha Whittelsey Fund, 1990 216
E.2 Adolphe-Léon Willette, *Revenge* (*Revanche*), 1895. New York, Metropolitan Museum of Art, Rogers Fund, 1922 217
E.3 G. Laplante after Gustave Doré, Frontispiece to Jacques Normand, *L'Émigrant alsacien, récit, avec une gravure de Gustave Doré* (Paris: Librairie du XIXe siècle, 1873). Strasbourg, Bibliothèque nationale et universitaire de Strasbourg 218
E.4 Aimé-Nicolas Morot, *The Captivity of the Jews in Babylon*, 1873. Paris, École nationale supérieure des Beaux-Arts 219
E.5 Paul Gauguin, *Vision of the Sermon* or *Vision after the Sermon* (*Jacob wrestling with the Angel*), 1888. Edinburgh, National Gallery of Scotland, Purchased 1925 225
E.6 Georges Rouault, *Christ Mocked by Soldiers*, 1932. New York, Museum of Modern Art, Given anonymously 227

Acknowledgments

As befits a book built around loss, I wish first to remember those who will not turn its pages. Having lost my father, Irving Ribner, a half-century ago, I can only hope that his love of literature and history lives on in what follows. My mother, Roslyn G. Ribner Reichler, gave me more than I can say and brought art into my life. My stepfather, Merton Reichler, who brightened her twilight years, would have been an eager reader. My doctoral advisor, Bob Rosenblum, showed me art history at its best; my other dissertation readers, Linda Nochlin and Gert Schiff, are also sorely missed. Without Frank Bowman, my first book might never have seen the light of day.

Long part of a marvelously collegial department, I give particular thanks for solidarity to Cynthia Becker, Jodi Cranston, Deborah Kahn, Becky Martin, Susan Rice, Kim Sichel, Alice Tseng, Greg Williams, and Michael Zell, never forgetting the critical support of Pat Hills. Having enjoyed stimulating conversation about my research, in and around BU, with Jeffrey Mehlman, Christopher Ricks, and Charles J. Rzepka, I regard the library science wizardry of Rhoda Bilansky and Ruth Thomas with wonder.

When acknowledging the friends who have stood by me, I must first mention Beth Nicklas and the late Mary C. Nicklas Buchert Tingley. My close friendship with Ken Simpson began when we were 15. My ties to Clifford S. Briggin, Sara Diaz, Howard Hebel, Robert Kaufmann, Chris Riopelle, John Schwab, Shauna Tannenbaum, Stefan Tessler, and Dan Weiner also have stood the test of time.

I received helpful advice from a number of scholars with whom I corresponded during the course of this project: Joseph Acquisto, Thomas W. Briggs, Daniel R. Guernsey, John M. Hunisak (whose teaching and mentoring at Middlebury College first sent me on my way), Mehdi Korchane, and Scott Sprenger.

My endnotes acknowledge numerous museum professionals who generously facilitated this project. Of these I offer particular thanks to Ágnes Horváth, Budapest Museum of Fine Arts—Hungarian National Gallery Reproductions Office; Anna Zsófia Kovács, Head of the Department of Art after 1800, Budapest Museum of Fine Arts; and Henrique Simoes, Chargé du Service images, Musée des Beaux-Arts de Lyon.

It is difficult to sufficiently express my gratitude to a group of uncommonly generous scholars to whom I reached out, requesting that they read draft chapters. That I had never met some of them makes their contribution all the more remarkable. First and foremost, my thanks go to Judy Sund, who read the entire manuscript and made countless, insightful suggestions, both large and small. My good fortune also extends to having benefitted from the expertise of Michael J. Call, Thomas Crow, Michèle

Hannoosh, Maurice Samuels, Richard Thomson, and Beth S. Wright. Tonic interventions by three anonymous readers for Routledge enhanced the argument's clarity and cohesion, while augmenting the bibliography. I remain grateful to my editor, Isabella Vitti, for welcoming my project, and to both her assistant, Katie Armstrong, and my project manager, Karthikeyan Subramaniam, for guiding the book to completion.

My labor would be of scant worth without the joy brought daily by my family: Lauren, Alex, Hanna, Norah, and my soulmate, Susan White.

Introduction

Exiled in Brussels, the middle-aged poet, politician, and historian of religion, Edgar Quinet (1803–75) reminisced about the national trauma that shaped his youth: "Thus, the great invasions of 1814 and 1815 left in my memory a core of impressions, of images through which I glimpsed all things. The collapse of a world was my first education."[1] Eleven years old when France fell to Napoleon's adversaries, and 12 when the emperor suffered his final defeat at Waterloo, the young Quinet was probably less politically aware than his long-after-the-fact memoir (1857) would suggest.[2] At the same time, his recollection persuasively evokes the acute sense of loss the polymath author shared with others who came of age in France during the first half of the nineteenth century. Nor was the double defeat that collapsed Quinet's world the sole dark legacy inherited by the Romantics. French Catholicism, ridiculed by Voltaire and persecuted under the revolutionary regime of de-Christianization, was reinstated by Napoleon amid the ruins of vandalized churches. Evidence that the faith reemerged deeply scarred is provided by nostalgia for the Catholic past, as expressed by François-René de Chateaubriand (1768–1848); by rage at religious indifference in the present, as voiced by Félicité Robert de Lamennais (1782–1854); and by unconventional Christian paintings suited to neither ecclesiastical settings nor private devotion.

Displacement from the firm ground of belief and its traditional imagery had a counterpart in painful separation from the fatherland. Exile was suffered by many Catholics, from French émigrés heading for the English Channel or central Europe, to Polish patriots seeking refuge in Paris in the wake of a doomed revolt against Russian hegemony. This experience was not visited solely upon believers. The dominant French artist of the late eighteenth century, Jacques-Louis David (1748–1825), also knew proscription. Having voted for Louis XVI's execution, the former radical and imperial propagandist had no choice but to live out his post-Napoleonic years in the same city that later harbored Quinet. These forced departures were revisited in a cycle of banishment and return that outstripped the lifespan of Romanticism—in the captivity of Napoleon on the island of Saint Helena (1815–21) and the repatriation of his remains (1840); in the exile of Victor Hugo (1802–85) on Jersey (1852–55) and Guernsey (1855–70), followed by triumphant homecoming at the ignominious close of the Second Empire; and in the deportation to the Pacific penal colony of New Caledonia or condemnation to death *in absentia* of surviving participants in the Paris Commune (1871) prior to their amnesty (1880). This painful history fed the burgeoning nationalism that constitutes a hallmark of the era. Nationalism, observed the expatriate Palestinian Edward Said (1935–2003), has an "essential association with

DOI: 10.4324/9781003184737-1

exile": "Indeed, the interplay between nationalism and exile is like Hegel's dialectic of master and servant, opposites informing and constituting each other."[3] Following his emigration to Paris in 1831, Heinrich Heine (1797–1856) gave this point a Romantic inflection. "It is an odd thing about patriotism, the true love of country," noted the Jewish German poet.

> A man can love his native land and never know that he loves it, though he live to be eighty—but then he must have stayed at home. You do not realize what spring means till it is winter; and the best songs of May are written behind the stove.[4]

Just as many were severed from their homeland, so too was colonial territory lost after the disastrous Seven Year's War (1756–63) established British hegemony in Canada and India at French expense. Though he built an empire on the European continent worthy of the Caesars, Napoleon presided over the loss of the most lucrative jewel in the French colonial crown, Saint-Domingue, where, since the late seventeenth century, the sickening brutality of slave labor underwrote world leadership in sugar and coffee production and prominence as a source of cacao, cotton, and indigo. In 1801, a French expeditionary force that included the father and uncle of Théodore Chassériau (1819–56) was dispatched to suppress the independence movement led by emancipated slave Toussaint Louverture (b. 1743) and to reinstate slavery, abolished during the Revolution.[5] In November 1803, following Louverture's death in captivity in April, the French forces, decimated by yellow fever, were defeated in battle; Saint-Domingue became independent Haiti in January 1804. With benefit from colonial commitment in North America a losing proposition (and anticipating a resumption of war with England, briefly halted by the Treaty of Amiens of 1802), Napoleon fostered good relations with the United States by offering, at an astounding discount, the vast territory comprising the Louisiana Purchase (1803). Reduced to a second-rate power following the Empire's collapse, the bereft nation was briefly buoyed by the Revolution of 1830, only to enter nearly two decades of disappointment and boredom. Starved for imperial glory, post-Waterloo France aggressively pursued colonial conquest in North Africa. Preoccupied by a heritage of defeat, Quinet and others besotted with *la patrie* (the fatherland) sought transcendence in the cult of Napoleon, the century's most prominent exile.[6]

The following pages address the consequences for visual culture of a series of national crises—from the assault on Catholicism and the flight of émigrés during the Revolution of 1789, to the collapse of the Empire and the dashing of hope raised by the Revolution of 1830. My central claim is that imaginative response to these politically charged experiences of loss constitutes a major shaping force in French Romantic art, and that pursuit of this theme in light of parallel developments in literature and political debate reveals a pattern of disenchantment transmuted into cultural capital. Starting from the premise that, in the age of Romanticism, a sense of loss was overdetermined, I argue that the depressive vectors impacting artists and writers were interrelated, such that hunger of the soul intersected with the pain of exile, the fury of nationalism, and the shame of defeat—each of which found expression in imagery marked by traces of adversity that have largely escaped notice.

So fundamental are loss, exile, and defeat to post-revolutionary culture that these overarching topics can—paradoxically—fade into invisibility. What might seem commonplace to scholars of nineteenth-century French literature and political history becomes startlingly vivid when texts conveying strong sentiments are set beside emotionally freighted works of art. Focusing on imagery that spoke in visual and verbal idioms particular to France in the aftermath of the Revolution and Empire, the interdisciplinary approach of this study yields a double reward. Heretofore hidden aspects of canonical works by major figures such as Chassériau, Eugène Delacroix (1798–1863), and Camille Corot (1796–1875) become visible, and long-forgotten artifacts of visual culture loaded with significance for nineteenth-century viewers return to life. In addition to the public space of propaganda—so often a preoccupation in studies of nineteenth-century art—my argument visits private sites of ferment. Attuned to the political charge of the material, I am no less interested in its lyrical aspects. Bolstering Henri Peyre's insistence on Romanticism's tenacity, what follows links word and image to reconstruct a cycle of creativity and grief.[7]

Loss is grounded in a tradition of inductive, contextual art history, which includes the work of, among others, Nina Athanassoglou-Kallmyer, Robert Rosenblum, Richard Thomson, and Beth S. Wright.[8] Moreover, it is indebted to publications by specialists in French literature oriented toward the history of ideas and politics (in particular, Paul Bénichou, Frank Paul Bowman, Ceri Crossley, and Maurice Samuels).[9] Michèle Hannoosh has provided an admirable model for approaching the intersection of art and writing in the Romantic era; and Pierre Nora's hefty compendium, *Les Lieux de mémoire* is, itself, a monument to the study of French national memory and symbolism.[10] Headquartered in the city designated by Walter Benjamin as the capital of the nineteenth century, the narrative passes through Lyon, samples the writing of exiles resident in Paris (e.g., Adam Mickiewicz, 1798–1855), and includes guest appearances by Lord Byron (1788–1824), whose work was translated and imitated in Paris. Shuttling between image and text, the argument follows the rhythm of creativity in the Romantic age, when artists and writers consorted, treated common subjects, and read the same journals. At the same time, evidence gleaned from canvas and page is not marshaled with an eye toward symmetry. Affinities of theme and plot linking art to novels, poetry, religious polemic, and political debate serve to illuminate works handcrafted in the studio. Privileging works of art as subjects of inquiry, *Loss* also revels in visually evocative writing, for example that of Chateaubriand and Lamennais.

Any experience of loss implies awareness of time's passage, and heightened sensitivity to the palpable and irreversible effect of historical change is a salient trait of French Romantic culture.[11] Passionately interested in history, the Romantics doggedly researched bygone eras, which inspired countless literary and visual representations. As Stephen Bann observes,

> An irreversible shift had occurred, and history—from being a localized and specific practice within the cultural topology—became a flood that overrode all disciplinary barriers and, finally, when the barriers were no longer easy to perceive, became a substratum to almost every type of cultural activity.[12]

This development is manifest in "archive glutton" Jules Michelet's notion of the historian's sacred calling as prophetic raiser of the dead; the French appetite for the novels of Sir Walter Scott; and untold bolts of canvas, brushed with scenes culled from French history, sent to the Paris Salon or displayed on the walls of the Palace of Versailles.[13] A transformation of historical consciousness is also legible in reconstructions of the past by artists of the late eighteenth and nineteenth centuries. Descriptive particularity and attempted (if not always achieved) archaeological authenticity of setting, costume, and props sets French history painting of this era apart from that of Nicolas Poussin (1594–1665), with its standard-issue togas and generic architecture. It is unthinkable that the founding father of French classical painting would have engaged the master furniture-maker Georges Jacob (1739–1814) to craft a chair in the Roman style, as did David when gathering source material for *The Lictors Bring to Brutus the Bodies of His Sons* (1789; Paris, Musée du Louvre). Such relish in particularized renderings of the trappings of long-gone ages speaks of awareness of unbridgeable separation between past and present.

That the first half of the nineteenth century can lay claim to a measure of uniqueness in this regard is suggested by the reification—and passage into cliché—of that gnawing affliction visited upon sensitive souls ill at ease with the present, the *mal du siècle*. This was neither the first nor the last wave of torment by agitated inner emptiness or, in Chateaubriand's untranslatable terminology, *le vague des passions*. Widespread since at least the mid-eighteenth century, it had been a plague of the years around 1760–80.[14] But when the disorder returned to haunt Chateaubriand and the younger generations of the Bourbon Restoration and July Monarchy, cognizance of national catastrophe magnified the intensity and contagiousness of the malady. Tellingly, suicide became topical. In 1835, two prominent painters, Antoine-Jean Gros (b. 1771) and Gros's former student Léopold Robert (b. 1794), took their own lives; three weeks after Robert's death, *Chatterton*, a three-act play by Alfred de Vigny (1797–1863), staged the bitter end of the legendary outsider poet, dampening many handkerchiefs.[15] For Octave, the anxious narrator of *The Confession of a Child of the Century* (*La Confession d'un enfant du siècle*, 1836) by Alfred de Musset (1810–57), life in the present is unbearable, as the Reign of Terror and Napoleon's defeat had swept away the convictions of the past, leaving nothing in their place:

> The entire sickness of the present century comes from two causes; the people who passed through '93 and 1814 bear two wounds in their hearts. All that which was is no longer; all that which will be is not yet. Do not search elsewhere for the secret of our ills.[16]

Visionaries, from Quinet to Lamennais, so longed for the future (*l'avenir*), that the writing of the former has been characterized as conveying a "*mal de l'avenir*," and the impatient circle around the latter titled their short-lived journal *L'Avenir*.[17] "It is not the weakness of our thought that kills us," declared Quinet in 1833, "it is its excess... it is supporting the weight of the future in the void of the present."[18]

Mindful of the peril attending any attempt to historicize so universal and subjective a sentiment as loss, I join others who have argued for its particularity and ubiquity in the late eighteenth and early nineteenth centuries. Thus, a group of key paintings from this period interrogated by Darcy Grimaldo Grigsby "are strikingly preoccupied not with mastery and conquest ... but with loss, degradation, and failure ...."[19] Following the Revolution and Empire, historian Peter Fritzsche writes, "a sense of loss pooled in the folds of everyday life." For thoughtful people of that era who were "stranded in the present" and attuned to "the melancholy of history," the conception of time was fraught with regret. Accordingly, ruins—admired in the eighteenth century as poetic manifestations of a natural process of decline—became markers of historical acts of depredation.[20] Fritzsche is not alone in discerning depressive retrospection in post-revolutionary culture. Beth S. Wright's study of representations of history from the Bourbon Restoration demonstrates that the detailed objects and architectural settings of the Troubadour painters—whose meticulous reconstructions of sentimental and chivalric scenes from the French Renaissance and Middle Ages thrilled viewers in the early nineteenth century—are imbued with post-revolutionary bereavement.[21] There has been much discussion of the Musée des monuments français curated by Alexandre Lenoir (1761–1839); between 1795 and 1816, the museum offered a steady stream of visitors moody ensembles of displaced *ancien régime* tombs sheltered from further revolutionary vandalism.[22] And Suzanne Glover Lindsay documents the prominence of exhumation and reburial in Romantic culture, from the violation of the dynastic tombs in the Abbey church of Saint-Denis in 1793 to the return of Napoleon's remains to Paris in 1840.[23]

Measure of the political amperage of imagery pertaining to this tide of retrospection is provided by a painting commemorating the enactment of a Bourbon ordinance of 1816 calling for the salvage and replacement in the Abbey church of Saint-Denis of royal bones cast into a ditch by revolutionary vandals. The execution of this reverent task by torchlight was depicted by François-Joseph Heim (1787–1865) in *Transfer of the Bones of the Kings from the Place Called Cemetery of the Valois, in a Cave at Saint-Denis, 18 January 1817.* Begun in 1817 and exhibited in the Salon of 1822, it hangs in the sacristy of Saint-Denis.[24] Undertaken by the artist at his own initiative and completed as an official commission, the work is best viewed in a smaller version (1817), which dramatically situates the proceedings beneath gothic spires hauntingly silhouetted by moonlight (Figure I.1).[25] Commemorative group portrait as well as exemplar of counterrevolutionary piety, the painting is no less steeped in outrage than the elegiac pages of Chateaubriand's sensational breviary of loss, the *Génie du christianisme* (*Spirit of Christianity*, 1802), which evokes the desolation of the ravaged church:

> Saint-Denis is deserted; the bird has taken it for a thoroughfare, the grass grows on its broken altars; and in place of the hymn for the dead, which resounded under its vaults, one hears only the drops of rain that fall through its uncovered roof, the fall of some stone detached from its ruined walls, or the sound of its clock, which passes through the empty tombs and the devastated subterranean passages.[26]

As if to rebut this Catholic, royalist lamentation on the ruins, Chateaubriand was mocked from the Left in an anonymous lithograph, *Le Conservateur des ruines* (*The Guardian of Ruins*), which puns on the double meaning of *Le Conservateur*—both curator and political conservative (Figure I.2). The insult is personalized by invoking both the jeremiads of the *Génie du christianisme* and the name of the political journal, *Le Conservateur* (8 October 1818–30 March 1820), founded by Chateaubriand with ultra-royalist support. Portrayed as a religious pilgrim, the apologist for throne and altar is seated beside a candle snuffer, stock attribute of the reactionary. Archaically armored with breastplate, Chateaubriand shoulders a partisan in place of a pilgrim's staff and attempts to protect architectural fragments labeled with *ancien régime* abuses (e.g., "privileges," "intolerant fanaticism," "seigniorial rights"). Meantime, a fierce dog—standing in for Chateaubriand's nemesis, Élie Decazes (1780–1860),

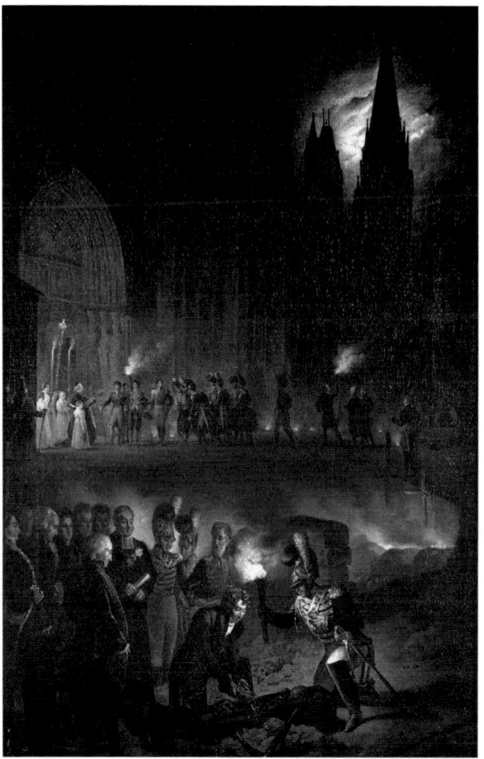

Figure I.1 François-Joseph Heim, *Transfer of the Remains of the Kings from the Place Called "Cemetery of the Valois," in a Cave, the Eighteenth of January 1817 at Saint-Denis*, 1817, oil on canvas, 66.5 × 44.5 cm. Sceaux, Musée du Domaine départemental de Sceaux. Photo: Agence Bulloz. © RMN-Grand Palais/Art Resource, NY.

minister of police, moderate royalist, and favorite of Louis XVIII (1755–1824)—pisses on a block labeled "feudal regime," outraging its would-be protector.[27] Garbed in a pilgrim's cloak adorned with an excessive number of scallop shells (traditional attribute of a believer who had made the pilgrimage to Santiago de Compostela) suspiciously resembling money bags, the target of this caricature cuts a figure unworthy of the veneration he commanded among vanguard Romantic poets of the Generation of 1820—including the teen-aged Hugo, who, precociously over-endowed with ego, famously recorded in a notebook his ambition to be "Chateaubriand or nothing."[28]

These contrasting images—one from the august realm of Catholic monarchism, the other from the low register of dissident print culture—are juxtaposed in a maneuver characteristic of this book—a braiding of art, writing, and politics (pertaining, respectively, to Catholicism, exile, and nationalism) around the theme of loss. If its level of engagement with literature is unconventional in scholarship on French Romantic art, aspects of the material under consideration have been studied by many others based in the precincts of French art and literature, as well as in the domains of political, social, religious, and intellectual history. In regard to Catholic art, I have found

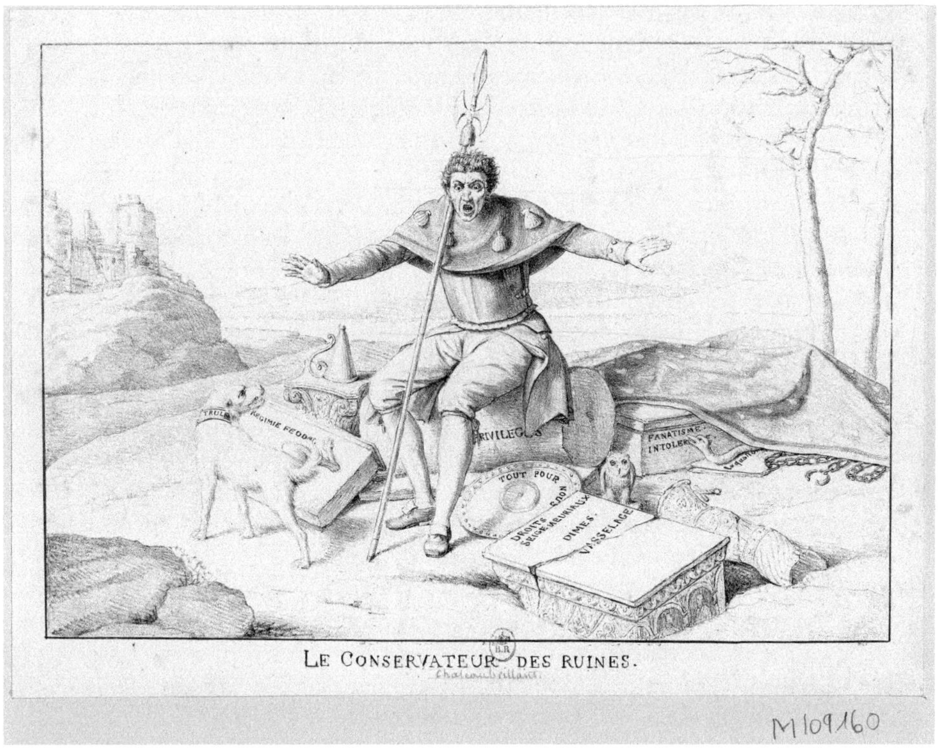

Figure I.2 *Le Conservateur des ruines*, 1819, lithograph. Paris, Bibliothèque nationale de France. Photo: BnF.

the dissimilar publications of Bruno Foucart and Michael Paul Driskel particularly useful, although I part company with both.[29] I regard nineteenth-century French religious art neither as comprising an overlooked renaissance (as per Foucart, who champions this largely forgotten or disdained corpus), nor as a topic whose interest resides primarily in its potential for theoretical modeling; in its wealth of ecclesiastical controversy and Church-State contestation; and as an arena for competition between naturalism and archaism (as per Driskel). Those studies neither share my preoccupation with loss nor plumb Romantic literature in comparable depth. Rather than dwelling on ecclesiastical patronage and doctrinal rifts, I highlight the urgency and cunning of spiritual craving among heirs to a faith that had suffered irreparable harm. Uninterested in the blandly sentimental religious paintings produced in quantity during the nineteenth century, this book traffics in innovative sacred imagery redolent of the uneasy legacy of de-Christianization.

The troubled discourse at the heart of this book emanates from the unprecedented disruption wrought by the Revolution. That shock continues to reverberate. As recently as 22 January 1993, Bourbon lilies were solemnly laid in the Place de la Concorde by throngs marking the bicentennial of Louis XVI's execution there (21 January 1793), with a repeat performance on 16 October to mourn Marie-Antoinette's guillotining at the same site. *Loss* opens with evidence of revolutionary violence against

Catholicism because the rupture with *ancien régime* faith was generative to French Romanticism; it was the very ur-disenfranchisement. Providing a base over which other losses were layered in the following century, the cataclysm represented, to borrow Michael S. Roth's felicitous phrase, "a charismatic wound, an injury that attracts everything to it."[30] With the culmination in 1905 of the official laicization of French society—all ecclesiastical buildings were nationalized and State financing of new churches and clerical salaries henceforth forbidden—the nation that once preened as the Eldest Daughter of the Church publicly acknowledged secularization's triumph. Tracking resistance to, and abetting of, the dereliction of Catholicism, this study is hardly the first to insist on the fertility of a relentless process that was constructive and metamorphic, as well as corrosive.[31] Where absent, Catholic worship was replaced by a pack of substitutes, some of astonishing eccentricity. No longer immured in chapels, sacred fervor migrated to the secular sphere. Long familiar to scholars of French intellectual history and literature, this pattern predates Romanticism and is imbricated with nationalism. David A. Bell indicates that France's religious heritage was vital to the cult of the nation as it developed over the course of the eighteenth century: "The sense of sacrality invested in the concept of *patrie* only enhanced the Church's influence, for the French approached this terrestrial object of adoration in what can only be called a deeply Catholic manner."[32] Despite antipathy toward the Church, the revolutionaries, according to Thomas Kselman, subscribed to a secularized version of the notion, originating in the late thirteenth century, that France is "a nation chosen by God to be his special instrument in history."[33] Revolutionary incursion into the domain of worship could be explicit, as in 1791, when Gilbert Romme (1750–95), who would later serve as deputy to the Legislative Assembly and the Convention, declared, "Law is the religion of the state, which must also have its ministers, its apostles, its altars, and its schools."[34]

Following the Revolution, syncretism became more evident. Thus, D.G. Charlton charted the efflorescence of "secular religions" among utopians and other exalted thinkers in a century plagued by doubt and attracted to grandiose, totalizing systems of redemption and belief; and Paul Bénichou set forth myriad examples of the investiture of French Romantic writers with priestly authority and prophetic vision (Hugo is a prime example).[35] Moreover, the seemingly self-evident notion that secularity is prerequisite to Modernism has been destabilized by revisionist histories of art. Illuminating the submerged spirituality of a substantial body of nineteenth- and twentieth-century art, Robert Rosenblum revealed affinity, for example, between the numinous, floating color fields of Mark Rothko (1903–70) and the sublimated religiosity of the northern Romantic tradition, as exemplified by the transcendent landscapes of Caspar David Friedrich (1774–1840).[36] More recently, Thomas Crow has discerned theological imperatives within a longer, ostensibly secular, artistic lineage. In this perspective, an enduring inheritance hails from the 1640s, when the fervently Catholic Jansenists began to profess uncompromising opposition to vainglorious displays of piety, earning the enmity of the Jesuits and alarming the monarchy. Long after 1713, when that tenacious sect's headquarters in the Abbey of Port-Royal des Champs was razed at the pleasure of Louis XIV, Jansenist radical humility and refusal of idolatry reappear in unexpected places, from a still life by Jean Siméon Chardin (1699–1779) to the Roden Crater project of James Turrell (b. 1943).[37] Further complicating the narrative of secularization, the present study brings salience to the revitalization of Christological motifs through an infusion of lyrical pessimism by artists and poets working in the heyday of the *mal du siècle*.[38] Depletion of devotional efficacy in imagery drawn from scripture and the lives of the saints, I argue, could be coupled with enhancement of longevity and expressive power—a paradox exemplified by the magisterial religious paintings of the nonbeliever Delacroix. That artist's work has been deeply mined since the epochal 1963 exhibition at the Louvre commemorating the centennial of his death; in addition to the catalogue raisonné of the paintings by Lee Johnson and Michèle Hannoosh's definitive edition of the *Journal*, there has been a spate of monographs, exhibition catalogs, and thematic studies for which I am grateful.[39]

After recounting examples of revolutionary vandalism and laying bare the aggressive assertion of state prerogative informing Napoleon's rescue of French Catholicism, Chapter 1 (Amid the Ruins of Our Temples) underscores the sense of loss coloring Chateaubriand's *Génie du christianisme*. Emphasizing the unorthodox aspect of Chateaubriand's privileging of feeling and beauty as the foundations of Christian worship, the chapter considers paintings by François Gérard (1770–1837), Jean-Victor Schnetz (1787–1870), and François-Joseph Navez (1787–1869) that feature "spectator Christianity"—that is, they convey fascination with the piety of others, rather than function as inducements to prayer. I then examine attempts to reclaim a lost past of Christian faith by means of stylistic archaism, as practiced by two pious painters from Lyon, Victor Orsel (1795–1850) and Hippolyte Flandrin (1809–64). Finally, I follow the political trajectory of Lamennais, who metamorphosed from militant enemy of religious tolerance and darling of the counterrevolution, to prophetic populist anathematized by the Church and adored by Parisian workers.

Chapter 2 (Agony in the Garden) explores the disparity between attraction to subjects pertaining to religion and the unorthodox aspects of such work. Having considered unconventional representations of Christ by Delacroix, Chassériau, and Pierre-Paul Prud'hon (1758–1823), I showcase the reliance by Louis Janmot (1814–92) on hermetically personal iconography. With this intriguingly eccentric artist, the narrative shifts from Paris to Lyon, a city brutalized during the Reign of Terror and steeped in Catholic mysticism. At issue is the conflict between private vision and didactic function informing Janmot's cycle of verse, drawings, and paintings, *The Poem of the Soul*—a key work of Lyonnais art that elicited Delacroix's admiration and dismay. Arguing that this hopelessly ambitious ensemble represents, no less than the religious paintings of Delacroix, a decisive break with pre-revolutionary Catholic tradition in the visual arts, the chapter reveals a surprising affinity between a fanatically devout student of Ingres and an un-converted Romantic.

Gauging emotional temperature in nineteenth-century France, the needle ticks when the topic of Chapter 3 (Banished) is raised. Consider, for example, the article "Exile" (1838) in the *Encyclopédie des gens du monde*:

> Everywhere a generous concern follows the steps of the exile; all who see him are moved, and it is then, above all, that you feel how much to be pitied is one who must drag out his existence on foreign soil, far from the tender mother who carried him in her womb and nourished him with her milk, far from the white-haired father who leans toward the tomb and who fears to die without having again seen his son![40]

That this tearful lament could be wrung from the dry pages of a reference work gives measure to a sensitivity toward exile bequeathed by the Revolution and kept alive in the nineteenth century, whether by Napoleonic, Bourbon, or Czarist tyranny. Given the sympathy exuded by the *Encyclopédie des gens du monde*, it is not surprising that its editor, the academician Alexis-François Artaud de Montor (1772–1849), had known banishment firsthand as an émigré. So had the counterrevolutionary political theorist Louis de Bonald (1754–1840), who regarded solidarity with exiles as a matter of common sense: "Injustice has so frequently been the cause of proscription, that, by itself, the noun exile (*proscrit*) implies presumption of innocence."[41]

For many who fled the guillotine, displacement from French soil brought spiritual as well as political reckoning. Fresh from exile, Chateaubriand attributed to providence the capacity of small things to instill attachment to one's birthplace (the "*instinct de la patrie*"), which is only strengthened by persecution:

> It is perhaps the smiles of a mother, of a father, of a sister; it is perhaps the memory of the old tutor who raised us, the young companions of our childhood... finally it is the simplest circumstances, if you will, the most trivial... the bell tower of the church visible above the trees, the yew of the cemetery, the gothic tomb....[42]

Nor was the link between Christianity and love of France newly forged by the émigrés. By the time of the Revolution, a religious aura had long encircled French patriotism. As David A. Bell points out, the growing attachment to the fatherland in eighteenth-century France had antique, sacred roots: "The Latin noun *patria* had strong religious connotations from the start, and after the fall of Rome, it survived mostly in religious usage: the Christian's true *patria* lay in the Kingdom of Heaven."[43] Just as the Emigration was the crucible of Chateaubriand's conversion—and in this he was hardly alone—so too did that experience lend immediacy to the ancient theological concept that life on earth is a period of exile.[44] Diffracting this trope through a Romantic lens, Chateaubriand attributed to Christianity a melancholy unknown to the ancients, fixed as they had been on the world before them: "The Christian always considers himself a traveler passing through a valley of tears, and who will only rest in the tomb."[45] It is hardly surprising that the earthly exile of the Christian was a favorite theme under the Bourbon Restoration, whose Catholic notables had shared Chateaubriand's involuntary experience abroad.[46]

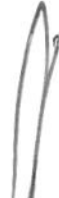

In accord with the prominence of exile in the history of the Revolution, art-historical investigation of the theme has been largely confined to the immediate aftermath of the Reign of Terror. Following the lead of James Henry Rubin, Mehdi Korchane and Thomas Crow have shed light on the key examples of exile imagery from that period, François Gérard's *Belisarius* and *The Return of Marcus Sextus* by Pierre-Narcisse Guérin (1774–1833).[47] Chapter three carries this inquiry into the Empire and beyond, claiming that sympathy with exiles remained ubiquitous, and that imaginative evocations of the victim's plight appear across a broad range of political persuasion. Having considered the effect of the author's exile on a popular novel by Germaine de Staël (1766–1817), *Corinne, or Italy* (1807), which inspired a sensational painting by Gérard, I argue that personal, rather than political, considerations drew Delacroix to exile motifs. This was in contrast to the expatriate poet Mickiewicz, who viewed the wandering of the Polish diaspora as a holy pilgrimage that would upend the European political order. The discussion then turns to innovative visual representations of two scriptural narratives pertaining to expulsion. Paintings of Hagar and Ishmael in the wilderness, by Navez, Corot, Jean Murat, (1807–63), and Jean-François Millet (1814–75), exhibit a sense of peril and desperation alien to old master antecedents; sculptures of Cain, by Antoine Étex (1808–98), and Henri de Triqueti (1803–74), offer contrasting interpretations of the first murderer's banishment. The chapter concludes with Hugo's cultivation of a public, heroic identity (in verse and in staged photographs) during the two decades, when (like Quinet) he chose exile over residence in Paris under the dictatorship (1852–70) of Napoleon III (1808–73).

Among the topics treated in this book, the hypnotic spell cast by Napoleon is the most familiar to historians of art. Addressing the shape-shifting capacity of imagery, whether in art or in print, that spoke to the void opened by his absence, the final chapters reconsider this phenomenon. Chapter 4 ("He's Not Dead!") sets forth the malleability and tenacity of the Napoleonic legend in the face of the emperor's defeat, exile, and death. It opens with contrast between the glamorizing of Napoleon in the fullness of his vitality and power (by Gros) and his vilification in defeat (by Byron and Chateaubriand). Separating the partisan sentimentality of Horace Vernet (1789–1863) from the compassionate curiosity of Théodore Géricault (1791–1824), the chapter adds its own stamp to the well-worked theme of Napoleon's unshakable grasp. Examining Napoleon's image in the aftermath of the ceremonial return of his remains to Paris in 1840, as embodied in the privately commissioned monument by François Rude (1784–1855), *Napoleon Awakening to Immortality* (1845–47), I consider other fictive guises in which the emperor appears in the 1840s. These manifest kinship between the cult of Napoleon and Catholic reverence, whether in the identification of the emperor as successor to Christ, or in fictive characterization of the exiled Bonaparte as a fervent Catholic. The chapter concludes with the resurgent triumph of Bonapartism through the coup d'état of the imperial nephew, Louis-Napoléon Bonaparte (1851), and the subsequent verse denunciations of the usurper by the exiled Hugo—formerly one of the principal voices of the Napoleon cult.

Having considered two famous works of fiction from the July Monarchy freighted with frustrated longing for imperial glory—Alfred de Vigny's *Military Servitude and Grandeur* (*Servitude et grandeur militaires*, 1836) and Musset's *La Confession d'un enfant du siècle*—Chapter 5 (Heroism Lost) proposes that the disaffection afflicting France between Waterloo and midcentury is embodied in a constellation of imagery that I term "the anti-heroic mode." Featuring self-absorbed, brooding, enervated, despairing, defeated, wounded, somnolent, or displaced figures, this mode is not limited to subjects that pertain to national loss, for example the 1812 retreat from Russia (a sensitive topic in post-Napoleonic France) treated by, among others, Théodore Géricault (Figure 5.2). An anti-heroic tenor is also conveyed by works seemingly unrelated to the recent past. An example is Étex's colossal group of the banished Cain and his disconsolate family, which caused a sensation as a plaster at the Salon of 1833 and was re-exhibited six years later in marble (Figures 3.18 and 3.19). Disdain for religion hardly dampened Heine's enthusiasm for the expressive character and timeliness of Étex's biblical sculpture:

> This is a group with symmetrical and even monumental beauty, full of antediluvian character, and at the same time with a completely modern meaning.

> Cain, with his wife and his child, is there, accepting destiny, absorbed, without thought, petrified in repose without consolation.[48]

That Heine discerned a "completely modern meaning" in a downbeat, inert portrayal of a fellow exile is a telling indication of the contemporaneity of the anti-heroic mode. Such linkage of images dissimilar in subject and style, yet fraternal in mood and period flavor, emulates an approach drawn from literary studies—the pursuit of intertextuality, whereby a text is commented on, imitated, parodied, or refuted in an alternate category of discourse.[49] This interdisciplinary analogy provides a useful conceptual framework for adumbrating unexpected kinship, such as that between a lithograph of the Grande Armée in bedraggled retreat and a sculpted evocation of the first murderer's dark inner life. Nor was religious art impervious to the anti-heroic mode, as Delacroix, Chassériau, and a host of others were drawn to a markedly unheroic episode in Christ's ministry—the ordeal at Gethsemane.

The anti-heroic mode's varied thematic and expressive repertoire distinguish it from a larger set with which it intersects—representations of melancholy. That stock motif has a long pre-Romantic genealogy extending well beyond Albrecht Dürer's *Melencolia I* (1514), into distant time.[50] William Hauptman's international compendium of melancholic images in late eighteenth- and nineteenth-century European art reveals a pervasiveness that borders on banality. Subsequently, the theme of melancholy in the visual arts was traced across a vast chronological expanse, reaching from antiquity to the present, in an ambitious exhibition organized by Jean Clair.[51] In contrast to the blue imagery gathered by Hauptman and by the Clair team, the term anti-heroic mode, as employed in this study, offers greater latitude of affect and circumstance, ranging from hypothermia to homesickness.

Despite its chameleon mutability, the anti-heroic mode is largely circumscribed by the late Revolution and the Second Republic; it cannot be mapped onto the far-flung temporal and geographic coordinates framing the surveys of Hauptman and Clair. Nor is the anti-heroic mode congruent with a kindred category: representations of mourning. Common coin in the history of art, these appear with particular frequency in the twilight of the long eighteenth century. As Margaret Fields Denton and Alison Hafera demonstrate, there was great interest in France, circa 1800, in sentimental portrayals of grief.[52] Coinciding with the reform of cemetery design and burial practice, the multiplication of such subjects represents the swansong of the Enlightenment taste for *la douce mélancolie* (sweet melancholy).[53] Gifted with *sensibilité*, connoisseurs of that bittersweet strain savored transparent effusion of sorrow. Thus, Denis Diderot (1713–84) delighted in the legible distress of *A Girl with a Dead Canary* exhibited by Jean-Baptiste Greuze (1725–1805) in the Salon of 1765 (Figure I.3): "When one first perceives this painting, one says: Delicious! If one pauses before it or comes back to it, one cries out: Delicious! Delicious!"[54] The anti-heroic mode, in contrast, favors opaque self-absorption, evoking tragedies that extend so far beyond the personal as to assume national or mythic import.[55] In view of the inductive, contextual research underlying its exposition, and given its inseparability from a troubled segment of French history, the concept of the anti-heroic mode is distant from Michael Fried's deductive, de-contextualized, and trans-historical model of an anti-theatrical, absorptive tradition stretching from the eighteenth century to Courbet and beyond.[56]

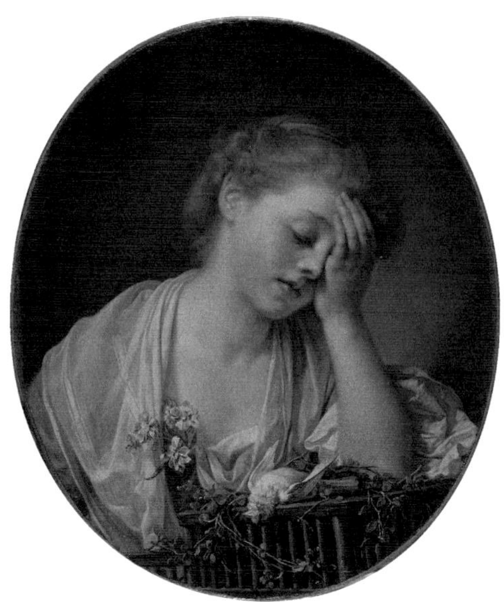

Figure I.3 Jean-Baptiste Greuze, *A Girl with a Dead Canary*, 1765, oil on canvas, 53.30 × 46 cm. Edinburgh, National Gallery of Scotland, Bequest of Lady Murray of Henderland, 1861. ©National Galleries of Scotland, Dist. RMN-Grand Palais/Art Resource, NY.

So timely was the anti-heroic mode, I contend, that its introversion and torpor could bleed into sensuous, escapist imagery remote from modern French history. From this unfamiliar vantage point, the chapter provides an entirely new reading of work from the 1830s and 1840s by Chassériau, a Franco-Caribbean Creole child of the century, whose work exhibits with unusual clarity the protean aspect of the anti-heroic mode.[57] Here, the argument takes a biographical turn. Drawing attention to the imperial heritage of the Chassériau family, and to the artist's painful childhood separation from his father (who had served Napoleon and remained dedicated to his memory), I reconsider a key painting exhibited in the Salon of 1842, *The Trojan Women* (*Les Troyennes*). I associate the destroyed painting with post-Waterloo elegiac discourse, revitalized two years earlier by the return of the emperor's remains. Viewed in relation to the anti-heroic mode, the long-recognized genealogical link between Chassériau and his Symbolist acolyte, Gustave Moreau (1826–98), appears in a fresh light.

Just as the imperial *tricolore* once flew over the lion's share of Europe, so too does the Napoleon bibliography seem boundless. Of this staggering list, the works most relevant to the present study are those addressing post-imperial mythologizing of the emperor.[58] The impact of the cult of Napoleon on visual culture is addressed in Michael Paul Driskel's monograph on the emperor's tomb and in Michael Marrinan's account of the political agenda of government initiative in the arts under the July Monarchy.[59] Sharing with those publications a contextual approach to a narrative in which partisan passions loom large, *Loss* departs from their overriding concern with official patronage, legitimization, and manipulation of popular sentiment. Delving deeply into Romantic literature, it explores sites of inner ferment as well as the public space of propaganda.

Returning to the topics of the book's preceding pages, an epilogue considers the renewed relevance acquired by the themes in question—as well as their transformation—during the late nineteenth and early twentieth centuries. In the foreground is a defeat no less devastating than those which collapsed Quinet's world. What Hugo termed *l'Année terrible* (*The Terrible Year*, 1870–71) featured catastrophic war with Prussia, loss of nearly all of Alsace and much of Lorraine, civil combat, mass execution, deportation, and exile. At issue are ways in which national calamity and disempowerment were reimagined, as in the prize-winning painting of the captive Hebrews in Babylon by Aimé-Nicolas Morot (1850–1913), and in the veneration of Napoleon as the "professor of energy" in *The Uprooted* (*Les Déracinés*, 1897)—the first installment in the trilogy, *The Novel of National Energy* by Maurice Barrès (1862–1923). Reopening the wound with which it began, *Loss* concludes with contrast between the harsh, world-weary, *fin-de-siècle* Catholic revival embodied in the suite of "Durtal" novels (1891–1903) by J.-K. Huysmans (1848–1907) and the post-revolutionary, sentimental return to faith advocated by Chateaubriand. Sketching the distinct ways in which the faith-famished Paul Gauguin (1848–1903) and the deeply Catholic Georges Rouault (1871–1958) each recoiled from the secularity and Positivism of the Third Republic, the book again exposes the indelible stain of modern France's founding trauma.

Motivated by an aspiration to extend the reach of interdisciplinary study of an era characterized by interchange among the sister arts and riven by political controversy, *Loss* engages a group of related questions: What visual and textual evidence—whether canonical or long forgotten—nuances our understanding of the sense of loss pervading French culture in the first half of the nineteenth century? How was religious art irrevocably altered following the Revolution's assault on Catholic tradition? What creative responses were elicited by exile in an era of intense nationalism? Do the collapse of the Empire and the absence of Napoleon resonate with art ostensibly unrelated to either national history or politics? These questions have led the research into uncharted territory. A study in national bereavement—an urgent theme at present—the book provides a new lens through which to view the coincidence of imagination and strife at the heart of French Romanticism.

Notes

1 "Ainsi les grandes invasions de 1814 et de 1815 avaient laissé dans ma mémoire un fond d'impressions, d'images à travers lesquelles j'entrevoyais toutes choses. L'écroulement d'un monde avait été ma première éducation." Edgar Quinet, *Histoire d'un enfant (Histoire de mes idées)* (Paris: Hachette, 1903), 154. Unless otherwise indicated, all translations herein are the author's.

2 For Quinet's reconsideration of his youth in light of the intense nationalism of his maturity, see Richard Howard Powers, *Edgar Quinet: A Study in French Patriotism* (Dallas, TX: Southern Methodist University Press, 1957), 8.

3 Edward Said, "Reflections on Exile" (1984), reprinted in *Altogether Elsewhere: Writers on Exile*, ed. Marc Robinson (New York: Harcourt Brace & Company, 1994), 139–40. I am grateful to Daniel R. Guernsey, for directing me to *The Phenomenology of Spirit* and to Hegel's lectures of the 1820s as sources for Said's reference.

4 From the preface (17 October 1833) to Heine's *The Salon*, reprinted in *Altogether Elsewhere*, ed. Robinson, 305.

5 For Toussaint Louverture, see Sudhir Hazareesingh, *Black Spartacus: The Epic Life of Toussaint Louverture* (New York: Farrar, Straus and Giroux, 2020); and David A. Bell, *Men on Horseback: The Power of Charisma in the Age of Revolution* (New York: Farrar, Straus and Giroux, 2020), chap. 4.

6 For a concise discussion of Quinet's exalted conception of France's historical destiny and religious mission, see Ceri Crossley, "Edgar Quinet and Messianic Nationalism in the Years Preceding 1848," in *1848: The Sociology of Literature, Proceedings of the Essex Conference on the Sociology of Literature, July 1977*, ed. Francis Barker et al., 265–76 (Essex: University of Essex, 1978).

7 See Henri Peyre, *What is Romanticism?* trans. Roda Roberts (University: University of Alabama Press, 1977, originally published 1971), chap. 9. For this topic, see also my "Resistance and Persistence: On the Fortunes and Reciprocal International Influences of French Romanticism," *Studies in Romanticism* 57, no. 4 (Winter 2018): 505–38.

8 See, for example, Nina M. Athanassoglou-Kallmyer, *Eugène Delacroix: Prints, Politics and Satire, 1814–1822* (New Haven, CT: Yale University Press, 1991); Robert Rosenblum, *Transformations in Late Eighteenth-Century Art* (Princeton, NJ: Princeton University Press, 1969); Richard Thomson, *The Troubled Republic: Visual Culture and Social Debate in France, 1889–1900* (New Haven, CT: Yale University Press), 2004; and Beth S. Wright, *Painting and History during the French Restoration: Abandoned by the Past* (Cambridge: Cambridge University Press, 1997).

9 See, for example, Paul Bénichou, *L'École du désenchantement: Sainte-Beuve, Nodier, Musset, Nerval, Gautier* (Paris: Gallimard, 1992); Frank Paul Bowman, *Le Christ des barricades (1789–1848)* (Paris: Les Éditions du Cerf, 1987); Ceri Crossley, *French Historians and Romanticism: Thierry, Guizot, the Saint-Simonians, Quinet, Michelet* (London: Routledge 2002); and Maurice Samuels, *The Spectacular Past: Popular History and the Novel in Nineteenth-Century France* (Ithaca, NY: Cornell University Press, 2004).

10 See, for example, Michèle Hannoosh, *Jules Michelet: Writing Art and History in Nineteenth-Century France* (University Park: Penn State University Press, 2019); and *Les Lieux de mémoire*, ed. Pierre Nora, 3 volumes in 7 parts (Paris: Gallimard, 1984–86).

11 "Independent of the individual, cultural or historical context in which melancholia appears, any idea of 'loss' always involves a temporal dimension...." *The Literature of Melancholia: Early Modern to Postmodern*, ed. Martin Middeke and Christina Wald (New York: Palgrave Macmillan, 2011), 4.

12 Stephen Bann, *Romanticism and the Rise of History* (New York: Twayne Publishers, 1995), 6–7.

13 The term "archive glutton" is employed by Frank Paul Bowman in *French Romanticism: Intertextual and Interdisciplinary Readings* (Baltimore, MD: Johns Hopkins University Press, 1990), 202. For Michelet's exalted conception of the historian's vocation, see Paul Bénichou, *Le Temps des prophètes: Doctrines de l'âge romantique* (Paris: Gallimard, 1977), 523–30. For the important place of the visual arts in Michelet's thought and writing, see Hannoosh, *Jules Michelet*. For a recent account of the Versailles commissions, see *Louis-Philippe et Versailles*, ed. Valérie Bajou (Versailles: Château de Versailles in association with Somogy, Paris, 2018).

14 For a discussion of this preromantic outbreak of spleen, see Peyre, *What is Romanticism?* 22–5. D.G. Charlton also cautions against viewing the *mal du siècle* as a uniquely Romantic phenomenon. See "Prose Fiction," in *The French Romantics*, ed. D.G. Charlton. (Cambridge: Cambridge University Press, 1984), 1: 169.

15 For the death of Gros, the artist's declining critical fortunes, and his position within the post-Napoleonic art world, see Sébastien Allard and Marie-Claude Chaudonneret, *Le Suicide de Gros: Les Peintres de l'Empire et la generation romantique* (Paris: Gourcuff Gradenigo, 2010). Vigny's play was an outgrowth of his philosophical novel, *Stello*, published in 1832.

16 "Toute la maladie du siècle présent vient de deux causes; le peuple qui a passé par 93 et par 1814 porte au coeur deux blessures. Tout ce qui était n'est plus; tout ce qui sera n'est pas encore. Ne cherchez pas ailleurs le secret de nos maux." Alfred de Musset, *La Confession d'un enfant du siècle*, ed. Sylvain Ledda (Paris: Flammarion, 2010), 80.

17 The phrase is from Ceri Crossley, *Edgar Quinet (1803–1875): A Study in Romantic Thought* (Lexington, KY: French Forum, 1983), 13.
18 "Ce n'est pas la faiblesse de notre pensée qui nous tue; c'est son excès ... c'est le poids de l'avenir à supporter dans le vide du present." Edgar Quinet, "Ahasvérus," *Revue des deux mondes* (October 1833): 10, quoted in Crossley, *Edgar Quinet*, 13.
19 Darcy Grimaldo Grigsby, *Extremities: Painting Empire in Post-revolutionary France* (New Haven, CT: Yale University Press, 2002), 4.
20 Peter Fritzsche, "The Melancholy of History: The French Revolution and European Historiography," in *The Literature of Melancholia*, ed. Middeke and Wald, 119, 122–3; and Fritzsche, *Stranded in the Present: Modern Time and the Melancholy of History* (Cambridge, MA: Harvard University Press, 2004), 8, 96–102. I am grateful to Michèle Hannoosh for bringing these publications to my attention.
21 See Wright, *Painting and History*, chap. 3.
22 A partial list includes *Un musée révolutionnaire: Le Musée des Monuments français d'Alexandre Lenoir*, ed. Geneviève Bresc-Bautier and Béatrice de Chancel-Bardelot (Paris: Musée du Louvre in association with Hazan, Paris, 2016); Alexandra Stara, *The Museum of French Monuments, 1795–1816: 'Killing Art to Make History'* (Farnham: Ashgate, 2013); Wright, *Painting and History*, 49–58; and Andrew McClellan, *Inventing the Louvre: Art, Politics, and the Origins of the Modern Museum in Eighteenth-Century Paris* (Cambridge: Cambridge University Press,1994), 155–97.
23 See Suzanne Glover Lindsay, *Funerary Arts and Tomb Cult—Living with the Dead in France, 1750–1870* (Farnham: Ashgate, 2012; and idem, "Mummies and Tombs: Turenne, Napoléon, and Death Ritual," *Art Bulletin* 82, no. 3 (September 2000): 476–502.
24 For the cycle of ten paintings, begun under Napoleon and completed under the Restoration (1811–22), see Todd Porterfield, "Resacralization through National History Painting: The Sacristy at Saint Denis, 1811–22," *Word and Image* 16 (January-March 2000): 31–44.
25 For this work, see Wright, *Painting and History*, 58–9 and n. 60; and Hugh Honour, *Romanticism* (New York: Harper & Row, 1979), 197–8 and 394.
26 "Saint-Denis est désert; l'oiseau l'a pris pour passage, l'herbe croît sur ses autels brisés; et au lieu du cantique de la mort, qui retentissait sous ses dômes, on n'entend plus que les gouttes de pluie qui tombent par son toit découvert, la chute de quelque pierre qui se détache de ses murs en ruine, ou le son de son horloge, qui va roulant dans les tombeaux vides et les souterrains d'dévastés." Chateaubriand, *Génie du christianisme*, ed. Maurice Regard (Paris: Gallimard, 1978), 939. In a note (XLVI to p. 939, on pp. 1195–208), Chateaubriand provides a detailed account of the exhumations that took place in Saint-Denis 6–8 August 1793, as recorded by a monk from the abbey. All quotations herein from the *Génie du christianisme* are from this edition.
27 For a gloss on the caricature, see Alix Chevallier et al., *Chateaubriand: Le Voyageur et l'homme politique* (Paris: Bibliothèque nationale, 1969), no. 342. The significance of the inscription on the dog's collar (TRUL) has yet to be deciphered.
28 "Whether or not Hugo actually wrote, in a notebook-diary he kept in 1816, 'I want to be Chateaubriand or nothing,' he certainly thought it." Maurice Z. Shroder, *Icarus: The Image of the Artist in French Romanticism* (Cambridge, MA: Harvard University Press, 1961), 69 and n.16, quoting Adèle Foucher *Hugo, Victor Hugo raconté par un témoin de sa vie* (Paris, 1868), 1: 339.
29 See Bruno Foucart, *Le Renouveau de la peinture religieuse en France (1800–1860)* (Paris: Arthéna, 1987); and Michael Paul Driskel, *Representing Belief: Religion, Art, and Society in Nineteenth-Century France* (University Park: Penn State University Press, 1992). For a study comparable in approach to that of Foucart, see Michel Caffort, *Les Nazaréens français: Théorie et pratique de la peinture religieuse au XIXe siècle* (Rennes: Presses Universitaires de Rennes, 2009).
30 See Michael S. Roth, *Memory, Trauma, and History: Essays on Living with the Past* (New York: Columbia University Press, 2012), xviii. For this point, and for alerting me to the publications of Roth, I am grateful to Scott Sprenger.
31 I thank Daniel R. Guernsey for this point.
32 David A. Bell, *The Cult of the Nation in France: Inventing Nationalism, 1680–1800* (Cambridge, MA: Harvard University Press, 2001), 43.

33 Thomas Kselman, "Religion and French Identity: The Origins of the *Union Sacrée*," in *Many Are Chosen: Divine Election and Western Nationalism*. Harvard Theological Studies 38, ed. William R. Hutchison and Hartmut Lehmann (Harrisburg, PA: Trinity Press International, 1994), 57–8.

34 Charles-Gilbert Romme, "Modèle des sentiments qui doivent animer les citoyens des campagnes," *Feuille Villageoise*, no. 43 (21 July 1791), 301, quoted in Albert Mathiez, *Les Origines des Cultes révolutionnaires (1789–1792)* (Paris; G. Bellais, 1904), 78.

35 See D.G. Charlton, *Secular Religions in France, 1815–1870* (Hull: University of Hull and London: Oxford University Press, 1963); and Paul Bénichou, *Le Sacre de l'écrivain, 1750–1830: Essai sur l'avènement d'un pouvoir spirituel laïque dans la France modern*, 2nd ed. (Paris: Librairie José Corti, 1985). See also Roger Pearson, *Unacknowledged Legislators: The Poet as Lawgiver in Post-Revolutionary France* (Oxford: Oxford University Press, 2016).

36 See Robert Rosenblum, *Modern Painting and the Northern Romantic Tradition: Friedrich to Rothko* (New York: Harper & Row, 1975); and idem, "The Abstract Sublime," *ARTnews* 59 (January 1961): 38ff.

37 See Thomas Crow, *No Idols: The Missing Theology of Art* (Sydney: Power Publications, 2017). I am grateful to the author for bringing this book to my attention.

38 For a thoughtful engagement with secularization from an international perspective, see Owen Chadwick, *The Secularization of the European Mind in the Nineteenth Century* (Cambridge: Cambridge University Press, 1975).

39 See Lee Johnson, *The Paintings of Eugène Delacroix: A Critical Catalogue*, 7 vols. (Oxford: Clarendon Press, 1981–2002); and Eugène Delacroix, *Journal*, ed. Michèle Hannoosh, 2 vols. (Paris: José Corti, 2009). For recent bibliographies, see Sébastien Allard et al., *Delacroix* (Paris: Musée du Louvre, in association with Éditions Hazan, Paris, 2018); and Barthélémy Jobert, *Delacroix*, new and expanded ed. (Princeton, NJ: Princeton University Press, 2018).

40 "Partout ... un intérêt généreux s'attache au pas de l'exilé; on s'émeut à sa vue, et c'est alors surtout qu'on sent combien il est à plaindre celui qui doit traîner son existence sur une terre étrangère, loin de la tendre mère qui le porta dans son sein et le nourrit de son lait, loin d'un père à cheveux blancs qui se penche vers la tombe et qui craint de mourir sans avoir revu son fils!" *Encyclopédie des gens du monde. Répertoire universel des sciences, des lettres et des arts, avec des notices sur les principales familles historiques et sur les personnages célèbres, morts et vivans. Par une société de savans, de littérateurs et d'artistes, français et étrangers* (Paris: Treuttel and Würtz, 1838), 10: 350.

41 This statement is attributed to Bonald in Pierre Larousse's *Grand Dictionnaire du XIXe siècle*, as quoted in Sylvie Aprile, "De l'émigration à la proscription, regards sur l'écriture de l'exil au XIXe," in *Mémorialistes de l'exil: Émigrer, écrire, survivre*, ed. François Jacob and Henri Rossi (Paris: L'Harmattan, 2003), 21. The *Grand Dictionnaire* was published 1866–76, with two supplements (1878 and 1888).

42 "C'est peut-être le souris d'une mère, d'un père, d'une soeur; c'est peut-être le souvenir du vieux précepteur qui nous éleva, des jeunes compagnons de notre enfance ... enfin ce sont les circonstances les plus simples, si l'on veut même, les plus triviales ... le clocher de l'église qu'on voyait au-dessus des arbres, l'if du cimetière, le tombeau gothique ...." Chateaubriand, *Génie du christianisme*, 601.

43 Bell, *The Cult of the Nation in France*, 38.

44 "It is good for us to encounter troubles and adversities from time to time, for trouble often compels a man to search his own heart. It reminds him that he is an exile here, and that he can put his trust in nothing in this world." Thomas à Kempis, *The Imitation of Christ*, trans. and ed. Leo Sherley-Price (Harmondsworth: Penguin Books, 1952), 39.

45 Chateaubriand, *Génie du christianisme*, 715.

46 See Fernand Baldensperger, *Le Mouvement des idées dans l'Émigration française (1789–1815)* (Paris: Plon-Nourrit, 1924), 1: 311.

47 See James Henry Rubin, "Oedipus, Antigone and Exiles in Post-Revolutionary French Painting," *Art Quarterly* 36, no. 3 (Autumn 1973): 141–71; Mehdi Korchane, *Pierre Guérin 1774–1833* (Paris: Mare & Martin, 2018), 64–84; idem, *Figures de l'exil sous la Révolution, De Bélisaire à Marcus Sextus* (Vizille: Musée de la Révolution française-Domaine de

Vizille, 2016); and Thomas Crow, *Emulation: David, Drouais, and Girodet in the Art of Revolutionary France*, rev. ed. (New Haven, CT: Yale University Press and Los Angeles: Getty Research Institute, 2006), 205–11; 232–6.

48 "C'est un groupe d'une beauté symétrique et même monumentale, plein du caractère antédiluvien, et en même temps d'une signification toute moderne. Caïn, avec sa femme et son enfant, est là, acceptant le destin, absorbé, sans pensée, pétrifié dans un repos sans consolation." Heinrich Heine, "Salon de 1833," in *Allemands et Français* (Paris: Michel Lévy, 1868), 231.

49 For an outstanding example of that approach in action, see Bowman, *French Romanticism*.

50 According to Matthew Bell, "the idea of melancholia is around 2,500 years old at least." *Melancholia: The Western Malady* (Cambridge: Cambridge University Press, 2014), 2.

51 See William Hauptman, "The Persistence of Melancholy in Nineteenth-Century Art: The Iconography of a Motif," 2 vols., Ph.D. diss., Pennsylvania State University, 1975; and *Mélancolie: Genie et folie en Occident*, ed. Jean Clair (Paris: Réunion des musées nationaux, in association with Gallimard, Paris, 2005).

52 See Margaret Fields Denton "Death in French Arcady: Nicolas Poussin's 'The Arcadian Shepherds' and Burial Reform in France c. 1800," *Eighteenth-Century Studies* 36, no. 2 (Winter 2003): 195–216; idem, "Antoine-Jean Gros' *Portrait de Christine Boyer* and Jean-Frédéric Schall's *Pensée sur la brièveté de la vie*: Private Grief and Public Rhetoric in Post-revolutionary French Painting," *Gazette des beaux-arts*, 6th ser. 128 (September 1996): 103–20; idem (under the name Margaret Denton Smith), "The Elegy of Death in French Painting at the End of the Eighteenth and Beginning of the Nineteenth Centuries." PhD diss., New York University, 1986; and Alison Hafera, "Visual Meditations on Mourning and Melancholia in France, 1790–1830," PhD diss., University of North Carolina, 2015.

53 See Guillaume Faroult, "'La Douce Mélancolie,' selon Watteau et Diderot: Représentations mélancoliques dans les arts en France au XVIIIe siècle," in *Mélancolie: genie et folie en Occident*, ed. Clair, 274–94.

54 *Diderot on Art*, trans. and ed. John Goodman, int. Thomas Crow (New Haven, CT: Yale University Press, 1995), 1: 98.

55 This point aligns with Lloyd Bishop's view that the Romantic *mal du siècle* transcends the personal and is inseparable from the facts of its historical context. See *The Romantic Hero and his Heirs in French Literature,* American University Studies, series 2: Romance Languages and Literature 10 (New York: Peter Lang, 1984), 9–12.

56 See Michael Fried, *Absorption and Theatricality: Painting & Beholder in the Age of Diderot* (Berkeley: University of California Press, 1980); and idem, *Courbet's Realism* (Chicago, IL: University of Chicago Press, 1990).

57 I was introduced to the work of Chassériau in a seminar on the art of the July Monarchy offered by Robert Rosenblum at the Institute of Fine Arts, New York University in 1979.

58 Sudhir Hazareesingh, *The Legend of Napoleon* (London: Granta, 2004) is especially pertinent. See also Philip Dwyer, *Napoleon: Passion, Death and Resurrection, 1815–1840* (London: Bloomsbury, 2018); Sylvain Pagé, *Le Mythe napoléonien: De Las Cases à Victor Hugo* (Paris: CNRS éditions, 2013); Natalie Petiteau, *Napoléon de la mythologie à l'histoire* (Paris: Éditions du Seuil, 1999); and the classic study, J. Lucas-Dubreton, *Le Culte de Napoléon, 1815–1848* (Paris: Albin Michel, 1960). For popular imagery, see Barbara Ann Day-Hickman, *Napoleonic Art: Nationalism and the Spirit of Rebellion in France (1815–1848)* (Newark: University of Delaware Press and London: Associated University Presses, 1999).

59 See Michael Paul Driskel, *As Befits a Legend: Building a Tomb for Napoleon, 1840–1861* (Kent, OH: Kent State University Press, 1993); and Michael Marrinan, *Painting Politics for Louis-Philippe: Art and Ideology in Orléanist France, 1830–1848* (New Haven, CT: Yale University Press, 1988). For an insightful account of the international artistic consequences of the eclipse of French hegemony, see Thomas Crow, *Restoration: The Fall of Napoleon in the Course of European Art, 1812–1820* (Princeton, NJ: Princeton University Press, 2018).

1 Amid the Debris of Our Temples

Vandalism and De-Christianization

Merely one year before First Consul Napoleon Bonaparte reestablished Catholicism in France, visitors to the Salon of 1800 could view a remarkable example of contempt for the nation's Christian heritage. Louis-François Petit-Radel (1739–1818), an architect with the title of inspector general of civil structures, exhibited a guide to the "Destruction of a Church in the Gothic Style, by Means of Fire":

> In order to minimize the dangers which this kind of operation entails, the piers are to be hollowed, near their bases, at a height of two stone courses. As stones are removed, half their volume is replaced by dry wood. This is continued throughout. Kindling is then inserted, and fire set to the wood. When enough of the wood has burned, it gives way under the weight of the masonry, and the whole structure collapses in less than ten minutes.[1]

This dispassionate language, so at odds with its latent fury, was of a piece with the detachment of the architect, whose entry above was accompanied by two others—an interior of an Egyptian temple and a Roman gallery leading up to a naumachia (i.e., an arena in which naval battles were staged). As noted in the Salon guidebook: "The author wished to present, in these three pictures, the parallel between Roman, Egyptian, and Gothic architecture."[2]

That a lesson in the destruction of a medieval monument could figure in a demonstration of archaeological erudition not only normalizes anti-ecclesiastical violence, but also speaks of hatred for the monarchy from which the Church was inseparable. In the autumn of 1793, great effort went into a brutal act of separation in central Paris. With the Reign of Terror dawning, scaffolding more than 15 meters high was erected to reach the 28 polychrome statues (each of 3.5 meters) of kings of Judah adorning the façade of Notre-Dame. Mistaken for French monarchs since the late thirteenth century, the Old Testament royals were zealously set upon.[3] When obliteration of the finials of crowns and scepters was deemed insufficient, the figures were removed and lowered—an arduous operation (December 1793–September 1794) supervised by the architect Bernard Poyet (1742–1824). In 1977, a cache of 21 severed heads of these ancestors of Christ was unearthed with more than 300 other sculptural fragments during excavation at the stables of the hôtel Moreau (20, rue de la Chaussée-d'Antin), which had belonged to Jean-Baptiste Lakanal-Dupuget (brother of the deputy to the Convention, Joseph Lakanal). I show one of the salvaged items (Figure 1.1).[4]

DOI: 10.4324/9781003184737-2

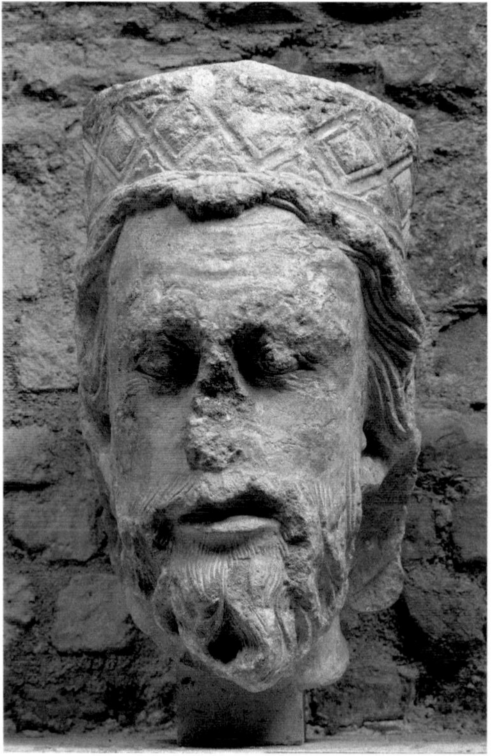

Figure 1.1 *King of Judah*, head no. 12, formerly Notre-Dame cathedral, Paris, West Façade, Gallery of Kings, 1220–30, limestone, 67 × 43 × 44 cm. Paris, Musée de Cluny, Musée national du Moyen-Âge. Photo: René-Gabriel Ojéda. © RMN-Grand Palais/Art Resource, NY.

Lakanal-Dupuget's architect apparently acquired the rubble as fill in March 1796. Previously, according to the Parisian chronicler Louis-Sébastien Mercier (1740–1814), it had remained heaped behind the cathedral, serving as a public latrine.[5] Bearing witness to anti-monarchic rage, the battered heads speak of tacit acknowledgment, on the part of Poyet and the mason he directed, of the symbolic power of these royal cathedral guardians.

In the year that Petit-Radel's leveling procedure was exhibited in the Salon, it was successfully tested on the early fourteenth-century Parisian church of Saint-Jean-en-Grève in the parish of the Hôtel-de-Ville. Taken out of ecclesiastical service in 1790, the church was demolished (1797–1800). Its demolition was recorded by the preeminent specialist in ruins, Hubert Robert (1733–1808; Figure 1.2).[6] Combustion glows and smokes at the base of an exposed pier as the asymmetrical bell towers of the west end await obliteration. Diminutive spectators occupying a shaded foreground *repoussoir* share our view from the east into the structure's receding bowels. Robert's conventionally scenic composition aestheticizes an event redolent with fanaticism. This sad memento anticipates the photographs of the charred remains of public buildings (such Saint-Jean-en-Grève's neighbor, the Hôtel de Ville) that would provide a tourist

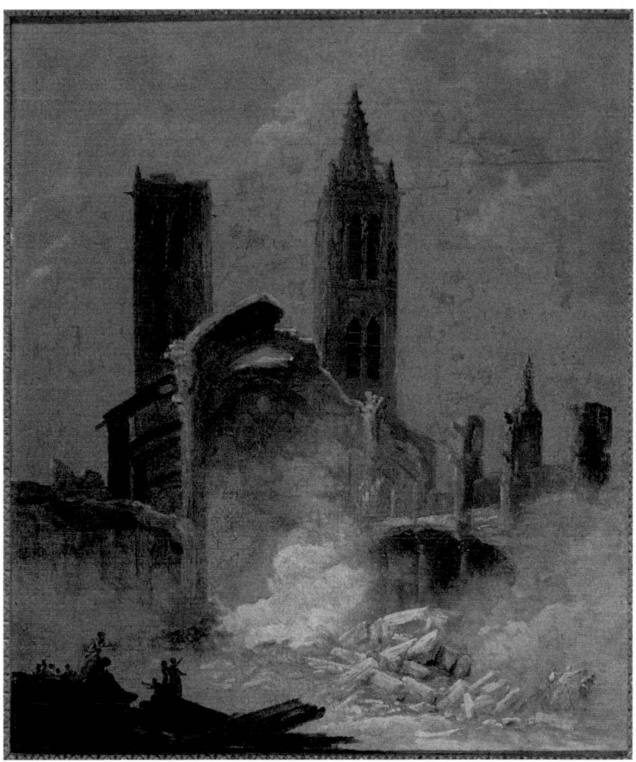

Figure 1.2 Hubert Robert, *The Demolition of the Church of Saint-Jean-en-Grève in 1800*, ca. 1800, oil on canvas, 80 × 71 cm. Paris, Musée Carnavalet. CCO Paris Musées/Musée Carnavalet.

attraction in post-Commune Paris. On 22 December 1801, a newspaper marveled at the efficiency and safety with which the bell tower of the church of Saint-André-des-Arts (where Voltaire had been baptized) had succumbed to the same technique: with minimal dispersion of stone, it was reported, the tower fell within its cramped setting 10 minutes after the fire was set.[7]

Petit-Radel's disregard for medieval architecture was longstanding. In response to an inquiry from the revolutionary government regarding the conservation of the Abbey church of Saint-Denis, he proposed demolition of the vaulted roof so as to permit conversion of the structure to a covered, enclosed market.[8] Even before the Revolution, he nursed antipathy toward the Gothic style. In 1784, he brought the late Gothic Parisian church of Saint-Médard up to date by fitting out the choir columns with neo-classical fluting and Doric capitals, sounding an anachronistic note beneath the groin vaulting.[9]

Anticipating the frightful recipe displayed in the Salon of 1800, Petit-Radel's remodeling of Saint-Médard also foreshadowed revolutionary de-Christianization. This campaign began in September 1793, climaxed in the spring of 1794, abated between February 1795 and the autumn of 1797, and resurged from September 1797 to December 1799.[10] In the heady days of the early Revolution, notwithstanding resentment of the wealth, dysfunction, and exploitative aspect of the clerical establishment, there was little evidence of either irreligion or denigration of Catholicism. Initially, government intrusion into Church affairs was guided by patriotic interest in state stewardship of worship, and a wish to respectfully position the established faiths within the new, revolutionary order. When, on 2 November 1789, the Constituent Assembly nationalized church property, the government assumed support of all aspects of ecclesiastical life, including churches, clergy, seminaries, teaching, and charity. Having dissolved all French monasteries and convents (February 1790), the Assembly promulgated the Civil Constitution of the Clergy (ratified 24 August 1790); this transformed French clerics into civil servants, henceforth to be elected by the laity, including nonbelievers. Well-meaning reform rapidly shaded into intolerance. Clergymen were compelled (by a decree, unwillingly signed by the king, 26 December 1790) to swear allegiance to the Civil Constitution.[11] Pursuant to a law of 26 August 1792, all *réfractaire* priests (i.e., those who refused the oath) were required to leave France within 15 days or be deported to French Guiana. Legal coercion preluded mob violence. Three bishops and 220 priests were among the victims when, amid war hysteria, some 1400 Parisian prison inmates suspected of opposition to the Revolution were massacred on 2–4 September 1792.

On 10 November 1793, shortly after a decree (23 October) required the complete removal of the sculptures of biblical kings from the facade of Notre-Dame, members of the Convention attended a Festival of Reason staged inside the cathedral that featured an opera actress personifying Liberty. A month later (23 November), the Commune of Paris ordered that all churches be closed. By the spring of 1794, most churches that remained open had been repurposed as temples of Reason. Representing the Convention in a crusade against religious fanaticism, superstition, and the "selfish rich" in the *départements* of Nièvre and Allier in central France, Joseph Fouché (1759–1820) considered de-Christianization essential to the Revolution's mission of moral regeneration.[12] Ever mindful of the importance of symbols, this former Oratorian led a dance in the town of Moulins around a bonfire of chasubles, copes and nun's veils; on 10 October 1793, he decreed that churches be stripped of their ornaments and that cemeteries be inscribed "DEATH IS AN ETERNAL SLEEP." In the *département* of Nord alone, 425 churches and 60 chapels were destroyed in two years.[13]

In view of this persecution, it is hardly surprising that the clerical corps was decimated during the 1790s. As many as 20,000 of the approximately 115,000 priests active before the Revolution are believed to have abandoned their ministry; another 30,000 either emigrated or were deported.[14] That so many managed to hold on speaks to the resilience of worship, whose imperatives are no less universal than those of sports, music, and picture making. De-Christianization met strong popular resistance, and the downfall of the radicals led by Maximilien Robespierre (1758–94) heralded a Catholic revival strengthened by the revolutionary ideals of popular sovereignty and religious liberty.[15] Nor was the Reign of Terror uniformly hostile to religion. Robespierre detested atheism, advocated religious tolerance, and, in accord with revolutionary precedent, venerated the Supreme Being—reference to whom was included in each iteration of the Declaration of Rights of Man and Citizen heading the Revolution's three ephemeral constitutions.[16]

The cult of the Supreme Being stemmed from the Enlightenment's deist legacy, most famously embodied in "The Profession of Faith of the Savoyard Vicar," which occupies a sizeable portion of Jean-Jacques Rousseau's *Émile, or On Education* (1762). There, reference to the Being (*Être*) is employed interchangeably with God (*Dieu*). Through the Savoyard vicar's exhortation of the young Émile, Rousseau (1712–78) proposed a tolerant, natural religion of the heart, unconcerned with transcendence, salvation or damnation. This theology (for which the author was condemned by the Sorbonne and the Parlement of Paris) was institutionalized by Robespierre in 1793. On 8 June 1794 (just weeks before the execution of "the Incorruptible"), the Cult of the Supreme Being was celebrated in a vast pageant staged by Jacques-Louis David.[17] Notwithstanding the magic of David's choreography, it is hardly surprising that a creed so intangible and doctrinally spare did not endure. The short-lived Cult of the Supreme Being was succeeded by a second monotheistic revolutionary religion, Theophilanthropy, first celebrated in January 1797. Neither this nor the *Culte décadaire* (established by laws and a decree in August and September 1798)—which marked the ten-day weeks of the revolutionary calendar with patriotic festivals celebrating stirring themes ranging from maternal tenderness to martyrs of liberty—could survive outside of the ideological hothouse of the 1790s.

The Concordat

Napoleon's coup d'état of 18 Brumaire (9 November 1799) put paid to the Revolution, and Catholicism officially returned to France on 15 July 1801 with the conclusion of secret negotiations for the Concordat.[18] Fruit of 21 drafts, this treaty between the first consul and Pope Pius VII (1742–1829) proclaimed Catholicism the religion of the great majority of the French people, but (to the pontiff's disappointment) denied that it was either the state religion or the sole protected faith. Guaranteeing liberty of religion, asserting the public nature of worship, and providing for state salaries to the clergy, the Concordat required all ecclesiastics to swear allegiance to the government; to report conspiracy against the state; and to lead solemn and public prayer for the Republic and the consuls. These assertions of governmental prerogative were accompanied by a provision making permanent a revolutionary legacy: the pope renounced all claim to nationalized Church property. All of this was consistent with the Janus-faced aspect of Napoleonic policy, which harkened back to *ancien régime* tradition while retaining innovations of the Revolution. Motivated by politics rather than piety, Napoleon's wish to establish official relations with the Holy See reflected the conviction of the first consul and his entourage that religion is a social necessity.

Notwithstanding its recognition of Catholicism, the Concordat initially appeared to repudiate a key French ecclesiastical tradition, Gallicanism. Attaining its apogee under Louis XIV, Gallicanism stood for royal prerogative in Church matters such that, for example, the pope could not intervene between king and clergy, and papal edicts and the rulings of Church councils could not be published without the monarch's approval.[19] In contrast, the Concordat invested the pope with the authority to dismiss all French bishops and archbishops, whether those who had taken the ultra-Gallican constitutional oath or *réfractaires* appointed prior to the Revolution. Yet any semblance of Vatican control over French Church affairs was illusory. Authority to dismiss high clerics was unwillingly accepted, as Pius VII was compelled to remove members of the flock who had suffered for their loyalty in face of the constitutional oath; this tabula rasa was demanded by Napoleon so that he could name an entirely new episcopacy. When the Concordat was announced (8 April 1802), it was accompanied by unilateral proclamation of Napoleon's 77 Organic Articles, which returned ecclesiastical autonomy to the French state with a vengeance and underscored the first consul's upper hand in the alliance. Accordingly, the Gallican Articles of 1682 were made an obligatory part of seminary curriculum.

During the course of his dictatorship, Napoleon would dominate the Vatican with increasing brutality. An uneasy witness of the imperial coronation (1804), Pius VII had little choice but to agree shortly before the ceremony that Bonaparte would break with tradition and place the crown on his own head—an arrogant gesture that David initially planned to include in his commemorative coronation painting (1805–07, Salon of 1808, Paris, Musée du Louvre).[20] The seriousness with which the artist considered the motif is indicated by a preparatory drawing squared-up for transfer to canvas (Figure 1.3).[21] Swathed in weighty robes, holding the crown aloft, and grasping his sword hilt, Napoleon projects heroic will. In contrast, the pope sits with hands in lap; his lightly delineated features and stooped posture speak of passive resignation—an attitude altered to one of blessing after the emperor purportedly remarked, "I didn't have him come all that way to do nothing."[22] In line with this expropriation of sacred authority, the *Imperial Catechism* (1806) proclaimed the emperor God's earthly representative; it demanded love and respect for Napoleon, as well as military service; and it declared that those who shirked their duties were transgressors of the divine order and worthy of eternal damnation. On 17 May 1809, Napoleon annexed the Papal States and the Vatican (accordingly, in 1811, the newborn imperial heir was named King of Rome). The pope responded with excommunication; in July, Pius VII literally

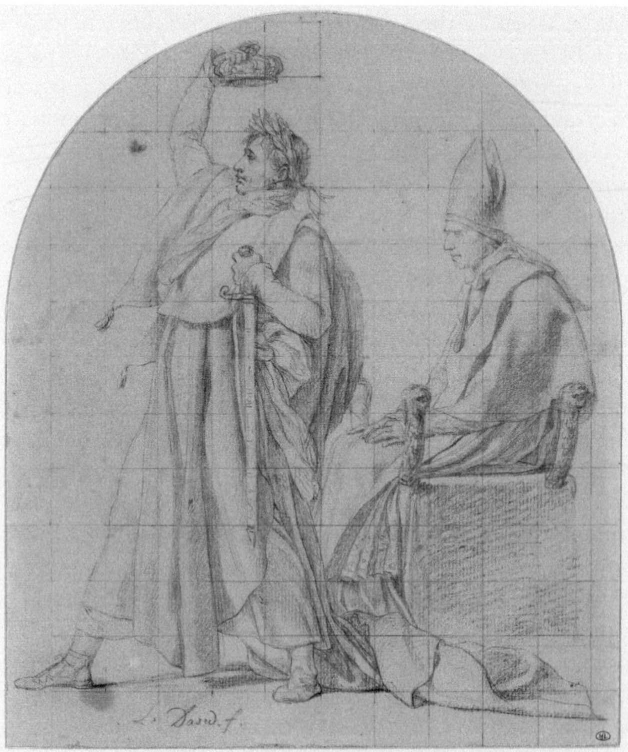

Figure 1.3 Jacques-Louis David, *Emperor Napoleon Crowning Himself*, ca. 1805, black crayon, black chalk, brown ink, graphite, squared, on beige paper, 29.2 × 25.2 cm. Paris, Musée du Louvre. Photo: Thierry Le Mage. © RMN-Grand Palais/Art Resource, NY.

became Napoleon's prisoner when, arrested and abducted from the Quirinale Palace, he was brought to Avignon, then Savona, and finally Fontainebleau, where he was compelled to accept a (soon-to-be-renounced) second Concordat (24 January 1813) that, among other provisions, required the pope's residence in France.

There was scant premonition of this troubled relationship on Easter, 18 April 1802, ten days after the proclamation of the Concordat. Jubilant piety was the official tone.

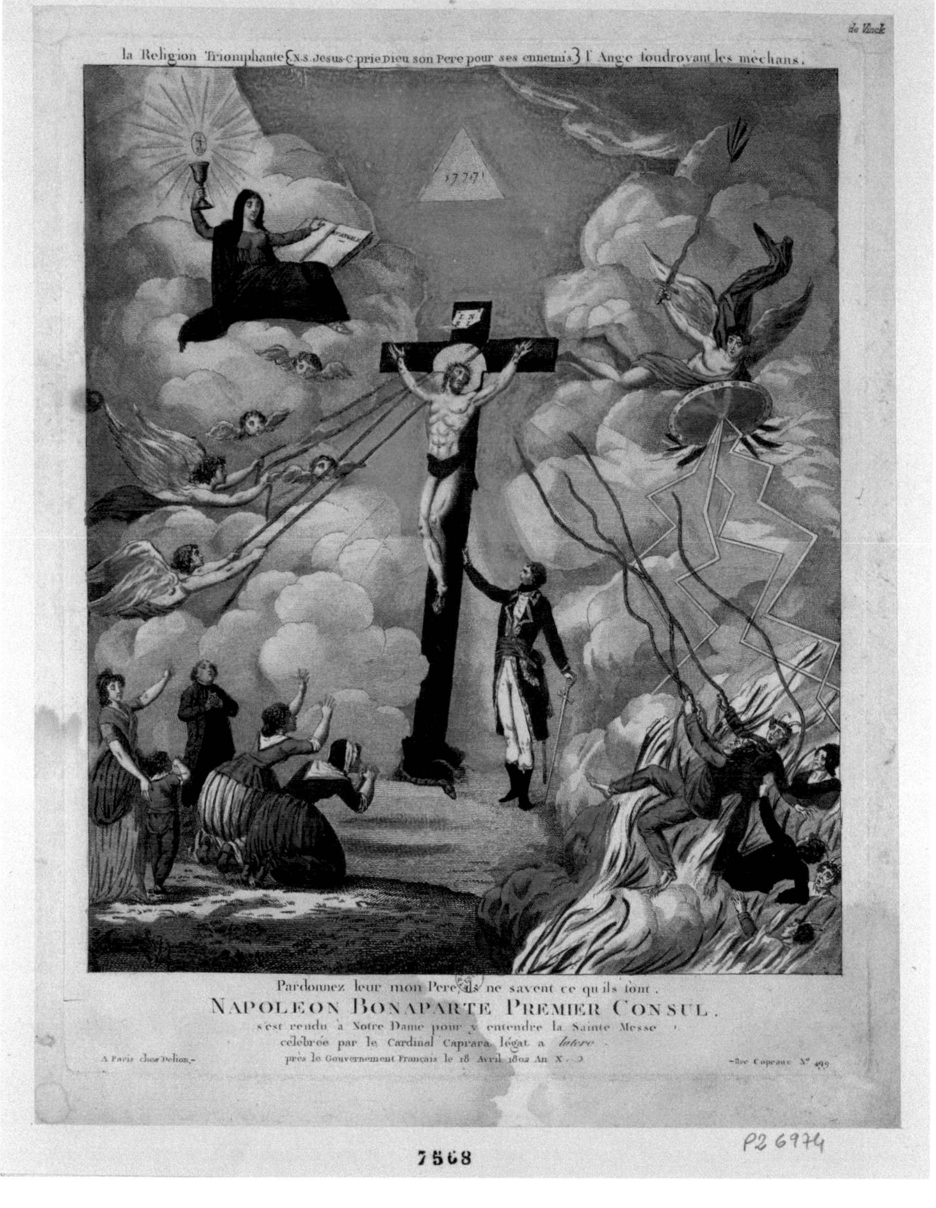

Figure 1.4 *Father Forgive Them, They Know Not What They Do*, ca. 1803, etching with watercolor and gouache, 26.9 × 22.8 cm. Paris, Bibliothèque nationale de France. Photo: BnF.

At a Mass in Notre-Dame said by the papal legate to the French government, Cardinal Giovanni Battista Caprara (1733–1810), and attended by the first consul, *Te Deum* was sung in gratitude for the Concordat and for the recent Treaty of Amiens, which had brought fragile peace with England. So profound a reversal of the dark years of de-Christianization left one of the speakers, the former émigré and Archbishop of Aix, Jean-de-Dieu Boisgelin de Cucé (1732–1804), recently appointed Archbishop of Tours, nearly breathless: "When providence calls me to fill a ministry long stifled in distance and silence, I look, I observe, I see this pulpit, this altar, this temple.... Oh heaven! What memories .... and on this day, what marvelous changes!"[23] The first consul's initiative in reestablishing the faith is allegorized in a hand-colored etching from the shop of Delion, which gives measure to the spiritual metamorphosis that had transpired since the Festival of the Supreme Being (Figure 1.4).[24] The crucified Christ, according to the text, prays for his foes: "Father forgive them, they know not what they do." Before a group of worshipers stands the elegantly costumed Bonaparte with drawn sword, effortlessly resting a supporting hand on the cross as it is raised by angels. At Christ's left (traditional site of the damned in representations of the Last Judgment), enemies of the faith are struck by lightning as they tumble into hellfire, their demolition ropes severed. Foremost among the condemned is a claw-footed sinner in green resembling Voltaire.[25] The haloed presence of Christ's body and blood, and the compellingly familiar format of the judgment of souls offer reassuring closure to an era of persecution.

Chateaubriand

On Good Friday, 14 April 1802, four days before the Mass at Notre-Dame, the *Spirit of Christianity, or Beauties of the Christian Religion* (*Génie du christianisme ou Beautés de la religion chrétienne*) was announced in the press and went on sale. This publication made a celebrity of Chateaubriand, a Breton aristocrat and former émigré, whose short novel, *Atala* (1801) had already created a sensation. Notwithstanding its ostentatious pedantry, the lengthy text was a best seller—a mark of the author's keen sense of timing. The book was conceived in exile. Following a sojourn in North America (April–December 1791) undertaken with aspirations of discovering the Northwest Passage, Chateaubriand joined the émigré forces and was wounded in the unsuccessful siege of Thionville staged by the Austrian and counter-revolutionary French coalition in 1792. The following year, he began a pinched residence in England, divided between misery in London and work as a French tutor in the Suffolk towns of Beccles and Bungay. Prior to his return to France, incognito, in early May 1800, he had undergone a religious conversion under the influence of fellow exile Louis de Fontanes (1757–1821).[26] With characteristic knack for drama, the author addressed an audience steeped in Rousseau when, in the preface to the first edition of the *Génie du christianisme,* he attributed (fictively, it seems) his conversion to the dying wish of his mother that he embrace the faith: "my conviction came from the heart: I wept, and I believed."[27]

Unqualified embrace of Catholicism separates the *Génie du christianisme* from the author's previous work written in exile, the *Historical Essay on the Relationship of Ancient and Modern Revolutions to the French Revolution* (1797), a monarchist critique of the French Revolution ambivalent toward faith. Heralding the end of Christianity, the *Essay* views religion as providing a necessary, palliative illusion. Chateaubriand's dedication of the *Essay* "to all the parties" did not please the ultra-royalist émigré community, which discerned insufficient condemnation of the Revolution—this despite the author's recoil from the Terror and his vehement denunciation of the baleful results of the monarchy's overthrow. In contrast, the pious *Génie du christianisme* was welcomed by the London émigrés, who may have heard Chateaubriand read excerpts from a draft as early as 1799.[28]

When the *Génie du christianisme* appeared," Chateaubriand explained at its reissue (1826–27) in his collected works,

> France was coming out of revolutionary chaos; all elements of society were thrown into confusion ....
>
> It was thus, so to speak, amid the debris of our temples that I published the *Génie du christianisme*, to summon back to those temples the ceremonies of worship and the servants of the altars.[29]

Haunted by loss of pre-revolutionary Catholic faith and institutions, the book appeals solely to the heart and the imagination, making little use of logical argument.[30] Abandoning the time-honored rationalist demonstration that Christianity is true, and that it is good because it comes from God, Chateaubriand holds that the divinity of the sole true religion is manifest in its benevolence, its appeal to tender feelings, and its fostering of beauty.[31] In accord with the sentimental and aesthetic basis of his argument, the author asserts the unparalleled inspirational force of the faith, contending that, as literature, the Old Testament is superior to Homer. Lacking first-hand familiarity with the Pentateuch and prophets, Chateaubriand's audience received this message as a revelation.[32] Chateaubriand was not alone in conveying enthusiasm for the Old Testament around 1800; David's faithful student Étienne-Jean Delécluze (1781–1863) later recalled that it was shared by the rebellious *Primitif* faction within the master's studio.[33] Unlike those pagan contemporaries, Chateaubriand extolled the Bible on ideological, as well as literary, grounds. Accordingly, the preface to the first edition of the *Génie du christianisme* draws a parallel between modern French and ancient Hebrew history. With feigned modesty, Chateaubriand compares himself to those who reconstructed the Temple following the Babylonian Captivity: "Obscure Israelite, I bring today my grain of sand."[34] This hopeful announcement of the return of *ancien régime* Catholicism was premature. Given that Napoleon regarded the Church as a malleable means to an imperial end, a genuine union of throne and altar remained chimerical until his fall brought the return of France's Catholic monarchy and an efflorescence of the sentiment conveyed by Chateaubriand.

As Ceri Crossley aptly puts it: "The France of the early nineteenth century was responsive to Chateaubriand's cocktail of Catholicism, royalism and Rousseauism."[35] Accordingly, the *Génie du christianisme* had talismanic potency for the young poets Alfred de Vigny, Victor Hugo, and Alphonse de Lamartine (1790–1869), who subscribed under the Bourbon Restoration to Chateaubriand's politically charged cult of the Old Testament. In Jeremiah, Isaiah, the psalms, and Job, these younger men found models of confessional lyricism.[36] Hugo was especially infatuated with the Breton author. The year after his idol was mocked in *Le Conservateur des ruines* (Figure I.2), he dedicated the ode "Le Génie" (July 1820) to Chateaubriand, contrasting the author's greatness with the pettiness of his critics.[37] Given Hugo's ultimate legacy—he died a republican with outsized stature as defender of liberty and champion of humanity—it is startling to realize how ostentatiously the young poet flaunted fealty to throne and altar in the early Restoration. Imitating the name of Chateaubriand's periodical (*Le Conservateur*), Hugo, with his brothers Abel and Eugène, founded a royalist (though not markedly Romantic) journal, *Le Conservateur littéraire* (1819–21), with which Vigny and Lamartine were also associated. Subsequently, royalism fused with full-blown Romanticism in the pages of *La Muse française* (July 1823–June 1824)—a journal in which Hugo, Vigny, and the other members of the circle gathered around Charles Nodier (1780–1844) professed an exalted conception of the poet's vocation as oracular guide to humanity.[38] Grounded in the paradigm of the divinely inspired Moses and the Hebrew prophets, this heady self-image was embraced by Hugo throughout his long career, notwithstanding his abandonment of royalism, around 1827, in favor of an alliance between Romanticism and liberty.[39]

Spectator Christianity

Hugo's investiture of the poet with prophetic authority is no more orthodox than Chateaubriand's defense of Catholicism on the basis of feeling and beauty. Other unexpected meetings of the sacred and the secular occur in a number of post-Napoleonic paintings that treat Christian subjects. A case in point is François Gérard's *Saint Theresa*, exhibited in the Salon of 1827–28 (Figure 1.5).[40] With expectation piqued by the open secret that the artist was working on a painting not to be included in the Salon, *Saint Theresa* made a dramatic appearance several days before the exhibition's closing. Gérard undertook the painting at the behest of Juliette Récamier (1777–1849), close friend of both the artist and the Chateaubriands. It was produced to adorn the main altar of the chapel of the Infirmary of Marie-Thérèse, established by Chateaubriand's wife, Céleste (1774–1847) in 1819 to serve elderly priests and destitute noblewomen. The institution's name had a touching Bourbon pedigree. The saint was patron to Princess Marie-Thérèse (1778–1851). Married to her cousin the Duc d'Angoulême (heir to the throne, as eldest son of Charles X), the princess was the sole child of Louis XVI and Marie-Antoinette to survive the Revolution.

Offering an admixture of piety and moody eroticism akin to that of *The Burial of Atala* (Salon of 1808; Paris, Musée du Louvre), by Gérard's fellow pupil from the David studio, Anne-Louis Girodet (1767–1824), the altarpiece was declared "incomparable" by Celeste's husband.[41] Antony Béraud (1791–1860), editor of an illustrated compendium of Salon entries), recognized the *Génie du christianisme* as the source of a work he regarded as "beyond praise": "The great artist owes a masterpiece to the great writer." Asking what "ravishing reverie" inspired Gérard, the critic extolled the "exquisite feeling in the melancholy expression of this adorable face!"[42] In contrast, Auguste Jal (1795–1873), no friend to the devout monarchy, mischievously suggested that the painter had endowed his subject with an allure more worldly than sacred: "The expression of the young saint is delightful … how pretty she is, this girl who loves with all the might of her Spanish soul! Here is certainly the mistress of the poet's dreams; but the saint?"[43] As in Girodet's *Burial of Atala*, erotic appeal is enhanced, rather than cooled, by Davidian chill. In contrast to the hot swoon of the enraptured nun, as famously portrayed by Bernini (1645–52; Rome, Cornaro Chapel, Santa Maria della Vittoria), Gérard's Theresa is tightly self-contained. Her concentrated, upward gaze confined by her habit (its contours restated in the pointed arch of the frame), the saint presses clasped hands close to the cold stone of a column that mirrors her steadfast

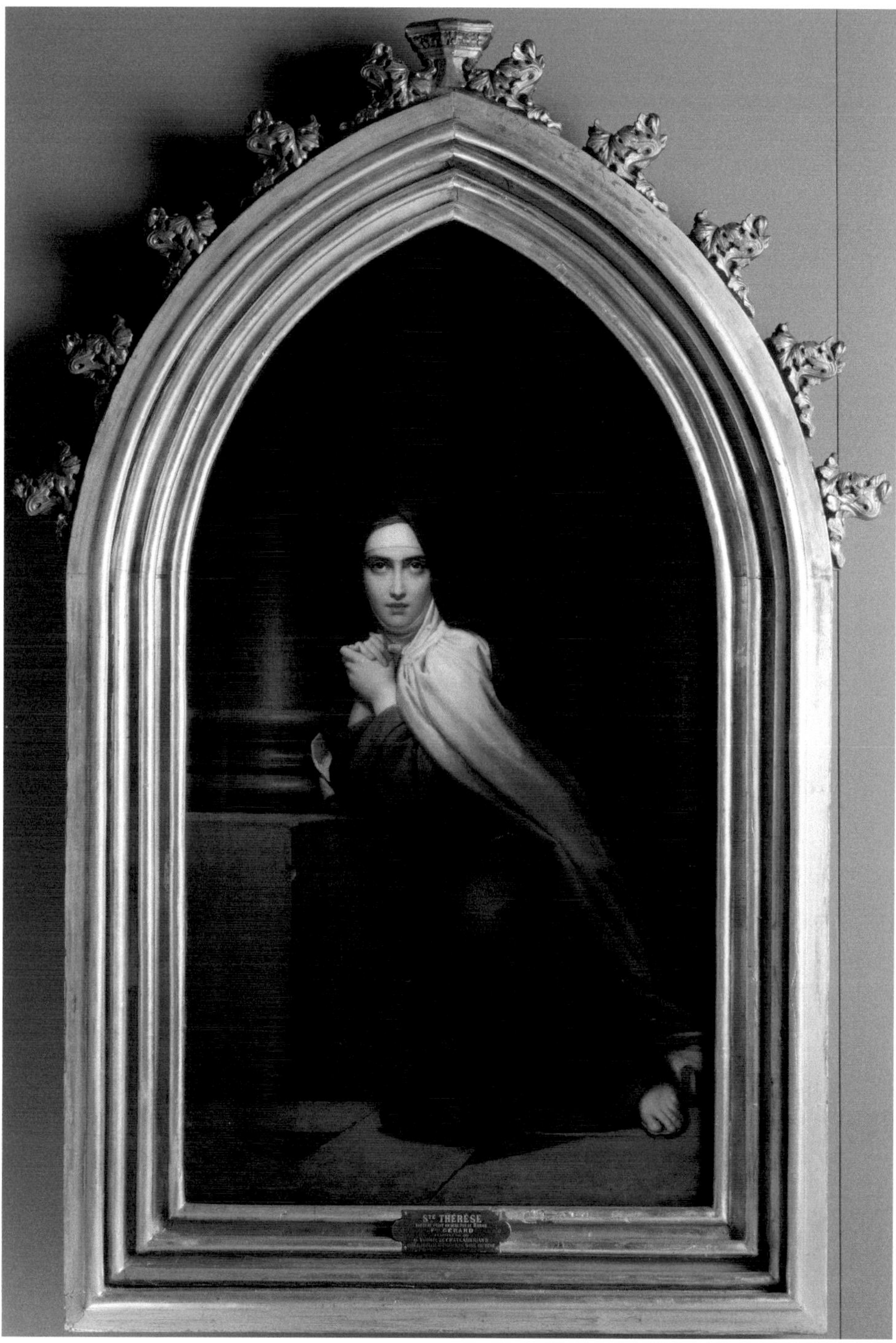

Figure 1.5 François Gérard, *Saint Theresa*, 1827, oil on canvas, 172 × 96 cm. Paris, Infirmerie Sainte-Thérèse. Photo: © RMN-Grand Palais /Art Resource, NY.

devotion. So magnetic was the painting that it even won over a Protestant liberal, François Guizot (1787–1874), who freely extrapolated a colorful scenario:

> Saint Theresa, after praying for a long time in the church ... has risen to leave. She has been walking slowly, profoundly meditative, preoccupied with the spirit, her heart moved by her pious and tender meditations. Suddenly, as she was passing before a column, the divine object of her ardent hope appeared to her .... A celestial joy floods her soul; suddenly, involuntarily, her body sags; she leans against the column and rests one knee on the ground; her hands are clasped, her head raised, her gaze is fixed upon the blissful vision; she is calm and yet beside herself, enraptured with joy and yet seized by a saintly terror ...."[44]

Bearing witness to the painting's evocative force, Guizot's enthusiasm should not be mistaken for devotion. Rather, he is overcome by empathy with the saint's fervor as portrayed by the painter. It follows that Gérard's conception is unlike that of its famous Baroque predecessor. In *The Ecstasy of Saint Theresa*, Bernini permits us to witness the illusionistic unfolding of a miracle in the company of the patron, Cardinal Federigo Cornaro, and his deceased forebears, portrayed in flanking balconies. We see the angelic instigator of cloud-borne Theresa's ecstasy, and the two are bathed in light emanating from a hidden window. Gérard, in contrast, depicts earth-bound worship in a dusky church interior. Representing piety, rather than instilling it in the viewer, Gérard's *Saint Theresa* bears witness to the enduring impact of de-Christianization. Abandoning the norms of devotional painting, Gérard's *Saint Theresa* is example of what Robert Rosenblum terms "spectator Christianity"—a representation of piety at arm's length that bears chameleon resemblance to conventional religious art.[45] Rather than soliciting prayer, such works appeal to the viewer's empathy with, and curiosity about, the faith of fictive characters, whose otherness is often signaled (as in later examples by Schnetz, Navez, and Gauguin) by alluringly exotic ethnographic trappings and by a religious fervor that was, for Parisians, disarmingly primitive. Implying anthropological remove on the part of both painter and viewer, spectator Christianity is shot through with nostalgia for irretrievably lost faith.[46] Given that Gérard's painting was crafted for the altar of a chapel, it is evident that the boundary separating works purveying spectator Christianity from religious art per se is not always clearly defined. In this regard, Gérard's *Saint Theresa* represents the French flipside of the issue famously raised by Caspar David Friedrich's *The Cross in the Mountains* (also known as *The Tetschen Altarpiece*; 1808; Dresden, Gemäldegalerie Neue Meister): whether a painting in a secular genre can function as a sacred image.[47]

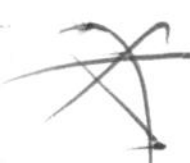

Another striking example of conflated genres is provided by *Saint Veronica of Milan*, painted in 1816 by David's Belgian follower François-Joseph Navez while under the exiled master's watch (Figure 1.6).[48] This is not the famous Veronica, whose *sudarium* captured the true image (i.e., the *vera icon*) of Christ's face on the way to Calvary, a standard motif of Christian art. Rather, Navez portrays an unusual subject: an Italian nun, born 1475, whose mystical attachment to Christ rivaled that of Saint Theresa. According to legend, she was told by the Virgin, in a vision, to meditate daily on the sufferings of Jesus. So single-mindedly did she follow this command that the young woman supposedly developed sympathetic wounds on hands and brow. Though the blood on her lap could have run from fingers holding a hazardously spiny crown of thorns, the absence of visible piercings suggests that the droplets are a miraculous apparition. The figures at either side are the saint's parents. Veronica's careworn mother presses her hands to her chest, her spread fingers echoing the thorns

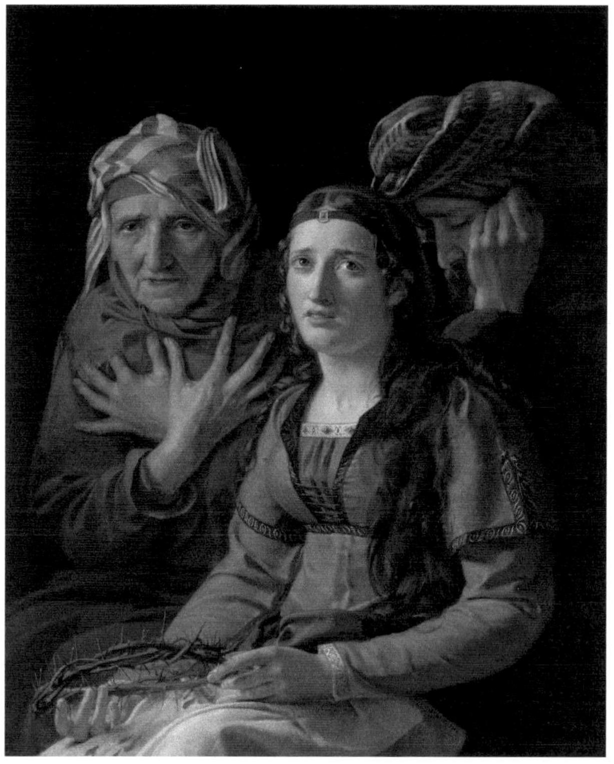

Figure 1.6 François-Joseph Navez, *Saint Veronica of Milan*, 1816, oil on canvas, 92 × 82 cm. Ghent, Museum of Fine Arts. Photo: Hugo Maertens, Museum of Fine Arts Ghent, www.artinflanders.be.

below; her father strikes the stock pose of melancholy.[49] As Thomas Crow indicates, there is ambiguity here: Either the parents share in Veronica's painful meditation or they are perturbed by her fanaticism. Convinced that they partake of their daughter's grief over Christ's suffering, I consider this inadvertent polysemy symptomatic of the painting's distance from traditional Catholic imagery. Navez represents religious transport, rather than a sacred event, and his painting's expressive charge upstages any invitation to worship. Deviation from devotional purpose coincides with a flair for picturesque costume; the saint is hardly clothed as a nun, and the parents sport eye-catching headwear. As in Gérard's *Saint Theresa*, secularity intrudes upon an ostensibly sacred subject. This hybridity reflects a connoisseurship of spirituality shared by the artist with the patron who commissioned and owned the painting, Navez's close friend, the distinguished Brussels pharmacologist Auguste-Donat de Hemptinne (1781–1854). Along with his sister, Navez lived in the Hemptinne home; the artist married his host's sister-in-law, and their families shared a cemetery crypt. Navez's dual allegiance to devotional purpose and artful display of sentiment is also manifest in the oscillation of his oeuvre between paintings with bona fide religious subjects (the Holy Family, for example) and genre pieces featuring devout Italian women—piety was gendered as female in the nineteenth century—whose exotic otherness corresponds with the aesthetic remove of the artist and his audience. Falling squarely within the domain of spectator Christianity, the latter are exemplified, for example, by *The Sick Child* (1844; Berlin, National Gallery), with its colorfully dressed women beseeching the Madonna (whose effigy stands in a nearby shrine) on behalf of a pathetically listless child adorned with a religious medal.

Jean-Victor Schnetz, a leading practitioner of this sentimental strain of spectator Christianity, shared with Navez a friendship originating in the David studio and cemented during an Italian sojourn (both artists traveled to Rome in 1817). Schnetz's *Vow to the Madonna* (La Rochelle, Musée des Beaux-Arts), which joined Gérard's *Saint Theresa* in the Salon of 1827–28, is a characteristic specimen.[50] Offering ingratiating description of fabric and accessories, Schnetz's representations of pious Italian peasantry, like those of Navez, are genre paintings; yet emphasis on the faith of the anonymous supplicants strains the limits of that category. It is a telling indication of metamorphosis within the field of sacred art that Schnetz produced another, very large *Vow to the Madonna* (nearly 3 × 5 meters) for a State religious commission. Intended for the Paris church of Saint-Étienne-du-Mont, this ambitious variation on the relatively small (100 × 75 cm.) La Rochelle *Vow to the Madonna* was exhibited to public acclaim in the early July Monarchy Salon of 1831 as *Unfortunates Imploring the Aid of the Virgin* (Figure 1.7), with reference, in the Salon guidebook, to the section of the litany of the Virgin that identifies her as *Consolatrix afflictorum* (Comforter of the Afflicted).[51]

Before an altar topped by an enthroned Virgin and decked with bouquets and votive offerings, a peasant couple pleads operatically for the health of an enfeebled young woman. Their fervor is seconded, on the right, by a pilgrim deep in prayer. At the left, a barefoot girl bearing flowers and candle adds a note of ingratiating charm. To post-revolutionary viewers hungry for faith, the unbridled and seemingly uncomplicated religiosity on view in this crowded Italian church could have seemed at once enviable and deliciously quaint. Delécluze was especially taken by the father, who "on his knees with joined hands, looks at and prays to the saint with all of his heart":

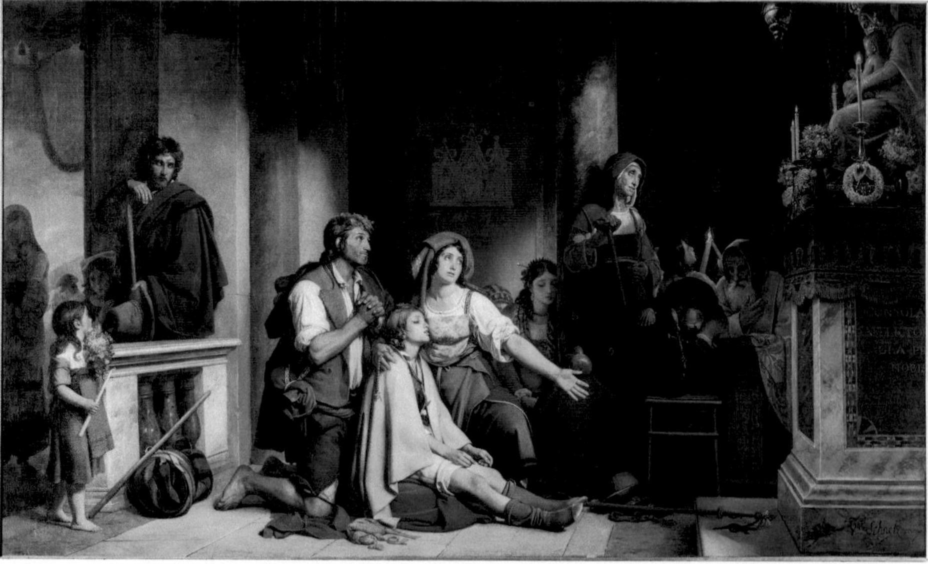

Figure 1.7 Jean-Victor Schnetz, *The Vow to the Madonna*, Salon of 1831, oil on canvas, 284 × 490 cm. Paris, Musée du Louvre. Photo: Jean Schormans. © RMN-Grand Palais /Art Resource, NY.

"On these rustic and naturally hard features, the painter has artfully placed a nuance of pain and hope, which render this character as touching as could be ...."[52] Unsympathetic to either Catholicism or to what he regarded as the painting's declamatory aspect, Heinrich Heine was less persuaded by its sacred pretentions: "rather than elevate my soul, he [Schnetz] lowers it to the level of the ground."[53] Given Schnetz's handling of a genre scene as if it were an ecclesiastical painting, the poet's putdown hits its mark.

Catholic Revival

When the Bourbon monarchy was restored in 1814, the fact that constitutional rule had been the political norm (in principle if not in practice) since 1791 made it inevitable that Louis XVIII would grant his subjects a *charte*. Echoing the Concordat, Article 5 of this Bourbon constitution guarantees that "Each professes his religion with equal liberty and receives the same protection for his worship." This tolerant provision is qualified in Article 6, which negates a key Napoleonic doctrine: "However, the Catholic, apostolic and Roman religion is the religion of the State."[54] This proviso was at the expense of other faiths, as bluntly set forth in a caricature by Pierre Langlumé (1790–1830), lithographed by Victor-Hippolyte Delaporte (1804–?), *Liberty of Religion under Charles X* (1827), dating from the reign (1824–30) of the ultra-Catholic, reactionary successor to Louis XVIII (Figure 1.8).

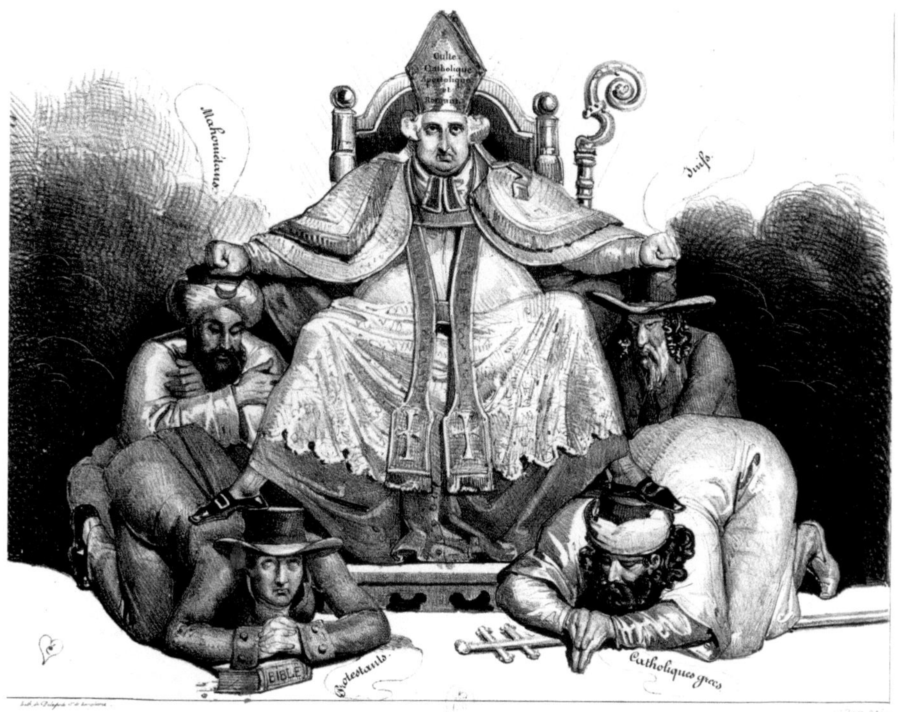

Figure 1.8 Pierre Langlumé, *Liberty of Religion under Charles X*, 1827, lithograph (by Victor-Hippolyte Delaporte). Paris, Bibliothèque nationale de France. Photo: BnF.

With comic resemblance to an enthroned Christ in Judgement, the archbishop of Paris, Hyacinthe-Louis de Quélen (1778–1839; in office 1821–39) dominates personifications of Catholicism's rivals, resting his fists on obeisant Islam and sinister Judaism, while planting his feet on groveling Protestantism and prostrate Greek Orthodoxy. The adjectives attached to the state religion as enshrined in the *Charte* of 1814 ("Catholic, Apostolic and Roman") are inscribed in the archbishop's miter.

Inflamed by State piety, such anti-clericalism was also conveyed by the songs of Pierre-Jean de Béranger (1780–1857); the pamphlets of Paul-Louis Courier (1772–1825); and reprints of Voltaire and Rousseau, as well as Molière's satire of religious bigotry and hypocrisy, *Tartuffe* (the latter issued in an edition of 50,000, popularly priced at 3 sous).[55] Nor did the July Monarchy open auspiciously for Catholicism. Indifference, if not outright hostility, toward the Church guided the government's passive response to the pillage and desecration of the Paris church of Saint-Germain-l'Auxerrois, its rectory, and the palace of Archbishop Quélen on 14–15 February 1831. Incited by a Mass mourning the assassination of the Duc de Berry (1778–1820; son of Charles X) 11 years earlier, and attended by Bourbon sympathizers, the violence was not halted by the National Guard. Denis-Auguste-Marie Raffet (1804–60) provided the dissident, satirical journal *La Caricature* (24 February 1831) with ribald commentary. Ransacking Quélen's wardrobe, a delighted National Guardsman with bayonetted musket dangles a suspiciously petite corset before his amused accomplices, one of whom displays rosaries (Figure 1.9)[56]

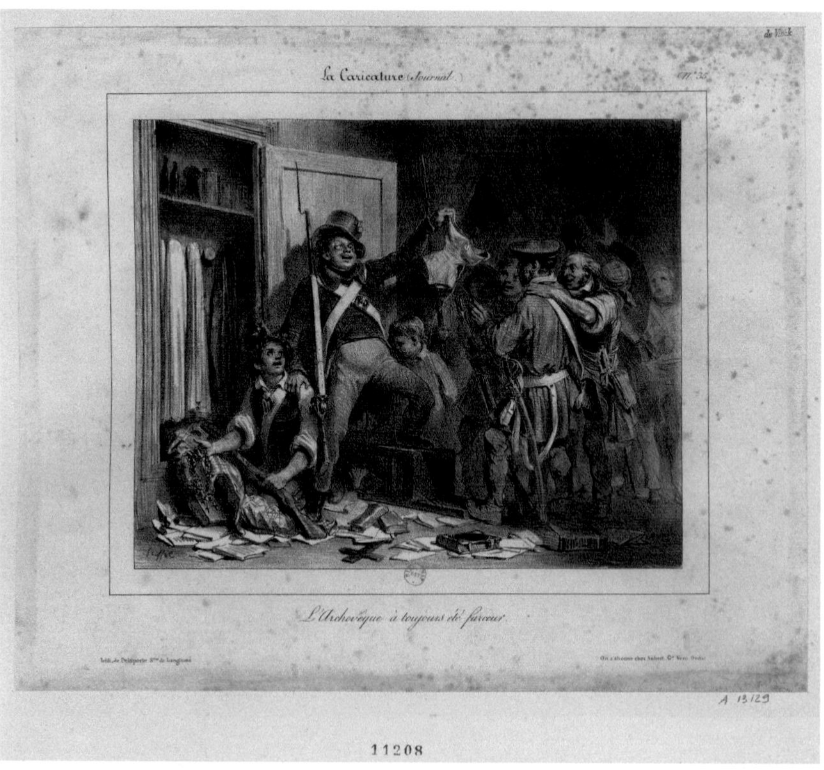

Figure 1.9 Denis-Auguste-Marie Raffet, "The Archbishop Was Always a Joker," lithograph (by Victor-Hippolyte Delaporte), 19.1 × 23.4 cm. In *La Caricature*, no. 35 (24 February 1831). Paris, Bibliothèque nationale de France. Photo: BnF.

"The Archbishop was always a joker" ("L'Archevêque à [sic] toujours été farceur") runs the caption.

By the mid-1830s, the beleaguered regime's militancy in the face of chronic insurrection—the sack of the archbishop's palace was but one example—dovetailed with a warmer embrace of the faith. Already, in 1832 (the year in which he was named minister of public instruction), Guizot, the earnest Protestant taken with Gérard's *Saint Theresa*, praised religion as an "eminently social principle that spreads and fortifies the love of order." Two years later, Alexis de Tocqueville (1805–59) spoke of "the political utility of a religion."[57] In 1837, crucifixes were installed in court rooms.[58] Whereas the period 1830–35 (years of maximum civil turbulence) saw an explosion of anti-clerical and anti-Christian publication, such discourse became rare in the 1840s.[59] Just as the Bourbon *Charte* of 1814 was the template for the July Monarchy's revised edition of 1830, so too did the regime (1830–48) of Louis-Philippe (1773–1850) continue the Restoration policy of ecclesiastical patronage, completing the churches of Notre-Dame-de-Lorette (1823–36) and Saint-Vincent-de-Paul (1824–44), both of which were ambitiously decorated.

A rough profile of Christian fervor is provided by the frequency with which religious subjects appeared in the Salon, helpfully quantified by Bruno Foucart.[60] Even in the most bountiful years, sacred images were vastly outnumbered by the more popular genres, especially portraiture. Within the modest percentiles of religious paintings on view, Foucart's research reveals noteworthy developments, including a considerable time lag between the Concordat and the appearance of religious subjects in significant quantity. In 1804, two years after the publication of the *Génie de christianisme,* 18 religious subjects (3.30% of the Salon total) were exhibited, a slight increase from 5 (1.39%) in the Salon of 1802. Following an elevation at the start of the Restoration, with 55 (5.67%) in 1814—up from 34 (3.32%) in 1812—there were banner years in 1819 (125; 10.36%) and 1827–28 (135; 12.83%). Unsurprisingly, there was a delayed decrease during the early, anti-clerical years of the July Monarchy, with 94 (4.33%) exhibited in 1831 and 54 (2.20%) in 1833. Sacred subjects began to multiply in 1836 (106; 5.71%), with a steady climb to a high plateau that reached 207 (10.18%) in 1841; 205 (10.88%) in 1842; 165 (13.86%) in the unusually small Salon of 1843; and a peak of 210 (11.61%) in 1844. Following 1845 (178; 10.63%) there was a fluctuating decline, with spikes in 1848 (252; 5.48%) and in the Salon held on the occasion of the Exposition universelle of 1855 (204; 10.93%).[61]

The enhanced presence of religious paintings in the Salon during the late 1830s and early 1840s belatedly reflects the religious revival of the first third of the century. Heralded by Chateaubriand, shadowed by spectator Christianity, and abhorred by anti-clericals, this return to faith was comparable in magnitude to Catholic resurgence in the first half of the seventeenth century.[62] Within this movement, there was pronounced regional variation in intensity. Piety (far more prevalent among women than men) was sufficiently robust to survive anti-clericalism under the Bourbons and in the early July Monarchy. Between 1815 and 1830, popular devotion was galvanized by over 1500 Catholic missions that, for weeks at a time, invoked national expiation of the Revolution's sins through processions, lectures, and sermons.[63] In addition to the missions (countered by performances of *Tartuffe*), there were mystical visitations. Catherine Labouré (1806–76; canonized 1947), a novice of the Daughters of Charity, experienced visions of the Virgin between April and December 1830 at her convent on the Rue du Bac.[64] In obedience to Mary's command to Catherine, a medal providing protection to the wearer was struck; during the cholera outbreak of 1832, some ten thousand were in circulation. By 1835, there were over one million, and the medals continued to multiply as belief in their protective power spread internationally. Jean-Marie Vianney (1786–1859, known as the Curé d'Ars), a priest renowned for uncommon piety, humility, simplicity, and mortification, attained cult status in the 1830s as faith healer and medical advisor. Born near Lyon to peasant parents and ordained in 1815, he was assigned in 1818 to a parish in the village of Ars (population 230) in the Combes, a marshy area some 40 kilometers from Lyon. There, he set an example of fervor recognized by canonization in 1925 and designation as patron saint of parish priests in 1929. Between 1830 and his death, an astonishing average of 70,000 pilgrims visited Ars annually.[65] Vianney subscribed to ultramontanism, a movement that would prove especially consequential to the Catholic revival. Its adherents—so named because their aspirations led them "beyond the mountains" (i.e., across the Alps to Rome)—believed in the absolute primacy of the pope in religious matters. Uncompromisingly committed to faith, they professed separation of Church and State, to the point of opposing government sponsorship of religious affairs. This was in square opposition to the Gallicanism of the post-revolutionary clerical establishment, which stood for ecclesiastical independence from the Holy See and for State management of religion.

Lamennais and Ultramontanism

Ultramontanism had an early, vehement advocate in a Breton priest born on the same street in Saint-Malo as Chateaubriand: Félicité Robert de La Mennais who, from the 1830s on, called himself Félicité Lamennais.[66] Volatile imagination inflames a work that predates not only Lamennais's emergence as a celebrity, but also his belated ordination at age 35; without seminary training, he became a priest on 9 March 1816, encouraged by his elder brother, the Abbé Jean-Marie de La Mennais (1780–1860). Invoking the preeminence of Saint Peter among the apostles, Félicité and Jean-Marie anonymously preached an ultramontane polemic in *Church Tradition Regarding the Appointment of Bishops,* published in August 1814. The authors indicate that, having spent six years gathering materials for the book, they completed it at end of 1813, only a few months before "the happy revolution, which permits us to freely publish it." That "happy revolution" is the return of the Bourbons, and the argument that follows is directed against the ecclesiastical order established by the Concordat and inherited by the restored monarchy. Here is no trace of the joy that had greeted Napoleon's treaty with the Vatican. Chateaubriand, for instance, had dedicated the second edition (1803) of the *Génie du christianisme* to the first consul and paid homage to Bonaparte as restorer of the faith: "One cannot but recognize in your destiny the hand of that Providence, which has marked you from afar, for the accomplishment of its wonderful designs."[67] The brothers, in contrast, indict the religious legacy of the dictator who (recently denounced by the politically reborn Chateaubriand in the anti-Napoleonic pamphlet *De Buonaparte et des Bourbons*) had run rough-shod over Pius VII.[68] Jean-Marie probably contributed the erudition underpinning the text; the rhetoric bears the searing touch of Félicité. At issue is nothing less than an apocalyptic battle between good and evil:

> Amid this black tempest, the faith of many totters, hope withers and is snuffed out: but a few moments and the very elect will be seduced.... A horrific apostasy

> menaces us; it afflicts the universe, which hesitates between you and the frightful idol of atheism.... Great God...! May the waves of your long-withheld anger burst forth upon your enemies and engulf them; may the sea reject from its midst their impure remains, and, like the miraculously rescued Israelites, we will sing on its shores the hymn of deliverance.[69]

Offering a glimpse of the prophetic idiom that would thrill Félicité's readers under the July Monarchy, *Church Tradition* makes its case with signature extremism.

In 1817, Félicité published his first solo work, volume one of the *Essay on Religious Indifference* (*Essai sur l'indifférence en matière de religion*). In a notice preceding this alarming critique of contemporary French spirituality, Lamennais (who again omitted his name, though his identity was an open secret) declared the urgency of publishing the first volume prior to completion of the entire work: "It is pressing to speak of truth, of order, of Religion, to the people, out of fear of resembling the doctor who expounds on life near a tomb."[70] Within a month, the first edition was depleted; by the end of 1818, 13,000 copies had been sold. Without Catholicism (the sole true religion), Lamennais argues, man and society are depraved. As proof, he adduces the horrors of the Enlightenment-born Revolution: "And when philosophy recently wished to establish a State without religion, it was compelled to give it cadavers for a base."[71] Indifference, he writes, is not solely a question of being lazy or lackadaisical regarding belief. It is also manifest in the pursuit of deistic natural religion; in the belief that religion is but a useful means of keeping the common herd in check; in the acceptance of fundamental aspects of Catholicism to the exclusion of those deemed superfluous; and in ecumenical tolerance (Protestantism receives particular animus). Diagnosing the malady, Lamennais resorts to medical metaphor:

> The sickest century is not the one impassioned for error, but the century that neglects, that disdains the truth. There remains strength, and consequently hope, where one perceives violent delirium: but when all movement is extinguished, when the pulse has ceased to beat, when cold has beset the heart, and when the breath of the dying one no longer tarnishes the mirror that an uneasy curiosity brings to his mouth, what can be awaited but an immediate and inevitable dissolution?
>
> In vain, one will try to hide that society, in Europe, is advancing rapidly toward this fatal end. The formidable noises that rumble in its breast, the jolts that shake it ... are not the most frightening symptom that it offers to the observer: these terrible convulsions might not be without remedy; but this lethargic indifference that we see it fall into, this profound drowsiness, this iron sleep, this mortal stupor, who will pull it from this? Who will breathe on these dry bones to reanimate them?[72]

A militantly Catholic counterpart to the post-Napoleonic discourse of lassitude and inertia (conveyed, as we will see, in the visual arts), this jeremiad employs characteristically concrete imagery.

That so lengthy an apology (500-plus pages) was a best seller reflects the compelling intensity of the author's bereavement. As Paul Bénichou observes, Lamennais's "ardent profession of faith is ... an incessant lamentation on the ruins. A hymn of mourning resounds throughout his first writings, a funeral oration of humanity divorced from the Spirit."[73] Chateaubriand was among Lamennais's enthusiastic readers, and both authors depart from French theological tradition in their deprecation of reason. At the same time, their texts are fundamentally dissimilar. Whereas his predecessor spoke of spiritual bereavement with accents of tender regret, and with nostalgia for lost institutions and ruined houses of worship, Lamennais' discourse is urgent and fiercely negative.

The *Essai sur l'indifférence* won praise from a leading theorist of counter-revolution, Joseph de Maistre (1753–1821), who hailed it as "a clap of thunder beneath a leaden sky."[74] Despite this reactionary imprimatur, Lamennais was uneasy, at the outset, with the Restoration's alliance of throne and altar. Viscerally opposed to the well-intentioned royal patronage of Catholicism that constituted a bulwark of Bourbon policy, Lamennais recoiled from the state's corruptingly secular reach into religious affairs. He voiced this dissident position in *Religion Considered in its Relations with the Political and Civil Order* (1826), which denounces Gallicanism as "the battle cry of all enemies of Christianity, of all men whom God weighs."[75] This inflammatory argument landed Lamennais in criminal court, which mandated seizure of the publication. Undeterred, the crusader produced *On the Progress of the Revolution and the War against the Church* (1829). Arguing that Catholicism can only be saved "by disengaging itself from any other interest but itself, by the firm resolution to endure all rather than to abandon the least part of the doctrine that Christ sealed with His blood," the irrepressible gadfly declares that "wherever is the spirit of God, there is liberty."[76] Thus, in the twilight of the Restoration, Lamennais broke with the Bourbon monarchy, metamorphosing into a devoutly Catholic liberal, who nonetheless abhorred individualism and rationalism.

The fatal contradiction between the progressive and retrograde aspects of Lamennais's thought is writ large in a remarkable episode involving the circle around the liberal ultramontane paper *L'Avenir* (*The Future*) in the early July Monarchy.[77] In print between 16 October 1830 and 15 November 1831, the journal was a mouthpiece for the ideas of Lamennais; the title was inadvertently ironic, given its contributors' nostalgia for papal preeminence. With an impact belying its modest circulation of two to three thousand subscribers, *L'Avenir* featured contributions from the vanguard literary Romantics Hugo, Lamartine, and Vigny. Writing under the motto "God and liberty," Lamennais collaborated with a group that included Comte Charles de Montalembert (1810–70), who helped finance the undertaking, the priest Henri Lacordaire (1802–61), and the economist Charles de Coux (1787–1864).

Championing separation of church and state, *L'Avenir* advocated liberty of education, association, and the press, and looked hopefully toward a future in which, freed from the moribund embrace of the monarchy, the papacy would reign supreme over a purified Catholic order. Undertaking an aggressive initiative to wrest control of education from the state, Lacordaire, Montalembert, and Coux established an illegal, independent school in May 1831, swiftly closed by the police. Hauled before the Chamber of Peers in September, the collaborators were fined one hundred francs.

Opposition from the Gallican ecclesiastical hierarchy and declining subscriptions having led to suspension of the paper, Lamennais, Lacordaire, and Montalembert made a pilgrimage to Rome (arriving 30 December 1831) to petition Pope Gregory XVI (1765–1846) to bless their liberal ultramontanism. The papal response was unlike that which had greeted Lamennais on his previous trip to Rome (1824), when the author of the *Essai sur l'indifférence* was warmly received by Leo XII (1760–1829). Following two audiences, the supplicants were given no reply until 15 August 1832 (Lamennais received the news on 30 August while in Munich). Without deigning to mention either the Lamennais circle or *L'Avenir*, Gregory XVI's encyclical *Mirari Vos* anathematized all that the liberal ultramontanes stood for. Rejecting separation of church and state, the pope denounced freedom of the press as "very disastrous and very detestable" and freedom of conscience as "a delirium, an error of the most contagious sort."[78] And this was on top of a papal brief of 9 June calling upon the bishops of Poland to exhort their flocks to submit to the Czar, repudiating a cause cherished by the Lamennais circle and other French liberals in the 1830s.

Following the debacle, Lamennais, as we will see, cast off allegiance to the pope and was radicalized. Lacordaire took a different path. A gifted orator, he delivered sermons, first at the Collège Stanislas in 1834, then at Notre-Dame (during Lent in 1835 and 1836, and again in 1843–51 during Advent.) His sermons were fashionable events which drew large audiences, including Chateaubriand, Lamartine, and Hugo. Lacordaire introduced a mode of preaching that, devoid of pomp and boilerplate, addressed his listeners with immediacy and simplicity and keyed into contemporary sentiment. Dedicated to the reestablishment of the Dominican order, banned in France since 1790, Lacordaire began to publicly advocate its restoration in 1839, when he spent the spring and summer in Italy, donning the Dominican habit and appending "Dominique" to his name.

Anticipating the attention to be garnered by painting a man of the hour, Théodore Chassériau visited Lacordaire in Rome. So impatient was the fiercely competitive young artist to seize this opportunity, that he was willing to usurp his elder classmate in the studio of Jean-Auguste-Dominique Ingres (1780–1867), Henri Lehmann (1814–82), who had naively shared his own plan to portray the celebrity cleric. Chassériau's portrait of Henri-Dominique in the cloister of the monastery of Santa Sabina, where the new monk was studying theology, hung in the Salon of 1841 (Figure 1.10). The unsettling stare is amplified by iconic frontality—an effect enhanced by the oblique view into the cloister and the asymmetrical crowding of the composition's right side. Light flooding in from the upper right suggests divine inspiration as it sets the head into bold relief. Effectively conveying intense inner life, the portrait displeased Lacordaire, who thought it "somewhat austere."[79] The forbidding gaze may have discomfited a cleric in quest of self-abnegation and mortification, who sought direct rapport with his flock.[80] Lacordaire's humility was on display even as Chassériau proposed the portrait: "At first," the artist reported, "he responded that he would reflect on my proposition, that he was insignificant in clerical rank, and that his portrait would be seen without interest, etc. etc."[81]

Nor did Lacordaire value art apart from its pastoral potential. On 21 July 1839, at the monastery of Santa Maria della Quercia in Viterbo, he set forth the regulations of a brotherhood of pious artists, the Confrérie de saint Jean, which took its name from the patron saint of the Dominican order; seven founding members signed on in Paris 23 January 1840.[82] The idea had been pitched to Lacordaire by Lyon-born painter and critic Claudius Lavergne (1815–87), apparently with the collaboration of another Lyonnais artist (about whom we will hear more soon), Louis Janmot.[83] Members were expected to devote their art entirely to the service of the faith. Lacordaire specified this in a letter (5 June 1839) to Lavergne, in which he insisted upon the

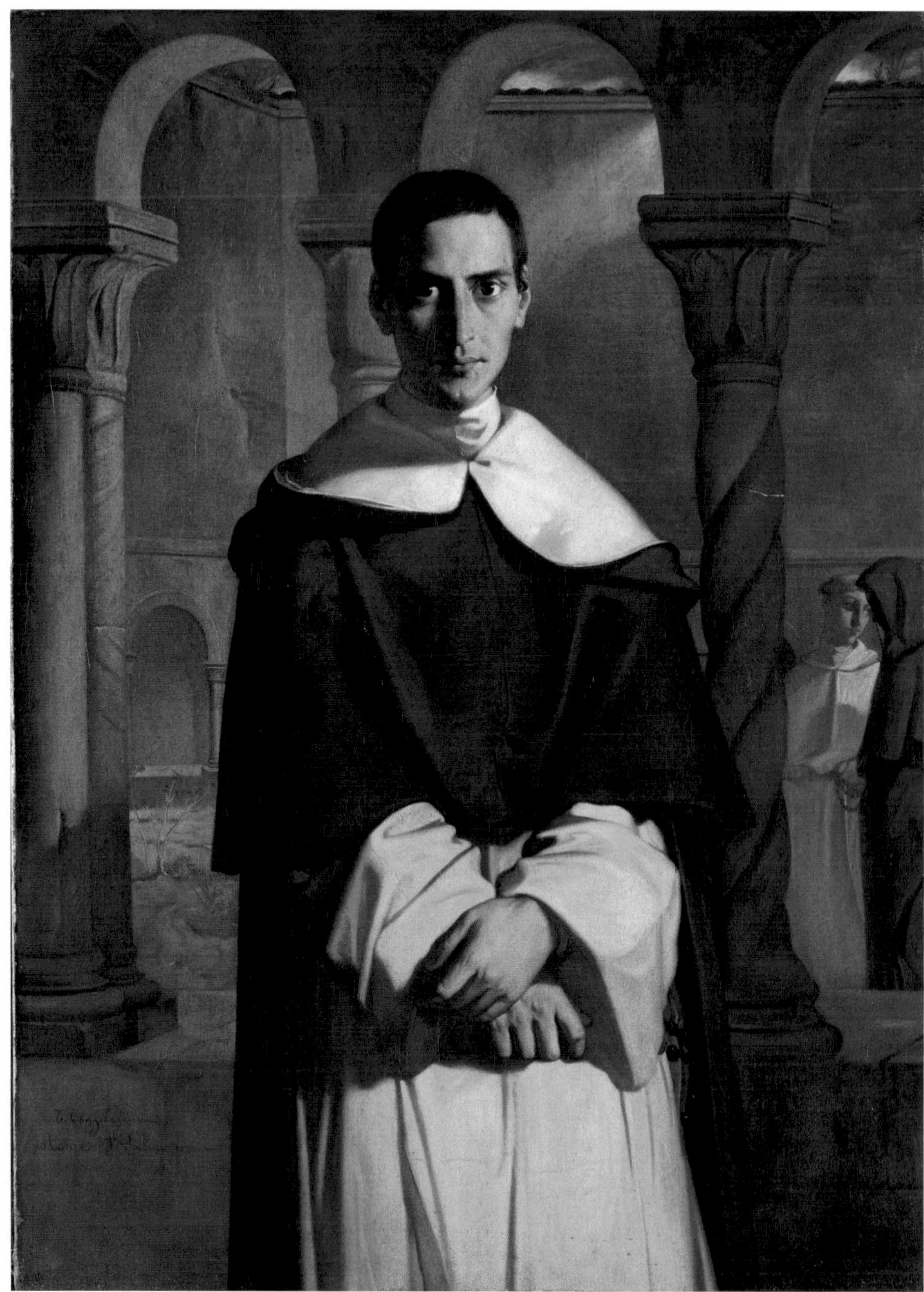

Figure 1.10 Théodore Chassériau, *Dominique Lacordaire, of the Order of Preaching Friars*, 1840, oil on canvas, 146 × 107 cm. Paris, Musée du Louvre. Photo: Franck Raux. © RMN-Grand Palais/Art Resource, NY.

> absolute necessity of giving to this association an unmistakable religious character, and to keep away all of those who do not call themselves Christians of faith and practice and blessed, among other things, with the need to proselytize. Nothing lax or middling is possible today. It is all or nothing. You must either want the establishment of the reign of God on Earth, or rest in peace at home.[84]

Apart from specifying that the artists should avoid using nude models (especially young girls), the Confrérie's rules do not address artistic practice, focusing instead on the state of members' souls. Declaring the confraternity open to artists, architects, and musicians, who make "an open and sincere profession of Catholic faith," the regulations demand adherence to a life of humility and prayer: their rooms will include images of Christ and the Virgin; they will wear only black, white, and gray; and meetings of the confraternity, to take place each Friday, will open with the kneeling members singing *Veni sancte spiritus* (the invitation to the Paraclete traditionally recited to celebrate the Pentecost) and with a sacred reading.

Sharing Lacordaire's conviction that painting should serve piety, Montalembert was a crusading preservationist who sought to save France's medieval architecture from the sort of demolition and disfigurement engineered by Petit-Radel. He brought strident militancy to the bereaved affection conveyed by Chateaubriand's commentary on the ruined church of Saint-Denis—a cause taken up by Hugo, whose denunciations of the abuse of medieval monuments include an ode of 1823, "La Bande noire."[85] Hugo's poem targets a company of speculators that, during the Restoration (notwithstanding the regime's piety toward pre-Revolutionary tradition) purchased and demolished old chateaux and disused abbeys in order to repurpose their materials.[86] Citing this poem, Montalembert seconded Hugo's efforts in a lengthy, passionate article, "Du vandalisme en France: Lettre à M. Victor Hugo" (1833) that expresses deep attachment to this threatened legacy:

> I contemplate these old monuments of Catholicism with as much love and respect as those who devoted their life and their wealth to found them: they do not merely represent for me an extinguished idea, epoch, or belief; these are the symbols of all that is most alive in my soul, of what is most august in my hopes. Modern vandalism is not only in my view brutal and stupid, but also, in addition, a sacrilege.[87]

Montalembert's preservationist fervor was of a piece with his enthusiasm for "primitive" late medieval and early Renaissance Italian painting. Convinced that flattened, hieratic compositions best convey piety, he extolled the art of Giotto and Fra Angelico, while decrying the materialism he discerned in the painting of Michelangelo, Titian, and the late Raphael. Montalembert's distaste for the ascendant naturalism of Italian Renaissance painting was shared by art historian Alexis-François Rio (1797–1874), who denounced its decadent tendencies in the first of a series of volumes on Christian art with an offputtingly pedantic title, *On Christian Poetry in Its Principle, in Its Subject and in Its Forms: The Art Form* (*De la Poésie chrétienne dans son principe, dans sa matière et dans ses forms. Forme de l'art,* 1836). There Rio signals defects in both the art and personal character of Fra Filippo Lippi and Andrea del Castagno while deploring the paganism, naturalism, and sensuality cultivated by Lorenzo de' Medici.[88] Though disappointed that Rio devoted insufficient attention to

Giotto's decoration of the Arena Chapel and the art of Fra Angelico and his historical moment, Montalembert approved of his Catholic critique of naturalism. Reviewing the volume in 1837, Montalembert set forth his own opinions on Italian art with a polemical verve absent from Rio's colorless text. In discussing the era of Fra Angelico, Montalembert equates primitive style with a bygone age "where nothing tarnishes the brilliance of the youthful attire with which religion clothed the world, where all that adorned and charmed the life of man brought heaven to his mind."[89] This pious nostalgia was akin to that of the German painters resident in Rome who styled themselves the Brotherhood of St. Luke in 1809, and were soon dubbed Nazarenes because of their Christian devotion, long hair, and robes; one of their founding members, Johann Friedrich Overbeck (1789–1869), opened his Roman studio each Sunday and was visited there by Rio and Montalembert in 1832.[90]

Underlying Montalembert's retrospection was a sense of loss. "There is no religious art in France," he opined in 1837, "that which bears the name is but a derisory parody."[91] Notwithstanding this pessimism, there were, in fact, French artists who (like the German Nazarenes) elicited devotion through stylistic archaism. Working in what Michael Paul Driskel terms "the hieratic mode," this pious cohort abandoned the sensuous surfaces, ingratiating detail, and cloying sentimentality typical of contemporaneous Salon painting in favor of austere frontality, immobility, and symmetry, which offered visual equivalents of their ultramontanism.[92] While much of their work was executed or exhibited in Paris, its spiritual center of gravity was the very Catholic city of Lyon.

Neo-Catholic Archaism

Victor Orsel's *Good and Evil* (Figure 1.11), conceived in Rome in 1829, completed in Paris in 1832, and exhibited in the Salon of 1833, is a founding work of the Lyonnais school.[93] Trained in Lyon under David's Troubadour student Pierre Révoil (1776–1842), Orsel began his studies in 1818 at the École des Beaux-Arts in Paris under Pierre-Narcisse Guérin. When Guérin was appointed director of the French Academy in Rome in 1822, Orsel joined him there, and spent the next eight years in Italy, supported by his inheritance. There, the notoriously slow-working painter abandoned his teacher's pagan neo-classicism, turning instead to religious didacticism and a self-conscious archaism that reflected his admiration for the work of the German Nazarenes, as well as for the Christian images from the late Middle Ages and the early Italian Renaissance that most moved Montalembert and Rio. The pseudo-altarpiece he conceived in Italy contrasts wise pursuit of virtue with foolish surrender to vice, each path personified by a young woman. On the left, a demure maiden in a simple pastel gown sits absorbed in a sacred book, shielded by a guardian angel. Her attractive counterpart, at right, wears a richly patterned red dress worthy of Lyon's famed silk industry. She rests her foot on a cast-off volume labeled "Sapientae Liber" [sic] (i.e., the *Liber Sapientae*, also known as *The Wisdom of Solomon*) and attends instead to the words of a demon, blown to her ear through a horn. Corresponding with this stark juxtaposition are vignettes of virtue and vice (replete with knights and demons) captioned in Latin. Above the central section, Christ sits in judgment, flanked on his right by the angel interceding for the virtuous maiden (identified, in Latin, by the inscription BEATITUDE) and, on his left, by the fallen one, who strains toward the Savior as she is yanked away by the demon (above the inscription DAMNATION). Enthusiastically praising *Good and Evil* when it was exhibited in Lyon

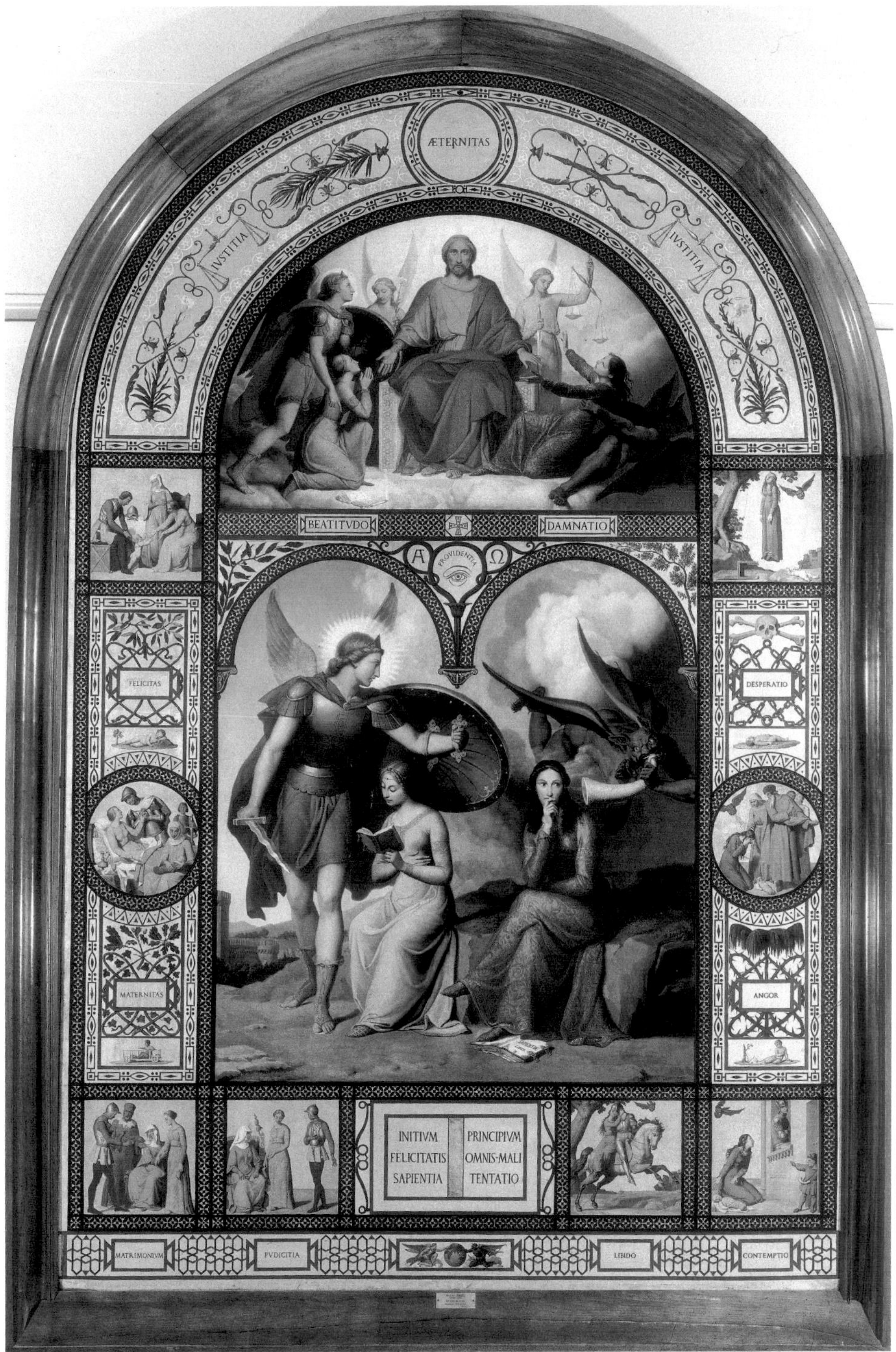

Figure 1.11 André-Jacques-Victor Orsel, *Good and Evil*, 1829–32, oil on canvas, 307 × 205 cm. Lyon, Musée des Beaux-Arts. Photo credit: HIP/Art Resource, NY.

in 1836 with the Société des Amis des Arts, the critic Alphonse Dupasquier floridly extrapolated Orsel's binaries into a tale of two sisters, which he set in Brittany or Normandy in 1250 or 1300:

> Blanche, the younger, timid girl, with blue eyes and blond hair, was the model of piety and gentleness. —Berthe, more beautiful, livelier, more piquant, already let show in her black eyes the fire of more lively passions, which yet slept in her thanks to the lessons and the good examples of her family.[94]

Blanche benefits from a good marriage, while Berthe, succumbing to temptation, is driven to infanticide and suicide: the wicked knight who seduced her discovers Berthe hanging from a tree beside their stabbed, illegitimate child.

Orsel's harsh lesson is resolutely retrograde in presentation. The retable format, the symmetrical multiplication of subsidiary narratives and inscriptions, the extensive use of gold ground, and the iconic, frontal Christ are flagrant archaisms. At the same time, there is nothing traditional about conflation of the Last Judgment, the choice of Hercules, and the parable of the wise and foolish virgins (Matthew 25). Nor is iconographic innovation the sole element that inadvertently points to departure from centuries of Church tradition. Illusionistic space in both the earthly and heavenly zones, as well as the suave modeling—Dupasquier singled out for praise Berthe's drapery "which unfolds on her body with such suppleness and in a manner so true and so natural"—speak of nineteenth-century academic training, with its dual commitment to idealism and persuasive mimesis. No less evident is the artist's self-conscious eclecticism, which omnivorously assimilates the trecento *Triumph of Death* frescos in Pisa's Camposanto and the Baroque classicism of Domenichino.[95] Opining that gold ground requires sharper contour, poet and critic Théophile Gautier (1811–72) wished that archaism had been carried further.[96] Despite the solemn sermonizing, there is something quaintly bourgeois about the melodrama of the judgment scene and the domesticity of the principal section below.

Orsel's attempt to turn the clock back to an era of fervent piety was taken up with a surer hand by the leading Lyonnais practitioner of the hieratic mode, Ingres's star pupil, Hippolyte Flandrin.[97] The mastery of academic convention that won Flandrin the Prix de Rome in 1832 is pointedly eschewed in a characteristic example of his religious art. *The Entry of Christ into Jerusalem*, a fresco painted on a sanctuary wall in the Parisian church of Saint-Germain-des-Prés (1842–44), places a rigidly profiled Jesus amidst a grave multitude, whose stylized attitudes of worship provide models for the viewer's devotion (Figure 1.12).[98]

Like *Good and Evil*, Flandrin's mural is a French counterpart to the forceful archaism and missionary fervor of German Nazarene painting. The radical planarity of the mounted Christ and his two-dimensional halo; the row of isocephalic worshipers; and the diminutive, simplified geometry of the architecture (set, without interval, behind the assembled figures) reconstruct a remotely distant era of Christian art. Gold ground further flattens this image, which offers only tentative invitations to enter a barely three-dimensional realm. Frozen attitudes suggest suspended motion, reinforcing the impression that the Gospel episode transpires in sacred space and time. Despite Flandrin's attempt to transport the viewer to the age of Giotto, there are tell-tale signs of his training (convincingly cast shadows, for example), which speak of kinship with Orsel. The critic Gustave Planche (1808–57) considered the eclecticism of Flandrin's decoration commendable: "Monsieur Flandrin has wished to reconcile the

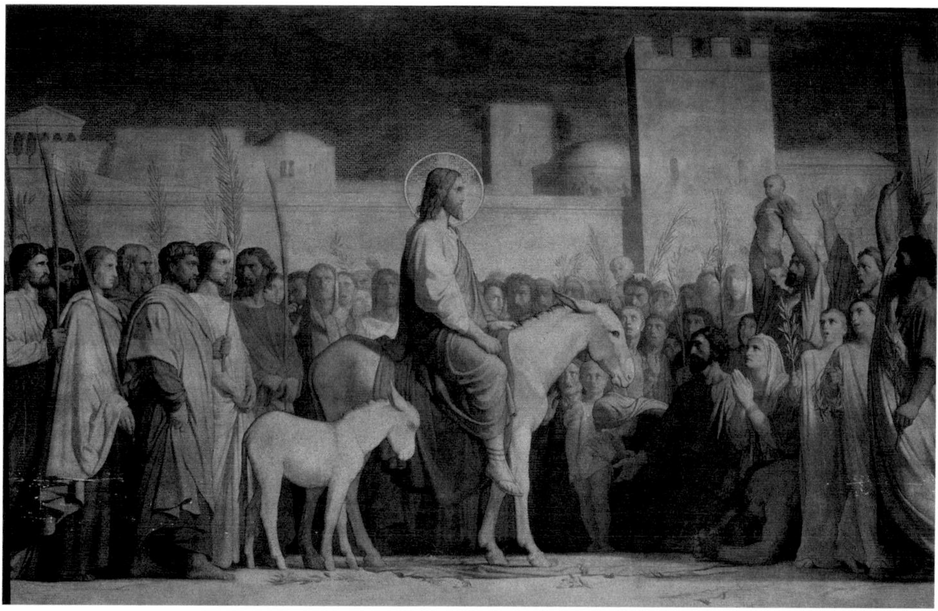

Figure 1.12 Hippolyte Flandrin, *Christ's Entry into Jerusalem*, 1842–44, fresco. Paris, Saint-Germain-des-Prés. Photo: Bulloz. © RMN-Grand Palais/Art Resource, NY.

Catholic sentiment of Giotto with the pagan science of Raphael. That's an initiative of which we highly approve."[99] Such appreciation of eclectic archaism—so comfortably at home in the nineteenth century—was not shared by an artist who lacked the faith of the devout Lyonnais painters. In a *Journal* entry of 1852, penned after a visit to Saint-Germain-des-Prés, Delacroix decried the "Gothic daubs with which they are covering the walls of that unhappy church."[100] No less steeped in his time than Orsel and Flandrin, Delacroix, as will be evident, imbued sacred subjects with an evocative power beyond their reach.

Lamennais in Revolt

The unshakable belief projected by the work of Orsel and Flandrin stands in contrast to the inner turmoil experienced by Lamennais in the wake of Gregory XVI's repudiation of liberal Catholicism and the cause of Polish independence. Going through the motions of joining Montalembert and Lacordaire in penitence, Lamennais renounced the priesthood, even as he signed (11 December 1833) an official submission to papal will. Casting off ultramontanism, he now identified Christ's mission with social justice rather than papal authority, a position set forth in his explosive *Words of a Believer* (*Paroles d'un croyant*). Written between February and July of 1833 and released 30 April 1834, this little book was published by Renduel (a purveyor of Romantic texts), who leaked the identity of the anonymous author. Going through eight editions in its first year alone, *Paroles d'un croyant* was pirated and internationally translated. Lines formed in reading rooms, and the text was declaimed in the jardin du Luxembourg.[101] Dedicated to "The People," it spawned a large number of pastiches, imitations, refutations, and satires—a corpus analyzed by Frank Paul Bowman, who indicates that "Lamennais's style and form were extremely contagious."[102] Borrowing the portentous rhetoric of the Hebrew prophets and the visionary format of the Book of Revelation, speaking in parables, continually referring to Christ, and heralding the reestablishment of the kingdom of God, Lamennais denounces social oppression, slavery, and monarchy in an apocalyptic diatribe propelled by dangerously exciting politics.

Under the Bourbon Restoration, the author's rage focused on the present and the recent past. Nineteenth-century indifference toward religion and the depression of papal authority in the ecclesiastical order established by the Concordat were his targets. Lamennais now conceived of loss in mystical, timeless terms, casting monarchy as a satanic invention that robbed an Edenic world of its innocence:

> And I was transported in spirit into ancient times, and the earth was beautiful, and rich, and fertile; and its inhabitants lived happily, because they lived as brothers.
>
> And I saw the Serpent slithering in their midst; he fixed his powerful gaze on several, and their soul was troubled, and they approached, and the Serpent spoke in their ears.
>
> And after having heard the word of the Serpent, they arose and said: We are kings.
>
> ...
>
> And there came to pass strange mysteries; and there were chains, tears and blood.
>
> ...
>
> And I understand that there must be a reign of Satan before the reign of God. And I will cry and I will hope.[103]

Representing Christ as friend to the poor and the oppressed, and the very model of a revolutionary, *Paroles d'un croyant* encouraged the adoption of Jesus by anti-clerical democratic socialists and workers in the years leading up the Revolution of 1848.[104] "The republicans of our time," Lamennais wrote to Montalembert (8 April 1835), "would have been, eighteen centuries ago, the most ardent disciples of Christ."[105]

Montalembert and Lacordaire were dismayed. The latter (already distanced from Lamennais since 1832) published a refutation. Predictably, there was papal condemnation. The encyclical *Singulari nos* characterized the book as "meager in volume but immense in perversity."[106] Between 1835 and 1836, at the very time that French religious painting began its ascent, Lamennais abandoned Catholicism. Like *Paroles d'un croyant*, his *Book of the People* (*Le Livre du peuple*, 1837) was immensely popular among working class readers. This denunciation of capitalist greed and enslavement went through seven editions in 1838, with more than 10,000 copies purchased during its first days on the market. Eventually, Lamennais moved so far to the Left that he was imprisoned in Sainte-Pélagie for a year (1841–42) for a pamphlet (*Le Pays et le gouvernement*) attacking the July Monarchy. Like Lacordaire, Lamennais embraced the Second Republic. The former was elected in 1848 to the Constituent Assembly (to which he wore his Dominican habit); Lamennais was sent twice to the republican legislature, the second time as a democratic socialist (albeit one who defended private property). A caricature (1850) by Cham (pseudonym for Amédé de Noé, 1818–79) shows the former priest at the rostrum of the Constituent Assembly of 1848, demanding on 15 July that he, rather than the manager of the journal *Le Peuple constituant*, be held legally responsible for a recent article attacking the government. An abandoned cassock hanging from thorny tendrils emblematizes the speaker's quest for martyrdom (Figure 1.13). In commentary accompanying the caricature, Auguste Lireux, (1810–70), a journalist for the satirical paper *Le Charivari,* attributes the speaker's bitterness to a physical inability to speak above a murmur:

> On that somber face, on the sinking line of that lip, in that forehead crease which tells of so much silently devoured gall, in that convulsive effort to blurt out the strident thought that invincibly dies in the paralyzed throat, it seems that we read all the past, all the present, all the life of this man ....[107]

Following the coup d'état of Louis-Napoléon Bonaparte, Lacordaire refused to preach in Notre-Dame and Lamennais abandoned public life. The author of *Paroles d'un croyant* began to translate the masterwork of a writer who had suffered exile for belonging to a faction opposed to the pope. Bearing a long, anti-papal introduction, the unfinished translation of Dante's *Divine Comedy* was published in 1855. In the

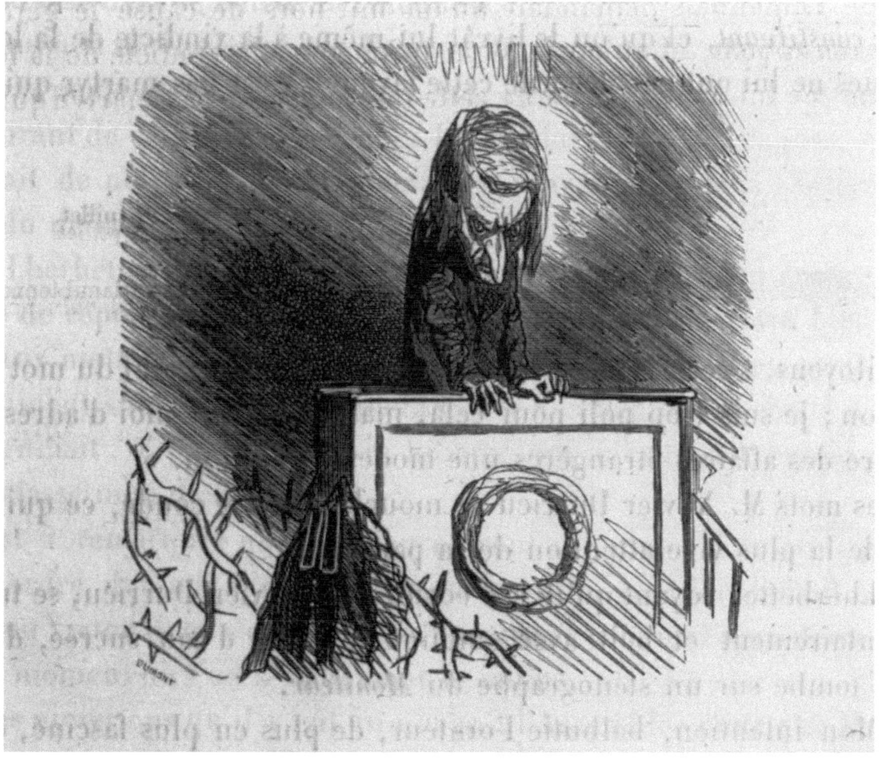

Figure 1.13 Cham (Amédé de Noé), Caricature of Lamennais, 1850. In Auguste Lireux, *Assemblée nationale comique, illustré par Cham* (Paris: Michel-Lévy Frères, 1850), 127. Paris: Bibliothèque nationale de France. Photo: BnF.

previous year, in accord with his last wishes, Lamennais was buried among the poor in a common grave, without Catholic rites. Mounted police enforced closure of Père-Lachaise Cemetery to the public. A crowd of workers forced its way into the cortege, with one determined mourner seriously wounded by a constable's sabre.

Lamennais claimed as a birthright the bilious discontent that remains constant throughout his vertiginous career. On more than one occasion, he confessed that his soul had been born with a gaping wound.[108] Yet his grief cannot be attributed solely to temperament. It was also a legacy of the spiritual crisis of national scope that opened with de-Christianization and continued after the Concordat, birthing literature and art as sensational as the *Génie du christianisme* and Gérard's *Saint Theresa*. That crisis was already running its inexorable course in the year that Lamennais turned 11 and the kings of Judah were taken from the façade of Notre-Dame.

Notes

1 Quoted in the classic anthology *Neoclassicism and Romanticism 1750–1850, Sources and Documents*, ed. Lorenz Eitner (Englewood Cliffs, NJ: Prentice-Hall, Inc., 1970), 1: 142. For vandalism during the Revolution, see Richard Clay, *Iconoclasm in Revolutionary Paris: The Transformation of Signs* (Oxford: Voltaire Foundation, 2012); François Souchal, *Le Vandalisme de la Révolution* (Paris: Nouvelles éditions latines, 1993); and Louis Réau, *Histoire du vandalisme: Les Monuments détruits de l'art français*, vol. 1 (Paris: Librairie Hachette, 1959).

2 *Explication des ouvrages de peinture et dessins sculpture, architecture et gravure, des artistes vivans, exposés au Muséum central des Arts, d'après l'Arrété du Ministre de l'Intérieur, le 15 Fructidor, an VIII de la République française* (Paris: De l'Imprimerie des Sciences et Arts, [1800]), reprint, *Catalogues of the Paris Salon, 1673 to 1881*, comp. H.W. Janson (New York: Garland, 1977), nos. 514–6.

3 For the Notre-Dame sculptures, their destruction, and restitution, see Alain Erlande-Brandenburg and Dominique Thibaudat, *Les Sculptures de Notre-Dame de Paris au Musée de Cluny* (Paris: Éditions de la Réunion des musées nationaux, 1982); and Clay, *Iconoclasm in Revolutionary Paris*, 217–20.

4 For this head (no. 12), see Erlande-Brandenburg and Thibaudat, *Sculptures de Notre-Dame*, no. 107

5 Mercier, who thought they were French kings, ironically remarked of the remains: "Tel est aujourd'hui dans Paris le nouveau St.-Denis, ou plutôt le muséum de ces antiques et royales statues. Le curieux le traversant, se pince les narines, et craint que ces effigies, plus puantes que des cadavres, n'engendrent la peste." ("Such, in Paris today, is the new Saint-Denis, or rather the museum of these ancient and royal statues. The curious passerby pinches their nostrils, and fears that these effigies—stinking more than cadavers—not give rise to plague.") Louis-Sébastien Mercier, *Le Nouveau Paris* (Paris: Fuchs, C. Pougens, and C. F. Cramer, [1797]), 6: 87. *Le Nouveau Paris* was begun in 1793.

6 For the artist, see Guillaume Faroult and Catherine Voiriot, *Hubert Robert, 1733–1808: Un peintre visionnaire* (Paris: Musée du Louvre in association with Somogy éditions d'art, Paris, 2016); and Margaret Morgan Grasselli and Yuriko Jackall, with Guillaume Faroult, Catherine Voiriot, and Joseph Baillio, *Hubert Robert* (Washington, DC: National Gallery of Art in association with Lund Humphries, London, 2016). Two paintings and a drawing by Pierre-Antoine Demachy (1723–1807) of the church's demolition are also in the collection of the Musée Carnavalet, Paris.

7 Réau, *Histoire du vandalism*, 2: 22. Closed in 1791 and sold in 1797, the church (whose choir dated from the thirteenth century and its façade from the seventeenth) was demolished 1800–08.

8 See Adolphe Lance, *Dictionnaire des architectes francais* (Paris: V.A. Morel, 1872), 2: 201–2, n. 2.

9 For Petit-Radel's renovation of Saint-Médard, with reference to his method of destroying Gothic churches, see Robert Rosenblum, *Transformations in Late Eighteenth Century Art* (Princeton, NJ: Princeton University Press, 1969), 111–2, nn. 14–16, and fig. 116.

10 For de-Christianization, with attention to regional variation, see Michel Vovelle, *The Revolution against the Church: From Reason to the Supreme Being*, trans. Alan José (Columbus: Ohio State University Press, 1991, originally published 1988); and John McManners, *The French Revolution and the Church* (New York: Harper & Row, 1969), chap. 10.

11 For the French clergy in the aftermath of this legislation, see Joseph F. Byrnes, *Catholic and French Forever: Religious and National Identity in Modern France* (University Park: Penn State University Press, 2005), chap. 1.

12 See Elizabeth Liris, "Vandalisme et régénération dans la mission de Fouché à l'automne 1793," in *Révolution française et "vandalisme révolutionnaire": Actes du colloque international de Clermont-Ferrand 15–17 Decembre 1988*, ed. Simone Bernard-Griffiths et al., 217–28 (Paris: Universitas, 1992).

13 These figures are from Gérard Cholvy and Yves-Marie Hilaire, *Histoire religieuse de la France contemporaine* (Toulouse: Bibliothèque historique Privat, 1985), 1:17.

14 Thomas A. Kselman, *Miracles & Prophecies in Nineteenth-Century France* (New Brunswick, NJ: Rutgers University Press, 1983), 12.

15 For the Catholic revival of the late 1790s, see Suzanne Desan, *Reclaiming the Sacred: Lay Religion and Popular Politics in Revolutionary France* (Ithaca, NY: Cornell University Press, 1990). Focusing on the laity in the department of the Yonne (and emphasizing the leading role taken by women in this popular movement), Desan argues for the cross-fertilization of revolutionary and Catholic revival culture and maintains that the political orientation of the Catholic revival was not exclusively counterrevolutionary.

16 The first Declaration, that of 1791, established the practice by stating: "The National Assembly recognizes and declares, in the presence and under the auspices of the Supreme Being, the following rights of Man and Citizen." *Les Constitutions de la France depuis 1789*, ed. Jacques Godechot (Paris: Flammarion, 1979), 33. The constitutions of 1793 and 1795 followed suit. Neither this clause, nor a Declaration of Rights of Man and Citizen, are included in Napoleon's post-coup d'état Constitution of 13 December 1799.

17 For the Festival of the Supreme Being, see Mona Ozouf, *Festivals and the French Revolution*, trans. Alan Sheridan (Cambridge, MA: Harvard University Press, 1988, originally published 1976), 106–18. For the temporary décor designed by David for the festival, see James A. Leith, *Space and Revolution: Projects for Monuments, Squares, and Public Buildings in France, 1789–1799* (Montreal, QC: McGill-Queen's University Press, 1991), 211–3.

18 For the Concordat, see A. Latreille and R. Rémond, *La Période contemporaine*, in A. Latreille et al., *Histoire du Catholicisme en France*, 3: 165–78 (Paris: Editions Spes, 1962). A concise account of the issues at hand is provided in Steven Englund, *Napoleon: A Political Life* (New York: Scribner, 2004), 180–5.

19 For the relationship of the French crown and the Church prior to the Revolution, see McManners, *The French Revolution and the Church*, chap. 2.

20 For the painting, see Todd Porterfield and Susan L. Siegfried, *Staging Empire: Napoleon, Ingres, and David*. (University Park: Penn State University Press, 2006).

21 See also two nude studies of the self-crowning (Paris, Bibliothèque Thiers, Fondation Dosne-Thiers and Cambridge, MA, Fogg Art Museum, Harvard University, respectively), reproduced in Dorothy Johnson, *David: Art in Metamorphosis* (Princeton, NJ: Princeton University Press, 1993), 187–8; see also the discussion of the Louvre drawing (RF 4377), p. 200.

22 As reported in Antoine Schnapper, *David* (New York: Alpine Fine Arts Collection, 1980), 22.

23 "Quand la providence m'appelle, à remplir un ministère si long-temps étouffé dans l'éloignement et le silence, je regarde, j'observe: je vois cette chaire, cet autel, ce temple ..... oh ciel! quels souvenirs ..... et dans ce jour, quels merveilleux changemens!" Jean de Dieu-Raymond Boisgelin de Cucé, *Discours sur le rétablissement de la religion, Prononcé à Notre-Dame, le jour de Pâques 1802*, in *Oeuvres du cardinal de Boisgelin, de l'Académie française* (Paris: F. Guitel, 1818), 205 (extended ellipses in original).

24 Marcel Roux, *Bibliothèque nationale, Département des estampes. Un siècle d'histoire de France par l'estampe, 1770–1871. Collection De Vinck, Inventaire analytique*, vol. 4: *Napoléon et son temps (Directoire, Consulat, Empire)* (Paris: Bibliothèque nationale, 1969), 243, no. 7568. Variants of this print, whether featuring Cardinal Caprara alone, or including the first consul, are in the Cabinet des estampes of the Bibliothèque nationale de France. For an example (Paris, Musée Carnavalet), which features rays of glory emanating from the crucified Christ, see Jean-Paul Clément and Marc Fumaroli, *Un livre, un siècle: Le Bicentenaire du 'Génie du Christianisme,'* (Vallée-aux-Loups: Maison Chateaubriand, 2002), no. 15. In a pendant print, *The Triumph of Religion* (deposited 5 May 1803),

> Pope Pius VII and the Clergy pray to the Holy Spirit to enlighten with its beneficent rays the unfortunates who have strayed and bring them back to the Catholic religion ... recognized and protected by the First Consul on 18 April 1802 Year X.

Roux, *Napoléon et son temps,* 242–3, no. 7567.

25 For hatred of Voltaire, and its place within anti-*philosophe* discourse predating the Revolution, see Darrin M. McMahon, *Enemies of the Enlightenment: The French Counter-Enlightenment and the Making of Modernity* (Oxford: Oxford University Press, 2001), chaps. 1, 2. I thank Scott Sprenger for this reference.

26 For Chateaubriand's relationship with Fontanes, see Marc Fumaroli, *Chateaubriand: Poésie et terreur* (Paris: Gallimard, 2003), part 1, chap. 4. Jeffrey Mehlman drew my attention to this publication.

27 Chateaubriand, *Génie du christianisme,* 1282. For this famous confession, see the editor's commentary (pp. 1580–2); Jean-Marie Roulin, *Chateaubriand: L'Exil et la gloire,* Bibliothèque de la littérature modern 26 (Paris: Honoré Champion, 1994), 159–60; and Béatrice Didier, *Chateaubriand* (Paris: Ellipses, 1999), 14.

28 The kernel of the *Génie du christianisme* was contained in a 48-page manuscript, *La Religion chrétienne par rapport à la morale et à la poésie,* proposed by the author (5 April 1799) to a publisher of works by émigrés, Pierre François Fauche (1763–1814), residing in Hamburg, publication capital of the Emigration. See Didier, *Chateaubriand,* 14. For the development of Chateaubriand's ideas and the response of the émigré community, see Kirsty Carpenter, *Refugees of the French Revolution: Émigrés in London, 1789–1802* (New York: St. Martin's Press, 1999), 146–50.

29 "Lorsque le *Génie du christianisme* parut, la France sortait du chaos révolutionnaire; tous les éléments de la société étaient confondus ....[new paragraph] Ce fut donc, pour ainsi dire, au milieu des débris de nos temples que je publiai le *Génie du christianisme,* pour rappeler dans ces temples les pompes du culte et les serviteurs des autels." Chateaubriand, *Génie du christianisme,* 459.

30 For this point, see Bernard M.G. Reardon, *Religion in the Age of Romanticism: Studies in Early Nineteenth Century Thought* (Cambridge: Cambridge University Press, 1985), 4.

31 For a lucid analysis of the aesthetic basis of Chateaubriand's apology, see Frank Paul Bowman, *Le Christ romantique,* Histoire des idées et critique littéraire 134 (Geneva: Droz, 1973), 232–4.

32 Though key Old Testament episodes were ensconced in the catechism, direct reading of the text by parishioners was not traditionally encouraged by the Catholic clergy.

33 See Étienne-Jean Delécluze, *Souvenirs de soixante années* (Paris: Michel Lévy, 1862), 59–60; and idem, *Louis David, Son École & son temps. Souvenirs* (Paris: Didier, 1855), 428.

34 "Obscur Israélite, j'apporte aujourd'hui mon grain de sable." Chateaubriand, *Génie du christianisme*, 1283. For the preface to the Ballanche (1809) and Ladvocat (1826–27) editions of *Génie du christianisme*, the author elaborated: "Pour moi, obscur Israélite, j'apporte aujourd'hui mon grain de sable, afin de hâter, autant qu'il est en mon pouvoir, la reconstruction du Temple." ("As for myself, an obscure Israelite, today I bring my grain of sand, in order to hasten, as much as it is within my power, the reconstruction of the Temple"). See the editor's commentary, in Chateaubriand, *Génie du christianisme*, 1283, note a (on p. 1958).

35 Ceri Crossley, *French Historians and Romanticism: Thierry, Guizot, the Saint-Simonians, Quinet, Michelet* (London: Routledge 2002), 20.

36 Old Testament references, borrowings, and imitations by the three writers are cataloged in Abraham Albert Avni, *The Bible and Romanticism: The Old Testament in German and French Romantic Poetry* (The Hague: Mouton, 1969), chaps. 6–9.

37 "Quand ton nom doit survivre aux âges, / Que t'importe, avec ses outrages, / A toi, géant, un people nain?" ("Given that your name will survive the ages, / What do you, a giant, care about the outrages / of a dwarf populace?") Victor Hugo, *Odes et ballades*, ed. Pierre Albouy (Paris: Gallimard, 1964), 222. The *Ballades*, which were joined to the *Odes*, date from 1823–28.

38 For the circle around *La Muse française,* see Paul Bénichou, *Le Sacre de l'écrivain, 1750–1830: Essai sur l'avènement d'un pouvoir spirituel laïque dans la France modern*, 2nd ed. (Paris: Librairie José Corti, 1985), 288–300.

39 The concluding lines of the preface (August 1828) to the 1828 edition of *Odes et ballades* declare: "Espérons qu'un jour le dix-neuvième siècle, politique et littéraire, pourra être résumé d'un mot: la liberté dans l'ordre, la liberté dans l'art," ("Let us hope that one day the nineteenth century—political and literary—will be able to be condensed into a word: liberty in [the political] order, liberty in art." Hugo, *Odes et ballades*, 41.

40 See the catalog entry by Isabelle Julia, in idem, Jean Lacambre, and Sylvain Boyer, *Les Années romantiques: La Peinture française de 1815 à 1850* (Paris: Éditions de la Réunion des musées nationaux, 1995), no. 96; the catalog entry by Geneviève Lacambre, in Frederick J., Cummings, Pierre Rosenberg, and Robert Rosenblum, *French Painting, 1774–1830: The Age of Revolution* (Detroit: Detroit Institute of Arts, 1975), no. 70; and Jennifer Marie Langworthy, "On Shifting Ground: The Revolutionary Career of François Gérard" (PhD Diss., University of Illinois at Urbana-Champaign, 2012), 333–4.

41 From a letter (29 April 1828), quoted by Julia, in Julia et al., *Les Années romantiques,* 388. For Girodet's painting (based on Chateaubriand's novella *Atala* of 1801, later appended to the *Génie du christianisme*), see the catalog entry by Sylvain Bellenger, in idem, Marc Fumaroli, and Bruno Chenique, *Girodet, 1767–1824* (Paris: Éditions Gallimard / Musée du Louvre Éditions, 2006), no. 51.

42 Antony Béraud, *Annales de l'école française des Beaux-Arts*, first year (Paris: Pillet aîné, 1827), 137–8.

43 Auguste Jal, *Esquisses, croquis, pochades ou Tout ce qu'on voudra sur le Salon de 1827* (Paris, 1828), 372–88, quoted by Geneviève Lacambre, in Cummings et al., *French Painting 1774–1830*, 439.

44 *Le Globe* (5 March 1828) quoted by Geneviève Lacambre, in Cummings et al., *French Painting 1774–1830*, 438.

45 For spectator Christianity, see Robert Rosenblum, *Paintings in the Musée d'Orsay*, frwrd. Françoise Cachin (New York: Stewart, Tabori & Chang, 1989), 31; and Rosenblum, *Jean-Auguste-Dominique Ingres* (New York: Harry N. Abrams, 1967, reprint, 1985), 100–3.

46 This current is also manifest in the granular account of seminary life in the novel *Volupté* (1834) by Charles-Augustin Sainte-Beuve (1804–69), who later devoted untold hours to research for a lecture series and subsequent multi-volume book, *Port-Royal* (1840–59) on the Jansenists.

47 Its carved frame replete with eucharistic emblems, Friedrich's representation of a crucifix on a north German peak surrounded by evergreens at sunset was exhibited in Dresden at Christmas time in 1808, in a chapel-like setting, as if it were an actual altarpiece intended to elicit prayer. The classicist Wilhelm Basilius von Ramdohr (1757–1822) famously attacked the mock devotional painting as a pernicious blending of genres—in which landscape had "crept into the church and crawled onto the altar"—foreshadowing the equivocal position of Gérard's altarpiece. See the discussion of the controversy in William Vaughan, *Friedrich* (London: Phaidon, 2004), 105–12.

48 See the deft analysis of this painting in Thomas Crow, *Restoration: The Fall of Napoleon in the Course of European Art, 1812–1820* (Princeton, NJ: Princeton University Press, 2018), 133–5. See also Denis Coekelberghs et al., *François-Joseph Navez (Charleroi 1787-Bruxelles 1869): La Nostalgie de l'Italie* (Charleroi: Musée des Beaux-Arts de Charleroi, in association with Snoeck-Ducaju & Zoon, Ghent, 1999), 29–31, and 72–4 for a later version, in which the mother, who solely accompanies her daughter, looks

heavenward (ca. 1822, private collection). I thank Sofie Corneillie and Bart de Sitter, of the Museum of Fine Arts, Ghent for assistance in obtaining a reproduction of *Saint Veronica of Milan*.

49 The kinship between the saint's parents and expressive heads drawn by David in the late 'teens and 1820s while exiled in Brussels is indicated by Crow and Coekelberghs. For examples of the David drawings, see Crow, *Restoration*, 138–40, and Coekelberghs et al., *François-Joseph Navez*, 76.

50 See the catalog entry by Geneviève Lacambre, in Cummings et al., *French Painting 1774–1830*, no. 166.

51 For this painting, see Bruno Foucart, *Le Renouveau de la peinture religieuse en France (1800–1860)* (Paris: Arthéna, 1987), 287–9.

52 Le père ... à genoux les mains jointes, regarde et prie le sainte de tout son coeur. Sur cette physionomie agreste et naturellement dure, le peintre a eu l'art d'y mettre une nuance de douleur et d'espérance qui rend ce personage on ne peut plus touchant ...." Étienne-Jean Delécluze, "Salon de 1831 (Schnetz et Robert)," *L'Artiste* 1 (1831), 189.

53 Heinrich Heine, *De la France*, new ed. (Paris: Michel Lévy, 1873), 354.

54 *Les Constitutions de la France depuis 1789*, ed. Godechot, 219.

55 See Latreille and Rémond, *La Période contemporaine*, 3: 262–2. For the prolific reprinting of works by the *philosophes* under the Bourbon Restoration (and their burning by opponents of the Enlightenment), see McMahon, *Enemies of the Enlightenment*, 172–82. McMahon (p. 183) indicates that anti-clericalism rose precipitously in the wake of the coronation of Charles X, with its ultra-royalist, Catholic pageantry. Sheryl Kroen's research demonstrates that the 1820s saw an explosion of interest in *Tartuffe* in the French provinces, with performances of the play serving as vehicles for hostility toward missionaries determined to eradicate the revolutionary heritage. See Sheryl Kroen, *Politics and Theater: The Crisis of Legitimacy in Restoration France, 1815–1830* (Berkeley: University of California Press, 2000), chap. 6.

56 Nicole Villa, *Bibliothèque nationale, Département des estampes. Un siècle d'histoire de France par l'estampe, 1770–1871. Collection De Vinck. Inventaire analytique*, vol. 6: *La Révolution de 1830 et La Monarchie de Juillet* (Paris: Bibliothèque nationale, 1979), 56, no. 11.208.

57 Guizot and Toqueville are quoted in Cholvy and Hilaire, *Histoire religieuse de la France contemporaine*, 1: 204.

58 Ibid., 1: 35.

59 For this point, see Frank Paul Bowman, *Le Christ des barricades, (1789–1848)* (Paris: Les Éditions du Cerf, 1987), 114–6.

60 For this topic, see also Elisabeth Kashey, "Religious Art in Nineteenth Century France," in *Christian Imagery in French Nineteenth-Century Art, 1789–1906*, ed. Martin L.H. Reymert and Robert J.F. Kashey, 1–30 (New York: Shepherd Gallery, 1980).

61 Foucart, *Le Renouveau de la peinture religieuse*, 76–7.

62 For this opinion, see Latreille and Rémond, *La Période contemporaine*, 251–2. For popular devotion, see Kselman, *Miracles & Prophecies*.

63 McMahon, *Enemies of the Enlightenment*, 176.

64 For the visions and the cult to which they gave rise, see Richard D.E. Burton, *Blood in the City: Violence and Revelation in Paris, 1789–1945* (Ithaca, NY: Cornell University Press, 2001), chap. 6.

65 This figure is from Byrnes, *Catholic and French Forever*, 94.

66 For the career and writings of Lamennais, see Reardon, *Religion in the Age of Romanticism*, chap. 7; idem, *Liberalism and Tradition: Aspects of Catholic Thought in Nineteenth-Century France* (Cambridge: Cambridge University Press, 1975), chaps. 4, 5; Paul Bénichou, *Le Temps des prophètes: Doctrines de l'âge romantique* (Paris: Gallimard, 1977), chap. 4; Guy Peeters, "Lamennais, l'irréductible croyant," *Nineteenth-Century French Studies* 14, nos. 1–2 (Fall–Winter 1985–86): 80–102; and the introduction to *Lamennais: A Believer's Revolutionary Politics*, trans. Richard A. Lebrun and Jerry Ryan, ed. Richard A. Lebrun and Sylvain Milbach, int. and annotat. Sylvain Milbach, Studies in the History of Political Thought 13 (Leiden: Brill, 2018), which includes translated selections from his publications of the 1830s.

67 On ne peut s'empêcher de reconnaître dans vos destinées la main de cette Providence qui vous avait marqué de loin, pour l'accomplissement de ses desseins prodigieux." Chateaubriand, *Génie du christianisme*, 1284.

68 This position represented an about-face analogous to that of Chateaubriand. In a short publication, *Réflexions sur l'état de l'Eglise en France pendant le XVIIIe siècle, et son situation actuelle* (1808), Lamennais had lauded the emperor for his contribution to the revival of Catholicism. As the author's call for strengthening the Church ran afoul of Napoleon's aggressive posture vis-à-vis the Pope, *Réflexions* was seized by the police. See Reardon, *Religion in the Age of Romanticism*, 178.

69 "Au milieu de cette noire tempête, la foi d'un grand nombre chancèle, l'espérance se flétrit et s'éteint: encore quelques momens [sic] et les élus même seront séduits.... Une effroyable apostasie nous menace; l'univers est en attente; il hésite entre vous et l'affreuse idole de l'athéisme .... Grand Dieu ...! Que les flots de votre colère long-temps retenus se débordent sur vos ennemis et les engloutissent; que la mer rejette de son sein leurs dépouilles impures, et, comme les Israélites miraculeusement sauvés, nous chanterons sur ses bords l'hymne de la déliverance." *Tradition de l'église sur l'institution des évêques* (Liege: Le Marié and Duvivier; and Paris: Société typographique, 1814), 3: 410–1.

70 "[I]l faut se presser de parler de vérité, d'ordre, de Religion, aux peuples, de peur de ressembler au médecin qui disserteroit sur la vie près d'un tombeau." Lamennais, *Essai sur l'indifférence en matière de religion*, vol. 1 (Paris: Tournachon-Molin and H. Seguin, 1817). The work eventually comprised four volumes (1817–23); the subsequent volumes did not renew the sensation created by the first. For a discussion of the first volume, see A. Latreille and R. Rémond, *La période contemporaine*, 3: 265–8.

71 "Et quand la philosophie récemment a voulu fonder un Etat sans religion, elle a été forcée de lui donner pour base des cadavres ...." Lamennais, *Essai sur l'indifférence* 1: 25.

72 "Le siècle le plus malade n'est pas celui qui se passionne pour l'erreur, mais le siècle qui néglige, qui dédaigne la vérité. Il y a encore de la force, et par conséquent de l'espoir, là où l'on aperçoit de violens [sic] transports: mais lorsque tout mouvement est éteint, lorsque le pouls a cessé de battre, que le froid a gagné le coeur, et que l'haleine du moribond ne ternit plus le miroir q'une curiosité inquiète approche de sa bouche, qu'attendre alors qu'une prochaine et inevitable dissolution. [new paragraph] En vain l'on essaierait de se le dissimuler, la société, en Europe, s'avance rapidement vers ce terme fatal. Les bruits formidables qui grondent dans son sein ... ne sont pas le plus effrayant symptôme qu'elle offre à l'observateur: ces terribles convulsions peuvent n'être pas sans remède; mais cette indifférence léthargique où nous la voyons tomber, ce profond assoupissement, ce sommeil de fer, cette stupeur mortelle, qui l'en tirera? Qui soufflera sur ces ossemens arides pour les ranimer?" Lamennais, *Essai sur l'indifférence*, 1: i–ii.

73 Bénichou, *Le Temps des prophètes*, 126.

74 Quoted in Reardon, *Religion in the Age of Romanticism*, 180.

75 Lamennais, *De la religion considerée dans ses rapports avec l'ordre politique et civil* (Paris: Bureau du mémorial catholique, 1826), 2: 31.

76 "On ne peut désormais le sauver qu'en se dégageant de tout autre intérêt que lui-même, que par la résolution ferme de tout endurer plutôt que d'abandonner la moindre partie de la doctrine que le Christ a scellée de son sang ...." Lamennais, *Des progrès de la Revolution et de la guerre contre l'Église* (Paris and Brussels: Belin-Mandar and Devaux, 1829), 267, 33.

77 For *L'Avenir*, see Latreille and Rémond, *La Période contemporaine*, 282–6.

78 Quoted in Cholvy and Hilaire, *Histoire religieuse de la France contemporaine*, 1:88. In a letter of 8 May 1833 to Abbé Vuarin, Lamennais stated that Gregory XVI had been sent by Providence '"to show the world just how low the human part of the divine institution can sink." Quoted in Reardon, *Religion in the Age of Romanticism*, 188.

79 See the perceptive discussion of the portrait in Michael Paul Driskel, *Representing Belief: Religion, Art, and Society in Nineteenth-Century France* (University Park: Penn State University Press, 1992), 31; and the catalog entry by Stéphane Guégan, in idem, Vincent Pomarède, and Louis-Antoine Prat, *Chassériau: Un autre romantisme* (Paris: Réunion des musées nationaux, 2002), no. 47, which quotes a displeased critic writing for a Catholic paper: "On ne saurait imaginer quelque chose ... de plus luthérien que l'aspect de ce

portrait." ("One could not imagine anything ... more Lutheran than the aspect of this portrait.") G.D., "Salon de 1841," *L'Univers* (5 June 1841).

80 The official biography by the Dominican Bernard Chocarne, *Le R.P. Lacordaire de l'ordre des Frères Precheurs* (1866), which went through seven reeditions and five translations, details the extremes to which Lacordaire carried self-immolation. It was his custom to request flagellation at the hands of a novice: "He ended up covered with bruises, but remained a long time, his lips glued to the feet of the person who had beaten him, expressing his gratitude in the strongest possible terms." Quoted in Frank Paul Bowman, *French Romanticism: Intertextual and Interdisciplinary Readings* (Baltimore, MD: Johns Hopkins University Press, 1990), 88.

81 "D'abord il m'avait répondu qu'il réfléchirait à ma proposition, qu'il était peu de chose comme rang dans le clergé et que son portrait serait vu sans intérêt, etc. etc." Letter to the artist's brother Frédéric, from Rome (9 September 1840), reprinted in Léonce Bénédite, *Théodore Chassériau, sa vie, son oeuvre*, ed. André Dezarrois (Paris: Braun, 1931), 1:136. See also the chronology by Bruno Chenique in Guégan et al., *Chassériau: Un autre romantisme*, 179.

82 For the Confrérie de saint Jean and its regulations, see Foucart, *Le Renouveau de la peinture*, 45–8; and Michel Caffort, *Les Nazaréens français: Théorie et pratique de la peinture religieuse au XIXe siècle* (Rennes: Presses Universitaires de Rennes, 2009), 21. In 1844, the confraternity was absorbed by a Dominican lay order.

83 Lavergne concluded his proposal to Lacordaire (written prior to June 1839): "Janmot et moi nous embrassons notre très cher Dominicain." ("Janmot and I embrace our very dear Dominican.") Quoted in Elisabeth Hardouin-Fugier, *Louis Janmot 1814–1892* (Lyon: Presses universitaires de Lyon, 1981), 48.

84 Lacordaire insists upon the

> nécessité absolue de donner à cette association un caractère religieux auquel on ne puisse se méprendre et d'écarter par là tous ceux qui ne se disaient pas chrétiens de foi, de pratique et doués, entre autre du besoin de prosélytisme. Rien de lâche ou d'intermédiaire n'est possible aujourd'hui. C'est tout ou rien. Il faut vouloir l'établissement du règne de Dieu sur la terre, ou bien rester tranquille chez soi.

Quoted, from the Archive Lacordaire, Paris, in the catalog entry by Elisabeth Hardouin-Fugier, in *Les Peintres de l'âme: Art lyonnais du XIXe siècle* (Lyon: Musée des Beaux-Arts, 1981), 176, no. 88.

85 For this poem, published in *La Muse française* (January 1824), and the poet's preservationist crusade, see Hugo, *Odes et ballades*, 115 n.1; and Constance Sherak, "Investing in the Past: Victor Hugo's La Bande noire," *Romance Languages Annual* 10, no. 1 (1999): 157–63.

86 The poem includes the mournful voice of an elegist who declaims: "'O débris! ruines de France / Que notre amour en vain defend ...." ("'Oh debris! ruins of France / That our love defends in vain ....") Hugo, *Odes et ballades*, 116.

87 "Je contemple ces vieux monuments du catholicisme avec autant d'amour et de respect que ceux qui dévouèrent leur vie et leurs biens à les fonder: ils ne représentent pas seulement pour moi une idée, une époque, une croyance éteinte; ce sont les symboles de ce qu'il y a de plus vivace dans mon âme, de plus auguste dans mes espérances. Le vandalisme moderne est non-seulement à mes yeux une brutalité et une sottise, c'est de plus un sacrilège." "Du vandalisme en France: Lettre à M. Victor Hugo," *Revue des deux mondes* 1 (March 1833), reprinted in Comte Charles Forbes de Montalembert, *Mélanges d'art et de littérature, in Oeuvres de M. le comte de Montalembert* (Paris: Jacques Lecoffre, 1861), 6:8–9.

88 Three additional volumes were published (as *De l'art chrétien*), 1855–67. Notwithstanding Chateaubriand's impact on the revival of Christian painting, his taste in the visual arts was conventional; Rio was disappointed that the author did not share his enthusiasm for the Italian primitives. See Bruno Foucart, "Chateaubriand et le renouveau de la peinture religieuse après la Révolution," in *Chateaubriand et les arts,* ed. Édouard Bonnefous and Marc Fumaroli (Paris: Éditions de Fallois, 1999), 153–62.

89 "L'âme sincèrement et logiquement catholique se repose avec délices sur cette époque si belle et si pure, où rien ne vient ternir l'éclat de la jeune parure dont la religion vêtait le

monde, où tout ce qui ornait et charmait la vie de l'homme lui rappelait le ciel." "De la peinture chrétienne en Italie, à l'occasion du livre de M. Rio," reprinted in Montalembert, *Mélanges d'art et de littérature*, in *Oeuvres*, 6: 97.

90 For the Nazarenes, see Cordula Grewe, *The Nazarenes: Romantic Avant-Garde and the Art of the Concept* (University Park: Penn State University Press, 2015); idem, *Painting the Sacred in the Age of Romanticism* (Farnham: Ashgate, 2009); and for a concise account, William Vaughan, *German Romantic Painting*, 2nd ed. (New Haven, CT: Yale University Press, 1994), chap. 8.

91 *De l'état actuel de l'art religieux en France*, quoted in Alain Daguerre de Hureaux, *Delacroix* (Paris: Hazan, 1993), 213 and n. 323 (on p. 293).

92 For the hieratic mode, see Driskel, *Representing Belief*, chap. 4. For practitioners of this mode, see also Foucart, *Le Renouveau de la peinture religieuse*; and Caffort, *Les Nazaréens français*.

93 For the painting, see Gilles Chomer, "Le Séjour en Italie (1822–1830) de Victor Orsel," in *Lyon et Italie: Six etudes d'histoire de l'art*, ed. Gilles Chomer, Marie-Félice Pérez, and Daniel Ternois (Paris: Éditions du Centre National de la Recherche Scientifique, 1984), 201–8; Henri Dorra, "'Le Bien et le Mal' d'Orsel: Tableau de manière symbolique au musée des Beaux-Arts de Lyon," *Bulletin des musées et monuments lyonnais* 5, no. 1 (1975): 291–302; Sylvie Ramond et al., *Le Temps de la peinture, Lyon 1800–1914* (Lyon: Éditions Fage, 2007), no. 89, with a discussion by Yuriko Anne Baccon, 214–5; and Caffort, *Les Nazaréens français*, 159–60. For a close reading of *Le Bien et le Mal*, see Grewe, *Painting the Sacred in the Age of Romanticism*, chap. 3. For Orsel, see also Foucart, *Le Renouveau de la peinture religieuse*, 202–5.

94 "Blanche, le plus jeune, timide fille aux yeux bleus, à la chevelure blond, était un modèle de piété et de douceur. —Berthe, plus belle, plus vive, plus piquante, laissait déjà percer dans son oeil noir le feu des plus vives passions, qui dormaient encore en elle grâce aux leçons et aux bons exemples de sa famille." [Alphonse Dupasquier], *L'Art à Lyon en 1836. Revue critique de la première exposition de la Société des Amis des Arts* (Lyon: Gabriel Rossary, 1837), 41.

95 For Orsel's sources, see Chomer, "Le séjour en Italie."

96 Théophile Gautier, "Salon de l'artiste, 1833," *La France littéraire* 6, no. 1 (1833), 159, quoted in Dorra, "'Le Bien et le Mal' d'Orsel," 293.

97 For Flandrin, see Foucart, *Le Renouveau de la peinture religieuse*, 205–11.

98 For this painting, see Driskel, *Representing Belief*, 126–8; and for Flandrin's four separately commissioned decorative ensembles in the church, carried out under the direction of the chief architect of the city of Paris, Victor Baltard (1805–74), see Bruno Horaist, "Saint-Germain-des-Prés (1839–1863)," in Jacques Foucart et al., *Hippolyte, Auguste et Paul Flandrin: Une Fraternité picturale au XIXe siècle*, 125–53 (Paris: Musée du Luxembourg, in association with Éditions de la Réunion des musées nationaux, 1984). These comprise the sanctuary (1842–46); the choir, also known as the Chapel of Apostles (1846–48); the nave (1856–63); and the transcept (1864). For *Christ's Entry into Jerusalem*, see also, in the same publication, the catalog entry by Jacques Foucart, no. 53. According to Horaist, (pp. 125–6), Hippolyte's brother Paul painted the two donkeys in *Christ's Entry into Jerusalem*.

99 "Monsieur Hippolyte Flandrin a voulu concilier le sentiment catholique de Giotto avec la science païenne de Raphaël. C'est là une tentative que nous approuvons hautement." Gustave Planche, "Peinture monumentale: M.M. Eugène Delacroix et Hippolyte Flandrin," *Revue des deux mondes*, new ser. 15 (July 1846), 157, quoted in Foucart et al., *Hippolyte, Auguste et Paul Flandrin*, catalog no. 53, entry by Jacques Foucart.

100 "Le lendemain de ce jour, mardi 6, en revenant de Saint-Sulpice, entré à Saint-Germain des Prés, où j'ai vu les barbouillages gothiques dont on couvre les murs de cette malheureuse église. Confirmation de ce que je disais à mon ami: j'aime mieux les imaginations de Lehmann que les contrefaçons de Baltard, Flandrin et Cie." ("The next day, Tuesday the 6th, returning from Saint-Sulpice, entered Saint-Germain-des-Prés, where I saw the gothic daubs with which they are covering the walls of that unhappy church. Confirmation of what I told my friend: I prefer the fancies of Lehmann over the fakeries of Baltard, Flandrin and company.") On 5 April, Delacroix had listened to his friend

Michel-Augustin Varcollier (1795–1882) rail against the paintings of the Ingres pupil Henri Lehmann in the Hôtel de Ville. Eugène Delacroix, *Journal*, ed. Michèle Hannoosh (Paris: José Corti, 2009), 1: 586–7 (5 April 1852), and see Hannoosh's commentary, n. 88. Flandrin's work was not in progress when Delacroix visited the church.

101 Reardon, *Religion in the Age of Romanticism*, 193.

102 See Bowman, *French Romanticism*, 65.

103 "Et je fus transporté en esprit dans les temps anciens, et la terre était belle, et riche, et féconde; et ses habitants vivaient heureux, parce qu'ils vivaient en frères. / Et je vis le Serpent qui se glissait au milieu d'eux: il fixa sur plusieurs son regard puissant, et leur âme se troubla, et ils s'approchèrent, et le Serpent leur parla à l'oreille. / Et après avoir écouté la parole du Serpent, ils se levèrent et dirent: Nous sommes rois.... Et il se passa là des mystères étranges; et il y eut des chaînes, des pleurs et du sang.... Et je compris qu'il devait y avoir un règne de Satan avant le règne de Dieu. Et je pleurai et j'espérai." Félicité Robert de Lamennais, *Paroles d'un croyant; Divers écrits pour le peuple*, int. Alphonse Séché (Paris: Nelson, n.d.), 34–5.

104 For this development, see Bowman, *Le Christ des barricades*, chap. 6; idem, *Le Christ romantique*, chap. 2; Edward Berenson, *Populist Religion and Left-Wing Politics in France, 1830–1852* (Princeton, NJ: Princeton University Press, 1984), chap. 3; and Driskel, *Representing Belief*, 135–9, 178–80. Bowman (*Le Christ des barricades*, p. 271) indicates that the notion of Christ as revolutionary was not unanimous, meeting resistance on the Left as well as from Catholic conservatives.

105 Quoted in Bénichou, *Le Temps des prophètes*, 166.

106 Quoted in Cholvy and Hilaire, *Histoire religieuse de la France contemporaine*, 1: 89.

107 "Sur ce sombre visage, sur cette lèvre dont le pli s'affaisse, dans cette ride du front qui accuse tant de fiel sourdement dévoré, dans cet effort convulsive pour jeter en éclats la pensée stridente qui expire invinciblement dans le gosier paralysé, il nous semble que nous lisons tout le passé, tout le present, toute la vie de cet homme...." Auguste Lireux, *Assemblée nationale comique, Illustré par Cham* (Paris: Michel-Lévy Frères, 1850), 127.

108 See Henri Peyre, *What is Romanticism?*, trans. Roda Roberts (Tuscaloosa.: University of Alabama Press, 1977, originally published 1971), 74, 115.

2 Agony in the Garden

In 1860, Delacroix wrote to the ministry in charge of arts management requesting that his *Christ on the Cross*, which had been purchased by the State at the Salon of 1835 and relegated to a damp chapel in the church of Saint-Paterne, Vannes, be moved to another, more salubrious location. In support of his request, the artist specified that he had produced this painting "without intending for it to be placed in a church."[1] A sympathetic critic (possibly Jules Janin, 1804–74) recognized the worldly aspect of that painting at the time of the Salon: "M. Delacroix's Calvary is both grand and solemn; it may not be a Christian Calvary, but there is no doubt that it is the Calvary of a great artist."[2] The disparity between Delacroix's attraction to sacred subjects—he represented them more than 70 times between 1835 and his death—and his resolutely secular devotion to his art exemplifies the phenomenon with which this chapter is concerned: the sacrifice of public, devotional function to private concerns in Christian art dating from the first half of the nineteenth century. It was, in the words of Chateaubriand, "amid the debris of our temples" that the Concordat reestablished Catholic worship; that debris formed an impassible barrier between the Old Masters and those such as Delacroix, who represented Christ and the saints in the age of Romanticism.

Gethsemane

Delacroix's unconventional approach to Catholic subjects was evident as early as 1824, when he received his first official commission from Comte Gaspard de Chabrol (1773–1843), prefect of the Seine. Exhibited in the Salon of 1827–28, *Christ in the Garden Olives* was sent to the Paris church of Saint-Paul-Saint-Louis (Figure 2.1).[3] As documentation of the commission has not been located, it is unknown whether Delacroix chose the subject; in any case he produced one of his most moving interpretations of the Gospels. Despite his radiant halo, Christ's humanity is emphasized, and the artist gives almost equal play to the tender sympathy of a trio of distressed, gorgeous angels. Seeming to refuse their commiseration, Delacroix's Christ projects sorrowful resolution rather than the resigned obedience to the Father's will and acknowledgement of the loneliness of the task before him, as specified in Matthew 26:39, Mark 14:36, and Luke 22:42. Here is Mark's version:

> When they reached a place called Gethsemane, he said to his disciples, 'Sit here while I pray.' And he took Peter and James and John with him. Horror and dismay came over him, and he said to them, 'My heart is ready to break with grief; stop here, and stay awake.' Then he went forward a little, threw himself on the

DOI: 10.4324/9781003184737-3

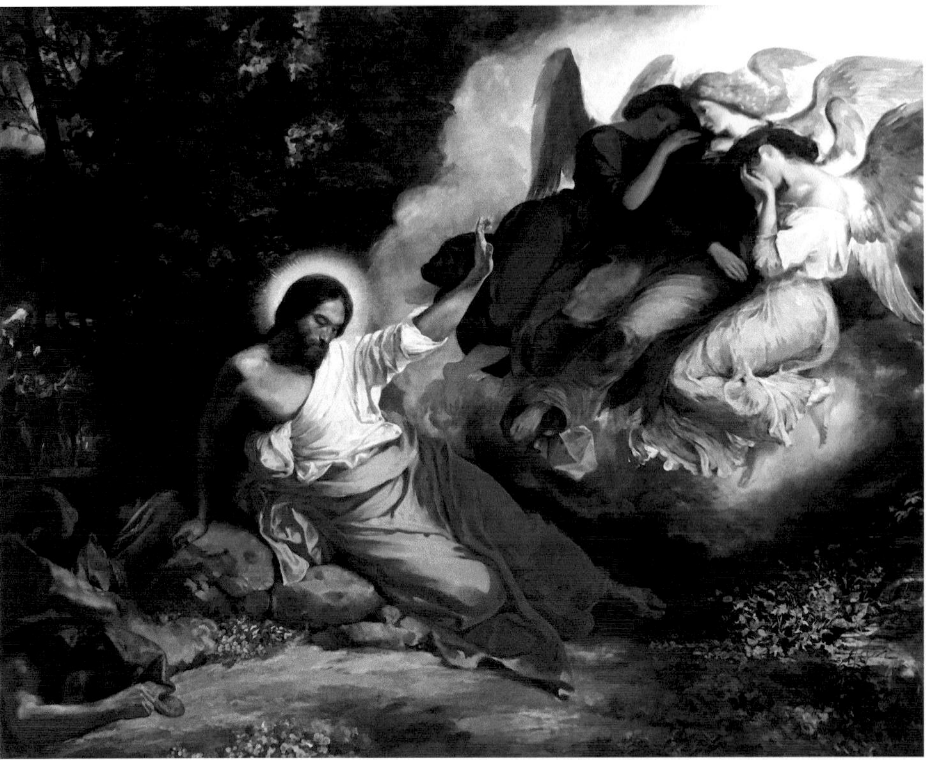

Figure 2.1 Eugène Delacroix, *Christ in the Garden of Olives*, 1824–26, oil on canvas, 294 × 362 cm. Paris, Saint-Paul-Saint-Louis. Photo: Jonathan P. Ribner.

> ground, and prayed that, if it were possible, this hour might pass him by. 'Abba, Father,' he said, 'all things are possible to thee; take this cup away from me. Yet not what I will, but what thou wilt.'
>
> He came back and found them asleep....[4]

Delacroix's initial intent to emphasize isolation and human frailty is laid bare in a watercolor and graphite study featuring Christ slumped on a rock and bereft of angelic consolation, his halo a nebulous glow (Figure 2.2).[5] Prophetic of later representations of the subject in French Romantic art and literature, this depressing early conception was revised in favor of what the artist's later admirer Charles Baudelaire (1821–67) characterized as "feminine tenderness and poetic unction."[6] At the expense of fidelity to scripture, Delacroix offers the pleasure of rich color (recently restored to life by a masterful cleaning), as well as suave, rhythmic composition. Draped in white and vivid coral, this handsome Christ is set in dramatic relief against nocturnal foliage.[7]

Delacroix offers neither the sentimental appeal and erotic edge that drew crowds to Gérard's *Saint Theresa*, nor the colorful exoticism of Schnetz's *Vow to the Madonna*. In contrast to those examples of spectator Christianity, *Christ in the Garden of Olives* represents a Gospel narrative. Although that qualifies the work as a religious painting, both the visual evidence and *Journal* entries suggest that connoisseurship of

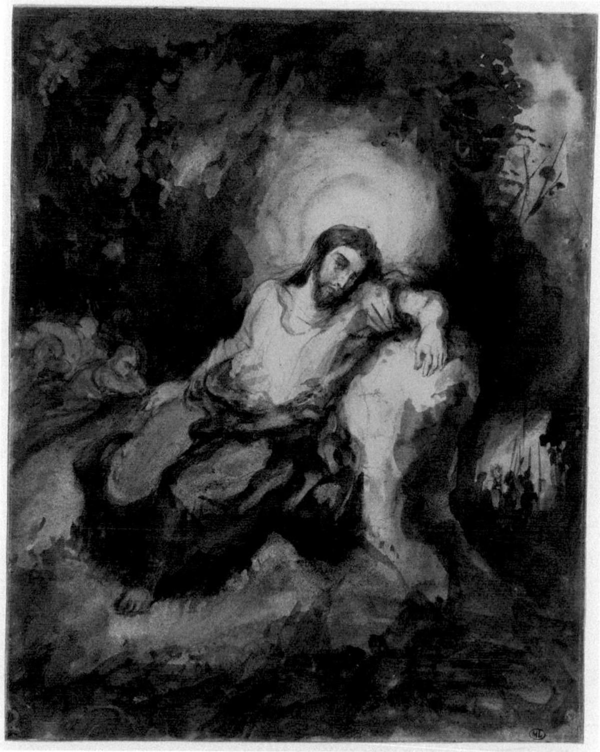

Figure 2.2 Eugène Delacroix, Study for *Christ in the Garden of Olives*, ca. 1824, watercolor and graphite, 25.2 × 20.5 cm. Paris, Musée du Louvre. Photo: Franck Raux. © RMN-Grand Palais/Art Resource, NY.

grief and of art, rather than Catholic fervor, guided Delacroix's brush. Accordingly, he was especially concerned with the expressions and appearance of the angels. On 30 April 1824, he noted, "For my painting of Christ, the sad and severe angels of death cast upon him their melancholy gaze."[8] An entry of 3 May invokes (with a note of desire) paintings of female saints by Zurbarán that he had seen in Marshal Jean-de-Dieu Soult's collection of Spanish art, as the artist adjures, "Think, when doing my angels for the prefect, of those beautiful and mystical figures of women ...."[9] Attuned to his own impulsive creativity rather than the needs of worshipers, the artist recorded on 1 May 1824, "I was in a kind of frenzy of creation at the studio this morning, and recaptured my feeling for the *Christ*, which I have not been in the mood for."[10] Professional ambition also loomed large. Hungry for future commissions, the young artist abandoned his early, bleak interpretation, all the while hawking his mastery of sensuous hue and touch no less flamboyantly than in the *Still Life with Lobsters* (Paris, Musée du Louvre), which also hung in the Salon of 1827–28. Both convey a conviction stated in his final *Journal* entry (22 June 1863): "The chief merit of a painting is to be a feast for the eye."[11]

Christ's bitter vigil in the Garden of Olives has a modest place in the Old Master repertoire; it is not even listed among the New Testament subjects represented in the seventeenth and eighteenth centuries, as catalogued by Andor Pigler.[12] Yet we know, thanks to the statistical research of Bruno Foucart, that it had enormous popularity in nineteenth-century France. Sixty-one examples appeared in the Salon between 1800 and 1861, with 39 in the period 1831–48.[13] The sole episode from the life of Christ exhibited with greater frequency is one pertaining to exile, the Flight into Egypt. That portrayals of Christ's dread and isolation had Romantic appeal was recognized by the critic Auguste Jal, who praised Delacroix's version as "a poem which Chateaubriand or Nodier might analyze, which Lamartine might translate."[14] The emotional pull of the theme was experienced in 1819 by Aurore Dupin (1804–76)—the future George Sand, who would become a close friend to Delacroix—when, as a 15-year-old worshiping in the dark chapel of the Parisian convent of the Augustinian nuns on the rue des Fossés-Saint-Victor, she meditated on a murky painting (that she thought was by Titian) representing Christ kneeling in the Garden of Olives, falling into the arms of an angel:

> While mechanically analyzing those grandiose and confused masses, I searched for the sense of this agony of Christ, the secret of this searing, voluntary pain, and I began to ascertain something larger and more profound than what had been explained to me; I became deeply sad myself, and distressed by extraordinary pity and suffering. Several tears came to the edge of my eyelid, I furtively wiped them, being ashamed to be so moved without knowing why.[15]

Imbued with the tender spirituality encouraged by Chateaubriand, this remarkable passage gives measure to the potency of the motif in the age of Romanticism, for a young, gifted viewer who could barely discern its lineaments.

Sand's response has a period flavor that also infuses the work of those painters whom Foucart designates the "School of Sentiment."[16] Within this category, he assembles a disparate cohort, including crowd pleasers, such as the exactingly descriptive Paul Delaroche (1797–1856) and the sentimental Dutch Protestant Ary Scheffer (1795–1858); the less popular and more daring Delacroix and Chassériau; and the poet Alfred de Vigny, author of the best-known verse interpretation of the Agony in the Garden. Identifying heightened emotionality and confessional lyricism as this school's common denominator, Foucart later separated Chassériau's representations of Christ in the Garden of Olives from those by his contemporaries on the grounds of the artist's singular conformity to Catholic tradition.[17] Yet as I will argue, Chassériau twice imbued the Gospel narrative with a downbeat moodiness that is less conducive to prayer than steeped in the *mal du siècle.*

Chassériau portrayed *Jesus in the Garden of Olives* in two large paintings of nearly identical dimensions, each sent to a provincial church.[18] The first (Figure 2.3), exhibited in the Salon of 1840 with reference in the guidebook to Mark's account, was commissioned by the Ministry of the Interior at an unknown date (perhaps after January 1839, when studies of the subject appear).[19] The oppressive gloom of this painting dramatizes the bleakness of Christ's predicament, rather than resignation to divine volition. Despondency is writ large in a chroma-starved color scheme that was not well received at the Salon. Heavenly light bleaches into pallid tints the drapery of three angels, two of whom bear attributes of the Passion as a third strikes the stock attitude of melancholy. This harsh illumination is set off by a curtain of blackened sky hovering above captors approaching in the distance. The classicist

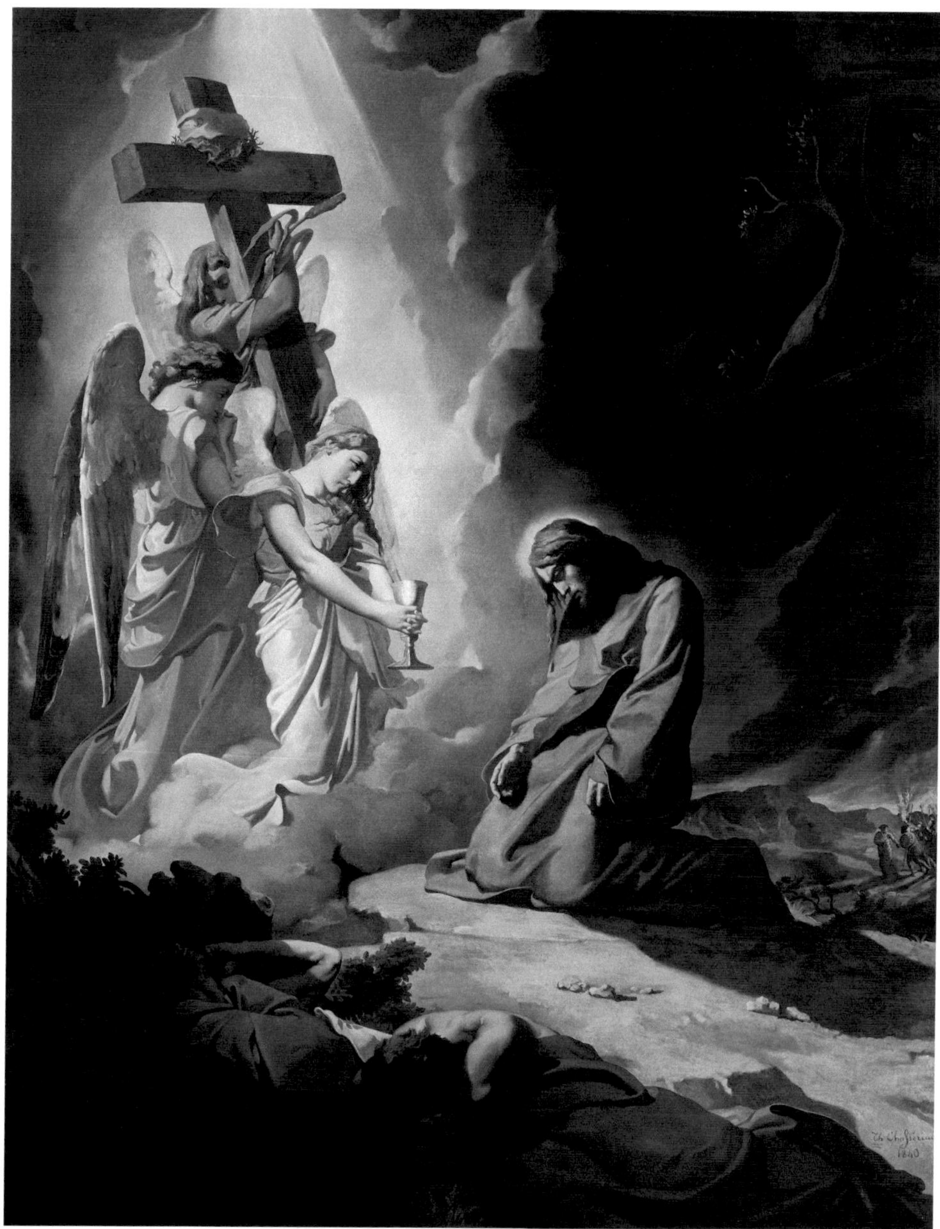

Figure 2.3 Théodore Chassériau, *Jesus in the Garden of Olives*, ca. 1839–40, oil on canvas, 452 × 357 cm. Lyon, Musée des Beaux-Arts, formerly in the church of Saint-Jean-d'Angély. Image © Lyon MBA-Photo Alain Basset.

Etienne-Jean Delécluze complained that "the brown tone of the painting is too uniform," and Prosper Haussard (1802–66) was put off by its mournful ambience: "the earth is desolate, the light is livid, the darkness atrocious... and an Olive tree twists its black, naked branches in a funereal fog."[20] Foucart notes that the attributes of the sorrowful trio of angels align the painting with Counter-Reformation doctrine; accordingly, he argues, it is closer in content to Baroque versions of the subject by Poussin, Le Brun, and Jouvenet than it is to representations of the Gospel narrative by contemporaries that belong to the tradition of *le Christ romantique,* as identified by Frank Paul Bowman.[21] Yet the crushing grief evoked by Chassériau's lugubrious canvas has no equivalent in the Baroque examples adduced by Foucart, with their supporting angels and heavenward gazes.

Undertaken at his initiative, Chassériau's second version of *Jesus in the Garden of Olives*, exhibited in the Salon of 1844, was purchased by the State in 1848, at a time when Jesus was in vogue among democratic socialists (Figure 2.4).[22] It shows a later moment in the narrative. Following Christ's resignation to God's will, his loneliness is brought home by the slumber of the disciples he had asked to remain awake. Retaining the first version's proclivity toward deep shadow and monochrome, Chassériau now opts for a pyramidal composition wherein stasis and symmetry recall the hieratic severity of his recent mural, in the Parisian church of Saint-Merri, of Saint Mary of Egypt's conversion (1842).[23] Standing on an incline behind the recumbent disciples, Jesus towers above them, haloed and seeming to illuminate the ground behind him. Likening this figure to an Early Christian Christ in Majesty (the artist copied an example while in Rome), Foucart interprets the hand gestures as signaling

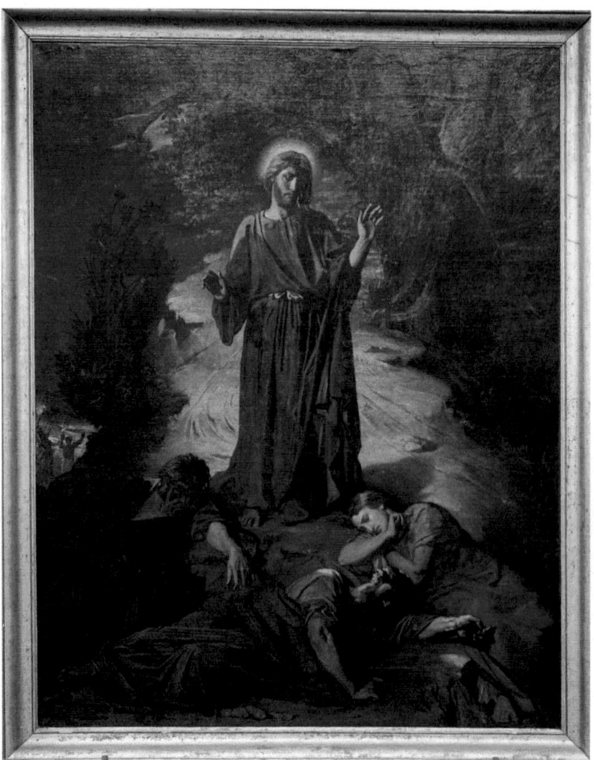

Figure 2.4 Théodore Chassériau, *Jesus in the Garden of Olives*, Salon of 1844, oil on canvas, 500 × 340 cm. Souillac, Sainte-Marie. Photo: Studio Guy. By permission of the Mairie, Souillac.

invocation, benediction, and pardon of the sleeping disciples.[24] I find the gestures ambiguous. Despite Christ's halo and aura, his hands could alternatively suggest the very human response of dismayed recognition of the disciples' weakness. Moreover, the self-absorption of this Jesus—alien to anterior representations of Christ, whether Early Christian or Baroque—suggests that he shares the humanity of the sleepers at his feet. Despite the iconographic features eruditely catalogued by Foucart to demonstrate that doctrinal orthodoxy separates Chassériau's two renditions of *Jesus in the Garden of Olives* from the flagrantly Romantic interpretations in paint and verse by his contemporaries, I contend that, in both paintings, the artist was more interested in establishing a somber emotional ambience than in transmitting dogma.

That overriding concern matches the tendency, evident throughout Chassériau's production of the 1830s and 1840s, to subordinate narrative to mood. An example is the solemn *Susanna Bathing* (Figure 5.16; Paris, Musée du Louvre) exhibited in the Salon of 1839, whose air of self-absorption is reinforced not only by the transfixed, deeply shaded voyeurs, but also by large areas of dusky green that, as in the case of the second version of *Jesus in the Garden of Olives*, gives way to an illuminated slope behind the figure. Nor is there certainty regarding the artist's religious convictions. Though he frequently depicted Christ, angels, and saints, the record of Chassériau's faith is no less equivocal that the gestures of the 1844 Jesus. When in Rome in 1840, he sent rosaries to his mother and sisters, with Lacordaire as courier; the artist wanted the rosaries, which Lacordaire had had blessed, delivered in time for Christmas.[25] Yet a year later, Lacordaire's correspondence registers unease at having been informed of Chassériau's negative change in attitude toward religion and the clergy, speculating that this was prompted by, among other factors, the lack of critical success of the Dominican's portrait in the Salon of 1841 (Figure 1.10).[26]

There is also the matter of professional drive, so evident in Chassériau's ruthless grasp at an opportunity to portray Lacordaire. That the artist would undertake, on his own initiative, so ambitious a painting as the 1844 *Jesus in the Garden of Olives* does not indicate concern with doctrinally-sound propagation of the faith. His motivation was more credibly determined pursuit of a state purchase in a year when the number of religious paintings exhibited at the Salon exhibition was at its height. In 1840, an official commission had given Chassériau free rein to present startling visual and emotional effects; four years later he opted for restraint. Notwithstanding Chassériau's attempt to garner official favor, his painting was only awarded a second-class medal at the Salon of 1844, where it was not well received by the critics. An exception was Gautier, who would remain a steadfast supporter. Whereas Delécluze complained that the artist seemed to have "an appetite for sadness," Gautier praised the contemporaneity of the painting's affect: "These are the tears of our time that run from his eyes ... our melancholy pours out in tears in this hair... this intelligent and fatigued figure... this is the uneasy suffering of our age."[27]

Diffraction of the gospel episode though Romantic sensibility is yet more pronounced in Vigny's "Le Mont des Oliviers."[28] The first version of the poem was completed on 12 November 1839 and published in the *Revue des deux mondes* 1 June 1843; its subject had interested the poet as early as 1824. Though Vigny's poem has been compared to the interpretations by Delacroix and Chassériau, among others,[29] Vigny's articulation of Christ's misery transcends the language of the brush. Envisioning perversion of his message as his most terrible torment to come, Christ declares that he had hoped to bring the world certitude and hope but has left instead doubt and evil. God remains silent as Christ begs for answers about such mysteries of life as the injustice "of undeserved misfortune, of the death of children." Throughout, Christ's human vulnerability is underscored, as the author skirts blasphemy by suggesting that God the Father has abandoned his son:

> Il se courbe, à genoux, le front contre la terre;
> Puis regarde le ciel en appellant: "Mon Père!"
> —Mais le ciel reste noir, et Dieu ne répond pas.
> ....
> Il eut froid. Vainement il appela trois fois:
> "Mon père!" Le vent seul répondit à sa voix.
> Il tomba sur le sable assis, et, dans sa peine,
> Eut sur le monde et l'homme une pensée humaine.
> He bends down, on his knees, his brow against the earth, / Then looks at the sky while calling: "My Father!" / —But the sky stays black, and God does not answer.... / He was cold. Vainly he called three times: / "My father!' Only the wind responded to his voice. / He fell on the sand, seated and, in his pain, / Had a human thought about the world and man.[30]

As Frank Paul Bowman observes, Vigny transposes to the Agony in the Garden the unsettling vision of a godless world set forth in "A Dream," Germaine de Staël's truncated translation of a chilling prose fragment by the German author Jean Paul Richter (1763–1825)—a text widely read and imitated in nineteenth-century France.[31] Though more complete translations were available, it was best known through that of Staël in *De l'Allemagne* (London, 1813; Paris, 1814), by far the most frequently reprinted version. "A Dream" recounts a nightmare of awakening at 11 PM in a cemetery amid open graves, with all but the children arising from their tombs as the earth quakes. Accompanied by the ghosts of the dead, the terrified dreamer enters a shaking church. Inside, the horror of this gothic set piece assumes a cosmic dimension:

> Then a radiant, noble, grand figure bearing the mark of perpetual sorrow descended upon the altar from on high; the dead cried out: —Oh Christ! Is there no God? —He responded: —There is none. —All the shades began to violently tremble, and Christ continued thus: — I traversed the worlds, I rose above the suns, and there, too, there is no God; I descended to the very limits of the universe, I looked into the abyss, and I cried: —Father, where are you?—But I only heard the rain that fell drop by drop into the abyss....

Then, the dead children leave their graves and prostrate themselves before the figure on the altar, asking: "Jesus, have we no father?—And he responded with a torrent of tears:—We are all orphans; me and you, we have no father."[32] French readers were all the more susceptible to this bleak vignette given that it was unaccompanied by the original's comforting conclusion in which the dreamer awakens, grateful for his sustained belief.[33] To Richter's dismay, Staël's partial translation occluded the point of his text, intended to frighten those complacent toward atheism. Vigny's tone of doubt and his humanizing of Christ also reflect awareness of the controversy, which broke out in 1836, surrounding the publication of *Das Leben Jesu kritisch bearbeitet* (*The Life of Jesus, Critically Examined*, Tübingen, 1835–36) by the German

Protestant theologian David Friedrich Strauss (1808–74). Translated into French by Émile Littré (1801–81) as *La Vie de Jésus* (1839–40), this book views Jesus as a historical figure, whose purported miracles are but myths predicated on Jewish messianic expectations.[34] Following the lead of Strauss, Ernest Renan (1823–92) popularized this historical, humanizing perspective in his *Vie de Jésus* (1863). Denying the miraculous aspects of the Gospel narrative, Renan created an uproar among the faithful.

Vigny, who knew Strauss' work well, raised the hopelessness of his poem yet another register when, around April 1863, dying of stomach cancer (and having read Renan's *Vie de Jésus*), he added a final stanza to "Le Mont des Oliviers" entitled "Silence," which remained unpublished in the poet's lifetime:

> S'il est vrai qu'au jardin sacré des Écritures,
> Le Fils de l'Homme ait dit ce qu'on voit rapporté;
> Muet, aveugle et sourd au cri des créatures,
> Si le Ciel nous laissa comme un monde avorté,
> Le juste opposera le dédain à l'absence,
> Et ne répondra plus que par un froid Silence
> Au silence éternel de la Divinité.
> If it is true that in the sacred garden of the Scriptures, / The Son of Man had said what you see reported; / If mute, blind and deaf to the cry of the living, / Heaven abandoned us like an aborted world, / The righteous man will set disdain against want / And will no longer respond except with a cold silence / To the eternal silence of God.[35]

Despite this biter defiance, Vigny (unlike Lamennais) insisted that Catholic rites attend his death. Like the renditions of the Agony in the Garden by Delacroix and Chassériau, Vigny's poem undermines the later assertion of Lyonnais poet (and newly-minted member of the Académie française) Victor de Laprade (1812–83) in a Catholic paper (1859) that reminders of Christ's human frailty are effective spurs to piety:

> It is in the most human hours of the history of the Redeemer, in those in which he puts himself the most on our level, in which his strength can serve as an example for our weakness, in which we can walk with the same step as he in his Calvary, that the poet must take the subjects of his tableaux.[36]

If Vigny's pessimism outstrips that conveyed by visual representations of the subject so far considered, Delacroix, too, plumbed the depths of despair in a small version of *Christ in the Garden of Olives* of 1851 (Figure 2.5).[37] In contrast to the public scale of the earlier, commissioned canvas, this private meditation is intimate in size as well as tone. In 1827, the young artist had used his first official commission to display dazzling command of painterly resources; here, in the twilight of his career, Delacroix focused on the betrayed Christ's isolation and pain. No trace remains of the elegance of the Saint-Paul-Saint-Louis canvas, with its attractive Christ and lovely angels. Bereft of halo, prostrate and alone, Christ crawls beneath a murky sky, the divine presence diminished, rather than asserted, by a muffled aureole.[38] In the Louvre hanging of the 2018 Delacroix retrospective, this startling reduction

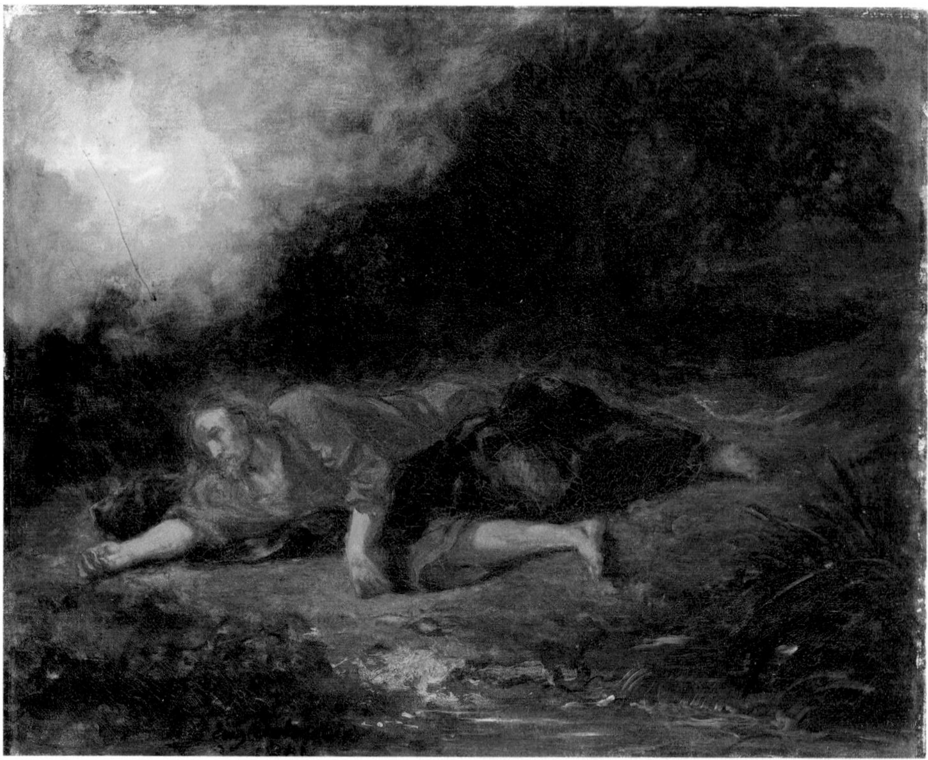

Figure 2.5 Eugène Delacroix, *Christ in the Garden of Olives*, 1851, oil on canvas, 34 × 42 cm. Amsterdam, Rijksmuseum, on deposit in Amsterdam, Van Gogh Museum. Photo: Rijksmuseum, Amsterdam.

of Christ to a state of abject animality was cleverly hung beside another small canvas, *A Mortally-Wounded Shepherd of the Roman Campagna Drags Himself to the Edge of Stream to Quench His Thirst* (also known as *A Mortally Wounded Brigand*) of ca. 1825.[39] In both paintings, the figure is reduced to a nearly sub-human state. Cynthia Bland associates Delacroix's humanization of Christ in the 1851 painting with the controversial position articulated by Strauss in *Das Leben Jesu* (which, as we have seen, stirred debate in France in the decades following Littré's translation, and was likely familiar to the artist).[40] Consideration of this connection demands tact. Contending that this is a matter of affinity rather than influence, I do not view the disparity between Delacroix's Restoration and mid-century interpretations as driven by theology.[41] Rather than attributable to a particular source, the dismal aspect of the 1851 canvas is overdetermined; German historical biblical criticism was hardly necessary to the genesis of a work whose desperation is anticipated by the watercolor study for the Saint-Paul-Saint-Louis *Christ in the Garden of Olives*. Nor, as we have seen, was Delacroix alone in emphasizing the human frailty of Christ. Despite their evident differences, Delacroix's two versions the Agony in the Garden both reveal an appetite for sorrow expressed in a letter to Baron Charles Rivet (15 February 1838): "My tragic inclinations always dominate me, and the Graces rarely smile on me."[42]

Having served the Romantics as a vehicle for pathos and pessimism, the Agony in the Garden later provided a confessional outlet to the financially and emotionally needy Paul Gauguin (whose investment in spectator Christianity will be addressed in the epilogue). Considering himself betrayed and his art unappreciated, Gauguin projected his own features onto the solitary, miserable protagonist of his *Christ in the Garden of Olives* (1889; West Palm Beach, FL, Norton Museum of Art).[43]

Prud'hon

Empathy with Christ's human vulnerability was also conveyed by the third most common religious subject included in the Salons between 1800 and 1859: his death on the cross. Those six decades saw a total of 55 Crucifixions presented at the Salon, with their numbers increasing significantly in the century's second quarter; from a single instance in the period 1800–1814, and five between 1817 and 1827, the examples reach 30 between 1831 and 1848.[44] This rise corresponds with a larger tendency discerned by Frank Paul Bowman: "If the theology and spirituality of the period were disproportionately centered on the Crucifixion, this is because of the conviction that religion was a response to the tragic sentiment of life."[45] Under the pressure of Romantic subjectivity, this conventional subject occasioned some markedly personal interpretations. These were led by the 1822 version exhibited by Pierre-Paul

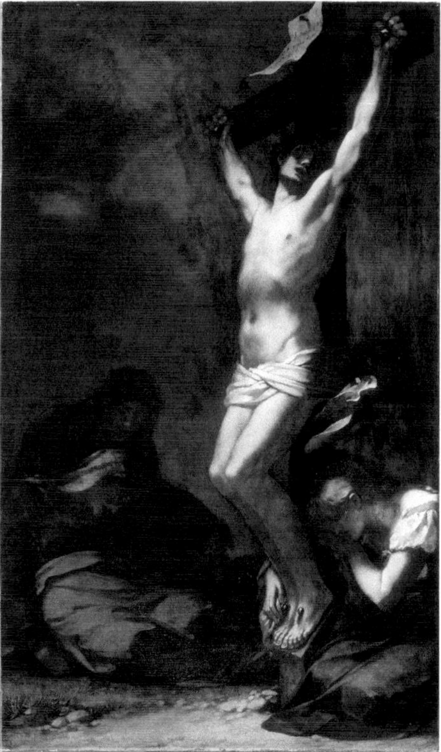

Figure 2.6 Pierre-Paul Prud'hon, *Christ on the Cross*, 1822, oil on canvas, 278 × 165 cm. Paris, Musée du Louvre. Photo: Gérard Blot. © RMN-Grand Palais/Art Resource, NY.

Prud'hon at the Salon of 1824 (Figure 2.6), which according to Foucart's statistics was among the paintings most copied by artists between 1815 and 1850.[46]

The beguiling eroticism of Prud'hon's mythological paintings, such as *A Young Zephyr Balancing above Water*, (1814, Dijon, Musée des Beaux-Arts, on permanent loan from the Musée du Louvre) hardly prepares us for the bludgeoning impact of his *Christ on the Cross*, commissioned by the State in 1821 for the cathedral of Strasbourg. As divergent from conventional religious painting as Schnetz's *Vow to the Madonna*, Prud'hon's *Christ on the Cross* was acquired for the Louvre after the artist's death.[47] Whereas Prud'hon's *Young Zephyr* showcases study of Correggio and taste for Leonardo's *sfumato*, *Christ on the Cross* is a tenebrous howl of despair. This was not the first time Prud'hon used exaggerated tonal contrast to heighten drama; he had done so to great effect in *Justice and Vengeance Pursuing Crime* (1808; Paris, Musée du Louvre), commissioned for the Palais de Justice, where it hung in the criminal courtroom until replaced in 1819, by order of Louis XVIII, with an image of Christ.[48] But the liquid, lunar chiaroscuro of that public melodrama is replaced, in Prud'hon's Crucifixion, by warm shadows and harsh highlights set against a cold backdrop of blackened green. The encroaching darkness (deepened by pigment deterioration and other conservation issues) foregrounds the martyred Christ, lending the image disquieting intimacy.[49] The oblique view from below, which sacrifices the iconographic clarity of the standard frontal composition in the interest of dramatic immediacy, lends salience to the strained left arm and pulls from the engulfing shadow just enough of the face to show that it is open-mouthed in torment. The surprisingly short cross lowers to the level of the Magdalene the feet that she anointed; nearly illegible in the dark background, the Virgin swoons in sorrow.[50] In expressive power, Prud'hon's painting foreshadows the era's most extreme rendition of Christ's agony, the monumental wooden crucifix (1840–46) by Auguste Préault (1809–79) in the Paris church of Saint-Gervais-Saint-Protais.[51] Prud'hon's audience was primed to see in his *Christ on the Cross* the painter's heart laid bare; it was popularly believed to be the work of a bereaved man reeling from the suicide of his collaborator, pupil, and lover, Constance Mayer (26 May 1821).[52] Mindful of the painter's personal tragedy, Delacroix likened the canvas to a final confession:

> Following this catastrophe, life became for him an unbearable burden....The Christ, on which he worked almost while dying is like the last glimmer of his soul. Dissatisfied with this work, which he left incomplete, he begged his friends to get rid of it after his death.[53]

Delacroix

Notwithstanding his sympathy for the artist, Delacroix only reservedly admired Prud'hon's *Christ on the Cross*, preferring the "suavity and grace" of works akin to *A Young Zephyr Balancing above Water*—traits that, in Delacroix's assessment "remain the singular characteristics of his talent." He regretted that the only works by Prud'hon on view in the Louvre were *Justice and Vengeance Pursuing Crime* and *Christ on the Cross,* works "that stand out by virtue of severity of subject and manner."[54] Still, in a *Journal* entry of 1853, Delacroix recalled having seen, "with the greatest of pleasure, a copy of the *Christ* of Prud'hon at Saint-Philippe du Roule; I think it was at the burial of M. de Beauharnais [François, Marquis de Beauharnais, died 3 March 1846]." Characteristically conflating the religious and the aesthetic, the artist attributed his pleasure to the capacity of church music to enhance his appreciation of the sacred painting: "Never, to be sure, did this composition, which is not above criticism, look better. The touching aspect of the painting seemed to emanate and reach me on the wings of the music."[55]

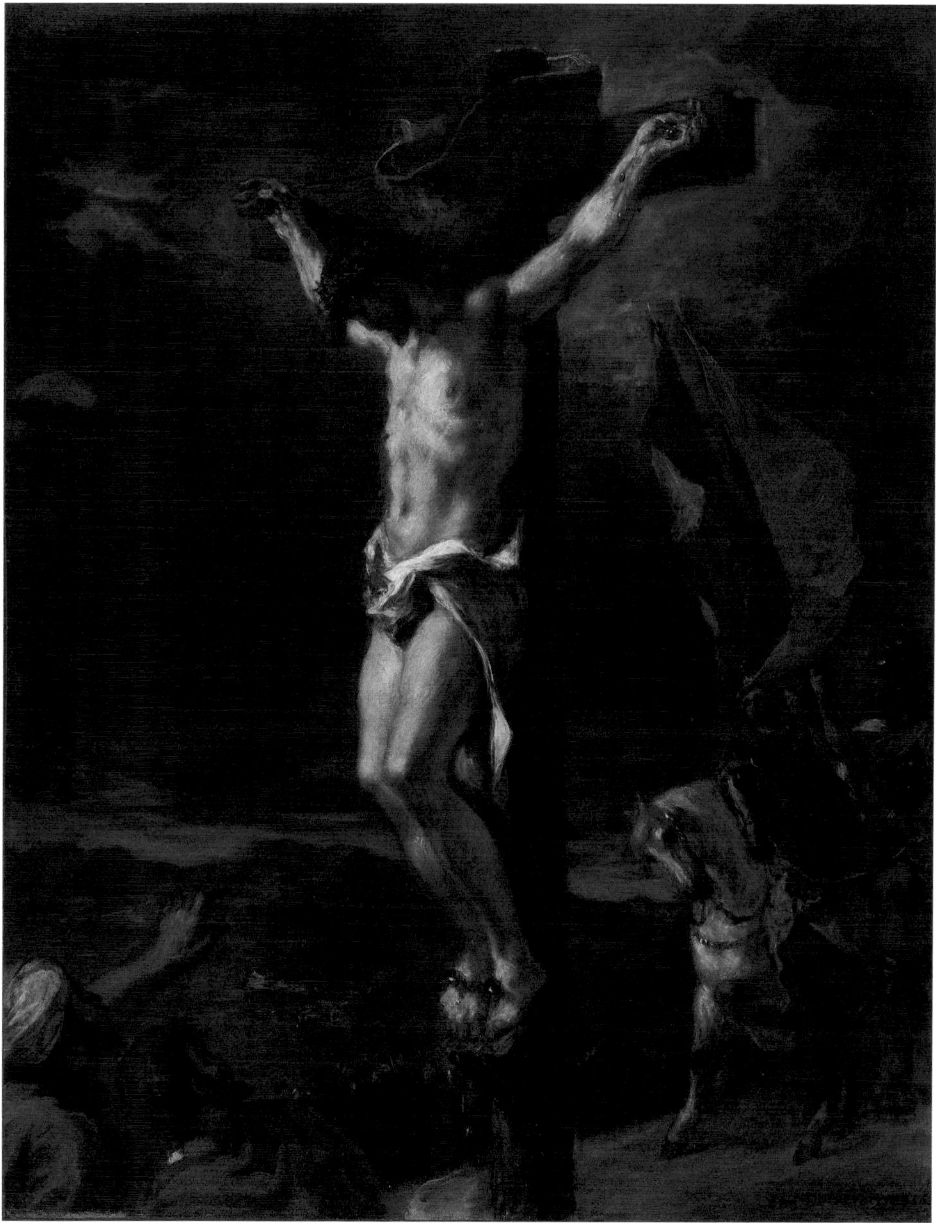

Figure 2.7 Eugène Delacroix, *Christ on the Cross*, 1846, oil on canvas, 80 × 64.2 cm. Baltimore, The Walters Art Museum. Photo: Susan Tobin. Credit: The Walters Art Museum, Baltimore.

In his own *Christ on the Cross* from 1846 (Figure 2.7), exhibited in the Salon the following year, Delacroix tempered the emotional pitch of Prud'hon's version and muted the wrenching grief of his own recent *Pietà* mural (1844; Paris, Saint-Denys-du-Saint-Sacrement).[56] Despite its modest size, the solemn canvas monumentalizes the elevated, hanging Christ, his half-illuminated, bleeding flesh set against somber hills and a sky whose churning murk recalls the scriptural account of daytime darkness.[57] Fluttering banners and a handsome brace of horses impart a note of colorful spectacle, linking it to two secular works of 1840 that blend visual delight with tragedy, *The Justice of Trajan* (Rouen, Musée des Beaux-Arts) and *The Entry of the Crusaders into Constantinople* (Paris, Musée du Louvre).

Like the Saint-Paul-Saint-Louis *Christ in the Garden of Olives*, the Crucifixion of 1846 is redolent of museum rather than church. Eliciting dismay rather than prefiguring resurrection, this *Christ on the Cross* contributed to the ubiquity of Jesus in the twilight of the July Monarchy. This vogue was not solely a function of the accelerated production of religious paintings that began in the late 1830s; it was also linked to the following decade's burgeoning cult of Jesus among democratic socialists, who embraced Him as friend to, and prototype of, the exploited worker—a conceit that ran against the grain of Delacroix's convictions. Disdaining utopian aspirations founded on belief in the fundamental goodness of man, the pessimistic aristocrat (of temperament if not of title) would detest the Revolution of 1848, complaining that its partisans apparently thought that "it would bring equality of talent as well as equality of wealth."[58] Yet Delacroix's leftist admirer Théophile Thoré (1807–69) projected humanitarian aspirations onto the Crucifixion exhibited in the Salon of 1847, though the fundamentally conservative painter had no such intent. According to Thoré, Delacroix's *Christ on the Cross*

> has a terrible aspect, as is fitting with the death throes of a God; nature is agitated from the earth to the sky, and you can hear passing in the air legions of spirit who cast a veil on the old world and celebrate the new destinies of man.[59]

Thoré's hopeful reading seems willfully arbitrary, particularly in view of the unmitigated gloom of Delacroix's contemporary *Lamentation* (Figure 2.8).[60] Amid the optimism of the juryless Salon that followed the fall of the July Monarchy in February 1848, this canvas must have struck a discordant note. His moribund flesh set off by a white shroud, a very dead Christ lies in a landscape so devoid of light that its oppressive flatness is relieved solely by a chilling glimmer around three crosses and by the red cloak of a tiny, distant figure. Characteristically, Delacroix understates facial expression, despite the appalling circumstances. Instead, he offers touching vignettes: the prostrate Virgin, who seems drained of tears; the Magdalene, who cradles a pierced foot beneath lifted shroud; and Saint John—whose mournful self-absorption is suggested by immersion in shadow—cautiously grasping the crown of thorns resting inches from Christ's lifeless fingers. No less expressive are the painting's larger features. Gautier was particularly struck by the effect of Saint John's drapery: this

> scarlet spot … lends an immense sadness to the general locality of the painting. It makes all of the other tones muddy, sickly, livid and greenish. Thanks to this rude dissonance, nothing is more lugubrious than this heavy, thick, grayed sky, in which shredded clouds creep.[61]

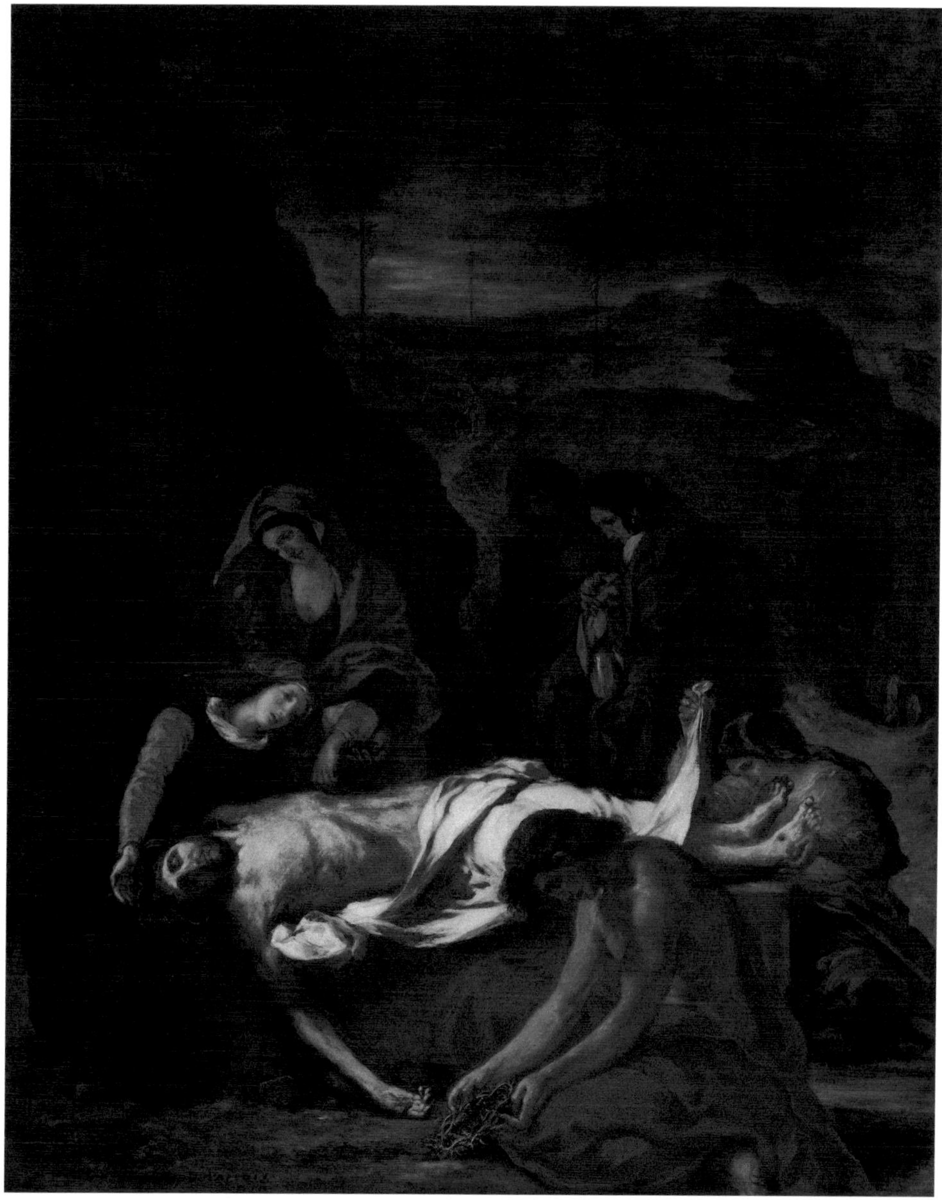

Figure 2.8 Eugène Delacroix, *The Lamentation* (*Christ at the Tomb*), 1847–48, oil on canvas, 162.6 × 132.1 cm. Boston, Museum of Fine Arts, Gift by contribution in memory of Martin Brimmer, 96.21. Photograph © 2021 Museum of Fine Arts, Boston.

Immersed in the chill of nearly impenetrable darkness, that red accent brings heat to the saint's face and glints in the wound in Christ's ashen side. Just as despair is conveyed by dark tonality, so too is bereaved fellowship written into the composition's oblong circuit. Viewing a lithographic copy (made by Jules Laurens in 1855) of his own reprise of the Boston painting, Delacroix was struck, on 11 December 1855, by an emotional power undiminished by negligent finishing:

> In general, the details are mediocre and don't stand up to inspection. At the same time, the ensemble inspires an emotion that astonishes me. You cannot take your eyes from it, and not a single detail stands out to be admired or to distract attention. This is, at its most perfect, that skill, whose object is to produce a simultaneous effect.[62]

Nor was this the only time that the artist thrilled to loss of detail in a Catholic context. A year earlier (12 September 1854), the obscurity of a church in Dieppe stirred similar thoughts:

> In the quarter of Saint-Rémy, seeing the door open, I entered and enjoyed the most grandiose spectacle, that of the dark and lofty Church, illuminated by a half-dozen smoking candles placed here and there. I challenge the adversaries of *vagueness* to produce, with precision and with well-defined lines, a comparable sensation.[63]

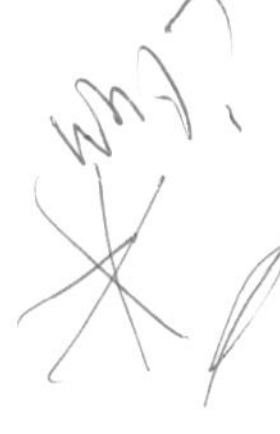

Delacroix's willingness to sacrifice detail to the effect of the whole reminds us that he stands apart from other nineteenth-century French painters of Christian subjects—and, indeed, from most of his contemporaries—not solely on the grounds of quality and painterly execution, but also by virtue of his expressive use of formal elements. In his inaugural Salon, he had shown himself adept at operatic physiognomy, fitting out the writhing damned of *The Barque of Dante* (Salon of 1822; Paris, Musée du Louvre) with melodramatic facial contractions.[64] He soon abandoned stock theatrics in favor of what would become signature expressive maneuvers: resonant color chords and the rhythmic pulse of undulating anatomy (be it human, equine, or feline), agitated drapery, and dynamic backdrop features, such as rocks, hills, and waves.

This distinctive mode of expression (which would earn the fierce respect of Van Gogh) imbues Delacroix's religious imagery with a power that Baudelaire found unique, and which he praised at the expense of pious artists such as Victor Orsel and Hippolyte Flandrin:

> Perhaps he alone, in our incredulous century, has conceived religious paintings that are neither empty or cold like competition pieces, nor pedantic, mystical or neo-Christian, like those of all the philosophers of art who make of religion a science of archaism, and believe it necessary above all to lay claim to symbolism and primitive traditions in order to move and make sing the religious chord.[65]

Explaining why "Delacroix alone knows how to handle religion," Baudelaire pointed to a fertile correspondence between the artist's temperament and Catholicism:

> The serious sadness of his talent accords perfectly with our religion, a religion profoundly sad, a religion of universal sorrow, and which, because of its very Catholicity, allows full liberty to the individual and asks no more than to be celebrated in the language of each—if he knows sorrow and he is a painter.[66]

Baudelaire's verdict was seconded by the American novelist Henry James (1843–1916), who viewed Delacroix's *Lamentation* when it was displayed in Paris, along with *The Death of Sardanapalus* (1827; Paris, Musée du Louvre), at the Durand-Ruel gallery in 1876. Ambivalent toward the latter––a youthful, Byronic extravaganza––the author declared that the *Lamentation*

> is one of the author's masterpieces, and is a work of really inexpressible beauty; Delacroix is there at his best, with his singular profundity of imagination and his extraordinary harmony of colour. It is the only modern religious picture I have seen that seemed to me painted in good faith....[67]

The chasm separating Romantic religious art from that of the Renaissance and the Counter-Reformation opens at our feet when, mindful of the opinions of Baudelaire and James, we realize that the very features compromising the devotional efficacy of the Christs of Delacroix, Chassériau, and Prud'hon bring to them a vitality missing from the bulk of nineteenth-century French religious painting. This paradox has a literary counterpart. Doubt, according to Bowman, underlies the best French Romantic writing pertaining to the sacred:

> For them [the leading Romantics], the return to dogma and faith was not sufficient to inspire; it was the subsequent loss of faith that generated literature.... Religious doubt is the force which leads to religious poetry and the creation of myths and a new symbolism.[68]

Delacroix's demand that his *Christ on the Cross* (Salon of 1835) be removed from the church of Saint-Paterne, Vannes revealed, at this chapter's opening, the artist's scant concern with the capacity of his religious paintings to induce prayer. From the fervent perspective of Durtal, the converted protagonist of J.-K. Huysmans' autobiographical novel *La Cathédrale* (1898), this was troubling: Delacroix's superiority as an artist—evident in his murals in the Chapel of the Holy Angels in Saint-Sulpice (1849–61)—made him no more successful as a painter of sacred subjects than his rivals. Contemplating the irreparable decline in religious art since Rembrandt, Durtal opines:

> In modern times, there is nothing to look for; the Overbecks, the Ingreses, the Flandrins were pale nags hitched to pious commissioned subjects; in the church of Saint-Sulpice, Delacroix crushes all the daubers who surround him, but his feeling for Catholic art is nil.[69]

Writing of the Saint-Paul-Saint-Louis *Christ in the Garden of Olives* in a Catholic paper in 1907, Alphonse Germain similarly discerned that it was at the expense of the faith that Delacroix shone as an artist: "One can contest the religious value of the *Agony,* and every Catholic will regret that the Angels there are disconsolate spectators while they should be consoling helpers, but no one can deny its tragic grandeur and its artistic character."[70] Without sharing such concerns, Barthélémy Jobert rightly considers the religious canvases that Delacroix exhibited in the Salon and executed on his own initiative "paintings, not devotional objects."[71] To the question as to why Delacroix so often treated sacred subjects, especially in his mid- and late career, Jobert proposes that, apart from meeting official commissions and requests from collectors and dealers, the artist aspired to surpass esteemed old master prototypes.[72] This was but one factor. Professional ambition aside, the prodigious output signals a timely spiritual hunger whetted by Delacroix's position as outsider to the faith.

Apart from the fact that Mass was said at Saint-Germain-des-Prés before his burial, Delacroix left no evidence that he was a believing Catholic, though *Journal* entries from the late years show him mindful of the positive aspects of religion and deeply moved by Catholic ritual and music.[73] Peerless among nineteenth-century French artists in his ability to imbue Christian subjects with expressive force, Delacroix also drew ribald, anti-clerical caricatures in his youth, consistent with liberal resentment of ecclesiastical resurgence under the Bourbon Restoration.[74] Several commentators concur on the non-sectarian aspect of the artist's view of religion. Alain Daguerre de Hureaux characterizes Delacroix's personal religion as "a mélange of Voltairean skepticism, of aesthetic sensibility, and of diffuse spirituality."[75] For Jobert, "Delacroix's spirituality"

> was never circumscribed within the strict beliefs of any church or practices of any religion: it extends, in a vague and diffuse way, to the whole world. He was not a materialist; as heir to Voltaire and eighteenth-century philosophy, he was perhaps a deist, but not a believer.[76]

Similarly, Patrick Noon discerns in the Boston *Lamentation* "a non-sectarian view of universal sadness and suffering that characterized Delacroix's religious beliefs."[77]

Consideration of Delacroix's investment in spectator Christianity provides purchase on the elusive topic of his spirituality; for it was as a spectator that, in his late years, Delacroix was attracted to the trappings of Catholicism. Thus, on a Sunday visit to the Parisian church of Saint-Eustace (26 June 1853), he briefly glimpsed the joys of piety from a distance lengthened by aesthetic appreciation:

> Stopped for a long time at Saint-Eustace, to hear Vespers: that made me understand, for several moments, the pleasure that comes from being devout ... I saw all the personnel of the church going to and fro, from the lame distributer of holy water, fitted out like a figure from Rembrandt, to the priest in his canon's hood and his ceremonial cope.[78]

As suggested by a *Journal* entry dating from a later Sunday (21 May 1854), even the promptings of guilt could not dislodge the artist from his removed vantage point. Hosted by his cousin, the pious, royalist lawyer and politician Pierre-Antoine Berryer (1790–1868) at his château in Augerville, Delacroix wrote of his esteem for another guest, the bishop of Orléans, Monsignor Félix Dupanloup (1802–78), whose doctrine would soon exert decisive influence on Gauguin's childhood education. Noting that the company had attended Mass, Delacroix admitted: "I felt a little ashamed on their return at not having gone with them."[79] The following day, he recounted his delight at the spectacle that had followed the bishop's celebration of a Confirmation:

> After the ceremony and the Monseigneur's exhortation, we attended the blessing of the tombs in the cemetery: very beautiful. The bishop, bare headed and in his vestments, the crozier in one hand and the aspergillum in the other, walked with

> great strides and sprinkled holy water, to the right and left, on the humble graves. Religion is beautiful when it is like this. The consolations and the counsels that the prelate gave in the church to these simple men, burnt by country labors and chained to harsh necessities, hit their true mark.[80]

Delacroix's enthusiasm reveals a capacity for arm's-length enjoyment of the faith of others; he shared this with Salon visitors drawn to Schnetz's scenes of peasant piety (such as that witnessed in the Augerville church) and to Gérard's *Saint Theresa*. At the same time, Delacroix's pathos-charged representations of sacred subjects are neither nostalgic nor sentimental. Rather, they reflect the artist's uncommon, dual empathy with his holy protagonists and with the Old Masters, whose paintings, informed by Christian belief, nourished his secular creativity.

Like other members of the generation of 1820, Delacroix came of age attuned to Chateaubriand's seductive invitation to view religion through an aesthetic lens. An oft-quoted passage written in a notebook at Augerville (12 October 1862) several months before the artist's death suggests tenacious adherence to the *Génie du christianisme*'s conflation of faith, and the good that it inspires, with beauty:

> God is in us; it is this inner presence that makes us admire beauty, that gladdens us when we have done well and consoles us for not sharing in the joy of the wicked. It is he, without doubt, who inspires men of genius and who warms them at the sight of their own creations. There are men of virtue as there are men of genius; both are inspired and favored by God.[81]

Though Delacroix resisted being called a Romantic, his conviction that "men of genius ... are inspired and favored by God" squares with a belief in the sacred investiture of the writer that is central to French Romanticism, an article of faith copiously documented by Paul Bénichou.[82] Less common in Delacroix's epoch was the relentlessly vital visual imagination that sustained his devotion to the religion of art.

Lyon

Baudelaire' s admiration of Delacroix's religious paintings was paired with scorn for the self-conscious archaicism encouraged by the writing of Montalembert and Rio and put into practice by the Lyonnais painters Orsel and Flandrin. Having lived in Lyon as a child, while his step-father, General Jacques Aupick (1789–1857), kept vigilance over civil unrest, the poet and critic wrote that it is a

> singular city, bigoted and commercial, Catholic and Protestant, full of fogs and embers, ideas are disentangled there with difficulty. All that comes from Lyon is meticulous, slowly elaborated and timid.... You could say that brains there are stuffed up like a nose.[83]

If this dyspeptic passage shows Baudelaire blinkered to Lyon's rich cultural particularity, his observation that "ideas are disentangled there with difficulty" is characteristically perceptive. In addition to nurturing the art of Orsel and Flandrin (wherein stylistic archaism provided the vehicle for what was intended to be legible content), Lyon was home to a tradition of arcane mysticism.[84]

Two legacies contributed to this unique intellectual climate. In 1773–76 and again in September 1785–early January 1786, Louis-Claude de Saint-Martin (1743–1803) sojourned in Lyon, finding a receptive audience among fellow Freemasons. Known as "the unknown philosopher," Saint-Martin was an apostle of Illuminism. This nebulous movement, which influenced Joseph de Maistre, Sand, Hugo, and Baudelaire, among others, sought knowledge of the divine mysteries to which mankind was blinded by the Fall. It is associated with an affinity toward the occult, a belief in the necessity of expiation and initiation, and a conviction that man, a fallen divine creature, has a responsibility to redeem matter and restore harmony and unity to the universe. Saint-Martin embraced a proto-Romantic belief in the poet as prophetic seer and a conviction that a holy person (the "man of desire") is charged by God with realizing the good and the absolute both in the spiritual realm and on earth.[85] Directly subsuming human affairs to providence, Saint-Martin viewed the French Revolution as a divinely orchestrated expiation visited upon the benighted clergy.[86]

Saint-Martin influenced the leading representative of Lyon's visionary tradition, Pierre-Simon Ballanche (1776–1847), author of a counter-Enlightenment defense of religious sentiment as the font of aesthetic inspiration that closely anticipated the *Génie du christianisme.* Little noticed at the time, *On Sentiment Considered in its Relationship with Literature and the Arts* (1801) was published in Lyon by the Ballanche family press and clandestinely distributed from just one Parisian source.[87] Extolling feeling at the expense of reason, Ballanche declared that his intention was

> to depict the Catholic religion lending to history the sole torch that can illuminate it, realizing the ideal morality that the author of our being has engraved in our hearts, warming genius by elevating it to a great height and giving life to all modern masterpieces.[88]

Ballanche's shorter and less pretentiously erudite book was known to Chateaubriand, with Fontanes acting as likely intermediary.[89] Speculating that Chateaubriand consulted *On sentiment* for the final draft of the *Génie du christianisme*, Bernard M.G. Reardon identifies a mystical, theosophical strain in Ballanche's volume absent from Chateaubriand's text. Whereas Chateaubriand employs images, Ballanche adduces symbols, which he locates in both antiquity and the present.[90] The overshadowing of *On sentiment* was inevitable, given Chateaubriand's rhetorical brilliance and thirst for renown; the relatively self-effacing Ballanche contributed to Chateaubriand's fame (his family press produced several editions of the *Génie du christianisme*, starting in 1804).

During the Bourbon Restoration and July Monarchy, the Catholic royalist Ballanche was, in Paul Bénichou's formulation, the "Janus of a progress-oriented counter-revolution."[91] The Lyonnais author held that the religion to which he adhered needed to transform as part of a process of social regeneration, which would be guided by a prophetic poet-priest (a role to which he aspired). He attempted to set forth his vision of mankind's past, present, and future in a vast, multi-part epic, conceived in 1827, under the title *Social Regeneration* (*Palingénésie sociale*)—an undertaking realized only in part. He influenced a younger Lyonnais generation that included the poet Victor de Laprade (we have met him previously as an advocate of representations of Christ at His most human); Antoine Blanc de Saint-Bonnet (1815–80), a philosopher eagerly read by the Catholic revivalists at the end of the century; and Louis Janmot, a pious artist who attempted to translate an idiosyncratic theology into an elaborate cycle of paintings, drawings, and poetry.

If this counter-Enlightenment current encouraged Lyon's mystical proclivities, the cruel facts of recent history were no less decisive. Political radicalization during the Revolution was resisted in Lyon. The radical Marie Joseph Chalier (b. 1747), having attempted to bring the Reign of Terror to Lyon, was arrested and guillotined (17 July 1793). During the summer and autumn of 1793, the city was subjected to siege and bombardment by the revolutionary army. After Lyon fell on 9 October 1793, it was decreed in the Convention that the rebel city be razed and commemorated by a column inscribed "LYON MADE WAR AGAINST LIBERTY. LYON IS NO MORE." Though the city was spared total destruction, more than 1860 Lyonnais were executed, including clergy—a ghastly dress rehearsal for the repression of the Commune in 1871. The reprisals were directed in part by the same Fouché who enforced de-Christianization in Nièvre and Allier (and who would later serve as minister of police during the Directory, the Consulate, and the Empire). Among the survivors was Fontanes (later Chateaubriand's friend and mentor), whose wife, Chantal Cathelin (1768–1829)—like Mary sheltered from the Massacre of the Innocents — gave birth to their first child in a barn during the havoc. Ballanche, who fled the siege at age 17, returned to this dark period when considering the role of sentiment in literature and art: "Oh what hand will engrave the actions and the courage of the generous defenders of Lyon? Will posterity ever know that, isolated amid enslaved France, they would dare to make heard the tones of true liberty?"[92] As a child, Orsel was deeply affected by the recollections of his mentor, Abbé Lacombe, who had survived the ordeal. Nor does Orsel's stylistic archaism constitute the sole instance of artistic recoil from the heritage of the Revolution and Enlightenment. As Marie-Claude Chaudonneret observes, Lyon's trauma contributed to the rise of the Troubadour style of painting.[93] In the vanguard of that retrospective trend were two friends of Ballanche: the devout, Lyonnais pupils of David, Pierre Révoil (Orsel's teacher, prior to Guérin) and Fleury François Richard (1777–1852). With Chateaubriand, the Troubadours shared a yearning for pre-revolutionary Catholicism as evoked by the ruins of vandalized churches.[94]

Janmot

Given the complexity of Lyon's Catholic culture—evident no less in the forward-looking humanitarian mysticism of Ballanche than in the retrospection of Orsel, Flandrin, and the Troubadours—it is fitting that the work of Janmot, a distinctly Lyonnais artist, offers examples of hazardous tension between devotional intent and private content.[95] Raised in a fervently Catholic family, Janmot, like Orsel, was initially trained at the Lyon École des Beaux-Arts, which he entered in 1831. Having moved to Paris in 1833, he continued his studies under Orsel and Ingres, and traveled to Rome in 1836 to rejoin the latter (who had assumed directorship of the French academy). Yet Janmot was drawn to neither Ingres's chilled sensuality nor Orsel's archaism and legibility. Whereas the simple binaries of Orsel's *Good and Evil* have the public reach of a sermon, Janmot sought to convey his convictions though hermetically personal imagery. Of the artist's piety, there can be no doubt. As a student at the Collège Royal de Lyon (until the summer of 1831), he became close friends with Frédéric Ozanam (1813–53), mentee of a revered professor of philosophy and aesthetics, Abbé Joseph Matthias Noirot (1793–1880). Noirot would begin class on his knees at the foot of the rostrum, beseeching descent of the Holy Ghost by reciting the *Veni Sancte Spiritus* (the liturgy sung at each meeting of Janmot and his fellow members of Lacordaire's Confrérie de saint Jean). Ozanam, who would have a distinguished career as a professor of foreign languages and history, founded the Conférences de Saint-Vincent-de-Paul, devoted to charity and to spiritual vigilance of the poor. Janmot, along with other Lyonnais artists in Paris, was a member. Like Ozanam, Janmot greatly admired the trio of *L'Avenir*, Lamennais, Lacordaire, and Montalembert; as a liberal ultramontane, he initially welcomed the Revolution of February 1848. Shocked by the class warfare that erupted in June, he retreated inward, and (counter to the leftward tracking of Lamennais) the Lyonnais painter abandoned his liberal convictions and embraced anti-republican, monarchic legitimism (an orientation characteristic of ultramontanism in the second half of the century).

If Janmot's apostolic commitment is unmistakable, his willingness to stray from orthodoxy is evidenced by his startling *Christ in the Garden of Olives* (Figure 2.9).[96] Like Delacroix and Chassériau, Janmot invested the subject with an anxiety absent from the Gospel narrative, though their versions appear almost conventional by comparison. Excluded from the 1840 Salon, then admitted to the more democratic Second Republic Salon of 1849 (whose jury, traditionally made up of academicians was elected by artists), this fascinatingly peculiar work pairs Christ's anguish with a surfeit of emotionally-charged historical reference. Visualizing the simile (Luke 22:43–4) that compares Christ's sweat to "clots of blood falling to the ground," Janmot shows Jesus literally sweating blood.[97] Rather than emphasizing Christ's solitude, Janmot introduces, beneath a pair of pitying angels (stiff counterparts to Delacroix's trio in

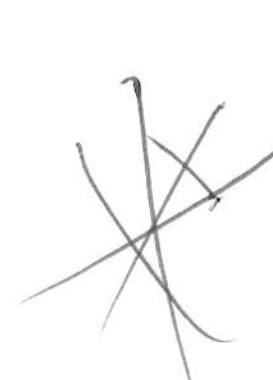

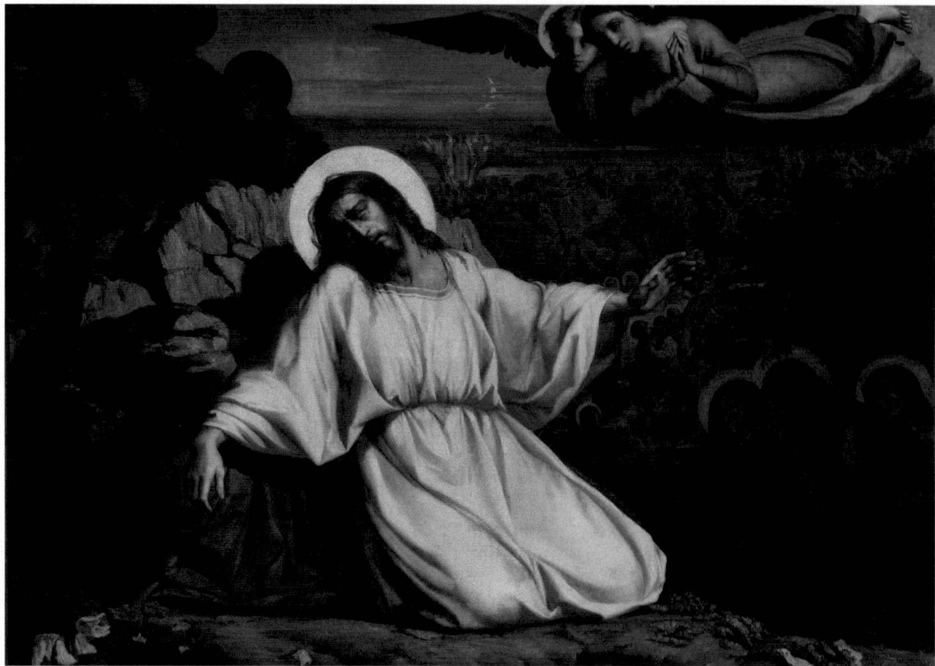

Figure 2.9 Louis Janmot, *Christ in the Garden of Olives*, 1840, oil on canvas, 182.3 × 258.7. Lyon, Musée des Beaux-Arts. © Lyon MBA-Photo Alain Basset.

Saint-Paul-Saint-Louis), a multitude that nearly crowds out the impossibly diminutive, sleeping disciples. The canvas is packed with a jaw-dropping roster of heretics, enemies of the Church, and crimes against the faith, specified in the Salon guidebook. To the left of Christ are, among others, Nero, Julian the Apostate, Henry VIII, Luther, Calvin, Voltaire, and Marat. On the right, behind the apostles, the first Christians are massacred. Further away are those who topple crosses, those who worship the golden calf, and those who take their own lives, "believing nothing and loving nothing." Sharing Rio's and Montalembert's admiration of the anti-humanist friar Savonarola, Janmot depicts, in the distance, the Dominican's fiery death at the stake in 1493, a martyrdom occasioned by his opposition to "the oppressors of the homeland and to the retrograde ideas of the Renaissance."[98] Finally, to the left of the burning Savonarola, are "Poles dying for defending their religion and nationality"—solidarity with whom was the great liberal cause of the 1830s, championed by Lamennais and Montalembert.[99] Before this iconographic onslaught, the militantly Catholic Louis Veuillot (1813–83) recognized good intentions, yet was disconcerted: "M. Janmot, who has talent and faith... loses himself and plunges into we don't know what kind of metaphysics." He cannot be faulted for lacking ideas, acknowledged Veuillot; "But you take up pen and paper when you want to write a book."[100] One wonders whether the Dominican friars at the Collège Lacordaire de Sorèze (directed by Lacordaire at the end of his life), from which the Lyon Musée des Beaux-Arts acquired the painting in 1981, were any less puzzled by Janmot's transhistorical litany of loss. In contrast to the versions of the subject by Delacroix and Chassériau, this *Christ in the Garden of Olives* makes no appeal to an audience touched by the *mal du siècle*. Its unorthodox aspect is a function, rather, of a proselytizing zeal in which aesthetics are of as little concern as spatial coherence.

Janmot did take up pen and paper when composing the text accompanying his life's work: *The Poem of the Soul* (*Le Poème de l'âme*): a cycle of 18 strangely beautiful paintings (1835–54) and 16 large, detailed charcoal drawings, some with highlights in color (1872–81). These are complemented by 2814 lines of verse (completed 10 September 1880). Only some of the verse, whose tendency toward triteness belies the lofty visual imagery to which it is joined, has a clear connection to the paintings and drawings. The cycle charts the growth, travails, and redemption of a soul. In the paintings, the soul is represented in the form of a male child clothed in dusky red (who grows into a young man) accompanied in most of the canvases by a virginal consort draped in white. The paintings and drawings comprise but a fragment of the original conception; the artist intended to include two additional series of images, one showing "the active life of the soul on earth" and the other "its active life beyond time."[101] Though the paintings follow a narrative arc, from the soul's infancy to its adult bereavement, they were not sequentially executed. Nor do inscribed dates consistently correspond with the year of execution. In the present context, space will permit consideration of only a sampling; sequential discussion and reproduction of the entire cycle and its accompanying text are available elsewhere.[102]

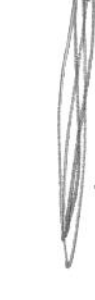

Encouraged by the approbation of visitors when he revealed the paintings in his Lyon studio on 1 April 1854, Janmot rented space in the covered arcade of the Passage du Saumon at the foot of Montmartre, where he exhibited the cycle 22 April–7 June. It received largely positive reviews from two Parisian critics, Alphonse de Calonne (1808–1902)—who did wonder who would possibly buy the paintings, and where they could be hung—and Gautier. Janmot was bitterly disappointed by the neglect of the cycle when it returned to Paris for the Exposition universelle the following year, purportedly through the intercession of Delacroix.[103] Poorly hung between architectural drawings, the paintings were, according to Baudelaire, "the object of august disdain."[104] Following the artist's publication in 1881 of 150 copies of a bound photographic facsimile of the complete cycle, together with its accompanying verse, the ensemble was forgotten until it was exhibited in Lyon in 1950. Installed in the Lyon Musée des Beaux-Arts since 1976, *The Poem of the Soul* represents an endeavor comparable in dizzying ambition to the religious and philosophical epics that tempted a number of French Romantics.[105] Among those was Ballanche, whom Janmot knew from the circle that gathered at the Abbaye-aux-Bois, the Parisian home of Chateaubriand's close friend, the Lyonnaise Juliette Récamier. In visionary scope, Janmot's cycle also has an affinity to the vast, abortive decorative cycle planned by Paul Chenavard (1808–95) for the interior of the Panthéon (the two Lyonnais artists became friends in 1854).[106] According to Janmot expert Élisabeth Hardouin-Fugier, the program of *The Poem of the Soul* is of the artist's invention, and replete with references to the convictions of the painter and his circle. Substituting melodrama for the tenderness that marks some of the earlier paintings, the drawings convey shrill hatred of the Third Republic in the reactionary spirit of the late nineteenth-century Catholic revival, whose beginnings this long-lived artist was able to witness.

As in Orsel's *Good and Evil*, bourgeois naturalism intrudes upon the remote spirituality of Janmot's cycle. Its sixth painting, *The Paternal Roof* (Figure 2.10) features

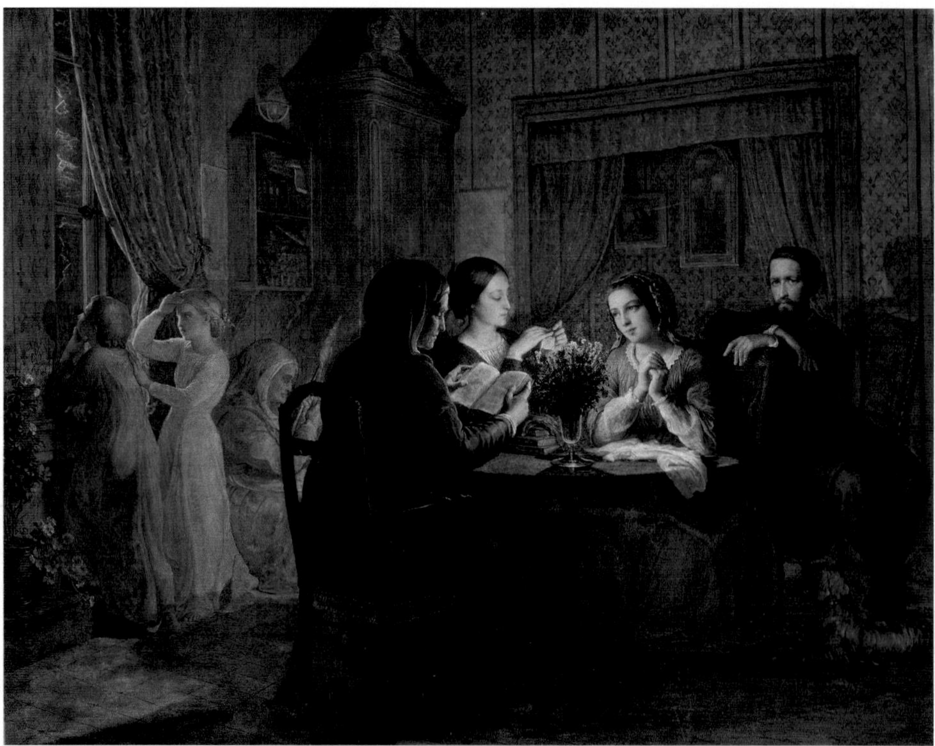

Figure 2.10 Louis Janmot, *The Paternal Roof* (*Le Toit paternel*), from *The Poem of the Soul*, ca. 1848; signed and dated 1854, oil on canvas, with graphite, 112.5 × 144 cm. Lyon, Musée des Beaux-Arts. Photo: René-Gabriel Ojéda. © RMN-Grand Palais/Art Resource, NY.

a cozy gathering sheltered from a storm (emblematic of the Revolution of 1848), watched at the window by the musing soul while his innocent, white-clad companion shows concern. Behind them, an elderly woman holding a distaff portentously recalls the classical motif of the three Fates. In reassuring contrast to the threat outside the heavily draped window, parted curtains on the rear wall reveal paintings of the Crucifixion and a seated Madonna; they hang on wall fabric that could have been woven by Lyonnais silk workers. Rendered in pale tones and relegated to the margin, the soul and his companion are upstaged by the boldly lit foreground group. At a table adorned with a bouquet, the artist's wife sews as a companion listens with rapt attention to an elder reading a psalm. Neither candle nor lamp is visible; piety suffices for illumination. Seated apart is Janmot. His look of anxiety (echoed by the alert dog at his feet) registers awareness of the threat to familial security posed by republican divorce legislation.[107] Janmot's inclusion of himself as uneasy witness brings to this wholesome and innocent domestic scene a troubling, confessional note. Gautier declared *The Paternal Roof* the only painting in the series that he considered "precisely human." This aspect stems from the descriptive particularity of the setting and accessories, and the individuation of the portraits of the artist and his wife; this earthliness is at odds with the obtrusive, yet ambiguous, symbolism.

Like many in Lyon, Janmot was no less hostile to state-sponsored, secular education than had been the circle around *L'Avenir* at the dawn of the July Monarchy. He

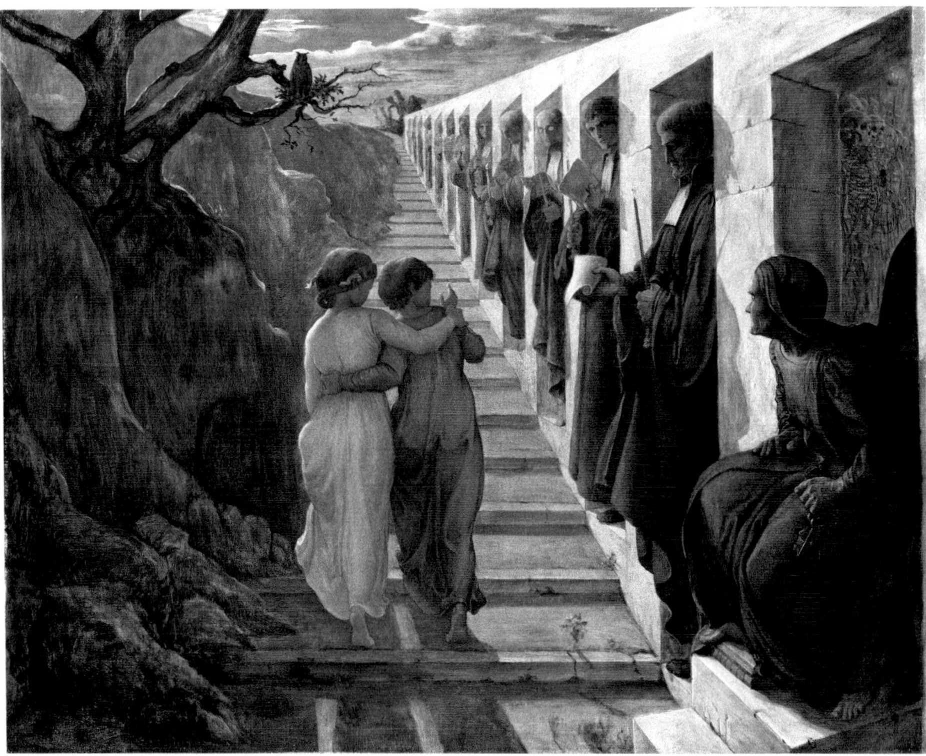

Figure 2.11 Louis Janmot, *The Evil Path* (*Le Mauvais sentier*), from *The Poem of the Soul*, 1850, oil on canvas, with graphite, 112.6 × 143.4 cm. Lyon, Musée des Beaux Arts. Image © Lyon MBA—Photo RMN/René-Gabriel Ojéda.

gave this pedagogy sinister form in the ensemble's most disturbing episodes, *The Evil Path* and *The Nightmare,* numbers seven and eight, respectively. These date from 1850, when the question of the place of religion in French education was passionately debated. That year, the controversial Falloux Law favored religious instruction at the primary and secondary levels and placed primary education under clerical control, leaving higher education to the State. This reform squared with the strongly Catholic leanings of the bill's original sponsor, Count Frédéric-Alfred-Pierre de Falloux (1811–86), monarchist deputy to the Legislative Assembly and former minister of public instruction and religion; Bishop Félix Dupanloup (who would later impress Delacroix at Augerville) helped craft the bill. In *The Evil Path* (Figure 2.11), the innocent youngsters, grown to collegians, clutch each other in fear as they ascend a vertiginous stairway flanked by a gauntlet of forbidding figures set in rectangular niches and bearing lit tapers. These are university professors offering the poisonous alternative to Catholic education; their perversion of wisdom is signaled by an owl nesting in the gnarled branches of a dead tree.[108] Watching the youths from the first niche is a darkly clad, malevolent mother who, like the professors, represents the false knowledge that destroys faith.

In *The Nightmare* (Figure 2.12), the vulnerable, young protagonists have entered her lair, stricken by the despair that comes from believing solely in reason. Bearing

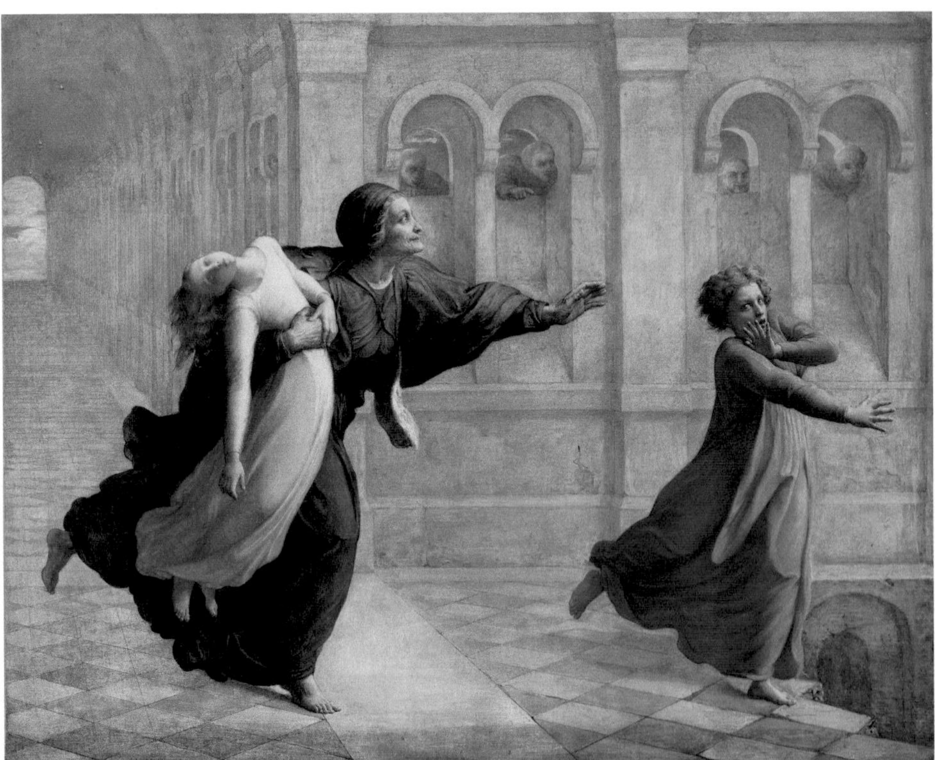

Figure 2.12 Louis Janmot, *The Nightmare*, from *The Poem of the Soul*, 1850, oil on canvas, with graphite, 113 × 144.3 cm. Lyon, Musée des Beaux Arts. Photo: René-Gabriel Ojéda/Thierry Le Mage. © RMN-Grand Palais/Art Resource, NY.

away the soul's companion (who hangs from her grip like a limp doll), the predator chases the youth to the brink of an abyss, watched by gnomic figures peering from arched windows. Primal terror is enhanced by the swift recession of an inclined corridor that suctions the viewer toward a drop into the clouded sky. Violating the stable harmonies of Albertian perspective, the settings of this image and *The Evil Path* anticipate the disquieting spaces of Giorgio De Chirico.[109] Like Jean Paul's gothic dream vignette (publicized in Germaine de Staël's sensational translation), *The Nightmare* is intended to bring home the terrifying prospect of loss of faith—a theme to which the artist returned in one of the cycle's large-scale drawings, *Without God* (1867; Lyon, Musée des Beaux-Arts). Formed in the crucible of Janmot's odd, religiously obsessed imagination, *The Nightmare* is so obscure in content that its didactic message is upstaged by sheer horror.

These frightful imaginings were meant to share wall space with sweetly naïve evocations of serenity and purity. In the cycle's fourteenth canvas, *On the Mountain* (Figure 2.13; 1851), for example, the couple's spiritual ascent takes the form of a climb up a hill, their gendered innocence mirrored in flowering plants, one upright (before the soul) and one bending (behind his companion). The soul's androgynous features temper the note of desire in his rapt gaze. The accompanying verse reminds us that this delightful excursion transpires in the presence of God:

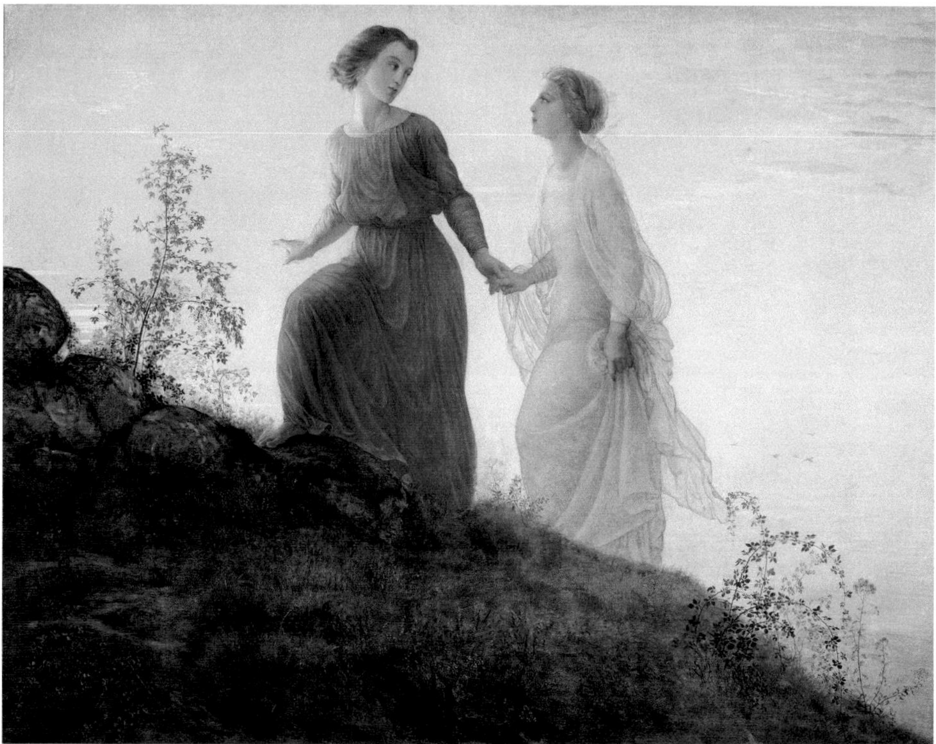

Figure 2.13 Louis Janmot, *On the Mountain,* from *The Poem of the Soul,* 1851, oil on canvas, 113 × 145.9 cm. Lyon, Musée des Beaux Arts. Photo: René-Gabriel Ojéda. © RMN-Grand Palais/Art Resource, NY.

Passons, sans les cueillir, près de ces fleurs si belles;
Aux parfums pénétrants d'autres fleurs plus vermeilles
  Nous attendent plus loin,
Qui, pour s'epanouir, cherchent les pics sauvages,
Une atmosphère vierge, un soleil sans nuages
  Et Dieu seul pour témoin.

Let us pass, without gathering them, near these flowers so beautiful; / With keen fragrances other more vermilion flowers / Await us further on, / Which, to bloom, seek out wild peaks, / a virgin atmosphere, sun without clouds / And God alone as witness (lines 1032–37).

When he viewed the paintings in Paris in 1854, Gautier voiced amazement that an artist would attempt to convey, in the "eminently plastic" medium of painting, such inaccessible subjects: "Swedenborg, Saint-Martin and Novalis captured on canvas! One never expected that."[110] Discerning in the painter's verse "a certain stiffness of touch and an intelligence expressing itself in a less familiar art," the critic expressed fascinated bewilderment before the paintings. Regarding the second canvas, *The Passage of Souls* (Figure 2.14), in which infant souls are carried to Earth by angels, the critic wondered at the inclusion of the suffering Prometheus—raising the issue of illegibility that vexes the cycle.[111] His complaint that he consulted the text to no avail

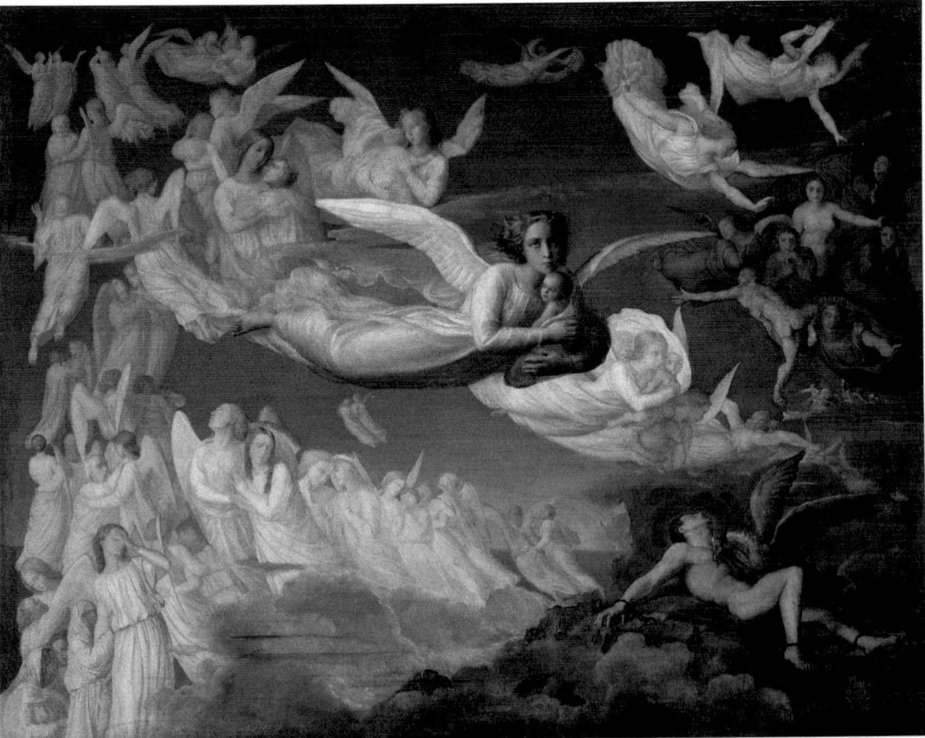

Figure 2.14 Louis Janmot, *The Passage of Souls*, from *The Poem of the Soul*, ca. 1838; signed and dated 1854, oil on canvas, 112.6 × 145.5 cm. Lyon, Musée des Beaux Arts. Image © Lyon MBA—Photo RMN/René-Gabriel Ojéda.

is well taken. While the verse identifies figures watching the titan's torment as evil spirits that torture mankind, the suffering of Prometheus is mentioned in the form of a question:

> Quel est donc ce géant et ce vautour cruel
> Qui lui ronge le coeur? En vain il le dépèce:
> Sans cesse dévoré, le coeur renaît sans cesse
>   Pour souffrir immortel.
> Who is this giant and this cruel vulture / That preys upon his heart? In vain it carves him up: / Ceaselessly devoured, the heart is ceaselessly reborn / To everlasting suffering. (lines 69–72)

Notwithstanding this obscurity, Gautier observed that:

> It is difficult to paint the immaterial in a more suave and delicate manner. M. Janmot has found for these scenes of the other world deathly pallors, tones of wax and the host, past grays and future blues unknown to human palettes. One would say the shadow of a dream caught by daguerreotype in those regions of the infinite beyond the light of stars.[112]

This was just the kind of prose—at once nebulous and self-consciously clever—that made Gautier's art criticism annoying to Delacroix, who mentioned his irritation when writing of Janmot's paintings the following year. His own ambivalent response to the cycle deserves to be quoted at length:

> There is a remarkable Dantesque fragrance in Janmot. He brings to mind those angels from the purgatory of the famous Florentine; I love those dresses, green as the meadow grass in the month of May, those inspired or dreamt heads that are like reminiscences of another world. This naïve artist will never be accorded a particle of the justice to which he is due. His barbarous execution unfortunately places him at a rank which is neither second nor third, nor last; he speaks a language which no one else will ever speak; it is not even a language; but one perceives his ideas through the confusion and the naïve barbarism of his means of rendering them. This is an entirely singular talent in our place and time; the example of his master Ingres, so proper for fertilizing, by imitation pure and simple of his technique, that crowd of followers devoid of any ideas of their own, will have been powerless to convey a manner of execution to this natural talent, which, however, knows not how to leave his swaddling clothes, who will be for all of his life like a bird that still drags the shell in which it was born and which still drags itself smeared with the mucus in which it was formed.[113]

Notwithstanding his disapproval of Janmot's "barbarous" technique and condescension toward an apparent incapacity for growth, Delacroix appreciated this exception to the tendency of Ingres's students to mindlessly ape their master (an accusation that could not be aimed fairly at Flandrin or Orsel). No less than Gautier, Delacroix delights in Janmot's capacity to bring visual form to visionary imaginings. At the same time, both viewers were thwarted by a hermetic language that renders the program inaccessible even to receptive eyes.

Neither Gautier nor Delacroix lived to see the cycle's sequel: a series of charcoal drawings in which the soul is embodied in a grown man whose temptation, transgression, and doubt lead the protagonist to temporarily abandon Christianity. Following this dismal turn, the suite concludes with uplift. The title of the final drawing, *Sursum Corda* (1879), is taken from the response to the *Sanctus* hymn in the Mass: "Let us elevate our hearts" (Figure 2.15). Here, the sinner is redeemed in the presence of virtues and angels bearing the features of Janmot's children. Above, in a heavenly zone, Christ (as the Good Shepherd) is worshiped by a blessed host, which includes Janmot's deceased wife, Léonie (in the guise of Saint Mary Magdalene), Lacordaire, and the Curé d'Ars. Notwithstanding this pious, optimistic conclusion, Janmot's decades of labor hardly produced an effective guide to Christian devotion. This was despite Ozanam's assertion that his friend's cycle would serve "the benediction of God and the instruction of mankind."[114] Like other radical, Romantic innovations in picturing the sacred (e.g., those of William Blake and Philip Otto Runge), Janmot's masterwork sacrifices public comprehension and Christian orthodoxy to the dictates of private vision.

Accordingly, the paintings were criticized at the time of the 1855 Exposition universelle in the Catholic paper *L'Univers*. Having "unfortunately strayed into the

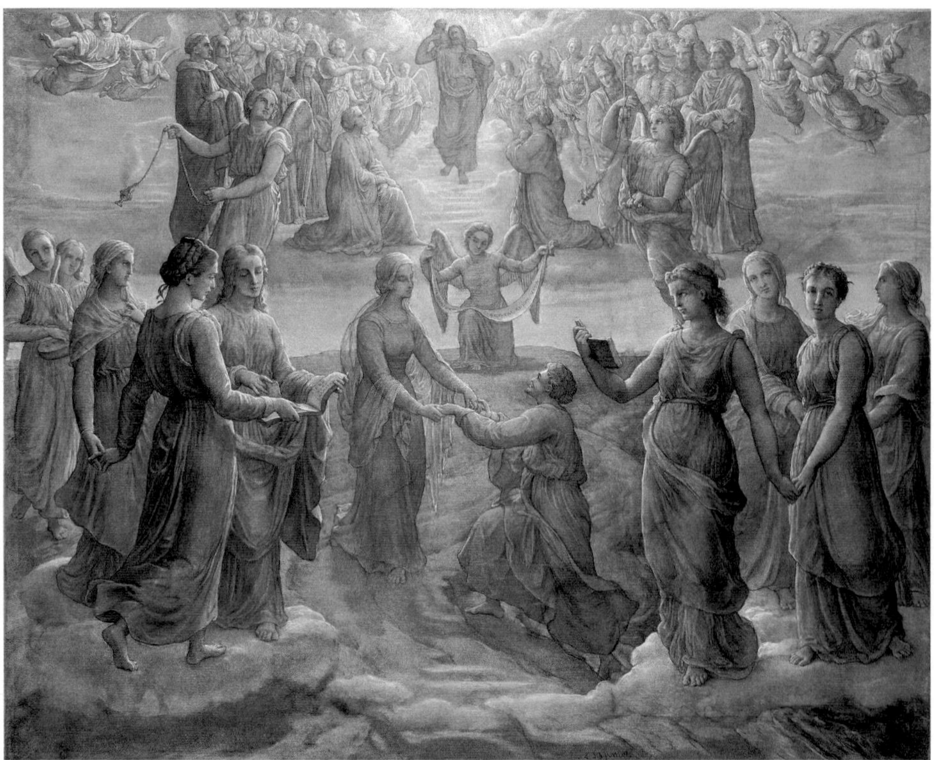

Figure 2.15 Louis Janmot, *Sursum Corda*, from *The Poem of the Soul*, 1879, charcoal with white and blue gouache on paper, 114 × 144 cm. Lyon, Musée des Beaux Arts. Image © Lyon MBA-Photo Alain Basset.

nebulous and abstract conceptions of Idealism," the artist was taken to task for considering "neither original sin, nor baptism, nor the temptations and the trials that comprise the life of man."[115] This critique must have been especially painful (and Janmot did address it in the drawings) for it came from a close friend, a Lyonnais disciple of Lacordaire, Claudius Lavergne, with whom Janmot had been an instigator of the Dominican's Confrérie de saint Jean. In their youth, the artists had traveled together to Rome; when Lavergne fell ill, Janmot cut short his stay to see his companion home. That Lavergne was driven to break with Janmot speaks of the radically wayward character of the cycle. In this regard, it is telling that Gautier and Delacroix appreciated the paintings for reasons that had nothing to do with their intended didactic purpose.

This was also the case with Baudelaire, who admitted that, on a purely artistic level,

> there is in the composition of these scenes, and even in the bitter color in which they are arrayed, an immense charm that is difficult to describe, something of the sweet savor of solitude, of the sacristy, of the church and of the cloister; an unconscious and childish mysticism.[116]

The Nightmare, in particular, struck this translator of Poe as "distinguished by a remarkable understanding of the fantastic" ("*où brillait une remarquable entente du fantastique*"). At the same time, he considered *The Poem of the Soul* "muddy and obscure" ("*trouble et confuse*") in content; he was understandably unsure whether it represented a male and female soul or twin counterparts of one soul. This criticism did not stem from disdain for belief; Baudelaire was disgusted by the vulgar disregard for religion he witnessed during a late-life residence in Belgium (1864–66). Yet he was hostile to the Lyonnais fervor of *The Poem of the Soul*, and Janmot, in his opinion, was characteristically Lyonnais: "This is a religious and elegiac spirit, he must have been marked from youth by Lyonnais bigotry."[117] Whereas Baudelaire considered Delacroix uniquely capable, in his secular era, of representing religious subjects, he judged Janmot's pious pursuit of the sacred a failure, partly redeemed by "an immense charm" unrelated to Catholic dogma.

The Naturalist authors Edmond and Jules de Goncourt (1822–96 and 1830–70, respectively) considered any attempt to produce Christian art in the nineteenth century futile. Commenting on the 1855 Exposition universelle (which featured a record number of sacred subjects), the brothers proclaimed the genre doomed by the rationalist spirit of the time: "Religious painting no longer exists.... How could it spring forth, with its ardors and its former naïvetés, from these triumphs of logic, from these apotheoses of science which constitute our very century."[118] With comparable pessimism, Vigny had previously doubted the authenticity of Catholic art produced without belief: "The artists illuminate it [Catholicism] like a precious medal, and immerse themselves in its dogmas as if it were an epic source of poetry; but how many of them kneel in the church that they decorate?"[119] Yet belief hardly guaranteed the vitality of sacred art in nineteenth-century France. The Saint-Paul-Saint-Louis *Christ in the Garden of Olives* provided a dazzling frontispiece to the Metropolitan Museum of Art's hanging of the 2018 Delacroix exhibition. It is unlikely that Orsel, Flandrin, or Janmot—who certainly knelt in the churches they decorated—will ever receive a world-class retrospective. *The Poem of Soul* was appreciated by few in its creator's lifetime and is little-known today outside Lyon and the small cohort of scholars of nineteenth-century French religious art. Notwithstanding its pious intent, Janmot's visionary, salvific program is no less intensely personal (and no more doctrinally sound) than Delacroix's pessimistic interpretations of the Crucifixion, the Lamentation, and the ordeal in the Garden of Olives. This shared trait of the art of Janmot and Delacroix stemmed from divergent sources. Irrevocably severed from the age in which his idol, Rubens, brought forth Herculean Saviors with brawn sufficient to brave torment on the cross, Delacroix projected empathy onto humanly vulnerable Christs. When representing subjects drawn from the Gospels and the lives of the saints, he gave free rein to the imperatives of his art, at the cost of providing stimulus to prayer. Steeped in the mysticism of a city traumatized by the Revolution, and heedless of the comprehension of his audience, Janmot strove to achieve nothing less than the reinvention of sacred art. Despite their obvious differences, Delacroix and Janmot each aspired to rival the great religious artists who worked in the centuries before Chateaubriand published the *Génie du christianisme* "amid the debris of our temples." In this perilous enterprise, advantage went to the non-believer—a telling indication that both artists were heirs to a legacy of loss.

Notes

1 Lee Johnson, *The Paintings of Eugène Delacroix: A Critical Catalogue* (Oxford: Clarendon Press, vol. 3, 1986), no. 421. The painting, also known as *Calvary*, is in La Cohue—Musée des Beaux-Arts, Vannes. The incident is recounted, and the artist is quoted, in Alain Daguerre de Hureaux, *Delacroix* (Paris: Hazan, 1993), 216.

2 Quoted from "Salon de 1835," *L'Artiste* 9, no. 8 (1835), 89–90, in Barthélémy Jobert, *Delacroix*, new and expanded ed. (Princeton, NJ: Princeton University Press, 2018), 290.

3 See Johnson, *Paintings of Eugène Delacroix*, vol. 1: *1816–31* (Oxford: Clarendon Press, 1981), no. 154; Sébastien Allard et al., *Delacroix* (Paris: Musée du Louvre, in association with Éditions Hazan, Paris), 2018, no. 115; and the catalog entries by Emmanuelle Federspiel, in *Une lutte moderne, de Delacroix à nos jours*, ed. Dominique de Font-Réaulx and Marie Montfort (Paris: Musée national Eugène-Delacroix, 2018), nos. 24 and 25.

4 *The New English Bible, with the Apocrypha* (New York: Oxford University Press, 1971), Mark 14:32–7.

5 Maurice Sérullaz, Arlette Sérullaz, Louis-Antoine Prat, and Claudine Ganeval, *Musée du Louvre, Cabinet des dessins. Inventaire général des dessins, École française. Dessins d'Eugène Delacroix, 1798–1863* (Paris: Éditions de la Réunion des musées nationaux, 1984), vol. 1, no. 93 (RF23325).

6 "Un de ses tableaux de jeunesse, le *Christ aux Oliviers* ("Seigneur, détournez de moi ce calice") ... ruisselle de tendresse féminine et d'onction poétique." "Salon de 1859," reprinted in Charles Baudelaire, *Critique d'art, suivi de Critique musicale*, ed. Claude Pichois, int. Claire Brunet (Paris: Gallimard, 1992), 292.

7 According to the artist's friend Adolphe-Ferdinand Moreau, *père* (1800–59), the landscape was partially the work of the skilled specialist Paul Huet (1803–69). See Daguerre de Hureaux, *Delacroix,* 214 and n. 326 (on p. 293).

8 "Pour mon tableau du *Christ*, les anges de la mort tristes et sévères portent sur lui leurs regards mélancoliques." Eugène Delacroix, *Journal,* ed. Michèle Hannoosh (Paris: José Corti, 2009), 1: 150. All quotations from the *Journal* herein are from this authoritative edition.

9 "Penser, en faisant mes anges pour le préfet, à ces belles et mystiques figures de femmes ...." Delacroix, *Journal* 1: 152 and n. 241.

10 "J'ai eu un délire de composition ce matin à mon atelier et j'ai retrouvé des entrailles pour le tableau du *Christ* qui ne me disait rien." Delacroix, *Journal*, 1: 150.

11 "Le premier mérite d'un tableau est d'être une fête pour l'oeil." Delacroix, *Journal*, 2: 1412.

12 See Andor Pigler, *Barockthemen: Eine Auswahl von Verzeichnissen zur Ikonographie des 17. und 18. Jahrhunderts*, 2 vols. (Budapest: Verlag der Ungarischen Akademie der Wissenschaften, 1956).

13 Bruno Foucart, *Le Renouveau de la peinture religieuse en France (1800–1860)* (Paris: Arthéna, 1987), 101–2. See also the extensive list of nineteenth-century French examples provided by Foucart, in "Chassériau et le thème du Christ au jardin des Oliviers: Entre romantisme et orthodoxie," in *Chassériau (1819–1856): Un autre romantisme, Actes du colloque organisé par le Musée du Louvre, le 16 mars 2002*, ed. Stéphane Guégan and Louis-Antoine Prat (Paris: La Documentation française / Musée du Louvre, 2002), 52 n. 17.

14 Quoted from Auguste Jal, *Esquisses ... sur le Salon de 1827* (1828), in Hugh Honour, *Romanticism* (New York: Harper & Row, 1979), 51 n. 57.

15 "En interrogeant machinalement ces masses grandioses et confuses, je cherchais le sens de cette agonie du Christ, le secret de cette douleur voluntaire si cuisante, et je commençais à y pressentir quelque chose de plus grand et de plus profound que ce qui m'avait été expliqué; je devenais profondément triste moi-même, et comme navrée d'une pitié, d'une souffrance inconnues. Quelques larmes venaient au bord de ma paupière, je les essuyais furtivement, ayant honte d'être émue sans savoir pourquoi." George Sand, *Histoire de ma vie*, ed. Brigitte Diaz (Paris: Librairie générale française, 2004), 394–5. Foucart cites this text to indicate the emotional force of the subject, in "Chassériau et le thème," 43.

16 See Foucart, *Le Renouveau de la peinture religieuse*, 244–7.

17 See Foucart, "Chassériau et le thème," 39–79.

18 For these paintings, see Stéphane Guégan, "Entre Paris et Alger: un croyant obstiné," in Stéphane Guégan, Vincent Pomarède, and Louis-Antoine Prat, *Chassériau: Un autre romantisme* (Paris: Réunion des Musées Nationaux, 2002), 41–5, and Guégan's essays accompanying catalog entries nos. 16–19 and 79. The Salon guidebook notices for both paintings refer to the Gospel of Mark.

19 For evidence regarding the timing of work on the project, see Guégan's essay accompanying catalog entries nos. 16–19, in idem, Pomarède, and Prat, *Chassériau: Un autre romantisme*; and the biographical chronology by Bruno Chenique, in ibid., 176–7. For providing access to images of this painting and of other works in the Lyon Musée des Beaux-Arts, and for granting reproduction rights, I am grateful to Henrique Simoes, Chargé du Service images, Musée des Beaux-Arts de Lyon.

20 Étienne-Jean Delécluze, "Salon de 1840," *Journal des débats* (12 March 1840) and Prosper Haussard "Salon de 1840," *Le Temps* (12 April 1840), both quoted by Guégan, in idem, Pomarède, and Prat, *Chassériau: Un autre romantisme*), 94 nn.14 and 17.

21 See Foucart, "Chassériau et le thème," 44–9; and Frank Paul Bowman, *Le Christ romantique*, Histoire des idées et critique littéraire 134 (Geneva: Droz, 1973).

22 For assistance with obtaining a reproduction of, and reproduction rights for, this painting, I am grateful to Claude Bardet, Présidente, Les Amis du Vieux Souillac; Studio Guy; François David, Premier Adjoint au Maire de Souillac; and Jérôme Billetat, État Civil, Mairie de Souillac.

23 Michael Paul Driskel underscores the hieratic aspect of the mural, in *Representing Belief: Religion, Art, and Society in Nineteenth-Century France* (University Park: Penn State University Press, 1992), 136.

24 See Foucart, " Chassériau et le thème," 50–1.

25 See the letter from Théodore to his brother Frédéric (23 November 1840), reprinted in Léonce Bénédite, *Théodore Chassériau, sa vie, son oeuvre*, ed. André Dezarrois (Paris: Braun, 1931), 1: 140. See also the chronology by Chenique, in Guégan, Pomarède, and Prat, *Chassériau: Un autre romantisme* (Réunion des musées nationaux), 180.

26 See the letter (27 September 1841) from Lacordaire to the Baronne Hortense de Prailly (née Chevandier de Valdrôme, sister of Paul Chevandier, with whom the artist had a stormy friendship), reprinted in Bénédite, *Théodore Chassériau*, 1: 156. See also the chronology by Chenique, in Guégan, Pomarède, and Prat, *Chassériau: Un autre romantisme* (Réunion des musées nationaux), 183. Contrary evidence is provided by the testimony of Arsène Houssaye (*Les Confessions; Souvenirs d'un demi-siècle, 1830–1880* [Paris: Dentu, 1885], 2: 28–9), director of *L'Artiste* (who knew the artist well), to the effect that Chassériau was *"un croyant obstiné"* (a steadfast believer), quoted in Guégan, "Entre Paris et Alger," 45.

27 "M. Chassériau a l'air d'être friand du *triste* ...." Étienne-Jean Delécluze, "*Journal des débats* (2 April 1844), quoted by Guégan, in idem, Pomarède, and Prat, *Chassériau: Un autre romantisme* (Réunion des musées nationaux), no. 79 (emphasis in original)."[C]e sont les larmes de notre temps qui coulent par ses yeux ... notre mélancolie s'épanche dans ces cheveux in pleurs ... cette figure intelligente et fatiguée ... c'est la souffrance inquiète de notre âge." Théophile Gautier, "Le Salon de 1844," *La Presse,* quoted in Foucart, *Le Renouveau de la peinture religieuse*, 250.

28 For Vigny's reinterpretation of the Gospel account, see Paul Bénichou, "Un Gethsémani romantique ('Le Mont des Oliviers' de Vigny)," *Revue d'histoire littéraire de la France* 98, no. 3 (May–June 1998): 429–36.

29 See Foucart, *Le Renouveau de la peinture religieuse*, 246–7; and Guégan, "Entre Paris et Alger," 41–5. Delaroche, friends with Vigny since the 1830s, produced a number of versions of the subject (in 1846 and 1852–5). For these, see Stephen Bann, *Paul Delaroche: History Painted* (Princeton, NJ: Princeton University Press, 1997), 259–62.

30 Alfred de Vigny, *Oeuvres complètes*, vol. 1: *Poésies* (Paris: Alphonse Lemerre, 1883), 249–50. For the evolution and sources of the poem see idem, *Oeuvres complètes*, vol. 1: *Poésie, théâtre*, ed. François Germain and André Jarry (Paris: Gallimard, 1986), 1102–9.

31 For the impact of Staël's translation of this text on French Romantic literature, see Frank Paul Bowman, *Le Christ des barricades (1789–1848)* (Paris: Les Éditions du Cerf, 1987), 158–64; and Claude Pichois, *L'Image de Jean-Paul Richter dans les les lettres françaises* (Paris: José Corti, 1963), part 2, chap. 7. That Staël was terrified by the text is indicated by Simone Balayé, in *Madame de Staël: Lumières et liberté* (Paris: Éditions Klincksieck, 1979), 188–90.

32 "Alors descendit des hauts lieux sur l'autel une figure rayonnante, noble, élevée, et qui portait l'empreinte d'une impérissable douleur; les mort s'écrièrent: —O Christ! n'est-il point de Dieu? —Il repondit: —il n'en est point. —Toutes les ombres se prirent à trembler avec violence, et le Christ continua ainsi: —J'ai parcouru les mondes, je me suis élevé au-dessus des soleils, et là aussi il n'est point de Dieu; je suis descendu jusqu'aux dernières limites de l'univers, j'ai regardé dans l'abime, et je me suis écrié: —Père, où est-tu? —Mais je n'ai entendu que la pluie qui tombait goutte à goutte dans l'abime .... Jésus, n'avons-nous pas de père? —Et il répondit avec un torrent de larmes: —Nous sommes tous orphelins; moi et vous, nous n'avons point de père." Anne-Louise-Germaine de Staël, *De l'Allemagne,* new ed. (Paris: G. Charpentier, 1890), 379–80.

33 Thus, the awakened dreamer declares: "My soul wept for joy that it could again worship God ... and out of the whole nature around me flowed forth peaceful strains, as from distant evening bells." "Speech of the Dead Christ Down from the Universe, That: There is No God," in Jean Paul Richter, *The Death of an Angel and Other Pieces Translated from the Works of Jean Paul Friedrich Richter*, trans. A. Kenney (London: Black and Armstrong, and Dresden and Leipzig: Chr. Arnold, 1839), 71–2.

34 For the *"querelle Strauss" in France, see Bowman, Le Christ des barricades*, 128–35.

35 Vigny, *Oeuvres complètes* (1883), 1:255. See Vigny, *Oeuvres completes* (1986), 1:1102–4, which indicates that the documentary evidence for dating the stanza "Le Silence" is ambiguous. Of two possible dates, the editors favor April 1863 over 2 April 1862, which is given in the 1883 Lemerre edition quoted above. That Vigny was an avid reader of Strauss, and that he read Renan's book prior to writing "Le Silence," are indicated in Pichois, *L'Image de Jean-Paul Richter*, 275.

36 "C'est aux heures les plus humaines de l'histoire du Rédempteur, à celles où il se met le plus à notre portée, où sa force peut servir d'exemple à notre faiblesse, où nous pouvons marcher du même pas que lui sur son calvaire, que le poète doit emprunter les sujets de ses tableaux." Quoted from Victor de Laprade, "Un Chapitre de la poétique chrétienne," *Le Correspondant* (November 1859), in Bowman, *Le Christ romantique*, 248.

37 Johnson, *Paintings of Delacroix*, vol. 3, no. 445. According to Johnson, this painting was possibly executed with the help of an assistant and is an inferior variant of a lost painting with the same composition (no. 438) executed ca. 1849—a judgement that underestimates the expressive power of the small, signed canvas. For the painting, see also Allard et al., *Delacroix*, no. 116 and pp. 181 and 185. Iris Labeur, account manager at the Rijksmuseum, Amsterdam kindly facilitated my obtaining a reproduction of this painting.

38 In its depressing mood, this painting is akin to a pastel of the same subject drawn for the private oratory of Mme Roché (1850), reproduced in Marie-Pierre Salé, "Facilité, rapidité, fragilité: Delacroix et le pastel," in Allard et al. *Delacroix*, 368. This pastel was preceded, in turn, by a wash drawing (ca. 1849), which features a solitary, downcast Christ, whose prone position announces that featured in the 1851 canvas. See Ashley E. Dunn, with contributions by Colta Ives and Marjorie Shelley, *Delacroix Drawings: The Karen B. Cohen Collection* (New York: Metropolitan Museum of Art, in association with Yale University Press, New Haven, CT, 2018), no. 96.

39 For this painting, exhibited in Salon of 1827–28 and located in the Öffentliche Kunstsammlung, Kunstmuseum, Basel, see Allard et al., *Delacroix*, no. 27; and Johnson, *The Paintings of Eugène Delacroix*, vol. 1, no. 162. Paul Joannides persuasively links this motif to a passage from the second canto of Byron's *Lara*. See "Delacroix and Modern Literature," in *The Cambridge Companion to Delacroix*, ed. Beth S. Wright (Cambridge: Cambridge University Press, 2001), 145–6.

40 See Cynthia Bland, "Du divin à l'humain: La Transfiguration du Christ dans Le Christ au jardin des Oliviers," *Bulletin de la Société des Amis du Musée Eugène-Delacroix*, no. 7 (2009): 11–8.

41 Accordingly, I subscribe to neither Bland's linkage of Delacroix's ideas regarding religion to the theology of Friedrich Daniel Ernst Schleiermacher nor Joyce Carol Polistena's invocation of Lamennais and Johann Adam Möhler as influences on the artist's religious paintings. In addition to Bland, "Du divin à l'humain," see idem, "Inspiration, Innovation, and Emotion: The Early Religious Paintings of Eugène Delacroix," PhD diss., University of Iowa, 2002; and Joyce Carol Polistena,"The 'Agony in the Garden' by Eugène Delacroix," *Van Gogh Museum Journal* (2001): 125–38.

42 *Correspondance générale d'Eugène Delacroix*, ed. André Joubin (Paris: Plon, 1936), 2: 5.

43 For this work, see Debora Silverman, *Van Gogh and Gauguin: The Search for Sacred Art* (New York: Farrar, Straus and Giroux, 2000), 295–301.

44 This is according to Foucart, *Le Renouveau de la peinture religieuse*, 101–2.

45 Frank Paul Bowman, "Illuminism, Utopia, Mythology," in *The French Romantics*, ed. D.G. Charlton (Cambridge: Cambridge University Press, 1984), 1: 78.

46 For a table quantifying copies of the most copied paintings, see Foucart, *Le Renouveau de la peinture religieuse*, 95–6.

47 Prud'hon's *Christ on the Cross* was complete by 21 January 1823 but remained unpaid for at the artist's death (16 February). It was acquired for the Louvre at the behest of the Comte de Forbin, Director of the Royal Museums, with a copy (destroyed 1830) by Prud'hon's student, Charles-Pompée Le Boulanger de Boisfremont, sent to the cathedral of Strasbourg. For *A Young Zephyr* and *Christ on the Cross*, see Sylvain Laveissière, *Pierre-Paul Prud'hon* (New York: Metropolitan Museum of Art, in association with Harry N. Abrams, New York; and Paris: Réunion des musées nationaux, 1998), nos. 182 and 211, respectively. For a grisaille study for *A Young Zephyr* (Paris, Musée du Louvre), see also the catalog entry by Jean Lacambre, in Frederick J. Cummings, Pierre Rosenberg, and Robert Rosenblum, *French Painting, 1774–1830: The Age Revolution* (Detroit: Detroit Institute of Arts, 1975), no. 143.

48 For *Justice and Vengeance Pursuing Crime*, see Laveissière, *Prud'hon*, 222 and nos. 165–71. The replacement is mentioned in Elisabeth Kashey, "Religious Art in Nineteenth Century France," in *Christian Imagery in French Nineteenth-Century Art, 1789–1906*, ed. Martin L.H. Reymert and Robert J.F. Kashey (New York: Shepherd Gallery, 1980), 5.

49 For the deterioration of *Christ on the Cross*, restored and perhaps prematurely varnished in 1831 (and permanently damaged by the artist's ill-judged addition of an ingredient intended to delay drying), see Laveissière, *Prud'hon*, no. 211.

50 The Virgin, supported by Saint John, is more visible in a preparatory drawing (Dijon, Musée des Beaux-Arts), reproduced in Laveissière, *Prud'hon*, 296.

51 For this remarkable work, barred entry (as a plaster) to the Salon of 1840 (the jury's vote was 14 to 6); carved in wood by Louis Buhot in 1846; and expulsed from the Parisian church of Saint-Paul, see Driskel, *Representing Belief*, 180–3. See also the monographic article, David Mower, "Antoine Augustin Préault (1809–1879)," *Art Bulletin* 63, no. 2 (June 1981): 295, in which the wood carving (attributed there to Préault) is dated 1849.

52 This point is made by Foucart, *Le Renouveau de la peinture religieuse*, 240.

53 "A partir de cette catastrophe, la vie devint pour lui un poids insupportable.... Le Christ auquel il travaillait presque en mourant est comme la dernière lueur de son âme. Mécontent de cet ouvrage, qu'il laissait imparfait, il suppliait ses amis de le faire disparaître après sa mort." "Prud'hon," *Revue des deux mondes* (1 November 1846), reprinted in Eugène Delacroix, *Oeuvres littéraires 2: Essais sur les artistes celèbres*, 6th ed. (Paris: G. Crès, 1923), 151.

54 Ibid., 155.

55 "Je me rappelle avoir vu ainsi, et avec le plus grand plaisir, une copie du *Christ* de Prud'hon, à Saint-Philippe du Roule; je crois que c'était pendant l'enterrement de M. de Beauharnais. Jamais, à coup sûr, cette composition, qui est critiquable, ne m'avait paru meilleure. La partie sentimentale semblait se dégager et m'arrivait sur les ailes de la musique." Delacroix, *Journal*, 1: 727 and n. 430.

56 For the Walters Art Museum *Christ on the Cross*, see Johnson, *The Paintings of Eugène Delacroix*, vol. 3, no. 433; and Allard et al. *Delacroix*, no. 112. For this work, and for other versions of the subject by Delacroix, see also the catalog entries by Vincent Pomarède, in Arlette Sérullaz et al., *Delacroix: The Late Work* Paris: Galeries Nationales du Grand Palais and Philadelphia: Philadelphia Museum of Art, in association with Thames and Hudson, New York, 1998, nos. 119–23. For assistance with obtaining a reproduction of the painting, I am grateful to Laura Seitter, Imaging and Rights Coordinator, The Walters Art Museum, Baltimore, MD.

57 In a study focussing on the formal underpinnings of the religious paintings' affective qualities, Susan Strauber perceptively analyzes the emotionally-charged handling of color in the Walters Art Museum canvas in a passage that deserves quotation:

> Above all else, it is the dark ground of the sky and mountains, the great sheet of deep green and blue-gray, which dominates and sets the key for the *Christ en croix*. It unifies the painting, creates an appropriately despondent, somber ambience, and provides the chromatic base for the most vivid contrast possible between the white-gray tones of Christ's flesh and drapery and the reds of his blood. By loading greens and marine blues into the dark grayed ground Delacroix heightens the visual force and dramatic impact of the globs of red blood which pour from his wound and of the translucent flesh, making it reverberate with an almost phosphorescent glow.

"The Religious Paintings of Eugène Delacroix," PhD diss., Brown University, 1980, 126–7.

58 Delacroix, *Journal* (16 April 1853), 1: 634 and n. 58.

59 "Tout cela est terrible d'aspect, comme il convient à l'agonie d'un Dieu; la nature est émouvée de la terre au ciel, et l'on entend passer dans l'air des légions d'esprit qui jettent un voile sur l'ancien monde, et célèbrent les nouvelles destinées de l'homme." ("Salon de 1847," in *Salons de T. Thoré, 1844, 1845, 1846, 1847, 1848, avec une preface par W. Bürger* (Paris, 1868), 453, quoted in Foucart, *Le Renouveau de la peinture religieuse*, 127–8.

60 Johnson, *The Paintings of Eugène Delacroix*, vol. 3, no. 434. Carolyn Cruthirds, Coordinator of Image Licensing, Boston Museum of Fine Arts kindly assisted me in obtaining rights to reproduce this painting.

61 This

> tache écarlate ... donne une tristesse immense à la localité générale du tableau. Elle rend terreux, malades, livides et verdâtres tous les autres tons. Grâce à cette rude dissonance, rien n'est plus lugubre que ce ciel lourd, épais, grisâtre, où rampent des nuages éventrés.

Quoted from "Salon de 1848," *La Presse*, 26 April 1848, in Daguerre de Hureaux, *Delacroix*, 224 and n. 343 (on p. 293).

62 "Les détails sont, en général, médiocres, et échappent en quelque sorte à l'examen. En revanche, l'ensemble inspire une émotion qui m'étonne moi-même. Vous restez sans pouvoir vous détacher, et pas un détail ne s'élève pour se faire admirer ou distraire l'attention. C'est la perfection de cet art-là, dont l'objet et de faire un effet simultané." Delacroix, *Journal*, 1: 732. For the complex sequence of Delacroix's rereading and reediting of this passage, whose core idea—that details should be subordinate to the entirety of a

composition—dates from 30 December 1853, see the commentary by Hannoosh, in Delacroix, *Journal*, 1: 731 n.448; and for the fact that the entry was written in light of Laurens's lithograph, itself copied from Delacroix's own copy of the Boston *Lamentation*, see idem, in Delacroix, *Journal*, 1: 732 n. 449. For a discussion of the artist's quest for unity in this painting, see Sébastien Allard and Côme Fabre, "Delacroix: l'art et la matière," in Allard et al., *Delacroix*, 178–80.

63 "Dans le quartier de Saint Remy, voyant la porte ouverte, je suis entré et ai joui du spectacle le plus grandiose, celui de l'Église sombre et élevée, éclairée par une demi-douzaine de chandelles fumeuses placées ça et là. Je demande aux adversaires du *vague* de me produire une sensation qu'on puisse comparer à celle-là avec de la précision et des lignes bien définies." Delacroix, *Journal*, 1:831 (emphasis in original).

64 For a discussion of the painting, see Elizabeth A. Fraser, *Delacroix, Art and Patrimony in Post-Revolutionary France* (Cambridge: Cambridge University Press, 2004), chap. 1.

65 "Lui seul, peut-être, dans notre siècle incrédule, a conçu des tableaux de religion qui n'étaient ni vides ni froids comme des oeuvres de concours, ni pédants, mystiques ou néo-chrètiens, comme ceux de tous ces philosophes de l'art qui font de la religion une science d'archaïsme, et croient nécessaire de posséder avant tout la symbolique et les traditions primitives pour remuer et faire chanter la corde religieuse." Baudelaire, "Salon de 1846," in Charles Baudelaire, *Critique d'art, suivi de Critique musicale*, ed. Claude Pichois, int. Claire Brunet (Paris: Gallimard, 1992), 95. For a discussion of this passage, see Driskel, *Representing Belief*, 8–11. Regarding Van Gogh's admiration of Delacroix, I am indebted to Jennifer Sichel's outstanding undergraduate Senior Independent Work for Distinction paper, "Cézanne, Van Gogh and the Legacy of Delacroix" (Boston University, 2005–06).

66 "[L]a tristesse sérieuse de son talent convient parfaitement à notre religion, religion profondément triste, religion de la douleur universelle, et qui, à cause de sa catholicité même, laisse une pleine liberté à l'individu et ne demande pas mieux que d'être célébrée dans la langage de chacun,—s'il connaît la douleur et s'il est peintre." Baudelaire, "Salon de 1846," in *Critique d'art*, 96.

67 Henry James, "Two Pictures by Delacroix," *New York Tribune* (19 February 1876), reprinted in *The Painter's Eye: Notes and Essays on the Pictorial Arts by Henry James*, ed. John L. Sweeney (London: Rupert Hart-Davis, 1956), 113. According to Johnson, *The Paintings of Eugène Delacroix*, vol. 3, no. 434 and vol. 1, no. 125, respectively, *The Lamentation* and *The Death of Sardanapalus* were both included in the 1878 exhibition at the Durand-Ruel gallery in Paris (*Exposition rétrospective de tableaux et dessins des maîtres modernes*). I am grateful to Judy Sund for bringing to my attention that this exhibition, devoted to the School of 1830, featured 380 works, of which 32 were by Delacroix. The notice by James indicates that the paintings were on view at the gallery prior to the exhibition.

68 Bowman, "Illuminism, Utopia, Mythology," 81.

69 "Dans le moderne, il n'y a non plus rien à chercher; les Overbeck, les Ingres, les Flandrin furent les blêmes haridelles attelées à des sujets de commande pieux; dans l'église Saint-Sulpice, Delacroix écrase tous les peinturleurs qu l'entourent, mais son sentiment de l'art catholique est nul." *La Cathédrale*, in J.-K. Huysmans, *Le Roman de Durtal*, pref. Paul Valéry (Paris: Bartillat, 2015), 929.

70 Quoted from Alphonse Germain "L'Art religieux au XIXe siècle en France," *Le Correspondant* (1907), 244, in Foucart, *Le Renouveau de la peinture religieuse*, 247.

71 Jobert, *Delacroix*, 288.

72 See Jobert, *Delacroix*, 87–92.

73 Delacroix's appreciative references to religion have been helpfully gathered in Joyce Carol Polistena, *The Religious Painting of Eugène Delacroix (1798–1863): The Initiator of the Style of Modern Religious Art* (Lewiston, New York: Edwin Mellen Press, 2008); and Bland, "Inspiration, Innovation, and Emotion." Bland (p. 71) argues that, though the artist was an independent thinker in regard to religion, "he certainly was not a non-believer." For a critique of this position, see Stéphane Guégan, *Delacroix: Peindre contre l'oubli* (Paris: Flammarion, 2018), 227–31; and idem, "Liturgie de l'absence," in *Une lutte moderne*, ed. Font-Réaulx and Montfort, 56–67.

74 See the discussion of these drawings, from the period 1818–20, in Nina M. Athanassoglou-Kallmyer, *Eugène Delacroix: Prints, Politics and Satire, 1814–1822* (New Haven, CT: Yale University Press, 1991), 15–8.

75 Daguerre de Hureaux, *Delacroix*, 222–3.
76 Jobert, *Delacroix*, 288.
77 See Patrick Noon and Christopher Riopelle, *Delacroix and the Rise of Modern Art* (London: National Gallery and Minneapolis: Minneapolis Institute of Art, in association with Yale University Press, New Haven, CT, 2015), no. 37.
78 "Arrêté longtemps à Saint-Eustace, à entendre les vêpres: cela m'a fait comprendre, quelques instants, le plaisir qu'il y a à être dévot... J'ai vu passer et repasser tout le personnel de l'église depuis l'éclopé donneur d'eau bénite, affublé comme un personnage de Rembrandt, jusqu'au curé dans son camail de chanoine et sa chape de cérémonie." Delacroix, *Journal*, 1: 673 (ellipsis in original).
79 "Berryer et ces messieurs avaient été à la messe; j'ai été un peu honteux à leur retour de ne les avoir pas suivis." Delacroix, *Journal*, 1:768.
80 "Après la cérémonie et l'exhortation de Monseigneur, nous avons assisté à la bénédiction des tombes dans le cimetière: c'est fort beau. L'évêque, tête nue, et dans ses habits, la crosse d'une main, le goupillon de l'autre, marche à grands pas et lance à droite et à gauche l'eau bénite sur les humbles sépultures. La religion est belle ainsi. Les consolations et les conseils que le prélat donnait dans l'église à ces hommes simples, brûlés par les travaux de la campagne et enchaînés à de dures nécessités, allaient à leur véritable adresse." Delacroix, *Journal*, 1: 770.
81 "Dieu est en nous; c'est cette présence intérieur qui nous fait admirer le beau, qui nous réjouit quand nous avons bien fait et nous console de ne pas partager le bonheur du méchant. C'est lui sans doute qui fait l'inspiration dans les hommes de génie et qui les échauffe au spectacle de leurs propres productions. Il y a des hommes de vertu comme des hommes de génie; les uns et les autres sont inspirés et favorisés de Dieu." Delacroix, *Journal*, 2: 1819–20.
82 See Bénichou, *Le Sacre de l'écrivain.*
83 "Ville singulière, bigote et marchande, catholique et protestante, pleine de brumes et de charbons, les idées s'y débrouillent difficilement. Tout ce qui vient de Lyon est minutieux, lentement élaboré et craintif.... On dirait que les cerveaux y sont enchiffrenés." Baudelaire, *Critique d'art*, 261.
84 See Joseph Buche, *L'École mystique de Lyon, 1776–1847*, pref. Edouard Herriot (Paris: Librairie Félix Alcan, 1935). The quest for legibility was not always successful; the elaborate typological program of Flandrin's nave murals in Saint-Germain-des-Prés (1856–63) confused some viewers. See Bruno Horaist, "Saint-Germain-des-Prés (1839–63)," in Jacques Foucart et al., *Hippolyte, Auguste et Paul Flandrin: Une fraternité picturale au XIXe siècle* (Paris: Musée du Luxembourg and Éditions de la réunion des musées nationaux, 1984), 125–53.
85 For Saint-Martin and Illuminism, see Bowman, *Le Christ des barricades*, 45–8; idem, the entries, "Illuminism" and "Saint-Martin," in *The New Oxford Companion to Literature in French*, ed. Peter France (Oxford: Clarendon Press, 1995), 399, 734; Bowman, "Illuminism, Utopia, Mythology," 82–6; and Paul Bénichou, *Le Sacre de l'écrivain, 1750–1830: Essai sur l'avènement d'un pouvoir spirituel laïque dans la France modern*, 2nd ed. (Paris: Librairie José Corti, 1985), chap. 3.
86 In his providential conception of the Revolution, Saint-Martin was perpetuating a discourse predating 1789. For this, see Darrin M. McMahon, *Enemies of the Enlightenment: The French Counter-Enlightenment and the Making of Modernity* (Oxford: Oxford University Press, 2001).
87 Marc Fumaroli, *Chateaubriand: Poésie et terreur* (Paris: Gallimard, 2003), 488.
88 "J'essayerai donc de peindre la Religion catholique prêtant à l'histoire le seul flambeau qui puisse l'éclairer, réalisant l'idéal de morale que l'auteur de notre être a gravé dans nos coeurs, échauffant le génie par la grande élévation où elle le place et donnant la vie à tous les chefs d'oeuvre modernes." Pierre-Simon Ballanche, *Du sentiment considéré dans ses rapports avec la littérature et les arts* (Lyon: Ballanche et Barret and Paris: Calixte Volland, an IX, [1801]), 165–6.
89 Prior to the publication of *Du sentiment*, Ballanche evidently had some familiarity with Chateaubriand's manuscript (which had been conceived as early as April 1799). Ballanche quotes, with approval, a passage from the *Génie du christianisme* praising Bossuet as

historian, crediting "*Des Beautés poétiques du Christianisme* par Châteaubriant [sic]." The passage regarding Bossuet quoted by Ballanche (*Du sentiment*, 312, as a note to p. 169) begins without resemblance to that of Chateaubriand, but then copies the *Génie du christianisme* verbatim (cf. Chateaubriand, *Génie du christianisme*, ed. Maurice Regard (Paris: Gallimard, 1978), 846.

90 See Bernard M.G. Reardon, *Liberalism and Tradition: Aspects of Catholic Thought in Nineteenth-Century France* (Cambridge: Cambridge University Press, 1975), 54. For the Chateaubriand-Fontanes-Ballanche connection, see also Buche, *L'École mystique de Lyon*, chaps. 8 and 9.

91 For Ballanche, see Bénichou, *Le Sacre de l'écrivain*, 155–71; and idem, *Le Temps des prophètes: Doctrines de l'âge romantique* (Paris: Gallimard, 1977), chap. 2.

92 "Oh quelle main burinera les actions et le courage des généreux défenseurs de Lyon? La postérité saura-t-elle jamais qu'isolés au milieu de la France esclave ils osèrent faire entendre les accens [sic] de la vraie liberté ?" Ballanche, *Du sentiment*, 106.

93 See Marie-Claude Chaudonneret, *Fleury Richard et Pierre Révoil: La Peinture troubadour*, pref. Daniel Ternois (Paris: Arthéna, 1980), 19.

94 See the eloquent discussion of the bereavement informing this current in Beth S. Wright, *Painting and History during the French Restoration: Abandoned by the Past* (Cambridge: Cambridge University Press, 1997), chap. 3.

95 For the artist, see Hardouin-Fugier, *Louis Janmot 1814–1892* (Lyon: Presses universitaires de Lyon, 1981); and *Louis Janmot, Précurseur du symbolism, Avec le texte intégral du `Poème de l'âme' (1881)*, ed. Wolfgang Drost, Elisabeth Hardouin-Fugier, and Birgit Gottschalk (Heidelberg: Universitätsverlag C. Winter, 1994).

96 See Sylvie Ramond, et al., *Le Temps de la peinture, Lyon 1800–1914* (Lyon: Éditions Fage, 2007), no. 103; and the catalog entry by Élisabeth Hardouin-Fugier, in *Les Peintres de l'âme: Art lyonnais du XIXe siècle* (Lyon: Musée des Beaux-Arts, 1981), no. 71.

97 See *The New English Bible, with the Apocrypha* (New York: Oxford University Press, 1971), 106.

98 Janmot later produced a book of more than 500 pages, *Opinion d'un artiste sur l'art* (Lyon: Vite & Perrussel and Paris: Victor Lecoffre, 1887), in which he argues, in the spirit of Montalembert and Rio, that the Renaissance, with its love of pagan antiquity, was a period of decadence rather than renewal.

99 *Explication des ouvrages de peinture, sculpture, architecture, gravure et lithographie des artistes vivants, exposés au Palais des Tuileries le 15 juin 1849* (Paris: Vinchon, 1849), no. 1110, reprint in *Catalogues of the Paris Salon 1673 to 1881*, comp. H.W. Janson (New York: Garland, 1977).

100 "M. Janmot qui a du talent et de la foi ... se perd et s'enfonce dans nous ne savons quelle métaphysique .... Mais on prend une plume et du papier lorsqu'on veut faire un livre." Quoted by Elisabeth Hardouin-Fugier in *Les Peintres de l'âme*, 158.

101 Quoted from the preface to the 1881 publication of reproductions of the cycle with the verse text, reprinted in *Louis Janmot, Précurseur du symbolism*, ed. Drost et al., 18. All quotations from Janmot's text herein are from this edition.

102 See Élisabeth Hardouin-Fugier, *`Le Poème de l'âme' par Janmot: Étude iconologique* (Lyon: Presses universitaires de Lyon, 1977); idem, *`Le Poème de l'âme' par Louis Janmot (1814–1892)* (Châtillon-sur-Chalaronne: Éditions La Taillanderie, 2007); idem., *Le Poème de l'âme* (Lyon: Musée des Beaux-Arts, 1976 (a copy of which was kindly given to me by Christopher Riopelle); *Louis Janmot, Précurseur du symbolism*, ed. Drost et al.; and Dominique Brachlianoff, *Le Poème de l'âme* (Lyon: Musée des Beaux-Arts de Lyon and Paris: Éditions de la Réunion des musées nationaux, 1995). See also the discussion of the cycle in Foucart, *Le Renouveau de la peinture religieuse*, 268–71. For analysis of the verse, see Frank Paul Bowman, "Le texte du 'Poème de l'âme'," in *Louis Janmot, Précurseur du symbolisme*, ed. Drost et al., 185–95.

103 See Gautier, "L'Âme, par M. Louis Janmot," *Le Moniteur universel* (26–27 May 1854) and Calonne, "Le Poème de l'âme en peinture et en vers, par M. Louis Janmot," *Revue contemporaine* 14 (June–July 1854), 136–47, both reprinted in *Louis Janmot, Précurseur du symbolism*, ed. Drost et al., 140–1 and 145–8, respectively. According to Hardouin-Fugier, Delacroix was responsible for the inclusion of the cycle in the Exposition

universelle of 1855. See "Un souffle européen aux bords du Rhône: L'Illuminisme et le *Poème de l'âme* de Louis Janmot," in Ramond et al., *Le Temps de la peinture*, 128; and Hardouin-Fugier, *Louis Janmot 1814–1892*, 82.

104 Quotations from Baudelaire herein are from the notes (dating largely from 1858–60), for an unpublished article printed posthumously as "L'Art philosophique," reprinted in Baudelaire, *Critique d'art*, 258–65. The project is referred to under various other titles in the author's correspondence. See the explanatory note by Pichois, in Baudelaire, *Critique d'art*, 606–7.

105 For leading examples, see Léon Cellier, *L'Épopée humanitaire et les grands mythes romantiques* (Paris: Société d'édition d'enseignement supérieur, 1971).

106 Notwithstanding the Ballanche-inspired title of its principal image, *Social Palingenesis*, Chenavard's project (which would have included at least 63 murals), as Daniel R. Guernsey demonstrates, was anti-clerical and upended the Catholic philosopher's ideology. Commissioned (11 April 1848) by the republican minister of the interior, Alexandre-Auguste Ledru-Rollin (1807–74) amid the utopian aspirations of the Second Republic, Chenavard's project met with clerical opposition starting in early 1851 and was rejected in December when, shortly after his coup d'état, Louis-Napoléon returned the Panthéon to its former function as the Church of Sainte-Geneviève (6 December 1851). See Daniel R. Guernsey, *The Artist and the State, 1777–1855: The Politics of Universal History in British and French Painting* (Aldershot: Ashgate, 2007), chap. 3; and for Chenavard, see also Marie-Claude Chaudonneret, ed. *Paul Chenavard 1807–1895: Le Peintre et le prophète* (Lyon: Musée des Beaux-Arts and Paris: Réunion des musées nationaux, 2000); and Joseph C. Sloane, *Paul Marc Joseph Chenavard, Artist of 1848* (Chapel Hill: University of North Carolina Press, 1962). Chenavard was good friends with Ernest Meissonier, also from Lyon; there is substantial discussion of Chenavard in Marc J. Gotlieb, *The Plight of Emulation: Ernest Meissonier and French Salon Painting* (Princeton, NJ: Princeton University Press, 1996).

107 For this painting's references to the Revolution of 1848 and to divorce legislation, see Hardoin-Fugier, *'Le Poème de l'âme' par Janmot: Étude iconologique*, 122–4.

108 For a discussion of *The Evil Path* in the context of hostility toward secular education, see Driskel, *Representing Belief*, 41.

109 Hardouin-Fugier indicates that this painting brings to mind the work of Max Ernst. See *Le 'Poème de l'âme' par Janmot: Étude iconologique*, 126. In fact, the resemblance of a detail in Max Ernst's *Two Children Are Threatened by a Nightingale* (1924; New York, Museum of Modern Art) to Janmot's abduction motif suggests that the Surrealist was familiar with the published facsimile of *The Poem of the Soul*.

110 "Swedenborg, Saint-Martin et Novalis fixés sur la toile! on ne s'y attendait guère." Théophile Gautier, "L'Âme, Par M. Louis Janmot," reprinted in *Louis Janmot, Précurseur du symbolisme*, ed. Drost et al., 140.

111 Hardouin-Fugier explains that the representation of Prometheus' torment in *The Passage of Souls* prefigures the Passion of Christ. See *'Le Poème de l'âme'* (1976), 12.

112 "Il est difficile de peindre l'immatériel d'une manière plus suave et plus délicate. M. Janmot a trouvé pour ces scenes de l'autre monde des pâleurs mortes, des tons de cire et d'hostie, des gris passés et des bleus futurs inconnus sur les palettes humaines. On dirait l'ombre d'un rêve prise au daguerréotype dans ces régions de l'infini où la lumière des astres n'arrive pas." Théophile Gautier, "L'Âme, Par M. Louis Janmot," reprinted in *Louis Janmot, Précurseur du symbolisme*, ed. Drost et al., 140–1.

113 "Il y a chez Janmot un parfum dantesque remarquable. Je pense en le voyant à ces anges du purgatoire du fameux Florentin; j'aime ces robes vertes comme l'herbe des prés au mois de mai, ces têtes inspirées ou rêvées qui sont comme des réminiscences d'un autre monde. On ne rendra pas à ce naïf artiste une parcelle de la justice à laquelle il a droit. Son exécution barbare le place malheureusement à un rang qui n'est ni le second, ni le troisième, ni le dernier; il parle une langue qui ne peut devenir celle de personne; ce n'est pas même une langue; mais on voit ses idées à travers la confusion et la naïve barbarie de ses moyens de les rendre. C'est un talent tout singulier chez nous et dans notre temps; l'exemple de son maître Ingres, si propre à féconder, par l'imitation pure et simple de ses procédés, cette foule de suivants déporvus d'idées propres, aura été impuissant à donner une exécution à

ce talent naturel, qui pourtant ne sait pas sortir des langes, qui sera toute sa vie semblable à l'oiseau qui traîne encore la coquille natale et qui se traîne encore tout barbouillé des mucus au milieu desquels il s'est formé." Delacroix, *Journal*, 1: 912–3 (Champrosay, 17 June 1855); and see Hannoosh's commentary regarding Delacroix's opinion of Gautier's art criticism, ibid., 1:912, nn. 221 and 222.

114 It will be offered "à la bénédiction de Dieu et à l'instruction des hommes." Quoted, from Ozanam's correspondence (14 October 1849), in Hardouin-Fugier, *'Le Poème de l'âme' par Janmot: Étude iconologique*, 110.

115 Claudius Lavergne, "L'Exposition universelle de 1855: Beaux-arts," *L'Univers* (1855), 99–101, quoted in *Louis Janmot, Précurseur du symbolisme*, ed. Drost et al., 150.

116 "[I]l faut reconnaître qu'au point de vue de l'art pur il y avait dans la composition de ces scènes, et même dans la couleur amère dont elles étaient revêtues, un charme infini et difficile à décrire, quelque chose des douceurs de la solitude, de la sacristie, de l'église et du cloître; une mysticité inconsciente et enfantine." Baudelaire, "L'Art philosphique," in Baudelaire, *Critique d'art*, 264.

117 Ibid., 263.

118 "La peinture religieuse n'est plus.... Comment jaillirait-elle, avec ses ardeurs et ses naïvetés anciennes, de ces triomphes de logique, de ces apothéoses de la science qui sont notre siècle même." Quoted from *La Peinture à l'Exposition universelle de 1855*, in Daguerre de Hureaux, *Delacroix*, 213 and n. 322 (on p. 293).

119 "Les artistes le mettent en lumière comme une précieuse médaille, et se plongent dans ses dogmes comme dans une source épique de poésie; mais combien y en a-t-il que se mettent à genoux dans l'église qu'ils décorent?" *Servitude et grandeur militaires*, in Alfred de Vigny, *Oeuvres complètes*, vol. 2: *Prose*, ed. Alphonse Bouvet (Paris: Gallimard, 1993), 821.

3 Banished

During the Revolution, 100 to 150,000 men and women fled or were banished from France.[1] Dispossessed and barred from return on pain of death, the émigrés constituted a cross-section of society with various reasons for departure: "Most of the nobles who left France were deliberate expatriates; most of the clergy were ostracized; and most of the men and women of the masses were fugitives driven by fear, despair, or panic."[2] In relation to a national population of 26 million, the number of émigrés was relatively small. Yet the political and cultural impact of the Emigration was magnified by the elite status of vocal members of the cohort, including Comte Trophime-Gérard de Lally-Tolendal (1751–1830). Horrified that women were not spared persecution, the count thundered in January 1797:

> Women, great God! Women guilty of *cowardice* or *treason*! ... The *coward* is the one who abandons them; the *traitor* the one who denounces them; the monster, the one who, bearing the knife to the throat of a budding virgin, or an equally defenseless, venerable matron, cuts off, without pity as without peril, the life that he must protect at the price of his own.[3]

This stage rhetoric springs from sincere grievance in the face of a national wound healed neither by Napoleon's closing of the list of émigrés (3 March 1800, retroactively effective 25 December 1799), nor by the general amnesty granted any émigré returning prior to 23 September 1802—a law finalized in the Senate, 26 April 1802. Modern France's formative experience of exile, the Emigration was hardly its last. Long after 1825, when restitution of former émigrés for nationalized property was acrimoniously debated, the topic of banishment continued to generate rage and sorrow.

As is well known, the acclaim that greeted two narratives of unjust proscription exhibited, respectively, at the Salons of 1795 and 1799 (François Gérard's *Belisarius* and Pierre-Narcisse Guérin's *The Return of Marcus Sextus*) was driven by sympathy for those excluded from the homeland during the Revolution. What follows is concerned with the subsequent place of exile in art and literature dating from the first half of the nineteenth century. Heightened sensitivity to the bitterness of expulsion, I claim, informs a diverse range of imagery. Some of this is clearly freighted with political significance and shaped by personal experience (e.g., the writing of Germaine de Staël and Adam Mickiewicz). Other examples, such as paintings of Hagar and Ishmael in the wilderness by Camille Corot and Jean Murat and sculpted interpretations of the punishment of Cain by Antoine Étex and Henri de Triqueti, are devoid of partisanship. In either case empathy drives invention and lends the works period flavor. Concluding

DOI: 10.4324/9781003184737-4

with Victor Hugo's defiant embrace of exile as a source of empowerment and insight, the chapter sets forth a spectrum of imaginative response to a woeful predicament.

In the Wake of the Terror

Despite the reforms of Napoleon (who was unsympathetic toward the émigrés and motivated by self-interest), the Emigration continued until the Bourbon throne was reestablished. Long before that, some exiles hazarded illegal return. Following the fall of Robespierre and the radical faction of the revolutionary legislature on 27 July 1794, a cohort reentered France, generally with false names; most stayed briefly. As early as the following year, warmth toward victims of the Revolution was sufficient for visitors to the Salon to admire a painting offering a poignant historical parallel. In the lost *Belisarius*, François Gérard took up the well-known story of an unjustly punished Byzantine general banished and blinded. I show a smaller replica (1797) by Léonor Mérimée (1757–1836), executed as model for an engraving (1806) by Auguste-Gaspard-Louis Boucher-Desnoyers (1779–1857; Figure 3.1).[4] Like his teacher David, who depicted Belisarius receiving charity (Salon of 1781; Lille, Musée des Beaux-Arts), Gérard aimed for tears.[5] Yet the paintings are as dissimilar as the political contexts in which they were exhibited. Working in a pre-revolutionary climate conducive

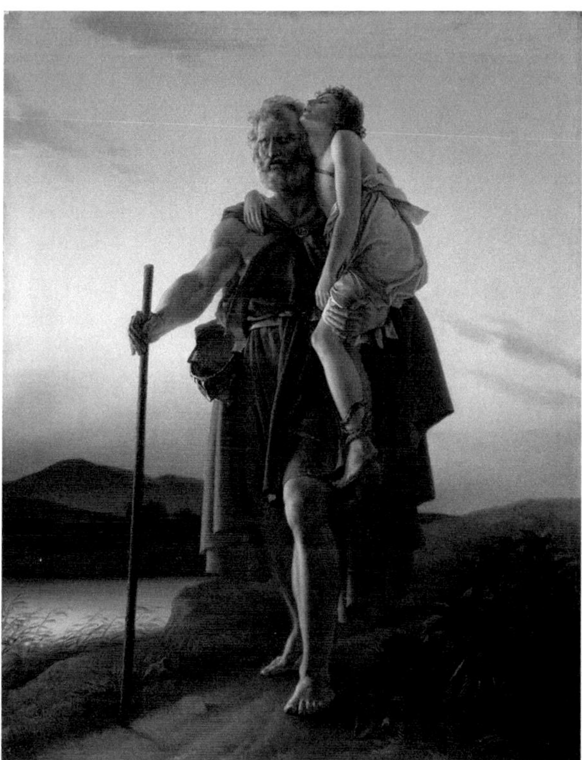

Figure 3.1 Léonor Mérimée after François Gérard, *Belisarius*, 1797, oil on canvas, 91.8 × 72.5 cm. Los Angeles, The J. Paul Getty Museum at the Getty Center. Digital image courtesy of the Getty's Open Content Program.

to earnest instruction, David invited the viewer to share a witnessing soldier's shock before the spectacle of his once formidable commander unjustly reduced to beggary, with a child as his sole advocate. Opting for uneasy introversion rather than emphatic expression, Gérard relocates Belisarius from the base of a monumental edifice to a perilous tract of rough land and open water that highlights the vulnerability of the wanderer. Blind to the brilliant sunset that sets off his imposing stature, the barefoot Belisarius tenderly carries his young guide. On the verge of death from the bite of a snake that remains hideously curled around his ankle, the child has gone limp, his androgyny redolent of innocence. As Thomas Crow indicates, Guérin's narrative invokes the misfortunes of the moderate Girondin faction, proscribed by the radicals in May of 1793, now permitted to return.[6]

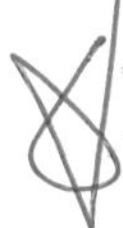

At the Salon of 1799, yet another portrayal of an ancient victim of proscription was enthusiastically received. Begun in 1797, Pierre-Narcisse Guérin's *The Return of Marcus Sextus* histrionically sets forth the cruelty of banishment (Figure 3.2).[7] Having portrayed *The Return of Belisarius to His Family* in a canvas featuring the reappearance of the blind general amid clamorous kin (ca. 1795–97),[8] Guérin imagined a grimmer homecoming for an imaginary Roman, Marcus Sextus, who returns from an exile imposed by the dictator Sulla only to discover that his wife has recently died. His features frozen in grief and rage, the stricken husband and father grasps the hand of

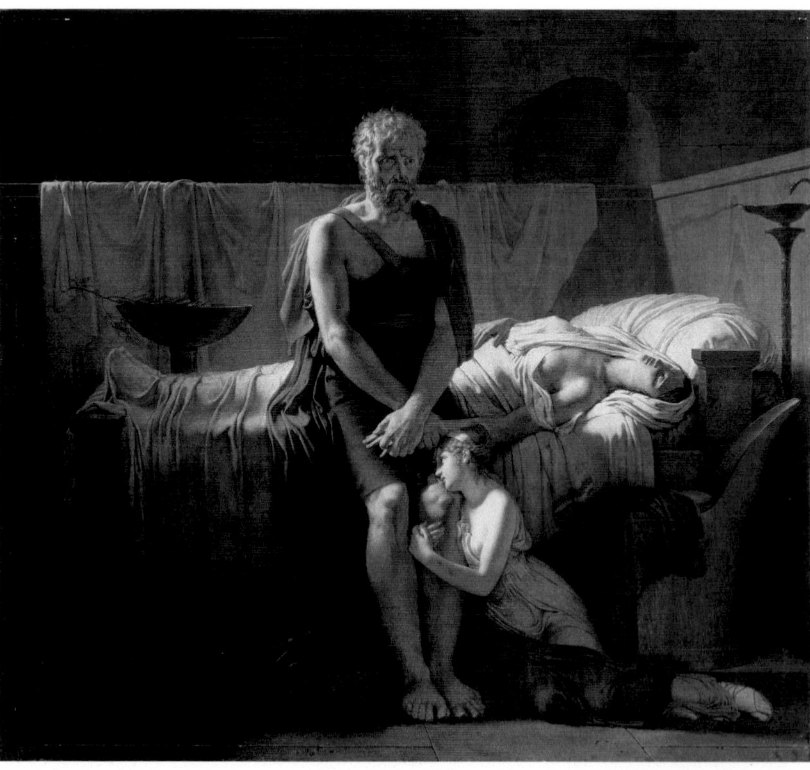

Figure 3.2 Pierre-Narcisse Guérin, *The Return of Marcus Sextus*, 1797–99, oil on canvas, 217 × 243 cm. Paris, Musée du Louvre. Photo: René-Gabriel Ojéda. © RMN-Grand Palais/Art Resource, NY.

his wife, tenderly separating her lifeless fingers. At his feet, their daughter languishes, overwhelmed by sorrow. Strong contrasts of light and shadow deepen the gloom; the deftly integrated figural composition speaks of familial unity, now rent by loss. While the terse (invented) narrative, harsh chiaroscuro, operatic physiognomy, and shallow stage space (replete with antique furniture) mimic David's severe tableaux dating from the eve of the Revolution, here the tragedy turns not on sacrifice of familial bonds in the name of virtue and *la patrie* (as in *Brutus* and *The Oath of the Horatii;* both Paris, Musée du Louvre), but on the destruction of a family by a tyrant. Stefan Germer observes that *The Return of Marcus Sextus* abandons the *exemplum virtutis* (the presentation of public exemplars of moral heroism), which held sway in French history painting prior to the fall of Robespierre and the radical Jacobins; Guérin replaces that didactic genre with a spectacle of private suffering addressed to an audience capable of sympathizing with victims of the Revolution.[9]

Cognizant of the evident reference to recent French history offered by *The Return of Marcus Sextus,* Mehdi Korchane argues persuasively that the topical immediacy of the subject does not fully account for the extraordinary sensation surrounding Guérin's painting from the moment of its dramatically late entrance into the Salon, 11 days after the exhibition's opening on 18 August 1799.[10] At the urging of Guérin's fellow students from the studio of Jean-Baptiste Regnault (1754–1829), David's pupil Philippe-Auguste Hennequin (1762–1833) attached a laurel wreath to the frame—a remarkable gesture from a rival, whose revolutionary allegory, *The Triumph of the French People on August 10th* (which had previously been officially awarded a wreath) faced *The Return of Marcus Sextus* in the Salon hanging.[11] By the exhibition's close, the frame was encumbered with admiring verse, and at least three banquets—including one both David and Regnault attended—were held in Guérin's honor between 3 and 22 October.[12] Orchestrated by Regnault's pupils, this hyperbolic reception was led by Charles-Paul Landon (1761–1826), whose acumen as art-world publicist and critic would later serve him well in his prolific production of illustrated anthologies of key Salon works.[13] That a painting offering a moving parallel to the plight of those expulsed during the Revolution was honored by the revolutionary propagandist Hennequin and the chastened radical David suggests that its appeal transcended both the machinations of the Regnault students and the political passions of the moment.

Whereas Hennequin's turgid allegory conveyed a schematic political message, Guérin's painting traffics in human misery. In departing from the *exemplum virtutis* in favor of forceful appeal to sympathy, Guérin was pursuing a strategy pioneered in images of exile by two David pupils, Gérard in *Belisarius* and Fulchran-Jean Harriet (1776–1805) in *Oedipus at Colonus* (1797–98; Cleveland, Cleveland Museum of Art)—an approach whose time was dawning.[14] This development represents a transformation of the teacher's legacy by his students. The immobile self-absorption of Marcus Sextus established a prototype for post-Napoleonic responses to the sense of loss besetting France between Waterloo and the demise of the July Monarchy—an anti-heroic mode to which we will return.

Protrayal of ancient exemplars of the suffering exile—whether historical (Belisarius), fictional (Marcus Sextus), or mythological (Oedipus)—fed the late eighteenth-century appetite for parallels between antiquity and the present. In the wake of the Revolution, scripture offered an alternate strain of historical analogy. As we have seen, Chateaubriand postured, in the preface to the *Génie du christianisme*, as an "obscure Israelite" bringing his grain of sand to rebuild the Temple. This counter-revolutionary typology also figures in *Sorrow and Pity* (*Le Malheur et la Pitié*) by the tireless *ancien régime* versifier, Abbé Jacques Delille (1738–1813).[15] In 1795, this former revolutionary, having been asked to provide lyrics to a "Hymn to the Supreme Being," fled France for Germany, Switzerland, and finally London, where he reigned as poet laureate of the Emigration. *Le Malheur et la Pitié*, which offers page after page of lamentation over exilic heartbreak and revolutionary crime, first appeared in censored form in France (1802), and in full the following year in London. Delille elevates the tribulations of the émigrés by invoking Psalm 137, the lament of the Hebrew captives in Babylon with its classic opening, "By the rivers of Babylon we sat down and wept / when we remembered Zion. / There on the willow-trees / we hung up our harps …."[16] Beloved in French literary tradition, the psalm is plaintively echoed by the chorus of Racine's *Esther*; during the eighteenth century, it was imitated by Jean-Baptiste Rousseau (1669–1741) and Jacques-Charles-Louis Clinchamps de Malfilâtre (1732–67).[17] Recent French history lent it fresh immediacy. Having paraphrased the psalm, Delille moves seamlessly from ancient Israel to modern France:

> Ainsi pleuroit l'Hébreu; mais du moins par ses frères
> Il n'étoit point banni du séjour de ses pères.
> Ah! combien du Français le sort est plus cruel!
> Chassé par des Français loin du sol paternel,
> Il fuit sous d'autres cieux; et, pour comble de peine,
> De sa patrie ingrate il emporte la haine.
>
> So wept the Hebrew; but at least by his brothers / He was not banished from the place of his fathers, / Ah! How much crueler is the fate of the Frenchman! / Chased by Frenchmen far from paternal ground, / He flees under foreign skies; and to top off his pain, / He bears the hate of his ingrate fatherland.[18]

Another émigré, Archbishop Boisgelin (who would later address the joyous audience at the Mass celebrating the Concordat) had the Revolution's victims in mind when, in the introduction to his verse translation of the psalms from Latin into French (1799), he commented on Psalm 137 in the first-person plural:

> With what sweet affection do bitter memories of the holy city arise in the heart of the captive Israelite! On the banks of the river of Babylon, immobile, seated under the reeds, with suspended harp, we think of ancient Zion, and we weep in silence over her misfortune and her glory.[19]

"Death in Miniature"

Heartfelt response to the pain of exile was hardly exclusive to the voices of counterrevolution. Between the expulsion from Paris of her father, Louis XVI's finance minister Jacques Necker (1732–1804), in 1787 and the fall of the Empire in 1814, the liberal author Anna-Louise-Germaine Necker, baronne de Staël-Holstein (1766–1817), conventionally known as Madame de Staël, spent nearly half of her life of 51 years in exile, largely at the behest of Napoleon.[20] Yet this experience nurtured Staël's creativity, just as it shaped her political convictions. According to biographer Angelica Goodden, "Exile led Staël to freedom, though it was meant to make her captive."[21] Initially thrilled by Napoleon's exploits in Italy and by what she viewed as his potential to bring peace, Staël soon irritated the dictator. On 5 January 1800, Staël's lover, the Swiss liberal political theorist Benjamin Constant (1767–1830), recently named to the Tribunat, delivered a startling speech defending that organ's independence and criticizing the authoritarian tendencies of the government.[22] The gesture was more than audacious, given that the Tribunat merely discussed laws emanating from the Conseil d'État (whose members were selected and coddled by First Consul Bonaparte) prior to their submission for vote by the Corps législatif. Staël was held complicit by society and in the press, and Constant was eventually expelled from the Tribunat (17 January 1802). Staël's novel *Delphine* (published December 1802) offended Bonaparte, who regarded the text as anti-social in its elevation of individual liberty at the expense of Catholic morality. The following year Staël was forbidden from entering Paris. At her Swiss château in Coppet on Lake Geneva, the author presided over a brilliant circle (which reached its apogee in 1807 and sometimes required table setting for 30); she sojourned in Germany (1803–04) and Italy (1804–05), acquiring material for her two most significant publications (*D'Allemagne* and *Corinne*). Such liberty was temporary. In 1810 Staël was placed under house arrest and imperial surveillance in Coppet, with travel to Geneva solely permitted. This was in retribution for *On Germany* (*De l'Allemagne*). That hallmark of nineteenth-century literature would do nothing less than introduce French readers to German Romanticism (as well as frighten them with Jean Paul's chilling dream fragment, whose echoes in the Garden of Olives we have considered). Denounced as "un-French" by Napoleon's minister of police (the emperor had thought the same of *Corinne*), the copies were seized and pulped. On 23 May 1812, Staël fled Coppet armed with a fan. Visiting Austria (including its Polish territory), Russia, Finland, and Sweden, the author arrived in England (June 1813) where, fêted as the nemesis of Bonaparte, she published *De l'Allemagne*. Despite these benefits of being away from Paris, banishment was nearly unbearable for the urbane author:

> My taste for society made me vulnerable.... For my whole life, I have been pursued by the phantom of ennui; my terror of this would have made me capable of bending before tyranny, if the example of my father, if his blood, which flows through my veins, had not overcome this weakness.[23]

Accordingly, Staël's writing is shadowed by exile, a condition that she characterized in a letter to her father (18 October 1803) as "death in miniature."[24]

The tenaciously popular novel *Corinne, or Italy* (*Corinne, ou l'Italie*, written 1805–06, published 1807) saw 32 editions between 1830 and 1870. "Exile," C.W. Thompson observes, "is centrally inscribed" in the novel.[25] Pointing to the ubiquity of exile in both the writing and life of Staël, Simone Balayé reminds us that it is not always possible to distinguish lived from fictive experience, so autobiographical are Staël's protagonists.[26] Such was the author's identification with her heroine, that "strangers, friends, and Staël herself routinely called the author Corinne after 1807."[27] Set in the winter of 1794–95, before the Italian campaign of Bonaparte, and concluding in 1803, *Corinne* is the tale of a beautiful, multitalented, and multilingual poet born in Italy of a Roman mother and English father. Following the death of her mother, Corinne was moved at age 15 to a provincial town in Northumberland, where her bigoted stepmother attempted to eradicate any traces of Italian heritage. Recalling her years in England, Corinne voices sentiments well known to the author:

> I was gripped by homesickness, the most unsettling sorrow that can take hold of the soul. For the lively and sensitive, exile is sometimes a torment much crueler than death; the imagination takes displeasure in all surroundings—climate, land, language, customs, life in general, life in its details; there is a pain for every moment as for each situation: because the fatherland gives us a thousand habitual pleasures of which we are unaware prior to having lost them....[28]

After the death of her father, Corinne returned to Italy at the expense of losing her legal name, which she replaced with that of the Greek poet Corinne. Staël contrasts the passionate, forthright, southern spirit of the heroine with the phlegmatic reserve of Corinne's (platonic) lover, the virtuous, melancholic Scot Sir Oswald Nelvil. As brave, practical, and dutiful as Corinne is inspired, natural, and spontaneous, Oswald (whose late, adored father intended him to marry Corinne's conventional half-sister, Lucile Edgermond) is swept off his feet at first sight of the poet as she is crowned with myrtle and laurel at the Roman Capitol before an adoring multitude. Readers were especially captivated by an episode in which Corinne improvises verse at Cape Miseno, beside the Gulf of Naples. Citing examples of ancient Roman injustice, she laments the cruelty of exile:

> The islands brought from the sea by volcanos sheltered, almost from their birth, the crimes of antiquity; the unhappy ones banished to these solitary rocks, amid the waves, viewed their fatherland from afar, trying to breathe in its aromas from the air, and sometimes, after a long exile, a death sentence informed them that at least their enemies had not forgotten them.[29]

Resonating with the author's own lot, Corinne's poem at Cape Miseno rehearsed before a large readership the theme of ancient proscription previously dramatized, under different political circumstances, by Gérard and Guérin.

This stirring vignette inspired one of the most reproduced paintings of the 1820s, Gérard's *Corinne at Miseno* (Figure 3.3).[30] Commissioned in 1819 by Prince Augustus of Prussia (1779–1843) at the suggestion of Staël's close friend, Juliette Récamier (whom the prince assiduously courted), it created a sensation at the Salon of 1822, as well as in Germany. Around 1821, the prince gave the painting to Récamier; it presided over gatherings in the salon of her home, the Abbaye-aux-Bois, in the aristocratic Faubourg Saint-Germain, where Chateaubriand would read his memoirs to admirers; it ended up in the Musée des Beaux-Arts of Lyon, the city of Récamier's origin.[31] Gérard's Prussian patron had asked that it show Corinne "as a better-looking version of Mme de Staël." Having previously portrayed the author—and wishing "to make Corinne as beautiful and interesting as the eloquent pen of the authoress has described her"—the artist turned to the beauty of Staël's writing, rather than to her physical features.[32] Corinne is shown holding forth before a visibly moved audience, her stormy thoughts mirrored by a dark, hovering cloud. Tormented by the thought that his late father would have condemned his love for Corinne, Oswald gazes in adoration, grasping his wrist in an effort to master passion about to overflow like the smoke of Mount Vesuvius rising above his head.

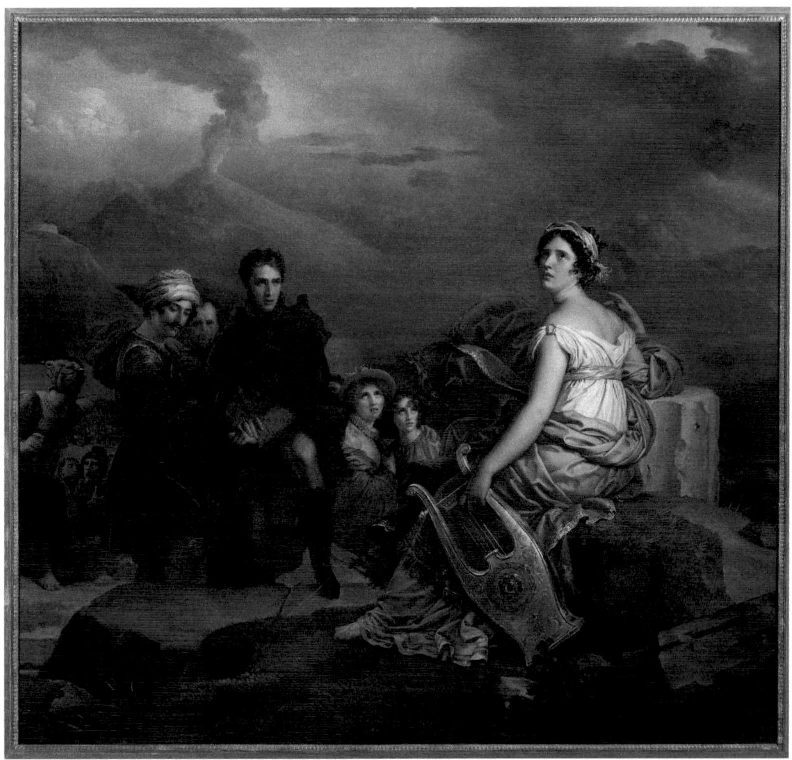

Figure 3.3 François Gérard, *Corinne at Cape Miseno*, ca. 1819–21, oil on canvas, 256.6 × 277.5 cm. Lyon, Musée des Beaux-Arts. © Lyon MBA-Photo Alain Basset.

Staël's writing signals a change in attitude toward exile that occurred at the border separating the Enlightenment from Romanticism. As Roy Porter and Mikuláš Teich observe, "When the *philosophes* migrated, they saw themselves more as cosmopolitans than as exiles."[33] The demise of that optimistic perspective in the face of the guillotine and imperial tyranny is legible, in the early nineteenth century, in a reversal of opinion regarding punitive exile. The ancient practice had been condoned by Montesquieu in *De l'Esprit des Lois* (1748) and by Rousseau in *Du contrat social* (1762), notwithstanding the latter's concern with matters of the heart. It is hardly surprising that the author of *Corinne* thought otherwise, stating her belief that it is "simple to show that exile is perhaps, of all the powers with which a sovereign is invested, the most dangerous by its ease and the most catastrophic by its consequences."[34] Her father's banishment from Paris by *lettre de cachet* (the *ancien régime* instrument that conveyed condemnation without accusation or trial) clearly shaped her opinion that of "all the attributes of authority, the one most favorable to tyranny is the power to exile without judgment."[35] For this former refugee from the Terror, even execution was less fearsome than exile: "In the end, scaffolds can awaken courage; but the domestic griefs of all sort that result from banishment weaken resistance, and only lead to fear of disgrace by the sovereign who can inflict on you such an unhappy existence."[36]

Staël's horror of exile anticipates the cooption of this pathos-ridden theme by the liberal opposition under the Bourbon Restoration. In "The Exile" ("L'Exilé"), dated January 1817, the immensely popular dissident poet and song writer, Pierre-Jean de Béranger, laments the cruel lot of a banished defender of the fatherland. A colored lithograph by Henry Monnier (1799–1877) represents Béranger's exile weeping beside a brook flowing toward France from an uncultivated site emblematic of the inhospitable wilderness in which this solitary nostalgic wanders (Figure 3.4). "Rendons une patrie, / une patrie / Au pauvre exile" ("Give back a fatherland, / a fatherland / To the poor exile.") runs the refrain.[37] Similarly, progressive sympathies galvanized in the 1820s by the Greek struggle for independence were stirred by invocations of exile. Solidarity with the cause—which pitted the Christian descendants of Homer against Ottoman hegemony—is exemplified by the liberal monarchist poet Casimir Delavigne's elegiac collection, the *Messéniennes,* which went into four editions during its first year (1822). Delavigne (1793–1843) invokes analogy to the captivity of the

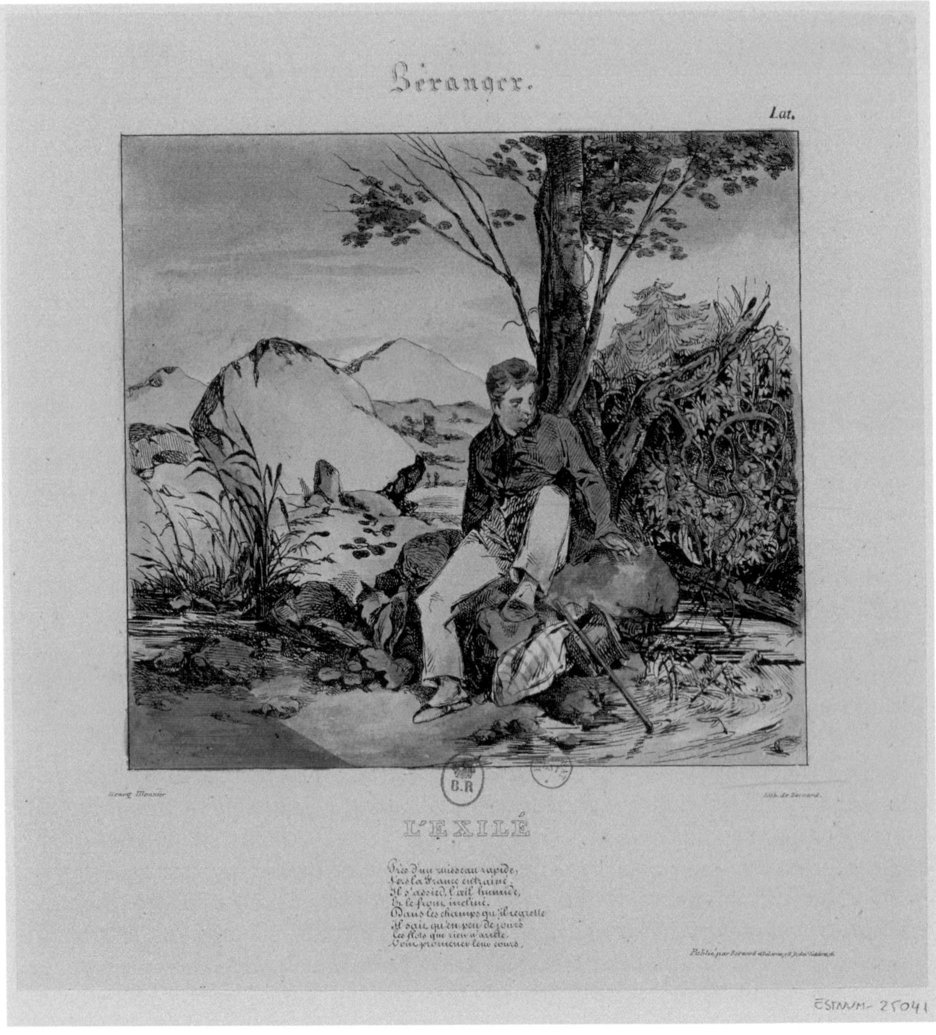

Figure 3.4 Henry Monnier, *The Exile* (*L'Exilé*) after Béranger, 1828, colored lithograph. Paris, Bibliothèque nationale de France. Photo: BnF.

ancient Hebrews, echoing the émigrés Delille and Boisgelin. It occurs in a poem that especially touched Delavigne's readers, "The Young Deacon, or Christian Greece" ("Le Jeune diacre, ou La Grèce chrétienne"), which recounts the death by an enemy bullet of a patriotic young Greek who had been singing of his people's sorrows from a boat.[38] In the manner of "David and the prophets," the singer, a deacon, compares himself to the captives of Psalm 137:

> "Et je pleure sur nos revers,
> "Comme les Hébreux dans les fers,
> "Quand Sion descendit du trône,
> "Pleuraient au pied des saules verts,
> "Près les fleuves de Babylone.
> And I weep over our defeat, / Like the Hebrews in irons, / When Zion fell from the throne, / Wept at the foot of the green willows, / By the rivers of Babylon.[39]

The motif was also taken up, around 1825, by a liberal, Dutch painter active in Paris, Ary Scheffer. In *Greek Exiles on a Rock Look over at their Lost Fatherland* (Figure 3.5), Christian refugees from the Ionian town of Parga (destroyed by the Ottomans in 1819) gather on Corfu's rocky shore and gaze across the water like Hebrews beside the Euphrates.[40]

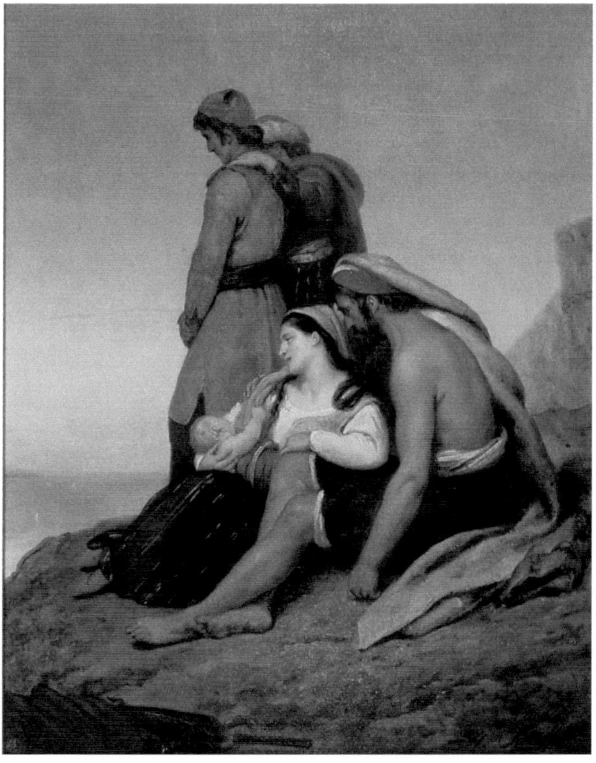

Figure 3.5 Ary Scheffer, *Greek Exiles on a Rock Look over at their Lost Fatherland*, ca. 1825, Oil on canvas, 40.5 × 32 cm. Enschede, Rijksmuseum Twenthe, on deposit from Amsterdam, Amsterdam Museum, C.J. Fodor Bequest. Collectie Rijksmuseum Twenthe, Enschede. Bruikleen Amsterdam Museum, Amsterdam, legaat C.J. Fodor (fotografie R. Klein Gotink). © Rijksmuseum Twenthe.

Poland's Martyrdom

Enthusiasm for Greek self-determination foreshadowed international adhesion to the great cause of the following decade. In 1830, Polish patriots staged the ill-fated November Insurrection against Russian rule. The ensuing ten-month war saw the fall of Warsaw in September 1831, Russian imposed as national language, and Poland's currency (the zloty) usurped by the ruble. These developments inflamed opinion in France, where connection to francophone, Catholic Poland was longstanding, from Louis XV's marriage to the well-liked, pious Marie Leczinska (or Leszczynska, 1703–68), to the heroic death of Napoleon's ally Prince Józef Antoni Poniatowski (1763–1813) in the Battle of Leipzig. In the aftermath of the Insurrection, some 10,000 Poles emigrated to France (mostly to the provinces), greeted by a nation nostalgic for the imperial alliance and hostile toward the adversary that hounded the Grande Armée westward across the steppes in 1812.[41] Like the Greek cause, Polish independence was warmly championed by liberals (including Scheffer), with the septuagenarian Marquis de Lafayette (1757–1834) chairing a Franco-Polish committee advocating military response.[42] Though commemorative demonstrations were permitted in Paris each November, the government of Louis-Philippe was hardly open to intervention on behalf of Poland, and the July Monarchy police surveilled activists.

Exiled Poles regarded poets as the guardians of their nation's spirituality and independence. Foremost among these was Adam Mickiewicz (1798–1855), the dominant figure of Polish Romantic literature and the post-Insurrection diaspora.[43] Mickiewicz's embodiment of Polish culture has a vicarious aspect; he never set foot in either Krakow (where he would be reinterred, with national honors, in 1890) or Warsaw, and spent his final 32 years abroad. Educated in the capital of the Grand Duchy of Lithuania at the University of Vilnius, Mickiewicz was born in what is now western Belarus, three years after the culturally Polish territory had been annexed by Russia from the defeated Polish-Lithuanian Commonwealth following the Russo-Polish war (1792–93) and suppression of an uprising led by Poland's national hero, Tadeusz Kościuszko (1746–1817) in 1794. After the retreating remnant of the Grande Armée passed through his town in 1812, the future poet added "Napoléon" to his name in honor of Poland's would-be savior. At university, Mickiewicz joined a morally-earnest, secret society, the Philomaths. Devoted to literature and social issues, the apolitical student group was steeped in Polish heritage. Publication of his *Ballads and Romances* (1822)—which extolled feeling, faith, and peasant oral tradition—brought celebrity and marked a turn away from the classical, Enlightenment texts in which Mickiewicz had been educated. In 1823 (at age 25), he was arrested with fellow Philomaths by Czarist authorities alarmed by agitation in the city's student societies. Initially imprisoned in a local monastery, the poet was sentenced to exile in Russia.

Residing, respectively, in Saint Petersburg, Moscow, and Odessa, Mickiewicz enjoyed remarkable liberty during five years of captivity. Lionized as Poland's star poet, he consorted with Russian aristocracy, befriended Pushkin, attended operas, published, and eventually headed west. Warmly received by the large Polish émigré community in Berlin, Mickiewicz heard (without pleasure) Hegel lecture. He visited Dresden and made a pilgrimage to Bonn to meet August Wilhelm Schlegel (formerly Staël's mentor in things German), whom he admired. In Weimar, Mickiewicz not only met an idol, Goethe, but also became friends with the sculptor Pierre-Jean David d'Angers (1788–1856), who had arrived there to commemorate the *Dichter* on the occasion of his eightieth birthday.[44] The sculptor would devote one of his many portrait medallions to Mickiewicz (an example of 1829 is in the Musée de la vie romantique, Paris) and provide him entry to the salons of Paris. Sightseeing across Italy, Mickiewicz spent the winters of 1829–30 and 1830–31 in Rome, undergoing Catholic conversion (first confessing 8 December 1830) and reading, with enthusiasm, the early work of Lamennais. After considering passage to Poland to join the Insurrection, he settled in Dresden in March 1832. Five months later, he sacrificed his Russian passport and illegally moved to Paris, previously visited in the spring of 1831. Disgusted by the July Monarchy's neutrality in regard to the Polish question, he would nevertheless stay in Paris for most of his remaining years. Ever the wanderer, Mickiewicz occupied 14 different Parisian addresses and cycled through at least three coteries. In early 1833, he became close to Lamennais and frequented his circle of liberal, ultramontane Catholics, but by the mid-1830s, this friendship gave way to association with Alfred de Vigny and with George Sand. In 1840, the philosopher Victor Cousin (1792–1867), minister of education, together with his associate, the liberal economist Léon Faucher (1803–54, married to the poet's sister-in-law) established a chair in Slavic literature expressly for Mickiewicz at the prestigious Collège de France. There, the devoutly Catholic poet bonded with the two most popular faculty members, Jules Michelet and, especially, Edgar Quinet (whom Mickiewicz met in 1837)—both fervently nationalist, anti-clerical Leftists. Such was popular enthusiasm for the Polish cause, that Mickiewicz's lectures initially drew

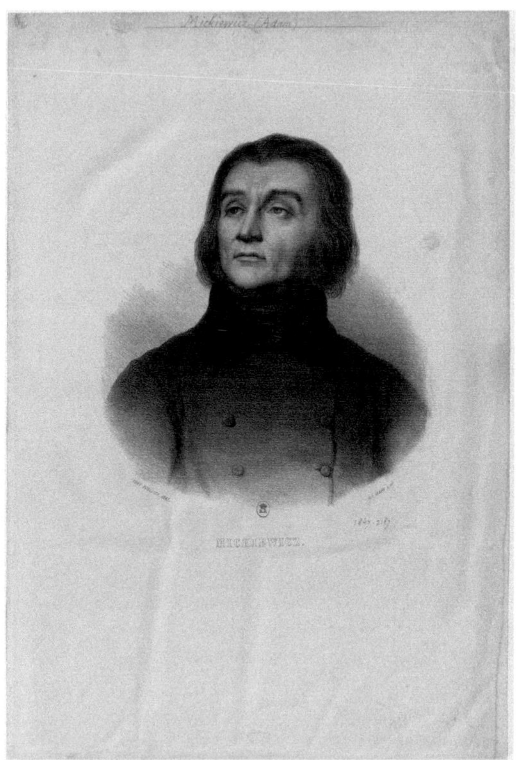

Figure 3.6 Tony Toullion, *Mickiewicz*, 1847, lithograph. Paris, Bibliothèque nationale de France. Photo: BnF.

crowds (including the rapt Aleksandr Turgenev), despite tangential ramblings, misquotations, and gaffes. Attendance picked up again in the second year of lectures when the poet gave free rein to his messianic leanings. Enthralled by the Lithuanian visionary Andrzej Towiański (of whom more soon), the speaker invoked Napoleon, Christ, and the providential missions of Poland and France—until his course was cancelled by government order in May 1844.[45]

Mickiewicz's identity as charismatic prophet-in-exile is captured in a lithographic portrait of 1847 by Tony Toullion, in which heavily lidded eyes suggest both inspiration and nobly borne suffering, while the military cut of his jacket signals militant dedication to Polish independence (Figure 3.6). Two years before his death, the poet sat for a photograph in the same dress (Figure 3.7). Grasping a staff, he poses as a Catholic counterpart to the Wandering Jew—a role in line with the Jewish lineage of his wife, Celina Szymanowska (1812–55). Allegedly scornful of anti-Semitism, Mickiewicz never refuted a rumor that his mother was part Jewish. Moreover, by the time of the portrait, the Wandering Jew had been elevated from demeaning folk trope to mythic emblem; in Quinet's drama of 1833, *Ahasvérus* (to which we will return), he represents humanity.

The staff also befits the poet's view of his exiled people as participants in a sacred pilgrimage, a conception dating from the decade of the November Insurrection. Prior to editing a political journal, *The Pilgrim* (April–June 1833), Mickiewicz set forth

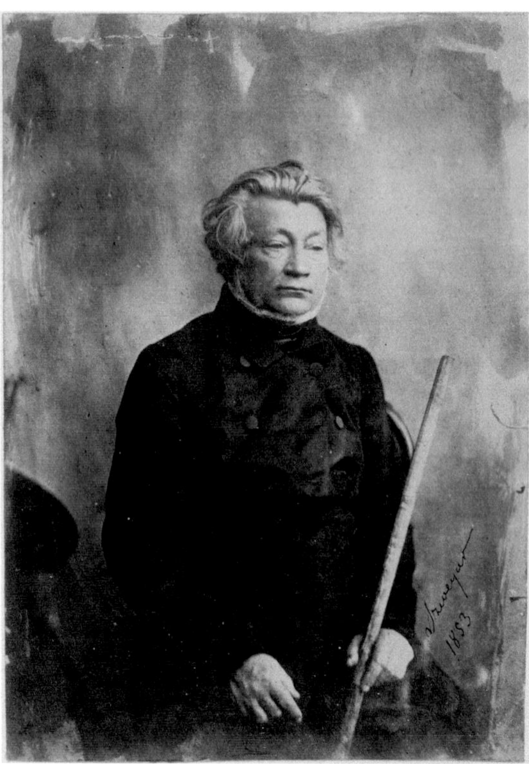

Figure 3.7 *Adam Mickiewicz*, 1853, photograph. Paris, Bibliothèque nationale de France. Photo: BnF.

an apocalyptic vision of national destiny in *The Books of the Polish Nation and the Polish Pilgrimage*. Published December 1832, it was distributed gratis; a French "translation" by Montalembert (who knew little Polish) was released the following year as *Book of the Polish Pilgrims*. With scriptural phrasing, Mickiewicz proclaimed that the travails of his people were a prelude to reversal of the world order. Moving

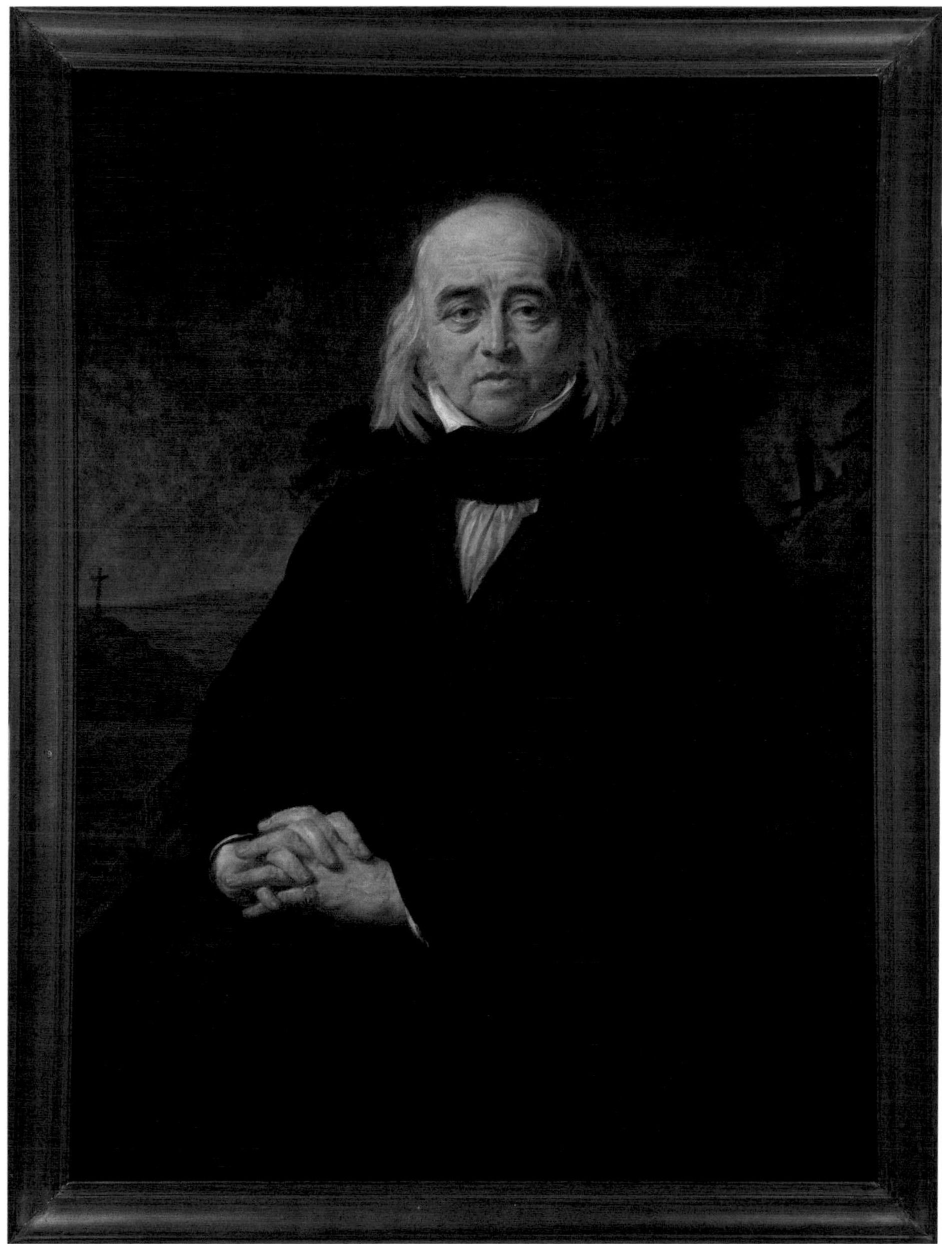

Figure 3.8 Antoine-Jean Gros, *Portrait of Julian Ursyn Niemcewicz*, 1833–34, oil on canvas, 128 × 98 cm. Krakow, National Museum/Princes Czartoryski Museum. Photo: Laboratory Stock National Museum in Krakow.

seamlessly between the timeless space of scripture and the political geography of the present, he exhorted the Polish diaspora:

> I tell you this in truth, your pilgrimage will be a stumbling block for the powers of the earth .... And of the grand political edifice of current Europe, there will not remain stone upon stone .... A day of great oppression will come for Judah and Israel.

The forthcoming resurrection of his homeland is identified with that of Christ, whose redemptive ministry prefigures the salvific role of Poland: "Because the Polish nation is not dead .... And in three days she will return to her body, and the Polish nation will revive, and she will liberate from slavery all the people of Europe."[46] Mickiewicz's prophetic posturing and willful simplicity would be imitated in *Paroles d'un croyant* by Lamennais, whose "Hymn to Poland," written in Rome in April 1832 (shortly before Gregory XVI's letter to the Polish faithful demanding their fealty to the Czar) is appended to Montalembert's translation.[47]

A more pessimistic view of Poland's destiny informs a somber portrait (1833–34) by Antoine-Jean Gros of Julian Ursyn Niemcewicz (1758–1841), an elder friend of Mickiewicz recently arrived in Paris (Figure 3.8).[48] Gros's painting of this veteran of the 1794 uprising and author of beloved patriotic ballads was conceived in friendship that originated in 1793, when the artist gave Niemcewicz drawing lessons in Florence. Jan Bialostocki insightfully views the portrait as affirming the bond between a bereaved exile and a disillusioned painter, whose glory as a Napoleonic propagandist was as much in eclipse as the neo-classical legacy of his deceased teacher, David. Seated in a bleak landscape before a burning building, Niemcewicz is cast as an uneasy wanderer in his mid-seventies. A cross atop a distant hill forms a dark and diminutive silhouette against the murky sky, and suggests the personal Calvary of the sitter, who had recently learned of the confiscation of his property at Ursynow, near Warsaw. Boldly illuminated against this gloomy backdrop, the care-worn features and tightly clasped fingers convey a sorrow that, for Gros's disciple J.-B. Delestre, transcend the particularity of the subject, representing "the sublime personification of an exile who remembers, suffers, and resigns himself ... a symbol of humanity summarized in an individual man."[49] The portrait's melancholy mood matches that of the Parisian diary kept by the francophone Pole, who lamented on 23 January 1834: "Du lever du soleil jusqu'à la nuit noire / Toujours des raisons nouvelles de désespoir." ("From sunrise to black night / Always new reasons for despair.")[50] Even the work's subsequent provenance is doleful. When Gros offered the painting to his friend, Niemcewicz declined; following the 1835 suicide, the poet accepted it from the artist's widow.

Delacroix: from Chopin to Ovid

In early 1838, Delacroix entered into close friendship with another distinguished Polish émigré. Frédéric Chopin (1810–49), born in the Duchy of Warsaw of a French father and Polish mother, regarded himself as thoroughly Polish. Having left Poland several weeks prior to the November 1830 Insurrection, he settled in Paris the following year. Notwithstanding dismay at the plight of his people, indignation at French neutrality, and friendship with Mickiewicz, the composer distanced himself from the popular rage on behalf of his homeland publicly vented each November. His allegiance was to the cultivated, aristocratic wing of the Parisian Polish community. This was a cohort

Delacroix knew well.[51] Within the artist's circle were the Chopin-trained pianists Princess Marcelline Czartoryska (1817–94) and Countess Delphine Potocka (born Komar-Korczak, 1807–77), and Delphine's sister Princess Charles-Juste de Beauvau (born Ludmille de Komar, 1820–81), to whom Chopin dedicated his *Polonaise in F# Minor*, op. 44 (1841). There were also two heroes of the national cause. Prince Adam-Georges Czartoryski (1770–1861) had served as president of the provisional Polish government in 1830, and then took up arms. With property confiscated and marked for capital punishment, Czartoryski emigrated to Paris in 1833. Known as the "uncrowned king of Poland" and as the "one-man great power," he organized international opposition to Czar Nicholas I.[52] In 1844, Delacroix was in charge of the restoration of decorative paintings by Le Brun and Le Sueur in the hôtel Lambert, property of Czartoryski's wife, Anna Sapieha Czartoryska (1799–1864). The prince was probably introduced to Delacroix by a close friend of Chopin and Mickiewicz, Count Albert Grzymala (1793–1870), whose patriotic resume included service in the Russian campaign of 1812 (in which he was wounded and then held prisoner for three years), followed by deportation to Saint Petersburg (until 1829) for support of the Kingdom of Poland's reestablishment. The former insurrectionist and director of the Polish bank came to Paris on a diplomatic mission in 1831 and remained there as an expatriate admirer of Delacroix.

From 1838 until 1847, Chopin had a famous liaison with the artist's friend Georges Sand. Unlike Sand and her lover, Delacroix appears to have had little contact with Mickiewicz. Nor did Delacroix produce, on behalf of Poland, anything comparable to his pro-Hellenic canvases of the 1820s. If the artist's friendships could only have nurtured sympathy for exiles, he viewed the theme through a lens at once private and broadly humanistic. Thus, for his decoration of the cupola of the library of the Chamber of Peers in the Luxembourg Palace (1840–46), in which Dante is introduced by Virgil to Homer and the greats of antiquity, Delacroix modeled the features of Dante on those of Chopin. The artist prized and kept for his own a graphite drawing inscribed "Cher Chopin" that portrays the banished Florentine with the unmistakable, profiled features of his friend (Figure 3.9).[53] This conflation of expatriate composer and exiled poet is as witty as the rebus with which Delacroix signed the sheet: a number two (*deux*), a musical note (*la*), and a cross (*croix*). The inside joke is enriched by historical analogy. Just as Dante's proscription arose from his anti-papal political allegiance, so too had Pope Gregory XVI (the nemesis of Lamennais) anathematized the national cause in 1832 by admonishing the Polish faithful to accept Russian rule.

Perhaps thinking of the love of *la patrie* prerequisite for the legislators of the Chamber of Deputies who assembled in the Palais-Bourbon, Delacroix represented exile thrice when decorating the five cupolas and two hemicycles of their library (1838–47).[54] In the cupola devoted to theology he included *The Babylonian Captivity* and *The Expulsion of Adam and Eve;* that pertaining to poetry includes *Ovid among the Barbarians*. Characteristic of the pessimism and penchant toward tragedy ubiquitous in the *oeuvre* (and on display throughout the library, most prominently in the hemicycle featuring *Attila Trampling Italy and the Arts*), these subjects are neither politically partisan nor topical in the manner of the earlier *Scenes from the Massacres at Chios: Greek Families Awaiting Death or Slavery, etc.* (Salon of 1824; Paris: Musée du Louvre). Rather, they are consistent with the artist's mid- and late-career quest for gravity and pathos in subjects drawn from the public domain and unattached to modern French history.

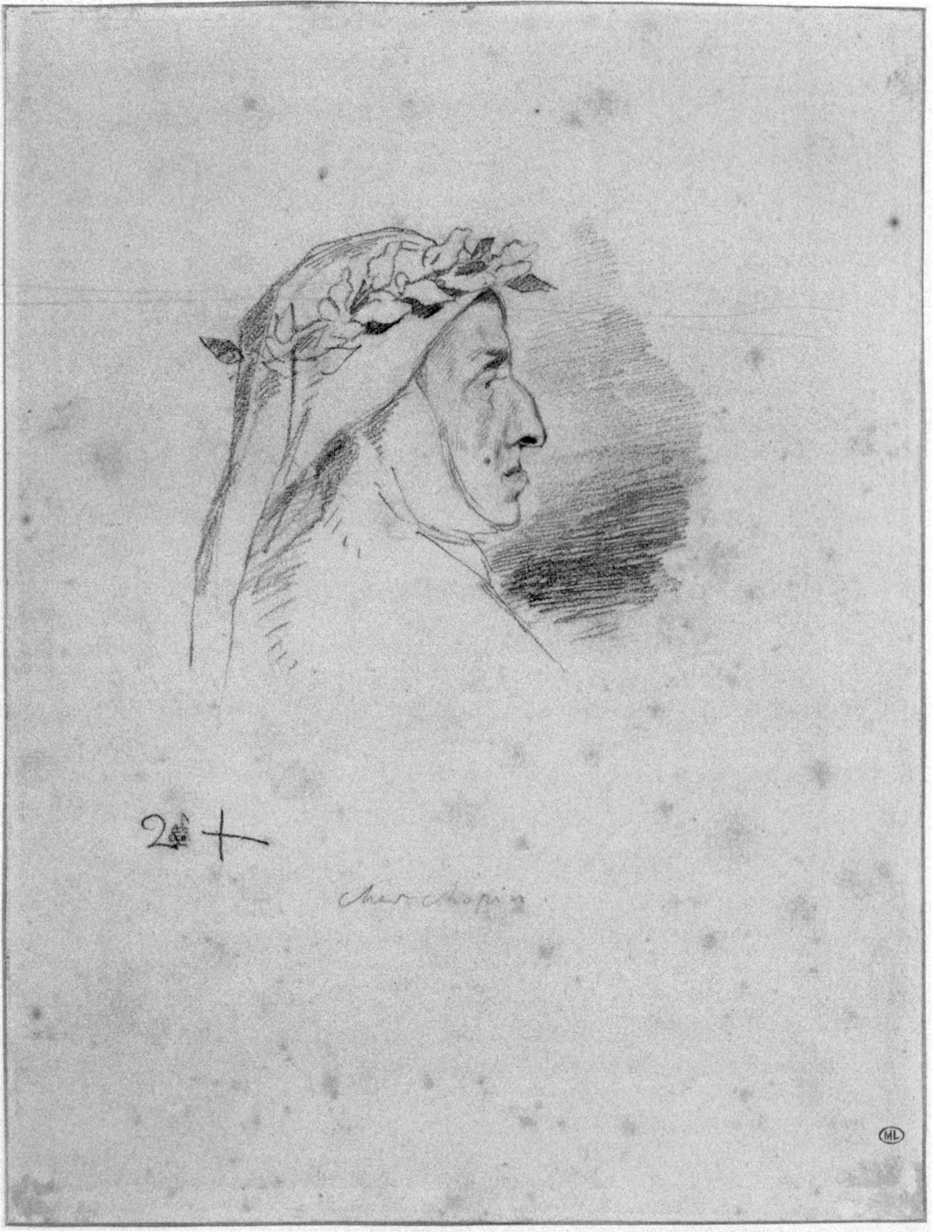

Figure 3.9 Eugène Delacroix, *Portrait of Frédéric Chopin as Dante*, ca. 1843–46, black lead on paper, 27.1 × 21.1 cm. Paris, Musée du Louvre. Photo: Thierry Le Mage © RMN-Grand Palais/Art Resource, NY.

If Delacroix's attraction to the theme of exile was neither unique nor partisan, he treated it with unparalleled poignancy. Among the library paintings, he apparently attached particular importance to *The Babylonian Captivity* (ca. 1843–45), which he executed himself, rather than delegating it to his assistants. According to

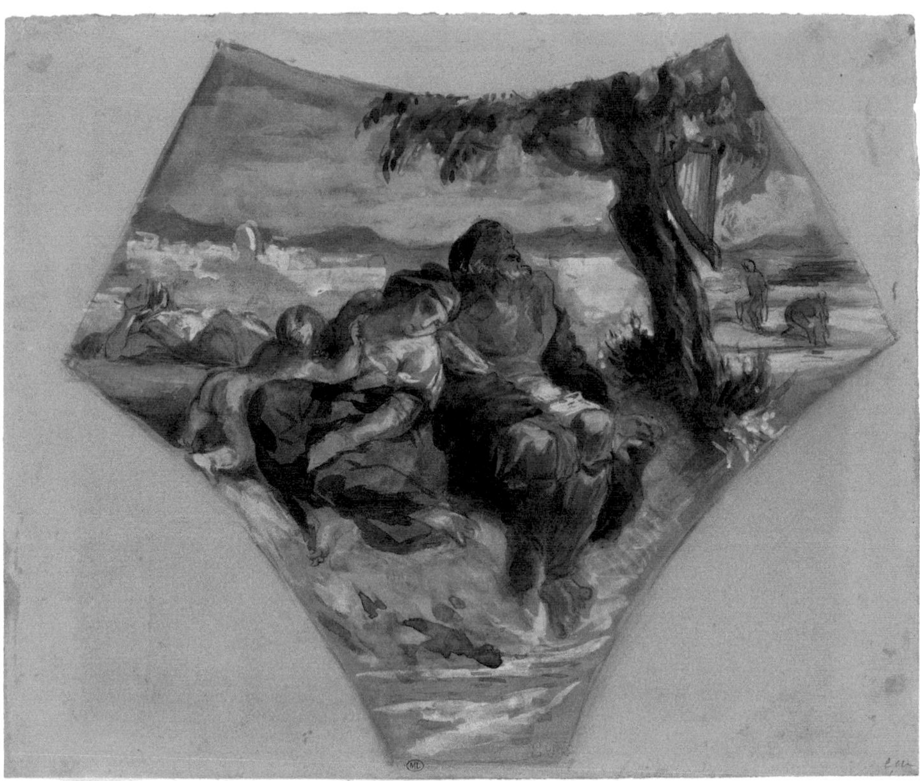

Figure 3.10 Eugène Delacroix, *The Babylonian Captivity*, ca. 1842, watercolor over black ink on brown paper, 24.9 × 31.3 cm. Paris, Musée du Louvre. Photo: Frank Raux. © RMN-Grand Palais/Art Resource, NY.

the description published by Théophile Thoré (and probably supplied by the artist), "A weeping family, seated on the bank of a river, sadly contemplates the water while thinking of the distant fatherland."[55] A study from the artist's hand in watercolor, gouache, and graphite on brown paper (Figure 3.10) of the well-worn motif from Psalm 137 has an expressively restless touch missed when the pendentive is viewed in situ.[56] Beside an idle harp hung on a willow, a Hebrew family languishes: "How could we sing the Lord's song / in a foreign land?" (Psalms 137:4). Fluid wash reinforces the cohesion of the group, whose undulating rhythms project captive vitality. Delacroix's breadth of handling and understated physiognomy lend a timeless aura to a timely motif.

No less impressive is Delacroix's reprise of *Ovid among the Barbarians* as an easel painting, a project considered as early as April 1849. In 1856, he received a commission for such a work from a friend, the Jewish banker and former member of the Chamber of Deputies, Benoît Fould (1792–1858; Figure 3.11)[57] Fould died before its completion; the painting was delivered to his widow and exhibited in the artist's final Salon in 1859. It was described (apparently by Delacroix) in the Salon guidebook as a portrayal of "Ovid in exile among the Scythians / Some regard him with curiosity,

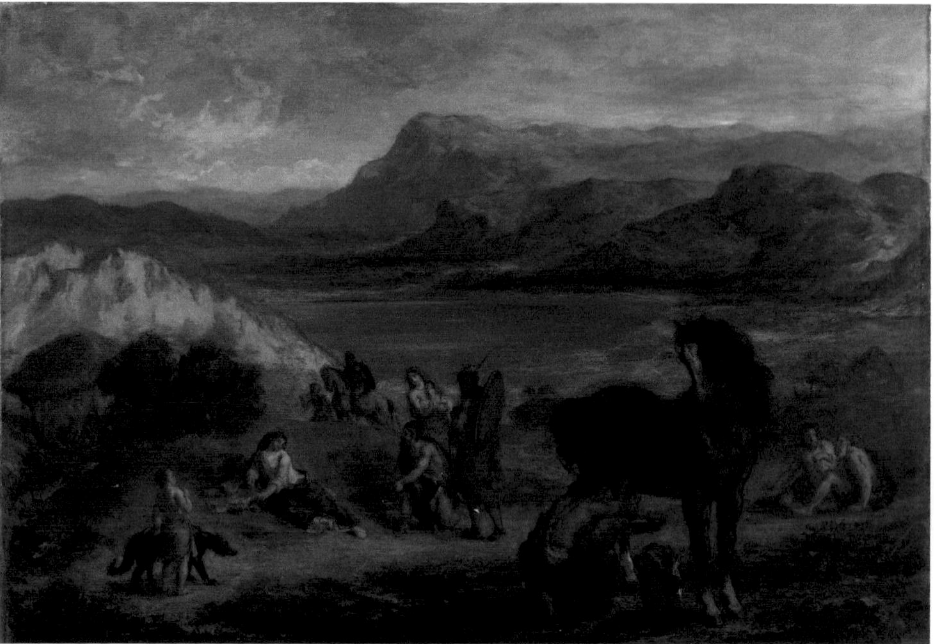

Figure 3.11 Eugène Delacroix, *Ovid among the Scythians*, 1859, oil on canvas, 87.6 × 130.2 cm. London, National Gallery. © National Gallery, London/Art Resource, NY.

others welcome him in their manner and offer him wild fruit, mare's milk, etc., etc." The confining pendentive format of the library's *Ovid* has been replaced by a rectangle, providing space for a broad vista; the bold, simple configuration aloft in the library—well suited to a reader's brief, upward glance—gives way to subtleties of atmospheric hue and delicate compositional rhythms befitting the touching encounter of the poet and his generous hosts.

Just as the imperatives of art outweigh fidelity to the Gospel narrative in Delacroix's renditions of *Christ in the Garden of Olives*, so too does *Ovid among the Scythians* depart from ancient history and literature. Delacroix's portrayal of the poet receiving Scythian hospitality is his own invention; it is found neither in Ovid's writings nor in any classical source (though Strabo, a geographer of the first century BCE, refers to Homer's admiration of Scythian mores).[58] Banished from Rome in 8 CE on account of a poem viewed as sanctioning adultery, Ovid exaggerated the discomfort of life in Tomis, now the Black Sea resort of Constanta in Romania.[59] As David O'Brien indicates, contrary to Ovid's disdain for Scythian savagery, Delacroix conveys approval of their unspoiled, primitive ways.[60] Consonant with the painting's visual charm, this positive characterization of Ovid's hosts points to the underlying paradox of an image that visualizes the advantages, as well as the sorrows, of exile, as Delacroix's Ovid is well cared for in an enticing setting.[61] This ambivalence toward the exiled poet's bitter-sweet idyll matches the artist's own dual identity as both insider and outsider. Notwithstanding unparalleled success in obtaining official commissions—of which the decoration of the Palais-Bourbon library was the most spectacular—Delacroix remained the butt of conventional opinion.[62] In the twilight of his career he faced repeated failures to enter the

Académie des Beaux-Arts, with seven abortive candidacies preceding success in 1857, one year following the commission from Fould and six years before the artist's death. To Delacroix's disappointment, the honor was not supplemented by a professorship at the École des Beaux-Arts. If, as Henri Loyrette claims, Delacroix transformed the motif of the banished poet into "an autobiographical meditation,"[63] then it was a meditation not only on this elitist's professional struggle in the face of mediocrity, but also on the solace of having received state patronage that richly awarded him with contracts for monumental paintings—this in addition to having enjoyed support from enlightened clients such as Fould, as well as from discerning critics (e.g., Thoré, Gautier, and Baudelaire). At the Salon of 1859, Baudelaire was especially taken with *Ovid among the Scythians,* which he praised in resolutely aesthetic terms:

> I will certainly not try to translate with my pen the sad, sensual pleasure exhaled by this verdant *exile*.... All that is delicate and fertile in Ovid has entered the painting of Delacroix; and, just as exile gave to the brilliant poet the sadness he lacked, melancholy has coated in its magical varnish the lush landscape of the painter. It is impossible for me to say: Which painting by Delacroix is the best of his paintings ... but one can say that *Ovid among the Scythians* is one of those astonishing works that Delacroix alone knows how to conceive and to paint.[64]

Devoid of reference to politics, Baudelaire's praise underscores the enduring appeal of the subject, even as the legacies of revolutionary injustice, Napoleonic tyranny, and the Polish insurgency faded into the past.

Despair in the Wilderness

The enhanced emotional charge carried by the theme of exile in nineteenth-century France is further suggested by pronounced changes in the interpretation of two familiar narratives from Genesis—the near-death experience of Hagar and Ishmael in the wilderness and the banishment of Cain following the first murder.[65] Though it concludes happily, the story of the expulsed mother and son does not begin well. Prior to the birth of Isaac, Abraham had a son, Ishmael, with his Egyptian servant, Hagar. After Sarah (the patriarch's 91-year-old wife) miraculously gave birth, conflict between wife and servant led to Abraham casting out Hagar and Ishmael to fend for themselves in the wilderness of Beersheba. Their water depleted and Ishmael nearing death,

> God heard the child crying, and the angel of God called from heaven to Hagar, 'What is the matter, Hagar? Do not be afraid: God has heard the child crying where you laid him. Get to your feet, lift the child up and hold him in your arms, because I will make of him a great nation.' Then God opened her eyes and she saw a well full of water; she went to it, filled her waterskin and gave the child a drink (Gen. 21:14–19).[66]

A stock Old Master subject, the rescue was represented, for example, by Claude Lorrain (Claude Gellée, 1600–82; Figure 3.12). All is well; the ordeal has ended, the angel has arrived, and the thirsting Ishmael is kept decorously from sight. Hagar is not alone in this verdant setting; in the middle ground, a boat plies calm waters and buildings crown a cliff. In accord with seventeenth-century classical landscape tradition, the

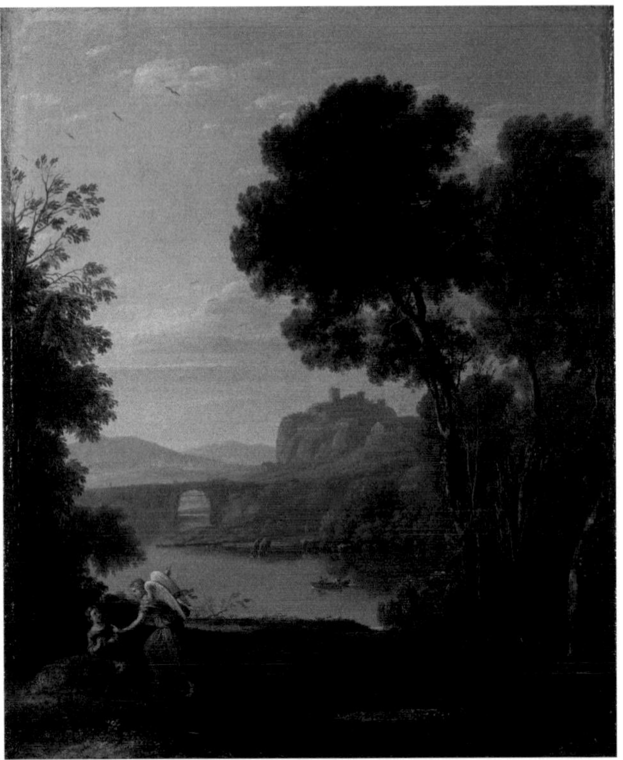

Figure 3.12 Claude Lorrain (Claude Gellée), *Landscape with Hagar and the Angel*, 1646, oil on canvas mounted on wood, 52.2 × 42.3 cm. London, National Gallery, Presented by Sir George Beaumont, 1828 (NG 61). © National Gallery, London/Art Resource, NY.

lucid order of idealized space offers a visual equivalent to the blessings of providence. Interpretation of the narrative as an exemplar of divine grace remained intact when Félicité de Genlis (1746–1830), the future, beloved tutor of Louis-Philippe, included *Hagar in the Desert, Comedy in Prose and in One Act* (1779) in her moralizing *Theater for the Use of Young People* (1779–80). Genlis represents Hagar as a paragon of virtue. With only passing mention of the cruelty of Sara, the outcast selflessly pities her suffering son while inculcating the need for submissive adoration of the benevolent Supreme Being. In the second scene, the angel transforms the desert into a paradise and concludes the script with an edifying speech: "That your example, Hagar, may forever serve as a lesson; may it halt the murmurs of foolish mortals; and may it teach that God knows how to reward patience, submission, courage, and virtue."[67]

Staël clearly had this short play in mind when she sojourned in Geneva during the winter of 1805–06 and composed an even more brief staging of the episode from Genesis, *Hagar in the Desert*.[68] Telltale details indicate direct borrowing from her rival, Genlis. In both versions, just prior to the angel's entrance, Hagar accidentally spills the remaining water while attempting to shield Ishmael from the sun with her veil, and the angel brandishes a palm frond to miraculously bring forth water. No less evident is Staël's departure from the earnest sermonizing of her predecessor.

Rather than provide, as does Genlis, an additional scene for the angel's intervention, Staël allots to the *deus ex machina* a mere moment of a narrative given over almost entirely to the spectacle of the mother and son dying of thirst beneath the desert sun. Refusing to blame Abraham, Staël's heroine is no less reverent than the Hagar of Genlis. Yet Staël decries injustice, whether through the innocent Hagar's references to Sara's jealousy, or by having Ishmael recollect that his kindness toward Isaac was met with his half-brother's demeaning reference to his slave status. In Staël's play, Hagar pleads that her innocent son be spared the misery of exile:

> O my God! Protect Ishmael! If I was too proud of your gifts in the days of my prosperity ... punish me; but spare this poor child, the sincerest, the gentlest, the most innocent of all beings; make him breathe that sweet air, that beneficial air that you provide in Egypt to the inhabitants of my fatherland. This burning sky, this brazen sky is not the image of your paternal kindness.[69]

Whereas the biblical story of banishment provided Genlis with a pretext for preaching obedience, Staël drew from it a transparently autobiographical, anti-Napoleonic parable of suffering and deliverance. This disparity corresponds with the different audiences for whom the authors wrote, as well as with the distinct function of each play. Genlis conveyed to young readers a thinly masked treatise of universal moral truth. Yearning to exit unjust banishment, Staël addressed the sympathetic circle of

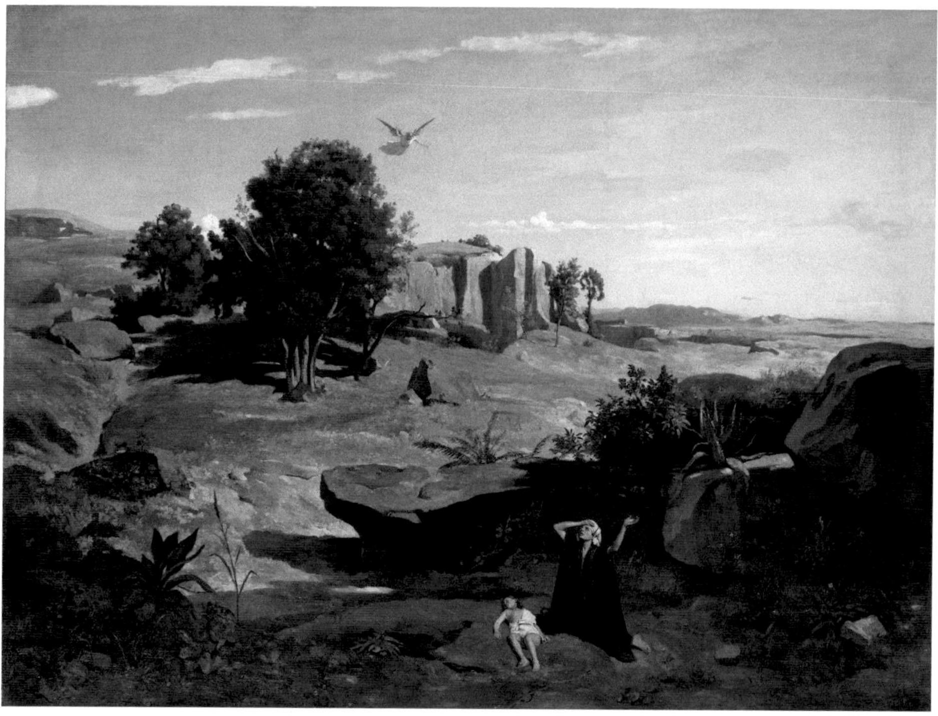

Figure 3.13 Jean-Baptiste-Camille Corot, *Hagar in the Wilderness*, 1835, oil on canvas, 180.3 × 270.5. New York, Metropolitan Museum of Art, Rogers Fund (38.64). Image copyright: © The Metropolitan Museum of Art. Image source: Art Resource, NY.

friends that attended her productions in Coppet and Geneva. Performing as Hagar (with her children, Albert and Albertine, in the supporting roles), Staël concludes her play on an upbeat note. Exhorting Hagar to raise her son in fear and love of God, Staël's angel offers glad tidings ("Receive, O woman, the lesson of happiness, after having experienced that of misfortune"), foretelling that Ishmael would be "the stem of a great people," who will rule the deserts of Arabia.

Staël's emphasis on the suffering of mother and son foreshadows increasingly forceful evocations of peril in two paintings that lack the partisan tenor stemming from the author's plight. A large depiction of Hagar and Ishmael in extremis was exhibited in the Salon of 1835 by Corot (Figure 3.13).[70] As early as 1833, prior to departing for Italy in 1834, the artist had begun to consider a painting of the subject. Showing the mother in despair and the child unconscious, the executed work was praised by Gautier as "the most beautiful landscape, perhaps, of the modern school."[71] Unaware of the distant angel, Hagar is surrounded by arid terrain, whose expanse is brought home by the imposing dimensions of the canvas. An anonymous reviewer for *L'Artiste* (possibly Jules Janin), observed that

> the earth is barren and burnt, the rocks are bare, and a few meager clumps of trees can be seen in the distance—a sterile, useless shadow giving neither shade nor fruit. And even this shadow is quite distant, and poor Hagar will never manage to drag herself that far....[72]

To authenticate the forbidding setting, the painter combined on-site studies widely separated in time and place. The stony cliffs rely on renderings made at Cività Castellana during an Italian sojourn of 1825–28; the aloe might have been spotted in Paris, at the Jardin des plantes; and the trees and foreground boulders are taken from an open-air study made in the Fontainebleau forest during the summer of 1832 or 1833 (New York, Metropolitan Museum of Art).[73] The displaced, shade-casting Fontainebleau oaks speak mockingly of a moist habitat remote from this parched ground. So persuasive is Corot's evocation of heat, thirst, and solitude, that the critic and archaeologist Charles Lenormant (1802–59) declared that the painting's painful effect could be felt even before the viewer became aware of its subject. His point squares with the artist's employment of the human motif as an accessory to the landscape that remains his principal concern. At the same time, the dry wasteland lends poignancy to the vulnerability of the protagonists. Lenormant approvingly recognized this relationship: "That is the particular merit of historical landscapes: the harmony between the setting and the passion or suffering that the painter chooses to depict in it."[74] As Susan Greenberg observes, Corot replaces the lucid order and spatial unity traditional in French historical landscapes with a sense of disorientation and discontinuity suggestive of the aimless wandering of Hagar and Ishmael.[75]

Yet Corot's painting seems optimistic in comparison to a life-sized rendition of *Hagar and Ishmael* exhibited by Jean Murat (1807–63) in the Salon of 1842 (Figure 3.14).[76] In 1837, Murat had won the Prix de Rome with a *Sacrifice of Noah* replete with expostulations of awe-stricken devotion (Paris, École nationale supérieure des Beaux-Arts).[77] Devoid of academic bromide, the later painting startles with its unflinching account of a near-fatal experience. Divine grace is absent; nor is any sign of assistance forthcoming. Beside her expiring son, Hagar beseeches the heavens with tearful eyes, the penitent-Magdalene pose clashing with an expression suggestive of bitterness rather than contrition. Bifurcation of the canvas according to hue

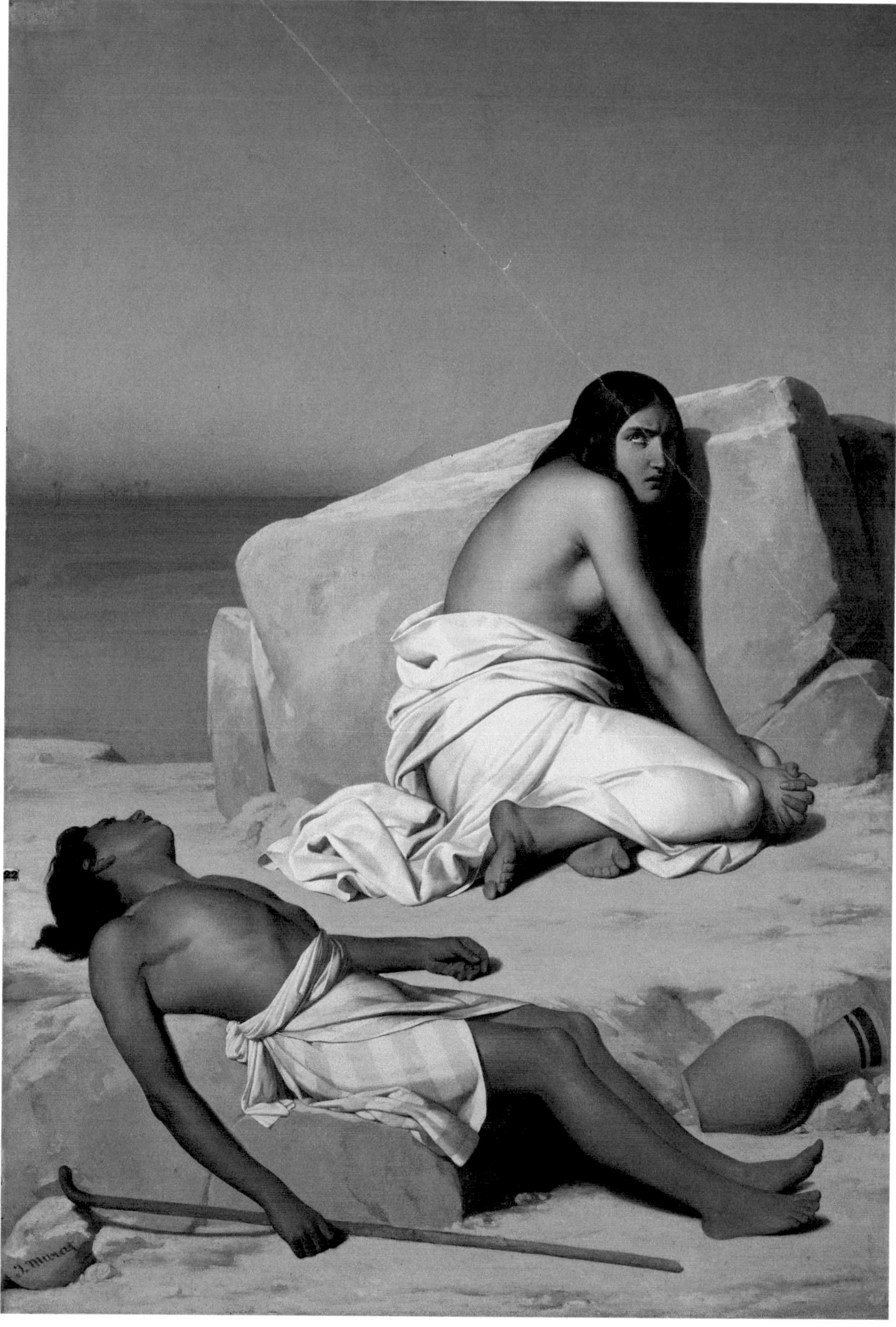

Figure 3.14 Jean-Gilbert Murat, *Hagar in the Desert*, ca. 1842, oil on canvas, 231 × 169 cm. Guéret, Musée d'Art et d'Archéologie. Photo: Benoît Touchard. © RMN-Grand Palais/Art Resource, NY.

temperature brings home the prospect of death by thirst, as the cold blue of the desert sky accentuates the dry heat of sand, rock, and sunbaked flesh. Panic is written into the contrast between particularized description—of walking stick, dusty feet, and empty jug—and the measureless expanse of the rear ground, in which a faint line of palms offers meager promise of drink.

Under the July Monarchy, the narrative of Hagar and Ishmael acquired topical interest in light of the nation's aggressive, popular colonial initiative in North Africa, which had an early success in the conquest of Algiers (5 July 1830, just prior to the advent of Louis-Philippe). Named in the Quran as a prophet, Ishmael was traditionally identified in France as the progenitor of the Arabs; in Genesis, God promises that "I will make of him a great nation."[78] Nurtured by the incursion into North Africa, fascination with Arab mores—as manifest, for example, in the work of two visitors, Horace Vernet (1789–1863) and Delacroix—was inseparable from the Orientalist conception that these ethnic others live outside of time. Accordingly, Delacroix admired North Africans as living analogs to the ancient Romans, and Vernet (the pre-eminent chronicler of French military exploits in North Africa) believed that Arabs offer an unchanged record of the appearance of characters from scripture—a notion embodied in the detailed Arab costume of Vernet's *Hagar Expulsed by Abraham* (1837; Nantes, Musée des Beaux-Arts), exhibited in the Salon of 1839.[79] The unconventionally defiant attitude of Vernet's Hagar in the face of Abraham's command of expulsion was approvingly noted at the Salon by the author and archaeologist Prosper Mérimée (1803–70).[80] Vernet's innovation suggests that the artist's zeal for the colonial cause was paired with admiration of an adversary that fiercely resisted the invaders until the surrender of the French military's nemesis, Emir Abdelkader ibn Muhieddine (1808–83), on 21 December 1847.

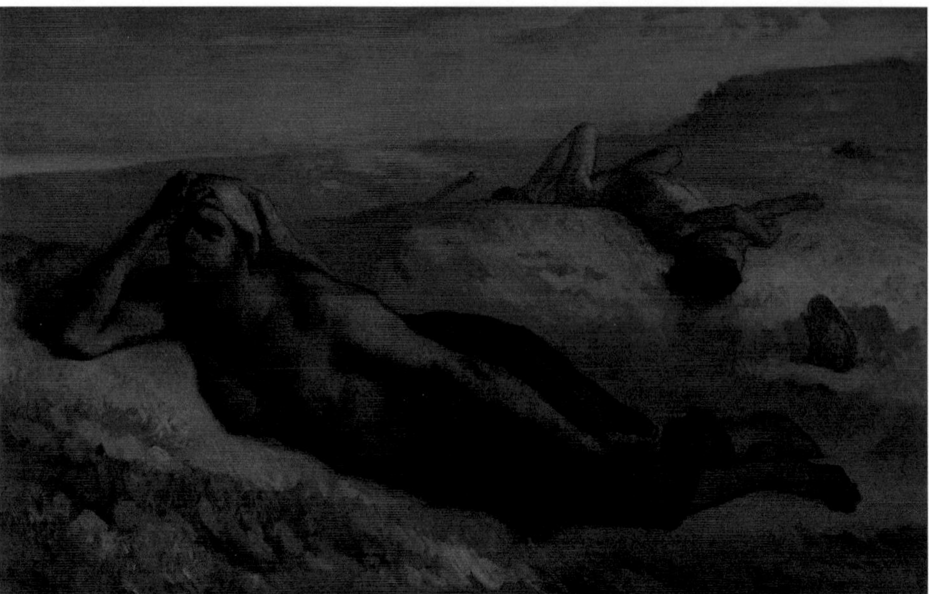

Figure 3.15 Jean-François Millet, *Hagar and Ishmael*, 1848–49, oil on canvas, 147 × 236.5 cm. The Hague, Rijksmuseum H.W. Mesdag. Photo: The Mesdag Collection, the Hague.

Murat's shocking canvas is a forgotten prelude to an unfinished painting of Hagar and Ishmael by Jean-François Millet (1814–75), who chose the subject to fulfill a commission from the fledgling Second Republic (Figure 3.15).[81] Forcefully evoking thirst and paralysis, Millet separates the victims in an additive, graceless composition—the largest of his career. Brutalized by want, their prone bodies are subsumed by parched ground in a space whose ambiguity, as T.J. Clark points out, evokes the desert's emptiness.[82] Bold anatomical simplification is enhanced by the unfinished state of the canvas, lending tragic generality to the harrowing situation. Nearly as close to death as her expiring son, Millet's over-life-size Hagar conveys despair not by means of tightly rendered physiognomic expression (in the manner of Murat), but rather by broad brushwork that lends a subhuman aspect to the prostrate mother.

Having suffered homesickness when he left his native Normandy for the capital, Millet was drawn to biblical subjects imbued with loss. This biographical significance was signaled by the artist's friend and patron Alfred Sensier (1815–77), who claimed that Millet's *Hagar and Ishmael* was an "allusion to his own sorrowful predicament, and also to Paris, which to him was also the Sahara."[83] Previously, in the Salon of 1848, Millet had exhibited a painting inspired by scripture and no less relevant to his status as uprooted provincial. Now overpainted, the canvas showed the Hebrew exiles of Psalm 137 refusing to sing their national songs in the face of mistreatment by Babylonians.[84] The significance of these images of dislocation is not solely biographical. Bringing to mind the poverty and social disruption that drove the Revolution of 1848, *Hagar and Ishmael* offers an Old Testament counterpart to Millet's pessimistic canvas *The Wanderers* (*Les Errants*), which places a vagabond mother and child in an inhospitable, featureless landscape (1848–49; Denver, Denver Art Museum)—an image associated by Robert L. Herbert with the mass, mid-century flight of the unemployed from France's rural provinces into economically depressed Paris.[85]

The timeliness of Millet's representations of displacement is further suggested by a painting exhibited in the Salon of 1849, *The Exiles* (*Les Exilés*) by Charles-Adolphe Richard-Cavaro (1819–c.1890), a pupil of Ingres and Léon Cogniet (1794–1880; Figure 3.16).[86] Executed in a style remote from Millet's Realism, *The Exiles* is an academic pastiche of *The Trojan Women* exhibited in the Salon of 1842 by Richard-Cavaro's exact contemporary, Chassériau. It was commissioned by the Ministry of the Interior headed by Alexandre-Auguste Ledru-Rollin three days before Paris erupted in the violence of the 1848 June Days insurrection. Brutally suppressed, that workers' revolt upended the idealism of the early Second Republic. The tone of the painting corresponds to the turbulent climate in which it was commissioned and executed. In a letter to the ministry from the following March, Richard-Cavaro specified that the canvas would have a "somber aspect" ("*Effet sombre.*").[87] At the water's edge, a group of classically-garbed figures strike attitudes of sorrow in this antique version of the Babylonian Captivity—an affiliation made obvious by the artist's quotation, in the Salon guidebook, of a verse imitation of Psalm 137 by the eighteenth-century poet Malfilâtre.[88] The critic Fabien Pillet was as sympathetic to the protagonists as he was impressed by the handling:

> Composition in a severe genre with half-life-sized, well-draped, tastefully drawn figures; mournful color, analogous to the subject; a pure and graceful touch; expressions all the more moving than if the artist had wished to exaggerate the sorrow of these noble, generous outcasts.[89]

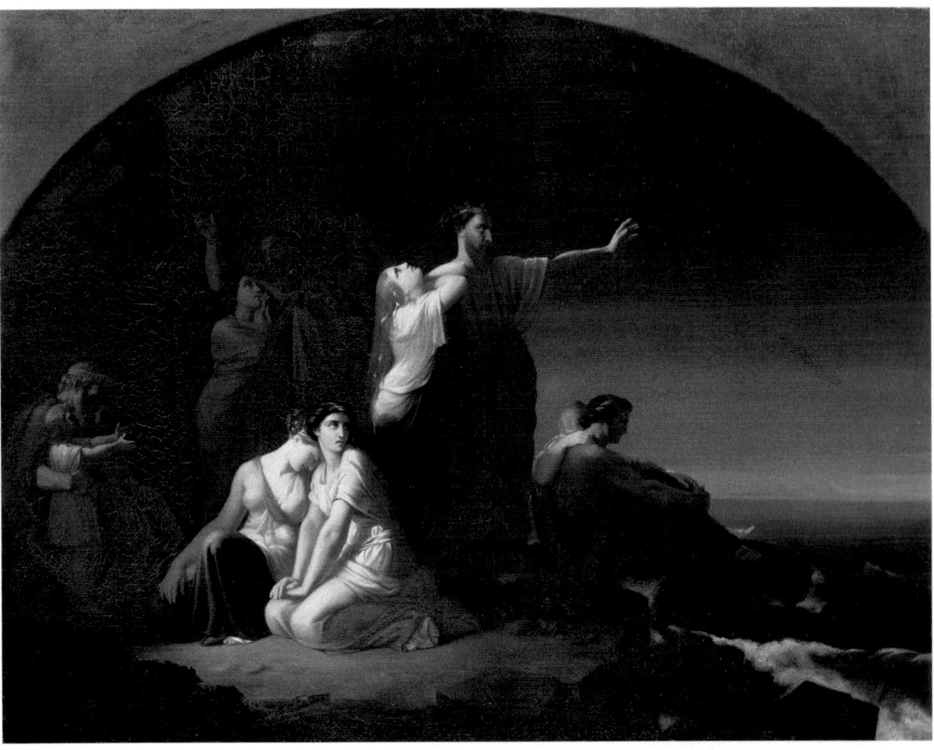

Figure 3.16 Charles-Adolphe Richard-Cavaro, *The Exiles* (*Les Exilés*), 1848–49, oil on canvas, 131 × 171 cm. Besançon, Musée des Beaux-arts et d'Archéologie. Photo: Charles Choffet. © Besançon, Musée des Beaux-arts et d'Archéologie.

Pillet's readiness to sympathize with these exiles (whom he assumes are noble and generous) is coupled with a taste for the representation of self-absorbed grief, such as that which Richard-Cavaro evidently admired in Chassériau's *Trojan Women*—a key example of the anti-heroic mode that had its heyday in the dispiriting years of the July Monarchy.

Cain Accursed

Given the flagrant injustice of Abraham's expulsion of Hagar and Ishmael, their predicament readily appealed to viewers sympathetic to exiles. Nineteenth-century French culture was sufficiently permeated with memory, whether personal or vicarious, of coercive displacement that receptivity to the suffering of the mother and son usurped traditional focus on their rescue. Modern history is less germane to the reevaluation of another, less innocent biblical exile. Empathy with Cain, rather, is symptomatic of Romantic identification with rebellious outsiders, as in the case of Milton's Satan and Hugo's Hernani. At the same time, we will see that Hugo turned to the motif of the banished Cain during his own exile, when his personal predicament was inseparable from his politics.

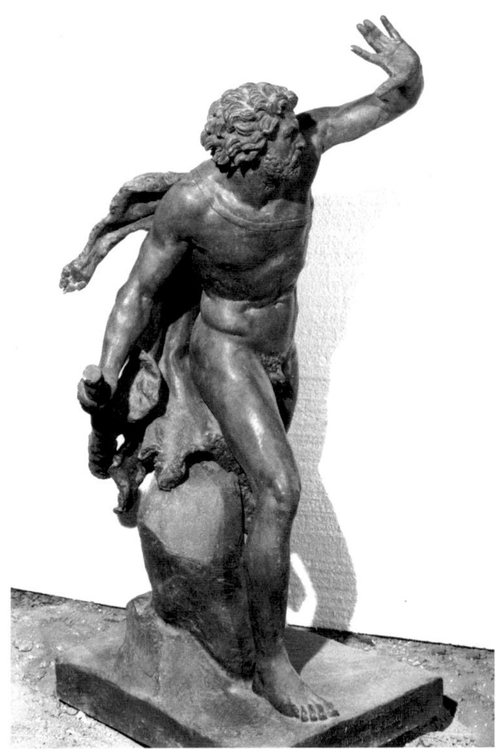

Figure 3.17 Georges Jacquot, *Cain Cursed by God* (*Caïn maudit*), 1820, bronze, 119 × 55 × 76 cm. Nancy, Musée des Beaux-Arts. Photo: Musée des Beaux-Arts, Nancy.

Interest in the troubled outcast from Genesis can be detected in Paris well before Lord Byron scandalously glamorized the first murderer as rebel against divine tyranny in *Cain, A Mystery* (1821; translated 1823).[90] By 1820, the subject was sufficiently conventional for *Cain Cursed by God* to be offered to sculptors competing for the Prix de Rome. I show a bronze cast of the winning entry by Georges Jacquot (1794–1874), given by the sculptor to the city of his origin (Figure 3.17).[91] Paying homage to the Louvre's *Borghese Gladiator*, Jacquot invested this skillfully modeled nude with a guilty agitation unknown to his heroic forebear.[92] Such noisy extroversion is absent from the work that put Cain at the center of the Parisian art world. Antoine Étex (1808–88) stunned visitors to the Salon of 1833 with a colossal (nearly two-meter-tall) plaster group, *Cain and His Race, Accursed of God* (*Caïn et sa race maudits de Dieu*), bringing full-blown Romanticism to the hidebound medium and winning a gold medal. I show the marble version of 1839 (Figure 3.18), as well as the sculptor's own lithographic reproduction (Figure 3.19), published in *L'Artiste*.[93]

The plaster was made in Rome, during a two-year Italian sojourn (1831–32) funded by a government stipend awarded to this ardently republican veteran of the July

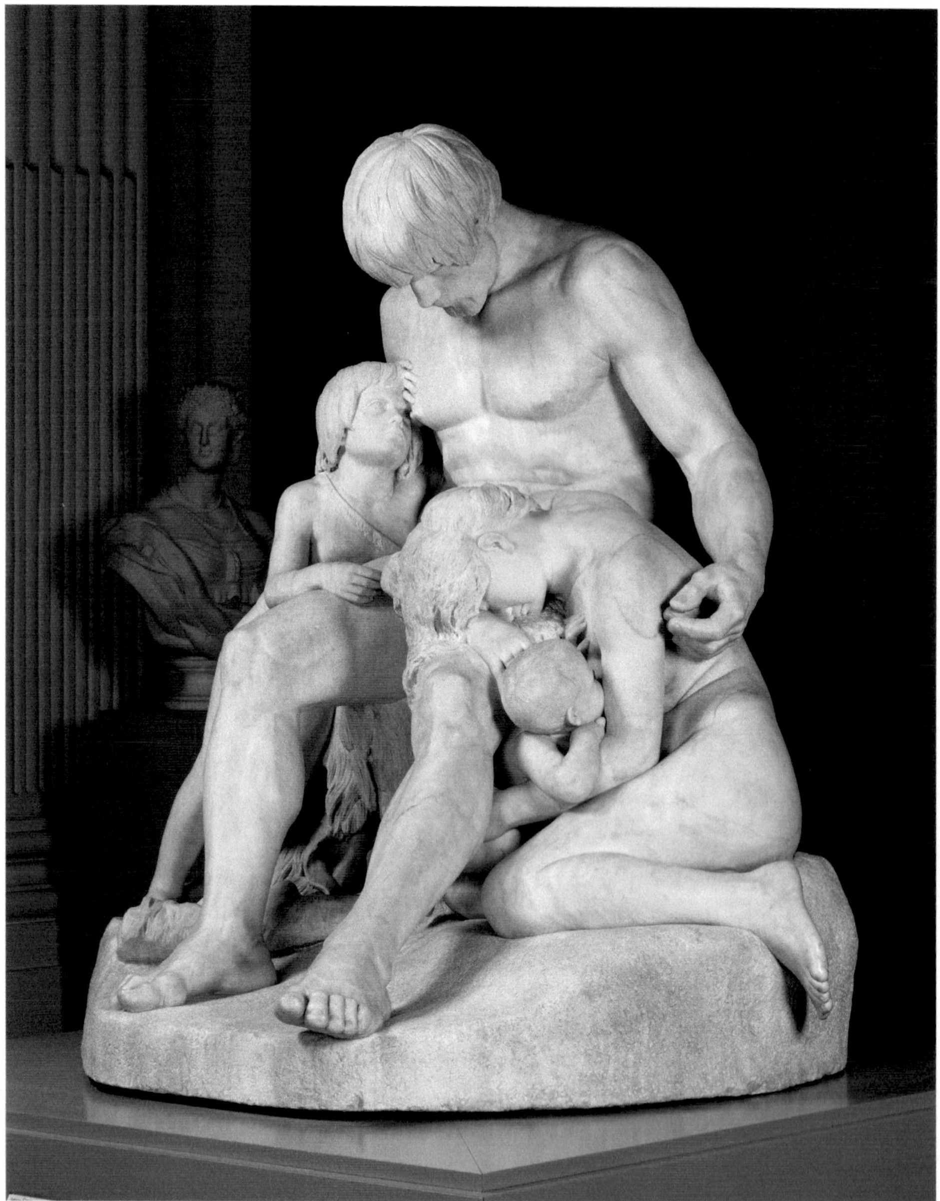

Figure 3.18 Antoine Étex, *Cain and His Race Accursed of God*, (*Caïn et sa race maudits de Dieu*) 1839 (after a plaster exhibited in the Salon of 1833), marble, 184 × 169 × 157 cm. Lyon, Musée des Beaux-Arts. Image © Lyon MBA-Photo Alain Basset.

Revolution. Antoinette Le Normand-Romain draws attention to the personal significance of the motif, arguing that Étex, embittered by failure in the Prix de Rome competition (which he attributed to the envy and intrigue of classmates and professors), projected onto Cain a self-image as cursed artist—a Romantic commonplace.[94]

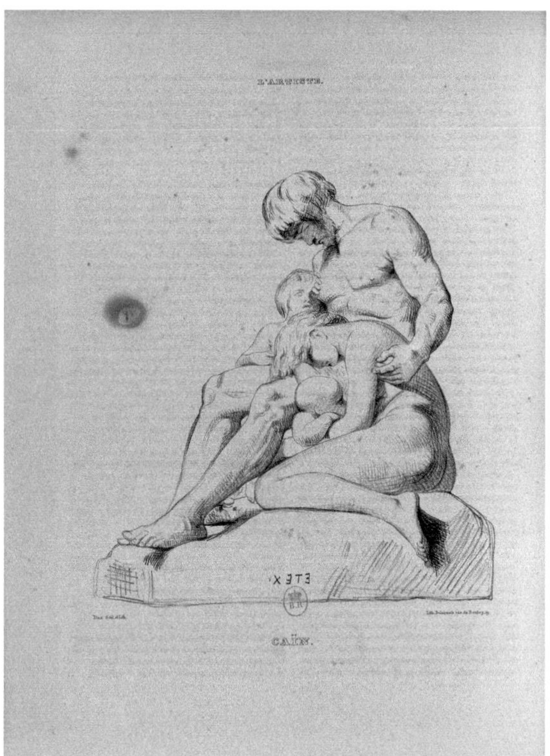

Figure 3.19 Antoine Étex, "Cain." In *L'Artiste*, 1st ser. 5 (1833), lithograph. Paris, Bibliothèque nationale de France. Photo: BnF.

There is an additional personal factor: the sculpture's emotional tenor aligns with the suicidal depression from which Étex suffered while in Rome.[95] Its self-absorbed gloom unnerved the critics Gabriel Laviron and B. Galbacio:

> The head of Cain is without doubt the most remarkable part of this sculpture. However, Genesis, in imparting to the murderer the haughty speech of a rebel against God, could have given the artist the motive for a less dejected face ... Cain looking at the sky would not have been less poetic.[96]

Gautier, in contrast, admired the novel interpretation: "This is, I believe, the first time that the outcast has been represented without grinding of teeth and without rebellion."[97] The critic for *L'Artiste* was also moved:

> It is neither remorse nor anger that animates the features of the murderer of Abel, it is a feeling of an invincible fatality; he is crushed, he has just said to the Lord: My iniquity is too great to obtain pardon.[98]

In his autobiography, the septuagenarian Étex recounts the ambivalent response of Ingres (whom Étex revered and considered one of his teachers) to the plaster group when it arrived in Paris. Impressed by the execution, Ingres found the work overly expressive, and advised the fledgling sculptor to secure a commission to execute it in marble, then destroy it. According to Étex, the painter counseled:

> Your group is superb, no one at this time is capable of modeling that; it's beautiful, very beautiful Canova; it is expressive sculpture (*c'est de la sculpture d'expression*); smash it, I repeat to you, but only when it has been commissioned.[99]

Since the brooding and distress conveyed by the sculpture are precisely what made it a Salon hit, it is hardly surprising that Étex did not follow Ingres's advice when he received a state commission to translate the group into marble.

Conceived for the public space of the Salon and magnified beyond life size, Étex's sculpture invests Cain and his despairing family with mythic amplitude. His appeal to the viewer's sympathy gains salience when the group is juxtaposed with a stylistically innovative, albeit conventionally Christian, interpretation of the subject by the devout Protestant sculptor, Henri de Triqueti (1803–74), a respectable Romantic who enjoyed official favor. Like his friend Delacroix, Triqueti served the July Monarchy well, having previously executed two monumental, allegorical relief sculptures with reassuring subjects, *Protecting Law* and *Avenging Law* (1833–34), in the Palais-Bourbon. For the Church of the Madeleine, directly across the Seine

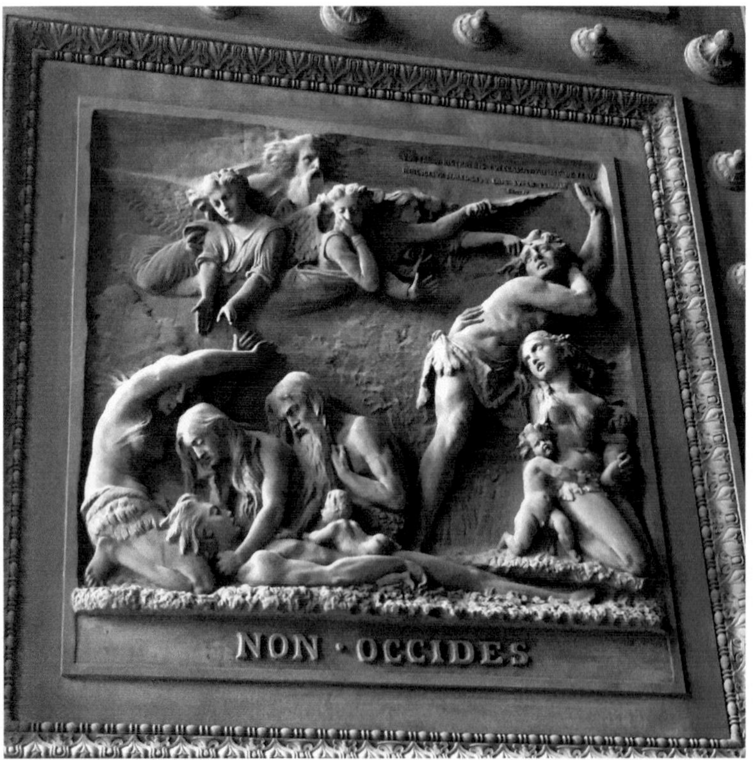

Figure 3.20 Henri de Triqueti, *Thou Shall Not Murder*, 1834–41, bronze. Paris, Church of the Madeleine. Photo: Susan White.

from the legislative palace, Triqueti provided colossal bronze doors adorned with a masterful sculptural program in high relief (1834–41). Visualizing the Ten Commandments through Old Testament narratives, the doors provide a biblical prototype for the constitutional *Charte* of 1830 undergirding the regime's legitimacy.[100] The panel representing the prohibition of murder shows the Cain family driven into exile by avenging angels in the company of God the Father while the slain Abel lies mourned by Adam, Eve, and Abel's family (Figure 3.20). The angel in highest relief reaches toward Abel's widow in pity; another holds hand to mouth in shock; a third brandishes a flaming sword, and a fourth points the way to exile. Piously chastening Étex's amoral conception, Triqueti replaces the anti-hero's brooding self-absorption with guilty recoil before the righteous machinery of divine justice. Instructive contrast between crime and punishment is woven into the composition: the encircling contours and tight grouping of the mourners speak of familial cohesion, while the diagonal rhythms of Cain and his family convey turmoil, their hemming in by the panel's frame a visual expression of the inexorable curse on the murderer.

Hugo in Exile

Just as there are autobiographical intimations in Étex's unconventional rendition of Cain, self-reference also informs Hugo's idiosyncratic poem "Conscience" ("La Conscience," composed 29 January 1853), which opens the first series (1859) of *La Légende des siècles*. There, Hugo casts the flight of Cain (the "somber man") from the open eye of God as an emblem of relentless guilt. Cain's family fruitlessly constructs defenses against God's eye, including a city with walls "the thickness of mountains," whose gateway bears a sign forbidding God to enter. Finally, the fugitive has himself placed in a tomb, but to no avail:

> Puis il descendit seul sous cette voûte sombre;
> quand il se fut assis sur sa chaise dans l'ombre
> et qu'on eut sur son front fermé le souterrain,
> l'oeil était dans la tombe et regardait Caïn.
> Then he descended alone under this somber vault; / when he was seated on his chair in the shadow / and when they had shut the subterranean vault, / the eye was in the tomb and looked at Cain.[101]

As implied by the title, there is a confessional aspect to the poem, which has been associated with remorse over the untimely death of Hugo's beloved eldest daughter Léopoldine, who drowned with her new husband in the Seine (4 September 1843) while her father was purportedly traveling with his mistress, Juliette Drouet (1806–83).[102] Grasping the poet's identification with his protagonist, François-Nicolas Chifflart (1825–1901), Hugo's ardent admirer and illustrator of a number of his works, portrayed the fleeing Cain with his idol's features in a charcoal drawing inspired by "La Conscience" that probably dates from the year of Hugo's state funeral (1 June 1885), when a sea of humanity attended the poet's Pantheonization (Figure 3.21).[103] A belated Romantic cousin to the *noirs* of Odilon Redon, Chifflart's nocturnal scene is lit by an immense, closely described eye from whose light Cain cringingly recoils, giving visual form to the oppressive guilt evoked in "La Conscience."[104]

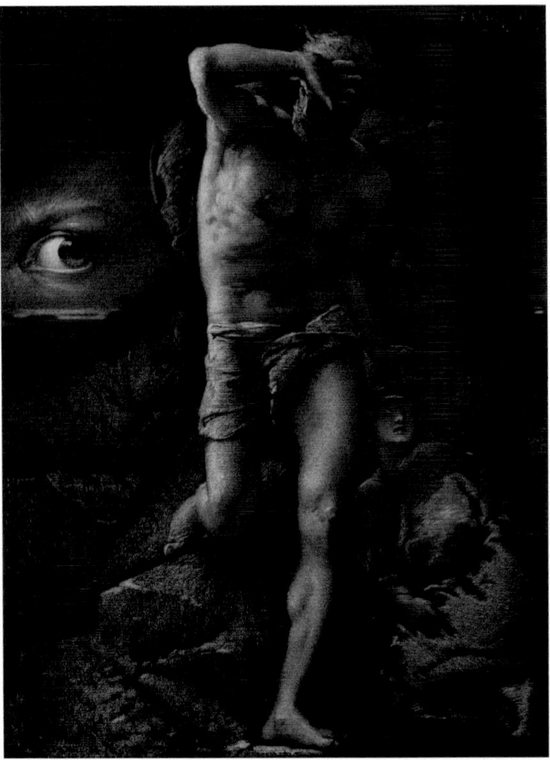

Figure 3.21 François-Nicolas Chifflart, *Conscience*, ca. 1885, charcoal, 61.6 × 47 cm. Paris, Maison de Victor-Hugo. CCO Paris Musées/Maisons de Victor Hugo Paris-Guernsey.

Hugo's identification with the outcast Cain is both personally and politically fraught. "La Conscience" was written while the poet shared the proscription of some 10,000 opponents of Louis-Napoléon Bonaparte, whose coup d'état on 2 December 1851 preluded elevation to the imperial throne as Napoleon III. Prior to the coup d'état, Hugo had been the pre-eminent bard of Napoleonic glory; in the late Restoration, his youthful infatuation with Catholic ultra-royalism had morphed into adulation of the late emperor. Initially a supporter of his hero's nephew, the poet was aghast at Louis-Napoléon's usurpation. From the islands of Jersey (1852–55) and Guernsey (1855–70), Hugo unleashed obsessive fury on the dictator in *Napoléon le petit* (1852) and *Les Châtiments* (1853), wrote his classic novel built around a sympathetic fugitive from injustice, *Les Misérables* (1862), and (like Ovid) personified the Romantic stereotype of the persecuted poet.

Hugo's view of exile oscillated between depression and elevation. He dramatized his martyrdom in more than 60 photographs taken by his son Charles (1826–71) in the period 1853–54 on Jersey, with settings chosen by the poet. This one, dating from the summer of 1853, features the exile perched on the Rocher des Proscrits (The Rock of the Proscribed) in the manner of Napoleon, captive on the rock of Saint Helena (Figure 3.22).[105] The heroic posture is of a piece with the poet's grandiose

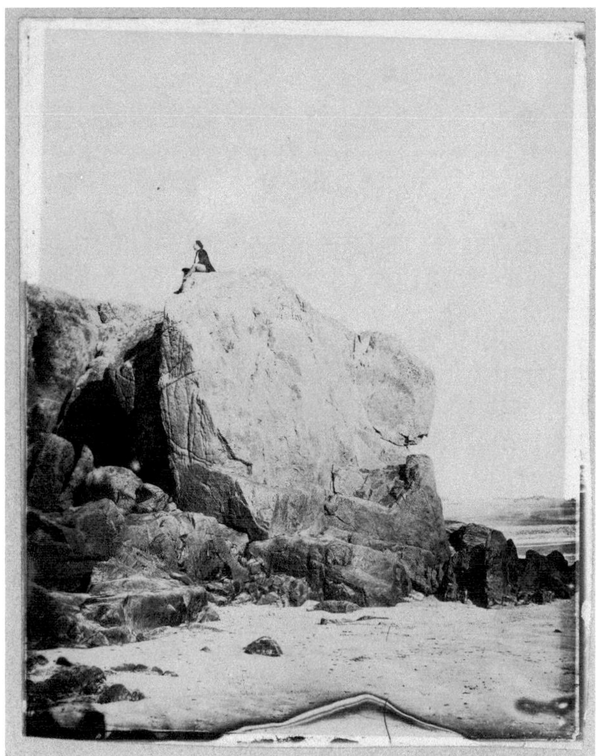

Figure 3.22 Charles Hugo, *Victor Hugo on the Rock of the Proscribed*, summer 1853, photographic print on salted paper, 23.5 × 15 cm. Guernsey, Maison de Victor Hugo-Hauteville House. CCO Paris Musées/Maisons de Victor Hugo Paris-Guernsey.

self-fashioning. Alerting the reader of the preface to his poetry collection *Les Contemplations* (1856) that "[t]his book must be read as one would read the book of someone dead," Hugo views his exile as representing both an aggrandizement of self and a state of radical selflessness:

> My life is yours, your life is mine, you live that which I live; destiny is one. So, take this mirror, and look at yourself in it. People sometimes complain of writers who say me. Speak to us of us, they cry out to them. Alas! When I speak to you of me, I speak to you of you. How can you not feel it? Oh, you fool, who believes that I am not you![106]

Hugo's preemptive irritation is not solely attributable to an ego as outsized as his shelf-bending literary output. For D.G. Charlton, this passage is characteristic of a pattern within French Romanticism especially apparent in the work of Hugo—a subsuming of the autobiographical and the personal within the universal. Similarly, Henri Peyre interprets the poet's claim as exemplifying an "evolution away from the narrowness of the ego lamenting … and toward the fraternity of mankind and social preoccupations...."[107] Convinced that he subsumes humanity, Hugo willingly embraced exile. In Brussels (22 January 1852), prior to embarking for the Channel Islands he confessed:

> I love proscription, I love exile ... I love poverty, I love adversity, I love all that I suffer for liberty, for the fatherland and for what is right; I have a joyful conscience; but it is always a sorrowful thing to walk on foreign soil.[108]

The pain of exile, then, is mitigated by the sufferer's noble self-sacrifice. Inseparable from this surprisingly buoyant outlook is Hugo's belief in his divine investiture. This he had shared with other members of the *Muse française* circle under the Bourbon Restoration, and it had been common coin among the utopian social thinkers who had theorized earthly paradises in the dog days of Louis-Philippe's reign: "In my occupation there is something of the sacred," he noted in 1853.[109] Divinely anointed, the poet is positioned to draw uncommon insight from the exile experience. In December 1854, he jotted in his journal:

> More and more I find exile good. One must believe that without their knowledge exiles are in proximity to a sun, because they ripen quickly. For three years now... I feel myself to be at the true summit of life, and I see the real lineaments of all of that which men call facts, history, events, success, catastrophes, huge mechanism of Providence. / Was it not from this perspective that I would need to thank M. Bonaparte who proscribed me and God who chose me[?] Perhaps I will die in exile, but I will die enlarged. / All is well.[110]

"No one has ever been a more satisfied exile than Hugo," concludes Maurice Z. Shroder.[111] And this satisfaction rests on a conviction that exile is empowering:

> it is enough that the collapsed man be a just man ... he is good whether he is condemned, ruined, despoiled, expatriated, ridiculed, insulted, repudiated, slandered and whether he epitomizes all forms of defeat and weakness; then he is all-powerful.... The emperor damns, the exile condemns.[112]

Accordingly, Hugo rejected the amnesty extended by the emperor to exiles (August 1859), declaring: "When liberty returns, I will return."[113]

A decade after Hugo's triumphant reentry into France (5 September 1870), his heroic posture was visualized in a full-length portrait (Figure 3.23) by the former Prix de Rome laureate Alphonse-Xavier Monchablon (1835–1907).[114] With arms crossed (as he often had been represented since 1848), Hugo stands foursquare on the rocky coast of Jersey, surrounded by crashing waves and illuminated against a stormy sky.[115] The imagery matches the poet's "Ultima verba," written on Jersey 2 December 1852, the anniversary of the coup d'état:

> Devant les trahisons et les têtes courbées,
> Je croiserai les bras, indigné mais serein.
> Before the betrayals and the bowed heads, / I will cross my arms, indignant but serene.[116]

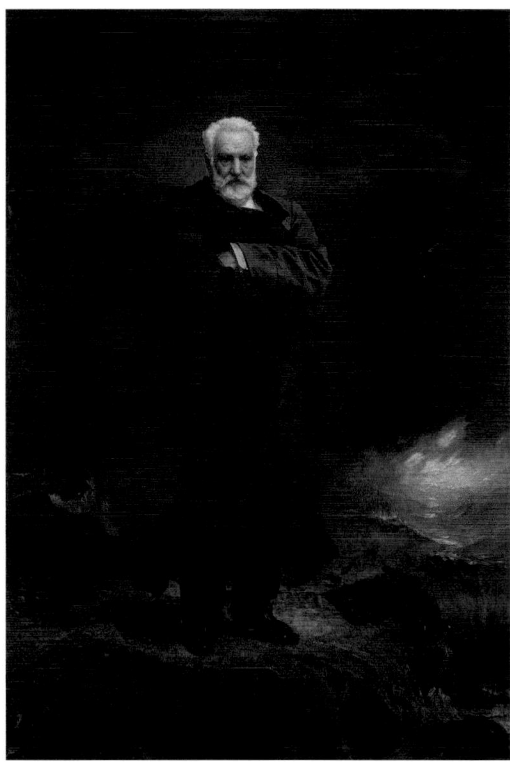

Figure 3.23 Alphonse-Xavier Monchablon, *Portrait of Victor Hugo*, 1880, oil on canvas, 257 × 177 cm. Épinal, Musée départmental d'art ancien et contemporain. ©Musée départmental d'art ancien et contemporain—Épinal (France), cliché Claude Philippot.

Like Charles Hugo's photograph of his father seated atop the Rock of the Proscribed, Monchablon's portrait invokes Napoleon's exile on Saint Helena. Painted nearly 60 years after the emperor's death, it testifies to the longevity of his spell.

Notes

1 These figures are from Sylvie Aprile, *Le Siècle des exiles: Bannis et proscrits de 1789 à la Commune* (Paris: CNRS Éditions, 2010), 21. An estimated total of 150,000 exiles, of which 129,099 were official émigrés, is adduced in Donald Greer, *The Incidence of the Emigration during the French Revolution,* Harvard Historical Monographs 24 (Cambridge, MA: Harvard University Press, 1951), 20. For the Emigration, see also Ghislain de Diesbach, *Histoire de l'Émigration 1789–1814* (Paris: Bernard Grasset, 1975); and Jean Vidalenc, *Les Émigrés français, 1789–1825* (Caen: Association des Publications de la Faculté des Lettres et Sciences Humaines de l'Université de Caen, 1963).

2 Greer, *The Incidence of the Emigration*, 91.

3 "Les femmes, grand Dieu! les femmes coupables de *lâcheté* ou de *trahison*! ... Le *lâche*, c'est celui qui les abandonne; le *traître*, celui qui les livre; le monstre, celui qui, portant le couteau dans la gorge d'un vierge naissante, ou d'une matrone vénérable, également indéfendues, tranche, sans pitié comme sans péril, la vie qu'il devait protéger au prix de la

sienne." Trophime-Gérard de Lally-Tolendal, *Défense des émigrés français. Addressée en 1797 au peuple français*, new ed. (Paris: Delaunay, 1825), 35–6 (emphasis in original).

4 For this painting, its political context, and its critical reception, see Thomas Crow, *Emulation: David, Drouais, and Girodet in the Art of Revolutionary France*, rev. ed. (New Haven, CT: Yale University Press and Los Angeles, CA: Getty Research Institute, 2006), 205–11; Mehdi Korchane, *Figures de l'exil sous la Révolution, De Bélisaire à Marcus Sextus* (Vizille: Musée de la Révolution française-Domaine de Vizille, 2016), 55–9; and Jennifer Marie Langworthy, "On Shifting Ground: The Revolutionary Career of François Gérard" (PhD Diss., University of Illinois at Urbana-Champaign, 2012), 187–203.

5 For David's painting, and for the theme of Belisarius, see Thomas E. Crow, *Painters and Public Life in Eighteenth-Century Paris* (New Haven, CT: Yale University Press, 1985), 198–209. For additional representations of Belisarius, see Korchane, *Figures de l'exil*, chap. 1.

6 Clemency for this cohort had been advocated by *La Décade philosophique,* in which Charles-Alexandre Amaury-Duval enthusiastically praised Gérard's painting: "What a simple yet captivating subject! It has been rendered with expression and feeling. We can read in the admirable head of Belisarius his great nobility of soul, his resignation in misery; and this poor child, how he suffers!" Quoted in Crow, *Emulation*, 206.

7 For the painting, see Mehdi Korchane, *Pierre Guérin 1774–1833* (Paris: Mare & Martin, 2018), 64–85; idem, *Figures de l'exil,* chap. 4; Stefan Germer, "In Search of a Beholder: On the Relation between Art, Audiences, and Social Spheres in Post-Thermidor France," *Art Bulletin* 74 (March 1992), 28–31; Josette Bottineau, "De *Bélisaire* à *Marcus Sextus*: Genèse et histoire d'un tableau de Pierre Guérin (1774–1833)," *Revue du Louvre et des Musées de France* 43, no. 3 (June 1993): 41–53; Robert Rosenblum, *Transformations in Late Eighteenth-Century Art* (Princeton, NJ: Princeton University Press, 1969), 90; James Henry Rubin, "Oedipus, Antigone and Exiles in Post-Revolutionary French Painting," *Art Quarterly* 36, no. 3 (Autumn 1973), 154–6; and the biographical notice by Jacques Vilain in Frederick J. Cummings, Pierre Rosenberg, and Robert Rosenblum, *French Painting, 1774–1830: The Age Revolution* (Detroit: Detroit Institute of Arts, 1975), 477.

8 The painting is reproduced in Korchane, *Pierre Guérin*, 63, fig. 39.

9 See Germer, "In Search of a Beholder." The classic discussion of the *exemplum vertutis* is Rosenblum, *Transformations*, chap. 2.

10 See Korchane, *Pierre Guérin*, 72ff.

11 For a discussion of *The Return of Marcus Sextus* in relation to *The Triumph of the French People on August 10th*, see Germer, "In Search of a Beholder." Hennequin's painting was dismembered under the Bourbon Restoration. The largest of the remaining fragments is in the Rouen Musée des Beaux-Arts.

12 Eyewitness accounts of the banquet (3 October 1799) for some 50 guests, including David and Hennequin, and another banquet (21 October) held by 30 women artists (together with Salon criticism, verse, and a dramatic fragment inspired by the painting), are collected in Korchane, *Figures de l'exil*, 134–54.

13 For Landon, whose *Annales du Musée de l'école moderne des beaux-arts* ran, in its first edition (1801–9) to 17 volumes, and in its second, mostly posthumous, edition (1823–35), to 44 volumes, see the biographical entry by Jacques Vilain, in Cummings, Rosenberg, and Rosenblum, *French Painting, 1774–1830*, 522.

14 Analysis of such images in their political context was pioneered in Rubin, "Oedipus, Antigone and Exiles."

15 For Delille, see Fernand Baldensperger, *Le Mouvement des idées dans l'Émigration française (1789–1815)* (Paris: Plon-Nourrit, 1924), 1: 256–68; and Kirsty Carpenter, *Refugees of the French Revolution: Émigrés in London, 1789–1802* (New York: St. Martin's Press, 1999), 145. For a painting by Henri-Pierre Danloux inspired by *La Pitié* (cut into two pieces; both Paris, Musée du Louvre), see the discussion by Olivier Meslay, in Korchane, *Figures de l'exil*, 96–103.

16 *The New English Bible with the Apocrypha* (New York: Oxford University Press, 1971), 735.

17 For Malfilâtre and other members of this cohort, see Paul Bénichou, *Le Sacre de l'écrivain, 1750–1830: Essai sur l'avènement d'un pouvoir spirituel laïque dans la France moderne*, 2nd ed. (Paris: José Corti, 1985), 84.

18 Jacques Delille, *La Pitié, poëme* (Paris: Giguet et Michaud, 1803), 129. For the prevalent theme of longing for the homeland in émigré verse, see Baldensperger, *Le Mouvement des idées* 1: 307–12.

19 "Avec quelle douce affection s'élèvent dans le coeur de l'Israélite captif les souvenirs amers de la sainte cité! Sur les bords du fleuve de Babylone, immobiles, assis sous les roseaux, la harpe suspendue, nous pensons à l'antique Sion, et nous pleurons en silence son infortune et sa gloire." *Le Psalmiste* (originally London, 1799), in Jean de Dieu-Raymond Boisgelin de Cucé, *Oeuvres du cardinal de Boisgelin de l'Académie française* (Paris: F. Guitel, 1818), 384.

20 For the life and work of Germaine de Staël, see Michel Winock, *Madame de Staël* (Paris: Fayard, 2010); Angelica Goodden, *Madame de Staël: The Dangerous Exile* (Oxford: Oxford University Press, 2008); Simone Balayé, *Madame de Staël: Lumières et liberté* (Paris: Éditions Klincksieck, 1979); and Ghislain de Diesbach, *Madame de Staël* (Paris: Librairie Académique Perrin, 1983). For the author's political opinions, see Biancamaria Fontana, *Germain de Staël: A Political Portrait* (Princeton, NJ: Princeton University Press, 2016).

21 "Just as she found a space for literature in all her exiles so her exile itself became literature, the written declaration of what her mind conceptualized, and as a means to effective protest that overrode local, national, and even international constraints." Goodden, *Madame de Staël,* 293–4.

22 For Constant's political theories, see Biancamaria Fontana, *Benjamin Constant and the Post-revolutionary Mind.* (New Haven, CT: Yale University Press, 1991).

23 "J'etais vulnérable par mon goût pour la société.... Le fantôme de l'ennui m'a poursuivie toute ma vie; c'est par cette terreur que j'aurais été capable de plier devant la tyrannie, si l'exemple de mon père, si le sang de lui qui coule dans mes veines ne l'emportait pas sur cette faiblesse." Germaine de Staël, *Dix années d'exil,* ed. Simone Balayé and Mariella Vianello Bonifacio (Paris: Arthème Fayard, 1996), 85. For Staël's unfinished *Dix années d'exile,* heavily edited and published (1821) by the author's son after her death, see Christopher W. Thompson, *French Romantic Travel Writing: Chateaubriand to Nerval* (Oxford: Oxford University Press, 2011), 248–60.

24 Quoted in Balayé, "Absence, exil, voyage," in *Madame de Staël: Écrire, lutter, vivre*, pref. Roland Mortier, postface, Frank Paul Bowman, Histoire des idées et critique littéraire 334 (Geneva: Droz, 1994), 57 and n. 46.

25 "Exile is centrally inscribed, since Corinne originally chooses disappearance from her family and anonymous exile in Rome, 'l'asile des exilés du monde', and since both she and Oswald are morally crippled by ambivalent relations to the countries of their birth, as well as by loss of, and differences with, parents." Thompson, *French Romantic Travel Writing*, 29. For the impact of the author's exile experience on *Corinne,* see Carpenter, *Refugees of the French Revolution*, 136–40; and Patrick Coleman, "Exile and Narrative Voice in *Corinne*," *Studies in Eighteenth-Century Culture* 24 (1995): 91–105. For an analysis of *Corinne* from the perspective of gender, see Margaret Waller, *The Male Malady: Fictions of Impotence in the French Romantic Novel* (New Brunswick, NJ: Rutgers University Press, 1993), chap. 3.

26 Simone Balayé, "Absence, exil, voyage," 48.

27 John Isbell, introduction to Anne-Louise-Germaine de Staël, *Corinne, or Italy,* trans. and ed. Sylvia Raphael (Oxford: Oxford University Press, 1998), xv.

28 "[J]e me sentais saisie par la maladie du pays, la plus inquiète douleur qui puisse s'emparer de l'âme. L'exil est quelquefois, pour les caractères vifs et sensibles, un supplice beaucoup plus cruel que la mort; l'imagination prend en déplaisance tous les objets qui vous entourent, le climat, le pays, la langue, les usages, la vie en masse, la vie en detail; il y a une peine pour chaque moment comme pour chaque situation: car la patrie nous donne mille plaisirs habituels que nous ne connaissons pas nous mêmes avant de les avoir perdus ...." Germaine de Staël, *Corinne, ou l'Italie* (Paris: H. Nicolle, 1807), 2: 155.

29 "Les îles que les volcans ont fait sortir de la mer servirent, presqu'en naissant, aux crimes du vieux monde; les malheureux rélégués sur ces rochers solitaires, au milieu des flots, contemplaient de loin leur patrie, tâchaient de respirer ses parfums dans les airs, et quelquefois, après un long exil, un arrêt de mort leur apprenait que leurs ennemis du moins ne les avaient pas oubliés." Ibid., 2:112.

30 For the painting, see Robert Rosenblum, *Transformations*, 118; and Madeleine Vincent, *La Peinture des XIXe et XXe siècles*, Catalogue du Musée de Lyon 7: (Lyon: IAC, Les Éditions de Lyon, 1956), 14–17.

31 For Récamier's salon and the fame of Gérard's canvas, see Daniel Harkett, "Mediating Private and Public: Juliette Récamier's Salon at l'Abbaye-aux-Bois," in *Women, Femininity and Public Space in European Visual Culture, 1789–1914*, ed. Temma Balducci and Heather Belnap Jensen (Farnham: Ashgate, 2014), 55–6.

32 Quoted in *The Romantic Movement* (London: Arts Council of Great Britain, 1959), no. 174.

33 *Romanticism in National Context*, ed. Roy Porter and Mikuláš Teich (Cambridge: Cambridge University Press, 1988), 4.

34 "Je crois [that it is] … facile de montrer que l'exil est peut-être de tous les pouvoirs laissés à un souverain, le plus dangereux par la facilité qu'il lui présente et le plus funeste par les effets qui doivent en résulter." Staël, *Dix années d'exil*, 155.

35 "Parmi toutes les attributions de l'autorité, l'une des plus favorables à la tyrannie, c'est la faculté d'exiler sans jugement." Germaine de Staël, *Considérations sur les principaux événements de la Révolution française, Publiées en 1818 par M. le duc de Broglie et M. le baron de Staël*, in *Oeuvres posthumes de Madame la baronne de Staël-Holstein, Précédees d'une Notice sur son caractère et ses écrits* (Paris, 1861; reprint, Geneva: Slatkine, 1967), 219.

36 "Les échafauds peuvent à la fin réveiller le courage; mais les chagrins domestiques de tout genre, résultat du banissement, affaiblissent la résistance, et portent seulement à redouter la disgrâce du souverain qui peut vous infliger une existence si malheureuse." Staël, *Considérations sur les principaux événements*, 219. Constant also vehemently denounced banishment, which he regarded as no different from arbitrary arrest and imprisonment. See Benjamin Constant, *Réflexions sur les constitutions et les garanties, avec une Esquisse de constitution* (1814–1818), in *Cours de politique constitutionnelle et collection des ouvrages publiés sur le gouvernement représentatif*, ed. Édouard Laboulaye, 2nd ed. (Paris: Guillaumin, 1872, reprint, Geneva: Slatkine, 1982), 1: 371.

37 *Chansons choisies de P.-J. de Béranger* (Bielefeld: Velhagen & Klasing, 1846), 68. For Béranger, see Jean Touchard, *La Gloire de Béranger*, 2 vols. (Paris: Armand Colin, 1968), a rich source for the political culture of the Restoration and the July Monarchy.

38 For representations of this poem, see the authoritative source regarding the impact of the Greek War on visual culture, Nina M. Athanassoglou-Kallmyer, *French Images from the Greek War of Independence 1821–1830: Art and Politics under the Restoration* (New Haven, CT: Yale University Press, 1989), 15–19, 25.

39 Casimir Delavigne, *Messéniennes et poésies diverses*, 11th ed. (Paris: Ladvocat, 1824), 1:97.

40 For this painting, exhibited in the Salon of Douai in 1825 as *Les Parganinotes*, see the catalog entry by Francis Ribemont, in Claire Constans et al., *La Grèce en révolte: Delacroix et les peintres français* (Bordeaux: Musée des Beaux-Arts, 1996), no. 79; and Athanassoglou-Kallmyer, *French Images*, 84–5. After acquisition in the Thevenin sale (27 January 1851), the painting entered the Fodor collection in Amsterdam as *Banished Greeks on a Rock, Viewing in the Distance Their Lost Fatherland*.

41 In 1839, of the 13,502 residents fitting the French legal definition of refugee (foreigners without protection of their government and without passport), three-quarters were Poles. Aprile, *Le Siècle des exiles*, 87.

42 Scheffer represented, in watercolor and black pencil, a bare-breasted *Polonia* trampled by an equestrian Cossack, her elbow resting on a slain Polish eagle (ca. 1831, Dordrecht, Dordrechts Museum). For this work, see *Ary Scheffer 1795–1858, Dessins, aquarelles, esquisses à l'huile* (Paris: Institut Néerlandais, 1980), no. 60.

43 For Mickiewicz, see the detailed biography, Roman Koropeckyj, *Adam Mickiewicz: The Life of a Romantic* (Ithaca, NY: Cornell University Press, 2008); idem., "Adam Mickiewicz and the Shape of Polish Romanticism," in *A Companion to European Romanticism*, ed. Michael Ferber (Malden, MA: Blackwell Publishing, 2005), 326–44; Lloyd S. Kramer, *Threshold of a New World: Intellectuals and the Exile Experience in Paris, 1830–1848* (Ithaca, NY: Cornell University Press), 1988, chap. 4; and Donald Pirie, "The Agony in

the Garden: Polish Romanticism," *Romanticism in National Context*, ed. Porter and Teich, 317–44. For analysis of the written *oeuvre*, see David Welsh, *Adam Mickiewicz* (New York: Twayne Publishers, 1966). I am grateful to Hans Henning Hahn for bringing Mickiewicz to my attention at a chance meeting over breakfast in the early 1980s.

44 For the sculptor, see Jacques de Caso, *David d'Angers: Sculptural Communication in the Age of Romanticism,* trans. Dorothy Johnson and Jacques de Caso (Princeton, NJ: Princeton University Press, 1992).

45 Mickiewicz professed: "Our intervention is political-religious, our tone is Christological-Napoleonic." ("Notre action est politico-religieuse, notre ton est christico-napoléonien.") Quoted in Jeremy Lambert, "Le Towianisme en France; La France dans le Towianisme," *Slavica bruxellensia*, 3 (2009): 61–73. https://doi.org/10.4000/slavica.274.

46 Adam Mickiewicz, *Livre des pèlerins polonais, traduit du polonais d'Adam Mickiewicz, par le comte Ch. de Montalembert, suivi d'Un hymne à la Pologne par F. de La Mennais* (Paris: Eugène Renduel), 1833), 147–48, 29–30.

47 Echoing Mickiewicz's prophecy of national resurrection, Lamennais's lullaby opens: "Sleep, O my Poland! Sleep in peace in what they call your tomb; I know, myself, that it is your cradle." Mickiewicz, *Livre des pèlerins*, 171.

48 For the portrait, see Jan Bialostocki, "Gros et Niemcewicz," *Gazette des beaux-arts*, 6th ser. 64 (December 1964): 363–72. Robert Rosenblum brought this painting to my attention. I am grateful to Sylwia Łopatecka, of the National Museum in Krakow/Princes Czartoryski Museum in Krakow for providing an image of the painting and granting reproduction rights.

49 Quoted from J.-B. Delestre, *Gros et ses ouvrages* (Paris, 1845), in Bialostocki, "Gros et Niemcewicz," 369.

50 Quoted in Bialostocki, "Gros et Niemcewicz," 363.

51 For the artist's relations with Polish émigrés, see André Joubin, "Delacroix, Chopin et la société polonaise," in "La France et la Pologne dans leurs relations artistiques," special issue, *Annuaire historique de la Bibliothèque polonaise de Paris* 2, nos. 1–2 (January–June 1939): 3–70.

52 Jürgen Osterhammel, *The Transformation of the World: A Global History of the Nineteenth Century,* trans. Patrick Camiller (Princeton, NJ: Princeton University Press, 2014), 137.

53 Maurice Sérullaz et al., *Musée du Louvre, Cabinet des dessins. Inventaire général des dessins, École française. Dessins d'Eugène Delacroix, 1798–1863* (Paris: Éditions de la Réunion des musées nationaux, 1984), vol. 1, no. 579 (RF 20 recto). This entry endorses the opinion of Hélène Toussaint that the artist's notation (verso), which states that, on 25 July 1857, he bequeathed the drawing to the housekeeper and companion of his later years, Jenny Le Guillou (1801–69), with instructions that it ultimately be passed along to the Louvre, actually refers to a self-portrait also given by Delacroix to the Louvre. For RF 20, see also "Delacroix, Eugène, École française, *Portrait de Chopin en Dante*," in *Louvre, Les Collections du département des arts graphiques*, accessed 2 November 2020, http://arts-graphiques.louvre.fr/detail/oeuvres/1/111545-Portrait-de-Chopin-en-Dante.

54 For the appropriateness of the decorative program to the legislative function of the Palais-Bourbon, see my *Broken Tablets: The Cult of the Law in French Art from David to Delacroix* (Berkeley: University of California Press, 1993), chap. 5. For other aspects of the cycle, see David O'Brien, *Exiled in Modernity: Delacroix, Civilization, and Barbarism* (University Park: Penn State University Press, 2018), chap. 2; Daniel R. Guernsey, *The Artist and the State, 1777–1855: The Politics of Universal History in British and French Painting* (Aldershot: Ashgate, 2007), chap. 2; and Michèle Hannoosh, *Painting and the 'Journal' of Eugène Delacroix* (Princeton, NJ: Princeton University Press, 1995), 131–47.

55 "Les Peintures de la Bibliothèque de la Chambre des deputes," *Le Constitutionnel* (31 January 1848). The subject had been previously treated by Delacroix's assistant, Louis de Planet, in *The Last Stop of the Jews Led into Captivity in Babylon*, (1842–43; Toulouse, Musée des Augustins). For other nineteenth-century French examples, see my *Broken Tablets*, 124–8; and my "On a Repainting by Millet," *Nineteenth-Century Art Worldwide* 13,

no. 1 (Spring 2014). http://www.19thcartworldwide.org/index.php/spring14/ribner-on-a-repainting-by-millet. A reproduction of a German prototype for French representations of the subject, the Dusseldorf painter Eduard Bendemann's despondent *The Captive Jews in Babylon* (1832; Cologne, Wallraf-Richartz Museum and Fondation Corboud) is included in the first volume of the Romantic era's authoritative French publication on contemporary German art, Comte Athanse Raczynski, *Histoire de l'art moderne en Allemagne*, 3 vols. (Paris: J. Renouard, 1836–41). For that painting's celebrity, and for a smaller version (ca. 1832) in a private collection, see Cordula Grewe, *The Nazarenes: Romantic Avant-Garde and the Art of the Concept* (University Park: Penn State University Press, 2015), 265–71, 285–7.

56 Sérullaz et al., *Dessins d'Eugène Delacroix*, vol. 1, no. 298 (RF 4774).

57 Lee Johnson, *The Paintings of Eugène Delacroix: A Critical Catalogue,* vol. 3: *1832–1863, Movable Pictures and Private Decorations* (Oxford: Clarendon Press, 1986), no. 334. For the London painting, see also Sébastien Allard and Côme Fabre, "Delacroix, l'art et la matière," in Sébastien Allard et al., *Delacroix* (Paris: Musée du Louvre, in association with Éditions Hazan, Paris, 2018): 301–4; the catalog entry by Patrick Noon, in Patrick Noon and Christopher Riopelle, *Delacroix and the Rise of Modern Art* (London: National Gallery and Minneapolis: Minneapolis Institute of Art, in association with Yale University Press, 2015), no. 56; and the catalog entry by Vincent Pomarède, in Arlette Sérullaz et al., *Delacroix: The Late Work* (Paris: Galeries Nationales du Grand Palais and Philadelphia: Philadelphia Museum of Art, in association with Thames and Hudson, New York, 1998), no. 95.

58 For this point, see Henri Loyrette, "Delacroix's *Ovid in Exile*," *Burlington Magazine* 137, no. 1111 (October 1995): 682–3.

59 "This is the worst possible fate: not just to be forced out of Rome, but to have to live among barbarians.... Nothing could be more alien to me than the cold of this place, or the hostile tribes, or the sea which freezes over.... While the Caesars rule Rome, a man of Latin blood must never be the prisoner of savages." *Tristia* 1, reprinted in *The Oxford Book of Exile*, ed. John Simpson (Oxford: Oxford University Press, 1995), 7–8.

60 See O'Brien, *Exiled in Modernity*, 1–6.

61 I do not share Maurice Sérullaz's negative view of Ovid's predicament, as represented in the painting: "Small in size, the characters appear lost in the arid mountains of this desolate region. The prostrate attitude of the poet, lying on the ground, translates his despair ...." *Eugène Delacroix* (New York: Harry N. Abrams, [1971], 156.

62 For Delacroix's critical fortunes, see Catherine Méneux, "Delacroix face à la critique," in Allard et al., *Delacroix,* 347–55.

63 See the catalog entry by Loyrette, in Gary Tinterow and Henri Loyrette, *Origins of Impressionism* (New York: Metropolitan Museum of Art, in association with Harry N. Abrams, New York, 1994), no. 69.

64 "Certes je n'essayerai pas de traduire avec ma plume la volupté si triste qui s'exhale de ce verdoyant *exil*.... Tout ce qu'il y a dans Ovide de délicatesse et de fertilité a passé dans la peinture de Delacroix; et, comme l'exil a donné au brillant poète la tristesse qui lui manquait, la mélancolie a revêtu de son vernis enchanteur le plantureux paysage du peintre. Il m'est impossible de dire: Tel tableau de Delacroix est le meilleur de ses tableaux ... mais on peut dire qu'*Ovide chez les Scythes* est une de ces étonnantes oeuvres comme Delacroix seul sait les concevoir et les peindre." Charles Baudelaire, "Salon de 1859," in *Critique d'art, suivi de Critique musicale*, ed. Claude Pichois, int. Claire Brunet (Paris: Gallimard, 1992), 296 (emphasis in original).

65 What follows supplements my "Wandering in the Wilderness under Louis-Philippe," in *Moving Forward, Holding Fast: The Dynamics of Nineteenth-Century French Culture*, ed. Barbara T. Cooper and Mary Donaldson-Evans, 131–50 (Amsterdam: Rodopi, 1997).

66 *The New English Bible with the Apocrypha*, 21.

67 "Que votre exemple, Agar, serve à jamais de leçon; qu'il corrige les murmures des Mortels insensés; & qu'il apprenne que Dieu sait récompenser la patience, la soumission, le courage & la vertu" (spelling modernized). Comtesse Stéphanie-Félicité de Genlis, *Agar dans le désert, Comédie en prose & en un acte,* in *Théâtre à l'usage des jeunes personnes*, vol. 1 (Paris: Panckoucke, 1779), 28.

68 For Staël's theater productions of the 1805–06 season, including *Agar dans le désert*, see Winock, *Madame de Staël*, 267–8.

69 "O mon Dieu! protégez Ismaël! Si je fus trop fière de vos dons dans les jours de ma prospérité ... punissez-moi; mais épargnez ce pauvre enfant, le plus simple, le plus doux, le plus innocent de tous les êtres; faites-lui respirer cet air suave, cet air bienfaisant que vous accordez en Égypte, aux habitants de ma patrie. Ce ciel brûlant, ce ciel d'airain n'est pas l'image de votre bonté paternelle." *Agar dans le désert, Scène lyrique composée en 1806*, in *Oeuvres posthumes de Madame la baronne de Staël-Holstein, Précédees d'une Notice sur son caractère et ses écrits* (Paris, 1861, reprint, Geneva: Slatkine, 1967), 433–4.

70 See Gary Tinterow, Michael Pantazzi, and Vincent Pomarède, *Corot* (New York: Metropolitan Museum of Art, in association with Harry N. Abrams, New York, 1996), no. 61. See also Charles Sterling and Margaretta M. Salinger, *French Paintings, A Catalogue of the Collection of the Metropolitan Museum of Art*, vol. 2: *XIX Century* (New York: Metropolitan Museum of Art, in association with New York Graphic Society, Greenwich, CT, 1966), 48–50.

71 Théophile Gautier, "Beaux-Arts, Overture du Salon," *La Presse* (1 March 1837).

72 "Salon de 1835, 3rd article, "Les Peintres et les poètes," *L'Artiste* 9 (1835), 85–90, quoted in Tinterow, et al., *Corot*, no. 61.

73 For this study (*Fontainebleau: Black Oaks at Bas-Bréau*, ca. 1832–3, New York, Metropolitan Museum of Art), see Tinterow et al., *Corot*, no. 35.

74 Charles Lenormant, "L'École française en 1835," in Charles Lenormant, *Beaux-Arts et voyages, Précédés d'une letter par M. Guizot* (Paris: Michel-Lévy frères, 1861), 1:114, quoted in Tinterow et al., *Corot*, no. 61.

75 See Susan Greenberg, "Reforming *paysage historique:* Corot and the Generation of 1830," *Art History* 27, no. 3 (June 2004), 421–3.

76 Georges Monnet, *Musée de Guéret: Catalogue descriptive des tableaux* (Guéret: P. Amiault, 1889), 18.

77 For this painting and its rivals, see Philippe Grunchec, *Le Grand Prix de peinture: Les Concours des Prix de Rome de 1797 à 1863*, pref. Jacques Thuillier (Paris: École nationale supérieure des Beaux-Arts, 1983), 222–5.

78 "And remember in the Book Ishmael: Surely he was true to the promise, and he was a messenger, a prophet. He commanded his people with the prayer and the alms, and he was pleasing before his Lord." Sūra 19: 54–5. *The Qur'ān: A New Annotated Translation*, trans. and ed. A.J. Droge (Sheffield Equinox, 2013), 196. A play by the academician Népomucène-Louis Lemercier (1771–1840), written in 1801 and performed at the Odéon in 1818, was titled *Agar et Ismaël, ou L'Origine du peuple arabe, Scène orientale en vers, Représentée au Théâtre de l'Odéon, le 23 janvier 1818* (Paris: Nepveu, 1818). It was inspired, according to Lemercier, by the return of the French army from Egypt.

79 For this painting, see *Horace Vernet (1789–1863)* (Rome: Académie de France à Rome, 1980), no. 68. Vernet defended his theory in *Opinion sur certains rapports qui existent entre le costume des anciens Hébreux et celui des Arabes modernes (Lu à l'Académie en 1847)* (Paris: Bonaventure et Ducessois, 1856); and in "Des anciens Hébreux et des Arabes modernes," *L'Artiste*, 5th ser. 1 (15 August 1848): 232–5. For Vernet's paintings of the conquest of North Africa, see Katie Hornstein, *Picturing War in France, 1792–1856* (New Haven, CT: Yale University Press, 2017), 109–25. For Delacroix's observation that "Rome n'est plus dans Rome" ("Rome is no longer to be found in Rome") in a letter to the critic Auguste Jal (4 June 1832), see Todd Porterfield, *The Allure of Empire: Art in the Service of French Imperialism, 1789–1836* (Princeton, NJ: Princeton University Press, 1998), 135–7 and n. 50. For a nuanced discussion of Delacroix's view of North Africa that brings salience to the fact that his Orientalism was neither static nor monolithic, see the introduction by Michèle Hannoosh to *Eugène Delacroix, Journey to the Maghreb and Andalusia, 1832: The Travel Notebooks and Other Writings*, trans. Michèle Hannoosh (University Park: Penn State University Press, 2019), 1–8.

80 See Prosper Mérimée, "Salon de 1839," *Revue des deux mondes,* 4th ser. 18 (1 April 1839): 95.

81 See Fred Leeman and Hanna Pennock, with contributions by Saskia de Bodt and Ronald de Leeuw, *Museum Mesdag: Catalogue of Paintings and Drawings* (Amsterdam: Van

Gogh Museum, in association with Uitgeverij Waanders, Zwolle, 1996), no. 262; and Bruce Laughton, "Millet's *Hagar and Ishmael*," *Burlington Magazine* 121, no. 920 (November 1979): 705–11. In 1886, the American painter Will H. Low attested that he was told by Millet's son François that his father had painted over the image, and that his brother Charles had removed the overpainting in 1885. Laughton includes an evaluation (1977) by Dr. V. R. Mehra, Chief Conservator at the Central Research Laboratory for Objects of Art and Science, Amsterdam, which substantiates Low's account. For an updated conservation report reflecting a 2002 restoration (which indicates that the original painting remained remarkably intact despite Charles Millet's removal of the overpainting), see René Boitelle, Marion Bosc, and Klaas-Jan van den Berg, "Reflections on J.-F. Millet's *Agar et Ismaël*: Technical Analyses of an Unfinished Painting," *Art Matters: Netherlands Technical Studies in Art* 2 (2005): 7–21.

82 See T.J. Clark, *The Absolute Bourgeois: Artists and Politics in France 1848–1851* (Greenwich, CT: New York Graphic Society, 1973), 77.

83 Quoted from Alfred Sensier, *La Vie et l'oeuvre de J.-F. Millet* (Paris, 1881), 12, in Leeman et al., *Museum Mesdag*, 336. For the biographical significance of the subject, see also Laughton, "Millet's *Hagar and Ishmael*," which connects it to the artist's unhappiness at being compelled to produce salable nudes in order to support his partner, Catherine Lemaire, and their three children.

84 For Millet's *Captivity of the Jews in Babylon*, later painted over with a *Young Shepherdess* (ca. 1870–73; Boston, Museum of Fine Arts) and barely visible in an X-ray photograph, see my "On a Repainting."

85 See Robert L. Herbert, *Jean-François Millet* (London: Arts Council of Great Britain, 1976), no. 28. In "French Landscape at the Margins of Survival," a virtual lecture sponsored by the NYU Alumni Association and the Institute of Fine Arts (10 August 2020), Thomas Crow aptly associated a similar painting by Millet, *Retreat from the Storm*, (ca. 1846, New York, Metropolitan Museum of Art)—as well as Corot's painting of the desperate Hagar and Ishmael in the same collection—with the dispossession of the French rural population.

86 For providing access to an image of this painting, and for granting reproduction rights, I am grateful to Juliette Roy of the Centre de documentation-bibliothèque, Musée des Beaux-Arts et d'Archéologie, Besançon.

87 The commission, from the Ministry of the Interior (20 June 1848) for 1000 francs was for a painting, the subject and *esquisse* of which were to be submitted for approval. In a letter (27 March 1849), the artist submitted the subject as *Les Exilés*, together with a passage from Malfilâtre. Following the passage, Richard-Cavaro indicates: "Effet sombre. Demandé." ("Somber effect. Requested"). F^{21} 53, dossier 12, Paris, Archives Nationales (underscored in original). The annotation perhaps indicates that this aspect of the painting had been requested by the ministry headed by Ledru-Rollin.

88 Following Greek numbering, Malfilâtre refers to the Psalm as 136. For the text (1758), see "Imitation du Psaume 136: *Super flumina Babylonis*," in Jacques-Charles-Louis Clinchamps de Malfilâtre, *Oeuvres de Malfilâtre*, ed. M. L.*** (Paris: Jehenne, 1825), 205–8.

89 "Composition d'un genre sévère; figures demi-nature, bien drapés et d'un bon goût de dessin; couleur triste, analogue au sujet; touche pure et moelleuse; expressions beaucoup plus touchantes que si l'auteur avait voulu exagérer la douleur de ces nobles et généreux bannis." Fabien Pillet, "Exposition de 1849 au palais des Tuileries," *Le Moniteur universel* (7 August 1849).

90 Byron's drama was translated, with a lengthy refutation, by a visionary playwright taken with mysticism, the occult, and ancient languages and cosmogonies, Antoine Fabre d'Olivet (1768–1825). See Fabre d'Olivet, *Caïn, mystère dramatique en trois actes de Lord Byron, Traduit en vers français et réfutê dans une suite de remarques philosophiques et critique. Précédé d'une lettre addressee à Lord Byron, sur les motifs et le but de cet ouvrage* (Paris: Servier, 1823). At the Salon of 1812, Pierre-Félix Trézel (1782–1855) exhibited a life-sized, moon-lit painting of the exiled Cain family based on *Der Tod Abels* (*The Death of Abel*, 1758) by the Swiss poet Solomon Gessner (1730–88). Gessner's sentimental pastoral enjoyed great popularity in both England (through the translation by Mary Collyer, 1761) and France (where it was adapted to the stage by Gabriel-Marie

Legouvé, 1764–1812 in 1792). The unlocated painting is reproduced and described in C.P. Landon, *Annales du Musée et de l'école moderne des beaux-arts. Salon de 1812. Recueil de pieces choisies parmi les ouvrages de peinture et de sculpture exposés au Louvre le premier novembre 1812* (Paris: Chaignieau ainé, 1812), 2: 39 and plate 25.

91 Muriel Mantopoulos of the Centre de documentation, Musée des Beaux-Arts, Nancy kindly sent documentation regarding the bronze cast and permitted reproduction of a photograph of the work provided by the museum. The original of 1820 is in the École nationale supérieure des Beaux-Arts, Paris.

92 Representation of the Cain narrative as melodrama had a precedent in a large (270 × 370 cm) painting of *Cain after the Murder of Abel* by Jean-Baptiste Paulin Guérin (1783–1855) exhibited in the Salon of 1812 and acquired by the State for the Musée du Luxembourg (Toulon, Musée des Beaux-Arts, with a small, autograph copy in Rochefort-sur-Mer, Musées municipaux de Rochefort). I am grateful to Sébastien Leboucher, documentarian and registrar of the Musées municipaux de Rochefort, for providing a photograph of the copy (46 × 55.7 cm). In the same histrionic register is a large painting of Cain in an agitated, strenuous pose executed in Rome by Jean-Victor Schnetz (1817; Rome, Accademia di San Luca), reproduced in Hugh Honour, *Romanticism* (New York: Harper & Row, 1979), 375.

93 For Étex and *Cain and His Race Accursed of God*, see the catalog entry by Stéphanie Deschamps-Tan, in *Musée des Beaux-Arts de Lyon. Sculptures du XVIIe au XXe siècle* (Lyon: Musée des Beaux-Arts, in association with Somogy éditons d'art, Paris, 2017), no. 73. I am grateful to Gérard Bruyère, Chargé du Service de la Documentation, Musée des Beaux-Arts de Lyon, for bringing this publication to my attention and for providing information about the work. See also the catalog entries by Peter Fusco, in idem and H.W. Janson, *The Romantics to Rodin: French Nineteenth-Century Sculpture from North American Collections* (Los Angeles, CA: Los Angeles County Museum of Art, in association with George Braziller, New York, 1980), nos. 124 and 125. For the circumstances surrounding its creation, the development of the composition, and Étex's sources, see Antoinette Le Normand-Romain, "Le Séjour d'Étex à Rome en 1831–1832: Un carnet de dessins inédit," *Bulletin de la Société de l'Histoire de l'Art français* (1981): 175–88. For Étex's sources, see also Mechthild Schneider, " 'Kain und seine von Gott verfluchte Rasse,' Eine monumentale Gruppe von Antoine Etex im Salon von 1833," *Bruckmanns Pantheon* 53 (1995): 108–15.

94 See Le Normand-Romain, "Le séjour d'Étex à Rome," 181.

95 See Antoine Étex, *Souvenirs d'un artiste* (Paris: E. Dentu, 1878), 119–20.

96 G. Laviron and B. Galbacio, *Le Salon de 1833* (Paris: Abel Ledoux, 1833), 329–30.

97 Théophile Gautier, "Salon de 1833." *La France littéraire* 6 (1833), 141.

98 "Beaux-Arts. Salon de 1833 ... Sculpture," *L'Artiste* 1st series 5 (1833): 143.

99 Étex, *Souvenirs d'un artiste*, 183.

100 For the Palais-Bourbon reliefs, the Madeleine doors, and their contribution to the official glorification of law under the July Monarchy, see my *Broken Tablets*, chap. 4. The doors are also discussed in Anne Pingeot et al., *La Sculpture française au XIXe siècle* (Paris: Galeries nationales du Grand Palais and Éditions de la Réunion des musées nationaux, 1986), 202–4.

101 Victor Hugo, *"La Conscience" in La Légende des siècles*, ed. P. Berret (Paris: Hachette, 1920), 1: 51.

102 For the poet's guilt regarding the death of Léopoldine, see the editor's commentary, in Victor Hugo, *Les Contemplations*, ed. Pierre Albouy, pref. Léon-Paul Fargue (Paris: Gallimard, 1973), 15; and Bradley Stephens, *Victor Hugo* (London: Reaktion Books, 2019), 89–91.

103 For the drawing, see the commentary by Pierre Georgel, in *La Gloire de Victor Hugo*, ed. Pierre Georgel (Paris: Éditions de la Réunion des musées nationaux, 1985), 86. For the artist, see Valérie Sueur, *François Chifflart, graveur et illustrateur* (Paris: Éditions de la Réunion des musées nationaux, 1993); and Philippe-Gérard Chabert and Pierre Georgel, *François-Nicolas Chifflart 1825–1901* (Saint-Omer: Musée de l'hôtel Sandelin, 1972). A wood engraving by Joliet after Chifflart's drawing illustrates an edition of *La Légende des siècles* (Paris: Eugène Hugues, 1885). The likeness is based on a portrait (Paris, Musée

Maisons Victor-Hugo, exhibited by Chifflart in the Salon of 1868), for which the poet sat during the artist's trip to Guernsey (27 January–10 February 1868). The resemblance to Jacquot's Prix de Rome sculpture of 1820 is not fortuitous; Chifflart had ample opportunity to view it while a student at the École des Beaux-Arts, where he won the Prix de Rome in 1851.

104 In the Salon of 1880, Fernand A. Cormon (pseudonym of Fernand Piestre, 1845–1924) exhibited to acclaim a huge painting (384 × 700 cm) inspired by "La Conscience," quoted in the *livret*. It represents Cain, in advanced age, leading his progeny across a barren waste (Paris, Musée d'Orsay). See the catalog entry by Geneviève Lacambre, in *La Gloire de Victor Hugo*, ed. Georgel, no. 892, pp. 625–7.

105 I am grateful to Alexandrine Achille of the Maison de Victor Hugo, Paris for assistance in obtaining reproductions of this photograph and Chifflart's drawing, *Conscience* (Figure 3.21). The photograph is included in the website https://www.parismuseescollections.paris.fr/fr/maison-de-victor-hugo/oeuvres/victor-hugo-sur-le-rocher-des-proscrits#infos-principales, accessed 4 January 2021. For Charles' Jersey photographs of his father, see *La Gloire de Victor Hugo*, ed. Georgel, 106–7, 114, and 207; and *En collaboration avec le soleil: Victor Hugo, Photographies de l'exil*, ed. Françoise Heilbrun and Danielle Molinari (Paris: Musée d'Orsay and Maison de Victor Hugo, 1998), which includes a darker print (no. 116, reproduced p. 53, Paris, Musée d'Orsay) of the view featured here.

106 "Ce livre doit être lu comme on lirait le livre d'un mort.... Ma vie est la vôtre, votre vie est la mienne, vous vivez ce que je vis; la destinée est une. Prenez donc ce miroir, et regandez-vous-y. On se plaint quelquefois des écrivains qui dissent moi. Parlez-nous de nous, leur crie-t-on. Hélas! quand je vous parle de moi, je vous parle de vous. Comment ne le sentez-vous pas? Ah! insensé, qui crois que je ne suis pas toi!" *Les Contemplations*, 27–8.

107 See D.G. Charlton, "The French Romantic Movement," in ed. D.G. Charlton, *The French Romantics* (Cambridge: Cambridge University Press, 1984), 1: 27; and Peyre, *What is Romanticism?*, 113.

108 "J'aime la proscription, j'aime l'exil ... j'aime la pauvreté, j'aime l'adversité, j'aime tout ce que je souffre pour la liberté, pour la patrie et pour le droit; j'ai la conscience joyeuse; mais c'est toujours une chose douloureuse de marcher sur la terre etrangère." Victor Hugo. *Choses vues: Souvenirs, journaux, cahiers, 1849–1869,* ed. Hubert Juin (Paris: Gallimard, 1972), 221.

109 Ibid., 242.

110 "Je trouve de plus en plus l'exil bon. Il faut croire qu'à leur insu les exilés sont près de quelque soleil, car ils mûrissent vite. Depuis trois ans ... je me sens sur le vrai sommet de la vie, et je vois les linéaments réels de tout ce que les hommes appellent faits, histoire, événements, succès, catastrophes, machinisme énorme de la Providence. / Ne fût-ce qu'à ce point de vue, j'aurais à remercier M. Bonaparte qui m'a proscrit, et Dieu qui m'a élu. Je mourrai peut-être dans l'exil, mais je mourrai accru. / Tout est bien." Ibid., 287–8.

111 Maurice Z Shroder, *Icarus: The Image of the Artist in French Romanticism* (Cambridge, MA: Harvard University Press, 1961), 78.

112 Victor Hugo, "What Exile Is," in *Pendant L'Exil: 1853–1861* (Paris: J. Hetzel and Co., 1883), reprinted in *Altogether Elsewhere: Writers on Exile*, ed. Marc Robinson (New York: Harcourt Brace & Company, 1994), 80 (trans. Jeanine Herman).

113 Quoted in Stephens, *Victor Hugo*, 134.

114 For this painting, see *La Gloire de Victor Hugo*, ed. Georgel, no. 97, p. 114. For providing an image and reproduction rights, I am grateful to Carole Dufour, Chargée de la régie des oeuvres et de la photothèque, Service des sites culturels, Conseil départmental des Vosges. I also received assistance in this regard from Gaëlle Bigoni of the Service des Sites culturels. Monchablon was co-winner of the Prix de Rome competition of 1863, with *Joseph Revealing Himself to His Brothers* as subject. For this painting, see Grunchec, *Le Grand Prix de peinture*, 45 and 326–8.

115 For images of Hugo with crossed arms, see *La Gloire de Victor Hugo*, ed. Georgel, 113–5.

116 Victor Hugo, *Les Châtiments*, ed. René Journet (Paris: Gallimard, 1977), 266.

4 "He's Not Dead!"

Hero and Villain

According to a Parisian who knew everyone worth knowing—the novelist, playwright, painter, and salon hostess Virginie Ancelot (1792–1875)—Honoré de Balzac kept a statuette of Napoleon in his study. It was mounted on a little altar inscribed: "What he began by the sword, I will finish by the pen."[1] If true, this would not have been the sole instance in which the creator of *La Comédie humaine* associated literary genius with the emperor's military prowess. In 1830, Balzac (1799-1850) maintained that "Napoleon is as great a poet as Homer; he wrote poetry just as Homer waged battles."[2] Turning on both the outsized stature of Napoleon and a grandiose conception of his own vocation, the author's witty parallels occlude the sense of loss that constitutes a fertile legacy of a figure who loomed ever larger in the wake of his defeat, exile, and death.

Mythologizing of Napoleon as the embodiment of willful action began well before the coup d'état of 18 Brumaire (9 November 1799), when the young revolutionary general dispersed the Council of Five Hundred legislators by military drum and tossed the Constitution of Year Three into the dustbin of history. During the Italian campaign, Napoleon had focused on his public image with an audacity comparable to that displayed on the battlefield. In 1796, Antoine-Jean Gros sketched Bonaparte's features in preparation for a portrait that would show what was popularly believed to have been a dazzling episode in the recent expedition: General Bonaparte crossing the bridge at Arcole on 17 November 1796 (Figure 4.1).[3]

Calm in the midst of battle, the victor is lent dynamism by a twist of the neck that sets the three-quarter view of his handsome, lean features into counterpoint with a flag grasped in gloved hand. So restless was Bonaparte that Gros complained to his mother that,

> You couldn't even call the short time that he gives me a sitting. I don't have time to choose my colors; I am resigned to paint only the character of his features, and after that, to my best ability, to give it the look of a portrait.[4]

Haste abetted the nervous intensity with which Gros imbued his subject—an aspect muted in the final, full-length composition (Versailles, Musée national du Château) and its repetitions. Pleased with the finished portrait, Bonaparte financed a print reproduction (which sold well), handsomely rewarded the artist, and asked him to serve on the commission responsible for choosing and transporting to Paris art works plundered in the wake of French conquest. Like the painter's later Napoleonic propaganda

DOI: 10.4324/9781003184737-5

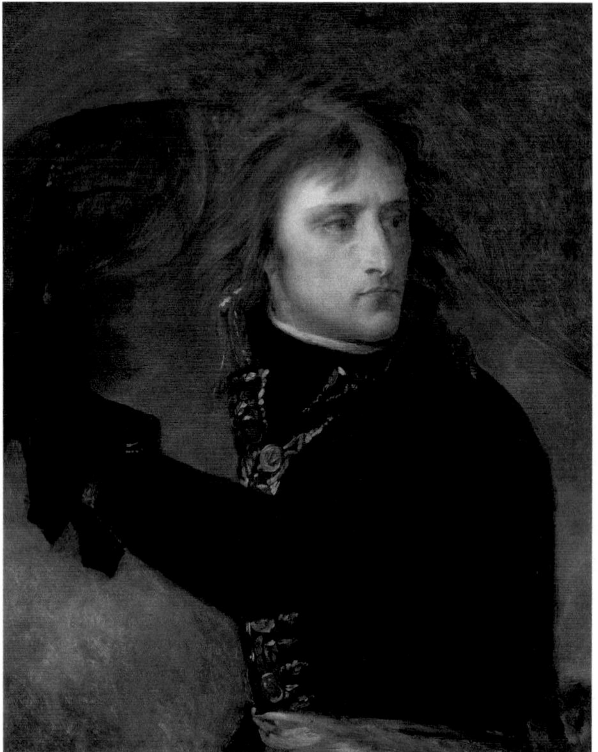

Figure 4.1 Antoine-Jean Gros, *Napoleon on the Bridge of Arcole,* 1796, oil on canvas, 73 × 59 cm. Paris, Musée du Louvre. Photo: Hérvé Lewandowski. © RMN-Grand Palais/Art Resource, NY.

machines, Gros's portrait of Bonaparte is a work of mythmaking. David O'Brien notes the extent to which the commemorated episode was fictive: attempting to lead a charge, the general actually halted before the bridge and fell into a ditch, from which he was pulled, covered in mud. That day's combat ended in stalemate, with two more days of fighting before the French traversed the bridge. Consigning these banal facts to oblivion, Gros persuasively glamorizes Bonaparte's lethal volition.

More than a half-century later, Étienne-Jean Delécluze, who entered David's studio after the elder Gros, recalled their teacher saying, "In short, my friends, this is a man to whom they would have raised altars in antiquity; yes, my friends; yes, my dear friends! Bonaparte is my hero!"[5] Delacroix, too, thought of ancient heroes when he considered Gros's mammoth *Napoleon on the Battlefield of Eylau* (Figure 4.2), in which the emperor strikes an attitude of clemency above the frozen dead and the reverent survivors of a savage winter battle.[6] Barely meriting designation as a French victory, the Battle of Eylau (7–8 February 1807) was horrifically costly to both sides, with as many as 30,000 French dead or wounded and more than 25,000 casualties among their adversaries (Russians, with Prussian support).[7] Boldly revising the historical record, Napoleon fostered the notion that it had been an imperial triumph.[8] So persuasive was the Napoleonic legend, that Delacroix—notwithstanding

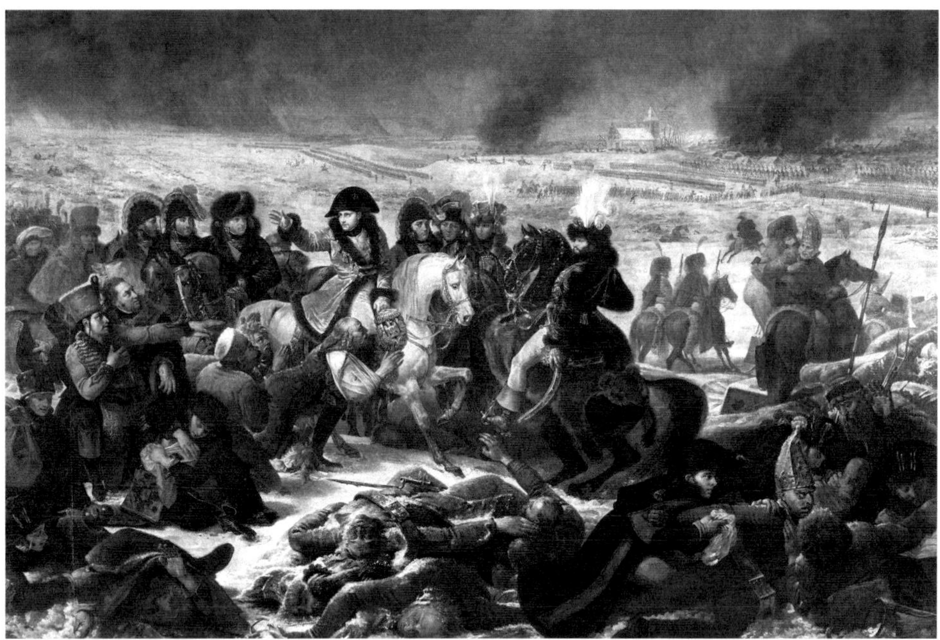

Figure 4.2 Antoine-Jean Gros, *Napoleon on the Battlefield of Eylau*, 1808, oil on canvas, 521 × 784 cm. Paris, Musée du Louvre. Photo: Franck Rau. © RMN-Grand Palais /Art Resource, NY.

his enthusiasm for Gros's canvas—did not think any artist equal to the challenge of conveying the emperor's heroism:

> This sinister painting, comprising a hundred paintings, seems to draw the eye and the mind from every side at once; yet this is but the setting for the sublime figure of Napoleon.... This is perhaps the most beautiful conception of the artist, and also the most magnificent, and surely the most exact, portrait that anyone has made of Napoleon.

Drawing a comparison in line with Balzac's, Delacroix asserts: "This personage, as poetic as Achilles, greater than all the heroes born of the imagination of poets, has not yet found his Homer, and Homer, himself, would have given up on painting him."[9] In Delacroix's case, admiration of Napoleon had family roots. His father supported Bonaparte's coup d'état and then loyally served the emperor as a prefect in Marseilles and Bordeaux. Of the artist's two brothers, the eldest, Charles-Henry (1779–1845), was wounded during the Russian campaign and imprisoned for two years; after he returned to France in 1814, Napoleon made him a general and a baron. Delacroix's other brother, Henry (1784–1807), was killed in the Battle of Friedland. The Musée Napoléon (as the Louvre was known in Delacroix's youth) served, even more than did the studio of Guérin, as the young artist's training ground; until Delacroix was 17, it was loaded with art looted from foreign collections. This trove, which Gros helped send to Paris, offered brilliant proof of the emperor's invincibility.

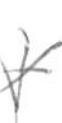

Aggrandizement of the despotic conqueror had a counterpart in a robust discourse of recrimination. Between the Egyptian campaign of 1797–98 and the emperor's death in 1821, more than 500 anti-Napoleonic pamphlets were published, concentrated in waves in 1814, 1815, and 1821.[10] Two famous indictments marking Napoleon's fall were as inflated as the imperial *bulletins* that trumpeted the triumphs of the Grande Armée. On 16 April 1814, ten days after the emperor abdicated, Byron anonymously published his "Ode to Napoleon Buonaparte," so quickly devoured that it reached its third edition by April 20. The opening sets Napoleon's former glory against his current ignominy: "Tis done—but yesterday a King! / And arm'd with Kings to strive—/ And now thou art a nameless thing / So abject—yet alive!" The poet is at once accusatory ("Thine evil deeds are writ in gore ....") and awestruck.[11] Such ambivalence also enters *Childe Harold's Pilgrimage* (1812–16), when the eponymous, world-weary protagonist visits Waterloo: "There sunk the greatest, nor the worst of men ... Extreme in all things!"[12] Captain Thomas Medwin (1788–1869), a poet who recorded his conversations with Byron, understandably remarked that he couldn't reconcile his friend's contradictory views of Napoleon. Byron's response: "Napoleon was his own antithesis (if I may say so). He was a glorious tyrant, after all."[13]

The British poet's "Ode to Napoleon Buonaparte" judges without invoking religion. In contrast, Chateaubriand's *De Buonaparte et des Bourbons* is couched in reference to divine will. Dated 30 March 1814, one day before the fall of Paris, this famous pamphlet was composed at night, behind bolted door, with two loaded pistols close at hand. Previously, the author had attributed to providence the first consul's reinstatement of French Catholicism; that was prior to the abduction and 21 March 1804 execution of Bonaparte's adversary, the Duc d' Enghien, which appalled Chateaubriand. In the emperor's defeat, the author again discerned the hand of God.[14] Claiming that Napoleon is not French (hence the Italian inflection, also signaled by Bryon, in "Buonaparte"), Chateaubriand attacked all aspects of the emperor-–even his military competence.[15] To that end he discharged a battery of hyperbole: "Born above all to destroy, Buonaparte bears evil in his breast naturally, as a mother carries her fruit, with joy and a sort of pride. He has a horror of the happiness of men..."[16] With Napoleon's foes closing in on the capital, Chateaubriand denounced the emperor's rule not only as a blight upon France, but as a disaster for Europe as a whole:

> The voice of the world declares you the guiltiest one who has ever appeared on the earth; for it was not upon barbaric peoples and degenerate nations that you spread so much ill; it was in the midst of civilization, in an enlightened century, that you wished to reign by the sword of Attila and the maxims of Nero.[17]

Reviving a vintage counter-Enlightenment discourse that attributed to providence the unleashing, and subsequent punishment, of the enemies of throne and altar, Chateaubriand was also mimicking recent English and royalist anti-Napoleonic publications.[18]

Indelible Memories

Having committed enormities, the emperor left to the brothers of Louis XVI a heritage too enormous to expunge. As prudence called for assimilation and alteration, the restored monarchy put a Bourbon stamp on some salient Napoleonic symbols. The order of the Legion of Honor, established by Napoleon, was maintained as a mark of distinction, whether military or civilian. At the same time, the medal was now adorned with the head of Henri IV, not that of Bonaparte; and the eagle on the medal's reverse was replaced by a trio of fleurs-de-lys. Comparable changes were made to the throne reserved for the emperor on official visits to the Palais-Bourbon to intimidate the Corps législatif. Presided over by Chateaubriand's mentor, Louis de Fontanes, it was nicknamed the "assembly of mutes," as its members were forbidden to discuss the laws on which they voted. Designed in 1804–05 by the same architect, Bernard Poyet, who oversaw the removal of the kings of Judah from the façade of Notre-Dame, and fashioned in 1805 by the master furniture maker François-Honoré-Georges Jacob-Desmalter (1770–1841), Napoleon's throne was as augustly suited to the new Caesar as the Palais-Bourbon's columnar Seine façade (1806–10), also designed by Poyet.

After the emperor's fall, the throne was refurbished for Louis XVIII (Figure 4.3).[19] A letter N, encircled by the beribboned laurel wreath framing the sitter's head, was deleted; flanking eagles were replaced by plump finials; and the crown at the summit was relieved of its imperial cross. Indelible reminders, however, resisted erasure. Fierce, leonine legs that once flanked the commander of the Grande Armée mocked the rotund monarch who had fled north in 1815 when the emperor suddenly returned from exile. And the throne's upholstery (embroidered by Augustin-François-André Picot), perhaps regarded as too richly wrought to discard, is replete with imperial motifs: the seat cushion features stylized eagles, and the backrest is adorned with twin coronation scepters superimposed on scales emblematic of the Code Napoléon.

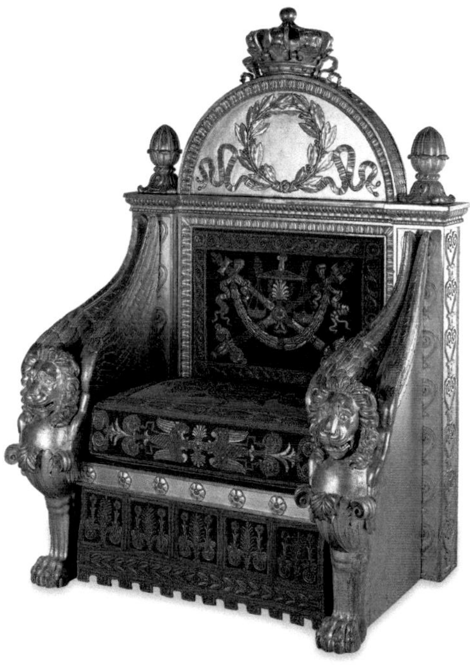

Figure 4.3 Bernard Poyet (design), François-Honoré-Georges Jacob-Desmalter (woodwork), and Augustin-François-André Picot (embroidery), Throne of Napoleon I for the Corps législatif, 1804–05, gilded wood, velvet, and silver embroidery, 160 × 110 × 82 cm. Paris, Les Arts Décoratifs, Musée des Arts décoratifs. Photo: © Paris, Les Arts décoratifs/Jean Tholance.

A more public remodeling was visited upon the column Napoleon had erected in the place Vendôme.[20] Cast from captured enemy cannon and topped by a sculpture of Napoleon in Roman imperial guise by Antoine-Denis Chaudet (1763–1810), this imitation of Trajan's Column was begun in 1806 and inaugurated in 1810 in commemoration of the victory at Austerlitz. In 1814, the Bourbon dynasty's fleur-de-lys-emblazoned white flag usurped the imperial effigy's place. Four years later, in accord with the political imperative that guided the revision of the Legion of Honor medal, Chaudet's emperor was melted to provide bronze for François Lemot's equestrian statue of Henri IV on the Pont Neuf (1818), which replaced the seventeenth-century original destroyed during the Revolution.[21] The Bourbons also recycled painters who had propagandized on behalf of the emperor. David's exile in Brussels following the collapse of the Empire was inevitable, given that, as a member of the Convention, he had voted for the death of Louis XVI, but his pupils were put to work by the brothers of the guillotined monarch. François Gérard, for example, whose *Battle of Austerlitz* won accolades at the Salon of 1810, painted the coronation of Charles X, and that reactionary king made Gros a baron in recognition of service to the restored monarchy.

Other, more recalcitrant, reminders of the recent past could be encountered following Napoleon's fall, disturbing the public silence that, as Satish Padiyar indicates, accompanied the twilight of the Empire and the advent of the Bourbon Restoration.[22] That royal regime saw a number of severely punished conspiracies. The period 1820–23 was the heyday of subversive activity by the Carbonari, a motley coalition of dissidents united in their hatred of the monarchy.[23] Organized plots were not the sole source of threat. The most spectacular act of violence against the restored dynasty was the work of a lone actor, Louis Pierre Louvel (1783–1820), a fanatical Napoleonic loyalist employed in the royal stables, who fatally stabbed the Duc de Berry (b. 1778), son of the heir to the throne, in 1820.[24] Sudhir Hazareesingh documents myriad manifestations of a nationwide current of hostility toward the Bourbons and attachment to Napoleon that found expression in subversive songs and placards, rumors that the emperor had returned from exile (or that the announcement of his death was premature), and a flood of Napoleonic knickknacks, coins, and busts.[25]

Among the purveyors of inflammatory rumors and objects were former imperial officers placed on inactive duty at half-pay when the army was demobilized following the emperor's abdication in 1814.[26] Left in uncertainty as to when and if they would be called to active duty, this thread-bare cohort (known as the *demi-solde*) was subject to restrictions spared veterans on pension, who enjoyed financial security and respect under the Bourbons, regardless of whether they had served the Revolution or Napoleon. Required to live in the *département* in which they had enrolled, prohibited from marrying unless enriched by a dowry of 12,000 francs, and unable, without official permission, to supplement their income with non-agricultural work, the *demi-solde* were subject to surveillance by provincial prefects on the lookout for political troublemakers. Their lot painfully contrasted with that of the lavishly funded Royal Military Household, which comprised around 6000 Swiss Guards and former émigrés. Vilified by ultra-royalists after Waterloo, the *demi-solde* received sympathy from liberals allied with Bonapartists and Republicans in opposition to the regime.[27] These discontents took pleasure in caricatures that ridiculed the opportunism and incompetence of aged aristocrats in uniform.[28]

Notwithstanding royalist alarm, the vast majority of the *demi-solde* were apolitical and sought only social reintegration; pervasive devotion to the glories of the Empire among veterans was largely a post-1830 phenomenon.[29] Of the total band of *demi-solde* (which receded from around 20,000 in 1815–16 to just over 3000 in 1828), only about 500–1000 seem to have been committed Bonapartists. Yet from the outset, this fact was upstaged in the public imaginary by the legend of the disaffected *demi-solde* devoted to the memory of the emperor and intoxicated with the elegiac patriotism made into song by Pierre-Jean de Béranger, generally referred to as the "national poet" from 1823 on. With airs such as "The Old Flag" ("Le Vieux Drapeau," 1820), in which an imperial veteran treasures a *tricolore* kept under his mattress like a holy relic (prefiguring Julien Sorel of Stendhal's *Le Rouge et le noir*, who stashes a portrait of Napoleon in his mattress), Béranger stirred sentiment that would be energized by the reinstatement of blue, white, and red for the national flag in 1830.

If the anxiety of the authorities was disproportionate to the numerical strength of dissident decommissioned soldiers, there were, indeed, *demi-solde* steadfastly loyal to the emperor and aflame with anti-Bourbon resentment. Lieutenant-Colonel Louis Bro (1781–1844), a cavalry veteran of Eylau, Moscow, and Waterloo was one such. Bro's truculence was shared by fellow members of the "Nouvelle Athènes" circle of the rue des Martyrs, which included Horace Vernet.[30] Twice tried and imprisoned (1821 and 1828) for songs conveying anti-clericalism and contempt for the crown, Béranger dropped by regularly. Like Bro, Vernet was a true believer in the cult of Napoleon. Nostalgic patriotism informs *La Barrière de Clichy, Defense of Paris on 30 March 1814* (Figure 4.4), which represents the occasion of the artist's sole experience

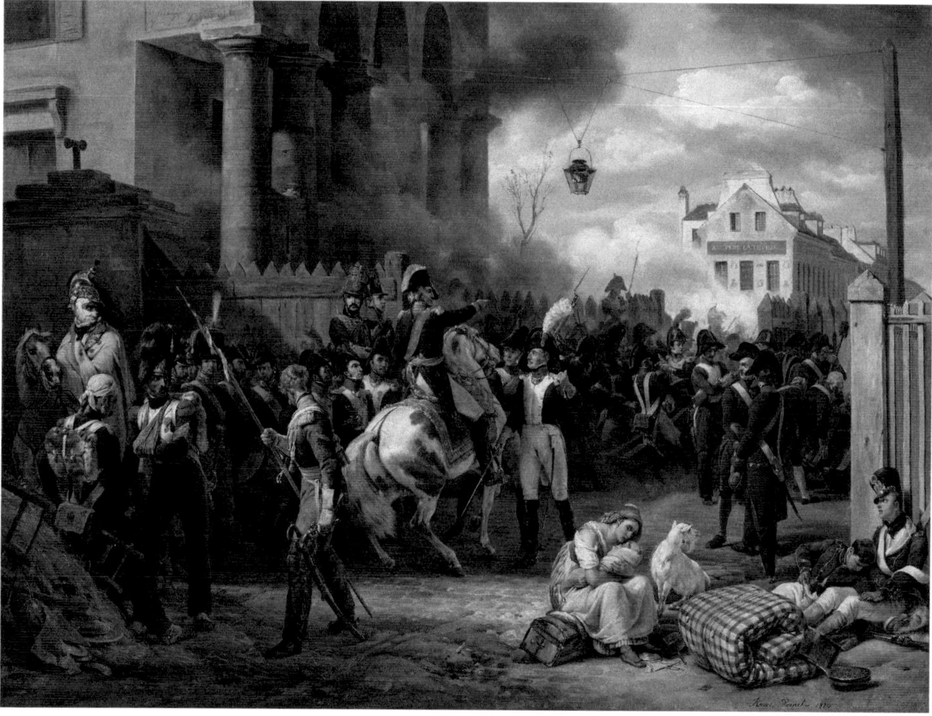

Figure 4.4 Horace Vernet, *The Barrière de Clichy, Defense of Paris on 30 March 1814*, 1820, oil on canvas, 97.5 × 130.5 cm. Paris, Musée du Louvre. Photo: Michel Urtado. © RMN-Grand Palais/Art Resource, NY.

under fire.[31] In March 1814, during the defense of Paris, Vernet joined the National Guard under the command of the 60-year-old Marshal Bon-Adrien Jeannot de Moncey (1754–1842). Responsible for guarding the northern and northeast frontiers of the capital, Moncey and his troops resisted the invaders until the armistice. The defenders also included the lithographer Nicolas-Toussaint Charlet (1792–1845), disabled veterans, and the artist's friend who commissioned the painting, the former imperial goldsmith Jean-Baptiste-Claude Odiot (1763–1850).[32] The middle-brow appeal of *La Barrière de Clichy* is enhanced by a descriptive specificity that would be at home in a genre piece—whether in the detailed rendition of Claude-Nicolas Ledoux's Neoclassical Clichy toll house or in the rolled mattress beside a vulnerable woman with infant. This touching image of the solidarity of common folk in the face of Napoleon's advancing foes carried an unsettling political charge for a regime indebted to France's conquerors. Consequently, along with Vernet's painting of the first victory (1792) of the revolutionary army, *The Battle of Jemappes*, *La Barrière de Clichy* was refused entry to the Salon of 1822. The prolific artist countered this politically motivated decision with a private studio exhibition that, in addition to the two proscribed canvases, comprised some 43 other works, including prints and drawings.[33]

Vernet pulled out the stops of bellicose nostalgia in another work included in that 1822 studio exhibition, *The Soldier Plowman* (*Le Soldat Laboureur*, Figure 4.5),

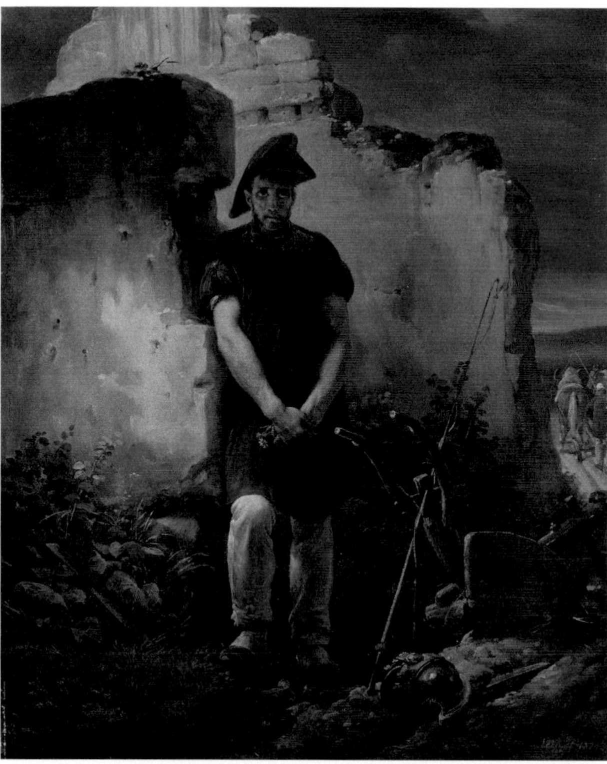

Figure 4.5 Horace Vernet, *Peace and War*, or *The Soldier Plowman* (*Le Soldat Laboureur*), 1820, oil on canvas, 55 × 45.8 cm. London, Wallace Collection. Photo credit: By kind permission of the Trustees of the Wallace Collection, London/Art Resource, NY.

also known as *Peace and War*. Vernet invites the viewer to share the pain of a former soldier of the Grande Armée, whose plow has unearthed an imperial helmet and a medal of the Legion of Honor amid ruins on the battlefield of Waterloo. Clutching the medal, he strikes an attitude of woeful retrospection redolent of longing not only for past military glory, but also for better times; the period between the Consulate and 1810--a golden age of worker's conditions--contrasted with the sharp economic decline between 1817 and 1820. As Nina Athanassoglou-Kallmyer demonstrates, the motif (first represented in a lost painting of 1818 by one Pierre-Roch Vigneron), was ubiquitous under the Restoration. The subject of prints, plays, bibelots, wallpaper designs, poems, ballads, and a novel, the image of the pacific and civic-minded veteran plowman was proffered by liberals (such as the future king, Louis-Philippe, who commissioned Vernet's painting) to counter the specter haunting the reactionaries—the resentful, plotting *demi-solde*.[34]

Vernet's friend (and Bro's tenant), Théodore Géricault (1791–1824), also lived on the rue des Martyrs. Géricault's work of the late 'teens reflects close contact with Vernet's dissident circle.[35] In Géricault's lithograph, *The Swiss Guard at the Louvre* (Figure 4.6), we witness a tense confrontation recently reported in the liberal opposition paper *Le Constitutionnel* (6 June 1819): a peg-legged veteran defiantly shows his Legion of Honor medal to a Swiss Guard (who challenges his passage into the Louvre's courtyard) while commanding the sentry to present arms.[36] An array of hats

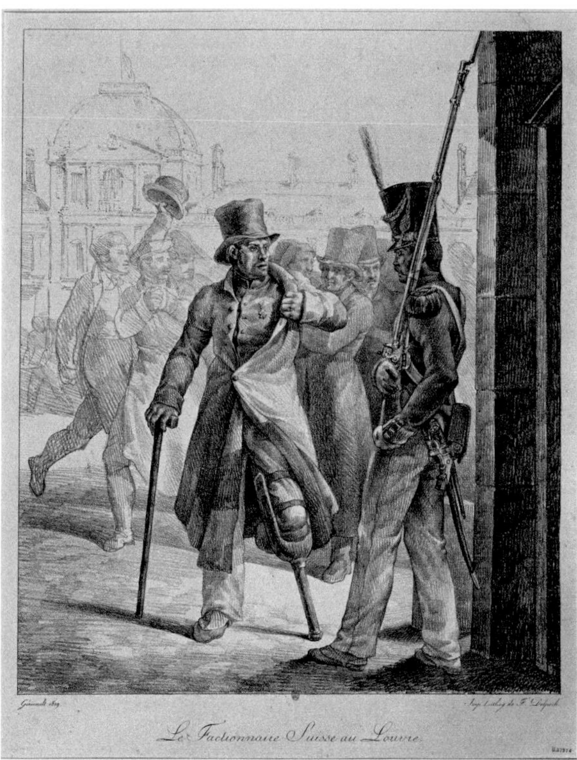

Figure 4.6 Théodore Géricault, *The Swiss Guard at the Louvre*, 1819, lithograph, 39.3 × 32.7 cm. Paris, Bibliothèque nationale de France. Photo: BnF.

emblematizes the politics at stake. In contrast to the guard's shako, the veteran wears a tall *bolivar,* which along with frock coat (*redingote*), were the characteristic attire of the *demi-solde.* To the right another man (apparently a *demi-solde*), also sporting a *bolivar,* observes with satisfaction, as the top-hatted bourgeois beside him glowers. In the left middle ground, a young man (whose stride counters the amputee's stance) holds aloft a civilian homburg, cheering the veteran's audacity.

Gericault's use of the print medium at this time for a Napoleonic subject registers influence from the seasoned lithographer Vernet, who provided the lightly rendered architectural background. Devoid of heroism, Géricault's image lacks the overtly partisan sentimentality of Vernet's *Barriére de Clichy* and *Solder Plowman.* Nor does it attempt to massage bruised pride in the manner of contemporary lithographs by Charlet representing imperial veterans in peacetime.[37] Instead, *The Swiss Guard at the Louvre* conveys curiosity—at once compassionate and detached—that anticipates Géricault's use of the medium for reportage on the street life of common people in a print series of 1821 inspired by his sojourn in London (1820–21). Even this most politically charged of Géricault's Napoleonic subjects makes no facile appeal to patriotic resentment.[38] Drawn to themes associated with liberalism and Bonapartism, the artist knowingly chose a subject embarrassing to the Bourbon regime when he painted *The Raft of the Medusa.* Yet the convictions informing Géricault's representation of a casualty of war fallen on hard times can only be inferred. And his record of military service suggests opportunism. If, by the late 'teens, Géricault sympathized with the liberal opposition, he contributed little to the imperial military effort nostalgically celebrated by the Vernet circle. On the contrary; in 1811, Géricault had been spared conscription by his affluent, royalist father's payment for a (subsequently slain) replacement. It was not until July 1814, following Napoleon's April abdication and the return of the royal family, that Géricault put on a uniform. He briefly served in the king's Mounted National Guard and then, until 31 September 1815, in the Grey Musketeers. As a member of this elite, royal guard corps, the artist joined the escort accompanying Louis XVIII on his flight to Belgium when Napoleon unexpectedly returned from exile in March 1815.[39] Moreover, in 1814 he made preparatory drawings for an unrealized project flattering to the Bourbons: *King Louis XVIII Reviews the Troops at the Champ de Mars.*[40] This trajectory from draft dodger, to defender of the crown, to master of imagery dear to liberal and Bonapartist sentiment suggests that Géricault's politics were subsidiary to an overweening preoccupation with artmaking and an ambitious quest for subject matter with trenchant topicality.

Posthumous Adulation

Prior to Napoleon's death on 5 May 1821, demonization of the emperor (by Byron and Chateaubriand, for example) was commonplace, but when news of his demise hit Paris two months later, denunciation fell silent before a torrent of adulation. Béranger, who had previously reserved the patriotic portion of his repertoire for the plight and the loyalty of the common soldier (and who had been reticent regarding imperial glory), now turned his talent to extolling the late emperor. In the preface to an 1833 collection of his songs, Béranger affirmed that Napoleon is "the greatest poet of modern times and perhaps of all time"—an opinion that would have been welcome in Balzac's study and Delacroix's studio.[41] Napoleon's mythic stature was enhanced by the appearance of several captivity narratives. Firsthand accounts were published by the emperor's attending physicians, the Irishman Barry Edward O'Meara (1822) and the Corsican François Antommarchi (1825), respectively. Portraying Napoleon as approachable, frank, entirely without pretention or arrogance, and a dedicated civil servant (sometimes working without interruption for meals or sleep), O'Meara (1786–1836) established the image of Napoleon as man of the people (that Béranger would popularize) and decried the prisoner's torment at the hands of his English warden, Sir Hudson Lowe (1769–1844). In addition, the emperor's memoirs were published (1823) by his companions on Saint Helena, the generals and aides-de-camp, Gaspard Gourgaud (1783–1852) and Charles-Tristan de Montholon (1783–1853). By far the most important of these remembrances—indeed, one of the century's greatest publishing successes—was the multi-volume *Mémorial de Sainte-Hélène* (1823) by Emmanuel de Las Cases (1766–1842), which reached 16 editions by the end of the century.[42] Stendhal possessed three editions, which he avidly reread.[43] A former émigré of old noble stock, Las Cases had participated in the abortive counter-revolutionary assault at Quiberon (June 1795) prior to his return to France from London in 1802. Rallying to Napoleon, Las Cases was named master of petitions in the Conseil d'état (1809) and in the following year became a chamberlain to the emperor with the title of count of the Empire. Such was the fervor of his political rebirth that, having once again taken up exile in London following the abdication of 1814, Las Cases returned to France during the One Hundred Days and, after Waterloo, obtained permission to accompany his hero to Saint Helena. There the author remained, recording the emperor's conversation, until his arrest (25 November 1816) and expulsion for intercepted clandestine letters addressed to Lucien Bonaparte and to Lady Clavering (whose children Las Cases had tutored in London)—a turn of events possibly orchestrated by Las Cases himself as a pretext to leave the island.[44] Confiscated and kept under seal by the English authorities, his journal was released to the author following the emperor's death.[45] Notwithstanding the impossibility of discerning to what extent their conversation was edited by Las Cases, the book is considered faithful to the self-vindication by which the emperor intended to persuade an international readership of the righteousness of his cause. The Additional Act (22 April 1815) drafted during the One Hundred Days by Napoleon's former adversary Benjamin Constant (and hastily appended to the imperial constitution to lend legitimacy to the resurrected Empire) proclaims: "Our goal is henceforth solely to increase the prosperity of France by strengthening public liberty."[46] In that spirit, Las Cases portrayed a conscientious liberal, whose recourse to war was an unavoidable response to aggression by France's adversaries. Above all, the Napoleon of Las Cases shines with impeccable patriotism. Quantitative analysis of the text reveals repetition of these stirring terms: "people," "army," "honor," "law," "nation," "national," "fatherland," "constitution," and "independence."[47] The appeal of the publication was guaranteed not only by its eyewitness account of the emperor's political metamorphosis; readers were also moved by its depiction of the exile's martyrdom. Subjected to the harsh climate of the rat-infested island, Napoleon remained a loving paterfamilias:

> Amid his suffering, thrown onto a scorched rock, a thousand leagues from his homeland, lacking everything, sick, tortured, obliged to defend his dignity step by step against a wretch [Sir Hudson Lowe], the greatest agony of the Emperor was to be separated from his wife and son.[48]

Apart from the wealth that Las Cases reaped from sales, evidence of surging sympathy for Napoleon in the wake of his death is provided by the transformation of

Victor Hugo from bard of Bourbon throne and Catholic altar to mythologizer of the emperor.[49] Although his father, Joseph Léopold Sigisbert Hugo (1773–1828), was an imperial general and count, the poet's youthful attitude toward Napoleon was hardly adulatory. The ode "Buonaparte" (March 1822) features the derogatory spelling employed by Byron and by Hugo's idol, Chateaubriand. Here, the poet recycled commonplaces of anti-Napoleonic discourse, characterizing the emperor as a despotic usurper sent by God to punish revolutionary France.[50] By February 1827, Hugo's opinion had undergone a sea change effected by a publicized incident that incensed French liberals. At a ball given by the Austrian ambassador, Antoine Apponyi (1782–1852), on 24 January 1827, four former imperial marshals were introduced bereft of the landed titles bestowed by Napoleon in honor of victories over Austria. Perceiving an affront to both France and his father, Hugo voiced affection for the most prominent Parisian monument to imperial military prowess.[51] His ode "À la colonne de la place Vendôme" resounds with pride: "O monument vengeur! Trophée indélébile! ... ruine triumphal / De l'édifice du géant!" ("Oh, avenging monument! Ineffaceable trophy! ... triumphant ruin / Of the giant's edifice!").[52] Hugo elegiacally reiterates the sentiment expressed in a popular song by Émile Debraux (1796–1831), "La Colonne" (1818): "Ah! qu'on est fier d'être français, / Quand on regarde la colonne!" ("Ah! How proud one is to be French / When one sees the column!").[53] Yet Hugo's welling nostalgia for imperial glory is devoid of the smoldering dissidence that allied the liberal Freemason Debraux, as well as Vernet and a minority of the *demi-solde*, to the political opposition under the Restoration. Hugo's nascent devotion to the Napoleonic legend was a function of a larger embrace of French history that extended to a sixteenth-century king venerated by the Bourbon regime. Joining the column to the equestrian statue of Henri IV on the Pont Neuf, the poet seems oblivious to the fact that Lemot's mounted monarch was cast from the melt of Chaudet's statue of the emperor, removed from the column by the restored monarchy.[54] In conclusion, Hugo voices discouragement that his generation was born too late for service in the Grande Armée: "Nous avons tous grandi sur le seuil de la tente. / Condamnés à la paix, aiglons bannis des cieux...." ("We have all grown up at the tent's threshold. / Condemned to peace, eaglets banished from the skies ....").[55] Precociously enunciated by Hugo, this theme would be developed during the July Monarchy by Alfred de Vigny and Alfred de Musset.

Later that year, Hugo's pride in the imperial heritage turned to adulation in "Him" ("Lui," December 1827), wherein Napoleon's greatness renders moral judgment irrelevant. "Tu domines notre âge; ange ou démon qu'importe! / Ton aigle dans son vol, haletans, nous emporte." ("You dominate our age: angel or demon, what does it matter? / Your eagle carries us away, breathless, in its flight.")[56] Set within a collection of Orientalist fantasies of violence, harems, despotic power, and genies (*Les Orientales*, 1829), the poem exoticizes the myth of Napoleon—thus, replaying the strategy of imperial propagandists such as Gros, painter of *Napoleon in the Pesthouse at Jaffa* (Salon of 1804; Paris, Musée du Louvre). In the language of overheated Romanticism, the bedazzled poet gives new life to the old imperial rhetoric of veneration:

> Toujours lui! Lui partout!—Ou brûlante ou glacée,
> Son image sans cesse ébranle ma pensée.
> Il verse à mon esprit le souffle créateur.
> Je tremble, et dans ma bouche abondent les paroles
> Quand son nom gigantesque entouré d'auréoles,

Se dresse dans mon vers toute sa hauteur.

> Always him! He is everywhere!—whether burning or frozen, / His image ceaselessly staggers my thought. / He pours creative breath into my spirit, / I tremble, and in my mouth the words abound / When his gigantic name, surrounded by glories, / Rises up to its full height in my verse.[57]

Given Hugo's exalted conception of his vocation—in the ode "Le Poète" (1823; published 1824) he identifies with Moses—his image of Napoleon pouring "creative breath into my spirit" at once divinizes the emperor and claims for himself the gift of prophecy.

The fall of the Bourbon monarchy in July 1830 saw an explosion of interest in Napoleon almost immediately reflected in the repertoire of Parisian theaters. Analyzing this phenomenon, Maurice Samuels contrasts Bourbon censorship of plays—a domain far more tightly controlled under the Restoration than prints or non-dramatic writing—with the incessant staging of the exploits of Napoleon and his troops in the July Monarchy's early years. In a paroxysm following the return of the tri-colored flag, the height of the craze fell between August 1830 and August 1831, when 27 such dramatizations opened on the Parisian boards.[58] Outside of Paris, during the first half of the 1830s, this popular enthusiasm was stoked by schematically rendered, colored woodblock prints featuring Napoleon (often represented as the Little Corporal in bicorne hat and overcoat) produced by the Pellerin publishing firm in Épinal.[59] Residing in Paris, the exiled Heinrich Heine wryly observed, in 1832, that adoration of Napoleon had become a national, secular creed:

> *Napoleon* is for the French a magical word, which electrifies them and bedazzles them. A thousand cannons sleep in this name, as they do in the column in the place Vendôme, and the Tuileries [the residence of King Louis-Philippe] will tremble if those thousand cannons awaken one day. Just as the Jews do not pronounce without necessity the name of their god, here one rarely designates Napoleon by his name, one almost always calls him the *man*, but you see his image everywhere in print, in plaster, in metal, in wood, and in all situations. On the boulevards and in the squares stand orators who celebrate the man, popular singers who retell his high deeds.... [T]his name is the most powerful incantation for the people. Napoleon is its god, its cult, its religion, and this religion becomes, in the end, banal like all the others."[60]

In contrast with Heine's ironic distance and disdain for religion, Balzac endorsed the sacred aspect of the cult of Napoleon in *The Country Doctor (Le Médecin de campagne)*. Written October 1832–July 1833 and published in September 1833, the novel enjoyed great popularity.[61] The narrative, set in 1829, largely comprises discourses by Benassis, the beloved physician and mayor of a once stagnant, squalid village in an isolated, rural valley near Grenoble. The country doctor recounts how, guided by paternalistic, entrepreneurial zeal, he has nearly single-handedly brought prosperity, industry, and social harmony to what has become a thriving region—this in spite of initial resistance by the inhabitants, who have come to esteem their benefactor. The doctor's interlocutor is Genestas, a battle-tested officer deeply loyal to the memory of Napoleon, from whom he received a tobacco box in gratitude. Impressing upon Genestas the fundamental importance of religion and its rituals to the social order of this model society, Benassis likens the townspeople's veneration of Napoleon to their Catholic faith:

> Neither political events nor revolution have reached this inaccessible region, which remains completely outside of social developments. Napoleon alone has left his name here; he is a religion here, thanks to two or three old local soldiers who have returned to their homes, and who, in evening gatherings, recount to these simple people, in fantastic terms, the adventures of this man and his armies.[62]

By popular demand, one such imperial veteran, the postman Goguelat, recounts the emperor's mythic exploits in the book's best known and most beloved chapter, "Le Napoléon du peuple"—an episode cited by all historians of the cult of Napoleon.[63] For Balzac, the cult of Napoleon is as nurturing as the benevolence of Benassis, whose selfless, energetic effort on behalf of his charges is at once Christ-like and Napoleonic. The author brings the point home at the novel's close when, following the doctor's funeral, Goguelat says of the deceased (whose name is carved into a rude wooden cross above his grave): "minus the battles, he is the Napoleon of our valley."[64]

Unlike the liberals Béranger, Debraux, Vernet (and Hugo, politically reborn in the late Restoration), Balzac contributed to the Napoleonic legend as a legitimist and anti-democrat, convinced of the need for paternalistic leaders and respectful of Catholicism. In the early 1830s (when, more than once, the National Guard battled insurgents), nostalgic attachment to the lost hero was more commonly professed by discontents on the Left. To safely channel popular enthusiasm for Napoleon—Heine predicted that "the Tuileries will tremble if these thousand cannons awaken one day"—the government of Louis-Philippe undertook a number of initiatives to honor the emperor's memory.[65] Colossal relief sculptures completed the Arc de triomphe de l'Étoile, begun in 1806 as a monument to the Grande Armée and inaugurated in July 1836. On the third anniversary of July Revolution (28 July 1833), shortly before the publication of *Le Médecin de campagne*, an effigy of Napoleon as the Little Corporal in bicorn hat and *redingote* by Charles Émile Seurre (1798–1858) was set atop the column in the place Vendôme.[66] A far cry from the imperial Roman represented by Chaudet, this was the people's Napoleon of Goguelat, Genestas, and the grandmother of Béranger's "Les Souvenirs du peuple," who recalls that, when she first saw her idol, "Il avait petit chapeau / Avec redingote grise" ("He had a little hat / with grey frock coat").[67]

Return

In his testament (published in ten editions between 1822 and 1833), the emperor stated: "I wish that my ashes rest on the banks of the Seine, in the midst of this French people whom I have so loved." In the early July Monarchy, this aspiration remained sufficiently controversial for dismissal, after only brief deliberation, of a petition (7 October 1830) to the Chamber of Deputies to reinter the imperial remains beneath the column in the place Vendôme. Two days later, the incensed Hugo returned to the column and to the image of the demi-god in "À la Colonne," included in *Les Chants du crépuscule* (1835). Amid breathless celebration of the emperor's military glory, his loading of the Louvre with stolen art, and his intimidation of kings, the poet voiced outrage before his compatriot's denial of the honor due their national hero.

Five years would pass before Hugo witnessed the solemn return of the imperial remains to Paris. The event is known as the Return of the Ashes (*le retour des Cendres*), though the body had not been cremated.[68] Initially opposed by the king, the initiative was zealously pursued by his prime minister and minister of foreign affairs, Adolphe Thiers (1797–1877), eager to distract from calls for parliamentary reform. On 12 May 1840, the project was abruptly proposed to the Chamber of Deputies (in the midst of a debate concerning sugar) by the prime minister's friend and ally, Minister of the Interior Charles de Rémusat (1797–1875). Rémusat requested a budget of one million francs to bring home the remains of Napoleon and to erect a durable monument to his memory. Deputy Alphonse de Lamartine, who was in the audience, confided that day to a friend, "Napoleon's ashes are not extinguished, and he is blowing on the sparks."[69] Two weeks later, the poet-legislator made his opinion public in an address to the Chamber received with a counterpoint of protest and approval befitting the controversial nature of the proposal spearheaded by Thiers and Rémusat:

> Though an admirer of this great man, mine is not an enthusiasm without memory and without foresight. I do not prostrate myself before this memory; I do not belong to this Napoleonic religion, to this cult of might that one wishes for some time now to substitute, in the spirit of the nation, for the serious religion of liberty. I do not believe it good to so ceaselessly deify war, to overexcite this boiling over of already-too-impetuous French blood, which one claims us to be impatient to spill after a reprieve of twenty-five years, as if peace, which is the happiness and the glory of the world, could be the shame of nations.[70]

So strong was the emotional pull of the imperial heritage that Lamartine concluded his address with support of funding for the project.

Shortly after one of Louis-Philippe's sons, François d'Orlèans, Prince de Joinville (1818–1900), departed on the frigate *Belle Poule* for the remote Atlantic island that held the exile's grave, the project assumed enhanced urgency in light of what was known as the Eastern Question.[71] On 15 July 1840, France's former enemies, England, Austria, Prussia, and Russia, entered into a protective alliance on behalf of the Ottoman Sultan, Abdulmejid I (1823–61), disregarding French interests in the Levant. In the previous year, the Ottomans had suffered defeat at the hands of France's ally Muhammad Ali, Pasha of Egypt (1769–1849), in a resumption of an earlier conflict (1831–33) over control of Syria and other Ottoman territories. The allies demanded that Muhammad Ali relinquish his territorial claims and acknowledge Ottoman hegemony. Aflame with resentment, France was prepared for war by Thiers, who initiated fortification of Paris; reservists were called to active duty, and emergency war credit authorized. For Edgar Quinet, the diplomatic marginalization of France reopened an old wound:

> the bonds of 1815 were suddenly refastened; the chain of the Titan was there, it had but to be bound tighter. France was plunged again into that mute solitude that the defeat had traced around her. As if she had lost the battle a second time, she again found herself in the aftermath of Waterloo.[72]

Quinet's metaphor of France plunged in mute solitude (a timely trope under the July Monarchy, as we will see) resounds in depressive counterpoint to the martial pride on parade when the body of the emperor traveled to the Invalides on 15 December 1840 –a pageant that drew between 700,000 and a million spectators.[73] Crowds lined the route of the funeral cortege, which was preceded by ranks of soldiers, sailors, and members of the National Guard. Barred from the official procession, imperial veterans could not be prevented from infiltration. François Guizot, ambassador to London during the preparations for the Return of the Ashes, had agreed to the undertaking as a symbol of Anglo-French *entente*. Yet his concern with enabling Bonapartist mischief led him to insist that the men who had been with the emperor on Saint Helena be excluded from official participation. So volatile a symbol required careful handling. Accordingly, the executed tomb complex is cold, remote, and placed below ground level.[74] Predictably, Hugo was among the multitude braving the frigid weather. "Yes, this is a festival," he noted, "the festival of an exiled coffin, which returns in triumph"—an observation prophetic of his own triumphant homecoming in 1870.[75] The poet was scandalized by the contrast between, on the one hand, the genuine enthusiasm of the common people and, on the other, the coldness of the bourgeoisie and the disrespect shown by the nation's legislators. Indignantly observing the tawdry, temporary decorations (plaster sculpture adorned the parade route), Hugo had scorn for what he viewed as the insincere machination of the regime.[76]

That the pageant of 15 December was both cautious and celebratory lends credence to a shrewd point made by Frédéric Bluche: inculcation of the *legend of Napoleon* was distinct from, and in some cases countervailing to, *Bonapartism*.[77] Sympathetic toward Napoleon as an individual and enthused by national glory (as embodied in the soldiers of the Grande Armée), the legend was fundamentally sentimental and retrospective. Popular after 1815 and in the wake of the White Terror (i.e., the wave of monarchist retribution toward Napoleonic loyalists following Waterloo), the legend was adopted by liberals under the Restoration. Bonapartism, in contrast, was political and focused on the perpetuation, in the present, of the doctrines of Napoleon I. These include a dynastic authoritarian regime with a populist, egalitarian base (i.e., legitimized by plebiscite, with intermediary parties and legislative bodies stripped of power), an uncompromising commitment to the maintenance of order, and a readiness to resort to military force in the national interest. Bluche concedes that the two currents overlapped after 1815 and between 1848 and the first years of the Second Empire. Thus, the publication of the *Mémorial*—a key event in the life of the legend—so forcefully conveyed Bonapartist ideology that it provided a conspiratorial roadmap for the imperial nephew. The death of Napoleon, which posed an existential threat to Bonapartism, enhanced the legend to the point of silencing the black discourse voiced by royalists and liberals (e.g., Chateaubriand and Staël, respectively) in the wake of the Empire's collapse. As Stanley Mellon points out, even Thiers cannot be considered a Bonapartist: he opposed the Second Empire and helped to destroy it.[78] The same could be said of Hugo, whose grandiose invocations of Napoleon I starkly contrast with the aspersions he cast on Napoleon III.[79]

Nor does this distinction between Bonapartism and the legend of Napoleon represent the full extent of Bluche's parsing. Closely linked to the legend is what Bluche calls the *Napoleonic myth*, which likewise appealed to the imagination and the emotions. Originating in 1797 during the Italian campaign (as in the portrait by Gros) and later sustained by imperial propaganda, the myth, unlike the legend, was initiated by Napoleon, himself. Having focused on the *proscrit* exiled on Saint Helena between 1815 and 1821, the myth assumed a literary voice in 1827, with Hugo at the cutting edge. Enduring for later generations, the myth cast the captive emperor as the chained Prometheus.[80] Rather than being concerned, as was Bonapartism, with the future, the myth either focused on the present or invoked a golden age of the past. There was also *Napoleonism*, as exemplified by Stendhal—admiration for Napoleon as persona, without approval of his politics. Finally, Bluche adduces the *cult of Napoleon*, whose adherents, nourished on the legend, adored the emperor like smitten lovers. Spreading contagiously in rural France in the years after 1815, this extreme form of Napoleonism was shared by imperial veterans such as Colonel Bro and Balzac's Goguelat.

This is not to say that Bluche's taxonomy—whose multiple categories reflect the omnipresence of Napoleon in the public imaginary—can be accepted without caveat. In this study, I opt for a more casual terminology, employing the legend, myth, and cult of Napoleon interchangeably; Bonapartism, however, demands more cautious handling. Taking issue with Bluche's notion that the Napoleonic legend was politically inert, Sudhir Hazareesingh persuasively argues that it was the lifeblood of Bonapartism, and that politically partisan Bonapartism is inextricably entwined with the cult of the emperor.[81] Bluche's allowance of overlap among the various currents is insufficient for Hazareesingh, who questions any separation between politics and popular infatuation. Both perspectives are illuminating. If Bluche's construct is more rigorous from the standpoint of the history of political ideas, Hazareesingh is supported by evidence from the domains of popular and material culture. Bluche's distinction between Bonapartism and the more emotionally fraught strains is especially convincing in regard to sophisticated Parisians (e.g., Thiers, Stendhal, Balzac, and Hugo), who trafficked, variously, in the myth, the legend, Napoleonism, and the cult of Napoleon—without being Bonapartists.[82] It has less traction with the nationwide, popular political culture represented, for example, by the huge, subversive trade in Napoleonic memorabilia during the Restoration (richly documented by Hazareesingh); the electoral victories of Louis-Napoléon in 1848; and the majority votes to legitimize his coup d'état and elevation to the imperial throne. Whereas Bluche considers the Restoration a period steeped in the Napoleonic legend but weak in Bonapartism, Hazareesingh documents a torrent of Bonapartist sentiment throughout the nation under the Bourbons, notes the contribution of Bonapartism to the Revolution of 1830, and regards Bonapartist dissidence between Waterloo and the July Monarchy as politically potent, notwithstanding its disorganization and diversity: "Napoleonic conspiracy was not so much goal-driven as expressive: it gave its participants an escape from the drab world of Restoration France, and opened up new prospects of adventure, heroism, mystery, and (above all) hope."[83] This analysis resonates with the culture of martial longing under the Restoration, fictionalized, during the July Monarchy, in Alfred de Vigny's *Servitude et grandeur militaires* and in Alfred de Musset's *La Confession d'un enfant du siècle* (to which we will soon return). Moreover, Hazareesingh demonstrates the tenacity of the Napoleonic cult under the Second Empire, when geriatric imperial veterans cherished the Médaille de Sainte-Hélène (established August 1857 to honor surviving soldiers of the Revolution and the Grande Armée) no less than the followers of Catherine de Labouré clung to her miraculous medal during the cholera plague of 1832.[84]

Resurrection

Employing Bluche's terms, it can be said that, just as the emperor's death gave decisive impetus to his legend, so too did the return of his remains open a transcendent phase in the cult of Napoleon. This current of the 1840s is famously represented by *Napoleon Awakening to Immortality* (*Le Réveil de Napoléon*) by François Rude (1784–1855).[85] This eccentric bronze monument (1845–47; I show the plaster model housed in the Musée de l'Armée) was unveiled on 19 September 1847 before some 18,000 imperial veterans and local dignitaries (Figure 4.7). It was commissioned by the sculptor's friend, the vintner and painter Claude Noisot (1787–1861), for his vineyard estate at Fixin, near Dijon. Both men hailed from Burgundy which, having prospered under the Empire, was strongly sympathetic to Napoleon. In 1814, Noisot (a veteran of Wagram, Spain, and Moscow) had accompanied the emperor into exile on the island of Elba, where he served as captain in the grenadiers of the Imperial Guard. Having seen action at Waterloo, Noisot was the very image of the dissident *demi-solde,* feared, surveilled, and maligned by the Bourbon regime. Contemptuous of the restored monarchy and fanatically loyal to the memory of the emperor, Noisot earned distinction in combat on the barricades during the July Revolution (he claimed to have escorted Lafayette en route to endorse Louis-Philippe at the Hôtel de Ville). Having married a wealthy, landed widow shortly before the Three Glorious

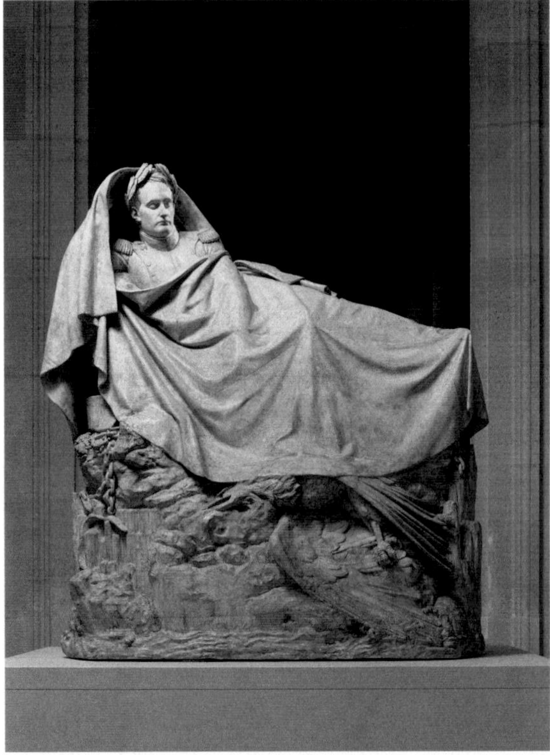

Figure 4.7 François Rude, *Napoleon Awakening to Immortality,* 1846 plaster, 220 × 205 × 116 cm. Paris, Musée du Louvre, on deposit in Paris, Musée de l'Armée. © Musée du Louvre, Dist. RMN-Grand Palais/Jean Schormans/Art Resource, NY.

Days, Noisot devoted his resources, and the remainder of his life, to the transformation of the Fixin estate into a symbolic space charged with Napoleonic significance.[86] Facing Italy and the Alps (theatres of Napoleonic conquest), the park features a hillside staircase with a step for each of the One Hundred Days; pines imported from Corsica; and a Fort of the Emperor (modeled on the military and civilian architecture of Elba) sheltering memorabilia to be watched over, according to Noisot's will, by a caretaker who, invested with a "religious mission," would preferably be an imperial veteran decorated with the Legion of Honor. Rude met his patron during the week of the Return of the Ashes, at which Noisot had shown uncommon zeal. In defiance of official protocol, the vintner (uniformed as a captain in the Imperial Guard and leading a contingent of Napoleonic veterans) forced his way into the cortège behind the massive funeral chariot. The sculptor, who shared Noisot's affection for the emperor, brought sterling patriotic credentials to the project, having crafted the colossal relief (1833–36), *The Marseillaise* (*The Departure of the Volunteers of 1792*) for the Arc de triomphe de l'Étoile. Working without charge on the Fixin monument (originally titled *Resurrection of Napoleon*), Rude displayed the plaster model in his studio in the spring of 1846. Crowned with laurel and shrouded in a camp cloak, the deceased Napoleon stirs into life on the wave-struck rock of Saint Helena, a broken eagle at his feet.[87] Conceived as a free-standing high relief, the format is no more conventional than the very notion of a secular monument featuring resurrection. In accord with the emperor's liminal state, the blocky composition is animated by diagonal rhythms of drapery folds and avian anatomy held in planar check—a muffled counterpart to the fanfare drama of *The Marseillaise*, in which dynamic anatomical contortion is subjected to severe planimetric restraint. Noisot referred to Napoleon as "the modern Christ" at the monument's inauguration, shortly before the bronze was revealed beneath a draped *tricolore* and *The Marseillaise* was sung.[88] A participant in the inauguration described the site in comparable terms: "One makes one's way toward a sharply rising hillside, covered with rocks, stark to the summit, a sort of Calvary, but that connects the Mount of Olives and the Garden of the Resurrection."[89]

Neither identification of Napoleon with Christ nor imagery of his resurrection were novel.[90] The former was common coin in the 1840s; familiar since the 1820s, the latter is represented, for example, by "La Colonne" (Rude had worked on the reliefs of the place Vendôme column while still a student) from Quinet's verse collection *Napoléon* (1836): "Il n'est pas mort! il n'est pas mort! De son sommeil / Le géant va sortir plus grand à son réveil." ("He's not dead! He's not dead! / Awakening from his sleep, the giant will be greater yet.")[91] In his packed inaugural lecture at the Collège de France in February 1842, Quinet again spoke of resurrection. To unanimous applause, he asked:

> Is it really true, as is repeated day in and day out, that here I have to do with a people who are finished ...? No, no, if they are exhausted, they will be refreshed; if they recline, they will rise up; if they are dead, they will be reborn.

Leaving the rostrum, Quinet was embraced by a close friend and colleague whose notion of national destiny was no less exalted, Mickiewicz.[92] It was an honor previously bestowed upon the Polish poet, himself; two years earlier, at the conclusion of his own first, crowded lecture at the Collége de France, the speaker had been kissed on the forehead by fellow exile Niemcewicz.

Catholic and Messianic Perspectives

In the previous decade, as we have seen, Mickiewicz equated Poland's suffering with the Passion in the *Book of the Polish Pilgrims* (1832). In the 1840s, this messianic nationalism melded with the cult of Napoleon. Having idolized Poland's ally since adolescence, Mickiewicz carried adoration to giddy heights under the influence of a Lithuanian visionary who, though not previously known to the poet, had also attended university in Vilnius, Andrzej Towiański (1799–1878, known in France as André Towiansky).[93] A self-proclaimed messenger from God, this charismatic believed that history would comprise seven epochs, opening with the coming of Christ; the second epoch was that of Napoleon, who had prepared the way for his successor—Towiański. Having arrived in France in May 1841, Towiański made an unannounced visit to Mickiewicz, who had experienced at the Return of the Ashes a vision of a man of destiny driving a one-horse carriage out of the depths of Lithuania. Convinced that his delusional wife had been cured of mental illness by Towiański, Mickiewicz accepted him as his Lord and Master and became a disciple in the cult figure's Circle of the Work of God. In Notre-Dame on 27 September 1841, Towiański exhorted an audience of Polish émigrés to embrace their divinely appointed mission to establish heaven on earth. The exile of the Poles, he insisted, is at once divine punishment and purification; they share with other Slavs exclusive stewardship of Christianity. Notwithstanding Mickiewicz's infatuation, Towiański's pan-Slavism alienated the Polish émigré community, which recoiled at his inclusion of Russia in the divine plan. Blending fervent Catholicism with mystical certainty of Napoleon's providential significance, Towiański's doctrine went dangerously beyond the regime's cautious memorialization of the emperor; he was expelled from France in July 1842. By late 1843, Mickiewicz's lectures at the Collège de France had become improvised, Towiański-inspired screeds. Under surveillance by the police for nearly two years, the course was shut down by the authorities in May 1844.

The messianic view of Napoleon conveyed by Mickiewicz and Towiański was encouraged by a book claiming to offer proof of the emperor's piety: *Napoleon's Religious Conversations, in which He Himself Reveals His Intimate Thoughts on Christianity*, by Robert Antoine de Beauterne (1803–46), first printed in 1840 and subsequently reissued in numerous editions with variant titles.[94] From eyewitness reports, Beauterne, son of a lieutenant in the Imperial Chasseurs, wove a fictive narrative of the heartfelt embrace of Catholicism in exile by a communicant whose patronage of the national religion hardly sprang from belief.[95] Vernet provided a touching frontispiece (1838) to Beauterne's volume. Softly illuminated, the bedridden emperor receives the viaticum, his idle sword hanging from the bedpost and a crucifix resting on his night table (Figure 4.8). The rite is administered by Abbé Angelo Paulo Vignali (1789–1836), a Corsican priest sent to the island in September 1819 by Napoleon's mother and his uncle, Cardinal Fesch, and ignored by the emperor until his death (he presided over Napoleon's burial). In his account of Napoleon taking the wafer, Beauterne gave voice to heartfelt sentiment that outstrips the documentary evidence, whose authenticity he was at pains to assert:

> Seeing Napoleon bow down with the trembling of faith before our mysterious and formidable host, wait with joined hands in deeply peaceful meditation, take and consume the food of the faith; may politics itself bow down and adore! ... Oh

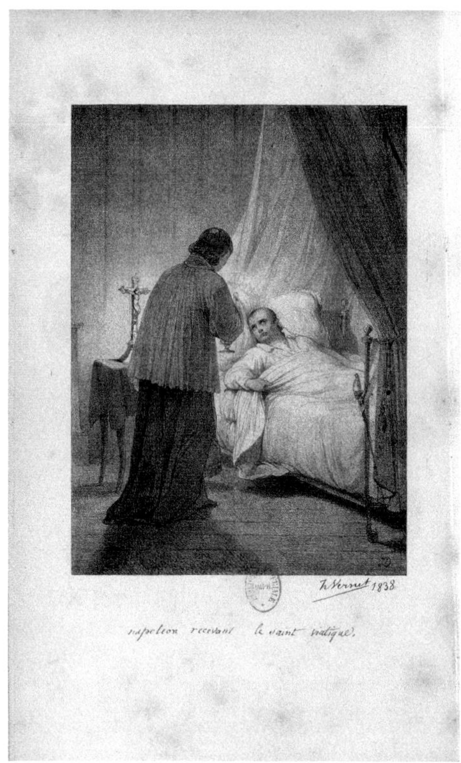

Figure 4.8 Horace Vernet, Frontispiece to Robert-Augustin Antoine de Beauterne, *Conversations religieuses de Napoléon, avec des Documents inédits de la plus haute importance où il révèle lui-même sa pensée intime sur le christianisme* (Paris: Chez l'auteur, Olivier-Fulgence, and Debécourt, 1841), lithograph. Paris, Bibliothèque nationale de France. Photo: BnF.

> elect of God, convert me, convert the impious one… while recounting to us, for our edification, the ideas and sentiment of your blessed communion.[96]

In the final chapter, Beauterne strays further into fantasy and sets forth a mystery play vignette, worthy of Quinet, in which Satan denounces Napoleon as an evil tyrant. At the behest of the Virgin, the emperor's guardian angel triumphantly provides defense:

> Satan, blinded by his hatred, was caught there as if in a trap. He admitted that he would be vanquished should I show him a single soul saved by Napoleon; and well! The sky opens: I see millions of the elect who wait for him as a second cause of their redemption: these are the soldiers dead on the fields of battle, instructed, converted by the example of this great man, [and] all the children baptized thanks to the concordat. And well! Satan, you are vanquished![97]

This astonishing scenario was entirely at home in the 1840s, which witnessed Mickiewicz's Towiański-inspired improvisations at the rostrum of the Collège de France.

It was also in the wake of the Return of the Ashes that, disillusioned with the lackluster July Monarchy, a diverse band of visionaries identified Napoleon with Christ and considered the defeat at Waterloo as the salvific equivalent to the Crucifixion. Their discourse could attain such peculiarity that (as Paul Bénichou writes) it would seem madness, were it not for the fact that these outlandish ideas had traction within the public sphere.[98] Insanity, to be sure, was sometimes clothed in imperial guise. In 1847, Alphonse Esquiros (1812–76), a Lamennais disciple who subscribed to Napoleonic messianism, reported that, in the year of the Return of the Ashes, 13 or 14 patients convinced that they were Napoleon were admitted to the Bicêtre asylum.[99] In 1841, when Gérard de Nerval (1808–55) underwent his first mental crisis, the poet (who believed himself to be related to Napoleon), began to exhibit a mystical obsession with the emperor.[100] The oddest of all Napoleonic apostles was a notorious eccentric known solely by his last name, Ganneau (variously spelled Gannau and Gannot). Ganneau called himself Le Mapah so as to identify with the bi-gendered deity of his self-proclaimed religion, Évadisme (i.e., Eve reunited with Adam).[101] His radical monism was wedded to belief in redemption through Napoleon. Thus, in a pamphlet of 1843 that identifies Napoleon with Cain, La Mapah partakes of Romantic empathy with the first murderer:

> Great Cain! On your brow are reflected all the Splendor and Majesty of Unity, all the Sorrows and all the Nothingness of individuality.... [E]ach of the terms of the human idea, be they Political, Social, or Religious, is summed up for the world by an immense cry, WATERLOO! That is the word of the great Labor of Adam, who called himself Abraham, Jacob, Moses, then Alexander, Socrates, Caesar, Muhammed, Charlemagne, finally Jesus and Napoleon: Jesus the Abel-Christ and Napoleon the Cain-Christ, great Beacons of the Centuries, living Synthesis, sublime forms through which Humanity has transformed so it can return to the Adamic Unity, from which it primitively departed.[102]

Such was the fringe of a popular cult of Napoleon that, following the fall of Louis-Philippe, was marshaled in support of the emperor's nephew, Louis-Napoléon Bonaparte.

The Imperial Nephew's Rise and Fall

At Strasbourg (October 1836) and at Boulogne-sur-Mer (August 1840, a year after Louis-Philippe inaugurated a huge, columnar monument to Napoleon in nearby Wimille), the imperial nephew had launched abortive attempts to dethrone the Orléans monarch.[103] In 1839, in preparation for his second attempted putsch, he offered to a wide readership a reinvention of his uncle's legacy that was no less politically expedient than Beauterne's Catholicizing of the exile of Saint Helena. *Napoleonic Ideas* echoes the apology mounted by the *Mémorial*, transforming his uncle into a bringer of peace and prosperity and defender of the liberties and aspirations of the French people. The Napoleonic idea, Louis-Napoléon argues,

> is not at all an idea of war, but a social, industrial, commercial, humanitarian idea. If for some men it appears forever surrounded by the thunder of combat, this is because it was, in effect, too long enveloped by cannon smoke and the dust of

> battles. But today the clouds have dissipated, and one perceives through the glory of arms a greater and more durable civil glory.[104]

Ascendance of this Bonapartist platform was abetted by the title (irresistible in the hungry 1840s) of his subsequent *The Eradication of Poverty* (*L'Extinction du paupérisme*, 1844). Key to Louis-Napoléon's success, of course, was the family name; its power was borne out by the surprise victory of the failed conspirator in three elections: that of 4 June 1848 (to the Constituent Assembly, from which he resigned in response to protest); that of 17–18 September (to the legislature); and that of 10–11 December, which carried him, by landslide, to the presidency of the Second Republic.

Empowered by universal suffrage (introduced under the Second Republic), the future Napoleon III held sufficient sway over popular sentiment to get the best not only of elections, but also the plebiscites on the legitimacy of his coup d'état and ascent to the imperial throne (21 December 1851 and 21 November 1852, respectively).[105] In the face of this popular appeal, intellectuals who had venerated the uncle were outraged by the nephew's betrayal of the Republic. The true believer Mickiewicz was not among these. Though he discarded Towiański's doctrine between 1846 and 1847, his reverence for the emperor persisted. Enthused by Louis-Napoléon's election and coup d'état, the poet was rewarded in 1852 by appointment as librarian of the Bibliothèque de l'Arsenal. His friend Quinet, in contrast, spent the Second Empire in exile after renouncing his enthusiasm for Napoleon in 1851; under the Third Republic, he dropped *Napoléon* from his collected works.[106] No about-face was more dramatic and public than that of Hugo. Two months before the presidential election, the candidacy of Louis-Napoléon was favored by *L'Événement*, a paper founded and directed by, among others, the poet's sons. Appalled by the coup d'état, Hugo became, as we have seen, the century's most famous exile apart from Napoleon. In Brussels, between 14 June and 12 July 1852, he produced *Napoléon le petit*, an attack on Louis-Napoléon which includes a jeremiad recalling the imagery of prostration (common under Louis-Philippe), to which we will return in the next chapter:

> Oh fatherland! It is at this hour when there you are bleeding, inanimate, with hanging head, eyes closed, mouth open and no longer speaking, the marks of the whip on your shoulders, the nails of the soles of the executioners imprinted all over your body, nude and soiled, and like unto a dead thing, object of hatred, object of ridicule, alas! It is at this hour, fatherland, that the heart of the exile abounds with love and respect for you![107]

From the Channel Islands, the poet hurled anathema at the despot and his minions in *The Castigations* (*Les Châtiments*, 1853), where exclamation has comic-strip abundance, as in the opening poem's evocation of the violent suppression of resistance to the coup d'état: "Que fait hors des maisons ce peuple? Qu'il s'en aille! / Soldats, mitraillez-moi toute cette canaille! … Que sur les boulevards le sang coule en rivières!" ("What are these people doing outside their houses! Let them be gone! / Soldiers, gun down for me this whole rabble! … Let rivers of blood spill on the boulevards!")[108] Incensed by Louis-Napoléon's cooption of his uncle's aura, Hugo points in accusation: "You there, filthy dwarf, crouched on that name!" ("Te voilà, nain immonde, accroupi sur ce nom!").[109] Unslaked by page after page of rhyming invective, the poet's animus continued to be shared by his readers after the fall of Napoleon III.

In 1879, for an illustrated edition of *Napoléon le petit,* Émile Bayard (1837–91) visualized the passage “Napoleon the Little Superimposes Himself on Napoleon the Great” (“Napoléon le Petit se superpose à Napoléon le Grand”) (Figure 4.9). An effigy of Louis-Napoléon, in the hat and *redingote* of the Little Corporal, stands atop a radically truncated version of the place Vendôme column, its battle reliefs replaced by inscriptions that invoke failure and civil war. Referring to the attempted putsches at Strasbourg, and Boulogne-sur-Mer, the illustrator also names Montmartre (birthplace of the Commune), and Satory (site of an infamous prison camp for captive Communards at Versailles).[110] Rising in ominous darkness, a ghostly silhouette of the original, full-length column seconds the dictator’s disgrace. The shattered pedestal and rubble also recall the destruction, eight years previously, of the actual column.

On 16 May 1871, shortly before it was suppressed with unspeakable brutality, the Paris Commune toppled the monument that, since its erection, had reliably indicated the changing fortunes of the Bonaparte name.

> Considering that the imperial column of the place Vendôme is a monument of barbarism, a symbol of brute strength and false glory, an affirmation of militarism, a negation of international law, a permanent insult by the victors to the

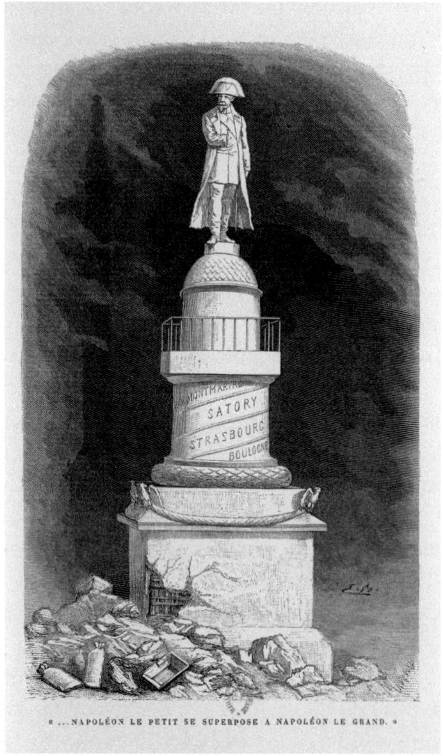

« ...NAPOLÉON LE PETIT SE SUPERPOSE A NAPOLÉON LE GRAND. »

Figure 4.9 Émile Bayard, “Napoleon the Little Superimposes Himself on Napoleon the Great,” from *Napoléon le petit, edition illustrée par MM. J.P. Laurens, É. Bayard, E. Morin, D. Vierge, Lix, Chifflart, Garcia, H. Scott, Brun, G. Bellenger* (Paris: Eugène Hugues, 1879), lithograph. Paris, Bibliothèque nationale de France. Photo: BnF.

> vanquished, a perpetual attack on one of the three great principles of the French Republic, Fraternity,

the Commune decreed its demolition on 12 April.[111] Gustave Courbet (1819–77), who was later accused of directing the demolition (a charge he vehemently denied), had proposed, six months prior to the Commune's formation, that the monument be "unbolted" and its metal repurposed for coinage.[112] The Communard Louis Barron bore witness:

> I saw the Vendôme Column fall, it collapsed all in one piece like a stage set on a nice bed of trash when the machinist's whistle blew.... This colossal symbol of the Grand Army—how fragile, empty, miserable it was! It seemed to have been eaten out from the middle by a multitude of rats, like France itself ....[113]

The act tacitly acknowledged the symbolic might of the Napoleonic legend; in pulling down the column, the Communards followed the example of the revolutionary vandals who stripped the kings of Judah from the façade of Notre-Dame in the belief that they were expunging the royal heritage with which they were obsessed.

One year after the column was laid low, Victor de Laprade (Ballanche's follower, Janmot's friend, member of Académie française, and Lyonnais deputy to the National Assembly) wrote the preface to a new edition of Chateaubriand's anti-Napoleonic diatribe, *De Buonaparte et des Bourbons*. He chose as the date of completion the anniversary of Louis-Napoléon's coup d'état. Despising Bonapartism (whether represented by uncle or nephew) no less than the Commune, Laprade faulted Chateaubriand's harsh judgement of the emperor for its "extreme indulgence." A liberal monarchist, Laprade acknowledged that he had admired Chateaubriand's text since his youth, when "political charlatanism returned his [the emperor's] ashes to the Invalides." For Laprade, the *Mémorial de Sainte-Hélène*—that bible of Bonapartism and of the cult of Napoleon—was but a "drawn-out display of shabbiness and lies." Yet more venom was reserved for the imperial nephew, whose coup d'état shocked Laprade less in "the villainy of its authors than the incommensurable stupidity of the nation, which wanted to believe itself saved by this crime."[114] The usurper, according to Laprade, bore responsibility for the Commune.

Like the destruction of the place Vendôme column, Laprade's fury toward the Bonaparte name inadvertently acknowledged Napoleon's outsized stature in the French imaginary. Having characterized the emperor as heir to Nero and Attila in *De Buonaparte et des Bourbons*, even Chateaubriand came to regard Bonaparte with awestruck admiration. Devoting a large portion of his voluminous memoirs to Napoleon, the author attempted to nuance the national adulation of the 1830s through criticism, as well as with recognition of Napoleon's greatness.[115] Death, in Chateaubriand's opinion, had brought immortality:

> The world belongs to Bonaparte; that which the ravager was unable to conquer, his renown usurped; while alive the world eluded him, dead he possesses it....Bonaparte was so strongly given to absolute domination, that after having submitted to the despotism of his person, we must submit to the despotism of his memory. This latter despotism is more domineering than the first, for if one sometimes fought against Napoleon while he was on the throne, there is universal consent in accepting the fetters that, dead, he casts upon us.[116]

This dispiriting outlook corresponds with the author's jaundiced view of the July Monarchy, to which his memoirs principally date.[117] Notwithstanding his disenchantment with the Bourbon regime during the late Restoration, Chateaubriand was committed to legitimate royalism, and would have no truck with Louis-Philippe. Gaping before Chateaubriand's disillusionment is the void left in the emperor's absence: "After Alexander, Roman power began; after Caesar, Christianity changed the world; after Charlemagne, the feudal night engendered a new society; after Napoleon, nothingness: the advent of neither empire, nor religion, nor barbarians is to be seen."[118] Here again, the aging author proved himself a peerless reader of signs of the times.

Notes

1 Marguerite-Louise-Virginie Ancelot, *Les Salons de Paris, Foyers éteints* (Paris: J. Tardieu, 1858), 96. The statuette or bust, if it actually existed, has not been located. It is possible that Ancelot was relying on hearsay rather than first-hand knowledge. The inscription had been previously published by Philarète Chasles in the *Journal des débats* (24 August 1850), as indicated in Beth Gerwin, "Révision et subversion: Balzac et le mythe de Napoléon," *Analyses: Revue des littératures Franco-Canadiennes et Québécoise* 8, no. 3 (Autumn 2013), 55–6 n. 12. https://uottawa.scholarsportal.info/ottawa/index.php/revue-analyses/issue/view/196. I am grateful to Thomas W. Briggs for bringing this publication to my attention.

2 Quoted in Maurice Z. Shroder, *Icarus: The Image of the Artist in French Romanticism* (Cambridge, MA: Harvard University Press, 1961), 95 and 262 n. 9.

3 The best discussion of the portrait is David O'Brien, *After the Revolution: Antoine-Jean Gros, Painting and Propaganda under Napoleon* (University Park: Penn State University Press, 2006), 31–7.

4 Quoted in Raymond Escholier, "Gros, peintre de Napoléon," *Europe* (April 1969), 242.

5 M.-E.-J. Delécluze, *Louis David, Son école & son temps. Souvenirs* (Paris: Didier, 1855), 203–4.

6 For this painting, see O'Brien, *After the Revolution*, 154–74; Robert Rosenblum, *Transformations in Late Eighteenth Century Art* (Princeton, NJ: Princeton University Press, 1969), 95–8; and Christopher Prendergast, *Napoleon and History Painting: Antoine-Jean Gros's 'La Bataille d'Eylau'* (Oxford: Clarendon Press, 1997).

7 These casualty figures are from Alexander Mikaberidze, *The Napoleonic Wars: A Global History* (New York: Oxford University Press, 2020), 224.

8 For Napoleon's insistence that the Battle of Eylau be publicized and recorded as a victory, see Michael Marrinan, "Literal/Literary/'Lexie': History, Text, and Authority in Napoleonic Painting," *Word & Image* 7, no. 3 (July–September 1991): 177–200, which reprints in an appendix (pp.194–5) the fictive, official account of the battle as published in an imperial *bulletin*.

9 "Ce tableau sinistre, formé de cent tableaux, semble appeler l'oeil et l'esprit de tous côtés à la fois; mais ce n'est encore que le cadre de la sublime figure de Napoléon.... C'est peut-être la plus belle conception de l'artiste, et aussi le portrait le plus magnifique et assurément le plus exact qu'on ait fait de Napoléon.... Ce personnage, aussi poétique qu'Achille, plus grand que tous les héros sortis de l'imagination des poètes, n'a point encore trouvé son Homère, et Homère lui-même eût renoncé à le peindre." "Gros," *Revue des deux mondes* (1 September 1848), reprinted in Eugène Delacroix, *Oeuvres littéraires 2: Essais sur les artistes célèbres*, 6th ed. (Paris: G. Crès, 1923), 184.

10 *L'Anti-Napoléon: La Légende noire de l'empereur*, ed. Jean Tulard (Paris: René Julliard, 1965), 32. See also Sylvain Pagé, *Le Mythe napoléonien: De Las Cases à Victor Hugo* (Paris: CNRS éditions, 2013), chap. 2.

11 Lord Byron [George Gordon], *Lord Byron: The Major Works*, ed. Jerome J. McGann (Oxford: Oxford University Press, 2000), 253, 256.

12 "Childe Harold's Pilgrimage" (canto 3, stanza 36, published 1816), in *Lord Byron: The Major Works*, ed. McGann, 114.

13 Thomas Medwin, *Medwin's Conversations of Lord Byron*, ed. Ernest J. Lovell, Jr. (Princeton, NJ: Princeton University Press, 1966), 184.

14 For Chateaubriand's changing views of Napoleon, see Marc Fumaroli, *Chateaubriand: Poésie et terreur* (Paris: Gallimard, 2003); Maurice Descotes, *La Légende de Napoléon et les écrivains français du XIXe siècle* (Paris: Lettres modernes Minard, 1967); and Jean Boorsch, "Chateaubriand and Napoleon," *Yale French Studies* 26 (Fall-Winter 1960–61): 55–62.

15 In February 1815, Lord Byron wrote to Lady Byron: "Bonaparte's conduct since his fall is to be traced entirely to the Italian character—for a Frenchman or Englishman would have shot himself." Quoted by Lovell in Medwin, *Medwin's Conversations of Lord Byron*, 185 n. 433.

16 "Né surtout pour détruire, Buonaparte porte le mal dans son sein, tout naturellement, comme une mère porte son fruit, avec joie et une sorte d'orgueil. Il a l'horreur du bonheur des hommes...." Chateaubriand, *De Buonaparte et des Bourbons*, pref. Victor de Laprade (Lyon: Félix Girard, 1872), 79. The full title is *De Buonaparte et des Bourbons, et de la nécessité de se rallier à nos princes légitimes pour le bonheur de la France et celui de l'Europe.*

17 "La voix du monde te déclare le plus grand coupable qui ait jamais paru sur la terre; car ce n'est pas sur des peuples barbares et sur des nations dégénérées que tu as versé tant de maux; c'est au milieu de la civilisation, dans un siècle de lumières, que tu as voulu régner par le glaive d'Attila et les maximes de Néron." Chateaubriand, *De Buonaparte et des Bourbons*, 81.

18 See Darrin M. McMahon, *Enemies of the Enlightenment: The French Counter-Enlightenment and the Making of Modernity* (Oxford: Oxford University Press, 2001). A principal purveyor of anti-Napoleonic tracts was Lewis Goldsmith, a former anti-British propagandist who had worked for Talleyrand before falling from grace and fleeing to England in 1809. For Goldsmith (ca. 1763–1846), see Descotes, *La Légende de Napoléon*, 72; and *L'Anti-Napoléon*, ed. Tulard, 230.

19 See the catalog entry by Odile Nouvel-Kammerer, in idem, *Symbols of Power: Napoleon and the Art of the Empire Style, 1800–1815* (Paris: Musée des Arts décoratifs and New York: American Federation of Arts, in association with Harry N. Abrams, New York, 2007), no. 58. The throne is modeled on the *Bacchus Throne* (Paris, Musée du Louvre), crafted (with the addition of some ancient Roman components) by the sculptor Francesco Antonio Franzoni in Rome in 1792. See Daniela Gallo, "On the Antique Models of the Empire Style," in ibid, 40–1. I am grateful to Flore Campestrini for providing an image of the throne, together with the corresponding file from the Musée des Arts décoratifs. I also thank Eve Briend, Pôle éditions et images, Photothèque for assisting me in obtaining reproduction rights.

20 For the changes wrought upon the Vendôme Column by subsequent regimes, see Michael Marrinan, *Romantic Paris: Histories of a Cultural Landscape, 1800–1850* (Stanford, CA: Stanford University Press, 2009), 114–21.

21 For Lemot's Henri IV (inaugurated 25 August 1818, the feast day of Saint Louis), see Anne M. Wagner, "Outrages: Sculpture and Kingship in France after 1789," in *The Consumption of Culture, 1600–1800: Image, Object, Text*, ed. Ann Bermingham and John Brewer (London: Routledge, 1995), 294–318.

22 See Satish Padiyar, *Chains: David, Canova, and the Fall of the Public Hero in Postrevolutionary France* (University Park: Penn State University Press, 2007), 44–5. I owe this reference to Thomas Crow.

23 See Alan B. Spitzer, *Old Hatreds and Young Hopes: The French Carbonari against the Bourbon Restoration* (Cambridge, MA: Harvard University Press, 1971).

24 For imagery generated by the assassination, including a sympathetic portrait of Louvel by Delacroix, see Nina M. Athanassoglou-Kallmyer, *Eugène Delacroix: Prints, Politics and Satire, 1814–1822* (New Haven, CT: Yale University Press, 1991), chap. 4.

25 See Sudhir Hazareesingh, *The Legend of Napoleon* (London: Granta, 2004), especially chap. 3. For dissident visual culture under the Bourbon Restoration, see also Barbara Ann Day-Hickman, *Napoleonic Art: Nationalism and the Spirit of Rebellion in France (1815–1848)* (Newark: University of Delaware Press and London: Associated University Presses, 1999), chap. 1.

26 The classic study is Jean Vidalenc, *Les Demi-solde: Étude d'une catégorie sociale* (Paris: Marcel Rivière, 1955). For the *demi-solde* and veterans under the Bourbon Restoration,

see also Isser Woloch, *The French Veteran from the Revolution to the Restoration* (Chapel Hill: University of North Carolina Press, 1979), 295–305.

27 In *Le Rouge et le noir* (*The Red and the Black*, 1830), Stendhal satirizes the tension underlying the Bonapartist-liberal alliance in a conversation between two friends, one a Bonapartist and the other a liberal. While the former waxes nostalgic on the reign of Napoleon, the latter blames the Concordat and the emperor's multiplication of the aristocracy for the priests and notables who have made his life in the provinces a living hell, compelling him to flee to Paris. See *Le Rouge et le noir*, ed. Anne-Marie Meininger, pref. Jean Prévost (Paris: Gallimard, 2000), 327–8. For the spectrum of liberal opinion regarding Napoleon and his legacy, see Sudir Hazareesingh, "Napoleonic Memory in Nineteenth-Century France: The Making of a Liberal Legend," *Modern Language Notes* 120, no. 4 (2005): 747–3.

28 For these caricatures, see Athanassoglou-Kallmyer, *Prints, Politics and Satire*, 34–41.

29 This, according to Vidalenc, *Les Demi-solde*, 207–11.

30 For the political orientation of Vernet and his circle, see Nina M. Athanassoglou-Kallmyer, "*Imago Belli:* Horace Vernet's *L'Atelier* as an Image of Radical Militarism under the Restoration," *Art Bulletin* 68, no. 2 (June 1986): 268–80; and *Horace Vernet and the Thresholds of Nineteenth-Century Visual Culture*, ed. Daniel Harkett and Katie Hornstein (Hanover, NH: Dartmouth College Press, 2017).

31 See the catalog entry by Philippe Durey, in *Horace Vernet (1789–1863)* (Rome: Académie de France à Rome, 1980), no. 34.

32 During the Empire, Odiot crafted exquisite confections, including a butterfly-handled milk cup (ca. 1810; Paris, Musée des Arts décoratifs) molded from a breast of Napoleon's sister, Pauline Borghese. See the catalog entry by Odile Nouvel-Kammerer, in idem, *Symbols of Power*, no. 157.

33 For Vernet's 1822 studio exhibition, see Daniel Harkett, "Revisiting Horace Vernet's Studio Exhibition," in *Horace Vernet*, ed. Harkett and Hornstein, 38–56; Katie Hornstein, *Picturing War in France, 1792–1856* (New Haven, CT: Yale University Press, 2017), 62; and Marie-Claude Chaudonneret, *L'État et les artistes: De la restauration à la monarchie de Juillet (1815–1833)* (Paris: Flammarion, 1999), 102–5. For *The Battle of Jemmapes* and three other battle scenes commissioned by the duc d'Orlèans (the future King Louis-Philippe), see Valérie Bajou, "Horace et monsieur de Valmy," in *Louis-Philippe et Versailles*, ed. idem (Versailles: Chatêau de Versailles, in association with Somogy, Paris, 2018), 55–9.

34 See Nina M. Athanassoglou-Kallmyer, "Sad Cincinnatus: The *Soldat Laboureur* as an Image of the Napoleonic Veteran after the Empire," *Arts Magazine* 60 (May 1986), 65–75; and idem, "Truth and Lies: Vernet, Vaudeville, and Photography," in *Horace Vernet*, ed. Harkett and Hornstein, 207–27. For the tenacity and popularity of the *soldat-laboureur* motif, from the Enlightenment through Vichy, see Gérard de Puymège, "Le Soldat Chauvin," in *Les Lieux de mémoire*, ed. Pierre Nora, vol. 2: *La Nation*, part 3 (Paris: Gallimard, 1986), 45–80.

35 See Nina Athanassoglou-Kallmyer, *Théodore Géricault.* (New York: Phaidon, 2010), chap. 3.

36 For this lithograph, see Robert Simon, "Géricault and the *fait divers*," in *Géricault*, ed. Régis Michel (Paris: La documentation française, 1996), 1: 259–62; Athanassoglou-Kallmyer, *Théodore Géricault*, 95–6; Lorenz Eitner, *Géricault: His Life and Work* (London: Orbis, 1983), 154–5; and the catalog entry by Sylvain Laveissière in idem et al., *Géricault* (Paris: Réunion des musées nationaux, 1991), no. 280.

37 For examples, see Athanassoglou-Kallmyer, *Théodore Géricault*, 92–5; and Stephen Bann, *Parallel Lines: Printmakers, Painters and Photographers in Nineteenth-Century France* (New Haven, CT: Yale University Press, 2001), 70–1.

38 In this I concur with Eitner, *Géricault*, 153–5.

39 For Géricault's brief service in the Grey Musketeers, see Eitner, *Géricault*, 72–5; Athanassoglou-Kallmyer, *Théodore Géricault*, 40; and the biographical chronology by Bruno Chenique, in Laveissière et al., *Géricault*, 270–4.

40 For this project, see Thomas Crow, *Restoration: The Fall of Napoleon in the Course of European Art, 1812–1820* (Princeton, NJ: Princeton University Press, 2018), 3, 40–1; Eitner, *Géricault*, 50–2; and Athanassoglou-Kallmyer, *Théodore Géricault*, 40.

41 Quoted in Jean Touchard, *La Gloire de Béranger* (Paris: Armand Colin, 1968), 1: 264.
42 For accounts of the emperor on Saint Helena, from O'Meara to Las Cases, see Natalie Petiteau, *Napoléon de la mythologie à l'histoire* (Paris: Éditions du Seuil, 1999), 57–60. For analysis of the literary aspects of the *Mémorial,* see Robert Morrissey, "The 'Mémorial de Sainte-Hélène' and the Poetics of Fusion," *Modern Language Notes* 120, no. 4 (September 2005): 716–32.
43 Hazareesingh, *The Legend of Napoleon*, 200 n. 87.
44 For the expulsion of Las Cases, and his predicament of desiring to leave the island without appearing to abandon the emperor, see Philip Dwyer, *Napoleon: Passion, Death and Resurrection, 1815–1840* (London: Bloomsbury, 2018), 83.
45 The text of the original manuscript, previously believed to have been lost, has been rediscovered (in a transcription by the British Colonial Office). Annotated by historians Peter Hicks, Thierry Lentz, François Houdecek, and Chantal Prévot, the text was published (2017) by Éditions Perrin and the Napoleon Foundation. It is shorter than the 1823 edition and devoid of some of the best known of the exiled emperor's aphorisms. See the notice by Sudhir Hazareesingh, in the *Times Literary Supplement* (17 November 2017), 14.
46 "Notre but n'est plus désormais que d'accroître la prospérité de la France par l'affermissement de la liberté publique." *Les Constitutions de la France depuis 1789*, ed. Jacques Godechot (Paris: Flammarion, 1979), 231.
47 Didier Le Gall, *Napoléon et 'Le Mémorial de Sainte-Hélène': Analyse d'un discours*, pref. Jean-Paul Bertaud (Paris: Éditions Kimé, 2003), 347.
48 Emmanuel de Las Cases, *Souvenirs de l'empereur Napoléon Ier, Extraits du Mémorial de Sainte-Hélène* (Paris: L. Hachette, 1854), 365.
49 For evolution of the conception of Napoleon in Hugo's poetry, see Keith Wren, "Victor Hugo and the Napoleonic Myth," *European Studies Review* 10 (1980): 429–58.
50 The poet offers a sinister parallel to the birth of Napoleon from the "regicide hydra" of the Revolution: "Telle souvent la mer qui gronde / Dévore un plaine féconde / Et vomit un sombre volcan." ("Thus, often the rumbling sea / Devours a fertile plain / And vomits a somber volcano.") Victor Hugo, *Odes et ballades*, ed. Pierre Albouy (Paris: Gallimard, 1964), 102–6.
51 For close readings of "À la colonne de la place Vendôme" and its sequel from the early July Monarchy, "À la colonne" (1830), see Kevin C. Smith, "Victor Hugo and the Vendôme Column: 'Ce fut le début de la rupture …'," *French Forum* 21, no. 2 (May 1996): 149–64. For the context of "À la colonne de la place Vendôme," see Albouy's commentary in Hugo, *Odes et ballades*, 187 n. 1 (on p. 454).
52 Hugo, *Odes et ballades*, 187.
53 For the popularity of this song, see Tulard, *Le Mythe de Napoléon*, 42–3.
54 "Au bronze de Henri mon orgueil te marie." ("My pride weds you to the bronze of Henri"). Hugo, *Odes et ballades*, 188. In 1819, Hugo won the Académie des jeux floraux competition with an essay honoring the reestablishment of the statue of Henri IV on the Pont Neuf, and he attended the ceremonial inauguration of the monument. See Bradley Stephens, *Victor Hugo* (London: Reaktion Books, 2019), 33.
55 Hugo, *Odes et ballades*, 193.
56 Victor Hugo, *Les Orientales, in Oeuvres de Victor Hugo*, 5th ed. (Paris: Charles Gosselin and Hector Bossange, 1829), 3: 380.
57 Ibid., 373–4.
58 See Maurice Samuels, *The Spectacular Past: Popular History and the Novel in Nineteenth-Century France* (Ithaca, NY: Cornell University Press, 2004), chap. 3 and the appendix, "Plays about Napoleon and the Empire, 1830–31."
59 For the Pellerin prints, see Day-Hickman, *Napoleonic Art.*
60 "*Napoléon* est pour les Français une parole magique qui les électrise et les éblouit. Mille canons dorment dans ce nom aussi bien que dans la colonne de la place Vendôme, et les Tuileries trembleront si ces mille canons s'éveillent un jour. De même que les juifs ne prononcent pas sans nécessité le nom de leur dieu, on désigne rarement ici Napoléon par son nom; on l'appelle presque toujours *l'homme*; mais on voit son image partout en estampe, en plâtre, en métal, en bois et dans toutes les situations. Sur les boulevards et dans les carrefours se tiennent des orateurs qui célèbrent l'homme, des chanteurs populaires

qui redisent ses hauts faits.... [C]e nom est pour le peuple la parole conjuratrice la plus puissante. Napoléon est son dieu, son culte, sa religion, et cette religion devient, à la fin, banale comme toutes les autres." Heinrich Heine, *De la France*, new ed. (Paris: Michel Lévy, 1873), 46–7 (19 January 1832; emphasis in original).

61 For the sources and biographical context of the novel—printed in seven editions between 1833 and 1846—see the preface by Pierre Citron, in Honoré de Balzac, *Le Médecin de campagne*, ed. Pierre Citron (Paris: Garnier-Flammarion, 1965). For the novel's contribution to the Napoleonic legend, see also Descotes, *La Légende de Napoléon*, 238–42. For Balzac and the legend of Napoleon, see also Gerwin, "Révision et subversion"; and Pierre Laubriet, "La Légende et le myth napoléoniens chez Balzac," *L'Année balzacienne* (January 1968): 285–302.

62 Balzac, *Le Médecin de campagne*, 56.

63 Such was the popularity of this episode, that it was republished separately as *Histoire de l'Empereur racontée dans une grange par un vieux soldat et recueillie par M. de Balzac* (Paris: Dubochet, 1842), as cited in Hazareesingh, *The Legend of Napoleon*, 238 n. 15.

64 Balzac, *Le Médecin de campagne*, 246.

65 For attempts by the July Monarchy to manipulate popular enthusiasm for the Napoleonic legend, see Michael Marrinan, *Painting Politics for Louis-Philippe: Art and Ideology in Orléanist France, 1830–1848* (New Haven, CT: Yale University Press, 1988), part IV; and Stanley Mellon, "The July Monarchy and the Napoleonic Myth," *Yale French Studies* 26 (fall-winter 1960–61): 70–8.

66 Inaugurated 28 July 1833 in the presence of Louis-Philippe, the sculpture is now in court of honor of the Church of the Invalides.

67 Pierre-Jean de Béranger, *Les Souvenirs du peuple. Chanson inédite de P.-J. de Béranger* (Paris: Badouin frères, 1827), 4.

68 For the *retour des Cendres*, see Driskel, *As Befits a Legend*, chap. 2; Marrinan, *Painting Politics for Louis-Philippe*, part IV; Suzanne Glover Lindsay, *Funerary Arts and Tomb Cult—Living with the Dead in France, 1750–1870* (Farnham: Ashgate, 2012), chap. 5; Jean Tulard, "Le Retour des Cendres," in *Les Lieux de mémoire,* ed. Pierre Nora, vol. 2: *La Nation*, part 3 (Paris: Gallimard, 1986), 81–110; and Jean Lucas-Dubreton, *Le Culte de Napoléon, 1815–1848* (Paris: Albin Michel, 1960), chap. 16.

69 Letter to Comte Léon de Pierreclos (12 May 1840), in *Correspondance de Lamartine*, ed. Valentine de Lamartine (Paris: Hachette, Furne, Jouvet, 1873–75), 5: 439.

70 "Quoique admirateur de ce grand homme, je n'ai pas un enthousiasme sans souvenir et sans prévoyance. Je ne me prosterne pas devant cette mémoire; je ne suis pas de cette religion napoléonienne, de ce culte de la force que l'on veut depuis quelque temps substituer dans l'esprit de la nation à la religion sérieuse de la liberté. Je ne crois pas qu'il soit bon de déifier ainsi sans cesse la guerre, de surexciter ces bouillonnements déjà trop impétueux du sang français, qu'on nous représente comme impatient de couler après une trêve de vingt-cinq ans, comme si la paix, qui est le bonheur et la gloire du monde, pouvait être la honte des nations." *La Politique de Lamartine: Choix de discours et écrits politiques*, ed. L. de Ronchaud (Paris: Hachette and Furne, Jouvet, 1878), 1:290. For a discussion of Lamartine's address, see Petiteau, *Napoléon de la mythologie à l'histoire*, 95–7; and, for opposition to the return of Napoleon's remains, see Driskel, *As Befits a Legend*, 17–21.

71 For a concise account of the crisis, see André Jardin and A.J. Tudesq, *La France des notables*, vol. 1: *L'Évolution générale, 1815–1848* (Paris: Éditions du Seuil, 1973), 185–90.

72 "[L]es liens de 1815 ont été subitement rattachés; la chaîne du Titan était là, il n'a été besoin que de la resserrer. La France a été replongée dans cette solitude muette que la défaite a tracée autour d'elle. Comme si elle avait perdu une seconde fois la bataille, elle s'est trouvée de nouveau au lendemain de Waterloo." Edgar Quinet, *1815 et 1840*, 2nd ed. (Paris: Paulin, 1840), 41–2.

73 This figure is from Dwyer, *Napoleon: Passion, Death and Resurrection*, 219.

74 Completion of the project outlasted the July Monarchy; interment of the emperor's remains in a massive porphyry sarcophagus occurred under the Second Empire (2 April 1861). Driskel, *As Befits a Legend* (pp. 176–7) associates the understated aspect of the burial ceremony with the less authoritarian, more liberal character assumed by the Second Empire in the fall of 1860.

75 "Oui, C'est une fête; la fête d'un cercueil exilé qui revient en triomphe." Victor Hugo, *Choses vues: Souvenirs, journaux, cahiers, 1830–1846*, ed. Hubert Juin (Paris: Gallimard, 1972), 179.

76 See ibid., 198–9.

77 See Frédéric Bluche, *Le Bonapartisme: Aux origines de la droite autoritaire (1800–1850)* (Paris: Nouvelles éditions latines, 1980), 168–72; and idem, *Le Bonapartisme* (Paris: Presses Universitaires de France, 1981), 42–60.

78 Mellon, "The July Monarchy and the Napoleonic Myth," 74. For Thiers's ambivalent attitude toward Napoleon, as conveyed in his 20-volume *Histoire du Consulat et de l'Empire* (1845–62), see Sudir Hazareesingh, "Napoleonic Memory," 765–70.

79 Similarly, Béranger—who maintained a warm correspondence with Louis-Napoléon during the six-year post-putsch incarceration at Ham (1840–46)—denied that he was a Bonapartist and never lent full-hearted support to the regime of Napoleon III (which, nevertheless, coopted the songwriter's popularity by staging a grandiose state funeral). See Touchard, *La Gloire de Béranger,* 2: 307–8, 343.

80 For identification of Napoleon with Prometheus, see Sylvain Pagé, *Le Mythe napoléonien: De Las Cases à Victor Hugo* (Paris: CNRS éditions, 2013), chap. 5.

81 See Hazareesingh, *The Legend of Napoleon.*

82 For a summary of the debate, see Dwyer, *Napoleon: Passion, Death and Resurrection,* 69 and n. 101. Dwyer accepts Hazareesingh's point regarding the integration of the emotionally charged legend with political partisanship, while allowing for cases in which Napoleonism and Bonapartism remain distinct.

83 Hazareesingh, *The Legend of Napoleon,* 124.

84 For this medal, see ibid., 242ff.

85 For this work, see Lucia Tripodes, "François Rude: The Importance of Sculpture" (PhD diss., New York University, 2003), 246–79; Ruth Butler, "Long Live the Revolution, the Republic, and Especially the Emperor!: The Political Sculpture of Rude," in *Art and Architecture in the Service of Politics,* ed. Henry A. Millon and Linda Nochlin (Cambridge, MA: MIT Press, 1978): 92–107; Lindsay, *Funerary Arts and Tomb Cult,* 166–72; and Bertrand Tillier, *Napoléon, Rude et Noisot: Histoire d'un monument d'outre-tombe* (Paris: Les Éditions de l'Amateur, 2012).

86 The symbolic program is detailed in Tillier, *Napoléon, Rude et Noisot,* chap. 5.

87 Jacque de Caso maintains that a study by Rude for a monument to Napoleon, which shows the emperor as a prone corpse, cannot be tied by documentation to the Fixin monument, and that it was from a separate project. See Jacques de Caso, *David d'Angers: Sculptural Communication in the Age of Romanticism,* trans. Dorothy Johnson and Jacques de Caso (Princeton, NJ: Princeton University Press, 1992), 207–10. This corrects the notion that the *gisant* was an early, rejected conception for the Fixin monument, a claim made in the catalog entry for *The Imperial Eagle Watching Over the Dead Napoleon* (Dijon, Musée des Beaux-Arts), in *The Romantic Movement* (London: Arts Council of Great Britain, 1959), no. 501.

88 Butler, "Long Live the Revolution," 100. For the text of the speech, see Tillier, *Napoléon, Rude et Noisot,* 144–5. On a ceremonial visit to Fixin on 13 August 1850, President Louis-Napoléon Bonaparte (dedicated to the vitality of Bonapartism) was not pleased by Rude's monument, with its dead eagle. Conversely, despite his worship of Napoleon, Noisot was opposed to the reestablishment of the Empire. Along with Rude, Noisot unsuccessfully ran, under the aegis of Lamartine, in the April 1848 elections to the Constituent Assembly. He harbored bitterness toward the Second Empire, which showed him scant favor. See Tillier, *Napoléon, Rude et Noisot,* 147–53.

89 "On se dirige vers un côteau-rapide, couverts des rochers, nu jusqu'au sommet, sorte de Calvaire, mais auquel se lient le Mont des Oliviers et le Jardin de la Résurrection." Quoted from M.J. Trullard, *Souvenirs de l'inauguration du monument érigé à Napoléon en Bourgogne, 1847* (Dijon: Guasco-Jobard, 1847), 6, in Day-Hickman, *Napoleonic Art,* 140 n. 12 (Day-Hickman's translation).

90 See Frank Paul Bowman, *French Romanticism: Intertextual and Interdisciplinary Readings* (Baltimore, MD: Johns Hopkins University Press, 1990, chap. 3 ("Napoleon as a Christ Figure"). For representations of the resurrected emperor, including Horace Vernet's

painting *The Apotheosis of Napoleon* (1823, London, Wallace Collection), see Alissa R. Adams, "French Depictions of Napoleon I's Resurrection (1821–48)" (PhD diss., University of Iowa, 2018), chap. 2. https://doi.org/10.17077/etd.vdzokygw.

91 Edgar Quinet, *Napoléon, poème* (Paris: Ambroise Dupont, 1836), 399.

92 The episode is recounted in Richard Howard Powers, *Edgar Quinet: A Study in French Patriotism* (Dallas, TX: Southern Methodist University Press, 1957), 107–8.

93 For Towiański's doctrine and his influence on the poet, see Jeremy Lambert, "Le Towianisme en France. La France dans le Towianisme," *Slavica bruxellensia*, 3 (2009): 61–73. https://doi.org/10.4000/slavica.274. Open Edition Journals; Roman Koropeckyj, *Adam Mickiewicz: The Life of a Romantic* (Ithaca, NY: Cornell University Press, 2008); Frank Paul Bowman, *French Romanticism*, 42–8; Lloyd S. Kramer, *Threshold of a New World: Intellectuals and the Exile Experience in Paris, 1830–1848* (Ithaca, NY: Cornell University Press, 1988), 209–12; and Tulard, *Le Culte de Napoléon*, chap. 7.

94 For Beauterne's influence on Mickiewicz, Towiański (and on another Pole who subscribed to Napoleonic messianism, the mathematician Josef Hoëné Wronski, 1776–1853), see Bowman, *French Romanticism*, 37–48.

95 On Saint-Helena, Napoleon told General Bertrand that he doubted that there was "anything after death." "I'm lucky not to believe," he asserted, "for I don't have chimerical fears about death." Quoted in Steven Englund, *Napoleon: A Political Life* (New York: Scribner, 2004), 454. For skepticism regarding Napoleon's embrace of Catholicism in captivity, see also Dwyer, *Napoleon: Passion, Death and Resurrection*, 115.

96 "En voyant Napoléon s'incliner avec le tremblement de la foi, devant notre mystérieuse et redoutable hostie, attendre les mains jointes, dans un recueillement profond, prendre et consommer l'aliment de la foi; que la politique s'incline elle-même et adore! ... ô élu de Dieu, convertissez-moi, convertissez l'impie ... en nous racontant, pour notre édification, les idées et les sentimens de votre communion bienheureuse." Robert-Augustin Antoine de Beauterne, *Conversations religieuses de Napoléon, avec des Documents inédits de la plus haute importance où il révèle lui-même sa pensée intime sur le christianisme* (Paris: Chez l'auteur, Olivier-Fulgence, and Debécourt, 1841), 241.

97 "Satan, aveuglé par sa haine, s'y est pris comme dans un piège. II se confesse vaincu, si je lui montre une seule âme sauvée par Napoléon; eh bien! le ciel s'ouvre: je vois des millions d'élus qui l'attendent comme une cause seconde de leur rédemption; ce sont les soldats morts sur les champs de bataille, instruits, convertis par l'exemple de ce grand homme, tous les enfants baptisés, grâce au concordat. Eh bien! Satan, te voilà donc vaincu!" Beauterne, *Conversations religieuses*, 299.

98 See Paul Bénichou, *L'École du désenchantement: Sainte-Beuve, Nodier, Musset, Nerval, Gautier* (Paris: Gallimard, 1992), 310, which associates the current with post-1830 disillusionment. See also Bowman, *French Romanticism*, chap. 3.

99 For Esquiros, Bicêtre, and Napoleonic messianism, see Bowman, *French Romanticism*, 34, 51–3. See also Dwyer, *Napoleon: Passion, Death and Resurrection*, 211 and n. 1.

100 For Nerval's four strange, unpublished Napoleonic sonnets (1841), see Bénichou, *L'École du désenchantement*, 311–22. Bowman underscores Nerval's inconsistency in regard to this subject: "Nerval is caustic and comic about Napoleonic messianism in his journalism, appropriates it seriously via figural thinking in his sonnets." *French Romanticism*, 207.

101 For Ganneau and his disciple Charles Caillaux, see Bowman, *French Romanticism*, 48–50; and Paul Bénichou, *Le Temps des prophètes: Doctrines de l'âge romantique* (Paris: Gallimard, 1977), 429–35.

102 Grand Caïn! Sur ton front se sont réfléchis tout la Splendeur et la Majesté de l'Unité, toutes les Douleurs et tout le Néant de l'individualité....[C]hacun des termes de l'idée humaine, qu'elle soit Politique, Sociale, ou Religieuse, vient se résumer par un immense cri, WATERLOO! C'est que là est le mot du grand Labeur d'Adam qui se nomma Abraham, Jacob, Moïse, puis Alexandre, Socrate, César, Mahomet, Charlemagne, enfin Jésus et Napoléon: Jésus le Christ-Abel, Napoléon le Christ-Caïn, grands Phares des Siècles, Synthèse vivante, sublimes forms par lesquelles l'Humanité est passé pour retourner à *l'Unité Adam*, d'où elle est primitivement sortie." Le Mapah, *Waterloo. À Vous, beaux fils de France, morts pour l'honneur. Salut et glorification! L'Honneur, c'est l'Unité!!*

(Paris: Au bureau des publications Évadiennes, 1843), 3–8 (emphasis in original). See the commentary on this text in Bowman, *French Romanticism*, 49–50.

103 For the Wimille column, see Tillier, *Napoléon, Rude et Noisot*, 107–11.

104 "[L]'idée napoléonienne n'est point une idée de guerre, mais une idée sociale, industrielle, commerciale, humanitaire. Si pour quelques hommes elle apparaît toujours entourée de la foudre des combats, c'est qu'elle fut en effet trop longtemps enveloppée par la fumée du canon et la poussière des batailles. Mais aujourd'hui les nuages se sont dissipés, et on entrevoit à travers la gloire des armes une gloire civile plus grande et plus durable." Louis-Napoléon Bonaparte, *Des idées napoléoniennes* (Paris: Paulin, 1839), 200.

105 For the contribution of the cult of Napoleon to the ascent of his nephew, see Hazareesingh, *The Legend of Napoleon*, chaps. 7 and 8.

106 For Quinet's intellectual contacts and the diffusion of his ideas while in exile, see Laure Lévêque, "Banni soit qui mal y pense: l'histoire en exil. Le cas Quinet," *Babel: Littératures plurielles* 29 (2014): 289–314. https://doi.org/10.4000/babel.3734

107 O patrie! c'est à cette heure où te voilà sanglante, inanimée, la tête pendante, les yeux fermés, la bouche ouverte et ne parlant plus, les marques du fouet sur les épaules, les clous de la semelle des bourreaux imprimés sur tout le corps, nue et souillée, et pareille à une chose mort, objet de haine, objet de risée, hélas! c'est à cette heure, patrie, que le coeur du proscrit déborde d'amour et de respect pour toi!" *Napoléon le petit* (London: Jeffs and Brussels: A. Mertens, 1852), 374.

108 "Nox" (Jersey, November 1852), in Victor Hugo, *Les Châtiments*, ed. René Journet (Paris: Gallimard, 1977), 28.

109 "Napoléon III" (Jersey, December 1852), in Hugo, *Les Châtiments*, 180.

110 The motif previously appeared in a satirical print from 1848, which has the truncated column inscribed "Boulogne, Suisse, Strasbourg, sergent de ville à Londres" and which shows Louis-Napoléon as largely reduced to a pair of boots, with his mouth padlocked. See Nicole Villa, Denise Dommel, and Jacques Thirion, *Bibliothèque nationale, Département des estampes. Un siècle d'histoire de France par l'estampe, 1770–1871. Collection De Vinck. Inventaire analytique*, vol. 7: *La Révolution de 1848 et La Deuxième République* (Paris: Bibliothèque nationale, 1955), 542, no. 15189.

111 "La Commune de Paris, considérant que la colonne impériale de la place Vendôme est un monument de barbarie, un symbole de force brute et de fausse gloire, une affirmation du militarisme, une négation du droit international, une insulte permanente des vainqueurs aux vaincus, un attentat perpétuel à l'un des trois grandes principes de la République française, la Fraternité, décrète:... La colonne de la place Vendôme sera démolie." Quoted in Victor Hugo, *L'Année terrible*, ed. Yves Gohin (Paris: Gallimard, 1985), 141 n. 1 (on p. 305).

112 According to Laurence des Cars, in Dominique de Font-Réaulx et al., *Gustave Courbet* (New York: Metropolitan Museum of Art, in association with Hatje Cantz, Ostfildern, 2008), 409–10.

113 Quoted in Richard D.E. Burton, *Blood in the City: Violence and Revelation in Paris, 1789–1945* (Ithaca, NY: Cornell University Press, 2001), 87.

114 Chateaubriand, *De Buonaparte et des Bourbons*, 5, 11, 21.

115 For this point, see Charles A. Porter, *Chateaubriand: Composition, Imagination, and Poetry*, Stanford French and Italian Studies 9 (Saratoga, CA: Anma Libri, 1978), 76. Porter (p. 77 n.15) observes that, in the much more sympathetic treatment of Napoleon in the *Mémoires d'outre-tombe*, Chateaubriand replaces the derogatory (i.e., un-French) "Buonaparte" with "Bonaparte" when referring to *De Buonaparte et des Bourbons*. For the satanic aspect of Napoleon's grandeur, as viewed by the author, see Fumaroli, *Chateaubriand: Poésie et terreur* part 4, chap. 3. For Chateaubriand's commentary on Napoleon, see also Tom Conner, *Chateaubriand's 'Mémoires d'outre-tombe': A Portrait of the Artist as Exile*, The Age of Revolution and Romanticism Interdisciplinary Studies 7, ed. Gita May (New York: Peter Lang, 1995), chap. 2.

116 "Le monde appartient à Bonaparte; ce que le ravageur n'avait pu achiever de conquérir, sa renommée l'usurpe; vivant il a manqué le monde, mort il le possède.... Bonaparte appartenait si fort à la domination absolue, qu'après avoir subi le despotisme de sa personne, il nous faut subir le despotisme de sa mémoire. Ce dernier despotism est plus dominateur

que le premier, car si l'on combattit quelquefois Napoléon alors qu'il était sur le trône, il y a consentement universel à accepter les fers que mort il nous jette." Chateaubriand, *Mémoires d'outre-tombe*, ed. Jean-Claude Berchet (Paris: Garnier, 2001), 2: 731.

117 Written largely after 1830 and published posthumously (1849–50), the *Mémoires d'outre-tombe* were conceived in 1803, begun in 1809, and completed in 1847.

118 "Après Alexandre, commença le pouvoir romain; apres César, le christianisme changea le monde; après Charlemagne, la nuit féodale engendra une nouvelle société; après Napoléon, néant: on ne voit venir ni empire, ni religion, ni barbares." Chateaubriand, *Mémoires d'outre-tombe,* 3: 290. The terminus post quem of this passage is 8 July 1833, as evidenced by reference to the Treaty of Unkiar Skelessi, signed by Russia and the Ottoman Empire on that date.

5 Heroism Lost

"France is a Bored Nation"

In Honoré Daumier's lithograph "France at Rest" ("Repos de la France"), published in *La Caricature* (28 August 1834), Louis-Philippe ignominiously slouches, his features hidden by the brim of a bourgeois hat (Figure 5.1).[1] Dozing in a throne surmounted by a pear-topped crown, the pudgy Citizen-King is accompanied by a desolate, Phrygian-capped woman with bound wrists—a sorry counterpart to the robust Liberty who leads the People over a barricade in Delacroix's classic celebration of the July Revolution (1830, Paris, Musée du Louvre). The captive is also a far

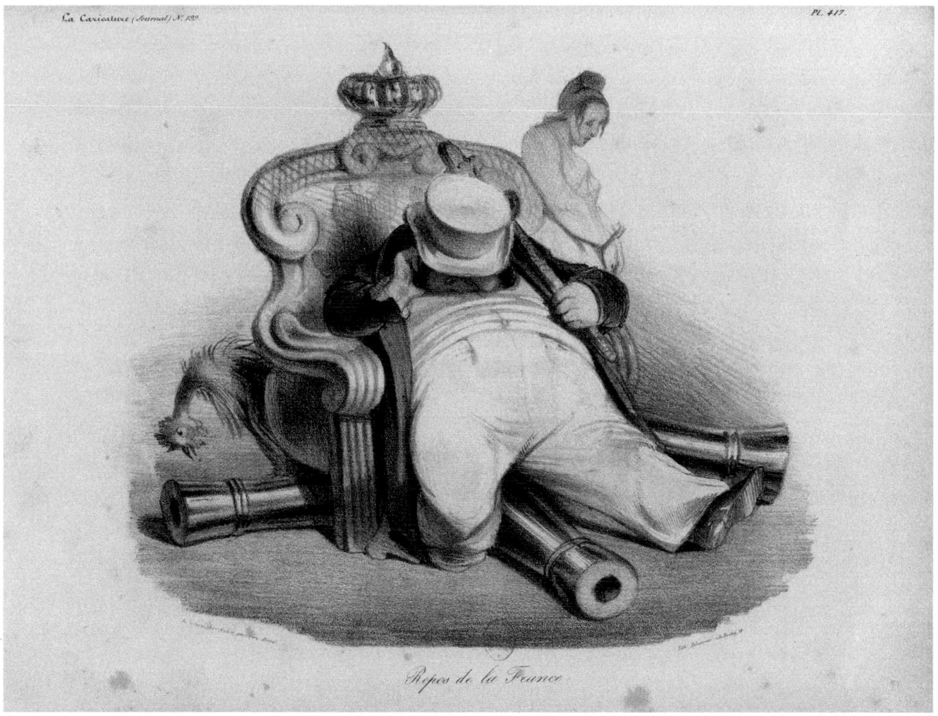

Figure 5.1 Honoré Daumier, "France at Rest" ("Repos de la France"). In *La Caricature* (28 August 1834), lithograph, 262 × 216 cm. Paris, Bibliothèque nationale de France. Photo: BnF.

DOI: 10.4324/9781003184737-6

cry from the fierce allegory of the Republic that François Rude was then sculpting for Napoleon's unfinished Arc de triomphe de l'Étoile at the behest of an embattled government avid for emblems of national glory. Three disused cannon barrels are accusatory reminders of past valor, whether that of the Grande Armée or of the revolutionary troops beside whom the young Louis-Philippe had seen action as a lieutenant-general in the battles of Valmy and Jemmapes (20 September and 6 November 1792, respectively). A drooping *coq gaulois* and the idled barrel between the monarch's legs add sexual insult to this image of royal impotence and national shame. Aimed at a regime that sought peace with the Empire's mortal foes, all the while aggressively pursuing a domestic campaign of law and order, *France at Rest* is characteristic of the dark satire that poured obsessively from *La Caricature* until its raging columns and cruelly clever illustrations were gagged by the censorship laws of September 1835.

Disgust with the July Monarchy's somnolence was not limited to the radical Left. Though appalled by the brutal *ad hominem* that was the stock and trade of Daumier (1808–79) and his dissident colleagues—and not at all nostalgic for imperial bellicosity—Lamartine famously declared to his fellow deputies in the Palais-Bourbon on 10 June 1839: "France is a bored nation" ("*La France est une nation qui s'ennuie*"). Targeting the tedium of life under a constitutional monarchy devoted to moderation and monetary gain, Lamartine's lament suggests that he shared the widespread disappointment that followed the hopeful Revolution of 1830. Having entered its second regime as a second-rate power confined to its hexagonal borders, France could only nostalgically yearn for the imperial might receding into an ever more distant past—a situation deemed dire by Lamartine's more truculent contemporaries.

Among those was Edgar Quinet. Considering France's post-Napoleonic descent into boredom a matter of cosmic significance, he invoked lost imperial glory in an idiosyncratic text that offers nothing less than a visionary exposition of human destiny, *Ahasvérus* (1833). Though the author was disappointed by the critical reception of this unstageable (and nearly unreadable) drama, it proved surprisingly popular, going into a second edition in 1843, and a fifth in 1876.[2] Predating Quinet's verse collection, *Napoléon* (1836) by three years, *Ahasvérus* is named after the protagonist of an international legend with medieval roots first popularized in print in Germany in 1602. Better known as the Wandering Jew, Ahasvérus is an apocryphal shoemaker who mocked Christ on his way to Calvary and was doomed to walk the earth until the Second Coming.[3] Familiar in France from popular prints known as *images d'Épinal* (in which Napoleon was a staple), the Wandering Jew personified the punishment meted out to the uncharitable and the unbelieving.[4] Crude, colored broadsides bearing his image provided provincial homes with a daily reminder of the sanctity of hospitality and the perfidy of Jews. Alongside this anti-Semitic folk tradition, a more positive view of the Wandering Jew emerged in the nineteenth century, when he was the subject of myriad literary reinterpretations.[5] In the best-known example, Eugène Sue's sensational serial thriller, *Le Juif errant* (1844–45), he is cast as an invulnerable, tragic hero. Spreading cholera in his wake, he defends the innocent heirs to a Protestant fortune against the diabolical machinations of a Jesuit mastermind and saves the life of a French general at the Battle of Waterloo.

Writing amid the exalted humanitarian and utopian rhetoric that burgeoned in the dispiriting aftermath of the July Revolution, Quinet's earlier publication invests

Ahasvérus with solemn grandeur. Accordingly, in *Ahasvérus*, the accursed wanderer "embodies mankind's unending quest for the Absolute."[6] As reinvented by Quinet, the Wandering Jew is Everyman; toward the end of *Ahasvérus*, God the Father says to Christ: "Ahasvérus is the eternal man. All others resemble him. Your judgment on him will serve as that for all."[7] Replete with Romantic empathy toward outcasts, Quinet's play has a characteristically nineteenth-century gigantism, featuring speaking appearances by figures drawn from history and scripture. Even geographical personifications, such as the Ocean and Babylon, deliver lines. Unfolding in four Days (Creation, the Passion, Death, and the Last Judgment) separated by interludes, this timeless spectacle is briefly tugged into the national present during the interlude of the Second Day. There, a chorus of old men decry France's decline since the fall of Napoleon and exhort the audience to return France to its position at the head of all nations:

> Men of Lodi, of Castiglione, of Marengo, where are you? Come out of the earth. You laid yourselves to rest an hour too soon. Come accomplish the task that your children do not have the heart to achieve.... Because, in my opinion, your greatest wrong is this: to have let your wicked enemies twice surround, flog, and plunder this great county.... My God! France, sweet France, flower of the sky sown on the earth, you have already, without knowing it, cost me tears that no one can repay! Beautiful ship without a rudder, many a time, in the black night, I have waited for you until the morning, no longer hoping that, all alone, you again locate your shore!... The earth is bored, it doesn't know what to do since your Emperor no longer keeps it hidden, just for fun, under a fold of his glory.[8]

Embedded in an epic of outsized ambition, this interlude is a grandiose counterpart to Daumier's contemptuous lithograph of the drowsing monarch and Lamartine's parliamentary address regarding national boredom. These disparate expressions of depressed national aspiration belong to an anti-heroic current that imparts period flavor to a broad range of post-Napoleonic art and literature. Imbued with a profound sense of loss, this discourse speaks to a legacy of defeat.

That troubled heritage inspired a refrain of the 1830s: the complaint of having been born too late to experience service in imperial uniform. Introducing the three stories that comprise Alfred de Vigny's *Military Servitude and Grandeur* (*Servitude et grandeur militaires*, 1835) the narrator (the author's mouthpiece) evokes the hunger for military glory he felt in youth:

> Toward the end of the Empire, I was a distracted lycéen [high school student]. The war was alive in the lycée, in my ears the drum stifled the voice of the instructors, and the mysterious voice of books spoke to us only a cold and pedantic language.... When one of our brothers, who had left the college several months before, reappeared in a hussar's uniform with his arm in a sling, we were ashamed of our books and we threw them at the heads of our instructors.[9]

These martial longings were frustrated by untimely birth:

> I belong to that generation born with the century, who, nourished on bulletins by the Emperor, always had a naked sword before its eyes, and went to seize it at the very moment when France replaced it in the scabbard of the Bourbons.[10]

This was the very predicament of the uncompromisingly ambitious Julien Sorel of Stendhal's *The Red and the Black* (*Le Rouge et le noir*, 1830). Nursing an obsession with Bonaparte inculcated by a provincial veteran of the Italian campaign, the *Mémorial de Sainte-Hélène*, and imperial war *bulletins*, Sorel judges his every audacious impulse in light of what Napoleon might have done in his place. Envious of the uniformed suitors and brother of the aristocrat Mathilde (whom he seduces), Julien rues his humble origin and ecclesiastical vocation:

> Me, poor peasant from the Jura ... condemned to always wear this sad black habit! Alas! Twenty years earlier, I would have worn the uniform like them! Then, a man like me was killed or a *general at thirty-three years*.[11]

Aged 17 in 1814, Vigny was also born too late; yet his military service was not, like that of Géricault, a passing fancy. The author bore arms from his enrollment in the Gendarmes du Roi at the opening of the Restoration (1814) until his resignation from the National Guard in the early July Monarchy (1832). This substantial time in uniform transpired in the Empire's wake; hence, the retrospective format of *Servitude et grandeur militaires*, which offers a trio of confessional tales, each recounted by an imperial veteran. Conceived as a military counterpart to *The Imitation of Christ*, Vigny's book is concerned with self-denial, which, for the soldier, can be a source of either heroic grandeur or bitter servitude.[12] Given the bleak interpretation of the Gospel narrative of Christ in the Garden of Olives Vigny later penned, it is unsurprising that spiritual trauma inflects the narrative voice of *Servitude et grandeur militaires*. In place of the immolation of self in imitation of Christ espoused by Thomas à Kempis, Vigny substitutes selfless devotion to Honor, "which keeps watch in us like a last lamp in a devastated temple."[13] Doggedly clinging to this secular cult as the sole remnant of the sacred amid "the universal shipwreck of beliefs," the author depicts situations fraught with ethical dilemma.[14] What infuses the book with period flavor is Vigny's elevation of the soldier's resignation and self-abnegation as virtues—he terms this "PASSIVE GRANDEUR"—as well as his characterization of the post-Napoleonic army as an inert entity, potentially perilous to the regime, and unbound by political allegiance:

> The dazzling Grandeurs of conquerors are perhaps extinguished forever. Their past radiance weakens ... as, in minds, disdain for war grows and, in hearts, disgust for its cold cruelties.... Each sovereign looks upon his Army with sadness; this colossus seated at his feet, immobile and mute, bothers and frightens him; he knows not what to do with it, and fears that it will turn against him. He sees it consumed with ardor and unable to move.[15]

This perception of frustrated inertia on the part of the "immobile and mute" post-Napoleonic military dovetails with the anti-heroic zeitgeist of France under Louis-Philippe.

Post-Napoleonic malaise is most famously conveyed by a novel contemporary to *Servitude et grandeur militaires*, Alfred de Musset's *The Confession of a Child of the Century* (*La Confession d'un enfant du siècle*). Begun in the summer of 1834, it was published on 1 February 1836 (four months after Vigny's ensemble, published in October 1835). The work was inspired by the author's amorous relationship with George

Sand, from whom Musset had recently parted, following a spell of passion, fever, and betrayal in Venice, during which Sand both succored the febrile Musset and became the lover of her paramour's physician, Pietro Pagello.[16] While most of the narrative concerns the protagonist's turbulent love life, the opening section (part 1, chapter 2) pertains to the turmoil visited upon his entire generation.[17] Mindful of the chapter's topicality and its brilliant style—and eager to promote a young, relatively unknown, promising author—François Buloz (1803–77), director of the *Revue des deux mondes*, published the excerpted chapter on 15 September 1835.[18] The opening confession of Octave (protagonist and narrator), is so well-known as to constitute a Romantic cliché:

> During the wars of the Empire, while husbands and brothers were in Germany, uneasy mothers brought into the world an ardent, pale, nervous generation. Conceived between two battles, raised in colleges to the roll of drums, thousands of children darkly glanced at each other, while trying out their sickly muscles. From time to time their blood-stained fathers appeared, lifted them to their gold brocaded chests, then replaced them on the ground and remounted their steeds.[19]

For this "generation of 1820"—whose ideas and passions under the Bourbon Restoration are lucidly chronicled by Alan B. Spitzer—the fall of Napoleon was catastrophic.[20] Formerly, he had dominated mankind: "In Europe at that time only one man was alive; the rest of the living tried to fill their lungs with the air that he breathed."[21] Subject to political reaction and piety during the Restoration, the vanquished nation was drained of energy:

> Just as a traveler, while on the road, runs night and day in rain and in sun, heedless of being on watch or in danger; but as soon as he has arrived in the midst of his family and sits down before the fire, he feels a boundless lassitude and can hardly drag himself to his bed; so too, France, widow of Caesar, suddenly felt her wound. She collapsed in exhaustion and slept such a deep sleep that her old kings, thinking her dead, wrapped her in a white [i.e., Bourbon] shroud.[22]

Notwithstanding its autobiographical genesis, Musset's novel is a trompe l'oeil period piece rather than a reminiscence. Paul Bénichou cautions that the generation Octave characterizes was not Musset's. The author was 13 years younger than Vigny, who was born 27 March 1797; Musset, born 11 December 1810, was less than four at the time of the Empire's collapse.[23] His fictive evocation of youthful yearning under the Restoration was possibly impacted by *Servitude et grandeur militaires* (Musset had known Vigny since 1828).[24] The disenchantment of Octave's generation, as Bénichou indicates, was not new. Yet *La Confession d'un enfant du siècle,* like Vigny's suite of military novellas, speaks to a sense of loss keenly felt at the time of publication. Present since the beginning of the century, and encouraged by the cult of Byron, this sentiment climaxed in the aftermath of the July Revolution.[25]

Thwarted martial ambition also troubles a novel published shortly before *Servitude et grandeur militaires* and *La Confession d'un enfant du siècle*: *Sensual Pleasure* (*Volupté*, 1834) by Charles-Augustin Sainte-Beuve (1804–69), who knew both Vigny and Musset and reviewed the latter's novel.[26] Set during the Consulate and Empire, Sainte-Beuve's glacially paced narrative offers scant fictional space outside of the thoughts of the indecisive, passive protagonist, Amaury, a convert to Catholicism. Tormented by his civilian status and transfixed by the military glory beyond his grasp, Amaury temporarily neglects his spiritual life, prayer, and acts of charity. Recounting the period in which hostilities resumed following the collapse of the Peace of Amiens, he confesses,

> I lived as if in an electric cloud, which hovered over my head and tempestuously enveloped me, discharging to the hills of the horizon its thunderclaps. My heart was swollen in my breast like the Ocean when the equinox moon lifts it, and I no longer found my level .... I fell into chaos ... dreaming solely of intoxication and glory ... to charge under cannon balls, and to die quickly.[27]

In an earlier novel, *Joseph Delorme* (1829), Sainte-Beuve spoke of suffocation when evoking the climate of the late Restoration: "In that time, every poor young man who had a heart, an ambition and vast thoughts, lacked air, withered in his garret and died of slow asphyxiation."[28] Later, the author attributed this oppressive languor to the absence of Napoleon:

> Our century, ... starting out in accord with the gigantic volition of the man with whom it identified, seems to have spent all at once its capacity to will, to have used it up in this first excess of material strength, and since then to have not rediscovered it.[29]

These pronouncements strike a common chord with a chorus of complaint, under Louis-Philippe, regarding somnolence, inertia, enervation, and boredom.

The Russian Campaign

Under both the restored Bourbons and the July Monarchy, the catastrophic Russian campaign of 1812 served as emblem of the Empire's collapse. Figures for Grande Armée casualties vary. The current authority on the Napoleonic wars, Alexander Mikaberidze, estimates that, of the approximately 600,000 invaders, about 500,000 were lost to either death, desertion (as many as 100,000), or capture (more than 120,000). Some 1,300 cannon and 200,000 horses were lost; the cavalry was virtually annihilated. Downplaying the role of the Russian climate, traditionally regarded as a principal cause of the disaster, Mikaberidze asserts that, when the cold arrived in November (after relatively mild weather had brought rain and mud), the campaign was already in shambles from combat casualties, disease, and desertion.[30] The retreat, which largely occurred in the autumn, was remembered solely as a winter event.

Ever attuned to the passions of the moment, Géricault made a lithograph of battered troops trudging homeward through Russian snow (Figure 5.2).[31] Blinkered by bandaging, his arm in a sling, a mounted cuirassier rests his hand on the shoulder of the stoical grenadier who guides him. Bending a handless arm to his chest, the grenadier, who wears a weather-beaten, fur *ourson*, grasps the reins of the cavalryman's exhausted, underfed mount with his remaining hand. A few paces away, his contours muffled by frosty air, another soldier (as if a Saint Christopher in shako) bears on his back a hatless comrade. The theme of loyalty and shared misery is reinforced by

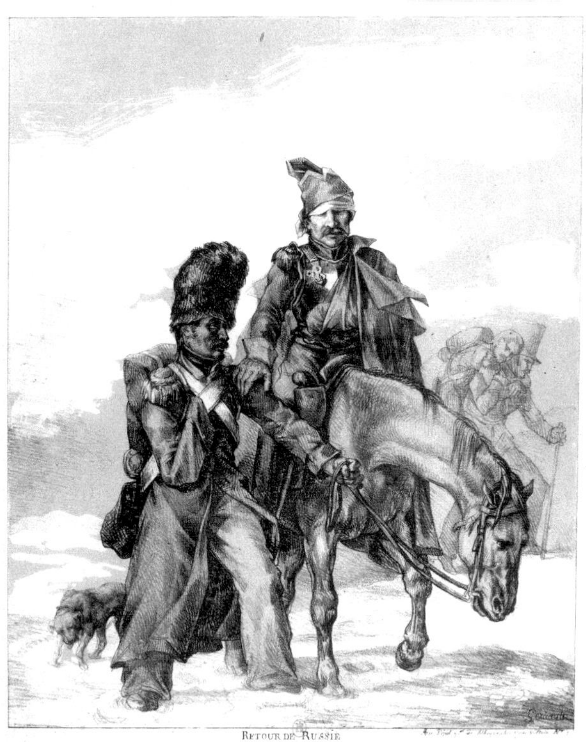

Figure 5.2 Théodore Géricault, *The Return from Russia*, 1818, lithograph, 44.4 × 36.2 cm. Paris, Bibliothèque nationale de France. Photo: BnF.

the shivering dog who trails behind. As in *The Swiss Guard at the Louvre* of the following year, Géricault eschews sentimentality in his treatment of a military subject of high pathos. This image of forlorn solidarity is energized by tension between the intimacy imparted by a close vantage point and the unexpected monumentality characteristic of the artist's work in small format. In his *Wounded Cuirassier Leaving the Field of Battle* (1814; Paris, Musée du Louvre), Géricault had enlarged an unheroic departure from combat to the dimensions of a Napoleonic propaganda piece, lending to the dismounted soldier the dynamism of a baroque horse trainer; despite the reportorial enumeration of mundane detail. *Return from Russia* is no less a work of high artifice.[32]

Six years after Géricault's lithograph, the decimation of the Grande Armée was emotionally detailed by a participant, Philippe-Paul de Ségur (1780–1873), in his *History of Napoleon and of the Grand Army During the Year 1812* (1824), which sold out its first of edition of 3,000 copies in several days. In his dedication to fellow veterans—the decorated, defiant *demi-solde* of Géricault's *The Swiss Guard at the Louvre* springs to mind—Ségur exhorts the survivors to proudly embrace a legacy all the more heroic for its disastrous end: "Alone against so many enemies, there was more glory in your fall than in their rise. Know then how to be vanquished without shame!"[33] In Ségur's account, the retreating Grande Armée was bereft of its former distinction: "Its most manly warriors, who had just proudly traversed so many fields of their victories, had lost their noble bearing: covered in rags, their feet naked and torn, leaning on pine branches, they dragged themselves, and all of the strength and perseverance that, until then, they had directed toward victory, they applied to flight."[34] Elsewhere, we see battle-ravaged soldiers reduced to "a trail of specters, covered in tatters, in women's fur-lined coats, in bits of carpet, or in dirty coats, scorched and perforated by gunfire, and whose feet were wrapped in every manner of rag…."[35]

Notwithstanding his imperial record and sympathies, Ségur rallied to the Restoration, served in its military, and occupied chairs in the Académie and the Chamber of Peers. His acclaimed chronicle was violently refuted by another imperial veteran, General Gaspard Gourgaud, whose heroism during the Russian campaign extended to swimming the icy Berezina. Gourgaud was fanatically loyal to Napoleon, whose life he saved in the Battle of Brienne during the campaign of France of 1814. As a parting gift, the defeated emperor gave him the sword he had worn at the Battle of the Pyramids in 1798, and Gourgaud, in turn, rejoined his idol for the One Hundred Days and fought at Waterloo. In contrast to Ségur, Gourgaud was shabbily treated under the Bourbon regime. Purged from the military and banished, he shared Napoleon's exile on Saint Helena for three years. He not only questioned Ségur's contention that the emperor was demoralized and stricken by ill health during the 1812 campaign but also rejected the author's claim to be a combatant brother-in-arms to the veterans. According to Gourgaud, Ségur was a lacky, a mere palace sergeant, bent on impugning the emperor and his commanders. So acrimonious was their disagreement that the pair dueled in the Bois du Boulogne; both suffered wounds, with Gourgaud garnering the sympathy of imperial enthusiasts and Ségur that of the aristocracy.

In the twilight of the Restoration, Balzac included a graphic vignette of the retreat in the touching novella, *Farewell* (*Adieu*), published in *La Mode* 15 May and 5 June 1830 as *Military Recollections, Farewell* (*Souvenirs soldatesques, Adieu*).[36] Here, a narrative set during the Restoration is haunted by the events of 29 November 1812 when, surrounded by corpses, the Grande Armée was caught in disarray between an overwhelming Russian advance and the Berezina. Whereas Gericault's *Return from Russia* represents esprit de corps prevailing in the bleakest of conditions, Balzac details the French army's reduction to subhuman indifference by cold, hunger, and sleep deprivation. Repetition brings home the numbing monotony of the daily round in a featureless waste:

> The apathy of those poor soldiers can only be comprehended by those who recall having traversed those vast deserts of snow, without any drink other than snow, without any bed other than snow, without any perspective other than a horizon of snow, without any food other than snow or some frozen beets, some handfuls of flour or horse flesh.[37]

Against this dismal backdrop, *Adieu*'s Stéphanie de Vandières (the wife of a French general) is separated from her selfless lover, Major Philippe de Sucy. She is driven insane by the experience, and by the time Sucy (now a colonel) encounters her seven years later, Stéphanie has descended to a state of animality comparable to that of the brutalized soldiers in retreat. In January 1820, Philippe attempts to cure her by staging a meticulous reenactment of the traumatic day—in the manner of the theatrical "moral cures" for insanity pioneered by the father of French psychiatry, Philippe Pinel (1745–1826).[38] Such is the shock of this spectacle that Stéphanie expires following a momentary return to sanity. Like Gericault's *Return from Russia, Adieu* is prophetic of the emotional charge carried by the Russian campaign in the first half of the July Monarchy, when dismal representations of the snow-bound retreat were as timely as the narratives of Vigny and Musset.

The subject's urgency is evidenced by the enthusiasm with which visitors to the Salon of 1836 greeted an *Episode from the Russian Campaign* (Figure 5.3) by Nicolas-Toussaint Charlet.[39] Having specialized, under the Restoration, in lithographs of disenfranchised imperial veterans, the fiercely patriotic artist here aspired to elevate the wounded nostalgia propagated in those popular, mass-produced sheets to the height of a unique Salon masterwork. In numbingly bleak weather, countless troops of the Grande Armée stumble past frozen corpses and broken wagons. According to the Salon guidebook, "a column of the wounded, harassed by Cossacks, repulses their attack."[40] Mention of counteroffensive was perhaps an attempt to give a heroic cast to what is actually a scene of abject retreat. The sole evidence of armed initiative is provided by three soldiers who point muskets at a bearded pillager with arms raised in surrender.[41] Imitating the sublime effects of the Briton John Martin's mezzotints of biblical cataclysm (then enjoying a Parisian vogue), Charlet reduces the column to an inchoate mass, enhancing the gloom by setting the march in fog, under a dark, lowering sky.[42] This somber ambience was viewed askance by one eyewitness to the debacle, a veteran officer brought to the exhibition by the artist Paul Chenevard: "After all, you painters, you need such things to move us. But the truth is that, in the retreat, we were blinded by the sun for a month."[43] Whereas, like Gourgaud, the skeptic bristled at subordination of fact to dramatic effect, no such reservation occurred to visitors

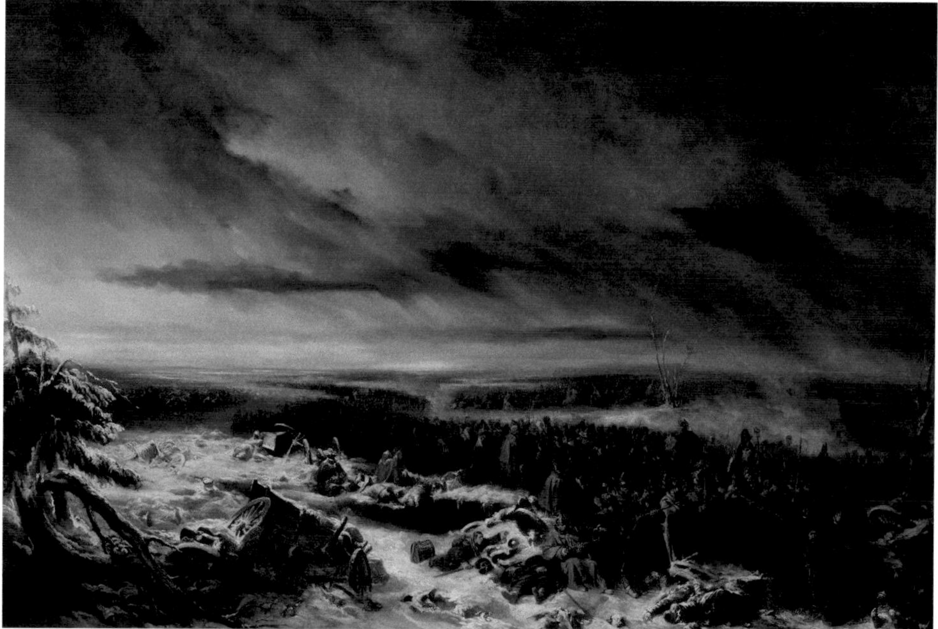

Figure 5.3 Nicolas-Toussaint Charlet, *Episode from the Russian Campaign,* 1836, oil on canvas, 194.7 × 294 cm. Lyon, Musée des Beaux Arts. © Lyon MBA-Photo Alain Basset.

with second-hand knowledge of imperial history. It was the painting's truth, "put on show for us in all its crudity, with all its horrors," that struck one critic.[44] Musset could not have been more impressed when he scrutinized the canvas at the Salon of 1836. As he reported,

> The *Retreat from Russia,* by M. Charlet, is a work of the highest importance. He has entitled it *episode*, and this is great modesty; it is an entire poem. In seeing it, one is at first struck with a vague and uneasy horror. What then does this painting represent? Is it the Berezina, is it the retreat of Ney? Where is the point that attracts the eyes, which one is accustomed to find in the battles of our museums? Where are the horses, the plumes, the captains, the marshals? There is none of that; this is the grand army, this is the soldier, or rather this is the man; this is human misery itself, under a foggy sky, on frozen ground, without guide, without leader, without distinction. This is despair in the desert .... [O]ne hundred thousand wretches march with equal step, head lowered, and death in the soul. This one stops, weary of suffering; he lies down and sleeps forever .... Everywhere the glance travels, it finds only horror, but horror without either ugliness or exaggeration. Outside of *The Medusa* of Géricault and *The Deluge* of Poussin, I know of no painting that makes a comparable impression, not that I compare these works, different in form and method; but the thought is the same in them, and (execution apart), stronger perhaps in M. Charlet.... This is certainly a work of these times, clear, audacious and original. I seem to see a page from an epic poem written by Béranger.[45]

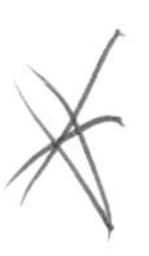

For Musset, then, Charlet's painting raises to epic amplitude the patriotic sympathies popularized in song by Béranger, and its sheer horror is enhanced by a bewildering lack of either narrative specificity or focal point. Musset's insistence that the painting "is certainly a work of these times" alerts us not only to the topical appeal of its subject, but also to its resonance with a national mood to which other lugubrious subjects spoke. We have seen, for example, that Corot, Murat, and Millet reinterpreted the traditionally reassuring narrative of Hagar and Ishmael as "despair in the desert." Musset's mention of a soldier who "stops, weary of suffering" and "lies down and sleeps forever" recalls Balzac's portrayal of imperial soldiers dying in their sleep in *Adieu*; Daumier's somnolent Citizen-King; and Octave's pessimistic metaphor of his defeated nation succumbing to deathly slumber in *La Confession d'un enfant du siècle*, published in the same year as Musset's Salon review.

Just as Musset's novel gave lasting shape to post-Napoleonic anguish, so too did his Salon review, like Charlet's painting and Ségur's narrative, endure.[46] Writing of Charlet's *Episode from the Russian Campaign* in *L'Artiste* in 1843, a critic referred approvingly to Musset's invocation of Poussin's *Deluge*, and added, "For Charlet, as well, the annihilation of our army amid the ice of Russia must have seemed like the end of the world"—an observation that inadvertently rings true to the affiliation of Charlet's painting with the apocalyptic biblical imagery of Martin.[47] Delacroix's essay on Charlet (1862) harmonizes with Musset's review, Balzac's *Adieu*, and Ségur's narrative:

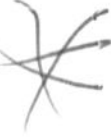

> Who does not recall this admirable Retreat from Russia...? The conception of this painting is truly frightening; the heart tightens before this immense solitude

> marked here and there by human forms buried under the snow, sinister landmarks of this desolate march. Charlet modestly entitles it Episode. This is not an episode, this is a complete poem; this is neither the retreat of Ney... nor Napoleon himself, already vanished from this dismal theater, carrying away his share of the horrible despair, which hurries on these one hundred thousand wretches: this is the army of Austerlitz and Iena become a hideous horde, without laws, without discipline, without bond other than shared misfortune.[48]

Dating from the reign of the emperor's nephew, the essay on Charlet honors the Napoleonic heritage of the Delacroix family while evidencing the strong and lasting impression made by the painting.

Whereas Charlet's elevated vantage point distances viewer from troops, whose immersion in fog renders them a measureless, miserable multitude, visitors to the previous Salon had been squarely faced with an unflinching representation of individuated suffering in *Episode from the Retreat from Moscow* (Figure 5.4) by Joseph-Fernand Boissard de Boisdenier (1813–66). The stunning power of Boissard de Boisdenier's grim rendering of two abandoned, unnamed members of the Grande Armée succumbing to hypothermia beside a dead horse and a dismembered cannon, stems from uncompromising realism. An uncomfortably close point of view suggests that we are leaning over these doomed soldiers, whose inadequate clothing is itemized in detail. Against this descriptive density, the summary indication of distant comrades tells of

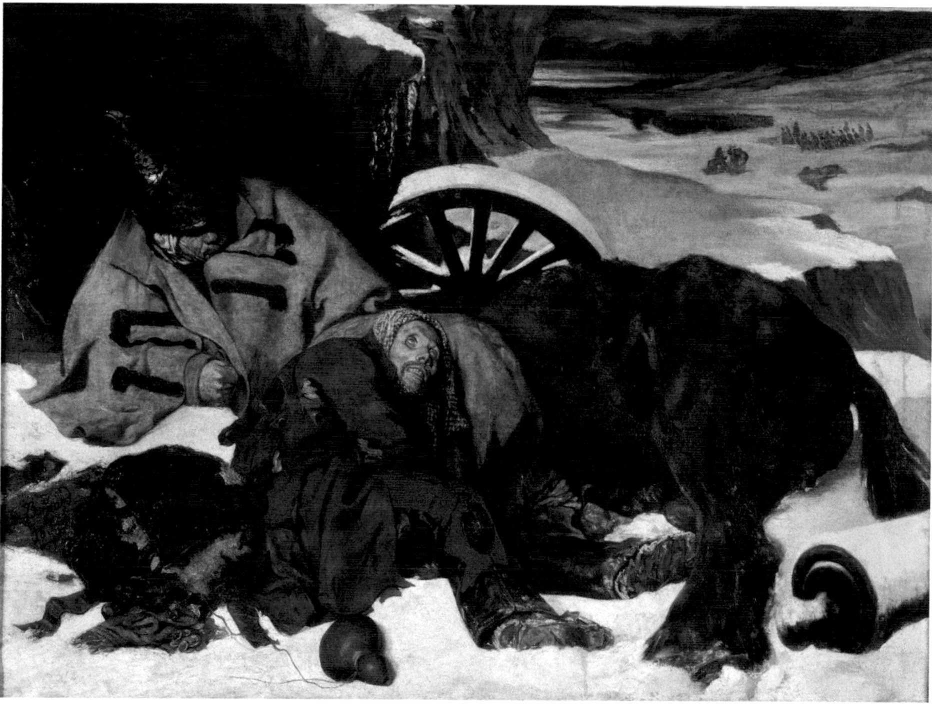

Figure 5.4 Joseph-Fernand Boissard de Boisdenier, *Episode from the Retreat from Moscow*, 1835, oil on canvas, 160 × 225 cm. Rouen, Musée des Beaux-Arts. Photo: Gérard Blot. © RMN-Grand Palais/Art Resource, NY.

the pair's fatal isolation. "The truth of this painting is frightful," exclaimed one critic. "A man and a horse, lying down and grouped as if they wanted to warm each other, are seized by death in a horrible state of deformation. What a subject!"[49] While he admired both the persuasive rendering of the snowy setting and the vigorous handling of detail, the critic Louis Viardot (1800–83) was similarly shocked:

> But good God! Why choose such types? Does M. Boissard think that he would have enfeebled the effect of his painting by placing, under these rags of uniforms, two beautiful military faces, such as our armies offer in profusion; while adding to the thoroughly physical and material pain some bitter regret for the fatherland, or the noble expression of a courage that nothing can demolish, and some resigned patience ...?[50]

In contrast, a critic writing in *L'Artiste* was impressed: "What profound desolation! M. de Ségur's saddest pages on the miseries of the grand army are surpassed!"[51] *Episode from the Retreat from Moscow* raises to an uncommon level of mimesis the convention of placing foreshortened casualties in the immediate foreground. This was a maneuver that Boissard de Boisdenier's teacher, Gros, deftly pulled off in *Napoleon on the Battlefield of Eylau* (so admired by Delacroix), wherein heaped corpses and

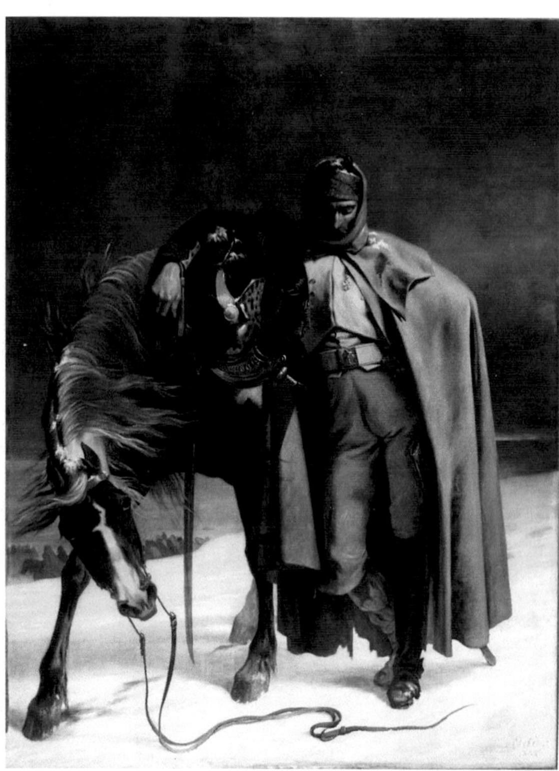

Figure 5.5 Édouard-Alexandre Odier, *Episode from the Retreat from Moscow (1812)—Dragoon of the Imperial Guard,* 1832, oil on canvas, 261 × 198 cm. Amiens, Musée de Picardie (photo Musée de Picardie) no inv.: M.P.2004.17.161.

frozen blood are subsidiary to the equestrian Emperor, whose augustly magnanimous presence justifies the carnage. Devoid of heroism, Boissard de Boisdenier's painting has no such division between major fiction and minor fact; there is nothing on show apart from inert victims beyond hope. Notwithstanding its pessimism, this chilling canvas was deemed an appropriate acquisition for the Rouen National Guard, which kept the painting until it became a prized acquisition of the Rouen Musée des Beaux-Arts in the early reign of Napoleon III (1853).

The brutal, earth-bound veracity of Boissard de Boisdenier's *Episode from the Retreat from Moscow* contrasts with the disarming sentimentality of an earlier *Episode from the Retreat from Moscow (1812)—Dragoon of the Imperial Guard* by Edouard-Alexandre Odier (1800–87), a Parisian artist born in Hamburg and fathered by a Genevan (Figure 5.5).[52] Tersely registered in the 1833 Salon guidebook as *Dragoon of the Imperial Guard; study*, this nearly six-foot painting was sufficiently well received to be purchased by the government for the Musée de Luxembourg,[53] the catalogue of which (1836) provides a more pathetic description: "A dragoon of the Imperial Guard, exhausted by his wounds, painfully makes his way forward, supporting himself on his horse."[54] Nursing a bloodied, bootless leg, the warrior is separated from the grey silhouette of a column on the move, forecasting a fate like that of Boissard de Boisdenier's abandoned comrades.[55] With lowered head and wind-blown mane, the horse staggers on. Its reins slack in the snow, the animal leaves a trail of blood from a right limb seemingly as compromised at that of its dismounted rider. Despite multiple wounds, Odier's dragoon leans on his faltering mount in graceful contrapposto—–an attitude no less crowd-pleasing than the parting of the blood-stained cloak to reveal a medal of the Legion of Honor.[56]

The Anti-Heroic Mode and Chassériau

Notwithstanding dissimilarity in affect and execution, the representations of the Russian retreat by Géricault, Charlet, Boissard de Boisdenier, and Odier all are examples of what I term the anti-heroic mode. [57] Such works feature withdrawn, vulnerable, enervated or defeated figures succumbing to despair, wounds, exposure, and/or the pain of exile. I employ "mode" to indicate that the term does not imply uniformity in either subject matter or style. This downbeat class of imagery had originated decades earlier, in the wake of the Terror and the Emigration. Pierre-Narcisse Guérin's show stopping entry in the Salon of 1799, *The Return of Marcus Sextus* is a trailblazing example, and this tendency gained a foothold under the Bourbon Restoration in masterworks by Guérin's students.[58] Featuring physical infirmity and somber emotional tone, Géricault's *Return from Russia* and *Wounded Cuirassier Leaving the Field of Battle*, as we have seen, are devoid of the valor glamorized in Napoleonic battle paintings; *The Raft of the Medusa* (1819; Paris, Musée du Louvre), with its dark tonality, its despondent father grasping his lifeless son, and its chain of desperate survivors, invests this depressive mode with a solemn monumentality commensurate with the maritime disaster's notoriety and the magnitude of the suffering depicted. Lacking heroic narrative, Géricault's entry in the Salon of 1819 prompted a critic writing in the *Gazette de France* to complain, "*all* is hideously passive."[59] Delacroix, who posed for one of the inert casualties on the raft, also avoided sentimentality, lending gravitas to the inert victims of *Scenes from the Massacres at Chios: Greek Families Awaiting Death or Slavery, etc.* Viewing that painting at the Salon of 1824, Margaret

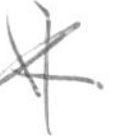

MacNamidhe indicates that critics were struck by the lassitude and enervation of the wounded, central male figure.[60] Gros's legendary remark that Delacroix had perpetrated "the massacre of painting" does not speak solely of daring breadth of handling and absence of compositional focus. It also gives measure to the distance of *Scenes from the Massacres of Chios* from the declamatory heroism of imperial propaganda pieces—this despite the younger artist's debt to the "affective" mode of battle painting represented by Gros's *Battle of Nazareth* (Salon of 1801; Nantes, Musée des Beaux-Arts), in which, as Susan Siegfried notes, the viewer is meant to feel as if amid the heat of combat.[61] Having gained traction after Waterloo, the anti-heroic mode flourished in the disappointing aftermath of the July Revolution. Under Louis-Philippe, the reach of the anti-heroic mode was sufficiently broad to span Daumier's caricature of the ignobly somnolent monarch and sympathetic representations of anonymous comrades suffering frosty martyrdom on the Russian steppes. Accusatory in the former, the anti-heroic mode is a vehicle for sympathy in the latter. And it presents in subjects without ostensible connection to recent French history. Attraction to Christ's moment of tormented introspection in the Garden of Olives (portrayed to particularly oppressive effect by Chassériau in 1840) attests to the pull of this dour idiom. We have seen examples culled from the Old Testament: Antoine Étex's brooding Cain and his devastated family and alarming representations of the expulsed Hagar and her prostrate son by Corot, Murat, and Millet.

So great was the appeal, in the 1830s and 1840s, of self-absorbed torpor, that this aspect of the anti-heroic mode could bleed into moody imaginings of sensuous, exotic bodies in works that, devoid of reference to modern history, offered escape from the discouraging banality of life under Louis-Philippe. Prime examples were produced by the short-lived Chassériau, whose obituary was written by his friend, Boissard de Boisdenier.

Recourse to the anti-heroic mode offers respite from the vexed question of Chassériau's originality—a preoccupation of writing about the artist, whether critical or defensive. The issue was acerbically raised by Baudelaire, who, in his review of the Salon of 1845, accused the Orientalist painter of *Ali-Ben-Hamet, Caliph of Constantine and Chief of the Haractas, Followed by His Escort* (1845; Versailles, Musée national du Château) of occupying an equivocal place between Ingres (Chassériau's teacher) and the artist Chassériau was trying to "rob"—Delacroix (the critic's favorite), whose *Sultan of Morocco and His Entourage* (1845; Toulouse, Musée des Augustins) hung in the same Salon.[62] Protesting Chassériau enthusiasts have since insisted upon the uniqueness of this markedly idiosyncratic artist who, disillusioned with Ingres during a visit to Italy in 1840, emulated Delacroix during the remaining years of his life.[63] Given the uneven quality of Chassériau's output, especially after the fall of Louis-Philippe, it is problematic to privilege singularity of style as his core accomplishment. Evaluation of the oeuvre from the perspective of connoisseurship is hampered by the mixed results of the artist's self-fashioning after the break with his teacher. Delacroix's dynamic, gestural, and volumetric mark-making resisted assimilation by the younger artist, whose rigidly two-dimensional draftsmanship, already evident in childhood artwork, was reinforced in the Ingres studio.[64] There, the fledgling painter imbibed a reliance on local color which, in comparison to Delacroix's ambient, sonorous hues, tends to render Chassériau's handling of the spectrum ornamental rather than expressive. Reconsideration of his work in light of its investment in, and transformation of, the anti-heroic mode sets into relief the fit between an undeniably unique sensibility and the era in which the artist worked.

Prior to exhibiting his grief-stricken *Jesus in the Garden of Olives* in the Salon of 1840, Chassériau was among those impressed by Étex's anti-heroic rendition of Cain and his family. Three years after Étex's entry in the Salon of 1833, the 17-year-old Chassériau made a respectable Salon debut with two biblical paintings and two portraits, landing a third-class medal. Drawing upon the fashion for Old Testament subjects, he exhibited *The Punishment of Cain*, or *Cain Accursed* (*Caïn maudit*; Figure 5.6).[65] Cain's pose mimics Étex's lithograph of his group published in *L'Artiste* (Figure 3.19)—a debt in line with the sculptor's esteem for Ingres. Although heavy-handedness betrays Chassériau's youth, *Caïn maudit* reflects an ambitious quest for grand, lugubrious effect. The first murderer and his family walk dejectedly into exile, a fate rendered all the more oppressive by a bituminous landscape that, in its lack of scale, reads alternately as flat backdrop and vast wasteland. At an indeterminate distance, the implausibly diminutive body of Abel lies beside a smoking altar. So bleak is the painting that fellow artist Alexandre-Gabriel Decamps (1803–60) felt that Chassériau had departed from the spirit of scripture: "M. Chassériau, wishing to express despondency and sorrow has passed his mark; his two figures do not stand and seem to stumble; this is certainly neither the Cain of the Bible, nor his gentle and resigned companion."[66] Chassériau sought to evoke shame through a rhetoric of introspection in which facial expression is largely masked or averted; the sole visible

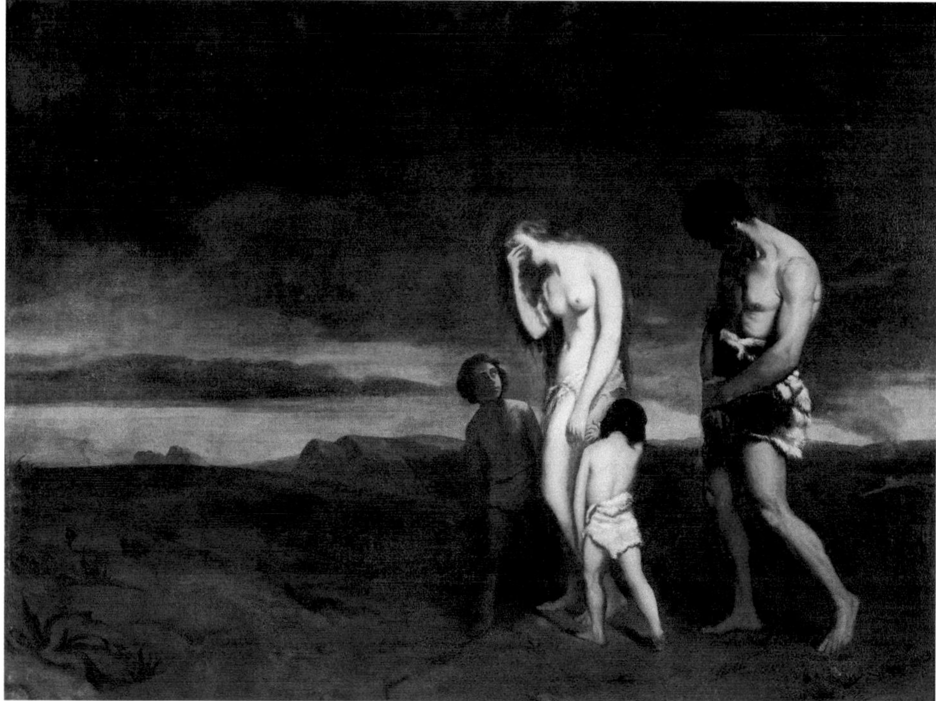

Figure 5.6 Théodore Chassériau, *The Punishment of Cain* (or *Cain Accursed*), 1836, oil on canvas, 120.7 × 162.6 cm. Cambridge, MA, Harvard Art Museums/Fogg Museum, Gift of Eric Seiler AB '78, AM '82, JD '82 and Darcy Bradbury AB '78, MBA '82 in honor of Matthew Rutenberg. Photo: © President and Fellows of Harvard College, 2020.296.

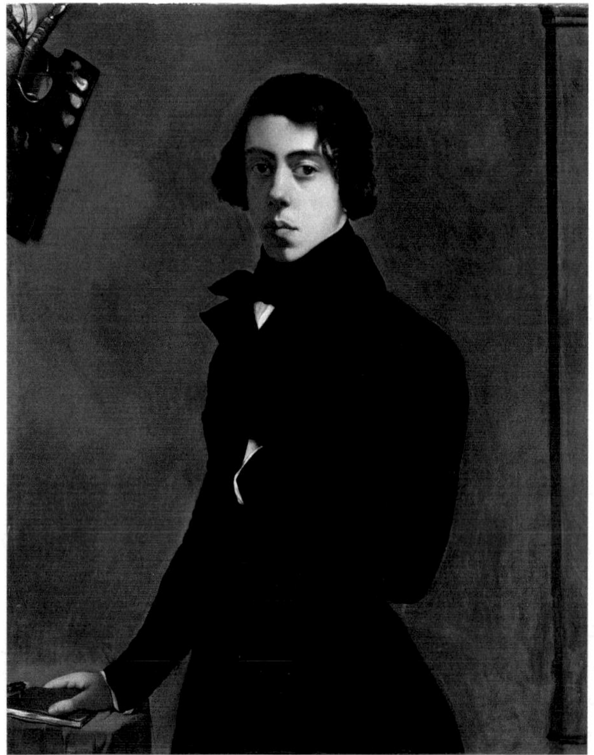

Figure 5.7 Théodore Chassériau, *Self-portrait*, 1835, oil on canvas, 99 × 82 cm. Paris, Musée du Louvre. Photo: Jean-Gilles Berizzi. © RMN-Grand Palais / Art Resource, NY.

face is that of the son, whose abrupt chiaroscuro and full lips recall a self-portrait of the previous year (Figure 5.7).

Chassériau's thick hair and prominent chin are discernible in the other biblical painting he exhibited in the Salon of 1836, *The Return of the Prodigal Son* (Figure 5.8).[67] Use of a mirror when portraying the son of Cain and the Prodigal Son would have been more than a matter of studio expediency. In regard to identification with Cain's child, there is, of course, the Romantic trope of the artist and poet as members of a cursed, elite cohort. At the same time, both subjects have pointedly personal implications. The Cain family walking into exile and the Prodigal Son embraced by his father exemplify family crisis—a theme relevant to the separation of the artist from his father, Benoît Chassériau (1780–1844), a diplomat in the Caribbean. Benoît's sojourns with his family in Paris were separated by long absences, for example during a three-year stay on the Danish island of Saint Thomas beginning in 1826, when the artist was seven. For much of his childhood, Théodore, with his mother, two sisters, and younger brother, were left in the care of the artist's elder brother, Frédéric-Victor-Charles (1807–81). Paternal absence is poignantly embodied in the contrast between the illuminated, articulated features of the Prodigal Son and the deeply shaded, schematic face of his father. This stereotypical patriarch, encircling

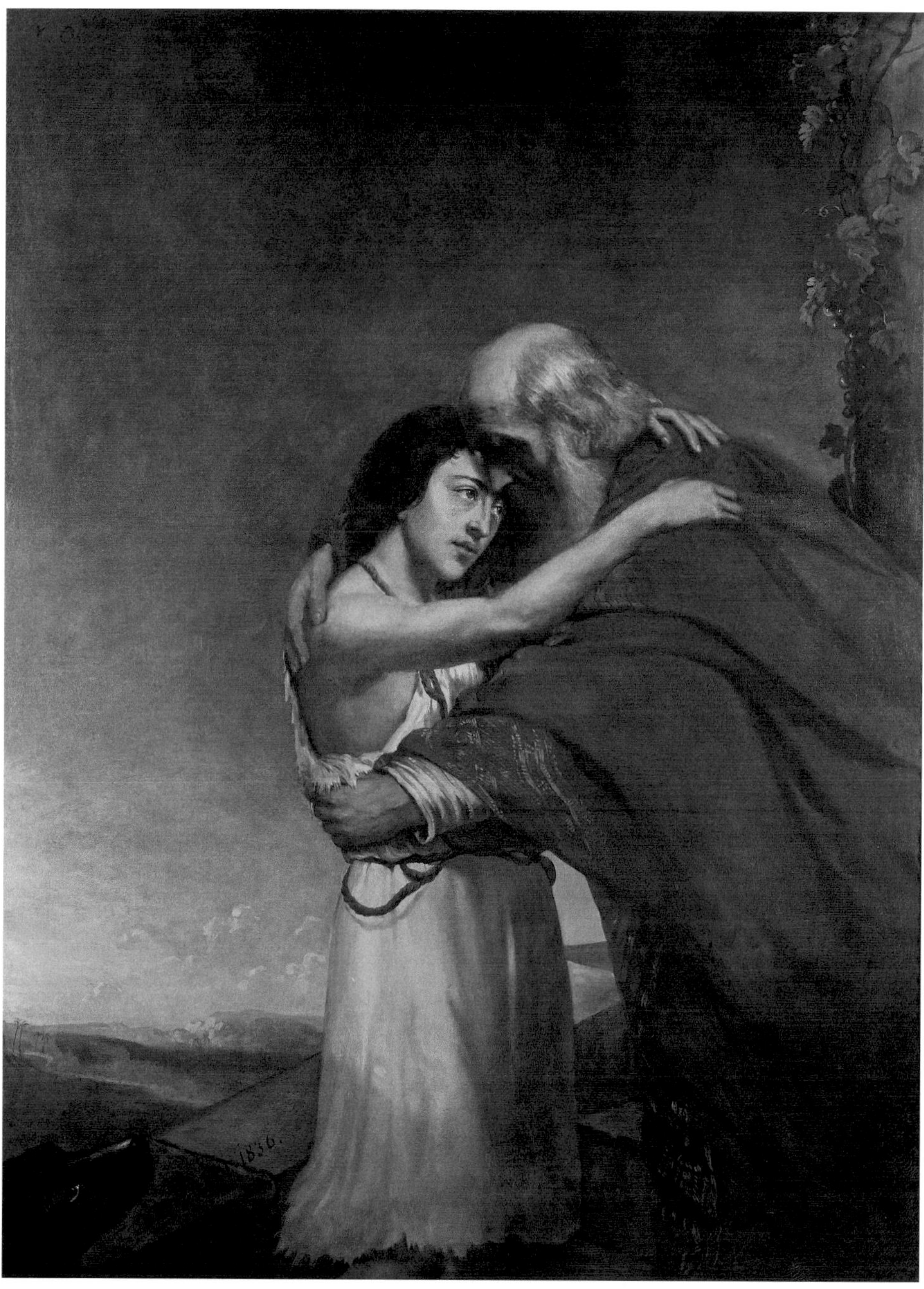

Figure 5.8 Théodore Chassériau, *The Return of the Prodigal Son*, 1836, oil on canvas, 170 × 129 cm. La Rochelle, Musée des Beaux-Arts. © Musées d'Art et d'Histoire de La Rochelle, Max Roy.

the youth like an empty shell, gives form to the abstract existence that the absent Benoît must have had for Théodore, who wrote pining childhood letters to his father. Lending an air of self-absorption to a motif calling for gratitude and penance, the artist sounds an unexpected, confessional note in this familiar biblical subject––even the loyal dog observes the reunion with a soulful expression.

Alignment of visual evidence with biography is perilous in the case of Chassériau, for whom documentation remains incomplete, despite the exhaustive chronology assembled by Bruno Chenique in the catalog of a 2002 retrospective exhibition. A cache of drawings and family documents pertaining to the artist, stored by his brother Frédéric in the basement of the Conseil d'Etat in the Palais d'Orsay, was destroyed when the building was torched during the Commune.[68] Enthused by the French conquest of Algeria, Chassériau otherwise focused his political energies on his career.[69] As a child, the precocious artist—he entered the Ingres studio around age 12—was troubled by the civil unrest of July 1830, as it disrupted his studies.[70] Mindful of the tact demanded by any attempt to infer affinities between an artist's life and oeuvre, I believe it possible to adduce some telling data points.

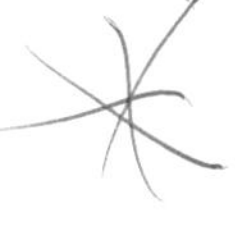

Chassériau's nearly fatherless childhood recalls the plight of the earlier generation characterized in *Servitude et grandeur militaires* and *La Confession d'un enfant du siècle*, both contemporary with the artist's Salon debut. Reared in a family with strong imperial ties, the young Chassériau (born four years after Waterloo) was well placed to experience the sense of post-Napoleonic belatedness Vigny and Musset evoke. And there was the example of his father. Benoît Chassériau had a glamorous youth in Napoleon's service, in which advancement came as preciously as his son's talent; there is also circumstantial evidence that Benoît's intrepid spirit was tainted by crime. Having joined the Egyptian campaign, Benoît was appointed comptroller to two Egyptian provinces at age 19. In 1802, when 22, he accompanied the (failed) French expedition to Saint-Domingue to suppress the independence and anti-slavery movement led by Toussaint Louverture, as did his brother, Victor-Frédéric, and was that year appointed treasurer of the colony.[71] In 1805, a year after Saint-Domingue (the western portion of the island of Hispaniola) attained independence as the Republic of Haiti—finalizing France's loss of its most valuable colonial possession—Benoît became secretary general of the eastern, formerly Spanish sector of the island. The following year, according to an anonymous note in the archives of the French Ministry of Foreign Affairs, he was imprisoned for embezzlement of public funds.[72] The same document alleges that Benoît sold his services to the English, and that he was released through the efforts of a wealthy planter eager that the prisoner marry his 14-year-old Creole daughter (eventually, mother to the artist, whose paternal grandmother and great-grandmother were also from the Antilles). Following Napoleon's invasion of Spain (1808), the eastern part of Hispaniola revolted, with English support, against French rule and Benoît's property on the Samaná peninsula (now part of the Dominican Republic) was seized. Pursuing adventures in the Caribbean and in Latin America, he was hired to serve the city of Cartagena, Columbia, first as captain major of engineering, and then with the unlikely title of commissioner general of police. Regaining his property in 1819 (the year of Théodore's birth), Benoît moved his family to Paris at the end of 1820. His departures began three years later, when, accompanied by the artist's elder brother, he left on a year-long diplomatic mission to Columbia at the behest of Chateaubriand, then minister of foreign affairs. His final destination was Puerto Rico, to which he was posted in 1834. A decade later, he committed suicide on the island amidst accusations of having swindled funds entrusted to him by two merchants. In contrast, Benoît's brother, Victor-Frédéric had died at Waterloo with the rank of general in the Grande Armée. Benoît's geographic distance from Paris provided ample space for Théodore to construct a family romance in which his scandal-ridden father was no less heroic than his valiant uncle.

From the outset, the young Chassériau associated artmaking with his father. Immensely proud of his son's talent, Benoît insisted that drawings by Théodore be enclosed in the family correspondence, and that they be dated so that he could judge the boy's progress. "My Dear papa," wrote Théodore wrote to his father (then in Saint Thomas) around 1827–28, "I am sending you some of my drawings and work and if I can send you something that will please you more, I will do so."[73] In a letter of 24 July 1830, on the eve of the revolution, Benoît counseled Théodore, in the spirit of Napoleonic meritocracy, "Apply yourself, my dear son, and remember that talent leads to everything."[74] Living in the disenchanted Paris of Louis-Philippe, this sheltered youth could aspire to emulate the heroism of his absent father and deceased uncle solely through art.

The uneasiness of that predicament is conveyed by a *Self-portrait Holding a Palette* painted in 1838 (Figure 5.9).[75] The fixity of the gaze and the pools of shadow about the eyes speak of private struggle. On the left, Chassériau's (currently unlocated) painting, *The Virgin*, introduces a note of warmth, contrasting with the cold sensuality of the figure study at the right. Immobilized between these competing images like an indecisive

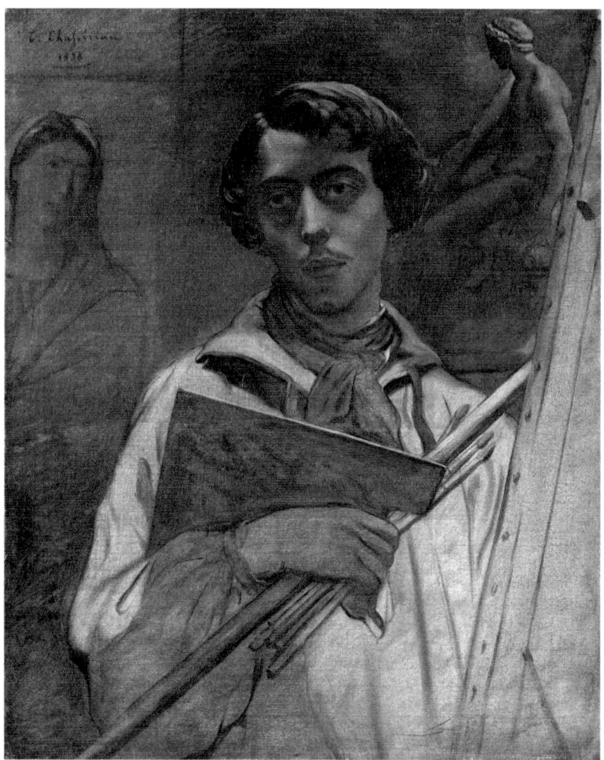

Figure 5.9 Théodore Chassériau, *Self-portrait Holding a Palette,* 1838, oil on canvas, 73 × 59 cm. Paris, Musée du Louvre. Photo: Philippe Fuzeau. © RMN-Grand Palais/Art Resource, NY.

Hercules, the artist exhibits a world-weariness that belies his youth.[76] In this regard, the *Self-portrait Holding a Palette* stands apart from the precociously poised *Self-portrait* of 1835, painted when Chassériau was 16, some four years after he had entered the studio of Ingres (cf. Figure 5.7). In that earlier canvas, with his wavy crown of dark hair and black frock coat setting off his brightly lit face, the artist strikes an attitude reminiscent of that in his teacher's own self-portrait at age 24 (1804; Chantilly, Musée Condé), which is similar in color, coiffure, and expression. The youngster's formal, reserved bearing, reinforced by the lean spatial setting, corresponds with his reputation as fastidiously proper. This restraint is tempered by a pool of shadow, which sets Chassériau's Creole features (later ridiculed through racist epithet by Hugo) into sensual relief and lends him an air of melancholy that, for a young artist in the 1830s, was as much a badge of his vocation as the palette affixed to the wall like a coat of arms.[77] That Chassériau signed and dated the later, grisaille canvas points to the Romantic taste for fragments, improvisation, and the incomplete. At the same time, its apparently unfinished condition suggests that it was executed following the discouraging rejection, early that year, of two paintings (including *The Virgin*) by the Salon jury (19 February 1838).

By that time, the competitive young artist's hunger for success had likely been whetted by a painting viewed the previous year. In 1837, Hippolyte Flandrin's *Nude Young Man Seated at the Edge of the Sea* was exhibited at the École des Beaux-Arts (Figure 5.10).[78] Completed in Flandrin's fourth year of study at the Académie de France à Rome—Ingres's star pupil had won a coveted Prix de Rome scholarship

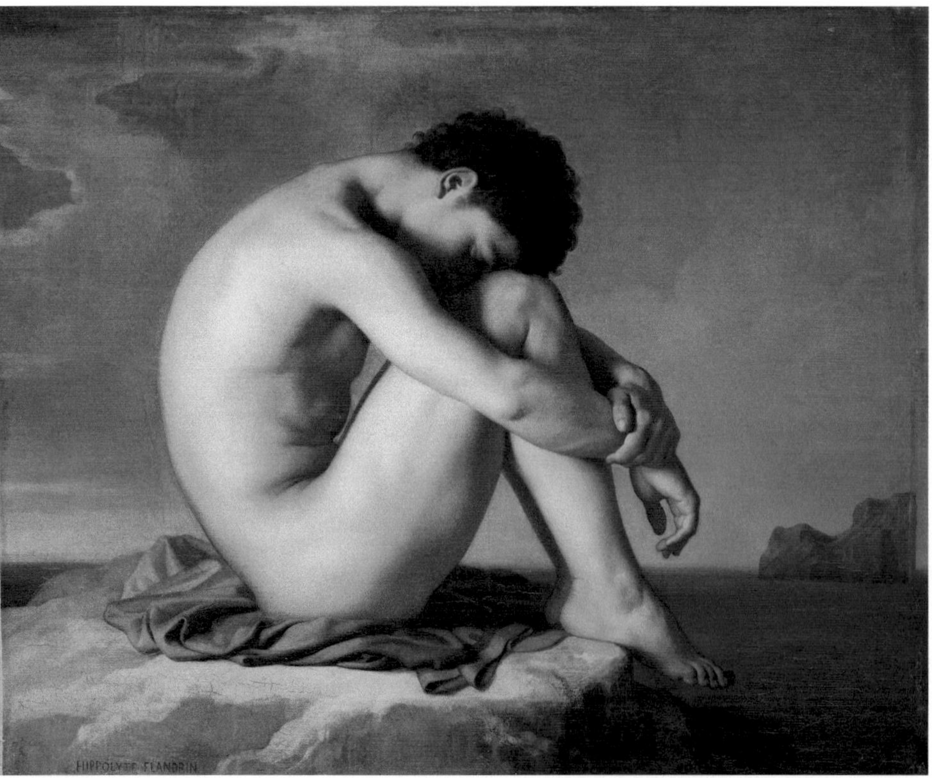

Figure 5.10 Hippolyte Flandrin, *Nude Young Man Seated at the Edge of the Sea*, 1835–36, oil on canvas, 98 × 124 cm. Paris, Musée du Louvre. Photo: Michel Urtado. © RMN-Grand Palais/Art Resource, NY.

in 1832—it is an outstanding example of the obligatory *envoi:* a painted *académie* (i.e., study of the male nude) executed in Rome and sent home to demonstrate academic progress. Silhouetted against the sky like a figure on a Greek vase, this flawless youth occupies a realm of remote idealism.[79] It is unthinkable that Chassériau did not spend time before Flandrin's canvas—a stunning achievement by an Ingres student, ten years his senior, working under the master's eye.

In the *Nude Young Man Seated at the Edge of the Sea*, the introversion characteristic of the anti-heroic mode is aestheticized and divested of any suggestion of lassitude or guilt, such as that conveyed by the sightless sinners portrayed in Flandrin's *Dante, Led by Virgil, Offers Consolation to the Shades of the Envious,* also executed in Rome and sent to Paris as the student's second year *envoi* (Figure 5.11). As Henri Dorra observes, there is an autobiographical aspect to that painting of damned souls, whom Dante compares to the blind who beg their bread in church; in 1834, Flandrin had been afflicted with eye problems.[80] When his condition improved, he began work on the painting, despite (as he wrote to his brother Auguste on 28 October 1834) a laziness that he attributed to "the torpor that one breathes in with the air of Rome" ("*cette torpeur qu'on respire avec l'air de Rome*")—a condition shared with the enervated denizens of the Inferno in his painting of Dante and Virgil.[81]

Like Prix de Rome entries, the *envoi* was intended to demonstrate mastery of idealized male nudity. In his *Nude Young Man Seated at the Edge of the Sea*, Flandrin went beyond that learning objective, investing the figure with an introverted moodiness

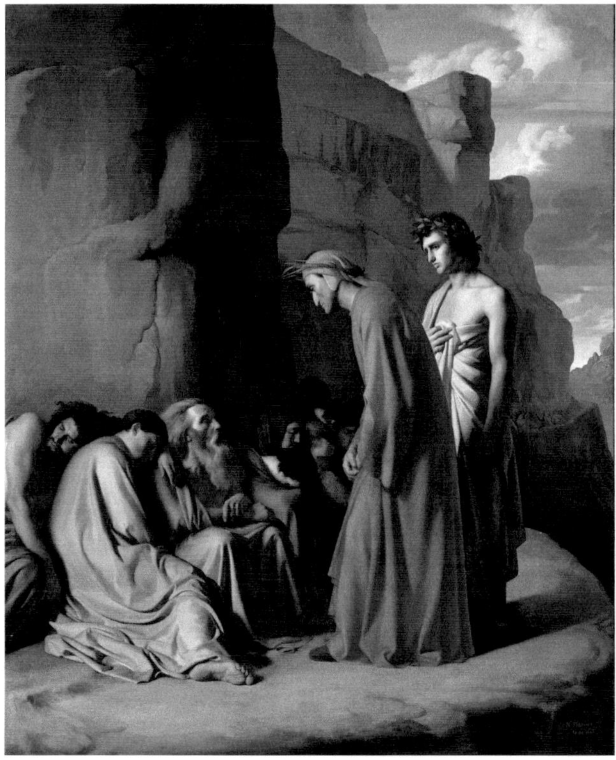

Figure 5.11 Hippolyte Flandrin, *Dante, Led by Virgil, Offers Consolation to the Souls of the Envious,* 1834–35, oil on canvas, 298 × 244.8 cm. Lyon, Musée des Beaux-Arts. Image © Lyon MBA-Photo Alain Basset.

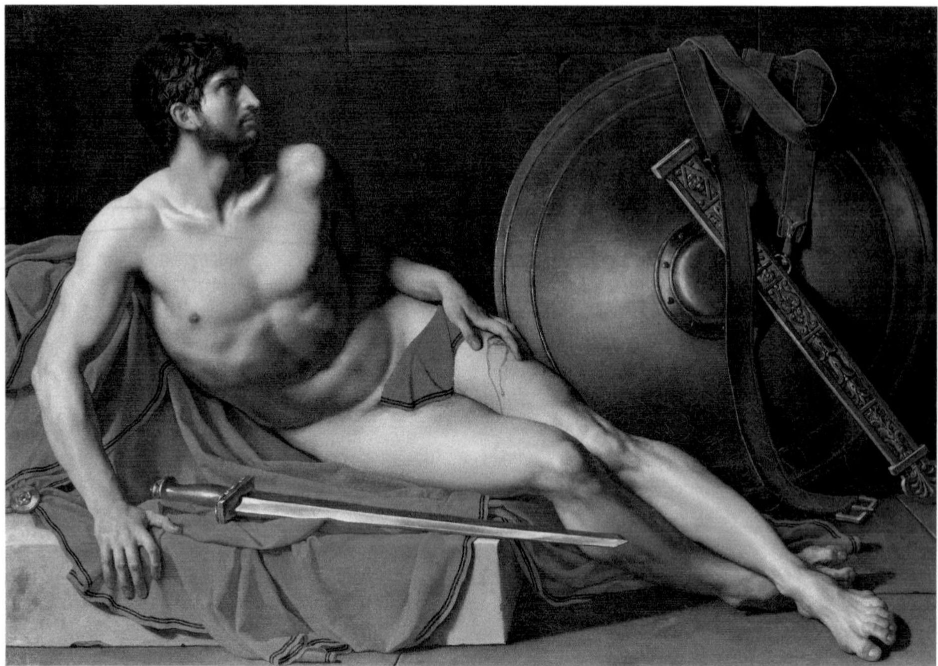

Figure 5.12 Jean-Germain Drouais, *The Dying Athlete,* 1785, oil on canvas, 125 × 182 cm. Paris, Musée du Louvre. © RMN-Grand Palais/Art Resource, NY.

that speaks a contemporary language. Its period flavor is brought out through comparison with *The Dying Athlete* (Figure 5.12) painted in 1785 as an *envoi* by Jacques-Louis David's pupil, friend, and collaborator, Jean-Germain Drouais (1763–88).[82] Stoically bearing a bleeding thigh wound, Drouais's figure displays martial toughness consonant with pre-revolutionary thirst for heroism and virtue. Conversely, Flandrin's withdrawn young man projects the spirit of a less heroic historical moment.

Evidence that the emotional tenor of Flandrin's *envoi* was in vogue is provided by the contemporary success of *Jeremiah on the Ruins of Jerusalem* by the Dusseldorf painter Eduard Bendemann (1811–89).[83] In 1836, a print after Bendemann's painting went on sale in Paris, and the following year the original, subsequently lost, was exhibited in the Salon, where it was awarded a first-class medal and earned the German artist knighthood in the Legion of Honor. I show a reproduction published in *L'Artiste* (Figure 5.13).[84] Prior to the Salon, the critic Alexandre Guyard de Saint-Chéron (1807–92) admired a reproduction of the painting in the shop of the print dealer Rittner: "As sad and fallen grandeur, as immense desolation, nothing could be better conceived and better executed; the prophet above all is magnificent in pose, in drapery, in severe character, in meditative absorption that is melancholic and deep."[85] This praise cannot be attributed solely to the admiration of contemporary German art professed by Catholics such as Saint-Chéron. It also signals the currency of imagery featuring melancholic withdrawal and catastrophic defeat. A wash drawing (ca. 1836–37) of Jeremiah weeping in chains amid the despairing inhabitants of Jerusalem (inscribed "Jérémie pleure Jérusalem—Jérémie") suggests that Chassériau was among the admirers of the downbeat German work (Figure 5.14).[86] If the attitude of

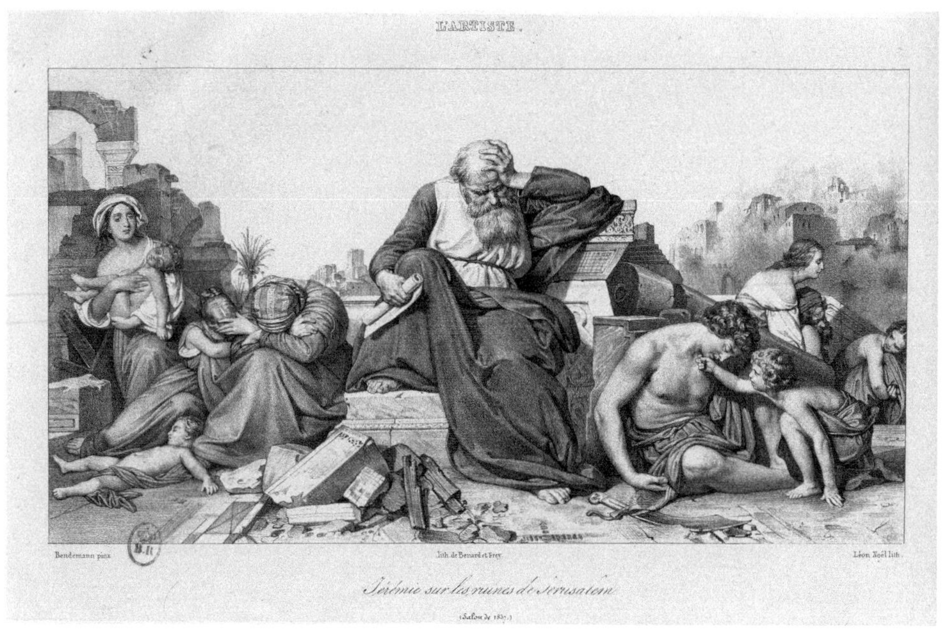

Figure 5.13 Léon Noël after Eduard Bendemann, "Jeremiah on the Ruins of Jerusalem." In *L'Artiste*, 1st ser. 13 (1837), lithograph. Paris, Bibliothèque nationale de France. Photo: BnF.

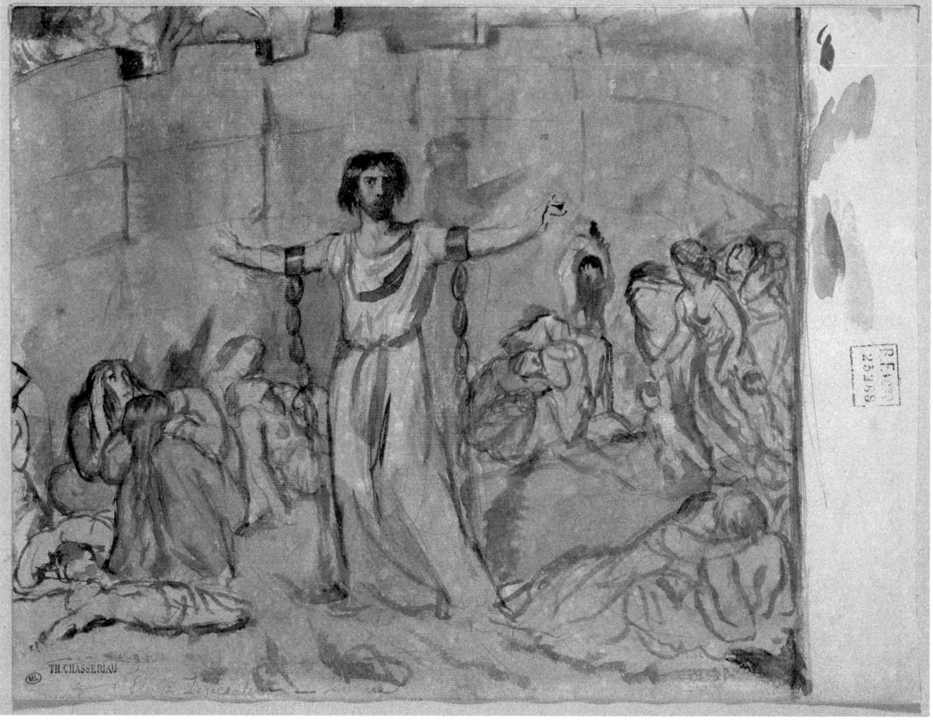

Figure 5.14 Théodore Chassériau, *Lamentations of Jeremiah*, ca. 1836–37, watercolor and graphite on paper, 24.8 × 33.4 cm. Paris, Musée du Louvre. Photo: Michel Urtado. © RMN-Grand Palais/Art Resource, NY.

Chassériau's prophet awkwardly mimics that of the hero of *The Martyrdom of Saint Symphorian* (1834; Autun, Cathedral of Saint-Lazare)—the monumental canvas with which his teacher was preoccupied during Chassériau's time in the Ingres studio—the dismal character of the drawing sets it apart.[87]

The *Nude Young Man Seated at the Edge of the Sea* was but an interlude for Flandrin, who moved on to the hieratic, Catholic painting for which he became celebrated. Yet its spell on Chassériau would endure. In 1838, Chassériau painted his own scene of classical nudity beside the sea. In a startling departure from the gloom

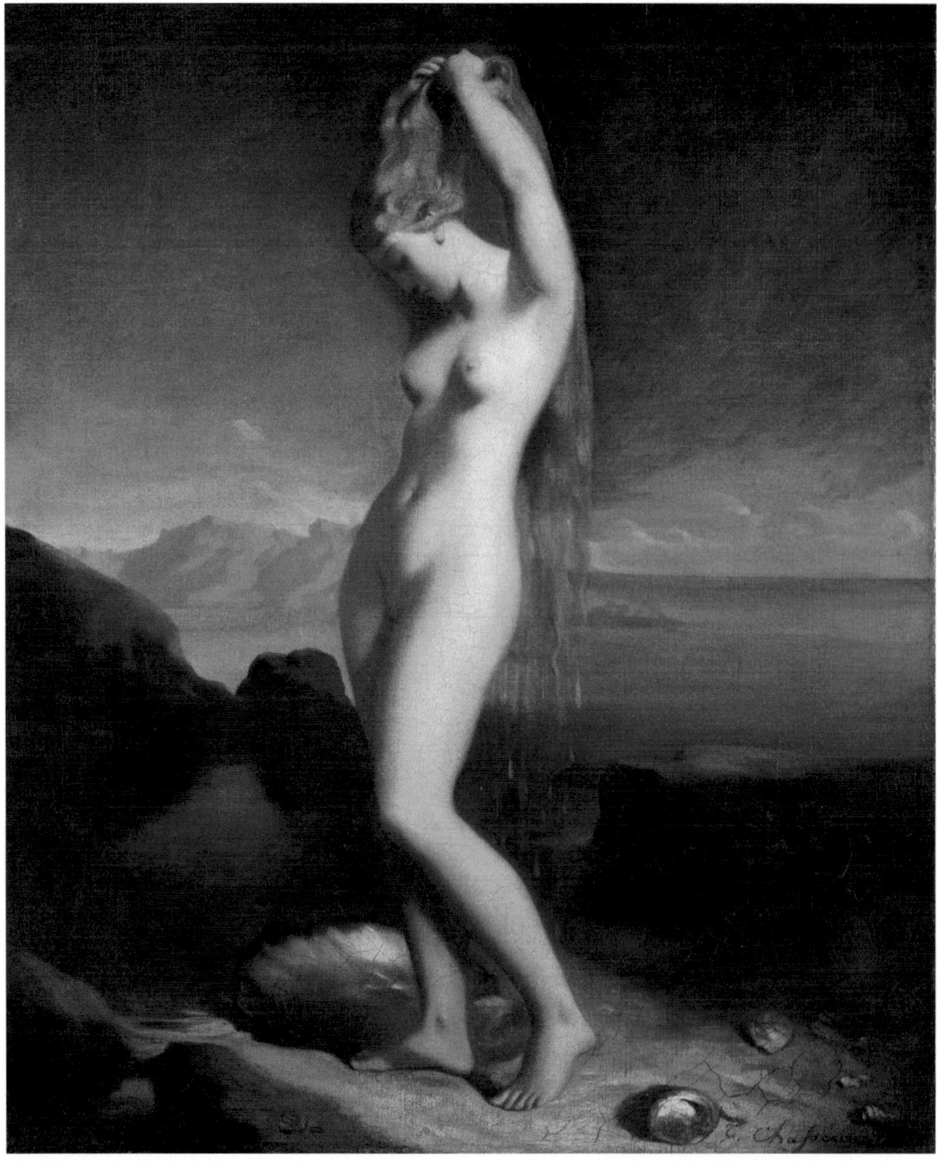

Figure 5.15 Théodore Chassériau, *Venus Anadyomene* (*Vénus marine*), 1838, oil on canvas, 65 × 55 cm. Paris, Musée du Louvre. Photo: Philippe Fuzeau. © RMN-Grand Palais/Art Resource, NY.

of *Cain Accursed,* his *Venus Anadyomene* (*Vénus marine*) offers escape to a contemplative space of exoticism and beauty that, following the artist's trip to North Africa in 1846, relocated to an imaginary Orient that flattered the artist's colonialist zeal (Figure 5.15).[88] With closed eyes, the self-absorbed goddess wrings the sea from her hair before a coastal landscape that seems simultaneously twilit and sun-struck. Fluid chiaroscuro, harkening back to Prud'hon, sensuously adumbrates her curves, imparting to this erotic subject an unexpected tincture of solemnity and introspection. This otherworldly effect is enhanced by the emblematic, flattened pose (compulsively repeated by the artist throughout the 1830s and '40s) in which bent neck parallels bent leg. It is also found in the moody *Susanna Bathing*, which the artist exhibited with *Venus Anadyomene* in the Salon of 1839 (Figure 5.16).[89] This Susanna is too self-absorbed to notice the voyeurs. Like her larger biblical cousin, *Venus Anadyomene* displays a signature feature of Chassériau's oeuvre, which Symbolist painter Ary Renan (1857–1900, son of Ernst Renan) would term "*la belle inertie*" (Ary Renan was born the year after Chassériau died).[90] This "beautiful inertia" has been savored by a legion of Chassériau connoisseurs, including Joseph C. Sloan and Léon Rosenthal. Sloan, for example, aptly viewed this lethargic inwardness as distinguishing Chassériau from Ingres and Delacroix, while constituting a formative legacy for Gustave Moreau and Pierre Puvis de Chavannes.[91]

Without abandoning the *belle inertie* of the *Venus Anadyomene* and *Susanna Bathing,* Chassériau returned to the anti-heroic mode in a remarkable canvas

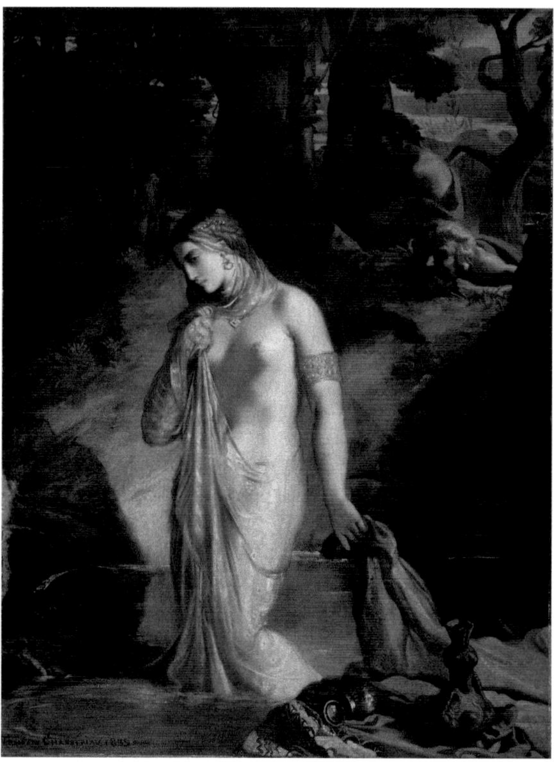

Figure 5.16 Théodore Chassériau, *Susanna Bathing,* 1839, oil on canvas, 255 × 196 cm. Paris, Musée du Louvre. Photo: Hervé Lewandowski. © RMN-Grand Palais /Art Resource, NY.

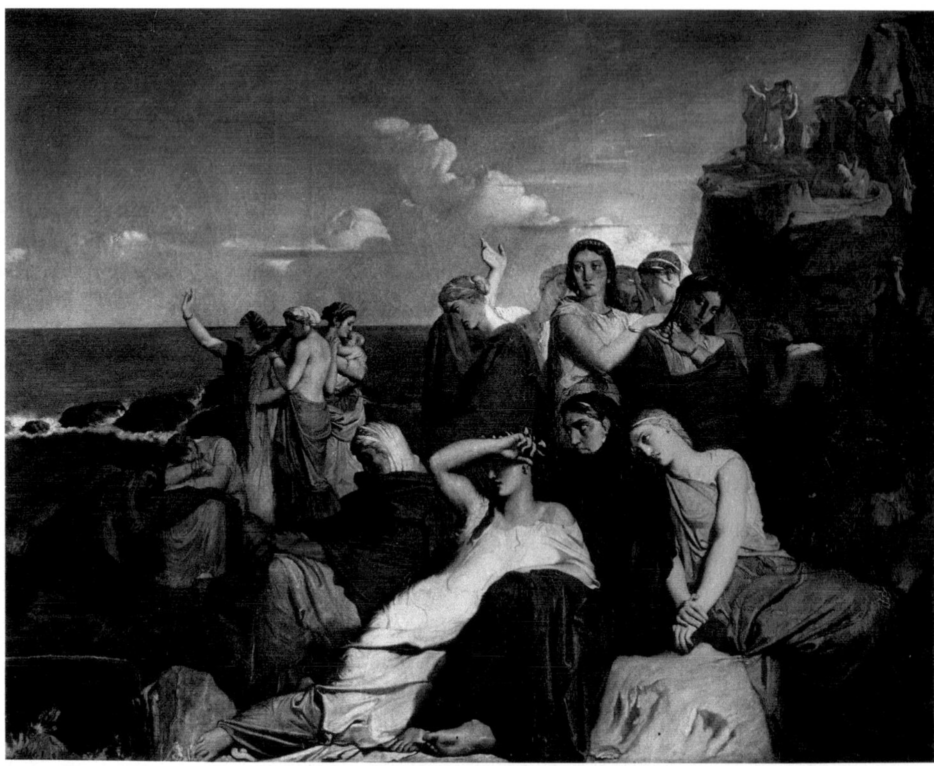

Figure 5.17 Théodore Chassériau, *The Trojan Women* (*Les Troyennes*), 1841. Destroyed, originally in the collection of Ferenc Hatvany, Budapest. Photo: Budapest, Museum of Fine Arts.

painted in 1841 and exhibited in the Salon of 1842. Acquired by the Hungarian collector Ferenc Hatvany, *The Trojan Women* (*Les Troyennes*) was destroyed during World War II, fortunately after having been photographed (Figure 5.17).[92] The photographic record of the lost painting is complemented by surviving studies, including a painted sketch (Figure 5.18).[93] The Salon guidebook indicates that the subject is taken from Book V of *The Aeneid*: "On a deserted, remote beach, the Trojan Women wept for the loss of Anchises, and weeping, they all looked at the deep sea."[94] Like Aeneas ("the man whom fate had sent / To exile from the shores of Troy"), these women are fugitives from their city, ravaged by the Greeks.[95] On the Sicilian shore, they mourn for their leader's father as the Trojan men commemorate his death with games. *The Trojan Women* brought together the artist's twin pursuits, whether to provide escapist contemplation of self-absorbed female figures or to represent the depths of grief. If the atmospheric, coastal setting of the painted sketch recalls the *Venus Anadyomene*, its clustered, bereft figures reestablish the depressed tenor of the drawing of Jeremiah and the painting of Cain and his family; the pyramidal group in the immediate foreground of the painted sketch (its central figure draped in red) suggests that Étex's *Cain and His Race* had made a lasting impression.

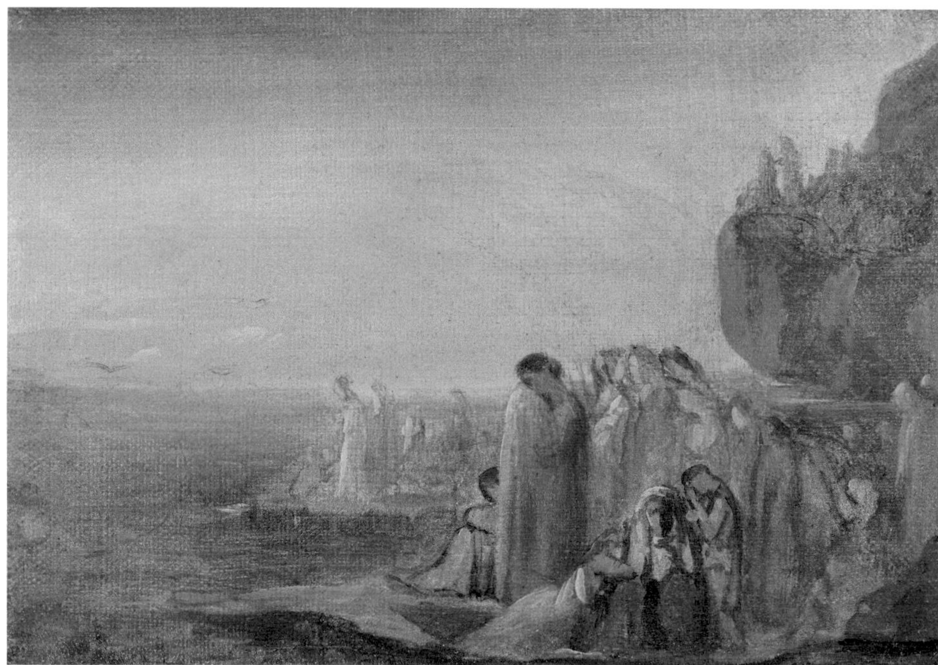

Figure 5.18 Théodore Chassériau, Study for *The Trojan Women,* 1840–41, oil on canvas, 26.5 × 18.5 cm. Beauvais, MUDO, Musée de l'Oise, Donation Chancerel-Gobineau, 1974. Photo: Adrien Didierjean. © RMN-Grand Palais/Art Resource, NY.

Like his *Susanna Bathing,* Chassériau's *Trojan Women* exemplifies the artist's tendency to enhance mood at the expense of narrative. This proclivity is a legacy of his tutelage under Ingres who, as Susan Siegfried observes, exhibits a "post-narrative" mode of history painting that minimizes action and emotional drama.[96] Rosenthal indicated that, regardless of the subject in question, Chassériau

> seems much less concerned with bringing heroes to life or developing characters than desirous of producing subtle and infinitely rich impressions suggested to him by the themes he chooses .... These paintings ... act like a charm or like an incantation ... they elicit fascinating, enervating dreams.[97]

Such preference for moody inertia over action (so fertile for the genesis of Symbolism) was anticipated by Ary Scheffer's *Greek Exiles on a Rock Look over at Their Lost Fatherland*, also an image of lamentation at the edge of the sea by exiles, but one whose tearfulness is alien to *The Trojan Women*, with its frozen poses and enigmatic groupings (cf. Figure 3.5).

Given the artist's proclivity for the imaginary and the exotic, it is only to be expected that the topicality of Chassériau's lost canvas has gone unnoticed. Notwithstanding the painting's proto-Symbolist remoteness, the group bereavement of *The Trojan Women* resonates with the bereft patriotism overdetermined since Waterloo and galvanized by the return of Napoleon's remains in 1840. The painting was possibly conceived as early as 1837, the year that Flandrin's *Nude* Young *Man Seated at the Edge of the Sea* and Bendemann's *Jeremiah on the Ruins of Jerusalem* were displayed; by the time that Chassériau completed *The Trojan Women*, his elegiac motif carried enhanced currency.[98] Whereas the Salon guidebook refers solely to *The Aeneid*, the patriotic dimension of the lost canvas is brought home by an overlooked source. I believe that Chassériau was also mindful of "The Trojan Women, Cantata" ("Les Troyennes, cantate"), a poem included in Casimir Delavigne's *Messéniennes*, published under the Restoration.[99] Opening with "Waterloo," Delavigne's popular collection must be read against the backdrop of recent French history. As the Trojan women of the poem nostalgically mourn for defeated Troy, the chorus intones a plaintive couplet: "D'un peuple d'exilés déplorable patrie, / Ton empire n'est plus, et ta gloire est flétrie." ("Wretched nation of an exiled people / Your empire is no longer, and your glory is withered.") The parallel with the Empire's fall is obvious. We have seen that in another of the collection's poems, "Le Jeune diacre, ou La Grèce chrétienne," a young Greek patriot equates the lot of his people with that of the captive Hebrews in Babylon, as evoked by Psalm 137. Delavigne also borrows from that psalm in "The Trojan Women, Cantata." Thus, the poem concludes with the women vowing to never sing their city's songs on foreign soil: "Sans cesse nous voulons pleurer notre misère, / Et les hymnes troyens / Ne retentiront pas sur la rive étrangère." ("We wish to ceaselessly weep over our misery, / And the Trojan hymns / Will not resound on the foreign

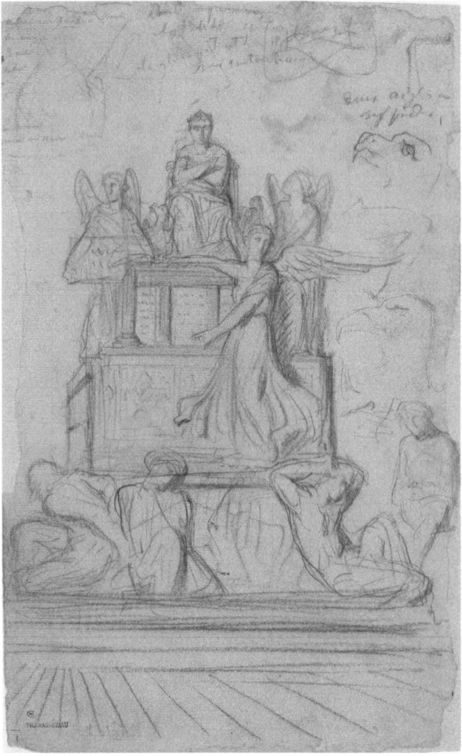

Figure 5.19 Théodore Chassériau, *Tomb Project for Napoleon I*, ca. 1840, red chalk and graphite on beige paper, 42 × 26.1 cm. Paris, Musée du Louvre. Photo: Michel Urtado. © RMN-Grand Palais/Art Resource, NY.

shore.") Similarly, Chassériau's lost painting is an antique variation on contemporary representations of the Babylonian Captivity.[100]

The imperial heritage of the Chassériau family sheds light on the lost painting's affinity with Delavigne's poem. Long after his Napoleonic service, Benoît remained devoted to the emperor's memory; in a letter to Théodore's elder brother Frédéric (28 July 1843), the artist's father wrote of a cherished stone and willow leaf from Saint Helena that he had recently received in tribute to his service in the Egyptian campaign.[101] Not surprisingly, Théodore worked on a design for Napoleon's tomb (Figure 5.19).[102] Deviating, like an afterthought, from the staid symmetry of this conventional funerary ensemble, with its winged allegories and bound captives, a seated figure on the right exhibits the artist's signature self-absorption—unexceptional in this context, yet of a piece with Chassériau's association of the anti-heroic mode with national grief in *The Trojan Women*. Excluded, by oversight, from the roster of contestants in the government's 1841 competition for the design of the tomb, Chassériau bitterly complained that, solely "to give proof of good will and zeal," he submitted a project that, though admired by connoisseurs, was not mentioned in the review of the competition in *L'Artiste*.[103] The lack of recognition must have been all the more galling, since the architect Charles-Frédéric Chassériau (1802–96), cousin to the painter and son of the general (Victor-Frédéric) killed at Waterloo, was one of officially recognized contestants.[104]

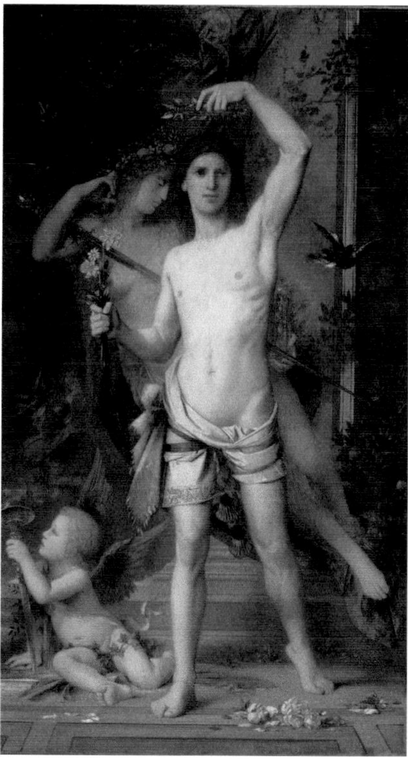

Figure 5.20 Gustave Moreau, *The Young Man and Death*, 1856–65, oil on canvas, 215.9 × 123.2 cm. Cambridge, MA, Harvard Art Museums/Fogg Museum, Gift of Grenville L. Winthrop, Class of 1886. Photo: © President and Fellows of Harvard College, 1942.186.

The precocious Symbolist Gustave Moreau (1826–98)—who met and became close to Chassériau around 1852—commemorated the elder artist's premature passing at age 37 with *The Young Man and Death* (Figure 5.20).[105] Above the inscription "A LA MÉMOIRE DE THÉODORE CHASSÉRIAU" ("TO THE MEMORY OF THÉODORE CHASSÉRIAU"), the "young victor" (as Moreau referred to his deceased friend), in the guise of a sleek, idealized androgyne—his Creole features expunged—transcends his mortality.[106] A winged hourglass, a flying bird, strewn petals, and a guttering torch signify the passing of an artist later described by Comte Robert de Montesquiou (1855–1921) as "privileged, deceased young, beloved by the gods."[107] To these conventional emblems of life's brevity is added a more personal motif. Enthroned behind the youth is a languid, female figure of Death, whose pensive profile identifies her as a cousin to the protagonists of the *Venus Anadyomene*, *Susanna Bathing*, and *The Trojan Women*. Holding a bouquet of cut flowers, the youth crowns himself with a gilded laurel wreath. Perhaps Moreau knew of an anecdote later conveyed by Chassériau's biographers Valbert Chevillard and Léonce Bénédite: before his elder students, Ingres predicted that the boy would be the "Napoleon of painting."[108] Paying homage to Chassériau's *belle inertie*, Moreau's memorial tribute forges a genealogical link between the enervation of the anti-heroic mode and the world-weariness of Symbolism.[109] This is not the sole instance in which a Romantic current born of loss had a post-Romantic reawakening. Because the heritage haunting the preceding pages assumed renewed urgency in the late nineteenth century, an epilogue is in order.

Notes

1 The lithograph is cataloged as "*Repos de la France*," *The Daumier Register*, no. 84, accessed 20 April 2019, http://www.daumier-register.org/werkview.php?key=84.

2 For a summary of *Ahasvérus*, see Léon Cellier, *L'Épopée humanitaire et les grands mythes romantiques*, 2nd ed. Paris: Société d'édition d'enseignement supérieur, 1971), chap. 4. For analysis, see Edgar Knecht, *Le Mythe du Juif errant: Essai de mythologie littéraire et de sociologie religieuse* (Grenoble: Presses Universitaires de Grenoble, 1977), chap. 4; and Paul Bénichou, *Le Temps des prophètes: Doctrines de l'âge romantique* (Paris: Gallimard, 1977), 460–8.

3 For the legend, see Knecht, *Le Mythe du Juif errant*; Eduard König, "The Wandering Jew: Legend or Myth?" in *The Wandering Jew: Essays in the Interpretation of a Christian Legend*, ed. Galit Hasan-Rokem and Alan Dundes (Bloomington: Indiana University Press, 1986), 11–26; and George K. Anderson, *The Legend of the Wandering Jew* (Providence RI: Brown University Press, 1965).

4 For the ubiquity of Napoleon in prints pulled from the presses of the Pellerin firm in Épinal, see Barbara Ann Day-Hickman, *Napoleonic Art: Nationalism and the Spirit of Rebellion in France (1815–1848)* (Newark: University of Delaware Press and London: Associated University Presses, 1999).

5 These are set forth in detail in Knecht, *Le Mythe du Juif errant*. See also Linda Nochlin, "Gustave Courbet's *Meeting:* A Portrait of the Artist as a Wandering Jew" (originally published 1967), in ed. Linda Nochlin, *Courbet*, 29–54 (New York: Thames & Hudson, 2007).

6 Ceri Crossley, *Edgar Quinet (1803–1875): A Study in Romantic Thought* (Lexington, KY: French Forum, 1983, 29.

7 Edgar Quinet, *Ahasvérus*, new ed. (Paris: Imprimeurs unis, 1843), 383.

8 "Hommes de Lodi, de Castiglione, de Marengo, où êtes-vous? Sortez de terre. Vous vous êtes couchés une heure trop tôt. Venez faire la tâche que vos enfants n'ont pas le coeur d'achever.... Car, à mon avis, votre plus grand tort, le voici: qui est d'avoir laissé deux fois environner, fouailler et fourrager ce grand pays par vos méchants ennemis.... Mon Dieu! France, douce France, fleur du ciel semée sur terre, que tu m'as déjà, sans le savoir,

coûté de larmes que personne ne me rendra! Belle barque sans rameur, que maintes fois, dans la nuit noire, je t'ai attendue jusqu'au matin, n'espérant plus que tu retrouves toute seule l'endroit de ton rivage!... La terre s'ennuie, elle ne sait plus que faire depuis que ton Empereur ne la tient plus cachée, pour s'amuser, sous un pan de sa gloire." Quinet, *Ahasvérus*, 128–30.

9 "Vers la fin de l'Empire, je fus un lycéen distrait. La guerre était debout dans le lycée, le tambour étouffait à mes oreilles la voix des maîtres, et la voix mystérieuse des livres ne nous parlait qu'un langage froid et pédantesque.... Lorsqu'un de nos frères, sorti depuis quelques mois du collège, reparaissait en uniforme de housard et le bras en écharpe, nous rougissions de nos livres et nous les jetions à la tête des maîtres." Alfred de Vigny, *Servitude et grandeur militaires*, in *Oeuvres complètes*, vol. 2: *Prose*, ed. Alphonse Bouvet (Paris: Gallimard, 1993), 688. All quotations herein are from this edition. In addition to this richly documented edition, see the commentary on *Servitude et grandeur militaires* in Paul Bénichou, *Les Mages romantiques* (Paris: Gallimard, 1988), 173–85.

10 "J'appartiens à cette génération née avec le siècle, qui, nourrie de bulletins par l'Empereur, avait toujours devant les yeux une épée nue, et vint la prendre au moment même où la France la remettait dans le fourreau des Bourbons." Vigny, *Servitude et grandeur*, 684.

11 "Moi, pauvre paysan du Jura ... condamné à porter toujours ce triste habit noir! Hélas! vingt ans plus tôt, j'aurais porté l'uniforme comme eux! Alors un homme comme moi était tué, ou *général à trente-six ans*." Stendhal, *Le Rouge et le noir*, ed. Anne-Marie Meininger, pref. Jean Prévost (Paris: Gallimard, 2000), 439, emphasis in original. See the illuminating discussion of the novel in Maurice Samuels, *The Spectacular Past: Popular History and the Novel in Nineteenth-Century France* (Ithaca, NY: Cornell University Press, 2004), chap. 6.

12 In December 1832, Vigny wrote to François Buloz, director of the *Revue des deux mondes*, asking him to announce a forthcoming historical novel of 42 chapters that would be "a book like the *Imitation*." Quoted by Bouvet, in Vigny, *Servitude et grandeur*, 1547. For Vigny's debt to *The Imitation of Christ*, see also, in the same edition, 695 n. 1 (note on p. 1562).

13 "Puisse ... la plus pure des Religions ne pas tenter de nier ou d'étouffer ce sentiment de l'Honneur qui veille en nous comme une dernière lampe dans un temple dévasté!" Vigny, *Servitude et grandeur*, 825.

14 "Que nous reste-il de sacré? [new paragraph] Dans le naufrage universel des croyances, quels débris où se puissant rattacher encore les mains généreuses?" Vigny, *Servitude et grandeur*, 821.

15 "Les Grandeurs éblouissantes des conquérants sont peut-être éteintes pour toujours. Leur éclat passé s'affaiblit ... à mesure que s'accroît, dans les esprits, le dédain de la guerre, et dans les coeurs le dégoût de ses cruautés froides.... Chaque souverain regarde son Armée tristement; ce colosse assis à ses pieds, immobile et muet, le gêne et l'épouvante; il n'en sait que faire, et craint qu'il ne se tourne contre lui. Il le voit dévoré d'ardeur ne pouvant se mouvoir." Vigny, *Servitude et grandeur*, 820.

16 For the author's biography, see Frank Lestringant, *Alfred de Musset* (Paris: Flammarion, 1999).

17 For a thoughtful discussion of this chapter as depiction of post-Napoleonic malaise, see Anita Brookner, *Romanticism and Its Discontents* (New York: Farrar, Straus and Giroux, 2000), chap. 3.

18 See Sylvain Ledda's comments in the introduction to *La Confession d'un enfant du siècle*, ed. Sylvain Ledda (Paris: Flammarion, 2010), 53. All quotations herein are from this edition. This is the original, uncut version of the novel, published 1 February 1836; this text was altered for the edition of 1840. See also the detailed account of the novel's genesis in Alfred de Musset, *Oeuvres complètes en prose*, ed. Maurice Allem and Paul-Courant (Paris: Gallimard, 1960), 1040–6. Since the time of our study at the Institute of Fine Arts, I have been indebted to Christopher Riopelle for bringing Musset's novel to my attention in connection with the mood in France after Napoleon's fall.

19 "Pendant les guerres de l'Empire, tandis que les maris et les frères étaient en Allemagne, les mères inquiètes avaient mis au monde une generation ardente, pâle, nerveuse. Conçus entre deux batailles, élevés dans les collèges aux roulements des tambours, des milliers

d'enfants se regardaient entre eux d'un oeil sombre, en essayant leurs muscles chétifs. De temps en temps leurs pères ensanglantés apparaissaient, les soulevaient sur leurs poitrines chamarrées d'or, puis les posaient à terre et remontaient à cheval." Alfred de Musset, *La Confession*, 60.

20 See Alan B. Spitzer, *The French Generation of 1820* (Princeton, NJ: Princeton University Press, 1987).

21 "Un seul homme était en vie alors en Europe; le reste des êtres tâchait de se remplir les poumons de l'air qu'il avait respiré." Musset, *La Confession*, 60.

22 "De même qu'un voyageur, tant qu'il est sur le chemin, court nuit et jour par la pluie et par le soleil, sans s'apercevoir de ses veilles ni des dangers; mais dès qu'il est arrivé au milieu de sa famille et qu'il s'assoit devant le feu, il éprouve une lassitude sans bornes et peut à peine se traîner à son lit; ainsi la France, veuve de César, sentit tout à coup sa blessure. Elle tomba en défaillance, et s'endormit d'un si profound sommeil que ses vieux rois, la croyant morte, l'enveloppèrent d'un linceul blanc." Musset, *La Confession*, 62.

23 See Paul Bénichou, *L'École du désenchantement: Sainte-Beuve, Nodier, Musset, Nerval, Gautier* (Paris: Gallimard, 1992), 177–8. The point is also made in Maurice Descotes, *La Légende de Napoléon et les écrivains français du XIXe siècle* (Paris: Lettres modernes Minard, 1967), 136.

24 For Musset's possible indebtedness to Vigny, see the editor's note in Vigny, *Servitude et grandeur*, ed. Bouvet, 688 n.1 (note on pp. 1558–9); and Alfred de Vigny, *Servitude et grandeur militaires*, ed. Auguste Dorchain (Paris: Garnier, 1955), 15 n. 1 (note on pp. 345–6).

25 For this point, see Bénichou, *L'École du désenchantement*, 178–9.

26 Sainte-Beuve's praise of the novel did not extend to part 1, chapter 2 (quoted above), "in which history and metaphysics are disguised beneath an incredible abuse of metaphors." C.-A. Sainte-Beuve, "La Confession d'un enfant du siècle, par M. Alfred de Musset," *Revue des deux mondes*, 4th ser. 5, no. 4 (15 February 1836), 492.

27 "[J]e vécus comme dans un nuage électrique, lequel planait sur ma tête et m'enveloppait orageusement, déchargeant aux collines de l'horizon ses coups de tonnerre. J'avais le coeur gonflé en mon sein comme l'Océan quand la lune d'équinoxe le soulève, et je ne retrouvais plus mon niveau .... Je retombai dans le chaos ... ne rêvant qu'ivresse et gloire, ... galoper sous les boulets, et vite mourir." Charles-Augustin, Sainte-Beuve, *Volupté*, ed. André Guyaux (Paris: Gallimard, 2011), 336–7.

28 Quoted in Robert Kopp, "'Les limbes insondés de la tristesse': Figures de la mélancolie romantique de Chateaubriand à Sartre," in *Mélancolie: genie et folie en Occident*, ed. Jean Clair (Paris: Réunion des musées nationaux, in association with Gallimard, Paris, 2005), 330.

29 "Notre siècle, ... en débutant par la volonté gigantesque de l'homme dans lequel il s'identifia, semble avoir dépensé tout d'un coup sa faculté de vouloir, l'avoir usée dans ce premier excès de force matérielle, et depuis lors ne l'a pas retrouvée." Sainte-Beuve, "L'Abbé de La Mennais," *Revue des deux mondes* (1832), 359–81, quoted by Ledda, in Musset, *La Confession*, 30.

30 See *The Napoleonic Wars: A Global History* (New York: Oxford University Press, 2020), 539–40. A variant estimate of French casualties is offered by Jean Tulard: some 380,000 dead, wounded, or deserted (40%–50% of officers and 80% to 90% of common soldiers), in *Napoleon: The Myth of the Saviour,* trans. Teresa Waugh. London: Methuen, 1985, 302–4, 436.

31 For the print, see Nina Athanassoglou-Kallmyer, *Théodore Géricault* (New York: Phaidon, 2010), 94–5; Lorenz Eitner, *Géricault: His Life and Work* (London: Orbis, 1983), 154–5; the catalog entry by Sylvain Laveissière, in idem et al., *Géricault* (Paris: Réunion des musées nationaux, 1991), no. 66; and James Cuno, "*Retour de Russie*: Géricault and Early French Lithography," in *Théodore Géricault, The Alien Body: Tradition in Chaos*, ed. Serge Guibault, Maureen Ryan, and Scott Watson (Vancouver, BC: Morris and Helen Belkin Art Gallery, 1997), 145–59.

32 Susan Siegfried observes that Géricault approached this lithograph, unusually rich in color and for which there are studies, as if it were a painting, in "Alternative Narratives." *Art History* 36, no. 1 (February 2013), 111.

33 "Seuls contre tante d'ennemis, vous tombâtes avec plus de gloire qu'ils ne se relevèrent. Sachez donc être vaincus sans honte!" Philippe de Ségur, *Histoire de Napoléon et de la Grande-Armée pendant l'année 1812* (Brussels: Arnold Lacrosse, 1825), 1: 3.
34 "Ses plus mâles guerriers, qui venaient de traverser fièrement tant de champs de leurs victoires, avaient perdu leur noble contenance: couverts de lambeaux, les pieds nus et déchirés, appuyés sur des branches de pin, ils se traînaient, et tout ce qu'ils avaient mis jusque là de force et de persévérance pour vaincre, ils l'employaient pour fuir." Philippe de Ségur, *Histoire de Napoléon et de la Grande-Armée pendant l'année 1812* (Paris: Baudouin frères, 1824), 2: 407–8.
35 Ségur, *Histoire de Napoléon*, 2:330.
36 For an insightful discussion of *Adieu*, see Samuels, *The Spectacular Past*, 208–24.
37 "L'apathie de ces pauvres soldats ne peut être comprise que par ceux qui se souviennent d'avoir traversé ces vastes déserts de neige, sans autre boisson que la neige, sans autre lit que la neige, sans autre perspective qu'un horizon de neige, sans autre aliment que la neige ou quelques betteraves gelées, quelques poignées de farine ou de la chair de cheval." Balzac, *Adieu*, in *Le Colonel Chabert, suivie de El Verdugo, Adieu, Le Réquisitionnaire*, pref. Pierre Gascar, ed. Patrick Berthier, 2nd revised ed. (Paris: Gallimard, 1974), 164.
38 For Pinel's moral cures, see Jan Goldstein, *Console and Classify: The French Psychiatric Profession in the Nineteenth Century* (Cambridge: Cambridge University Press, 1987), chap. 3.
39 For this work, see Stephen Bann, *Parallel Lines: Printmakers, Painters and Photographers in Nineteenth-Century France* (New Haven, CT: Yale University Press, 2001), 75–8; and Barthélémy Jobert, "Charlet, une carrière de peintre, de la Restauration à la monarchie de Juillet," in *Charlet: Aux origines de la légende napoléonienne 1792–1845* (Boulogne-Billancourt: Bibliothèque Paul-Marmottan, in association with Bernard Giovanangeli, Paris, 2008), 32–7. The painting is briefly discussed as an example of the artist's characterization of the soldier as proletarian representative of "the people," in Michael Paul Driskel, "The Proletarian's Body: Charlet's Representations of Social Class during the July Monarchy," in *The Popularization of Images: Visual Culture under the July Monarchy*, ed. Petra ten-Doesschate Chu and Gabriel P. Weisberg (Princeton, NJ: Princeton University Press, 1994), 73–4.
40 *Explication des ouvrages de peinture, sculpture, architecture, gravure et lithographie des artistes vivans, exposés au Musée royal le 1er Mars 1836* (Paris: Vinchon, 1836), no. 336, reprinted in *Catalogues of the Paris Salon 1673 to 1881*, comp. H.W. Janson (New York: Garland Publishing, 1977). Comparison with a lithograph by Charlet's pupil Raffet, *They Grumbled and Continued to Follow Him* (*Ils grognaient et le suivaient toujours*) of 1836 sets into relief the bleakness of the Charlet's painting. Representing the mounted emperor leading his retreating army, Raffet emphasizes the common soldiers' bond with their leader (as indicated by the title). For this print, see Day-Hickman, *Napoleonic Art*, 78 and n. 59.
41 Bann (*Parallel Lines*, 77) agrees with the catalog of the Lyon Musée des Beaux-Arts (1877), which identifies the pillager as a Jew.
42 For the French vogue for John Martin (1789–1854), see Jean Seznec, *John Martin en France* (London: Faber & Faber, 1964).
43 Quoted in Madeleine Vincent, *La Peinture des XIX*[e] *et XX*[e] *siècles,* Catalogue du Musée de Lyon 7 (Lyon: IAC, Les Editions de Lyon, 1956), 37.
44 Quoted from *L'Artiste*, in Léon Rosenthal, *Du romantisme au realisme: Essai sur l'évolution de la peinture en France de 1830 à 1848* (Paris: H. Laurens, 1914), 388.
45 "La *Retraite de Russie,* de M. Charlet, est un ouvrage de la plus haute portée. Il l'a intitulé *épisode,* et c'est une grande modestie; c'est tout un poème. En le voyant, on est d'abord frappé d'une horreur vague et inquiète. Que représente donc ce tableau? Est-ce le Bérésina, est-ce la retraite de Ney? Où est le groupe de l'état-major? Où est le point qui attire les yeux, et qu'on est habitué à trouver dans les batailles de nos musées? Où sont les chevaux, les panaches, les capitaines, les maréchaux? Rien de tout cela; c'est la grande armée, c'est le soldat, ou plutôt c'est l'homme; c'est la misère humaine toute seule, sous un ciel brumeux, sur un sol de glace, sans guide, sans chef, sans distinction. C'est le désespoir dans le desert.... [C]ent mille malheureux marchent d'un pas égal, tête baissée, et la mort

dans l'âme. Celui-ci s'arrête, las de souffrir, il se couche et s'endort pour toujours.... Partout où le regard se promène, il ne trouve qu'horreur, mais horreur sans laideur, comme sans exagération. Hors la *Méduse* de Géricault et le *Déluge* du Poussin, je ne connais point de tableau qui produise une impression pareille, non que je compare ces ouvrages, différens de forme et de procédé; mais la pensée en est la même, et (l'exécution à part) plus forte peut-être dans M. Charlet.... C'est bien une oeuvre de ce temps-ci, claire, hardie et originale. Il me semble voir une page d'un poème épique écrit par Béranger." Alfred de Musset, "Salon de 1836," *Revue des deux mondes,* 4th ser. 6 (15 April 1836): 152–4.

46 Musset's review was reprinted in 1865 and 1867 and was included in subsequent editions of the author's complete works from the publishing houses of Charpentier and Lemerre. See Maurice Tourneux, *Salons et expositions d'art à Paris (1800–1870): Essai bibliographique,* (Paris: Jean Schemit, 1919), 82.

47 *L'Artiste* 3rd ser. 3 (1843), 154.

48 "Qui ne se rappelle cette admirable *Retraite de Russie...*? La conception de ce tableau est vraiment effrayante; le coeur se serre devant cette immense solitude marquée çà et là par des formes humaines ensevelies sous la neige, sinistres jalons de cette marche désolée. Charlet l'intitule modestement *Episode.* Ce n'est pas un épisode, c'est un poème tout entier; ce n'est ni la retraite de Ney, ... ni Napoléon lui-même, déjà disparu de ce lugubre théâtre, emportant sa part de l'horrible désespoir qui précipite ces cent mille malheureux: c'est l'armée d'Austerlitz et d'Iéna devenue une horde hideuse, sans lois, sans discipline, sans autre lien que le malheur commun." "Charlet," *Revue des deux mondes* (1 January 1862), reprinted in Delacroix, *Oeuvres littéraires* 2: *Essais sur les artistes célèbres*, 6th ed. (Paris: G. Crès, 1923), 208.

49 Quoted from *Annales du Musée, Salon de 1835*, 4, in Rosenthal, *Du romantisme au réalisme*, 387.

50 Louis Viardot, "Salon de 1835," *Le National* (21 March 1835).

51 "Salon de 1835," *L'Artiste,* 1st ser. 9 (1835), 63. According to Maurice Tourneux, the review is either by Jules Janin or one of his imitators. See *Salons et expositions*, 76.

52 Bann indicates that the present title of the painting may reflect the sensation caused by Charlet's later *Episode from the Russian Campaign* (which, in turn, may have been motivated by Odier's painting). See *Parallel Lines*, 75. For Odier's painting, see also Hugh Honour, *Romanticism* (Harper & Row, 1979), 41 and 376. I am grateful to Catherine Renaux of the Musée de Picardie for sharing her research on Odier's painting. Gauthier Gillmann, of the Musée de Picardie's photograph library, kindly provided an image of the painting and facilitated my obtaining reproduction rights A small reproduction of the painting hangs over a piano in an early work by Ernest Hébert featuring an interior with Mademoiselle Buscoz, of Grenoble, and the father of the painter (deposited by the Musée du Louvre in the Musée Hébert in La Tronche). See Jacques Foucart, "À propos du peintre Odier: Note complémentaire à l'article de Marcel Roethlisberger,"*Genava: Revue d'histoire de l'art et d'archéologie* 37 (1989), 187. For the artist, see also Marcel G. Roethlisberger, "Edouard Odier (1800–1887): Sur les traces d'un peintre d'histoire romantique," *Genava: Revue d'histoire de l'art et d'archéologie* 36 (1988): 105–16.

53 Apart from the large format, the level of detail belies the characterization of the work as a "study." Rather than a study, observed a pair of commentators, it "seems to us a much more complete painting." Gabriel Laviron and B. Galbacio, *Le Salon de 1833* (Paris: Abel Ledoux, 1833), 266. Largely appreciative, Laviron and Galbacio criticize Odier's handling of the horse as "articulated in a dry and shrill manner: this is not necessary in order to render him wounded and suffering" (p. 266).

54 See *Explication des ouvrages de peinture et de sculpture de l'école moderne de France exposés dans le Musée royal du Luxembourg, destiné aux artistes vivans* (Paris: Vinchon, 1836), no. 106, in which the painting is titled *Episode de Moscou*. In 1846, Odier painted a larger version of *Episode from the Retreat from Russia*, which included the emperor and his army in the snow. Refused by the jury of the Salon of 1847, the painting was given to the museum of Caen by the artist's brother-in-law. It was destroyed in 1944. For this information, I am grateful to Catherine Renaux.

55 The dragoon's attitude is echoed in that of Odier's downcast *Genius Crying on the Ruins of Venice* (1837), reproduced in *Christian Imagery in French Nineteenth-Century Art,*

1789–1906, ed. Martin L.H. Reymert and Robert J.F. Kashey (New York: Shepherd Gallery, 1980), no. 56.

56 Other images based on the campaign of 1812 include a *Retreat from Russia* (Besançon, Musée des Beaux-Arts), exhibited in the Salon of 1838 by Édouard Swebach (1800–70), which features a despondent cavalryman seated on a dead horse, separated from a column of troops. See the catalog entry by Isabelle Julia, in idem, Jean Lacambre, and Sylvain Boyer, *Les Années romantiques: La Peinture française de 1815 à 1850* (Paris: Éditions de la Réunion des musées nationaux, 1995), no. 171 (on p. 437), plate 100. A similar *Episode from the Retreat from Moscow* had been exhibited in the Salon of 1835 by Henri-Félix-Emmanuel Philippoteaux (1814–84). In this painting (Versailles, Musée national du château, with a copy in Montauban, Musée Ingres), a wounded French soldier, seated with drawn pistol on a snowy mound beside a dead horse, shelters a dying bugle boy with his cloak. See Daniel Ternois, *Montauban, Musée Ingres, peintures. Ingres et son temps (artistes nés entre 1740 et 1830)*, Inventaire des collections publiques françaises 11 (Paris: Éditions Musées nationaux, 1965), no. 221.

57 I introduced the term "anti-heroic mode" in "Théodore Chassériau and the Anti-Heroic Mode under the July Monarchy," in *Chassériau (1819–1856): Un autre romantisme, Actes du colloque organisé par le Musée du Louvre, le 16 mars 2002*, ed. Stéphane Guégan and Louis-Antoine Prat, 11–38 (Paris: La Documentation française/Musée du Louvre, 2002).

58 For an early group of anti-heroic paintings inspired by *The Return of Marcus Sextus*, see Mehdi Korchane, *Figures de l'exil sous la Révolution, De Bélisaire à Marcus Sextus* (Vizille: Musée de la Révolution française-Domaine de Vizille, 2016), 112–27. These range from Fortuné Dufau, *The Death of Ugolino* (Salon of 1800; Valence, Musée des Beaux-Arts) to José Aparicio e Inglada (a Spanish student of David), *The Year of Hunger in Madrid* (1818; Madrid, Prado).

59 Quoted in Darcy Grimaldo Grigsby, *Extremities: Painting Empire in Post-revolutionary France* (New Haven, CT: Yale University Press, 2002, 219, emphasis in original.

60 See Margaret MacNamidhe, "Delécluze's Response to Delacroix's "Scenes from the Massacres at Chios" (1824)," *Art Bulletin* 89, no. 1 (2007), 66–7; and for further commentary on this figure, idem, *Delacroix and His Forgotten World: The Origins of Romantic Painting* (London: I.B. Tauris, 2015), 38–42.

61 See Susan Locke Siegfried, "Naked History: The Rhetoric of Military Painting in Postrevolutionary France," *Art Bulletin* 75, no. 2 (June 1993): 235–58.

62 For the portrait of *Ali-Ben-Hamet*, see the catalog entry by Stéfan Guégan, in idem, Vincent Pomarède, and Louis-Antoine Prat, *Chassériau: Un autre romantisme* (Paris: Réunion des Musées Nationaux, 2002), no. 134. For the critic's commentary, see Charles Baudelaire, *Critique d'art, suivi de Critique musicale*, ed. Claude Pichois, intro. Claire Brunet (Paris: Gallimard, 1992), 27.

63 The case for the artist's originality is made, for example, in Rosenthal, *Du romantisme au réalisme*, 163; and in Henri Focillon, "Chassériau, ou Les Deux romantismes," in *Le Romantisme et l'art,* pref. Edouard Herriot, ed. Louis Hautecoeur (Paris: H. Laurens, 1928), 161–85. For a historiographic synopsis of the Ingres-Delacroix theme in writing about the artist, see Guégan, Pomarède, and Prat, *Chassériau: Un autre romantisme*, 14–20.

64 For the artist's childhood work, see my "Chassériau's Juvenilia: Some Early Works by an *Enfant du Siècle*," *Zeitschrift für Kunstgeschichte* 57, no. 2 (1994): 219–38.

65 I am grateful to Jeff Steward and Britt Bowen, of Digital Imaging and Visual Resources, Harvard Art Museums, for kindly providing this image (and fig. 5.20 below) and for facilitating my obtaining reproduction rights.

66 "M. Chassériau, en voulant exprimer l'abattement et la douleur, a dépassé le but; ses deux figures ne posent pas et semblent trébucher; ce n'est certainement pas le Caïn de la Bible, ni sa douce et résignée compagne. Alexandre Decamps, "Salon de 1836," *Le National* (1 May 1836).

67 I am grateful to Barbara Favreau of the Musées d'Art et d'Histoire de La Rochelle for providing an image of the painting and facilitating my obtaining reproduction rights.

68 Léonce Bénédite, *Théodore Chassériau, sa vie, son oeuvre*, ed. André Dezarrois (Paris: Braun, 1931), 2: 341.

69 For Chassériau's support of the conquest of Algeria, manifest in the allegorical program of his murals for the staircase of the Cour des comptes (1844–48, largely destroyed in the Palais d'Orsay fire during the Commune, with fragments preserved in Paris, Musée du Louvre), see Peter Benson Miller, "By the Sword and the Plow: Théodore Chassériau's Cour des Comptes Murals and Algeria," *Art Bulletin* 86, no. 4 (December 2004): 690–718.

70 Apparently referring to the July Revolution, the artist wrote to his father, then in Saint Thomas: "I work all the time at drawing, the revolutions that have suddenly afflicted Paris have prevented me from continuing my customary studies, such that I can only send you a little drawing made in haste." ("je travaille toujours au dessin, les révolutions subitent qui ont affligé Paris mont empêchés de continuer mais études ordinaires, de sorte que je ne puis tenvoyer qu'un petit dessin fais à la hâte.") Louis-Antoine Prat, *Musée du Louvre, Cabinet des dessins. Inventaire général des dessins, École français. Dessins de Théodore Chassériau, 1819–1856* (Paris: Éditions de la Réunion des musées nationaux, 1988), 2: 974 (letter XVI, original spelling preserved). The letter is inscribed, by another hand, July 1830.

71 For the history of slave revolt and colonial repression in Saint-Domingue, see Grigsby, *Extremities*, chap. 1.

72 For Benoît's biography, see the commentary of Vincent Pomarède, in Guégan, Pomarède, and Prat, *Chassériau: Un autre romantisme*, 58–9. In the same exhibition catalog, see also the detailed chronology of the artist's life assembled by Bruno Chenique, especially pp. 163 and 271. The document in question is Archives du ministère des Affaires étrangères, dossier Personnel, 1re série, Benoît Chassériau 889, internal note.

73 "Mon Cher papa / je t'enbrasse de tout mon coeur. Je t'envoi de mes daissin et de mon travaille et si je pouvait t'envoyer quelque chose qui te fasse plus de plaisir je le ferai." Prat, *Dessins de Théodore Chassériau*, 2: 973 (letter IV, original spelling preserved).

74 "Cultive bien tes dispositions mon cher fils et rappelle toi bien que le talent conduit à tout." Prat, *Dessins de Chassériau*, 2: 974–5 (letter XX).

75 Guégan, Pomarède, and Prat, *Chassériau: Un autre romantisme*, no. 2, catalog entry by Pomarède.

76 I owe the reference to the choice of Hercules to Robert Rosenblum.

77 For Hugo's malicious caricature of Chassériau as "Serio," see *Choses vues: Souvenirs, journaux, cahiers, 1847–1848*, ed. Hubert Juin (Paris: Gallimard, 1972), 241–6 (23–24 February 1848). The poet has Chassériau's lover, Alice Ozy (1820–93), here called "Zubiri," refer to the Creole artist as a "sapajou" (Capuchin monkey).

78 See Jacques Foucart et al., *Hippolyte, Auguste et Paul Flandrin: Une fraternité picturale au XIXe siècle* (Paris: Musée du Luxembourg and Éditions de la Réunion des musées nationaux, 1984), no. 14, catalog entry by Jacques Foucart. For the painting's afterlife as an icon of gay visual culture, see Michael Camille, "The Abject Gaze and the Homosexual Body: Flandrin's *Figure d'Etude*," *Journal of Homosexuality* 27, no. 1–2 (1994): 161–88, published simultaneously in *Gay and Lesbian Studies in Art History*, ed. Whitney Davis, 161–88 (The Haworth Press, Inc., 1994).

79 The self-absorption and doubled-over pose of the Louvre canvas set it apart from an otherwise closely related work by Flandrin, executed in Rome in 1834 as his first-year *envoi*, *Polites, Son of Priam, Observing the Movements of the Greeks Toward Troy* (Saint-Étienne, Musée d'Art Moderne Saint-Étienne Métropole). For this see Sylvie Ramond et al., *Le Temps de la peinture, Lyon 1800–1914* (Lyon: Éditions Fage, 2007), no. 20; and Foucart et al., *Hippolyte, Auguste et Paul Flandrin*, no. 6, catalog entry by Jacques Foucart and Chantal Lanvin.

80 See Henri Dorra, "Dante et Virgile par Hippolyte Flandrin," *Bulletin des musées et monuments lyonnais* 5 (1976), 397. Dorra indicates (p. 399) that the pose of the foremost sinner was developed into that of the *Nude Young Man Seated at the Edge of the Sea*. See also Foucart et al., *Hippolyte, Auguste et Paul Flandrin*, no. 9, catalog entry by Jacques Foucart and Chantal Lanvin.

81 Quoted in Dorra, "Dante et Virgile," 395.

82 See the perceptive analysis of *The Dying Athlete* in Thomas Crow, *Emulation: David, Drouais, and Girodet in the Art of Revolutionary France*, rev. ed. (New Haven, CT: Yale University Press and Los Angeles, CA: Getty Research Institute, 2006), 49–57.

83 For the reception of this painting by German and French critics, and an analysis of preparatory studies, see Konrad Renger, "Eduard Bendemanns 'Jeremias': Vorzeichnungen und Würdigungen eines verlorenen Hauptwerkes der Düsseldorfer Malerschule" in *Ars naturam adiuvans: Festschrift für Matthias Winner: zum 11 März 1996*, ed. Victoria V. Flemming and Sebastian Shütze, 621–37 (Mainz am Rhein: Philipp von Zabern, 1996). The painting (ca. 1835), commissioned by the crown prince of Prussia (later Friedrich Wilhem IV), was apparently destroyed in 1945 in the Leineschloss in Hanover.

84 A reproduction of the painting is included in the first volume (1836) of Comte Athanse Raczynski, *Histoire de l'art moderne en Allemagne*, 3 vols. (Paris: J. Renouard 1836–41). The reproduction is bound into the album accompanying the full set of volumes.

85 "Rien de mieux conçu et de mieux exécuté comme grandeur triste et déchue, comme désolation immense; le prophète surtout est magnifique de pose, de draperie, de caractère sévère, d'absorption méditative pleine de mélancolie et de profondeur." S.-C., "Overbeck et l'école allemande," *L'Artiste*, 1st ser. 12 (1837): 51. For Saint-Chéron's militant Catholicism, see Michael Paul Driskel, *Representing Belief: Religion, Art, and Society in Nineteenth-Century France* (University Park: Penn State University Press, 1992), 77.

86 Prat, *Dessins de Chassériau*, 1: 59, no. 7 (RF 25288 R). Apart from sharing Bendemann's subject, Chassériau's *Jeremiah* drawing can be dated ca. 1836–7; a study for (or after) *The Prodigal Son,* exhibited in the Salon of 1836, appears on the drawing's verso.

87 For *The Martyrdom of Saint Symphorian,* see Susan L. Siegfried, *Ingres: Painting Reimagined* (New Haven, CT: Yale University Press, 2009), 337–71; and, for the controversy it generated at the Salon of 1834, see Andrew Carrington Shelton, *Ingres and His Critics* (Cambridge: Cambridge University Press, 2005), chap. 1.

88 Guégan, Pomarède, and Prat, *Chassériau: Un autre romantisme,* no. 13, catalog entry by Pomarède.

89 Ibid., no. 15, catalog entry by Pomarède.

90 Positing "la belle inertie" as a signal aspect of Gustave Moreau's work, Renan opens his discussion of this characteristic with reference to the influence of Chassériau on Moreau and Pierre Puvis de Chavannes. See Ary Renan, "Gustave Moreau" (2nd article), *Gazette des beaux-arts*, 3rd series 21 (1899), 200.

91 See Joseph C. Sloane, *French Painting between the Past and the Present: Artists, Critics and Traditions from 1848 to 1870* (Princeton, NJ: Princeton University Press, 1951), 129–31. See also Christine Peltre, *Théodore Chassériau* (Paris: Gallimard, 2001), epilogue.

92 For this photograph, I am grateful to Anna Zsófia Kovács, Head of the Department of Art after 1800, Museum of Fine Arts, Budapest and to Ágnes Horváth of the Reproductions Office, Museum of Fine Arts–Hungarian National Gallery.

93 The emotional tenor of the lost canvas is also anticipated by a study in pencil, with white highlights, on blue paper featuring a woman in a sorrowful attitude, with arms drawn in and neck bent (1840–41, Paris, Musée du Louvre). See Guégan, Pomarède, and Prat, *Chassériau: Un autre romantisme*, no. 39, catalog entry by Prat. For other studies, see Prat, *Dessins de Chassériau*, 1: nos. 97–119.

94 "Sur une plage déserte, écartée, les Troyennes pleuraient la perte d'Anchise, et, en pleurant, elles regardaient toutes la mer profonde." *Explication des ouvrages de peinture, sculpture, architecture, gravure et lithographie des artistes vivants, exposés au Musée royal le 15 mars 1842* (Paris: Vinchon, 1842), no. 347. Marc Sandoz noted that the passage from Virgil is quoted by Chateaubriand in the *Génie du christianisme* (part 2, book 2, chapter 10: "Parallel between Virgil and Racine"), as well as in *Les Martyrs* (book 10). See Marc Sandoz, *Théodore Chassériau, 1819–1856: Catalogue raisonné des peintures et estampes* (Paris: Arts et métiers graphiques, 1974), no. 90.

95 Virgil, *The Aeneid*, trans. David Ferry (Chicago: University of Chicago Press, 2017), 3.

96 See Siegfried, *Ingres.*

97 Rosenthal, *Du romantisme au réalisme*, 162.

98 That *The Trojan Women* was conceived around 1837 is indicated in Guégan, Pomarède, and Prat, *Chassériau: Un autre romantisme*, no. 39, p. 111, catalog entry by Prat, A drawing inscribed July 1838, which appears to feature mournful female figures at the edge of sea, suggests that *The Trojan Women* remained embryonic at this date. Prat, *Dessins de Chassériau*, 1:95–6, nos. 103 and 103v (RF 25.303).

99 Casimir Delavigne, *Messéniennes et poésies diverses*, 11th ed. (Paris: Ladvocat, 1824), 2: 89–101. An epigraph references Euripides, whose drama *The Trojan Women* is the poem's source.

100 See the representation of the subject by Ingres student Romain Cazes (1810–81) exhibited in the Salon of 1837 (Montauban, Musée Ingres) and another by Angel Joyard (1809–?), reproduced in *L'Artiste* 2d ser. 8 (1841), in my *Broken Tablets: The Cult of the Law in French Art from David to Delacroix* (Berkeley: University of California Press, 1993), 126–7.

101 For the letter, see Bénédite, *Théodore Chassériau: Sa vie et son oeuvre*, 1: 16.

102 Prat, *Dessins de Chassériau* 1:407–8, no. 999 (RF 25.797).

103 Bruno Chenique specifies November 1841 as the date and A.-H., Delaunay, editor of *L'Artiste*, as the addressee, of a note from Chassériau, discovered by Christine Peltre in La Rochelle (birthplace of the artist's father): "J'avais concouru sans autre intention que de prouver de la bonne volonté et du zéle [no punctuation] les amateurs m'ont fait des compliments du dessin. Mais c'est fini n'en parlons plus." ("I competed with the sole intention of giving proof of good will and zeal [no punctuation] the connoisseurs complimented the drawing. But it's done let's speak no further of it.") Quoted in Guégan, Pomarède, and Prat, *Chassériau: Un autre romantisme,* 183 (underscoring in original). See also Peltre, *Théodore Chassériau*, 149–50.

104 Théodore Chassériau is not included in the list of contestants, as reprinted in Michael Paul Driskel, *As Befits a Legend: Building a Tomb for Napoleon, 1840–1861* (Kent, OH: Kent State University Press, 1993), appendix C, 215.

105 For Moreau, see Peter Cooke, *Gustave Moreau: History Painting, Spirituality and Symbolism* (New Haven, CT: Yale University Press, 2014). For Moreau's collection of drawings and prints by Chassériau, as well as photographs and reproductions of his work, see Sylvie Patry, "Ma fidelité au souvenir de Chassériau, Gustave Moreau" in "Mélanges en homage à Dominique Brachlianoff," special issue of *Cahiers du Musée des beaux-arts de Lyon* (2003): 86–93.

106 Moreau thus described the principal figure in a letter (8 December 1856), to his friend Eugène Fromentin (1820–76), reprinted in *Gustave Moreau et Eugène Fromentin: Documents inédits*, ed. Barbara Wright and Pierre Moisy (La Rochelle: Quartier Latin, 1972), 86.

107 Robert de Montesquiou, "Alice et Aline (Une peinture de Chassériau)," in *Autels privilégiés* (Paris: Bibliothèque-Charpentier, 1898), 251. Comte Marie Joseph Robert Anatole de Montesquiou-Fézensac was the model for Des Esseintes, protagonist of the novel *À Rebours* by J.-K. Huysmans.

108 The sources of the anecdote are Valbert Chevillard, *Un peintre romantique, Théodore Chassériau* (Paris: Alphonse Lemerre, 1893), 13 and Bénédite, *Théodore Chassériau,* 1: 58. For these references, see the chronology by Bruno Chenique, in Guégan, Pomarède, and Prat, *Chassériau: Un autre romantisme*, 169. According to Bénédite, the anecdote was conveyed to the artist's nephew, Baron Arthur Chassériau, by the painter Alberto Pasini (1826–99), who studied under Théodore in 1854. Julius Kaplan observed similarity between the gesture of young man in Moreau's paining and that of Bonaparte in David's study for *The Coronation of Napoleon* (cf. fig. 1.3 above). See Kaplan, *The Art of Gustave Moreau: Theory, Style, and Content* (Ann Arbor, MI: UMI Research Press, 1982), 30.

109 Chassériau's subordination of narrative to mood deserves mention as having encouraged Moreau's tendency (as characterized by Peter Cooke) to replace with "contemplative immobility, evocation and mystery" the theatrical interaction of figures characteristic of French history painting since the seventeenth century. For this aspect of Moreau's work, see *Gustave Moreau*, chap. 2, especially p. 69; and idem, "Gustave Moreau and the Reinvention of History Painting," *Art Bulletin* 90, no. 3 (September 2008): 394–416. Reference to Chassériau is also missing when Scott C. Allan cites Ary Renan's employment of the term "la belle inertie" as characteristic of the painting of Gustave Moreau. See "Tyrannical Inopportunity: Gustave Moreau's Anti-narrative Strategies," in *Painting and Narrative in France: From Poussin to Gauguin*, ed. Peter Cooke and Nina Lübbren (London: Routledge, 2016), 145 n. 10.

Epilogue

After the Terrible Year

That the dark thread traced in the preceding pages runs through so rich a cultural fabric testifies to the fertility of the troubled religious and political inheritance of artists and writers who came of age or attained celebrity in the first half of the nineteenth century. Encompassing de-Christianization and the transformation of religious painting, the exile experience (whether personal or vicarious), the cult of Napoleon, and regret for lost glory, this study identifies the anti-heroic mode as a timely vehicle of expression hidden in plain sight. Embodying enervation, withdrawal, resignation, or vulnerability, the anti-heroic mode, I claim, is as germane to French Romantic visual culture as were exemplars of heroic virtue to the art of David and his contemporaries in the twilight of the eighteenth century. What follows is occasioned by the renewed urgency of the themes in question in the century's final decades, which saw a fresh series of national crises. A story of transformation as well as resurgence, this epilogue underscores differences separating the passions of two distinct eras. Whereas the Romantic imagination was imprinted by the legacies of de-Christianization and imperial glory, Waterloo, and post-1830 disenchantment, those who came of age after Romanticism's death had been prematurely tolled by mid-century Realism inherited new sources of unease and disenfranchisement.

Defeat and *Revanche*

Napoleon's magic persisted into the Third Republic, whose birth was overshadowed by a loss no less devastating than those of 1814 and 1815. Locked in a dispute with Prussia arising from the prospect that a German prince might succeed to the Spanish throne, the overly confident Napoleon III led France to war, anticipating that poetic justice would be delivered to one of his uncle's principal adversaries. On 2 September 1870, however, the emperor and 130,000 French soldiers were captured at Sedan by the Prussian army, bringing ignominious conclusion to the Second Empire, but not to the nation's sorrow. That which Hugo dubbed *The Terrible Year* (*L'Année terrible*) in an eponymous verse collection spanned the months from August 1870 to July 1871. During the fall and record cold winter of 1870, a brutal siege subjected Paris to shelling and rat-eating hunger until an armistice was signed on 28 January 1871, ten days after the coronation of Wilhelm I as Kaiser of Germany at Versailles, seat of the *grand siècle* and birthplace of the Revolution.[1] A new French government was formed the following month. In defiance of its septuagenarian chief executive, the moderate republican Adolphe Thiers (who had championed the return of Napoleon's remains to Paris), and the predominately monarchist legislature, dissidents in the well-armed capital proclaimed radical leftist rule on 28 March, choosing a name with revolutionary pedigree, the Paris

DOI: 10.4324/9781003184737-7

Commune. Overwhelmed by invading government troops headquartered at Versailles, the insurgents suffered the hideous carnage of the Bloody Week (21–28 May); at least 10,000 died, largely by firing squad, and some 40,000 were arrested.[2] The Communards, in turn, executed 24 hostages, including the archbishop of Paris and other clerics, and burnt a bevy of prominent buildings associated with the late Empire, including the Hôtel de Ville, the Tuileries Palace, and the Palais d'Orsay—the latter reduced to ruins adorned with the exposed remains of Chassériau's murals (1844–48) on the staircase of the bureau in charge of public finance and accounting, the Cour des comptes.

Daumier allegorized the defeat in a powerful lithograph published in *Le Charivari* (13 February 1871), "France-Prometheus and the Eagle-Vulture," of which I reproduce the artist's proof (Figure E.1).[3] Here, the satirist's characteristic mirth gives way to furious grief. France is personified as a female Prometheus, her arms spread, Christlike, in a breast-flattening stretch, as she endures assault by a frightful variation on the eagle emblems of Napoleon III and Prussia, the avian predator's flame-like wings echoed in the victim's shackled hand.

Surrender was formalized by the Treaty of Frankfurt (10 May 1871), which cost the nation nearly all of Alsace, much of Lorraine, and an indemnity of five billion francs. Until the lost territory was reclaimed after the Pyrrhic victory of 1918, the nation

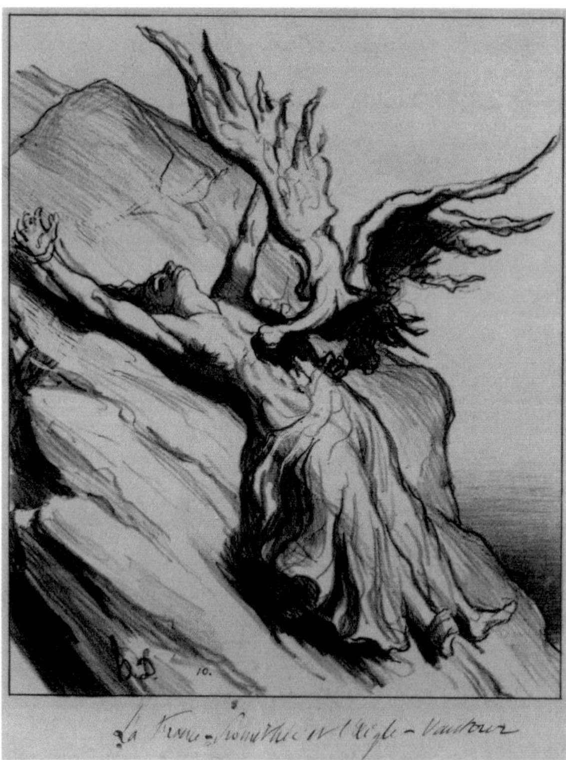

Figure E.1 Honoré Daumier, "France-Prometheus and the Eagle-Vulture." In *Le Charivari,* 13 February 1871 (artist's proof), lithograph, image 22.5 × 18.9 cm., sheet 33.4 × 24.9 cm. New York, Metropolitan Museum of Art, Elisha Whittelsey Collection, Elisha Whittelsey Fund, 1990 (1990.1027). Photo: The Metropolitan Museum of Art (Open Access).

experienced grief sufficient to transform French nationalism from its post-Waterloo form (nostalgic and bellicose, yet cosmopolitan and constitutional) into vengeful, xenophobic, anti-parliamentarian rage. Although this current became distinctly anti-Semitic with the eruption of the Dreyfus Affair in 1898, anti-Semitism had been embraced by many French nationalists well before Émile Zola (1840–1902) published "J'Accuse," his famous denunciation of the unjust condemnation for espionage (1894) of Alfred Dreyfus, a former Jewish captain on the general staff. In 1890, illustrator and poster designer Adolphe Willette (1857–1926)—who had run on the anti-Semitic ticket for the second district of the ninth arrondissement of Paris in the legislative election of September 1889—produced *Revanche* (*Revenge*), a lithograph that offers a terse remedy to the torment evoked by Daumier.[4] A mounted French officer has decapitated the German imperial eagle, whose orb and scepter lie beside its severed head (Figure E.2). Contentedly wiping his sword with the tail of his startled mount, the avenged victor is positioned beside toppled frontier markers that will no longer divide France from her stolen land. This print epitomizes the stridently patriotic imagery that, as Richard Thomson observes, permeates French visual culture of the 1890s, as the loss of Alsace-Lorraine continued to rankle, and the desire for *revanche* remained keen, despite marginalization of these grievances in contemporary political discourse.[5]

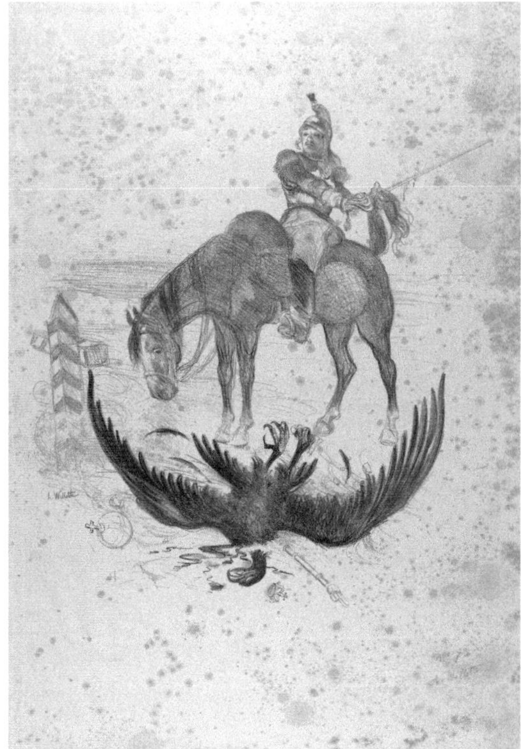

Figure E.2 Adolphe-Léon Willette, *Revenge* (*Revanche*), 1895, lithograph, image 40.2 × 37.1 cm., sheet 43.2 × 59.5 cm. New York, Metropolitan Museum of Art, Rogers Fund, 1922 (22.82.1–94). Image copyright © The Metropolitan Museum of Art. Image source: Art Resource, NY.

Some two decades earlier, with the defeat painfully fresh, anticipation of *revanche* figured in an exile's lament titled *The Alsatian Emigrant, A Narrative* (*L'Émigrant alsacien, Récit*, 1873)—a brief, early work by the poet and playwright Jacques Normand (1848–1931), a patriotic veteran of the Franco-Prussian War. Sold for one franc to benefit the needy of Alsace-Lorraine, this now rare publication saw two editions. A tale in verse, it is narrated by an old Alsatian, who recounts why he has emigrated to Paris in spite of longing for his native land. His two sons killed in the war and his wife long dead, he was reduced to wandering as a beggar. One day he met a young man paralyzed by sorrow near the French border; when his parents had been brutally killed by the Germans, the young man planned to join the French army, yet found himself unable to depart from his home and his fiancée. After encountering German occupying forces who mock and harass them, the old and young man join forces and travel to Paris—one regains a son, the other a father—and the young man joins the cavalry in anticipation of *revanche* of the sort imagined by Willette. In the frontispiece provided by Gustave Doré (1832–83), a patriotic Alsatian artist who served in the ambulance corps during the war with Prussia, and who had known, firsthand, the misery of the Siege of Paris, the pair hold hands in grim solidarity as the German troops pass (Figure E.3):

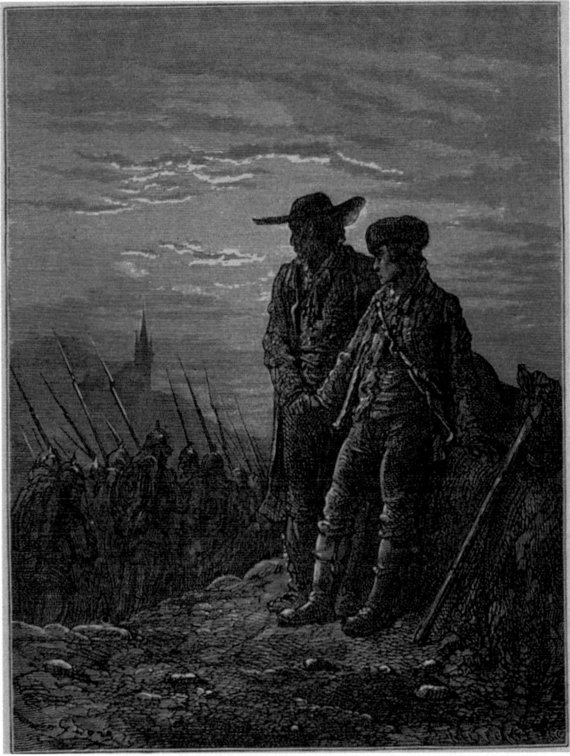

Figure E.3 G. Laplante after Gustave Doré, frontispiece to Jacques Normand, *L'Émigrant alsacien, récit, avec une gravure de Gustave Doré* (Paris: Librairie du XIXe siècle, 1873), engraving. Strasbourg, Bibliothèque nationale et universitaire de Strasbourg. Coll. and photo. BNU de Strasbourg.

> Rangés près du fossé pour leur laisser la place
> Nous regardions passer les maîtres de l'Alsace,
> Tête basse, et sentant résonner dans nos coeurs
> Ainsi qu'un glas de mort, le tambour des vainqueurs.
> Steady near the trench to make way for them / We watched the masters of Alsace go by, Head lowered, and feeling resonate in our hearts, / Like a death knell, the drum of the vanquishers.[6]

With word and image, Normand and Doré return us to the elegiac truculence running, in the wake of Waterloo, from Vernet to Quinet.

The loss of Alsace and Lorraine also returned currency to Psalm 137. In the same year that Normand and Doré collaborated on *L'Émigrant alsacien,* the captivity of the Hebrews in Babylon provided the subject of the Prix de Rome competition at the École des Beaux-Arts. It may have been considered appropriate that the winner, Jean-Léon Gérome's brother-in-law, Aimé-Nicolas Morot (1850–1913), was a native of Nancy, which remained French when other Lorraine territory was annexed. Whereas the competition traditionally called for emphatically expressive physiognomy and gesture, the downbeat topic prompted departure from conventional extroversion. Dusting off the anti-heroic mode, Morot represented two generations huddled in despair under armed

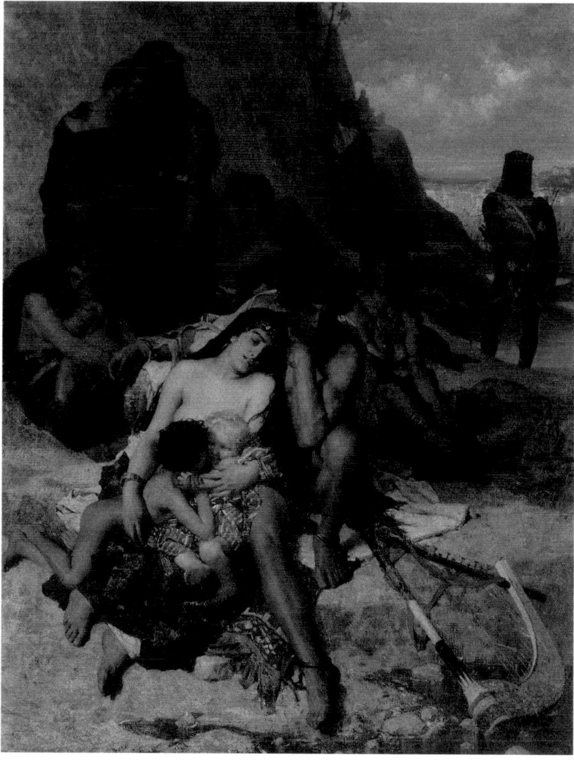

Figure E.4 Aimé-Nicolas Morot, *The Captivity of the Jews in Babylon*, 1873, oil on canvas, 145 × 113 cm. Paris, École nationale supérieure des Beaux-Arts. © Beaux-Arts de Paris, Dist. RMN-Grand Palais/Art Resource, NY.

guard (Figure E.4).[7] A swarthy, muscle-bound father sits in the foreground, his ankles and one wrist in shackles, an idle harp at his feet. Striking the stock attitude of melancholy, he supports a languishing, distinctly Caucasian mother. Young siblings squirm on her lap, their contrasting complexions matching those of their parents and recalling the contrast between Jacob and Esau. Morot's painting revives the parallel between the tribulations of the ancient Hebrews and the sorrows of modern France that had been employed by the émigrés Delille, Boisgelin, and Chateaubriand. This parallel had folk appeal in the aftermath of territorial loss, as suggested by a provincial publication by a cleric (Abbé Cl.-P. S.), *The Lamentations of the Prophet Jeremiah Translated into French Verse and Followed by Several Religious and Patriotic Songs Composed on the Occasion of the War of 1870–71 between France and Germany*. Printed in Troyes (1871), the collection bluntly sets forth the analogy: "Now, what could be more like the sorrows of France in 1870 and 1871 than the sorrows of Judea in the numerous invasions that so frequently ravaged and desolated it under several of its kings?"[8] In the spirit of the post-war Moral Order, which led the Catholic-dominated legislature to appropriate funds in 1873 so that the basilica of Sacré-Coeur (begun 1876) could be erected in leftist Montmartre in expiation of the nation's sins, *The Lamentations of the Prophet Jeremiah* attributes the defeat to atheism.

In the Wake of the Commune: Exile

Residents of Alsace and Lorraine were not the only French citizens painfully separated from the fatherland. Of the captive Communards who escaped execution, around 4,000 were deported to a location no less remote than Saint Helena: the archipelago of New Caledonia, some 800 miles east of Australia, which served as a French penal colony from 1863 to 1896.[9] Others fled into exile. Among the latter was Gustave Courbet's friend Jules Vallès (1832–85), who spent nine years in London.[10] Sentenced to death *in absentia*, the dissident journalist and novelist left a bitter record of the experience in correspondence and in a ferociously Anglophobic travelogue (*La Rue à Londres*), published in Paris four years after the general amnesty declared in July of 1880 permitted his return.[11] Attempting to persuade fellow ex-Communard exile Arthur Arnould (1833–95) to join him, Vallès held out the allure of living, as a detached observer, amid an abhorrent people. "I absolutely recommend to you the *black City*, London, the enormous London," Vallès wrote on 15 March 1877. "I hate, I hate, I hate the English, but what need would we have to bring them into our lives! We would be content before the moving spectacle of the battle and the view of the monster."[12] "Frankly speaking" he explained later that year, "it is commitment to observation, heroic love of my craft, and as an investigator of mores that I love ... the spectacle of this ferocious city."[13] "I would like," he proposed in December 1878, "to turn the misery of these silent, crushed people into a great social novel."[14] This ambition locates the author in a post-Romantic era of Naturalism and social consciousness. At the same time, expectation that exile would nurture his craft links Vallès to a genealogy running from Chateaubriand and Staël to Hugo.

Unlike Vallès, Courbet did not live to see amnesty. Charged, legally and financially, by the Third Republic with responsibility for the toppling of the place Vendôme column, the artist was imprisoned prior to emigrating across the French border.[15] The Realist lived out his remaining years in Switzerland, protesting his innocence. While in exile, he repeatedly painted a building well-known to travelers, the

Château de Chillon, on Lake Geneva, several kilometers from La Chaux-de-Fonds, his home since 1873. Sometimes engaging assistants, the artist based these views on photographs, perhaps never having visited the site.[16] The repetition reflected threadbare need; debts necessitated saleable representations of a location popular with sightseers. Its tourist appeal stemmed from the fabled imprisonment within its walls (1530–36) of François Bonivard (ca. 1496–1570), an ally of the Genevans in their resistance to the hegemony of Charles III, Duke of Savoy. The subject of Byron's *The Prisoner of Chillon* (1819)—which opens "Eternal spirit of the chainless mind! / Brightest in dungeons, Liberty!"—Bonivard's captivity had been represented by Delacroix (1835; Paris, Musée du Louvre).[17] In light of the cruel facts of Courbet's predicament, the Romantic legend assumed personal significance.

National Energy

Whereas Courbet and Vallès suffered exile from Paris, separation from Lorraine casts a pall over *The Uprooted* (*Les Déracinés*, 1897). First in the trilogy, *The Novel of National Energy* (*Le Roman de l'énergie nationale*), it was written by a key figure in the post-defeat metamorphosis of French nationalism, the novelist and politician from Nancy, Maurice Barrès.[18] Though Barrès is remembered as the very embodiment of bellicose French patriotism, his preoccupation with the Alsace-Lorraine question was delayed. His sentiments in this regard intensified in response to the Dreyfus Affair, in which he figured as Zola's anti-Semitic counterpart.[19] Published on the eve of the Affair, the novel recounts, in the unflinchingly candid idiom of Zola's Naturalism, the vicissitudes of life in the capital in the early 1880s for seven young men from Nancy. Embracing the deterministic insistence of Positivist historian Hippolyte Taine (1828–93) on the inescapable cultural and moral determinants of race, milieu, and moment, Barrès sets forth the baleful consequences of the young men's uprooting from their native soil.[20]

Such is the moral depression of the Third Republic that, even before leaving Nancy, the seven protagonists are stunted. Echoing the frustrated yearning of the earlier generation conveyed by *Servitude et grandeur militaires* and *La Confession d'un enfant du siècle*, Barrès contrasts the experience of these *lycée* students with those of Napoleon's time:

> At an age in which high school students of the first Empire heard the cannon of Marengo and sometimes the coupe of the Man crossing their city in haste, these children, grown up since the war, had no other general idea of an emotionally moving nature than defeated France and the struggle of the Republic against the dynastic parties.[21]

Barrès arrays the former students in a spectrum represented, at one end, by the intellectual seriousness of Maurice Roemerspacher and the idealism of François Sturel and, at the other, by the amoral abjection of Antoine Mouchefrin and Honoré Racadot. In a perversion of Barrès' cult of national energy, Mouchefrin and Racadot, desperate to save their bankrupt political journal— formerly an idealistic enterprise, now morphed into an instrument of blackmail—murder and rob of her jewelry Sturel's former lover, a beautiful Armenian cosmopolite, Astiné Aravian, whose name and exotic past are emblematic of Asiatic otherness.

"At the Tomb of Napoleon," a pivotal chapter of *Les Déracinés,* describes its young protagonists' meeting at the Invalides on 5 May, anniversary of the emperor's death. There, these uprooted grandchildren of soldiers of the Grande Armée experience a fleeting moment of transcendence around a redemptive symbol:

> The tomb of the Emperor, for twenty-year-old Frenchmen, is not at all the site of peace, the philosophical ditch where a pitiful body that was so restless gives itself up; it is the crossroads of all the energies that one calls audacity, will, appetite.... When the years will have destroyed the work of this great man and his genius no longer usefully counsels either the thinkers or the people ... something however will remain: his power to multiply energy.[22]

Napoleon's varied representations, we are told, coalesce in one irresistible persona: "Professor of energy! Such is his definitive physiognomy and his decisive formula, obtained by the superimposition of all the forms in which he is represented by the specialists, the artists, and the people."[23] Bearing witness to the tenacity of the cult of Napoleon (which resurged in the 1890s), this episode returns us to the malaise that had found expression, more than half-a-century earlier, in the torpid self-absorption of the anti-heroic mode. Just as those images of defeat and enervation elegized a lost heroism, whether in the aftermath of Waterloo or in the wake of the July Revolution, so too does Barrès conversely associate the entombed emperor with French vitality. Thus, the young men, who, at the Invalides, have become "a band of young tigers," take an oath proposed by Sturel: "At the tomb of Napoleon, professor of energy, let us swear to be men!"[24] In the brevity of this resolve—soon belied by the divergent destinies of the protagonists and the degradation and collapse of the journal they resolve to establish—there is a sense of loss that recalls national traumas predating the Third Republic. In this regard, Barrès's taste for Chassériau is telling. Having discovered Valbert Chevillard's quirky, fin-de-siècle monograph on the artist in late 1904, the nationalist author became a devotee, discerning affinity between *The Trojan Women* and his own cause.[25]

Catholic Revival

Like the renewed urgency of the theme of exile in the wake of the Terrible Year, invocation of the "professor of energy" returns us to earlier pages of this study. But what of Catholicism? In accord with the post-war demand for national expiation symbolized by the basilica of the Sacré-Coeur, the early 1870s brought an upsurge of apocalyptic prophecies and pilgrimages to shrines—a galvanization of popular piety that heralded a sea change in the sophisticated realm of high culture.[26] Between the late 1870s and early 1880s, and continuing beyond the close of the century, France saw a Catholic revival that even touched Barrès, a non-believer whose nationalism constituted a secular religion.[27] Having begun his political career espousing the anti-clericalism typical of the Left, Barrès—who, in a manner characteristic of late nineteenth-century French radicalism, embraced extreme positions of both Left and Right—eventually arrived at a respectable conservatism, seeing Catholicism as an integral part of the national heritage (as had Napoleon). Conversely, his contempt for the Third Republic impressed Catholic revival authors such as Joris-Karl Huysmans (1848–1907) and Léon Bloy (1846–1917). In the case of the latter, fervent belief coincided with mystical veneration of Napoleon. Whereas Barrès positioned the "professor of energy" as an inspiring foil to the dispiriting climate of late nineteenth-century Paris, Bloy considered the emperor nothing less than forerunner to the Second Coming:

> Napoleon is the most inexplicable of men because he is before all and above all the prefiguration of THE ONE who must come and who is perhaps not far away, a prefiguration and a precursor close to us, signified himself by all the extraordinary men who preceded him throughout time.[28]

That so outlandish an opinion (which would have been at home in the 1840s) could be expressed as late as 1912 gives measure to the emperor's enduring charisma.

Part of a larger repudiation of the Third Republic, the Catholic revival stood in opposition to the commitment to contemporaneity and empirical fact that had dominated the French artistic and literary avant-garde since mid-century. As the twentieth century approached, religion and mysticism were in vogue on the Paris art scene. Hardly uniform, this current encompassed the eclecticism of *Christ and Buddha* (ca. 1890; private collection) by the Nabi Paul Ranson (1861–1909); the mellow, decorative imagery of his fellow Nabi, the liberal Catholic Maurice Denis, (1870–1943); and the rarefied idealism purveyed in the Salons de la Rose + Croix (1892–97).[29] Vehemently opposed to anything tainted by Realism, and infatuated with all things occult, the Lyonnais writer Joseph-Aimé Péladan (1858–1918), who called himself the Sâr Mérodack Joséphin Péladan, presided over the Rose + Croix exhibitions. Professing a blend of mystical Catholicism and Rosicrucianism (a seventeenth-century German spiritual movement), the pronouncements of this exhibitionistic impresario harkened back to comparably arcane manifestations of Lyonnais faith; in 1887, six years after the still-living Janmot completed *The Poem of the Soul*, Péladan established a Parisian lodge devoted to the doctrine of Saint-Martin. While the Sâr dabbled on the fringe of the Catholic revival, others—contributors to what Richard Griffiths terms the reactionary revolution—stridently embraced Catholicism, raging at the Third Republic's individualism, Positivism, and official secularism (the latter pointedly manifest in the de-Christianizing of state education in 1882, and in the divorce of Church and state officially finalized in 1905).[30] This reawakening (known as the *ralliement*) was hardly akin to that heralded by the *Génie du christianisme*. In contrast to Chateaubriand's sentimental appeal to feeling and to aesthetic sensitivity (intended to win converts), Catholic revival authors espoused a harsh, hierarchical spirituality, reveling in features of worship that repelled the uninitiated. Chateaubriand elicited tears from readers nursed on Rousseau; impressed by *Pain* (*La Douleur*, 1849) by Antoine Blanc de Saint-Bonnet (a Lyonnais mentee of Ballanche), adherents of the *fin-de-siècle* Catholic revival thirsted for what Griffiths terms "vicarious suffering," that is, expiatory mortification on behalf of others. This could be pursued in the legends of saints or enacted in one's personal affairs—as when Huysmans, dying of jaw and throat cancer, refused morphine.

That writer stands as a telling example of the transformative power of the late nineteenth-century wave of faith.[31] Initially a disciple of Zola's hardscrabble Naturalism, Huysmans immersed the reader in the extravagantly decadent, hothouse world of Des Esseintes—amoral despiser of nature and connoisseur of the perversely exotic—in *À Rebours* (*Against Nature* or *Against the Grain*, 1884). Reviewing *À Rebours* in the *Constitutionnel* (28 July 1884), the Catholic dandy Jules Barbey d'Aurevilly (1808–89)—who had converted his neighbor, the young Bloy, in 1869—famously declared that the novel had left Huysmans with a choice "between the muzzle of a pistol and the foot of the cross." The latter alternative is embraced by Huysmans's autobiographical protagonist, Durtal, whose spiritual trajectory runs from the "black novel," *Down There* (*Là-bas,* 1891), which opens the Durtal tetralogy, to the tripartite "white novel" that followed the author's conversion in 1892 (when, turning his back on the secular Republic, Huysmans first confessed on 14 July and took communion the following day).[32] Fascinated and appalled by Satanism, Durtal attends a black mass in *Là-bas.* In the three subsequent novels, he surrenders to an ever more demanding Catholicism. This leads to an anxious sojourn in a Trappist monastery by this intensely introspective man of letters (*En Route*, 1895); heady absorption in the art and symbolism of Chartres (*La Cathédrale*, 1898); and finally, in *L'Oblat* (1903), commitment to the vocation of oblate (lay brother). Whereas Chateaubriand waxed nostalgic over monasteries that once might have sheltered an afflicted René (the troubled protagonist of an eponymous novella originally appended to the *Génie du christianisme*), Huysmans, like Durtal, was magnetically drawn to the most rebarbative aspects of monastic life. Moreover, the affliction had changed between the dawn and the twilight of the century. The *vague des passions* that drove the wandering of René and his author was replaced by a world-weariness that leads Durtal to religion:

> Ah! ... When I think of that horror, of that disgust with existence, which, for years and years, worsened in me, I understand that I inevitably sailed toward the sole port where I was able to find shelter, toward the Church.[33]

Yet a legacy of lost innocence underlies the embrace of Catholicism by Durtal, who wonders whether it would be permissible to bring volumes of Hugo, Baudelaire, and Flaubert to the monastery. It is hardly surprising that the Catholic novels of Huysmans gave devout readers pause.[34]

Durtal's fixation on the friars' unrelenting daily routine of self-denial and prayer updates the spectator Christianity manifest in Schnetz's versions of *Vow to the Madonna*, Navez's *Saint Veronica of Milan*, and Gérard's *Saint Theresa*. This preoccupation with extreme religiosity on the part of others is paralleled in the work of an artist who shared with Durtal an appetite for Christian mystery—Paul Gauguin. In the late 1880s, the artist was drawn to the intensely pious culture of Brittany, apparently sharing a proclivity attributed by Griffiths to Catholic revivalists, who professed respect for peasant wisdom and harbored a "sense of a lost paradise of truth, which must be sought again if man is to be saved ... intimately connected with the innocence of childhood."[35] It is not surprising that two Breton priests successively refused Gauguin's offer of a painting probably begun in mid-August and completed around mid-September 1888, *Vision of the Sermon* (as the artist referred to it; also known as *Vision after the Sermon (Jacob Wresting with the Angel)*; Figure E.5).[36] The artist proposed that it adorn their respective churches in the Breton villages of Pont-Aven and Nizon. Émile Bernard (1868–1941) later recalled that he and fellow artist Charles Laval (1861–94) accompanied Gauguin when he offered *Vision of the Sermon* to the priest at Nizon: "A silence filled with suspicion ensued after the artist's lengthy explanation of his painting; and then came a flat refusal."[37] The failure of Gauguin's overture was guaranteed by the painting's radically abstracted style, in which simplification of form and high saturation of hue offer visual equivalents to visionary experience. Yet the unsuitability of the painting to a church interior was not solely a matter of style. Although Gauguin referred to the work in correspondence as a "religious

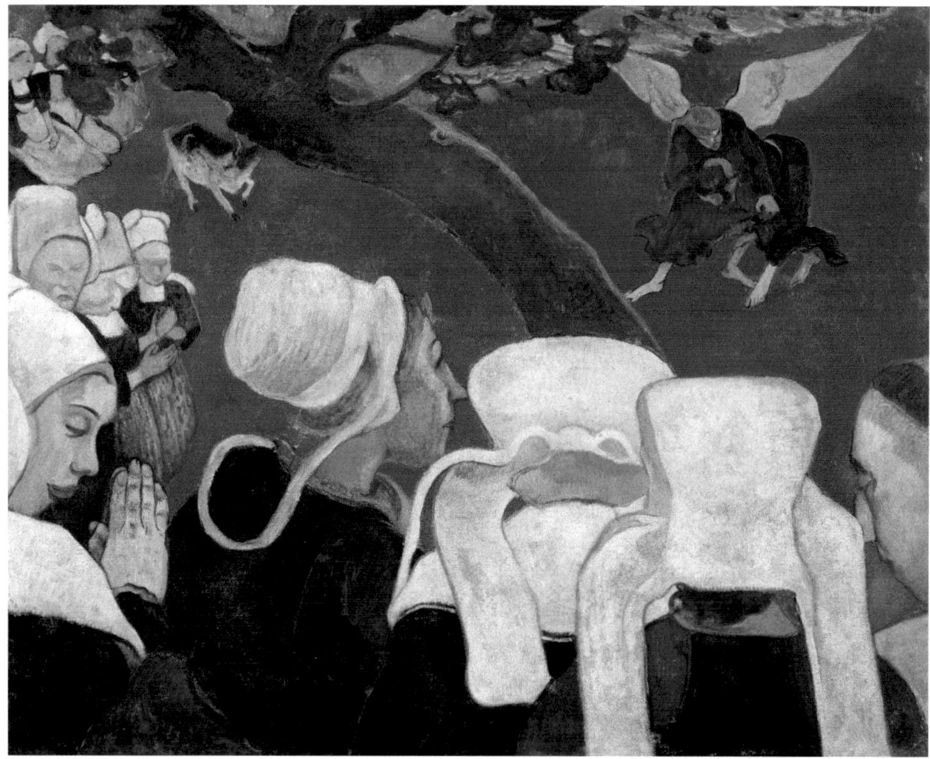

Figure E.5 Paul Gauguin, *Vision of the Sermon* or *Vision after the Sermon (Jacob wrestling with the Angel)*, 1888, oil on canvas, 72.2 × 93 cm. Edinburgh, National Gallery of Scotland, Purchased 1925. Photo: Antonia Reeve © National Galleries of Scotland, Dist. RMN-Grand Palais/Art Resource, NY.

painting" (letter to Vincent van Gogh, 25–27 September 1888) meant as a "painting for a church" (letter to Theo van Gogh 6 or 7 October 1888), *Vision of the Sermon* is hardly an inducement to worship.[38] It is an imaginative reconstruction of Breton religious transport rather than a religious painting in the traditional sense of the term. Perhaps, as Fred Orton and Griselda Pollock suggest, Gauguin was posturing as religious artist to win favor from Bernard's devout sister, Madeleine. Less persuasive is their view that Gauguin's association of the Bretons with superstition provides evidence of cynical disdain for religion.[39] I concur, instead, with Belinda Thomson, who is inclined to accept Gauguin's designation of the work as "religious" (if problematic), and characterizes the artist as at once anti-clerical and "a Catholic at heart."[40] As the examples of Quinet and Lamennais demonstrate, hunger for Christian spirituality could coexist with hostility toward the Church.[41] The abiding presence of Gauguin's Catholic heritage is brought home by Debora Silverman's convincing exposition of the pressure it tenaciously exerted. For at least four years (1859–62), starting at age 11, Gauguin studied at the Jesuit Petit séminaire de la Sainte-Chapelle in Orléans, where the teaching of Monseigneur Dupanloup, bishop of Orléans oriented the future artist toward disdain for the material world (it was Dupanloup's blessing of the graves that so impressed Delacroix in the Augerville cemetery in 1854).[42] Just as there is disjunction between Durtal's worldliness and his obsessive yearning for simple faith, so too does Gauguin's sophistication jar with his vicarious embrace of Breton devotion. The priests' refusals of the painting underscore the disparity between Gauguin's quest for spirituality and the utter unsuitability of his private, vanguard imagery to a public, nineteenth-century, devotional setting. Here then, at the close of the century, is a paradox no less keen than the preeminence as religious painter of the non-believer Delacroix: Gauguin's thwarted aspiration to produce "a painting for a church" resulted in a work scorned by the clergy and firmly ensconced in the canon of Modernism.

The work of Georges Rouault (1871–1958) stands apart from the overwhelming secularity of that canon.[43] His representations of a suffering world populated by sorrowing Christs, miserable clowns, grotesque prostitutes, and malevolent judges suggest that, in the very years Surrealism was conjuring private dream spaces and Picasso was biomorphically declaring his passion for Marie-Thérèse Walter, an ember of the Catholic revival stubbornly glowed. Rouault was born in Paris as the Commune was under bombardment by the *Versaillais*. In April 1901, still suffering from a depression brought on by the death of his teacher, Gustave Moreau, Rouault joined Huysmans in the village of Ligugé near Poitiers. Hoping to attract a circle of Catholic artists, the author and art critic had moved there to be near the Benedictine abbey of Saint-Martin (France's first abbey, founded by Saint Martin of Tours). In 1891, Bloy had broken with Huysmans over *Là-bas*, in which he saw himself caricatured.[44] Yet Huysmans' friend Rouault entered into a close bond with Bloy (initiated 12 April 1904) in Montmartre, despite the author's repulsion by what he considered the ugliness of Rouault's art.[45] "My dear Georges Rouault, we will see the glory of God!," Bloy concluded a letter to his friend (3 October 1904).[46] The artist also enjoyed friendship with two other members of the Bloy circle in Montmartre, the philosopher Jacques Maritain (1882–1973) and his wife, the poet and philosopher Raïssa Maritain (1883–1960), both of whom had converted under Bloy's influence. Championing Rouault's art from the outset, Jacques discerned in his friend:

> an intense religious sentiment akin to a vital hidden spring, a stubborn hermit's faith that brought him to Huysmans and to Léon Bloy, and which makes him discover the image of the divine Lamb in all the abandoned and rejected ones he pities.[47]

These contacts strengthened a devout Catholicism that found expression in the artist's characteristic, smoldering hues edged by dark, gestural bands. The effect, as in *Christ Mocked by Soldiers* (1932; Figure E.6), is akin to that of stained glass (from 1886 to 1892, the artist had been employed by a restorer of stained glass). Rouault's distressing images are visually distressed; their leprous *facture* and refusal of anatomical finesse evoke mortification of the flesh. Having exhibited amid the blazing summer hues of the 1905 Salon d'automne (he had previously shown with the Rose + Croix), Rouault was henceforth associated with the Fauves; one of his works was reproduced on the same page of the exhibition review in *L'Illustration* (4 November 1905) as *The Open Window, Collioure* (1905; Washington, D.C., National Gallery of Art) and *Woman with the Hat* (1905; San Francisco, San Francisco Museum of Modern Art) by fellow Moreau student Henri Matisse (1869–1954).[48] Yet there is a world of difference between the febrile joy and domestic calm of Matisse's paintings and the pained, pessimistic imagery of Rouault. Asked "How should modern art

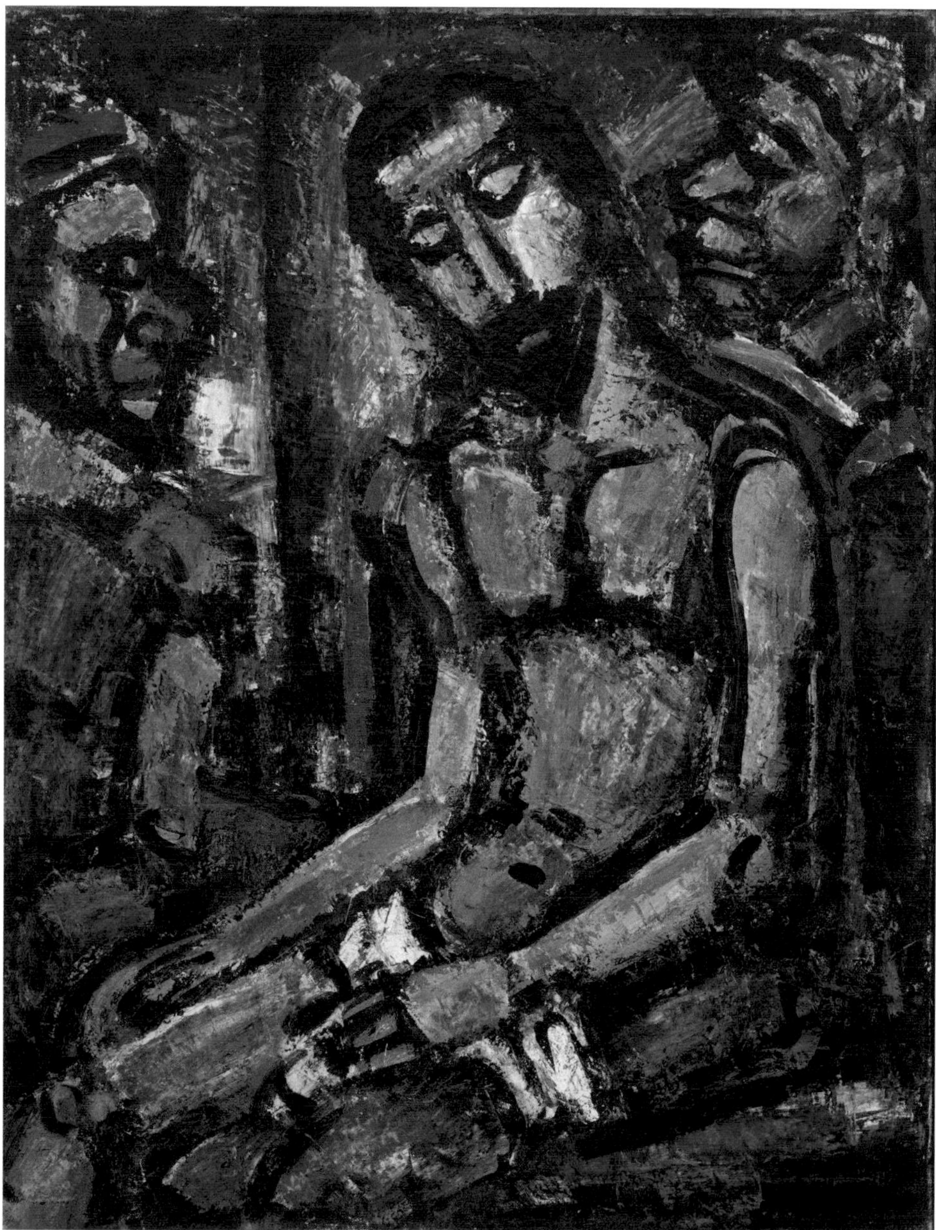

Figure E.6 Georges Rouault, *Christ Mocked by Soldiers*, 1932, oil on canvas, 92.1 × 72.4 cm. New York, Museum of Modern Art, Given anonymously. Photo: Kate Keller © 2021 Artists Rights Society (ARS), New York/ADAGP, Paris. Digital image © The Museum of Modern Art/Licensed by SCALA/Art Resource, NY.

enter the churches?" the Catholic artist replied: "On its knees, in silence."[49] Given the lonely conviction with which this Modernist odd-man-out represented sacred subjects deep into the twentieth century, Rouault stands as a belated exemplar of the bereaved creativity traced by this book.

Notes

1 For visual culture generated by the siege, see Hollis Clayson, *Paris in Despair: Art and Everyday Life under Siege (1870–71)* (Chicago, IL: University of Chicago Press, 2002). Among the Parisians braving the siege was Quinet, who returned to France from exile after Napoleon III was deposed in 1870.

2 This figure is from Robert Tombs, *France 1814–1914* (Abingdon: Routledge, 2014), 19. Quantification of the death toll varies wildly, going as high as 35,000.

3 Henri Loyrette et al., *Daumier 1808–1879* (Paris: Réunion des musées nationaux, 1999), no. 339, catalog entry by Ségolène Le Men. For Daumier's lithograph, see also John Milner, *Art, War and Revolution* in *France, 1870–1871: Myth, Reportage and Reality* (New Haven, CT: Yale University Press, 2000), 128–9.

4 See the discussion of this lithograph (first published in *Le Courrier français* in November 1890 and again in the ninth edition of a print album, *L'Estampe originale* in 1895), in Richard Thomson's superb study, *The Troubled Republic: Visual Culture and Social Debate in France, 1889–1900* (New Haven, CT: Yale University Press, 2004), 205–6.

5 See Thomson, *The Troubled Republic*, chap. 4.

6 Jacques Normand, *L'Émigrant alsacien, Récit, avec une gravure de Gustave Doré* (Paris: Librairie du XIXe siècle, 1873), 11. I am grateful to Thomas Bonnin of the Bibliothèque nationale et universitaire de Strasbourg for making this publication available. For Doré's patriotic imagery inspired by the national defeat, see Lisa Small, "L'Année Terrible and Political Imagery," in Eric Zafran, Robert Rosenblum, and Lisa Small, *Fantasy and Faith: The Art of Gustave Doré* (New York: Dahesh Museum of Art, in association with Yale University Press, New Haven, CT: 2007), 32–63; and *Gustave Doré, 1832–1883* (Strasbourg: Cabinet des dessins, Musée d'art moderne, 1983).

7 Kirk Varnedoe suggested the relevance of the recent defeat to this painting.

8 "Or, quoi de plus semblable aux malheurs de la France en 1870 et 1871, que les malheurs de la Judée dans les nombreuses invasions qui l'ont si souvent ravagée et désolée sous plusieurs de ses rois." *Les Lamentations du prophète Jérémie traduites en vers français et suivies de Quelques Chants religieux et patriotiques composés à l'occasion de la guerre de 1870–71 entre la France et l'Allemagne* (Troyes: P. Lambert, 1871).

9 For the ex-Communard deportees, see Alice Bullard, *Exile to Paradise: Savagery and Civilization in Paris and the South Pacific, 1790–1900* (Stanford, CA: Stanford University Press, 2000), which indicates that the deportation and colonization were intended to civilize the convicts and the indigenous Kanak people (both viewed by the French authorities as "savages").

10 For a portrait of Vallès by Courbet that coveys the writer's fierce energy (ca. 1861; Paris, Musée Carnavalet), see Dominque de Font-Réaulx et al., *Gustave Courbet* (New York: Metropolitan Museum of Art in association with Hatje Cantz Verlag, Ostfildern, 2008), no. 55. For Vallès's obituary for Courbet see Linda Nochlin, "The De-Politicization of Gustave Courbet: Transformation and Rehabilitation under the Third Republic" (originally published 1982), in ed. Linda Nochlin, *Courbet* (New York: Thames & Hudson, 2007), 126–7. For Vallès as an art critic, see Henriette Bessis, "La Chronique artistique de Jules Vallès," *Gazette des beaux-arts* 110 (September 1987): 73–80; and for affinities between two friends, see idem, "Courbet-Vallès: Réalisme et actualisme," *Revue d'Études vallésiennes* 16 (June 1993): 345–53. For the writer's biography, see Roger Bellet, *Jules Vallès* (Paris: Fayard, 1995).

11 For Vallès's exile experience, see my article "The London Sublime," *British Art Journal* 16, no. 2 (Autumn 2015): 76–88. A portion of the material in that article was presented in *Open Eyes and Open Mind: The Art History of Robert Rosenblum: A Symposium in Honor of the 50th Anniversary of Robert Rosenblum's Ph.D. from the Institute of Fine Arts, New York University*, New York University, New York City, 13–14 October 2006. See also *Jules Vallès: L'Exile à Londres (1871–1880)*, ed. Gérard Delfau (Paris: Bordas, 1971).

12 "Je te conseille absolument la *Ville noire*, Londres, l'énorme Londres.... Je hais, je hais, je hais les Anglais, mais qu'aurions-nous besoin de les mêler à notre vie! On se contenterait du spectacle émouvant de la bataille, de la vue du monstre." Letter of 15 March 1877, in Jules Vallès, *Jacques Vingtras*, vol. 4: *Le Proscrit. Correspondance avec Arthur Arnould*, ed. Lucien Scheler (Paris: Les Éditeurs français réunis, 1973), 172 (emphasis in original).

13 "A parler franc, c'est par conviction d'observateur, par amour héroïque du métier, comme fouleur de mœurs, que j'aime...le spectacle de cette ville féroce." Letter of 6 October 1877, in Vallès, *Jacques Vingtras,* 201.

14 "Je voudrais faire un grand roman social avec la misère de ces écrasés silencieux." Vallès, *Jacques Vingtras*, 257.

15 Prior to the Commune, as previously mentioned, the artist had recommended that the column be dismantled; Vallès advocated its destruction in an article of 4 April 1871 in the Communard *Cri du people.* The article in the *Cri du peuple* is mentioned in Gustave Courbet, *Letters of Gustave Courbet,* trans. and ed. Petra ten-Doesschate Chu (Chicago, IL: University of Chicago Press, 1992), 419–20 n. 4. According to Vallès, Courbet watched the column topple with foreboding: "It will crush me as it falls." ("Elle m'écrasera en tombant"). Quoted in Henriette Bessis, "Vallès et Courbet dans la tourmente de la Commune," *Revue d'Études vallésiennes* 15 (November 1992), 70.

16 For an exception to the uneven quality of the series (1874; Ornans, Musée Gustave Courbet), see the catalog entry by Dominique de Font-Réaulx, in idem et al., *Gustave Courbet*, no. 215. See also Sarah Faunce and Linda Nochlin, *Courbet Reconsidered* (Brooklyn, NY: Brooklyn Museum, 1988), no. 88, which references an unpublished manuscript by Tom Wolf, Bard College); and Alan Bowness et al., *Gustave Courbet 1819–1877* (London: Royal Academy of Arts, 1978), no. 125.

17 For the painting, commissioned by the Duc d'Orléans, see Lee Johnson, *The Paintings of Eugène Delacroix: A Critical Catalogue*, vol. 3*: Text, 1832–1863, Movable Pictures and Private Decorations* (Oxford: Clarendon Press, 1986), no. 254.

18 For the political career of Barrès, see *Zeev Sternhell, Maurice Barrès et le nationalisme français* (Brussels: Editions Complexe, 1985); idem, *La Droite révolutionnaire, 1885–1914: Les Origines françaises du fascisme* (Paris: Éditions de Seuil, 1978); and (with discussion of *Les Déracinés*) Eugen Weber, *My France: Politics, Culture, Myth* (Cambridge, MA: The Belknap Press of Harvard University Press, 1991), chap. 11.

19 This point is made by Sternhell, who indicates that Barrès's first published reference to the lost provinces is dated 21 February 1889. See *Maurice Barrès*, 217.

20 Taine makes an appearance in *Les Déracinés*, sagely admiring the slow growth of a plane tree—emblem of the organic paradigm of national destiny that the historian defended (at the expense of the republican legacy of constitutional law and the Rights of Man) in *Les Origines de la France contemporaine* (1875–93).

21 "Dans un âge où les lycéens du premier Empire entendaient le canon de Marengo et parfois le coupé de l'Homme traversant en hâte leur ville, ces enfants, grandis depuis la guerre, n'avaient d'autre idée générale de qualité émouvante que la France vaincue et la lutte de la République contre les partis dynastiques." Maurice Barrès, *Les Déracinés*, in *Romans et voyages*, ed. Vital Rambaud, pref. Éric Roussel (Paris: Robert Laffont, 1994), 497.

22 "Le tombeau de l'Empereur, pour des Français de vingt ans, ce n'est point le lieu de la paix, le philosophique fossé où un pauvre corps qui s'est tant agité se défait; c'est le carrefour de toutes les énergies qu'on nomme audace, volonté, appétit.... Quand les années auront détruit l'oeuvre de ce grand homme et que son genie ne conseillera plus utilement les penseurs ni les peuples ... quelque chose pourtant subsistera: sa puissance de multiplier l'énergie." Barrès, *Les Déracinés*, 606–9. This passage is adduced as evidence of the resurgence of the cult of Napoleon in the 1890s, in Michael Paul Driskel, *As Befits a Legend: Building a Tomb for Napoleon, 1840–1861* (Kent, OH: The Kent State University Press, 1993), 178–9. That there was a resurgence of the Napoleonic legend around 1890, when Bonapartism no longer represented a political danger, is indicated by Frédéric Bluche, *Le Bonapartisme: Aux Origines de la droite autoritaire (1800–1850)* (Paris: Nouvelles éditions latines, 1980), 172 n.11. For this point, see also Bernard Ménager, *Les Napoléon du peuple* (Paris: Aubier, 1988), 349.

23 "Professeur d'énergie! telle est sa physionomie définitive et sa formule décisive, obtenues par la superposition de toutes les figures que nous retracent de lui les spécialists, les artistes et les peuples." Barrès, *Les Déracinés*, 608–9.

24 "Au tombeau de Napoléon, professeur d'énergie, jurons d'être des hommes!" Ibid., 609–14.

25 See Valbert Chevillard, *Un peintre romantique, Théodore Chassériau* (Paris: Alphonse Lemerre, 1893; and for Barrès's thoughts on *The Trojan Women*, see Christine Peltre, "Résurrection et métamorphose: Chassériau autour de 1900," in Stéfan Guégan, Vincent

Pomarède, and Louis-Antoine Prat, *Chassériau: Un autre romantisme* (Paris: Réunion des musées nationaux, 2002), 52–3.

26 The authoritative source for such manifestations of popular fervor is Thomas A. Kselman, *Miracles & Prophecies in Nineteenth-Century France* (New Brunswick, NJ: Rutgers University Press, 1983).

27 For a cogent discussion of religious art of the 1890s in its political and social context, see Thomson, *The Troubled Republic*, chap. 3. For late nineteenth-century religious art, see also Michael Paul Driskel, *Representing Belief: Religion, Art, and Society in Nineteenth-Century France* (University Park: Penn State University Press, 1992); and Bruno Foucart, *Le Renouveau de la peinture religieuse en France (1800–1860)* (Paris: Arthéna, 1987).

28 "Napoléon est le plus inexplicable des hommes parce qu'il est avant tout et surtout le préfigurant de CELUI qui doit venir et qui n'est peut-être plus bien loin, un préfigurant et un précurseur tout près de nous, signifié lui-même par tous les hommes extraordinaires qui l'ont précédé dans tous les temps." Quoted from Léon Bloy, *L'Âme de Napoléon* (Paris: Le Mercure de France, 1912), 8–9, in Natalie Petiteau, *Napoléon de la mythologie à l'histoire* (Paris: Éditions du Seuil, 1999), 145.

29 For *Christ and Buddha*, see Robert Rosenblum and H.W. Janson, *19th-Century Art*, rev. and updated ed. (Upper Saddle River, NJ: Pearson Prentice Hall, in association with Laurence King Publishing, London, 2005), 448–9. For Denis, see Katherine M. Kuenzli, *The Nabis and Intimate Modernism: Painting and the Decorative at the Fin-de-Siècle* (Farnham: Ashgate, 2010), chap. 3, which underscores Denis's quest for balance between Fra Angelico's spirituality and sense-based experience. For the Rose + Croix exhibitions, see Vivien Greene, *Mystical Symbolism: The Salon de la Rose + Croix in Paris 1892–1897* (New York: Solomon R. Guggenheim Museum, 2017); and Thomson, *The Troubled Republic*, 160–1.

30 See Richard Griffiths, *The Reactionary Revolution: The Catholic Revival in French Literature, 1870–1914* (New York: Frederick Ungar, 1965).

31 For biography, see Robert Baldick, *The Life of J.-K. Huysmans* (Oxford: Clarendon Press, 1955).

32 For the author's conversion and the spiritual vicissitudes of Durtal, see Richard D.E. Burton, *Blood in the City: Violence and Revelation in Paris, 1789–1945* (Ithaca, NY: Cornell University Press, 2001), chap. 9.

33 "Ah! ... quand je songe à cette horreur, à ce dégoût de l'existence qui s'est, d'années en années, exaspéré en moi, comme je comprends que j'aie forcément cinglé vers le seul port où je pouvais trouver un abri, vers l'Église." *En Route*, in J.-K. Huysmans, *Le Roman de Durtal*, pref. Paul Valéry (Paris: Bartillat, 2015), 331.

34 "The anti-clericalism, naturalist language, and sensual aspects of his books caused more orthodox Catholics to doubt both his sincerity and the validity of such writing if it were meant to serve the cause." Christopher Lloyd, *J.-K. Huysmans and the 'Fin-de-siècle' Novel* (Edinburgh: Edinburgh University Press, 1990), 142.

35 Griffiths, *The Reactionary Revolution*, 59.

36 See the excellent discussion of this painting by Belinda Thomson, in idem et al., *Gauguin's Vision* (Edinburgh: National Galleries of Scotland, 2005). See also the catalog entry by Claire Frèches-Thory, in Richard Brettell et al., *The Art of Paul Gauguin* (Washington, DC: National Gallery of Art in association with Graphic Society Books, New York and Little, Brown and Company, Boston, 1988), no. 50. For Camille Pissarro's disapproval (1891) of the painting on ideological grounds, see Richard Thomson, *The Troubled Republic*, 117–8.

37 Quoted by Frèches-Thory, in Richard Brettell et al., *The Art of Paul Gauguin*, 103.

38 Quoted by Belinda Thomson, in idem et al., *Gauguin's Vision,* 15. Gauguin conveyed his satisfaction with the work in the letter to Vincent:

> I have just painted a religious picture, very clumsily but it interested me and I like it. I wanted to give it to the church of Pont-Aven. Naturally they don't want it.... I think I have achieved in the figures a great simplicity, rustic and superstitious.

Quoted in Thomson et al., *Gauguin's Vision,* 53.

39 See Fred Orton and Griselda Pollock, "Les Données Bretonnantes: La Prairie de Répresentation," *Art History* 3, no. 3 (September 1980): 314–44.

40 Thomson, in idem et al., *Gauguin's Vision*, 68–70.

41 For the centrality of religion within the thought of the anti-clerical Quinet (who believed that the message of Christianity is manifest in the principles of the French Revolution), see Ceri Crossley, "Edgar Quinet and Messianic Nationalism in the Years preceding 1848," in *1848: The Sociology of Literature, Proceedings of the Essex Conference on the Sociology of Literature, July 1977*, ed. Francis Barker et al., 265–76 (Essex: University of Essex, 1978).

42 See Debora Silverman, *Van Gogh and Gauguin: The Search for Sacred Art* (New York: Farrar, Straus and Giroux, 2000), especially chap. 3; and idem, "At the Threshold of Symbolism: Van Gogh's *Sower* and Gauguin's *Vison after the Sermon*," in *Critical Readings in Impressionism and Post-Impressionism: An Anthology*, ed. Mary Tompkins Lewis (Berkeley: University of California Press, 2007), 272 n. 4.

43 For the artist, see Dominique Bozo and Fabrice Hergott, *Rouault: Première période 1903–1920* (Paris: Musée national d'Art moderne, Centre Georges Pompidou, 1992); and Fabrice Hergott, Georges Rouault, "*Forme, couleur, harmonie*," (Strasbourg: Musée d'Art moderne et contemporain de Strasbourg, 2007). Other departures from the secularity of modern European art include the decoration of the church of Notre-Dame-de-Tout-Grâce at Assy, France (1939–49) by Rouault, Matisse, and other distinguished Modernists. For this see William S. Rubin, *Modern Sacred Art and the Church of Assy* (New York: Columbia University Press, 1961.

44 In regard to the novel, Bloy scornfully noted (12 May 1895): "The pages of *En Route* that attempt to be lyrical make you think of *artificial* flowers that one would offer to Mary in a chamber pot." ("Les pages *d'En Route* qui veulent être lyriques, font penser à des fleurs *artificielles* qu'on offrirait à Marie dans un pot de chambre"). Léon Bloy, *Journal*, vol. 1: *1892–1907*, ed. Pierre Glaudes (Paris: Robert Laffont, 1999), 144 (emphasis in original).

45 Having viewed his friend's entries in the 1905 Salon d'automne, Bloy lamented in his *Journal*, that "This artist who one would believe capable of painting seraphim, seems no longer to conceive anything besides atrocious and vengeful caricatures." ("Cet artiste qu'on croirait capable de peindre des séraphins, semble ne plus concevoir que d'atroces et vengeresses caricatures"). Quoted in Bozo and Hergott, *Rouault: Première période*, 192.

46 Quoted in ibid., 187–8.

47 "Il y a aussi en lui, comme une source vive cachée, un sentiment religieux intense, une foi d'ermite entêté, qui l'a conduit à Huysmans et à Léon Bloy, et qui lui fait découvrir l'image de l'Agneau divin en tous les abandonnés et tous les rejetés sur lesquels il s'apitoie." Quoted, from Jacques Maritain, "Georges Rouault," *La Revue universelle* 17, no. 4 (15 May 1924), 505–8, in Bozo and Hergott, *Rouault: Première période,* 223.

48 See the catalog entry by Ylinka Barotto (in Greene, *Mystical Symbolism*, 88–9) regarding Rouault's *The Holy Women Mourning Christ* (1895; Grenoble, Musée de Grenoble), exhibited in 1896 in the Salon des Artistes français and again in 1897 (with 12 more works by the artist) in the sixth Salon de la Rose + Croix. Executed under the influence of Moreau, this tenebrous, early work is not in Rouault's mature manner.

49 Quoted in Ileana Marcoulesco, *Georges Rouault: The Inner Light*, forwrd., Dominique de Menil (Houston: The Menil Collection, 1996), 5.

Bibliography

Adams, Alissa R. "French Depictions of Napoleon I's Resurrection (1821–1848)." PhD diss., University of Iowa, 2018. https://doi.org/10.17077/etd.vdzokygw.

Allan, Scott C. "Tyrannical Inopportunity: Gustave Moreau's Anti-narrative Strategies." In *Painting and Narrative in France: From Poussin to Gauguin*, edited by Peter Cooke and Nina Lübbren, 144–59. London: Routledge, 2016.

Allard, Sébastien and Côme Fabre, with contributions by Catherine Adam-Sigas, Dominique de Font-Réaulx, Michèle Hannoosh, Mehdi Korchane, Ségolène Le Men, Catherine Méneux, Asher Miller, and Marie-Pierre Salé. *Delacroix*. Paris: Musée du Louvre, in association with Éditions Hazan, Paris, 2018.

Allard, Sébastien and Côme Fabre, "Delacroix: l'art et la matière," in Sébastien Allard, and Côme Fabre, with contributions by Catherine Adam-Sigas, Dominique de Font-Réaulx, Michèle Hannoosh, Mehdi Korchane, Ségolène Le Men, Catherine Méneux, Asher Miller, and Marie-Pierre Salé. *Delacroix*, 20–311. Paris: Musée du Louvre, in association with Éditions Hazan, Paris, 2018.

Allard, Sébastien and Marie-Claude Chaudonneret. *Le Suicide de Gros: Les Peintres de l'Empire et la generation romantique*. Paris: Gourcuff Gradenigo, 2010.

Ancelot, Marguerite-Louise-Virginie. *Les Salons de Paris, Foyers éteints*. Paris: J. Tardieu, 1858.

Anderson, George K. *The Legend of the Wandering Jew*. Providence RI: Brown University Press, 1965.

Aprile, Sylvie. "De l'Émigration à la proscription, regards sur l'écriture de l'exil au XIXe." In *Mémorialistes de l'exil: Émigrer, écrire, survivre*, edited by François Jacob and Henri Rossi, 21–40. Paris: L'Harmattan, 2003.

———. *Le Siècle des exiles: Bannis et proscrits de 1789 à la Commune*. Paris: CNRS Éditions, 2010.

Ary Scheffer 1795–1858, Dessins, aquarelles, esquisses à l'huile. Paris: Institut Néerlandais, 1980.

Athanassoglou-Kallmyer, Nina M. *Eugène Delacroix: Prints, Politics and Satire, 1814–1822*. New Haven, CT: Yale University Press, 1991.

———. *French Images from the Greek War of Independence 1821–1830: Art and Politics under the Restoration*. New Haven, CT: Yale University Press, 1989.

———. "*Imago Belli:* Horace Vernet's *L'Atelier* as an Image of Radical Militarism under the Restoration." *Art Bulletin* 68, no. 2 (June 1986): 268–80.

———. "Sad Cincinnatus: The *Soldat Laboureur* as an Image of the Napoleonic Veteran after the Empire." *Arts Magazine* 60 (May 1986): 65–75.

———. *Théodore Géricault*. New York: Phaidon, 2010.

———. "Truth and Lies: Vernet, Vaudeville, and Photography." In *Horace Vernet and the Thresholds of Nineteenth-Century Visual Culture*, edited by Daniel Harkett and Katie Hornstein, 207–27. Hanover, NH: Dartmouth College Press, 2017.

Avni, Abraham Albert. *The Bible and Romanticism: The Old Testament in German and French Romantic Poetry.* The Hague and Paris: Mouton, 1969.

Bajou, Valérie, ed., *Louis-Philippe et Versailles.* Versailles: Chatêau de Versailles, in association with Somogy, Paris, 2018.

Balayé, Simone. *Madame de Staël: Écrire, lutter, vivre.* Preface by Roland Mortier, postface by Frank Paul Bowman. Histoire des idées et critique littéraire 334. Geneva: Librairie Droz, 1994.

———. *Madame de Staël: Lumières et liberté.* Paris: Éditions Klincksieck, 1979.

Baldensperger, Fernand. *Le Mouvement des idées dans l'Émigration française (1789–1815).* 2 vols. Paris: Plon-Nourrit, 1924.

Baldick, Robert. *The Life of J.-K. Huysmans.* Oxford: Clarendon Press, 1955.

Ballanche, Pierre-Simon. *Du sentiment considéré dans ses rapports avec la littérature et les arts.* Lyon: Ballanche et Barret and Paris: Calixte Volland, an IX, [1801].

Balzac, Honoré de. *Le Colonel Chabert, suivie de El Verdugo, Adieu, Le Réquisitionnaire.* Preface by Pierre Gascar. Edited by Patrick Berthier. 2nd revised ed. Paris: Gallimard, 1974.

———. *Le Médecin de campagne.* Edited by Pierre Citron. Paris: Garnier-Flammarion, 1965.

Bann, Stephen. *Parallel Lines: Printmakers, Painters and Photographers in Nineteenth-Century France.* New Haven, CT: Yale University Press, 2001.

———. *Paul Delaroche: History Painted.* Princeton, NJ: Princeton University Press, 1997.

———. *Romanticism and the Rise of History.* New York: Twayne Publishers, 1995.

Barbier, Auguste. "Salon de 1837." *Revue des deux mondes* (15 April 1837): 145–76.

Barrès, Maurice. *Les Déracinés.* In *Romans et voyages.* Edited by Vital Rambaud. Preface by Éric Roussel. Paris: Robert Laffont, 1994.

Baudelaire, Charles. *Critique d'art, suivi de Critique musicale.* Edited by Claude Pichois. Introduction by Claire Brunet. Paris: Gallimard, 1992.

Beauterne, Robert-Augustin Antoine de. *Conversations religieuses de Napoléon, avec des Documents inédits de la plus haute importance où il révèle lui-même sa pensée intime sur le christianisme.* Paris: Chez l'auteur, Olivier-Fulgence, and Debécourt, 1841.

"Beaux-Arts. Salon de 1833 ... Sculpture." *L'Artiste*, 1st ser. 5 (1833).

Bell, David A. *The Cult of the Nation in France: Inventing Nationalism, 1680–1800.* Cambridge, MA: Harvard University Press, 2001.

———. *Men on Horseback: The Power of Charisma in the Age of Revolution.* New York: Farrar, Straus and Giroux, 2020.

Bell, Matthew. *Melancholia: The Western Malady.* Cambridge: Cambridge University Press, 2014.

Bellenger, Sylvain, Marc Fumaroli, and Bruno Chenique. *Girodet, 1767–1824.* Paris: Éditions Gallimard/Musée du Louvre éditions, 2006.

Bellet, Roger. *Jules Vallès.* Paris: Fayard, 1995.

Bénédite, Léonce. *Théodore Chassériau, sa vie, son oeuvre.* Edited by André Dezarrois. 2 vols. Paris: Braun, 1931.

Bénichou, Paul. *L'École du désenchantement: Sainte-Beuve, Nodier, Musset, Nerval, Gautier.* Paris: Gallimard, 1992.

———. "Un Gethsémani romantique ('Le Mont des Oliviers' de Vigny)." *Revue d'histoire littéraire de la France* 98, no. 3 (May-June 1998): 429–36.

———. *Les Mages romantiques.* Paris: Gallimard, 1988.

———. *Le Sacre de l'écrivain, 1750–1830: Essai sur l'avènement d'un pouvoir spirituel laïque dans la France moderne.* 2nd ed. Paris: Librairie José Corti, 1985.

———. *Le Temps des prophètes: Doctrines de l'âge romantique.* Paris: Gallimard, 1977.

Béranger, Pierre-Jean de. *Chansons choisies de P.-J. de Béranger.* Bielefeld: Velhagen & Klasing, 1846.

———. *Les Souvenirs du peuple. Chanson inédite de P.-J. de Béranger.* Paris: Badouin frères, 1827.

Béraud, Antony. *Annales de l'école française des beaux-arts*, 1st year. Paris: Pillet aîné, 1827.

Berenson, Edward. *Populist Religion and Left-Wing Politics in France, 1830–1852*. Princeton, NJ: Princeton University Press, 1984.

Bessis, Henriette. "La Chronique artistique de Jules Vallès." *Gazette des Beaux-Arts* 110 (September 1987): 73–80.

———. "Courbet-Vallès: Réalisme et actualisme." *Revue d'études vallésiennes* 16 (June 1993): 345–53.

———. "Vallès et Courbet dans la tourmente de la Commune." *Revue d'études vallésiennes* 15 (November 1992): 67–72.

Bialostocki, Jan. "Gros et Niemcewicz," *Gazette des beaux-arts*, 6th ser. 64 (Dec. 1964): 363–72.

Bishop, Lloyd. *The Romantic Hero and his Heirs in French Literature*. American University Studies, 2nd ser.: Romance Languages and Literature 10. New York: Peter Lang, 1984.

Bland, Cynthia. "*Du divin à l'humain: La Transfiguration du Christ dans Le Christ au jardin des Oliviers.*" Bulletin de la Société des Amis du Musée Eugène-Delacroix 7 (2009): 11–8.

———. "Inspiration, Innovation, and Emotion: The Early Religious Paintings of Eugène Delacroix." PhD diss., University of Iowa, 2002.

Bloy, Léon. *Journal, 1: 1892–1907.* Edited by Pierre Glaudes. Paris: Robert Laffont, 1999.

Bluche, Frédéric. *Le Bonapartisme*. Paris: Presses Universitaires de France, 1981.

———. *Le Bonapartisme: Aux origines de la droite autoritaire (1800–1850)*. Paris: Nouvelles éditions latines, 1980.

Boisgelin de Cucé, Jean de Dieu-Raymond. *Oeuvres du cardinal de Boisgelin, de l'Académie française*. Paris: F. Guitel, 1818.

Boitelle, René, Marion Bosc, and Klaas-Jan van den Berg. "Reflections on J.-F. Millet's *Agar et Ismaël*: Technical Analyses of an Unfinished Painting." *Art Matters: Netherlands Technical Studies in Art* 2 (2005): 7–21.

Bonaparte, Louis-Napoléon. *Des idées napoléoniennes*. Paris: Paulin, 1839.

Boorsch, Jean. "Chateaubriand and Napoleon." *Yale French Studies* 26 (fall-winter 1960–61): 55–62.

Bottineau, Josette. "De *Bélisaire* à *Marcus Sextus*: Genèse et histoire d'un tableau de Pierre Guérin (1774–1833). *Revue du Louvre et des Musées de France* 43, no. 3 (June 1993): 41–53.

Bowman, Frank Paul. *Le Christ des barricades (1789–1848)*. Paris: Les Éditions du Cerf, 1987.

———. *Le Christ romantique. 1789: Le Sans-culotte de Nazareth. 1848: Le Christ au barricades. La "Confirmatio christianorum per Socratica." "Le Christ a mis fin à l'esclavage." Napoléon et le Christ. Les Harmonies de la religion chrétienne.* Théologie et esthétique. Histoire des idées et critique littéraire 134. Geneva: Droz, 1973.

———. *French Romanticism: Intertextual and Interdisciplinary Readings*. Baltimore, MD: Johns Hopkins University Press, 1990.

———. "George Sand, le Christ et le Royaume," *Cahiers de l'association internationale des études françaises* 28 (May 1976): 243–62.

———. "Le Texte du 'Poème de l'âme.'" In *Louis Janmot, Précurseur du symbolism, avec le Texte intégral du 'Poème de l'âme' (1881)*, edited by Wolfgang Drost, Elisabeth Hardouin-Fugier, and Birgit Gottschalk, 185–95. Heidelberg: Universitätsverlag C. Winter, 1994.

Bowness, Alan, Marie-Thérèse de Forges, Michel Laclotte, and Hèlène Toussaint, *Gustave Courbet 1819–1877*. London: Royal Academy of Arts, 1978.

Bozo, Dominique, and Fabrice Hergott. *Rouault: Première période 1903–1920*. Paris: Musée national d'Art moderne, Centre Georges Pompidou, 1992.

Brachlianoff, Dominique. *Le Poème de l'âme*. Lyon: Musée des Beaux-Arts de Lyon and Paris: Éditions de la Réunion des musées nationaux, 1995.

Bresc-Bautier, Geneviève, and Béatrice de Chancel-Bardelot, eds. *Un musée révolutionnaire: Le Musée des monuments français d'Alexandre Lenoir*. Paris: Musée du Louvre, in association with Hazan, Paris 2016.

Brettell, Richard, Françoise Cachin, Claire Frèches-Thory, Charles F. Stuckey, and Peter Zegers. *The Art of Paul Gauguin*. Washington, DC: National Gallery of Art, in association with Graphic Society Books, New York and Little, Brown and Company, Boston, 1988.

Brookner, Anita. *Romanticism and Its Discontents*. New York: Farrar, Straus and Giroux, 2000.

Brunel, Georges. "La Peinture religieuse: art officiel et art sacré." In Isabelle Julia, Jean Lacambre, and Sylvain Boyer, *Les Années romantiques: La Peinture française de 1815 à 1850*, 46–59. Paris: Éditions de la Réunion des musées nationaux, 1995.

Buche, Joseph. *L'École mystique de Lyon, 1776–1847*. Preface by Edouard Herriot. Paris: Librairie Félix Alcan, 1935.

Burton, Richard D.E. *Blood in the City: Violence and Revelation in Paris, 1789–1945*. Ithaca, NY: Cornell University Press, 2001.

Butler, Ruth. "Long Live the Revolution, the Republic, and Especially the Emperor! The Political Sculpture of Rude." In *Art and Architecture in the Service of Politics*, edited by Henry A. Millon and Linda Nochlin, 92–107. Cambridge, MA: MIT Press, 1978.

Byrnes, Joseph F. *Catholic and French Forever: Religious and National Identity in Modern France*. University Park: Penn State University Press, 2005.

Byron, Lord [George Gordon]. *Lord Byron: The Major Works*. Edited by Jerome J. McGann. Oxford: Oxford University Press, 2000.

Caffort, Michel. *Les Nazaréens français: Théorie et pratique de la peinture religieuse au XIXe siècle*. Rennes: Presses universitaires de Rennes, 2009.

Camille, Michael. "The Abject Gaze and the Homosexual Body: Flandrin's *Figure d'Etude*." *Journal of Homosexuality* 27, no. 1–2 (1994): 161–88. Published simultaneously in *Gay and Lesbian Studies in Art History*, edited by Whitney Davis, 161–88. Haworth Press, 1994.

Carpenter, Kirsty. *Refugees of the French Revolution: Émigrés in London, 1789–1802*. New York: St. Martin's Press, 1999.

Caso, Jacques de. *David d'Angers: Sculptural Communication in the Age of Romanticism*. Translated by Dorothy Johnson and Jacques de Caso. Princeton, NJ: Princeton University Press, 1992.

Cellier, Léon. *L'Épopée humanitaire et les grands mythes romantiques*. Paris: Société d'édition d'enseignement supérieur, 1971.

Černy, Václav. *Essai sur le Titanisme dans la poésie romantique occidentale entre 1815 et 1850*. Prague: Éditions Orbis, 1935.

Chabert, Philippe-Gérard and Pierre Georgel. *François-Nicolas Chifflart 1825–1901*. Saint-Omer: Musée de l'hôtel Sandelin, 1972.

Chadwick, Owen. *The Secularization of the European Mind in the Nineteenth Century*. Cambridge: Cambridge University Press, 1975.

Charlton, D.G., ed. *The French Romantics*. 2 vols. Cambridge: Cambridge University Press, 1984.

———. *Secular Religions in France, 1815–1870*. Hull: University of Hull and London: Oxford University Press, 1963.

Chateaubriand, François René de. *De Buonaparte et des Bourbons*. Preface by Victor de Laprade. Lyon: Félix Girard, 1872.

———. *Essai sur les révolutions, Génie du christianisme*. Edited by Maurice Regard. Paris: Gallimard, 1978.

———. *Mémoires d'outre-tomb*. Edited by Jean-Claude Berchet. 4 vols. Paris: Garnier, 2001–2002.

Chaudonneret, Marie-Claude. *L'État et les artistes: De la restauration à la monarchie de Juillet (1815–1833)*. Paris: Flammarion, 1999.

———. *Fleury Richard et Pierre Révoil. La Peinture troubadour*. Preface by Daniel Ternois. Paris: Arthéna, 1980.

———. ed. *Paul Chenavard 1807–1895: Le Peintre et le prophète.* Lyon: Musée des Beaux-Arts and Paris: Réunion des musées nationaux, 2000.

Chevillard, Valbert. *Un Peintre romantique, Théodore Chassériau.* Paris: Alphonse Lemerre, 1893.

Chevallier, Alix, Madeleine Cottin, and Roger Pierrot. *Chateaubriand: Le Voyageur et l'homme politique.* Paris: Bibliothèque nationale, 1969.

Cholvy, Gérard, and Yves-Marie Hilaire. *Histoire religieuse de la France contemporaine.* 3 vols. Toulouse: Bibliothèque historique Privat, 1985–88.

Chomer, Gilles. "Le Séjour en Italie (1822–1830) de Victor Orsel." In *Lyon et Italie: Six études d'histoire de l'art*, edited by Gilles Chomer, Marie-Félice Pérez, and Daniel Ternois, 181–211. Paris: Éditions du Centre National de la Recherche Scientifique, 1984.

Clair, Jean, ed. *Mélancolie: Génie et folie en Occident.* Paris: Réunion des musées nationaux and Gallimard, Paris, 2005.

Clark, T.J. *The Absolute Bourgeois: Artists and Politics in France 1848–1851.* Greenwich, CT: New York Graphic Society, 1973.

Clay, Richard. *Iconoclasm in Revolutionary Paris: The Transformation of Signs.* Oxford: Voltaire Foundation, 2012.

Clayson, Hollis. *Paris in Despair: Art and Everyday Life under Siege (1870–71).* Chicago, IL: University of Chicago Press, 2002.

Clément, Jean-Paul, and Marc Fumaroli. *Un livre, un siècle: Le Bicentenaire du 'Génie du Christianisme'.* Vallée-aux-Loups: Maison Chateaubriand, 2002.

Coekelberghs, Denis, Alain Jacobs, and Pierre Loze. *François-Joseph Navez (Charleroi 1787–Bruxelles 1869): La Nostalgie de l'Italie.* Charleroi: Musée des Beaux-Arts de Charleroi, in association with Snoeck-Ducaju & Zoon, Ghent: 1999.

Coleman, Patrick. "Exile and Narrative Voice in *Corinne*." *Studies in Eighteenth-Century Culture* 24 (1995): 91–105.

Conner, Tom. *Chateaubriand's 'Mémoires d'outre-tombe': A Portrait of the Artist as Exile.* The Age of Revolution and Romanticism Interdisciplinary Studies 7, edited by Gita May. New York: Peter Lang, 1995.

Constans, Claire, Dominique Cante, Marina Lambraki-Plaka, Francis Ribemont, Arlette Sérullaz, and Fani-Maria Tsigakou. *La Grèce en révolte: Delacroix et les peintres français.* Bordeaux: Musée des Beaux-Arts, 1996.

Constant, Benjamin. *Cours de politique constitutionnelle et collection des ouvrages publiés sur le gouvernement représentatif.* Edited by Édouard Laboulaye. 2nd ed., 2 vols. Paris: Guillaumin, 1872; rpt. Geneva and Paris: Slatkine, 1982.

Cooke, Peter. *Gustave Moreau: History Painting, Spirituality and Symbolism.* New Haven, CT: Yale University Press, 2014.

———. "Gustave Moreau and the Reinvention of History Painting." *Art Bulletin* 90, no. 3 (September 2008): 394–416.

Courbet, Gustave. *Letters of Gustave Courbet.* Translated and edited by Petra ten-Doesschate Chu. Chicago, IL: University of Chicago Press, 1992.

Crossley, Ceri. *Edgar Quinet (1803–1875): A Study in Romantic Thought.* Lexington, KY: French Forum, 1983.

———. "Edgar Quinet and Messianic Nationalism in the Years preceding 1848." In *1848: The Sociology of Literature, Proceedings of the Essex Conference on the Sociology of Literature, July 1977*, edited by Francis Barker, John Coombes, Peter Hulme, Colin Mercer, and David Musselwhite, 265–76. Essex: University of Essex, 1978.

———. *French Historians and Romanticism: Thierry, Guizot, the Saint-Simonians, Quinet, Michelet.* London: Routledge, 2002.

Crow, Thomas. *Emulation: David, Drouais, and Girodet in the Art of Revolutionary France.* Revised ed. New Haven, CT: Yale University Press and Los Angeles: The Getty Research Institute, 2006.

———. *No Idols: The Missing Theology of Art*. Sydney: Power Publications, 2017.
———. *Painters and Public Life in Eighteenth-Century Paris*. New Haven, CT: Yale University Press, 1985.
———. *Restoration: The Fall of Napoleon in the Course of European Art, 1812–1820*. Princeton, NJ: Princeton University Press, 2018.
Cummings, Frederick J., Pierre Rosenberg, and Robert Rosenblum. *French Painting, 1774–1830: The Age of Revolution*. Detroit: Detroit Institute of Arts, 1975.
Cuno, James. "*Retour de Russie*: Géricault and Early French Lithography." In *Théodore Géricault, The Alien Body: Tradition in Chaos*, edited by Serge Guibault, Maureen Ryan, and Scott Watson, 145–59. Vancouver, BC: Morris and Helen Belkin Art Gallery, 1997.
Daguerre de Hureaux, Alain. *Delacroix*. Paris: Hazan, 1993.
The Daumier Register, no. 84. "*Repos de la France*." Accessed 20 April 2019. http://www.daumier-register.org/werkview.php?key=84.
Day-Hickman, Barbara Ann. *Napoleonic Art: Nationalism and the Spirit of Rebellion in France (1815–1848)*. Newark: University of Delaware Press and London: Associated University Presses, 1999.
Decamps, Alexandre. "Salon de 1836." *Le National*, 1 May 1836.
Delacroix, Eugène. *Correspondance générale de Eugène Delacroix*. Edited by André Joubin. 5 vols. Paris: Plon, 1935–8.
———. *Journal*. Edited by Michèle Hannoosh. 2 vols. Paris: José Corti, 2009.
———. *Journey to the Maghreb and Andalusia, 1832: The Travel Notebooks and Other Writings*. Translated and edited by Michèle Hannoosh. University Park: Penn State University Press, 2019.
———. *Oeuvres littéraires 2: Essais sur les artistes celèbres*. 6th ed. Paris: G. Crès, 1923.
Delavigne, Casimir. *Messéniennes et poésies diverses*. 11th ed. 2 vols. Paris: Ladvocat, 1824.
Delécluze, Étienne-Jean. *Louis David, Son école & son temps. Souvenirs*. Paris: Didier, 1855.
———. "Salon de 1831(Schnetz et Robert)." *L'Artiste* 1, 15th livraison (1831): 187–9.
———. *Souvenirs de soixante années*. Paris: Michel Lévy, 1862.
Delfau, Gérard, ed. *Jules Vallès: L'Exil à Londres (1871–1880)*. Paris: Bordas, 1971.
Denton, Margaret Fields (see also Smith, Margaret Denton). "Antoine-Jean Gros' *Portrait de Christine Boyer* and Jean-Frédéric Schall's *Pensée sur la brièveté de la vie*: Private Grief and Public Rhetoric in Post-revolutionary French Painting." *Gazette des beaux arts*, 6th per. 128 (September 1996): 103–20.
———. "Death in French Arcady: Nicolas Poussin's 'The Arcadian Shepherds' and Burial Reform in France c. 1800." *Eighteenth-Century Studies* 36, no. 2 (Winter 2003): 195–216.
Desan, Suzanne. *Reclaiming the Sacred: Lay Religion and Popular Politics in Revolutionary France*. Ithaca, NY: Cornell University Press, 1990.
Descotes, Maurice. *La Légende de Napoléon et les écrivains français du XIX*[e] *siècle*. Paris: Lettres modernes Minard, 1967.
Diderot, Denis. *Diderot on Art*. Translated and edited by John Goodman, introduction by Thomas Crow. 2 vols. New Haven, CT: Yale University Press, 1995.
Didier, Béatrice. *Chateaubriand*. Paris: Ellipses, 1999.
Diesbach, Ghislain de. *Histoire de l'Émigration 1789–1814*. Paris: Bernard Grasset, 1975.
———. *Madame de Staël*. Paris: Librairie Académique Perrin, 1983.
Dorra, Henri. "'Le Bien et le Mal' d'Orsel: Tableau de manière symbolique au Musée des Beaux-Arts de Lyon." *Bulletin des musées et monuments Lyonnais* 5, no. 1 (1975): 291–302.
———. "'Dante et Virgile' par Hippolyte Flandrin." *Bulletin des musées et monuments lyonnais* 5 (1976): 391–402.
———. "Montalembert, Orsel, les Nazaréens et 'l'Art abstrait.'" *Gazette des beaux-arts* 6th per. 85 (April 1975): 137–46.

Driskel, Michael Paul. *As Befits a Legend: Building a Tomb for Napoleon, 1840–1861*. Kent, OH: Kent State University Press, 1993.

———. "The Proletarian's Body: Charlet's Representations of Social Class during the July Monarchy." In *The Popularization of Images: Visual Culture under the July Monarchy*, edited by Petra ten-Doesschate Chu and Gabriel P. Weisberg, 58–89. Princeton, NJ: Princeton University Press, 1994.

———. *Representing Belief: Religion, Art, and Society in Nineteenth-Century France*. University Park: Penn State University Press, 1992.

Drost, Wolfgang, Elisabeth Hardouin-Fugier, and Birgit Gottschalk, eds. *Louis Janmot, Précurseur du symbolism, avec Le Texte intégral du 'Poème de l'âme' (1881)*. Heidelberg: Universitätsverlag C. Winter, 1994.

Dunn, Ashley E., with contributions by Colta Ives and Marjorie Shelley. *Delacroix Drawings: The Karen B. Cohen Collection*. New York: The Metropolitan Museum of Art, in association with Yale University Press, New Haven, 2018.

[Dupasquier, Alphonse]. *L'Art à Lyon en 1836. Revue critique de la première exposition de la Société des Amis des Arts*. Lyon: Gabriel Rossary, 1837.

Dwyer, Philip. *Napoleon: Passion, Death and Resurrection, 1815–1840*. London: Bloomsbury, 2018.

Eitner, Lorenz. *Géricault: His Life and Work*. London: Orbis, 1983.

———. ed. *Neoclassicism and Romanticism 1750–1850, Sources and Documents*. 2 vols. Englewood Cliffs, NJ: Prentice-Hall, 1970.

Encyclopédie des gens du monde. Répertoire universel des sciences, des lettres et des arts, avec des notices sur les principales familles historiques et sur les personnages célèbres, morts et vivans. Par une société de savans, de littérateurs et d'artistes, français et étrangers. 22 vols. Paris: Treuttel and Würtz, 1833–44.

Englund, Steven. *Napoleon: A Political Life*. New York: Scribner, 2004.

Erlande-Brandenburg, Alain and Dominique Thibaudat. *Les Sculptures de Notre-Dame de Paris au Musée de Cluny*. Paris: Éditions de la Réunion des musées nationaux, 1982.

Escholier, Raymond. "Gros, peintre de Napoléon." *Europe* (April 1969): 241–51.

Étex, Antoine. *Souvenirs d'un artiste*. Paris: E. Dentu, 1878.

Explication des ouvrages de peinture et dessins, sculpture, architecture et gravure, des artistes vivans exposés au Muséum central des Arts, d'après l'Arrété du Ministre de l'Intérieur, le 15 Fructidor, an VIII de la République française. Paris; De l'Imprimerie des Sciences et Arts, [1800]. Reprinted in *Catalogues of the Paris Salon, 1673 to 1881*, compiled by H.W. Janson. New York: Garland, 1977.

Explication des ouvrages de peinture et de sculpture de l'école moderne de France exposés dans le Musée royal du Luxembourg, destiné aux artistes vivans. Paris: Vinchon, 1836.

Explication des ouvrages de peinture, sculpture, architecture, gravure et lithographie des artistes vivans, exposés au Musée royal le 1er Mars 1836. Paris: Vinchon, 1836. Reprinted in *Catalogues of the Paris Salon 1673 to 1881*, compiled by H.W. Janson. New York and London: Garland, 1977.

Explication des ouvrages de peinture, sculpture, architecture, gravure et lithographie des artistes vivants, exposés au Musée royal le 15 mars 1842. Paris: Vinchon, 1842.

Fabre d'Olivet, Antoine. *Caïn, mystère dramatique en trois actes de Lord Byron, Traduit en vers français et réfutê dans une suite de remarques philosophiques et critiques. Précédé d'une lettre addressee à Lord Byron, sur les motifs et le but de cet ouvrage*. Paris: Servier, 1823.

Faroult, Guillaume. "'La Douce Mélancolie,' selon Watteau et Diderot: Représentations mélancoliques dans les arts en France au XVIIIe siècle." In *Mélancolie: genie et folie en Occident*, edited by Jean Clair, 274–94. Paris: Réunion des musées nationaux and Gallimard, 2005.

Faroult, Guillaume and Catherine Voiriot. *Hubert Robert, 1733–1808: Un peintre visionnaire*. Paris: Musée du Louvre, in association with Somogy éditions d'art, Paris, 2016.

Faunce, Sarah, and Linda Nochlin. *Courbet Reconsidered.* Brooklyn: Brooklyn Museum, 1988.

Focillon, Henri. "Chassériau, ou Les Deux romantismes." In *Le Romantisme et l'art*, preface by Edouard Herriot, edited by Louis Hautecoeur, 161–85. Paris: H. Laurens, 1928.

Fontana, Biancamaria. *Benjamin Constant and the Post-revolutionary Mind.* New Haven, CT: Yale University Press, 1991.

———. *Germaine de Staël: A Political Portrait.* Princeton, NJ: Princeton University Press, 2016.

Font-Réaulx, Dominique de, Laurence des Cars, Michel Hilaire, Bruno Mottin, and Bertrand Tillier. *Gustave Courbet.* New York: Metropolitan Museum of Art, in association with Hatje Cantz, Ostfildern, 2008.

Font-Réaulx, Dominique de and Marie Montfort, eds. *Une Lutte moderne, de Delacroix à nos jours*. Paris: Musée national Eugène-Delacroix, 2018.

Foucart, Bruno. "Chassériau et le thème du Christ au jardin des Oliviers: Entre romantisme et orthodoxie." In *Chassériau (1819–1856): Un autre romantisme, Actes du colloque organisé par le Musée du Louvre, le 16 mars 2002*, edited by Stéphane Guégan and Louis-Antoine Prat, 39–79. Paris: La Documentation française / Musée du Louvre, 2002.

———. "Chateaubriand et le renouveau de la peinture religieuse après la Révolution." In *Chateaubriand et les arts*, edited by Édouard Bonnefous and Marc Fumaroli, 153–62. Paris: Éditions de Fallois, 1999.

———. *Le Renouveau de la peinture religieuse en France (1800–1860)*. Paris: Arthéna, 1987.

Foucart, Jacques. "À propos du peintre Odier: Note complémentaire à l'article de Marcel Roethlisberger." *Genava*: *Revue d'histoire de l'art et d'archéologie* 37 (1989): 187–93.

Foucart, Jacques and Bruno Foucart, with contributions by Bruno Horaist, Philippe Grunchec, and Chantal Lanvin. *Hippolyte, Auguste et Paul Flandrin: Une fraternité picturale au XIXe siècle*. Paris: Musée du Luxembourg and Éditions de la Réunion des musées nationaux, 1984.

Fraser, Elisabeth A. *Delacroix, Art and Patrimony in Post-Revolutionary France*. Cambridge: Cambridge University Press, 2004.

Fried, Michael. *Absorption and Theatricality: Painting & Beholder in the Age of Diderot.* Berkeley: University of California Press, 1980.

———. *Courbet's Realism*. Chicago, IL: University of Chicago Press, 1990.

Fritzsche, Peter. "The Melancholy of History: The French Revolution and European Historiography." In *The Literature of Melancholia: Early Modern to Postmodern*, edited by Martin Middeke and Christina Wald, 116–29. New York: Palgrave Macmillan, 2011.

———. *Stranded in the Present: Modern Time and the Melancholy of History*. Cambridge, MA: Harvard University Press, 2004.

Fumaroli, Marc. *Chateaubriand: Poésie et terreur*. Paris: Gallimard, 2003.

Fusco, Peter and H.W. Janson. *The Romantics to Rodin: French Nineteenth-Century Sculpture from North American Collections*. Los Angeles, CA: Los Angeles County Museum of Art, in association with George Braziller, New York, 1980.

Gallo, Daniela. "On the Antique Models of the Empire Style." In Odile Nouvel-Kammerer, *Symbols of Power: Napoleon and the Art of the Empire Style, 1800–1815*, 40–51. Paris: Musée des Arts Décoratifs and New York: American Federation of Arts, in association with Harry N. Abrams, New York, 2007.

Gautier, Théophile. "Beaux-Arts. Overture du Salon." *La Presse* (1 March 1837).

———. *Les Beaux-Arts en Europe, 1855*, 1st ser. Paris: Michel Lévy frères, 1856.

———. "Salon de 1833." *La France littéraire* 6 (1833): 139–66.

———. "Salon de 1839." *La Presse* (27 March 1839).

Genlis, Stéphanie-Félicité, comtesse de. *Agar dans le désert, Comédie en prose & en un acte*. In *Théâtre à l'usage des jeunes personnes*, vol. 1. Paris: Panckoucke, 1779.

Georgel, Pierre, ed. *La Gloire de Victor Hugo*. Paris: Éditions de la Réunion des musées nationaux, 1985.

Germer, Stefan. "In Search of a Beholder: On the Relation between Art, Audiences, and Social Spheres in Post-Thermidor France." *Art Bulletin* 74 (March 1992): 19–36.

Gerwin, Beth. "Révision et subversion: Balzac et le mythe de Napoléon." *Analyses: Revue des littératures Franco-Canadiennes et Québécoise* 8, no. 3 (Autumn 2013): 48–88. Accessed 11 November 2019. https://uottawa.scholarsportal.info/ottawa/index.php/revue-analyses/issue/view/196.

Godechot, Jacques, ed. *Les Constitutions de la France depuis 1789*. Paris: Flammarion, 1979.

Goldstein, Jan. *Console and Classify: The French Psychiatric Profession in the Nineteenth Century*. Cambridge: Cambridge University Press, 1987.

Goodden, Angelica. *Madame de Staël: The Dangerous Exile*. Oxford: Oxford University Press, 2008.

Gotlieb, Marc J. *The Plight of Emulation: Ernest Meissonier and French Salon Painting*. Princeton, NJ: Princeton University Press, 1996.

Gourgaud, Gaspard. *Napoléon et la Grande-Armée en Russie, ou Examen critique de l'ouvrage de M. le comte Ph. de Ségur*. Brussels: H. Tarlier, 1825.

Grasselli, Margaret Morgan and Yuriko Jackall, with Guillaume Faroult, Catherine Voiriot, and Joseph Baillio. *Hubert Robert*. Washington, DC: National Gallery of Art, in association with Lund Humphries, London, 2016.

Greenberg, Susan. "Reforming *paysage historique:* Corot and the Generation of 1830." *Art History* 27, no. 3 (June 2004): 412–30.

Greene, Vivien. *Mystical Symbolism: The Salon de la Rose+Croix in Paris 1892–1897*. New York: Solomon R. Guggenheim Museum, 2017.

Greer, Donald. *The Incidence of the Emigration during the French Revolution*. Harvard Historical Monographs 24. Cambridge, MA: Harvard University Press, 1951.

Grewe, Cordula. *The Nazarenes: Romantic Avant-Garde and the Art of the Concept*. University Park: Penn State University Press, 2015.

———. *Painting the Sacred in the Age of Romanticism*. Farnham: Ashgate, 2009.

Griffiths, Richard. *The Reactionary Revolution: The Catholic Revival in French Literature, 1870–1914*. New York: Frederick Ungar, 1965.

Grigsby, Darcy Grimaldo. *Extremities: Painting Empire in Post-revolutionary France*. New Haven, CT: Yale University Press, 2002.

Grunchec, Philippe. *Le Grand prix de peinture: Les Concours des Prix de Rome de 1797 à 1863*. Preface by Jacques Thuillier. Paris: École nationale supérieure des Beaux-Arts, 1983.

Guégan, Stéphane. *Delacroix: L'Enfer et l'atelier*. Paris: Flammarion, 1998.

———. *Delacroix: Peindre contre l'oubli*. Paris: Flammarion, 2018.

———. "Entre Paris et Alger: Un croyant obstiné." In Stéphane Guégan, Vincent Pomarède, and Louis-Antoine Prat. *Chassériau (1819–1856): Un autre romantisme*, 30–47. Paris: Réunion des musées nationaux, 2002.

Guégan, Stéphane, Vincent Pomarède, and Louis-Antoine Prat. *Chassériau: Un autre romantisme*. Paris: Réunion des musées nationaux, 2002.

Guernsey, Daniel R. *The Artist and the State, 1777–1855: The Politics of Universal History in British and French Painting*. Aldershot: Ashgate, 2007.

Gustave Doré, 1832–1883. Strasbourg: Cabinet des dessins, Musée d'Art moderne, 1983.

Hafera, Alison. "Visual Meditations on Mourning and Melancholia in France, 1790–1830." PhD diss., University of North Carolina, 2015.

Hannoosh, Michèle. *Jules Michelet: Writing Art and History in Nineteenth-Century France*. University Park, PA: Penn State University Press, 2019.

———. *Painting and the 'Journal' of Eugène Delacroix*. Princeton, NJ: Princeton University Press, 1995.

Hardouin-Fugier, Elisabeth. *Louis Janmot 1814–1892*. Lyon: Presses universitaires de Lyon, 1981.

———. *'Le Poème de l'âme'*. Lyon: Musée des Beaux-Arts, 1976.
———. *'Le Poème de l'âme' par Janmot: Étude iconologique*. Lyon: Presses universitaires de Lyon, 1977.
———. *'Le Poème de l'âme' par Louis Janmot (1814–1892)*. Châtillon-sur-Chalaronne: Éditions La Taillanderie, 2007.
_____. "Un souffle européen aux bords du Rhône: L' Illuminisme et le *Poème de l'âme* de Louis Janmot." In *Le Temps de la peinture, Lyon 1800–1914*, edited by Sylvie Ramond, Gérard Bruyère, Pierre Vaisse, and François Fossier. 124–33. Lyon: Éditions Fage, 2007.
Harkett, Daniel. "Mediating Private and Public: Juliette Récamier's Salon at l'Abbaye-aux-Bois." In *Women, Femininity and Public Space in European Visual Culture, 1789–1914*, edited by Temma Balducci and Heather Belnap Jensen, 47–64. Farnham: Ashgate, 2014.
———. "Revisiting Horace Vernet's Studio Exhibition." In *Horace Vernet and the Thresholds of Nineteenth-Century Visual Culture,* edited by Daniel Harkett and Katie Hornstein, 38–56. Hanover, NH: Dartmouth College Press, 2017.
Hasan-Rokem, Galit and Alan Dundes, eds. *The Wandering Jew: Essays in the Interpretation of a Christian Legend*. Bloomington: Indiana University Press, 1986.
Hauptman, William. "The Persistence of Melancholy in Nineteenth-Century Art: The Iconography of a Motif." 2 vols. Ph.D. diss. Pennsylvania State University, 1975.
Hazareesingh, Sudhir. *Black Spartacus: The Epic Life of Toussaint Louverture*. New York: Farrar, Straus and Giroux, 2020.
———. "Books of the Year." *Times Literary Supplement* (17 November 2017): 14.
———. *The Legend of Napoleon*. London: Granta, 2004.
———. "Napoleonic Memory in Nineteenth-Century France: The Making of a Liberal Legend." *Modern Language Notes* 120, no. 4 (September 2005): 747–73.
Heilbrun, Françoise and Danielle Molinari, eds., *En Collaboration avec le soleil: Victor Hugo, Photographies de l'exil*. Paris: Musée d'Orsay and Maison de Victor Hugo, 1998.
Heine, Heinrich. *De la France*. New edition. Paris: Michel Lévy, 1873.
———. "Salon de 1833." In *Allemands et Français*. Paris: Michel Lévy, 1868.
Herbert, Robert L. *Jean-François Millet*. London: Arts Council of Great Britain, 1976.
Hergott, Fabrice. *Georges Rouault, "Forme, couleur, harmonie."* Strasbourg: Musée d'Art moderne et contemporain de Strasbourg, 2007.
Honour, Hugh. *Romanticism*. New York: Harper & Row, 1979.
Horace Vernet (1789–1863). Rome: Académie de France à Rome, 1980.
Horaist, Bruno. "Saint-Germain-des-Prés (1839–1863)." In Jacques Foucart, and Bruno Foucart, with contributions by Bruno Horaist, Philippe Grunchec, and Chantal Lanvin. *Hippolyte, Auguste et Paul Flandrin: Une fraternité picturale au XIXe siècle*, 125–53. Paris: Musée du Luxembourg and Éditions de la Réunion des musées nationaux, 1984.
Hornstein, Katie. *Picturing War in France, 1792–1856*. New Haven, CT: Yale University Press, 2017.
Hugo, Victor. *L'Année terrible*. Edited by Yves Gohin. Paris: Gallimard, 1985.
———. *Les Châtiments*. Edited by René Journet. Paris: Gallimard, 1977.
———. *Choses vues: Souvenirs, journaux, cahiers, 1830–1846*. Edited by Hubert Juin. Paris: Gallimard, 1972.
———. *Choses vues: Souvenirs, journaux, cahiers, 1847–48*. Edited by Hubert Juin. Paris: Gallimard, 1972.
———. *Choses vues: Souvenirs, journaux, cahiers, 1849–1869*. Edited by Hubert Juin. Paris: Gallimard, 1972.
———. *Les Contemplations*. Edited by Pierre Albouy, preface by Léon-Paul Fargue. Paris: Gallimard, 1973.
———. *La Légende des siècles*. 2 vols. Edited by P. Berret. Paris: Hachette, 1920.
———. *Napoléon le petit*. London: Jeffs and Brussels: A. Mertens, 1852.

———. *Napoléon le petit, Édition illustrée par MM. J.P. Laurens, É. Bayard, E. Morin, D. Vierge, Lix, Chifflart, Garcia, H. Scott, Brun, G. Bellenger.* Paris: Eugène Hugues, 1879.

———. *Odes et ballades.* Edited by Pierre Albouy. Paris: Gallimard, 1964.

———. *Les Orientales.* In *Oeuvres de Victor Hugo*, 5th ed, vol. 3. Paris: Charles Gosselin and Hector Bossange, 1829.

Huysmans, J.-K. *Le Roman de Durtal.* Preface by Paul Valéry. Paris: Bartillat, 2015.

Jackson, Stanley W. *Melancholia and Depression from Hippocratic Times to Modern Times.* New Haven, CT: Yale University Press, 1986.

Jacob, François, and Henri Rossi, eds. *Mémorialistes de l'exil: Émigrer, écrire, survivre.* Paris: L'Harmattan, 2003.

James, Henry. *The Painter's Eye: Notes and Essays on the Pictorial Arts by Henry James.* Edited by John L. Sweeney. London: Rupert Hart-Davis, 1956.

Janin, Jules. "Beaux-Arts, Salon de 1839 (seventh article): Sculpture." *L'Artiste* (1839), 2:301–11.

Janmot, Louis. *Opinion d'un artiste sur l'art.* Lyon: Vite & Perrussel and Paris: Victor Lecoffre, 1887.

Jardin, André and A.J. Tudesq. *La France des notables*, vol. 1: *L'Évolution générale, 1815–1848.* Paris: Éditions du Seuil, 1973.

Joannides, Paul. "Delacroix and Modern Literature." In *The Cambridge Companion to Delacroix*, edited by Beth S. Wright, 130–53, 216–20. Cambridge: Cambridge University Press, 2001.

Jobert, Barthélémy. "Charlet, Une Carrière de peintre, de la Restauration à la monarchie de Juillet." In *Charlet: Aux origines de la légende napoléonienne 1792–1845*, 26–37. Boulogne-Billancourt: Bibliothèque Paul-Marmottan, in association with Bernard Giovanangeli, Paris, 2008.

———. *Delacroix.* New and expanded ed. Princeton, NJ: Princeton University Press, 2018.

Johnson, Dorothy. *David: Art in Metamorphosis.* Princeton, NJ: Princeton University Press, 1993.

Johnson, Lee. *The Paintings of Eugène Delacroix: A Critical Catalogue.* 7 vols. Oxford: Clarendon Press, 1981–2002.

Joubin, André. "Delacroix, Chopin et la société polonaise." In "La France et la Pologne dans leurs relations artistiques." Special issue, *Annuaire historique édité par la Bibliothèque polonaise de Paris* 2, nos. 1–2 (January–June 1939): 3–70.

Julia, Isabelle, Jean Lacambre, and Sylvain Boyer, *Les Années romantiques: La Peinture française de 1815 à 1850.* Paris: Éditions de la Réunion des musées nationaux, 1995.

Kaplan, Julius. *The Art of Gustave Moreau: Theory, Style, and Content.* Ann Arbor, MI: UMI Research Press, 1982.

Kashey, Elizabeth. "Religious Art in Nineteenth Century France." In *Christian Imagery in French Nineteenth-Century Art, 1789–1906*, edited by Martin L.H. Reymert and Robert J.F. Kashey, 1–30. New York: Shepherd Gallery, 1980.

Kempis, Thomas à. *The Imitation of Christ.* Translated and introduction by Leo Sherley-Price. Harmondsworth: Penguin Books, 1952.

Knecht, Edgar. *Le Mythe du Juif errant: Essai de mythologie littéraire et de sociologie religieuse.* Grenoble: Presses Universitaires de Grenoble, 1977.

König, Eduard. "The Wandering Jew: Legend or Myth?" In *The Wandering Jew: Essays in the Interpretation of a Christian Legend,* edited by Galit Hasan-Rokem and Alan Dundes, 11–26. Bloomington: Indiana University Press, 1986.

Kopp, Robert. "'Les Limbes insondés de la tristesse': Figures de la mélancolie romantique de Chateaubriand à Sartre." In *Mélancolie: genie et folie en Occident,* edited by Jean Clair, 328–40. Paris: Réunion des musées nationaux, in association with Gallimard, Paris, 2005.

Korchane, Mehdi. *Figures de l'exil sous la Révolution, De Bélisaire à Marcus Sextus.* Vizille: Musée de la Révolution française-Domaine de Vizille, 2016.

———. *Pierre Guérin 1774–1833.* Paris: Mare & Martin, 2018.

Koropeckyj, Roman. "Adam Mickiewicz and the Shape of Polish Romanticism." In *A Companion to European Romanticism,* edited by Michael Ferber, 326–44. Malden, MA: Blackwell Publishing, 2005.

———. *Adam Mickiewicz: The Life of a Romantic.* Ithaca, NY: Cornell University Press, 2008.

Kramer, Lloyd S. *Threshold of a New World: Intellectuals and the Exile Experience in Paris, 1830–1848.* Ithaca, NY: Cornell University Press, 1988.

Kroen, Sheryl. *Politics and Theater: The Crisis of Legitimacy in Restoration France, 1815–1830.* Berkeley: University of California Press, 2000.

Kselman, Thomas A. *Miracles & Prophecies in Nineteenth-Century France.* New Brunswick, NJ: Rutgers University Press, 1983.

———. "Religion and French Identity: The Origins of the *Union Sacré.*" In *Many Are Chosen: Divine Election and Western Nationalism,* edited by William R. Hutchison and Hartmut Lehmann, 57–97. Harvard Theological Studies 38. Harrisburg, PA: Trinity Press International, 1994.

Kuenzli, Katherine M. *The Nabis and Intimate Modernism: Painting and the Decorative at the Fin-de-Siècle.* Farnham: Ashgate, 2010.

Lally-Tolendal, Trophime-Gérard. *Défense des émigrés français. Addressée en 1797 au peuple français.* New ed. Paris: Delaunay, 1825.

Lamartine, Alphonse de. *Correspondance de Lamartine.* Edited by Valentine de Lamartine. 6 vols. Paris: Hachette, Furne, Jouvet, 1873–5.

———. *La Politique de Lamartine: Choix de discours et écrits politiques.* Edited by L. de Ronchaud. 2 vols. Paris: Hachette, Furne, Jouvet, 1878.

Lambert, Jeremy. "Le Towianisme en France; La France dans le Towianisme." *Slavica bruxellensia* 3 (2009): 61–73. https://doi.org/10.4000/slavica.274. Open Edition Journals.

Lamennais: A Believer's Revolutionary Politics. Edited by Richard A. Lebrun and Sylvain Milbach, translated by Richard A. Lebrun and Jerry Ryan, introduction and annotations by Sylvain Milbach. Studies in the History of Political Thought 13. Leiden: Brill, 2018.

[Lamennais, Félicité Robert de]. *Essai sur l'indifférence en matière de religion.* Vol. 1. Paris: Tournachon-Molin and H. Seguin, 1817.

———. *Paroles d'un croyant. Divers écrits pour le people.* Introduction by Alphonse Séché. Paris: Nelson, n.d.

Lamennais, Félicité Robert de. *De la religion considerée dans ses rapports avec l'ordre politique et civil.* 2 vols. Paris: Bureau du memorial catholique, 1825–6.

———. *Des progrès de la Révolution et de la guerre contre l'Église.* Paris and Brussels: Belin-Mandar et Devaux, 1829.

[Lamennais, Félicité Robert de, and Jean-Marie de La Mennais]. *Tradition de l'Église sur l'institution des évêques.* 3 vols. Liege: Le Marié and Duvivier; Paris: Société typographique, 1814.

Lance, Adolphe. *Dictionnaire des architectes francais.* 2 vols. Paris: V.A. Morel, 1872.

Landon, C.P. *Annales du Musée et de l'école moderne des beaux-arts. Salon de 1812. Recueil de pieces choisies parmi les ouvrages de peinture et de sculpture exposés au Louvre le premier novembre 1812.* 2 vols. Paris: Chaignieau ainé, 1812.

Langworthy, Jennifer Marie. "On Shifting Ground: The Revolutionary Career of François Gérard." PhD Diss., University of Illinois at Urbana-Champaign, 2012.

Las Cases, comte Emmanuel de. *Souvenirs de l'empereur Napoléon Ier, Extraits du Mémorial de Sainte-Hélène.* Paris: L. Hachette, 1854.

Latreille, A. and R. Rémond. *La Période contemporaine.* In *Histoire du Catholicisme en France,* edited by A. Latreille, R. Palanque, E. Delaruelle, and R. Rémond, vol. 3. Paris: Éditions Spes, 1962.

Laubriet, Pierre. "La Légende et le myth napoléoniens chez Balzac." *L'Année balzacienne* (January 1968): 285–302.

Laughton, Bruce. "Millet's *Hagar and Ishmael.*" *Burlington Magazine* 121, no. 920 (November 1979): 705–11.

Laveissière, Sylvain. *Pierre-Paul Prud'hon*. New York: The Metropolitan Museum of Art, in association with Harry N. Abrams, New York, and Réunion des musées nationaux, Paris, 1998.

Laveissière, Sylvain, Régis Michel, Bruno Chenique, and Yveline Cantarel-Bessin, *Géricault*. Paris: Réunion des musées nationaux, 1991.

Laviron, Gabriel, and B. Galbacio. *Le Salon de 1833*. Paris: Abel Ledoux, 1833.

Leeman, Fred and Hanna Pennock, with contributions by Saskia de Bodt and Ronald de Leeuw. *Museum Mesdag: Catalogue of Paintings and Drawings*. Amsterdam: Van Gogh Museum, in association with Uitgeverij Waanders, Zwolle, 1996.

Le Gall, Didier. *Napoléon et 'Le Mémorial de Sainte-Hélène': Analyse d'un discours*. Preface by Jean-Paul Bertaud. Paris: Éditions Kimé, 2003.

Leith, James A. *Space and Revolution: Projects for Monuments, Squares, and Public Buildings in France, 1789–1799*. Montreal, QC: McGill-Queen's University Press, 1991.

Lemercier, Népomucène-Louis. *Agar et Ismaël, ou L'Origine du peuple arabe, Scène orientale en vers, Représentée au Théâtre de l'Odéon, le 23 janvier 1818*. Paris: Nepveu, 1818.

Le Normand-Romain, Antoinette. "Le Séjour d'Etex à Rome en 1831–1832: Un Carnet de dessins inédit." *Bulletin de la Société de l'Histoire de l'Art français* (1981): 175–88.

Lestringant, Frank. *Alfred de Musset*. Paris: Flammarion, 1999.

Lévêque, Laure. "Banni soit qui mal y pense: l'histoire en exil. Le cas Quinet. *Babel: Littératures plurielles* 29 (2014): 289–314. https://doi.org/10.4000/babel.3734

Lindsay, Suzanne Glover. *Funerary Arts and Tomb Cult––Living with the Dead in France, 1750–1870*. Farnham: Ashgate, 2012.

———. "Mummies and Tombs: Turenne, Napoléon, and Death Ritual." *Art Bulletin* 82, no. 3, (September 2000): 476–502.

Liris, Elizabeth. "Vandalisme et régénération dans la mission de Fouché à l'automne 1793." In *Révolution française et "vandalisme révolutionnaire": Actes du colloque international de Clermont-Ferrand 15–17 Décembre 1988*, edited by Simone Bernard-Griffiths, Jean Ehrard, and Marie-Claude Chemin, 217–28. Paris: Universitas, 1992.

Lloyd, Christopher. *J.-K. Huysmans and the 'Fin-de-siècle' Novel*. Edinburgh: Edinburgh University Press, 1990.

Louvre, Les Collections du département des arts graphiques. "Delacroix, Eugène, École française, *Portrait de Chopin en Dante*." Accessed 2 November 2020. http://arts-graphiques.louvre.fr/detail/oeuvres/1/111545-Portrait-de-Chopin-en-Dante.

Loyrette, Henri. "Delacroix's Ovid in Exile." *Burlington Magazine* 137, no. 1111 (Oct. 1995): 682–3.

Loyrette, Henri, Michael Pantazzi, Segolène Le Men, Édouard Papet, Dominique Lobstein, and Michel Melot. *Daumier 1808–1879*. Paris: Réunion des musées nationaux, 1999.

Lucas-Dubreton, Jean. *Le Culte de Napoléon, 1815–1848*. Paris: Albin Michel, 1960.

MacNamidhe, Margaret. *Delacroix and His Forgotten World: The Origins of Romantic Painting*. London: I.B. Tauris, 2015.

———. "Delécluze's Response to Delacroix's 'Scenes from the Massacres at Chios' (1824)." *Art Bulletin* 89, no. 1 (2007): 63–81.

Malfilâtre, Jacques-Charles-Louis Clinchamps de. *Oeuvres de Malfilâtre*. Edited by M. L.***. Paris: Jehenne, 1825.

Le Mapah [Ganneau]. *Waterloo. À Vous, beaux fils de France, morts pour l'honneur. Salut et glorification! L'Honneur, c'est l'Unité!* Paris: Au Bureau des publications Évadiennes, 1843.

Marcoulesco, Ileana. *Georges Rouault: The Inner Light*. Forward by Dominique de Menil. Houston, TX: The Menil Collection, 1996.

Marrinan, Michael. "Literal/Literary/'Lexie': History, Text, and Authority in Napoleonic Painting." *Word & Image* 7, no. 3 (July–September 1991): 177–200.

———. *Painting Politics for Louis-Philippe: Art and Ideology in Orléanist France, 1830–1848*. New Haven, CT: Yale University Press, 1988.

———. *Romantic Paris: Histories of a Cultural Landscape, 1800–1850*. Stanford, CA: Stanford University Press, 2009.

Mathiez, Albert. *Les Origines des Cultes révolutionnaires (1789–1792)*. Paris: G. Bellais, 1904.

McClellan, Andre. *Inventing the Louvre: Art, Politics, and the Origins of the Modern Museum in Eighteenth-Century Paris*. Cambridge: Cambridge University Press, 1994.

McMahon, Darrin M. *Enemies of the Enlightenment: The French Counter-Enlightenment and the Making of Modernity*. Oxford: Oxford University Press, 2001.

McManners, John. *The French Revolution and the Church*. New York: Harper & Row, 1969.

Medwin, Thomas. *Medwin's Conversations of Lord Byron*. Edited by Ernest J. Lovell, Jr. Princeton, NJ: Princeton University Press, 1966.

Mellon, Stanley. "The July Monarchy and the Napoleonic Myth." *Yale French Studies* 26 (Fall–Winter 1960–61): 70–8.

Ménager, Bernard. *Les Napoléon du peuple*. Paris: Aubier, 1988.

Méneux, Catherine "Delacroix face à la critique." In *Delacroix*, edited by Sébastien Allard, and Côme Fabre, with contributions by Catherine Adam-Sigas, Dominique de Font-Réaulx, Michèle Hannoosh, Mehdi Korchane, Ségolène Le Men, Catherine Méneux, Asher Miller, and Marie-Pierre Salé, 347–55. Paris: Musée du Louvre, in association with Éditions Hazan, Paris, 2018.

Mercier, Louis-Sébastien. *Le Nouveau Paris*. 6 vols. Paris: Fuchs, C. Pougens, and C. F. Cramer, [1797].

Mérimée, Prosper. "Salon de 1839." *Revue des deux mondes*, 4th ser. 18 (1 April 1839), 83–103.

Michel, Régis, ed. *Géricault*. 2 vols. Paris: La Documentation française, 1996.

Mickiewicz, Adam. *Livre des pèlerins polonais, traduit du polonais d'Adam Mickiewicz, par le comte Ch. de Montalembert, suivi d'Un hymne à la Pologne par F. de La Mennais*. Paris: Eugène Renduel, 1833.

Middeke, Martin and Christina Wald, eds. *The Literature of Melancholia: Early Modern to Postmodern*. New York: Palgrave Macmillan, 2011.

Mikaberidze, Alexander. *The Napoleonic Wars: A Global History*. New York: Oxford University Press, 2020.

Miller, Peter Benson. "By the Sword and the Plow: Théodore Chassériau's Cour des Comptes Murals and Algeria." *Art Bulletin* 86, no. 4 (Dec. 2004): 690–718.

Milner, John. *Art, War and Revolution* in *France, 1870–1871: Myth, Reportage and Reality*. New Haven, CT: Yale University Press, 2000.

Monnet, Georges. *Musée de Guéret: Catalogue descriptive des tableaux*. Guéret: P. Amiault, 1889.

Montalembert, Charles Forbes, comte de. *Mélanges d'art et de littérature*. In *Oeuvres de M. le comte de Montalembert*, vol. 6. Paris: Jacques Lecoffre, 1861.

Montesquiou, Robert de. "Alice et Aline (Une peinture de Chassériau)." In *Autels privilégiés*, 251–67. Paris: Bibliothèque-Charpentier, 1898.

Moreau, Gustave, and Eugène Fromentin. *Gustave Moreau et Eugène Fromentin: Documents inédits*. Edited by Barbara Wright and Pierre Moisy. La Rochelle: Quartier Latin, 1972.

Morrissey, Robert. "The 'Mémorial de Sainte-Hélène' and the Poetics of Fusion." *Modern Language Notes* 120, no. 4 (Sept. 2005): 716–32.

Mower, David. "Antoine Augustin Préault (1809–1879)," *Art Bulletin* 63, no. 2 (June 1981): 288–307.

Musée des Beaux-Arts de Lyon. Sculptures du XVIIe au XXes siècle. Lyon: Musée des Beaux-Arts in association with Somogy éditons d'art, Paris, 2017.

Musset, Alfred de. *La Confession d'un enfant du siècle*. Edited by Sylvain Ledda. Paris: Flammarion, 2010.

———. "Salon de 1836. *Revue des deux mondes*. 4th ser. 6 (15 April 1836), 144–76.

The New English Bible, with the Apocrypha. New York: Oxford University Press, 1971.

Nochlin, Linda. "The De-Politicization of Gustave Courbet: Transformation and Rehabilitation under the Third Republic," In *Courbet*, edited by Linda Nochlin, 126–7. New York: Thames & Hudson, 2007 (originally published 1982).

———. "Gustave Courbet's *Meeting:* A Portrait of the Artist as a Wandering Jew" In *Courbet*, edited by Linda Nochlin, 29–54. New York: Thames & Hudson, 2007 (originally published 1967).

Noon, Patrick, and Christopher Riopelle. *Delacroix and the Rise of Modern Art*. London: National Gallery and Minneapolis: Minneapolis Institute of Art, in association with Yale University Press, New Haven, 2015.

Normand, Jacques. *L'Émigrant alsacien, Récit, avec une gravure de Gustave Doré*. Paris: Librairie du XIXe siècle, 1873.

Nouvel-Kammerer, Odile. *Symbols of Power: Napoleon and the Art of the Empire Style, 1800–1815*. Paris: Musée des Arts Décoratifs and New York: American Federation of Arts, in association with Harry N. Abrams, New York, 2007.

O'Brien, David. *After the Revolution: Antoine-Jean Gros, Painting and Propaganda under Napoleon*. University Park: Penn State University Press, 2006.

———. *Exiled in Modernity: Delacroix, Civilization, and Barbarism*. University Park: Penn State University Press, 2018.

Orton, Fred and Griselda Pollock. "Les Données Bretonnantes: La Prairie de Répresentation." *Art History* 3, no. 3 (September 1980): 314–44.

Osterhammel, Jürgen. *The Transformation of the World: A Global History of the Nineteenth Century*. Translated by Patrick Camiller. Princeton, NJ: Princeton University Press, 2014.

Ozouf, Mona. *Festivals and the French Revolution*. Translated by Alan Sheridan. Cambridge, MA: Harvard University Press, 1988 (originally published 1976).

Padiyar, Satish. *Chains: David, Canova, and the Fall of the Public Hero in Postrevolutionary France*. University Park: Penn State University Press, 2007.

Pagé, Sylvain. *Le Mythe napoléonien: De Las Cases à Victor Hugo*. Paris: CNRS éditions, 2013.

Pearson, Roger. *Unacknowledged Legislators: The Poet as Lawgiver in Post-Revolutionary France*. Oxford: Oxford University Press, 2016.

Peeters, Guy. "Lamennais, l'irréductible croyant." *Nineteenth-Century French Studies* 14, nos. 1–2 (Fall–Winter 1985–86): 80–102.

Les Peintres de l'âme: Art lyonnais du XIXe siècle. Lyon: Musée des Beaux-Arts, 1981.

Peltre, Christine. *Théodore Chassériau*. Paris: Gallimard, 2001.

Petiteau, Natalie. *Napoléon de la mythologie à l'histoire*. Paris: Éditions du Seuil, 1999.

Peyre, Henri. *What is Romanticism?* Translated by Roda Roberts. University: University of Alabama Press, 1977 (originally published 1971).

Pichois, Claude. *L'Image de Jean-Paul Richter dans les les lettres françaises*. Paris: José Corti, 1963.

Pigler, Andor. *Barockthemen, eine Auswahl von Verzeichnissen zur Ikonographie des 17. und 18. Jahrhunderts*. 2 vols. Budapest: Verlag der Ungarischen Akademie der Wissenschaften, 1956.

Pillet, Fabien."Exposition de 1849 au palais des Tuileries." *Le Moniteur universel* (7 August 1849).

Pingeot, Anne, Philippe Durey, Antoinette Le Normand-Romain, Isabelle Leroy-Jay, Laure de Margerie, and Véronique Wiesinger. *La Sculpture française au XIXe siècle*. Paris: Galeries nationales du Grand-Palais and Éditions de la Réunion des musées nationaux, 1986.

Pirie, Donald. "The Agony in the Garden: Polish Romanticism." In *Romanticism in National Context*, edited by Roy Porter and Mikuláš Teich, 317–44. Cambridge: Cambridge University Press, 1988.

Polistena, Joyce Carol. "The 'Agony in the Garden' by Eugène Delacroix." *Van Gogh Museum Journal* (2001): 125–38.

———. *The Religious Painting of Eugène Delacroix (1798–1863): The Initiator of the Style of Modern Religious Art*. Lewiston, NY: The Edwin Mellen Press, 2008.

Porter, Charles A. *Chateaubriand: Composition, Imagination, and Poetry*. Stanford French and Italian Studies 9. Saratoga, CA: Anma Libri, 1978.

Porter, Roy, and Mikuláš Teich, eds. *Romanticism in National Context*. Cambridge: Cambridge University Press, 1988.

Porterfield, Todd. *The Allure of Empire: Art in the Service of French Imperialism, 1789–1836*. Princeton, NJ: Princeton University Press, 1998.

———. "Resacralization through National History Painting: The Sacristy at Saint Denis, 1811–22." *Word and Image* 16 (January–March 2000): 31–44.

Porterfield, Todd and Susan L. Siegfried. *Staging Empire: Napoleon, Ingres, and David*. University Park: Penn State University Press, 2006.

Powers, Richard Howard. *Edgar Quinet: A Study in French Patriotism*. Dallas, TX: Southern Methodist University Press, 1957.

Prat, Louis-Antoine. *Musée du Louvre, Cabinet des dessins. Inventaire général des dessins, École française. Dessins de Théodore Chassériau, 1819–1856*. 2 vols. Paris: Éditions de la Réunion des musées nationaux, 1988.

Prendergast, Christopher. *Napoleon and History Painting: Antoine-Jean Gros's 'La Bataille d'Eylau'*. Oxford: Clarendon Press, 1997.

Puymège, Gérard de. "Le Soldat Chauvin." In *Les Lieux de mémoire*, edited by Pierre Nora, vol. 2: *La Nation*, part 3, 45–80. Paris: Gallimard, 1986.

Quinet, Edgar. *Ahasvérus*. New ed. Paris: Imprimeurs unis, 1843.

———. *1815 et 1840*. 2d ed. Paris: Paulin, 1840.

———. *Histoire d'un enfant (Histoire de mes idées)*. Paris: Hachette, 1903.

———. *Napoléon, poème*. Paris: Ambroise Dupont, 1836.

The Qur'ān: A New Annotated Translation. Translated and edited by A.J. Droge. Sheffield: Equinox, 2013.

Raczynski, comte Athanse. *Histoire de l'art moderne en Allemagne*. 3 vols. Paris: J. Renouard, 1836–41.

Ramond, Sylvie, Gérard Bruyère, Pierre Vaisse, and François Fossier. *Le Temps de la peinture, Lyon 1800–1914*. Lyon: Éditions Fage, 2007.

Reardon, Bernard M.G. *Liberalism and Tradition: Aspects of Catholic Thought in Nineteenth-Century France*. Cambridge: Cambridge University Press, 1975.

———. *Religion in the Age of Romanticism: Studies in Early Nineteenth Century Thought*. Cambridge: Cambridge University Press, 1985.

Réau, Louis. *Histoire du vandalisme: Les Monuments détruits de l'art français*. 2 vols. Paris: Librairie Hachette, 1959.

Renan, Ary. "Gustave Moreau" (second article). *Gazette des beaux-arts*, 3rd ser. 21 (1899): 189–204.

Renger, Konrad. "Eduard Bendemanns 'Jeremias': Vorzeichnungen und Würdigungen eines verlorenen Hauptwerkes der Düsseldorfer Malerschule." In *Ars naturam adiuvans: Festschrift für Matthias Winner: zum 11 März 1996*, edited by Victoria V. Flemming and Sebastian Shütze, 621–37. Mainz am Rhein: Philipp von Zabern, 1996.

Reymert, Martin L.H., and Robert J.F. Kashey, eds., *Christian Imagery in French Nineteenth-Century Art, 1789–1906*. New York: Shepherd Gallery, 1980.

Ribner, Jonathan P. *Broken Tablets: The Cult of the Law in French Art from David to Delacroix*. Berkeley: University of California Press, 1993.

———. "Chassériau's Juvenilia: Some Early Works by an *Enfant du Siècle.*" *Zeitschrift für Kunstgeschichte* 57, no. 2 (1994): 219–38.

———. "The London Sublime." *British Art Journal* 16, no. 2 (Autumn 2015): 76–88.

———. "On a Repainting by Millet." *Nineteenth-Century Art Worldwide* 13, no. 1 (Spring 2014). http://www.19thcartworldwide.org/index.php/spring14/ribner-on-a-repainting-by-millet

———. "Resistance and Persistence: On the Fortunes and Reciprocal International Influences of French Romanticism." *Studies in Romanticism* 57, no. 4 (Winter 2018): 505–38.

———. "Théodore Chassériau and the Anti-Heroic Mode under the July Monarchy." In *Chassériau (1819–1856): Un autre romantisme, Actes du colloque organisé par le Musée du Louvre, le 16 mars 2002*, edited by Stéphane Guégan and Louis-Antoine Prat, 11–38. Paris: La documentation française / Musée du Louvre, 2002.

———. "Wandering in the Wilderness under Louis-Philippe." In *Moving Forward, Holding Fast: The Dynamics of Nineteenth-Century French Culture*, edited by Barbara T. Cooper and Mary Donaldson-Evans, 131–50. Amsterdam: Rodopi, 1997.

Richter, Jean Paul. *The Death of an Angel and Other Pieces Translated from the Works of Jean Paul Friedrich Richter.* Translated by A. Kenney. London: Black and Armstrong, and Dresden: Chr. Arnold, 1839.

Robinson, Marc, ed. *Altogether Elsewhere: Writers on Exile.* New York: Harcourt Brace & Company, 1994.

Roethlisberger, Marcel G. "Edouard Odier (1800–1887): Sur les traces d'un peintre d'histoire romantique." *Genava: Revue d'histoire de l'art et d'archéologie* 36 (1988): 105–16.

The Romantic Movement. London: Arts Council of Great Britain, 1959.

Rosenblum, Robert. *Jean-August-Dominique Ingres.* New York: Harry N. Abrams, 1967, reprint, 1985.

———. "The Abstract Sublime." *ARTnews* 59 (January 1961): 38ff.

———. *Modern Painting and the Northern Romantic Tradition: Friedrich to Rothko.* New York: Harper & Row, 1975.

———. *Paintings in the Musée d'Orsay.* Foreword by Françoise Cachin. New York: Stewart, Tabori & Chang, 1989.

———. *Transformations in Late Eighteenth-Century Art.* Princeton, NJ: Princeton University Press, 1969.

Rosenblum, Robert and H.W. Janson. *19th-Century Art.* Revised and updated edition. Upper Saddle River, NJ: Pearson Prentice Hall, in association with Laurence King Publishing, London, 2005.

Rosenthal, Léon. *Du romantisme au realisme: Essai sur l'évolution de la peinture en France de 1830 à 1848.* Paris: H. Laurens, 1914.

Roth, Michael S. *Memory, Trauma, and History: Essays on Living with the Past.* New York: Columbia University Press, 2012.

Roulin, Jean-Marie. *Chateaubriand: L'Exil et la gloire.* Bibliothèque de la littérature moderne 26. Paris: Honoré Champion, 1994.

Roux, Marcel. *Bibliothèque nationale, Département des estampes. Un siècle d'histoire de France par l'estampe, 1770–1871. Collection De Vinck. Inventaire analytique.* Vol. 4: *Napoléon et son temps (Directoire, Consulat, Empire).* Paris: Bibliothèque nationale, 1969.

Rubin, James Henry. "Oedipus, Antigone and Exiles in Post-Revolutionary French Painting." *Art Quarterly* 36, no. 3 (Autumn 1973): 141–71.

Rubin, William S. *Modern Sacred Art and the Church of Assy.* New York: Columbia University Press, 1961.

S., Cl.-P., abbé. *Les Lamentations du prophète Jérémie traduites en vers français et suivies de Quelques Chants religieux et patriotiques composés à l'occasion de la guerre de 1870–71 entre la France et l'Allemagne.* Troyes: P. Lambert, 1871.

Sainte-Beuve, Charles-Augustin. "La Confession d'un enfant du siècle, par M. Alfred de Musset." *Revue des deux mondes* 4th ser. 5, no. 4 (1836): 483–93.

———. *Volupté*. Edited by André Guyaux. Paris: Gallimard, 2011.

Saint-Chéron, Alexandre de. "Overbeck et l'école allemande," *L'Artiste*, 1st ser. 12 (1836), 51–2.

Salé, Marie-Pierre, 'Facilité, rapidité, fragilité: Delacroix et le pastel." In Sébastien Allard and Côme Fabre, with contributions by Catherine Adam-Sigas, Dominique de Font-Réaulx, Michèle Hannoosh, Mehdi Korchane, Ségolène Le Men, Catherine Méneux, Asher Miller, and Marie-Pierre Salé. *Delacroix*, 367–73. Paris: Musée du Louvre, in association with Éditions Hazan, Paris, 2018.

Samuels, Maurice. *The Spectacular Past: Popular History and the Novel in Nineteenth-Century France*. Ithaca, NY: Cornell University Press, 2004.

Sand, George. *Histoire de ma vie*. Edited by Brigitte Diaz. Paris: Librairie générale française, 2004.

Sandoz, Marc. *Théodore Chassériau, 1819–1856. Catalogue raisonné des peintures et estampes*. Paris: Arts et métiers graphiques, 1974.

Schnapper, Antoine. *David*. New York: Alpine Fine Arts Collection, 1980.

Schnapper, Antoine and Arlette Sérullaz. *Jacques-Louis David 1748–1825*. Paris: Musée du Louvre and Versailles: Musée national des Châteaux de Versailles et de Trianon, 1989.

Schneider, Mechthild. "'Kain und seine von Gott verfluchte Rasse': Eine monumentale Gruppe von Antoine Etex im Salon von 1833." *Bruckmanns Pantheon* 53 (1995): 108–15.

Ségur, Philippe de. *Histoire de Napoléon et de la Grande-Armée pendant l'année 1812*, vol. 1. Brussels: Arnold Lacrosse, 1825.

Ségur, Philippe de. *Histoire de Napoléon et de la Grande-Armée pendant l'année 1812*, vol. 2. Paris: Baudouin frères, 1824.

Sérullaz, Arlette, with contributions by Lee Johnson, Joseph J. Rishel, Vincent Pomarède, Louis-Antoine Prat, and David Liot. *Delacroix: The Late Work*. Paris: Galeries Nationales du Grand Palais and Philadelphia: Philadelphia Museum of Art, in association with Thames and Hudson, New York, 1998.

Sérullaz, Maurice. *Eugène Delacroix*. New York: Harry N. Abrams, [1971].

Sérullaz, Maurice, Arlette Sérullaz, Louis-Antoine Prat, and Claudine Ganeval, *Musée du Louvre, Cabinet des dessins. Inventaire général des dessins, École française. Dessins d'Eugène Delacroix, 1798–1863*. 2 vols. Paris: Éditions de la Réunion des musées nationaux, 1984.

Seznec, Jean. *John Martin en France*. London: Faber & Faber, 1964.

Shelton, Andrew Carrington. *Ingres and His Critics*. Cambridge: Cambridge University Press, 2005.

Sherak, Constance. "Investing in the Past: Victor Hugo's La Bande noire." *Romance Languages Annual* 10, no. 1 (1999): 157–63.

Shroder, Maurice Z. *Icarus: The Image of the Artist in French Romanticism*. Cambridge, MA: Harvard University Press, 1961.

Siegfried, Susan L. "Alternative Narratives." *Art History* 36, no. 1 (February 2013): 100–27.

———. *Ingres: Painting Reimagined*. New Haven, CT: Yale University Press, 2009.

———. "Naked History: The Rhetoric of Military Painting in Postrevolutionary France." *Art Bulletin* 75, no. 2 (June 1993): 235–58.

Silverman, Debora. "At the Threshold of Symbolism: Van Gogh's *Sower* and Gauguin's *Vision after the Sermon*." In *Critical Readings in Impressionism and Post-Impressionism: An Anthology*, edited by Mary Tompkins Lewis, 271–85. Berkeley: University of California Press, 2007.

———. *Van Gogh and Gauguin: The Search for Sacred Art*. New York: Farrar, Straus and Giroux, 2000.

Simon, Robert. "Géricault and the *fait divers*." In *Géricault*, edited by Régis Michel, 2 vols. 1:259–62. Paris: La Documentation française, 1996.

Simpson, John, ed. *The Oxford Book of Exile*. Oxford: Oxford University Press, 1995.

Small, Lisa. "L'Année Terrible and Political Imagery." In Eric Zafran, Robert Rosenblum, and Lisa Small, *Fantasy and Faith: The Art of Gustave Doré*, 32–63. New York: Dahesh Museum of Art, in association with Yale University Press, New Haven, 2007.

Smith, Kevin C. "Victor Hugo and the Vendôme Column: 'Ce fut le début de la rupture...'." *French Forum* 21, no. 2 (May 1996): 149–64.

Smith, Margaret Denton (see also Denton, Margaret Fields). "The Elegy of Death in French Painting at the End of the Eighteenth and Beginning of the Nineteenth Centuries." PhD diss., New York University, 1986.

Souchal, François. *Le Vandalisme de la Révolution*. Paris: Nouvelles éditions latines, 1993.

Spitzer, Alan B. *The French Generation of 1820*. Princeton, NJ: Princeton University Press, 1987.

———. *Old Hatreds and Young Hopes: The French Carbonari against the Bourbon Restoration*. Cambridge, MA: Harvard University Press, 1971.

Staël, Anne-Louise-Germaine de. *De l'Allemagne*. New edition. Paris: G. Charpentier, 1890.

———. *Considérations sur les principaux événements de la Révolution française, Publiées en 1818 par M. le duc de Broglie et M. le baron de Staël*. In *Oeuvres posthumes de Madame la baronne de Staël-Holstein, Précédés d'une Notice sur son caractère et ses écrits*. Paris, 1861. Reprint. Geneva: Slatkine, 1967.

———. *Corinne, ou l'Italie*. 2 vols. Paris: H. Nicolle, 1807.

———. *Corinne, or Italy*. Translated and edited by Sylvia Raphael. Introduction by John Isbell. Oxford: Oxford University Press, 1998.

———. *Dix années d'exil*. Edited by Simone Balayé and Mariella Vianello Bonifacio. Paris: Arthème Fayard, 1996.

———. *Agar dans le desert, Scène lyrique composée en 1806*. In *Oeuvres posthumes de Madame la baronne de Staël-Holstein, Précédés d'une Notice sur son caractère et ses écrits*. Paris, 1861. Reprint. Geneva: Slatkine, 1967.

Stara, Alexandra. *The Museum of French Monuments, 1795–1816: 'Killing art to make history.'* Farnham: Ashgate, 2013.

Stendhal [Henri Beyle]. *Le Rouge et le noir*. Edited by Anne-Marie Meininger. Preface by Jean Prévost. Paris: Gallimard, 2000.

Stephens, Bradley. *Victor Hugo*. London: Reaktion Books, 2019.

Sterling, Charles and Margaretta M. Salinger. *French Paintings, A Catalogue of the Collection of the Metropolitan Museum of Art*, vol. 2: *XIX Century*. New York: Metropolitan Museum of Art, in association with New York Graphic Society, Greenwich, CT, 1966.

Sternhell, Zeev. *La Droite révolutionaire, 1885–1914: Les Origines françaises du fascisme*. Paris: Seuil, 1978.

———. *Maurice Barrés et le nationalisme français*. Brussels: Editions Complexe, 1985.

Strauber, Susan. "The Religious Paintings of Eugène Delacroix." PhD diss., Brown University, 1980.

Sueur, Valérie. *François Chifflart, graveur et illustrateur*. Paris: Editions de la Réunion des musées nationaux, 1993.

Ternois, Daniel. *Montauban, Musée Ingres, peintures. Ingres et son temps (artistes nés entre 1740 et 1830)*. Inventaire des collections publiques françaises 11: Paris: Éditions des musées nationaux, 1965.

Thompson, Christopher W. *French Romantic Travel Writing: Chateaubriand to Nerval*. Oxford: Oxford University Press, 2011.

Thomson, Belinda, Frances Fowle, and Lesley Stevenson. *Gauguin's Vision*. Edinburgh: National Galleries of Scotland, 2005.

Thomson, Richard. *The Troubled Republic: Visual Culture and Social Debate in France, 1889–1900*. New Haven, CT: Yale University Press, 2004.

Thoré, Théophile. "Les Peintures de la Bibliothèque de la Chambre des deputes." *Le Constitutionnel* (31 January 1848).

Tillier, Bertrand. *Napoléon, Rude et Noisot: Histoire d'un monument d'outre-tombe*. Paris: Les Éditions de l'Amateur, 2012.

Tinterow, Gary, and Henri Loyrette. *Origins of Impressionism*. New York: Metropolitan Museum of Art, in association with Harry N. Abrams, New York, 1994.

Tinterow, Gary, Michael Pantazzi, and Vincent Pomarède. *Corot*. New York: Metropolitan Museum of Art, in association with Harry N. Abrams, New York, 1996.

Tombs, Robert. *France 1814–1914*. Abingdon: Routledge, 2014.

Touchard, Jean. *La Gloire de Béranger*. 2 vols. Paris: Armand Colin, 1968.

Tourneux, Maurice. *Salons et expositions d'art à Paris (1800–1870): Essai bibliographique*. Paris: Jean Schemit, 1919.

Tripodes, Lucia. "François Rude: The Importance of Sculpture," PhD diss., New York University, 2003.

Tulard, Jean, ed. *L'Anti-Napoléon: La Légende noire de l'empereur*. Paris: René Julliard, 1965.

———. *La Mythe de Napoléon*. Paris: Armand Colin, 1971.

———. *Napoleon: The Myth of the Saviour*. Translated by Teresa Waugh. London: Methuen, 1985.

———. "Le Retour des Cendres." In *Les Lieux de mémoire*, edited by Pierre Nora, vol. 2: *La Nation*, part 3, 81–110. Paris: Gallimard, 1986

Vallès, Jules. *Jacques Vingtras*, vol. 4: *Le Proscrit: Correspondance avec Arthur Arnould*. Edited by Lucien Scheler. Paris: Les Éditeurs français réunis, 1973.

Vaughan, William. *Friedrich*. London: Phaidon, 2004.

———. *German Romantic Painting*. 2nd ed. New Haven, CT: Yale University Press, 1994.

Vernet, Horace. "Des anciens Hébreux et des Arabes modernes," *L'Artiste*, 5th ser. 1 (15 August 1848): 232–5.

———. *Opinion sur certains rapports qui existent entre le costume des anciens Hébreux et celui des Arabes modernes (Lu à l'Académie en 1847)*. Paris: Bonaventure et Ducessois, 1856.

Vidalenc, Jean. *Les Demi-solde: Étude d'une catégorie sociale*. Paris: Marcel Rivière, 1955.

———. *Les Émigrés français, 1789–1825*. Caen: Association des Publications de la Faculté des Lettres et Sciences Humaines de l'Université de Caen, 1963.

Vigny, Alfred de. *Oeuvres complètes*, vol. 1: *Poésie, théâtre*. Edited by François Germain and André Jarry. Vol. 2: *Prose*. Edited by Alphonse Bouvet. Paris: Gallimard, 1986–93.

———. *Poésies*. In *Oeuvres completes*, vol. 1. Paris: Alphonse Lemerre, 1883.

———. *Servitude et grandeur militaires*. Edited by Auguste Dorchain. Paris: Garnier, 1955.

———. *Servitude et grandeur militaires*, in *Oeuvres complètes*, vol. 2: *Prose*. Edited by Alphonse Bouvet. Paris: Gallimard, 1993.

Villa, Nicole. *Bibliothèque nationale, Département des estampes. Un siècle d'histoire de France par l'estampe, 1770–1871. Collection De Vinck. Inventaire analytique*, vol. 6: *La Révolution de 1830 et La Monarchie de Juillet*. Paris: Bibliothèque nationale, 1979.

Villa, Nicole, Denise Dommel, and Jacques Thirion. *Bibliothèque nationale, Département des estampes. Un siècle d'histoire de France par l'estampe, 1770–1871. Collection De Vinck. Inventaire analytique*, vol. 7: *La Révolution de 1848 et La Deuxième République*. Paris: Bibliothèque nationale, 1955.

Vincent, Madeleine. *La Peinture des XIXe et XXe siècles*. Catalogue du Musée de Lyon 7: Lyon: IAC, Les Éditions de Lyon, 1956.

Virgil. *The Aeneid*. Translated by David Ferry. Chicago, IL: University of Chicago Press, 2017.

Vovelle, Michel. *The Revolution against the Church: From Reason to the Supreme Being*. Translated by Alan José. Columbus: Ohio State University Press, 1991 (originally published 1988).

Wagner, Anne M. "Outrages: Sculpture and Kingship in France after 1789." In *The Consumption of Culture, 1600–1800: Image, Object, Text*, edited by Ann Bermingham and John Brewer, *294–318*. New York: Routledge, 1995.

Waller, Margaret. *The Male Malady: Fictions of Impotence in the French Romantic Novel.* New Brunswick, NJ: Rutgers University Press, 1993.

Weber, Eugen. *My France: Politics, Culture, Myth. Cambridge, MA: The Belknap Press of Harvard University Press, 1991.*

Welsh, David. *Adam Mickiewicz.* New York: Twayne Publishers, 1966.

Winock, Michel. *Madame de Staël.* Paris: Fayard, 2010.

Woloch, Isser. *The French Veteran from the Revolution to the Restoration.* Chapel Hill: University of North Carolina Press, 1979.

Wren, Keith. "Victor Hugo and the Napoleonic Myth." *European Studies Review* 10 (1980): 429–58.

Wright, Beth S., ed. *The Cambridge Companion to Delacroix.* Cambridge: Cambridge University Press, 2001.

———. *Painting and History during the French Restoration: Abandoned by the Past.* Cambridge: Cambridge University Press, 1997.

Index

Note: *Italic* page numbers refer to figures and page numbers followed by "n" denote endnotes.

Abdelkader ibn Muhieddine, Emir 122
Abdulmejid I, Ottoman Sultan 157
Additional Act 153
Amiens: Peace of 182; Treaty of 2, 26
Ancelot, Marguerite-Louise-Virginie 143, 168n1
The anti-heroic mode 11–13, 96–7, 101, 124, 179–80, 189–91, 201, 205–6, 215, 219, 222
anti-Semitism 110, 217
Antommarchi, François 153
Apponyi, Antoine 154
Artaud de Montor, Alexis-François 10
Athanassoglou-Kallmyer, Nina 3, 151
Augerville 74–5, 226
Augustus, Frederick William Henry, Prince of Prussia (Friedrich Wilhelm Heinrich August) 104
Aupick, Jacques 75
L'Avenir 4, 38–9, 53n77, 78, 81

Balayé, Simone 103
Ballanche, Pierre-Simon 76–7, 80, 167, 223; *On Sentiment Considered in Its Relationship with Literature and the Arts* 76
Balzac, Honoré de: *The Country Doctor (Le Médecin de campagne)* 155–6; *Military Recollections, Farewell (Souvenirs soldatesques, Adieu)* 184, 186
Bann, Stephen 3
Barbey d'Aurevilly, Jules 223–4
Barrès, Maurice 221–2; *The Novel of National Energy* (*Le Roman de l'énergie nationale*) 14, 221; *The Uprooted* (*Les* Déracinés) 221–2
Baudelaire, Charles 58, 72, 80, 87, 117, 190, 224
Bayard, Émile: *Napoleon the Little Superimposes Himself on Napoleon the Great* 166, *166*
Beauterne, Robert Antoine de: frontispiece by Vernet to 162, *163; Napoleon's Religious Conversations, in which He Himself Reveals His Intimate Thoughts on Christianity* 162–3
Bell, David A. 8, 10
Bendemann, Eduard: *Jeremiah on the Ruins of Jerusalem* 198, *199*, 204
Bénichou, Paul 3, 8, 37, 75–6, 164, 181
Benjamin, Walter 3
Béranger, Pierre-Jean de 34, 106, 149, 152, 156, 186
Bernard, Émile 224
Bernini, Gian Lorenzo 28, 30
Berry, Duc de (Charles-Ferdinand d'Artois) 34, 148
Berryer, Pierre-Antoine 74
Blanc de Saint-Bonnet, Antoine 76; *Pain* (*La Douleur*) 223
Bland, Cynthia 66, 91n41, 93n73
Bloy, Léon 222–3, 226
Bluche, Frédéric 158–9, 160
Boisgelin de Cucé, Jean-de-Dieu 26, 102
Boissard de Boisdenier, Joseph-Fernand 190; *Episode from the Retreat from Moscow* 187–9, *187*
Bonald, Louis de 10
Bonaparte, Louis-Napoléon 11, 130, 159, 164–7; *see also* Napoleon III
Bonaparte, Napoleon 1–2; Battle of Eylau 144, 168n8; Battle of Waterloo 148–9, 153, 157–60, 164, 178, 184, 190, 203–5, 215, 217, 219, 222; Concordat 19, 23–6, 170n27; cult of 2, 11, 13, 155, 156, 159, 160, 162, 164, 167, 215, 222; reference to, by Barrès 221–2; Return of the Ashes (*Le Retour des cendres*) 157–8, 161–2, 164, 172n68; Russian campaign 182–9, 211n56
Bonapartism 11, 152, 158–9, 167, 173n88, 229n22
Bonivard, François 221

Borghese Gladiator 125
Bourbon Restoration 4, 5, 10, 46, 74, 76, 132, 148, 181
Bowman, Frank Paul 3, 46, 62, 64, 67, 73
Bro,Louis 149
Buloz, François 181
Byron, Lord (George Gordon): *Cain, A Mystery* 125; "Childe Harold's Pilgrimage" 146; "Ode to Napoleon Buonaparte" 146; "The Prisoner of Chillon" 221

Call, Michael J. xv
Calonne, Alphonse de 79
Caprara, Giovanni Battista 26
Catholic revival 33–6, 222–7
Chabrol, Comte Gaspard de 57
Chalier, Marie Joseph 77
Cham (Amédé de Noé) 47; caricature of Lamennais by *47*
Chardin, Jean Siméon 8
Charles X, King of France 33, 52n55; *see also Bourbon Restoration*
Charlet, Nicolas-Toussaint 150, 189; *Episode from the Russian Campaign 185*, 185–7
Charlton, D.G. 8, 131
Charte of 1814 34–5
Charte of 1830 35, 129
Chassériau, Benoît 192–4, 205, 212n72
Chassériau, Charles-Frédéric 205
Chassériau, Frédéric-Victor-Charles 192–3
Chassériau, Théodore 2, 13, 39, 123, 216; and the anti-heroic mode 189–206; *Ali-Ben-Hamet, Caliph of Constantine and Chief of the Haractas, Followed by His Escort* 190; *Dominique Lacordaire, of the Order of Preaching Friars* 39, *40*; *Jesus in the Garden of Olives* 60–3, *61, 62*; *Lamentations of Jeremiah* 199, *199*; *The Punishment of Cain*, or *Cain Accursed* 191–2, *191*; *The Return of the Prodigal Son* 192–3, *193*; *Self-portrait* 192, 192, 195; Self-*portrait Holding a Palette* 195–6, *195*; *Susanna Bathing* 63, *201*, 201–2; *Tomb Project for Napoleon I 204*, 205; *The Trojan Women (Les Troyennes)* 113, 123–4, 202–4, *202*; study for *The Trojan Women* 202, *203; Venus Anadyomene (Vénus marine) 200*, 201; *The Virgin* 195–6
Chassériau, Victor-Frédéric 194, 205
Chateaubriand, Céleste 28
Chateaubriand, François-René de 1, 5, 9–10, 26–8, 152, 154, 167–8, 194, 220, 223–4; caricature of (*Le Conservateur des ruines*) 5–6, *7; De Buonaparte et des Bourbons* 146, 167; *Historical Essay on the Relationship of Ancient and Modern Revolutions to the French Revolution* 26–7; *Spirit of Christianity* (Génie du christianisme) 26–7, 35, 36, 76
Chaudet, Antoine-Denis 148
Chaudonneret, Marie-Claude 77
Chenavard, Paul 185, 96n106
Chenique, Bruno 193
Chifflart, François-Nicolas *La Conscience* 129, *130*
Civil Constitution of the Clergy 22
Clair, Jean 12
Clark, T.J. 123
Claude Lorrain (Claude Gellée) *Landscape with Hagar and the Angel* 117–8, *118*
Cogniet, Léon 123
Confrérie de saint Jean 39, 87
Le Conservateur littéraire 28
Constant, Benjamin 103, 153
Corot, Camille 3, 98; *Hagar in the Wilderness 119*, 120
Courbet, Gustave 12, 167, 220–1
Courier, Paul-Louis 34
Cousin, Victor 109
Coux, Charles de 38
Crossley, Ceri 3, 27
Crow, Thomas xv, 8, 10, 31, 100
Culte décadaire 23
Cult of the Supreme Being 23
Curé d'Ars *see* Vianney, Jean-Marie
Czartoryska, Marcelline 113
Czartoryski, Adam-Georges 113
Czartoryski, Anna Sapieha 113

Daguerre de Hureaux, Alain 74
Dante (Dante Alighieri) 47, 72, 85, 96–7, 113
Daumier, Honoré: "France at Rest" *("Repos de la France") 177*, 177–8; "France-Prometheus and the Eagle-Vulture" *216*, 216–7
David, Jacques-Louis 1, 4; *Belisarius* 99–100; *Emperor Napoleon Crowning Himself* 24, *24*; Festival of the Supreme Being 23; *The Lictors Bringing to Brutus the Bodies of His Sons 4*; *The Oath of the Horatii* 101; *Primitif* faction in the studio of 27, 101
David d' Angers, Pierre-Jean (Pierre-Jean David) 108–9
Debraux, Émile 154, 156
Decamps, Alexandre-Gabriel 191
Decazes, Élie 5–6
de-Christianization 1, 7, 215
Declaration of the Rights of Man and Citizen 22
Delacroix, Eugene 3, 59, 66, 85, 90, 117, 122, 139n79, 144–5, 186–7, 226; *The Babylonian Captivity* 113–15, *115*; *Christ in the Garden of Olives* 57–60, *58*, 65, 66, *66*, 67; *Christ on the Cross*

57, 68–70, *69*, 73; *The Entry of the Crusaders into Constantinople* 70; *The Expulsion of Adam and Eve* 113; *The Justice of Trajan* 70; *Lamentation* 70–3, *71*; A Mortally Wounded Shepherd of the Roman Campagna Drags Himself to the Edge of a Stream to Quench His Thirst 66; *Ovid among the Scythians* 115–16, *116*, 117; *Portrait of Frédéric Chopin as Dante* 113, *114*; *Scenes from the Massacres at Chios: Greek Families Awaiting Death or Slavery, etc.* 113, 189–90; and spectator Christianity 72, 74–5; *Still Life with Lobsters* 59; study for *Christ in the Garden of Olives* 58, *59*; *The Sultan of Morocco and His Entourage* 190
Delaroche, Paul 60, 90n29
Delécluze, Étienne-Jean 27, 61, 144
Delille, Abbé Jacques: *Sorrow and Pity* (*Le Malheur et la Pitié*) 102
Delion, shop of: *Father Forgive Them, They Know Not What They Do* *25*, 26
The *demi-solde* 148–9, 148–50, 151–2, 154, 160, 183
Denis, Maurice 223
Denton, Margaret Fields (also called Margaret Denton Smith) 12, 18n52
Diderot, Denis 12
Doré, Gustave: frontispiece to Normand, *L'Émigrant alsacien* by 218, *218*
Dreyfus, Alfred 217
Dreyfus Affair 217, 221
Driskel, Michael Paul 7, 13, 42
Drouais, Jean-Germain: *The Dying Athlete* 198, *198*
Drouet, Juliette 129
Dupanloup, Monsignor Félix 74, 82, 225
Dürer, Albrecht, *Melencolia I* 12

Eastern Question 157
The Emigration 98–9, 102, 133n1, 134n15
Esquiros, Alphonse 164
Étex, Antoine: *Cain and His Race, Accursed of God (Caïn et sa race maudits de Dieu)* 11, 98, 125–8, *126*, *127*, 202
Exposition universelle of 1855 35, 79

Flandrin, Hippolyte 9; *Dante, Led by Virgil, Offers Consolation to the Shades of the Envious* 197, *197*; *The Entry of Christ into Jerusalem* 44–5, *45*; *Nude Young Man Seated at the Edge of the Sea* *196*, 196–7, 200, 203
Fontanes, Louis de 26, 76–7, 147
Foucart, Bruno 7, 35, 60–3; statistics regarding copies of religious paintings, compiled by 68, 91n46; statistics regarding quantity of religious paintings exhibited at the Paris Salon, compiled by 35, 52n61
Fouché, Joseph 22, 77, 86–7
Franco-Prussian War 218
Friedrich, Caspar David 8; *The Cross in the Mountains* 30
Fritzsche, Peter 4–5

Galbacio, B. 127
Gallicanism 23, 36, 38
Gauguin, Paul 14, 30, 74; *Christ in the Garden of Olives* *67*; *Vision of the Sermon* 224–6, *225*
Gautier, Théophile 79, 84–5, 117, 120, 127
Genlis, Félicité de: *Hagar in the Desert* 118–9
Gérard, François 9, 148; *Belisarius* 10, 99, *99*; *Corinne at Cape Miseno* 104, *105*; *Saint Theresa* 28, *29*, 30–2, 58
Géricault, Théodore 11, 152, 180, 186; *King Louis XVIII Reviews the Troops at the Champ de Mars* 152; The *Raft of the Medusa* 152, 186, 189; *The Return from Russia* 182–5, *183*, 189; *The Swiss Guard at the Louvre* *151*, 151–2, 183, 189; *Wounded Cuirassier Leaving the Field of Battle* 183, 189
Germain, Alphonse 73
Girodet-Trioson, Anne-Louis: *The Burial of Atala* 28
Gourgaud, Gaspard 153, 184
Greenberg, Susan 120
Gregory XVI, Pope 38–9, 45
Greuze, Jean-Baptiste: *A Girl with a Dead Canary* 12, *13*
Griffiths, Richard 223
Grigsby, Darcy Grimaldo 4
Gros, Antoine-Jean 4, 143, 154, 190; *Napoleon on the Battlefield of Eylau* 144–5, *145*, 188; *Napoleon on the Bridge of Arcole* 143–4, *144*; *Napoleon in the Pesthouse at Jaffa* 154; *Portrait of Julian Ursyn Niemcewicz* 111–2, *111*
Grzymala, Count Albert 113
Guérin, Pierre-Narcisse: *The Return of Belisarius to His Family* 100; *The Return of Marcus Sextus* 10, 100, *100*, 189
Guernsey, Daniel R. 96n106
Guizot, François 30, 35, 158

Hafera, Alison 12
Hannoosh, Michèle xv–xvi, 3, 9
Hardouin-Fugier, Élisabeth 80
Harriet, Fulchran-Jean: *Oedipus at Colonus* 101
Hatvany, Ferenc 202
Hauptman, William 11
Haussard, Prosper 61

Hazareesingh, Sudhir 148, 159
Heim, François-Joseph: *Transfer of the Bones of the Kings from the Place Called Cemetery of the Valois, in a Cave at Saint-Denis, 18 January 1817* 5, *6*
Heine, Heinrich 2, 11–12, 155
Hemptinne, Auguste-Donat de 31
Hennequin, Philippe-Auguste: *The Triumph of the French People on August 10th* 101
Henri IV, King of France 147, 148, 154
Herbert, Robert L. 123
Homer 143, 145
Hugo, Charles: *Victor Hugo on the Rock of the Proscribed* 130, *131*, 133
Hugo, Joseph Léopold Sigisbert 154
Hugo, Victor 1, 6, 27, 99; "The Black Gang" ("La Bande noire") 41; *The Castigations* (*Les Châtiments*) 130, 165; *Contemplations* (*Les Contemplations*) 131; "Conscience"("La Conscience") 129–30; exile of 129–33; "Him" ("Lui") 154–5; *The Legend of the Centuries* (*La Légende des siècles*) 129; *Les Misérables 130; Napoleon the Little* (*Napoléon le petit*) 130, 166; *Odes and Ballads (*Odes et ballades) 51n37, 51n39, 54nn85–6, 171nn50–2, 171nn54–5; *The Orientals* (*Les Orientales*) 154; "The Poet"("Le Poète") 155; "Spirit" ("Le Génie") 27; *The Terrible Year* (*L'Année terrible)* 14, 215; "To the Column" ("À la Colonne") 156; "To the Column of the place Vendôme ("À la colonne de la place Vendôme") 154
Huysmans, J.-K. 14, 222; *Against Nature* or *Against the Grain* (*À rebours)* 223; *The Cathedral* (*La Cathédrale)* 73, 224; Durtal novels 224, 226

Illuminism 76
Imperial Catechism 24
Infirmary of Marie-Thérèse 28
Ingres, Jean-Auguste-Dominique 39, 44, 77, 85, 127–8, 190–1, 193, 195, 196, 200, 201; *The Martyrdom of Saint Symphorian* 200

Jacob, Georges 4
Jacob-Desmalter, François-Honoré-Georges: Throne of Napoleon I for the Corps législatif 147, *147*
Jacquot, Georges 125; *Cain Cursed by God* 125, *125*
Jal, Auguste 28, 60
James, Henry 73
Janmot, Louis 39, 76–88; *Christ in the Garden of Olives 78,* 78–9; Delacroix's opinon of 85; *The Evil Path 80,* 81, 82–3; *On the Mountain 83,* 83–4; *The Nightmare 82,* 82–3, 87; *The Passage of Souls 84,* 84–5; *The Paternal Roof 80,* 80–1; *The Poem of the Soul* 79–87; *Sursum Corda 86,* 86
The Jansenists 8
Jobert, Barthélémy 73–4
Johnson, Lee 9
Joinville, Prince de (François d'Orléans) 157
Joseph Delorme (Sainte-Beuve) 182
July Monarchy 4, 13, 34–5, 37, 46, 76, 122, 124, 128, 154–7, 159, 164, 168, 178, 180, 182, 185

Kempis, Thomas à: *The Imitation of Christ* 17n44, 80
Kościuszko, Tadeusz 108
Korchane, Mehdi 10, 101
Kselman, Thomas 8

Labouré, Catherine de 159
La Caricature 34, 177–8
Lacombe, Abbé 77
Lacordaire, Henri-Dominique 38–41, 45–7, 63, 78–9, 86; Chassériau's portrait of 39, *40*
Lally-Tolendal, Comte Trophime-Gérard de 98
Lamartine, Alphonse de 27, 157
La Mennais, Abbé Jean-Marie de: *Church Tradition Regarding the Appointment of Bishops* 36
Lamennais, Félicité Robert de 1, 36–42, 45–8, 52n66, 112; and *L'Avenir* 4, 38; Cham's caricature of 47, *47; Church Tradition Regarding the Appointment of Bishops* 36; *Essay on Religious Indifference* (*Essai sur l'indifférence en matière de religion*) 37–8; *On the Progress of the Revolution and the War against the Church* 38; *Religion Considered in its Relations with the Political and Civil Order* 38; *Words of a Believer* (*Paroles d'un croyant*) 45–6
La Muse française 28, 51n38, 132
Landon, Charles-Paul 101
Langlumé, Pierre: *Liberty of Religion under Charles X* 33, *33*
Laprade, Victor de 65, 76, 167
L'Artiste 120, 125, 127, 188
Lafayette, Marquis Gilbert du Motier de 108, 160
Las Cases, Emmanuel de *Mémorial de Sainte-Hélène* 153, 158, 167, 177n45
Laval, Charles 224
Lavergne, Claudius 39, 87
Laviron, Gabriel 127
Le Charivari 47, 216
Le Conservateur littéraire 28

Le Constitutionnel 151
Leczinska, Marie, Queen of France 108
Ledoux, Claude-Nicolas 150
Ledru-Rollin, Alexandre-Auguste 123
Lehmann, Henri 39
Lemot, François: *Henri IV* 148, 154, 171n54
Lenoir, Alexandre 5
Lenormant, Charles 120
Leo XII, Pope 38
Le Peuple constituant 47
Lindsay, Suzanne Glover 5
Littré, Émile: translation of Strauss, *The Life of Jesus, Critically Examined* (*Das Leben Jesu kritisch bearbeitet*) by 65
Louisiana Purchase 2
Louis XIV, King of France 8, 23
Louis XV, King of France 108
Louis XVI, King of France 1, 28, 102, 146, 148
Louis XVIII, King of France 6, 33, 68, 147, 152; *see also* Bourbon Restoration
Louis-Philippe d'Orléans, King of the French 118, 177–8; *see also* July Monarchy
Louvel, Louis Pierre 148
Louverture, Toussaint 2
Lowe, Sir Hudson 153
Loyrette, Henri 117
Lyon: Ballanche and 76; Baudelaire's opinions regarding 75–7; Janmot's education in 77; Saint-Martin's sojourn in 76; Siege of 77; Troubadour Style and 77

MacNamidhe, Margaret 190
Maistre, Joseph de 38
Malfilâtre, Jacques-Charles-Louis Clinchamps de 102, 123, 134n17, 140n88
Le Mapah (Ganneau) 164
Marrinan, Michael 13
Martin, John 185–6
Matisse, Henri 226
Mayer, Constance 68
Medwin, Thomas 146
Mellon, Stanley 158
Mercier, Louis-Sébastien 20
Mérimée, Léonor 99
Mérimée, Prosper 122
Michelet, Jules 3, 109
Mickiewicz, Adam 108–13, 136n43, 161–2; *Ballads and Romances* 108; *Book of the Polish Pilgrims* 162; portraits of *109*, *110*, 110
Mikaberidze, Alexander 182
Millet, Jean-François 11, 123; *Captivity of the Jews in Babylon* 123, 140n84; Hagar and Ishmael *122*, 122–3, 186, 190; *The Wanderers* (*Les Errants*) 123
Molière (Jean-Baptiste Poquelin): *Tartuffe* (*Le Tartuffe, ou l'Imposteur*) 34–5
Moncey, Bon-Adrien Jeannot de 150
La Mode 184
Monchablon, Alphonse-Xavier: *Victor Hugo* 132–3, *133*
Monnier, Henry: illustration to *The Exile(L'Exilé)* after Béranger by 106, *106*
Montalembert, Comte Charles Forbes René de 38, 41, 42, 45, 46, 75, 78, 79, 111, 112
Montesquieu, Charles Louis de Secondat, Baron de la Brède et de: opinion of practice of punitive exile in *Onthe Spirit of Laws* (*De l'Esprit des lois*) by 105
Montholon, Charles-Tristan de 153
Moreau, Gustave 13, 201, 226; *The Young Man and Death 205*, 206
Morot, Aimé-Nicolas: *The Captivity of the Jews in Babylon* 14, *219*, 219–20
Muhammad Ali, Pasha of Egypt 157
Murat, Jean-Gilbert 98; *Hagar in the Desert* 120, *121*, *122–3*
La Muse française 28, 51n38
Musset, Alfred de 159, 180, 186; *The Confession of a Child of the Century (La Confession d'un enfant du siècle)* 4, 11, 159, 180–1, 186, 193, 207n18, 221

Napoleon III, Emperor of France 130, 158, 165, 189, 215, 216; *see also* Bonaparte, Louis-Napoléon
Navez, François-Joseph 9, 30, 32; *Saint Veronica of Milan* 30–1, *31*, 224; *The Sick Child* 32
The Nazarenes 42
Necker, Jacques 102
Nerval, Gérard de 164
New Caledonia 1, 220
Nicholas I, Czar of Russia 113
Niemcewicz, Julian Ursyn 111–3, 161
Noirot, Abbé Joseph Matthias 78
Noisot, Claude 160–1
Noon, Patrick 74
Nora, Pierre 3
Normand, Jacques: *The Alsatian Emigrant, A Narrative (L'Émigrant alsacien, Récit)* 218; frontispiece by Doré to 218, *218*
Normand-Romain, Antoinette Le 126
Notre-Dame, Cathedral of 19, 22, 47–8; head of a *King of Judah*, formerly on façade of 19, *20*, 48n5; Lacordaire's sermons at 39
Notre-Dame-de-Lorette, Church of 35

O'Brien, David 116, 144
Odier, Édouard-Alexandre: *Episode from the Retreat from Moscow (1812)-Dragoon of the Imperial Guard 188*, 189

Odiot, Jean-Baptiste-Claude 150
O'Meara, Barry Edward 152–3
Orsel, Victor 9; *Good and Evil* 42–4, *43*, 77
Orton, Fred 225
Overbeck, Johann Friedrich 42
Ozanam, Frédéric 77–8

Padiyar, Satish 148
Pagello, Pietro 181
Paris Commune 1, 166–7, 215–16, 220–1
Péladan, Joseph-Aimé 223
Petit-Radel, Louis-François 19, 21, 41
Peyre, Henri 3, 131
Pigler, Andor 60
Pillet, Fabien 123
Pius VII, Pope 23–5, 36
Poland: Chopin and 112–13; exiles in Delacroix circle from 112–17; Mickiewicz and 108–12; Niemcewicz and 112; November Insurrection of 108, 110
Polistena, Joyce Carol 91n41, 93n73
Pollock, Griselda 225
Poniatowski, Prince Józef Antoni 108
Porter, Roy 105
Potocka, Delphine 113
Poussin, Nicolas 4
Poyet, Bernard 19; Throne of Napoleon I for the Corps législatif 147, *147*
Préault, Auguste 68, 91n51
Prud'hon, Pierre-Paul *Christ on the Cross* *67*, 67–70; *Justice and Vengeance Pursuing Crime* 68; *A Young Zephyr Balanching above Water* 68

Quélen, Monsignor Hyacinthe-Louis de 34
Quinet, Edgar 1–2, 109, 157, 178; *Ahasvérus* 178–9; *Napoléon* 161

Raffet, Denis-Auguste-Marie, "The Archbishop Was Always a Joker" *34*, 34–5
Ranson, Paul 223
Reardon, Bernard M.G. 76
Récamier, Juliette 28, 80, 104
Regnault, Jean-Baptiste 101
Rémusat, Charles de 157
Renan, Ernest: *The Life of Jesus* (*La Vie de Jésus*) 65
Révoil, Pierre 42, 77
Revue des deux mondes 63
Richard, Fleury-François 77
Richard-Cavaro, Charles-Adolphe: *The Exiles (Les Exilés)* 123–4, *124*
Richter, Jean Paul (also known as Jean Paul) 64, 83
Rio, Alexis-François 41–2
Robert, Hubert: *The Demolition of the Church of Saint-Jean-en-Grève in 1800* 20–1, *21*
Robert, Léopold 4
Robespierre, Maximilien 22–3, 99, 101
Romme, Gilbert 8
Rosenblum, Robert 3, 8, 30, 102
Roth, Michael S. 8
Rothko, Mark 8
Rouault, Georges 14; *Christ Mocked by Soldiers* 226–7, *227*
Rousseau, Jean-Jacques: *Émile, or On Education* 22; opinion of practice of punitive exile in *The Social Contract* (*Du contrat social*) by 105
Rubin, James Henry 10
Rude, François, *The Marseillaise* (*The Departure of the Volunteers of 1792*) 161, 178; *Napoleon Awakening to Immortality* (*Le Réveil de Napoléon*) 11, *160*, 160–1
Russo-Polish war 108

S., Cl.-P., *The Lamentations of the Prophet Jeremiah Translated into French Verse and Followed by Several Religious and Patriotic Songs Composed on the Occasion of the War of 1870–71 between France and Germany* 220
Said, Edward 1–2
Saint-André-des-Arts, Church of 21
Saint-Chéron, Alexandre Guyard de 198
Saint-Denis, Abbey church of 5, 21
Saint-Domingue 2, 194
Saint-Eustace, Church of 74
Saint-Germain-l'Auxerrois, Church of 34
Saint-Germain-des-Prés, Church of 44–5, 74
Saint-Jean-en-Grève, Church of 20
Saint-Martin, Louis-Claude de 76, 223
Saint-Médard, Church of 21
Saint-Paul-Saint-Louis, Church of 58, 66
Saint-Paterne, Vannes, Church of 57, 73
Saint-Sulpice, Church of 73
Saint-Vincent-de-Paul, Church of 35
Sainte-Beuve, Charles-Augustin: *Joseph Delorme* 182; review of Musset, *La Confession d'un enfant du siècle* by 181; *Sensual Pleasure (Volupté)* 181; and spectator Christianity 51n46
Salon of 1795 98
Salon of 1799 98, 100
Salon of 1800 19, 21
Salon of 1824 68
Salon of 1827–28 28, 29, 32, 57
Salon of 1836 185–6, 192
Salon of 1840 60
Salon of 1842 13
Salon of 1844 62, 63
Salon of 1849 78
Samuels, Maurice xv, 3, 155

Sand, George (Amantine Aurore Lucile Dupin) 60, 109, 113, 180–1
Scheffer, Ary 60; *Greek Exiles on a Rock Look over at Their Lost Fatherland* 107, *107*, 203
Schnetz, Jean-Victor 9; *The Vow to the Madonna* *32*, 32–3, 58
Scott, Sir Walter 3
Second Republic 165
Ségur, Philippe-Paul de: *History of Napoleon and of the Grand Army during the Year 1812* 183
Sensier, Alfred 123
Seurre, Charles Émile 156
Shroder, Maurice Z. 132
Siege of Paris 215, 218, 228n1
Siegfried, Susan 190, 203, 208n32
Silverman, Debora 225
Smith, Margaret Denton *see* Denton, Margaret Fields
spectator Christianity 9, 24, 28–33, 51n45, 51n46, 224
Spitzer, Alan B. 181
Staël, Germaine (Anne-Louise-Germaine Necker, Baronne de Staël-Holstein) 64, 83, 98, 102–7, 135n20; *De l'Allemagne* 64, 103; *Corinne, or Italy* 10, 103–4; *Hagar in the Desert* 118–20
Stendhal (Henri Beyle) 153, 159; *The Red and the Black* (*Le Rouge et le noir*) 149, 170n27, 180
Strauber, Susan 92n57
Strauss, David Friedrich: *The Life of Jesus, Critically Examined* (*Das Leben Jesu kritisch* bearbeite) 64–5
Sue, Eugène: *The Wandering Jew* (*Le Juif errant*) 178
Sund, Judy xv
Szymanowska, Celina 110

Taine, Hippolyte 221
Teich, Mikuláš 105
Theophilanthropy 23
Third Republic 215, 221–2
Thompson, C.W. 103
Thomson, Belinda 225
Thomson, Richard xvi, 3, 217
Thoré, Théophile (also known as William Bürger and Théophile Thoré-Bürger) 70, 115, 117
Tocqueville, Alexis de 35
Towiański, Andrzej 110, 162
Treaty of Frankfurt 216
Triqueti, Henri de 11, 98; *Protecting Law* and *Avenging Law* 128; *Thou Shall Not Murder* *128*, 129
Turrell, James 8

ultramontanism 36–42

Vallès, Jules 220–1
vandalism during the French Revolution 19–22, 48n1
Vendôme Column 161, 166–7, 169n20, 220, 169n20, 229n15
Vernet, Horace 122, 149–50, 156; *La Barrière de Clichy, Defense of Paris on 30 March 1814* *149*, 149–50, 152; frontispiece to Beauterne, *Religious Conversations of Napoleon* by 162, *163*; *Hagar Expulsed by Abraham* 122; *Peace and War* or *The Soldier Plowman* (*Le Soldat laboureur*) *150*, 150–2
Veuillot, Louis 79
Vianney, Jean-Marie (the Curé d'Ars) 36, 86
Viardot, Louis 188
Vignali, Abbé Angelo Paulo 162
Vigny, Alfred de 27, 60, 109, 159, 179; *Chatterton* 4; "Le Mont des Oliviers" 63–4, 90n29; *Military Servitude and Grandeur* (*Servitude et grandeur militaires*) 11, 159, 179–80, 221

The Wandering Jew 110, 178–9
The White Terror 158
Willette, Adolphe-Léon: *Revenge (Revanche)* *217*, 217
Wright, Beth S. xvi, 3, 5, 95n94

Zola, Émile 217, 221, 223–4